LANGUAGE INTERPRETATION AND COMMUNICATION

NATO CONFERENCE SERIES

I Ecology
II Systems Science
III Human Factors
IV Marine Sciences
V Air–Sea Interactions

III HUMAN FACTORS

Volume 1 Monitoring Behavior and Supervisory Control
Edited by Thomas B. Sheridan and Gunnar Johannsen

Volume 2 Biofeedback and Behavior
Edited by Jackson Beatty and Heiner Legewie

Volume 3 Vigilance: Theory, Operational Performance, and Physiological Correlates
Edited by Robert R. Mackie

Volume 4a Recent Advances in the Psychology of Language: Language Development and Mother–Child Interaction
Edited by Robin N. Campbell and Philip T. Smith

Volume 4b Recent Advances in the Psychology of Language: Formal and Experimental Approaches
Edited by Robin N. Campbell and Philip T. Smith

Volume 5 Cognitive Psychology and Instruction
Edited by Alan M. Lesgold, James W. Pellegrino, Sipke D. Fokkema, and Robert Glaser

Volume 6 Language Interpretation and Communication
Edited by David Gerver and H. Wallace Sinaiko

LANGUAGE INTERPRETATION AND COMMUNICATION

Edited by
David Gerver
University of Stirling
Stirling, Scotland

and
H. Wallace Sinaiko
Smithsonian Institution
Washington, D.C.

Published in coordination with NATO Scientific Affairs Division
PLENUM PRESS · NEW YORK AND LONDON

Library of Congress Cataloging in Publication Data

Nato Symposium and Language Interpretation and
Communication, Giorgio Cini Foundation, 1977.
Language interpretation and communication.

(NATO conference series: III, Human factors; v. 6)
"Proceedings of the NATO Symposium on Language Interpretation and Communication, held at the Giorgio Cini Foundation on the Isle of San Giorgio Maggiore, Venice, Italy, September 26–October 1, 1977, sponsored by the NATO Special Program Panel on Human Factors."
Includes bibliographic references and index.
1. Translating and interpreting — Congresses. 2. Congresses and conventions — Translating services — Congresses. 3. Sign language — Congresses. 4. Linguistics — Congresses. I. Gerver, David. II. Sinaiko, H. Wallace. III. Nato Special Program Panel on Human Factors. IV. Title. V. Series.
P306.N37 1977 418'.82 78-15105
ISBN 0-306-40051-0

Proceedings of the NATO Symposium on Language Interpretation and Communication held at the Giorgio Cini Foundation on the Isle of San Giorgio Maggiore, Venice, Italy, September 26–October 1, 1977, sponsored by the NATO Special Program Panel on Human Factors

A Division of Plenum Publishing Corporation
227 West 17th Street, New York, N.Y. 10011

Printed in the United States of America

PREFACE

Language Interpretation and Communication: a NATO Symposium, was a multi-disciplinary meeting held from September 26 to October 1st 1977 at the Giorgio Cini Foundation on the Isle of San Giorgio Maggiore in Venice. The Symposium explored both applied and theoretical aspects of conference interpretation and of sign language interpretation.

The Symposium was sponsored by the Scientific Affairs Division of the North Atlantic Treaty Organisation, and we would like to express our thanks to Dr. B. A. Bayrakter of the Scientific Affairs Division and to the Members of the NATO Special Programme Panel on Human Factors for their support. We would also like to thank Dr. F. Benvenutti and his colleagues at the University of Venice for their generous provision of facilities and hospitality for the opening session of the Symposium. Our thanks are also due to Dr. Ernesto Talentino and his colleagues at the Giorgio Cini Foundation who provided such excellent conference facilities and thus helped ensure the success of the meeting.

Finally, we would like to express our appreciation and thanks to Becky Graham and Carol Blair for their invaluable contributions to the organization of the Symposium, to Ida Stevenson who prepared these proceedings for publication, and to Donald I. MacLeod who assisted with the final preparation of the manuscript.

David Gerver

H. Wallace Sinaiko

CONTENTS

SECTION 1. CONFERENCE INTERPRETATION – AN INTRODUCTION

1. Language Interpretation and Communication: Introduction to the Proceedings 1
David Gerver and H. Wallace Sinaiko

2. How Conference Interpretation Grew 5
Jean Herbert

3. Selection and Training of Conference Interpreters 11
Walter Keiser

4. Reflections on the Training of Simultaneous Interpreters: A meta-linguistic approach 25
Claude Namy

5. Intercultural Communication and the Training of Interpreters at the Monterey Institute of Foreign Studies 35
Etilvia Arjona

6. An Integrated Programme for Training Interpreters 45
Patricia Longley

SECTION 2. SIGN LANGUAGE AND SIGN LANGUAGE INTERPRETATION

7. The Role of Oral Language in the Evolution of Manual Language 57
Harlan Lane and Robbin Battison

8. Sign Language Interpretation: The State of the Art 81
Rita L. Domingue and Betty L. Ingram

9. Research in Sign Language Interpreting at California State University, Northridge 87
Harry J. Murphy

10. Sign Language and Psycholinguistic Process: Fact, Hypotheses and Implications for Interpretation 99
Ryan D. Tweney

11. Sign Language Interpretation and General Theories of Language, Interpretation and Communication 109
Robert M. Ingram

SECTION 3. BILINGUALISM, TRANSLATION AND INTERPRETATION

12. Linguistic Abilities in Translators and Interpreters 119
John B. Carroll

13. Psychological Approaches to Bilingualism, Translation and Interpretation 131
Wallace E. Lambert

14. True Bilingualism and Second Language Learning 145
Christopher Thiery

15. Translating as an Innate Skill 155
Brian Harris and Bianca Sherwood

16. Four Generations of Machine Translation Research and Prospects for the Future 171
Yorick Wilks

SECTION 4. LINGUISTIC, SOCIOLINGUISTIC AND SOCIAL APPROACHES

17 On the Distinction between Linguistics and Pragmatics 185
E. M. Uhlenbeck

18. Language Meaning and Message Meaning: Towards a Sociolinguistic Approach to Translation 199
Maurice Pergnier

19. Contributions of Cross-Cultural Orientation Programs and Power Analysis to Translation/Interpretation 205
Richard W. Brislin

20. Interpreter Roles and Interpretation Situations: Cross-Cutting Typologies 217
R. Bruce W. Anderson

21. Behavioral Aspects of Liaison Interpreters in Papua New Guinea: Some Preliminary Observations 231
Ranier Lang

SECTION 5. PSYCHOLOGICAL APPROACHES

22. On the Representations of Experience 245
Paul A. Kolers

23. The Bilingual's Performance: Language Dominance, Stress, and Individual Differences 259
Stanislav Dornic

24. Summary and Recall of Text in First and Second Languages: Some Factors Contributing to Performance Differences 273
John Long and Edith Harding-Esch

25. Psychosemantics and Simultaneous Interpretation 289
Jean-François Le Ny

26. An Information-Processing Model of Understanding Speech 299
Dominic W. Massaro

SECTION 6. THEORY AND RESEARCH IN CONFERENCE INTERPRETATION

27. Human Factors Approach to Simultaneous Interpretation 315
H. McIlvaine Parsons

28. Simultaneous Interpretation – Units of Meaning and Other Features 323
Marianne Lederer

29. Language and Cognition 333
Danica Seleskovitch

30. Syntactic Anticipation in German-English Simultaneous Interpreting 343
Wolfram Wilss

31. Simultaneous Interpretation: A Hypothetical Model and its Practical Application 353
Barbara Moser

32. Adult Simultaneous Interpretation: A Functional Analysis of Linguistic Categories and a Comparison with Child Development 369
Annette Karmiloff-Smith

SECTION 7. CONCLUSION

33. The Contribution of Cognitive Psychology to the Study of Interpretation 385
G. B. Flores d'Arcais

Appendix A. Discussion Report 403

Appendix B. List of Participants 405

Name Index 413

Subject Index 421

Language Interpretation and Communication:

Introduction to the Proceedings

David Gerver
University of Stirling, Stirling, Scotland

H. Wallace Sinaiko
Smithsonian Institution, Washington D.C.

This volume is the record of a symposium Language Interpretation and Communication which was part of the NATO Human Factors Conference and Symposium Program for 1977. Ninety-six participants from 16 countries and 6 international organizations met at the Giorgio Cini Foundation on the Isle of San Giorgio in Venice during the last week of September, 1977 to take part in the first interdisciplinary forum on practical and theoretical aspects of conference interpretation. Those present included conference interpreters, sign language interpreters, and teachers of these skills, as well as representatives from the fields of psychology, linguistics, translation, anthropology, sociology, and psychiatry.

Techniques for mediating spoken communication among people who do not speak or understand the same natural language have long been in use, but contemporary society is becoming even more dependent on these techniques. The proliferation of international organizations, international meetings of professional and scientific bodies, the expansion of international travel, as well as the ever increasing capacities and use of telecommunication facilities (to name but a few factors) have all led to a greater interdependence among peoples, consequently there is a greater reliance on the skills of the interpreters and translators to facilitate communication across language boundaries. Indeed, the very survival of such bodies as the United Nations is crucially dependent upon language services. Similarly, international scientific communication at multilingual meetings is enhanced or degraded by the quality of language interpretation provided. In spite of the importance of the contribution made by conference interpreters to communication and understanding in the world today, relatively little research has been carried out in this field. The Venice symposium afforded a unique opportunity for professional interpreters, those involved in their training and employment, and workers in the other fields cited above to discuss theory and research, and outline future research needs.

The aims of the symposium were threefold: The dissemination and exchange of theory and research findings in the fields of psychology, linguistics, translation and sociology as they relate to language interpretation; the definition of points of contact between professional and research interests; and the planning of collaborative research.

These proceedings have been organized in seven sections. The first section provides an introduction to conference interpretation. The present chapter sets out the purpose of the symposium and sketches its contents. In the second chapter, the doyen of the conference interpreting profession Jean Herbert provides a personal summary of over sixty years observation of the growth of the profession. At the symposium a film on conference interpretation in the European Communities was presented by Madam van Hoof, Director of Interpretation and Conference Services at the Commission of the European Communities. In her introduction to the film, which also served as an introduction to the papers on selection and training, Madam van Hoof provided some useful background information as to the scope of the services provided by interpreters in a large multi-national organization such as the E.E.C. Some of the issues involved in training interpreters to meet the needs of such organizations were discussed in the following four papers, which were all written by practising interpreters who are also teachers of conference interpretation. In Chapter 3, Keiser stresses the need for further applied research on problems of training and selection. In Chapter 4, Namy outlines a sociolinguistic approach to the training of interpreters at the University of Geneva. In Chapter 5, Arjona describes the multi-disciplinary base of interpreters training at the Monterey Institute for Foreign Studies. In Chapter 6, Longley discusses the 6 months course in interpreter training at the Polytechnic of Central London.

A unique feature of the symposium was the bringing together of conference interpreters and sign language teachers and interpreters. As representatives from both fields found at the symposium, interpreters of sign and of spoken languages have much in common. Not only are there common theoretical issues insofar as interpretation of both oral and sign languages involves the transmission of messages in a code different from that in which they were received, but there are also common practical problems for interpreters in either medium. By way of introduction to the second section Lane and Battison discuss the history of American Sign Language, and its relation to spoken English (in Chapter 7). Domingue and Ingram discuss the growth and current status of sign language interpretation as a profession in the United States and other countries in Chapter 8. In Chapter 9, Murphy reviews recent research on information processing aspects of sign language interpretation from the point of view of both interpreters and their clients. Tweney, in Chapter 10, surveys current knowledge about linguistic and psycholinguistic aspects of sign language and discusses the implications for translation and interpretation of the unique properties of visual languages. In the final chapter in this section (Chapter 11), Ingram argues that research on sign language interpretation must be carried out within the framework of general theories of language, interpretation and communication.

The third section brings together discussions of aspects of bilingualism and of translation theory. In Chapter 12 Carroll draws on his experience in research on aptitude for foreign languages to suggest lines of research in language abilities that might prove of use in the selection and training of conference interpreters. Lambert, in Chapter 13, reviews recent advances in psychological approaches to bilingualism. In Chapter 14, Thiery discusses the phenomenon of what he terms "true bilingualism" among conference interpreters. Harris introduces the subject of translation in Chapter 15, but not from the technical aspect. Harris refers to "natural translation", or "the bilingual translation done in everyday circumstances by people who have had no special training for it". Theoretical aspects of translation are introduced in Wilk's chapter (Chapter 16) on machine translation and research in artificial intelligence.

Linguistic and social factors are the subject of section four. Uhlenbeck addresses the distinction between linguistics and pragmatics in Chapter 17, while Pergnier carries the discussion further in Chapter 18, in which he argues for a sociolinguistic approach to problems of translation and interpretation. Translators and interpreters are discussed within the context of cross-cultural orientation programs by Brislin in Chapter 19. Anderson gives a sociological analysis of interpreters' roles in Chapter 20. Finally, in this section Lang provides a detailed analysis of the interaction between a court interpreter and his clients in New Guinea (in Chapter 21).

Psychological issues bearing on bilingualism and interpretation are treated in the chapters in section five. In Chapter 22, Kolers discusses ways in which the study of bilingualism can shed light on the representation of knowledge in the mind. Dornic reviews research on the effects of language dominance, stress and inter-individual differences on performance of a number of tasks in a second language in Chapter 23. A specific example of decrement in performance in a second language is presented by Long and Harding-Esch in Chapter 24 where they describe an experiment on summary and recall of text in first and second languages. In Chapter 25, Le Ny analyses the role of semantic memory in simultaneous interpretation. In the final chapter of this section Massaro presents an information processing model of language processing (Chapter 26).

In the sixth section, research and theory in conference interpretation are discussed. In Chapter 27, Parsons describes a human factors approach to conference interpretation based on research carried out with interpreters at the United Nations in New York. Lederer provides, in Chapter 28, a detailed analysis of a portion of simultaneously interpreted text. In Chapter 29, Seleskovitch argues that interpreters need to go beyond the meanings of the words they hear if they are to adequately convey the ideas intended by source language speakers. Wilss discusses the role of anticipation in English-German interpretation in Chapter 30. Anticipation also plays a role in Moser's model of simultaneous interpretation discussed in Chapter 31. In Chapter 32, Karmiloff-Smith suggests that the study of simultaneous interpretation may well shed valuable light on ordinary language use and understanding.

In the final section Flores d'Arcais presents an evaluative summary of the issues raised in the symposium in Chapter 33. On the final morning of the Symposium participants were formed into a number of discussion groups in order to formulate plans for future action. The results of these discussions are outlined in Appendix A.

Discussion of previous psychological research in conference interpretation can be found in a review by Gerver (1976), which can be found together with a number of papers on related topics in Brislin (1976). Other issues in translation and conference interpretation are discussed in a volume edited by Kapp (1974). An extensive bibliography on interpretation and translation is available in Henry (1977).

REFERENCES

Brislin, R. W., (Ed.) *Translation: Application and Research.* New York: Gardner Press, 1976.

Gerver, D., Empirical studies of simultaneous interpretation: a review and a model. In: R. Brislin (Ed.), *Translation: Applications and Research.* New York: Gardner Press, 1976.

Henry, R., *A bibliography of interpretation.* Obtainable from: School of Translators and Interpreters, Laurentian University, Sudbury, Ontario, 1977.

Kapp, V. (Ed.), *Ubersetzer und Dolmetscher*, Heidelberg: Quelle und Meyer, 1974.

How Conference Interpretation Grew

Jean Herbert

Geneva

Of course interpreting is nothing new. In the remotest antiquity people met who did not know each other's language and still wanted to talk together; so there must have been interpreters. As we were reminded by Professor Stelling Michaud in his Preface to my "Interpreter's Handbook", Saint Paul advised the Corinthians to have recourse to them; in the beginning of the XIIth century a French lawyer advised his King to set up a school of interpreters for use in the Middle East and more particularly in the Holy Land during the crusades, and he even criticized Pope Boniface VIII for not speaking foreign languages. Two centuries later, Christopher Columbus sent young Indians to Spain to be trained as interpreters, and all Embassies in foreign countries have always had dragomen or other interpreters to make contacts possible with local people. But that was, and is, something totally different from what we now call conference interpretation. I suppose that the reason why I have been called upon to introduce this topic is that I am, of all living interpreters, the one with the longest experience, and that I witnessed the very birth of our profession sixty years ago. I shall therefore be able to illustrate with some personal recollections.

Conference interpretation only actually started during the first World War. Until then all international meetings of any importance had been held exclusively in French. That was the case of the famous Congress of Vienna in 1814 - 1815. All participants were either career diplomats for whom a perfect knowledge of French was a must, or else very high officials who had been selected mostly because they knew French, as was the case for instance in the World Postal Union. During the first World War, the fact that some of the topmost ranking negotiators from the U.S.A. and the United Kingdom were not sufficiently conversant with French made it necessary to resort to interpreters. The first one, Professor Paul Mantoux was for several years seconded to Lloyd George by the French Government, and interpreted between French and English at a number of meetings held at the highest level. I do not know what arrangements were then made for translation from and into Russian – if any – but I suppose that the only possibility was sentence-by-sentence consecutive interpretation.

It was at that time that I had my first experience of Conference interpreting. The French Finance Minister M. Thierry and the Governor of the Banque de France M. Luquet had to go to London in June 1917 to negotiate a loan. Professor Mantoux was not available and as a young Army officer I was then on a four-day home-leave from the front. So they decided to take me along as an interpreter, but since the word "interpreter" could not possibly apply to the holder of a diplomatic passport (which I was given) I was described as the Minister's Private Secretary. The meeting took place in Park Lane in Lloyd George's house, around the breakfast table, to the accompaniment of ham and eggs. I am grateful that my interpretations were not recorded, because if I heard them now I should certainly blush. However, that was the best that could be done at the time and, strange as it may sound, it was appreciated.

After the Armistice had been signed, a number of Armistice Commissions were set up to discuss all sorts of subjects between the representatives of the German Army and those of the Allied and Associated Forces, as they were then called. They were held in three languages, French, English and German. The German army provided the German interpreter, who was generally a young officer with excellent knowledge of French or English. The Allies provided army interpreters, or former liaison officers like myself, for translation from, and into, French and English. Of course, none of us had had any experience of conference interpreting, and we worked mostly sentence by sentence. However unsatisfactory according to modern standards, our performance was thought miraculous, largely I suppose because none of the high ranking officers on our side of the table was competent to check what we said. The atmosphere was very tense. I remember one day shaking hands with my German opposite number at the end of a meeting, for which impropriety the scandalised French General who presided threatened to have me reduced to the ranks.

During the Conference on the Preliminaries of Peace (there was never any Peace Conference as such), the Supreme Council and the various Committees held their meetings in Paris, mostly in French Ministères, exclusively in French and English, all delegates being conversant with either language. The meetings with the German delegation were held separately, and of course there was no Russian representative. We were about a dozen interpreters, who had by that time acquired a certain amount of experience, mostly in the Armistice Commissions, and we could do fairly creditable work. We interpreted in consecutive in teams of two, one Frenchman from English into French, one Englishman from French into English. We had to take down and translate *verbatim* speeches which occasionally lasted well over one hour. It may be said that that exacting exercise led us to develop for the first time in history a technique of consecutive interpretation, with taking of notes, etc., as we now know it. Evidently we all did fairly creditable work. We were then expected to turn up in morning-coats, striped trousers and butterfly collar, whatever the temperature might be.

The same process obtained throughout the life of the League of Nations family. In long and large meetings, such as those of the Assembly or the Council, the interpreter used to go to the rostrum to deliver his translation immediately after the speaker had come down. In smaller groups the interpreter could speak from his place. It was of course extremely hard work, such as most of our colleagues in the younger generation have never been trained to undertake. I still remember a fairly technical conference in London, which lasted one whole month and in which I was the sole interpreter, having to translate in consecutive, morning and afternoon, six days a week, from and into French, English and German. I was so tired that one day I actually fell asleep while speaking, but apparently I went on interpreting during my few moments of sleep and continued normally when I woke up. Nobody seemed to have noticed anything!

But that hard work also had its compensations. At that time the interpreter was seated on the rostrum next to the Chairman and the General Secretary and was both their confidant and their technical adviser in the matter of International Conference Procedure. Most Chairmen had little or no experience of presiding over international multilingual meetings, a matter in which the interpreter had become an expert.

A new problem arose with the International Labour Organisation in meetings where a number of delegates, trade-unionists for instance, knew neither English or French, nor any language other than their own. The first solution adopted was to supply each language group with a whispering interpreter who translated simultaneously to them and interpreted them in consecutive into French or English. A few years before the Second World War a first attempt was made to resort to simultaneous interpretation. We were then seated in something like an orchestra pit just below the restrum, trying our best to understand what came over loudspeakers and whispering into a sort of box called a Hushaphone. In addition to which, one of us was seated with the President and the Director and interpreted them into the other official language.

It was shortly before the outbreak of war that simultaneous interpretation as we know it was introduced in various meetings. For a long time, however, it was not trusted, because the speaker's delegation could not check the translation, and also (we must admit) because our performance was still far from faultless. We came very near a setback at the San Francisco Conference which drafted the Charter of the United Nations, since the organisers had not provided for any interpretation. At the beginning of the opening session in the San Francisco Opera House, our host, the Secretary of State of the United States, Mr Stettinius, made a long address in English and evidently thought it went without saying that all the proceedings would be conducted exclusively in the same language. However the French delegation headed by Foreign Minister, George Bidault had thought it safer to bring four highly experienced interpreters. As soon as Mr Stettinius had finished speaking, M. Bidault signalled to one of us who was sitting next to him to give a French translation. He got up, uninvited by the Chairman, and delivered his interpretation from his seat in the orchestra stalls. Mr Stettinius was clearly baffled, and asked his secretary what delegation the unknown delegate represented! The Secretary General was so impressed that he provided us with a very special rest-room equipped not only with comfortable armchairs, but also with four beds on which to relax.

In the Preparatory Commission of the United Nations which sat in London, in Church House, and also during the first months of the United Nations proper, the same procedure was followed. In spite of the rule laid down in the Charter, French and English were still the only two working languages and Spanish and Chinese were not used. When Soviet delegates spoke in Russian, as they usually did, a member of their delegation, who was never a trained interpreter, translated what they had said into French or English, and the same person whispered to them a translation of what was said in French or English, without any possibility of checking. That occasionally resulted in catastrophic misunderstandings!

The question of Spanish arose in the Committee which drafted the Constitution of the World Health Organisation. The many Spanish-speaking delegations insisted on having their language used in exactly the same conditons as French or English. With considerable difficulty, I managed to bring two interpreters from Mexico in a couple of days, and from then on, Spanish was gradually introduced in various meetings. The problem of interpretation became more and more acute as many delegates indulged in long speeches which had to be translated in consecutive, verbatim, into two other languages, which meant a considerable loss of time. That led to experimenting with simultaneous translation. An American, Colonel Dostert, who had worked with the US Armed Forces, started to train another team of interpreters in simultaneous interpretation. Very slowly, but surely, simultaneous interpretation gained ground, particularly as Spanish, Chinese and Russian were used more and more extensively. For a long time, however, and still now, in many cases it was not trusted wholeheartedly. For that reason consecutive interpretation continued for a number of years in meetings of the United Nations family, even after simultaneous equipment was installed. In the Security Council, until a few years ago, both methods were practiced at the same time, the consecutive interpreter delivering his translation after the original speech has been given *and* translated simultaneously. With improvement in the quality of the equipment available simultaneous interpretation also gained ground in an ever increasing number of Congresses and Conferences outside the United Nations family. One reason being that in many of these meetings, particularly scientific or medical ones, a large proportion of participants come with the sole purpose of reading long contributions and are not overmuch interested in what others have to say! In more or less political Assemblies, many delegates also speak mostly for the record, repeating what others have already said, merely to prove to their Government that they have taken an active part in the debate!

It is interesting to note that participants sometimes do not understand the process of simultaneous interpretation. I shall mention a couple of cases. It happened to me at least twice, and I am sure that some other interpreters have had the same experience, that the Chairman sent me a note while I was in the booth: "Please speak faster – or make it shorter – because we do not have much time left"! Once, during a medical conference, a French doctor was evidently much intrigued by what we were doing, so he came and sat behind the booth where I was working with a colleague. At a time when we were silent, he seized the opportunity and asked us: "Why are there two of you doing this work?" My colleague explained: "We must. One of us listens and the other one speaks." The doctor was deeply impressed and passed on this valuable information to other delegates!

Alongside the developments mentioned above, the number of working languages in the United Nations kept increasing. Arabic has now been adopted in many United Nations bodies. In addition to French, German, Italian and Dutch, the Common Market now uses English and Danish. In many meetings held in various countries the local language, whether German, Italian, Scandinavian, Thai or Japanese is used for the benefit of local participants. Simultaneous interpretation is, therefore, the only possible solution for the other delegates. For all these reasons, and also on account of the amazing proliferation of multilingual meetings throughout the world, the number of trained conference interpreters required has now probably increased to a thousand times what it was in 1919. Fortunately, a number of excellent schools, particularly in Universities, can now supply them, and it can no longer be said, as was formerly admitted, that an interpreter is born, not made.

This development has had serious psychological repercussions on the interpreter who now, more often than not, sits in his glass case, without any contact with the other participants, and translates mechanically what is said on subjects in which he is not interested by people whom he does not know. On the one hand, he often feels greatly humilitated. How often have we not heard people say: "After all interpreters are just like parrots, they merely repeat what other people say, they are never allowed to express their own opinion: talking machines could do the job." – which gives the interpreter an inferiority complex. At the same time, the interpreter – although he can no longer claim to be a prima donna, as some of our older colleagues were wont to consider themselves – may be overconscious of his own importance. If the Chairman is absent, a Vice-chairman can officiate in his place; if a delegate is absent, the meeting can nevertheless proceed. If the interpreters are absent, however, everything comes to a stop, as was beautifully illustrated a few years ago when the interpreters in the Common Market went on strike – so he may also have a superiority complex!

To my mind, neither of those two complexes is justified. A great catchword, nowadays, is "Communication". Now who is the best, the most highly specialised agent for "Communication", if not the interpreter? It is his own specific professional task to help people, whether individuals or groups, not only to know each other – which often merely leads to friction – but to understand each other, to talk constructively rather than fight. He thus holds a key position, if not *the* key position in the field of communications. How could he have an inferiority complex? Furthermore, in a Conference he is the only one who may freely express his own opinion to the delegates, in the lobbies, in social functions and elsewhere. The Chairman and the Secretary must, and should be, absolutely impartial. Delegates have their own instructions and must abide by them whatever their personal views may be. The interpreter is the only one free to say what he thinks. How could he have an inferiority complex? Of course there are limits to the use of that freedom. When in a meeting of a military or political alliance, or even of ecologists, he should not show himself as aggressive against the ideals of the participants, but he is under no obligation to accept work from organisations with whose goals he fundamentally disagrees.

On the other hand, he should not feel, as some of us more or less unconsciously do, that the conference is for the interpreter and not the interpreter for the conference. Just like the Chairman and the Secretary General, he is there to *serve* the Conference, and to do it to the very best of his ability, even if some of the work assigned to him is unpleasant and tiring. So how could he have a superiority complex?

REFERENCES

Herbert, J. *Manuel de l'Interprète*. Genève: Georg, 1952.

Selection and Training of Conference Interpreters

Walter Keiser

University of Geneva

Geneva

INTRODUCTION

Those concerned with the selection and training of conference interpreters must never lose sight of the eminently practical and professional gifts and skills that make a good interpreter. Interpreters are not trained for the purpose of scientific investigation. Selection and training must be conceived and organized so as to give the future interpreter a maximum of assurance that he will be fully prepared to successfully face the acid test of his first professional assignments. Theoretical studies, linguistic research in particular, will no doubt lead to the scientific confirmation of many of the pragmatic findings and methods now applied in this field. New ideas may emerge, leading to better tests and methods, and recent investigations have yielded new insights into the mental processes involved in conference interpreting, in the input-processing-output-sequence in the chain of oral communication. Much however remains to be done to shed more light upon this almost schizophrenic mental and physical exercise called high speed simultaneous interpretation.

The big difficulty when dealing with this type of plurilingual oral communication lies in the quasi-impossibility of experimentally reproducing the actual multilingual conference situation in which the professional interpreter works, the numerous material, visual and auditory aids and hints and feedback the interpreter constantly gets while he performs.

The quality of the interpreter's output depends on many factors: his own professional qualification as a result of his natural gifts, his training and professional experience; the quality of the technical environment (work-space, ventilation and lighting of his booth for simultaneous interpretation, seating arrangement and acoustics in consecutive interpreting); preparation of the subject matter by the interpreter before the meeting and documentation during the sessions; duration of the sittings and manning strength of the team; teamwork within each booth or consecutive team, and the understanding of the problem of language communication and willingness to co-operate on the part of the participants, in particular the chairman of the meeting; last but not least: the interpreter's fitness on that particular day.

To reproduce all this for purposes of scientific comparison and analysis is almost impossible. This is why most investigations published to this day have weaknesses as to the method employed and lacunae that are immediately spotted by professional interpreters. Ideally, one should obtain permission from one of the large organizations employing interpreters to get a long run of tests with several professional interpreters of the same language combination all working simultaneously from and into the same languages in a real meeting, doing the same speeches in identical technical conditions and with identical preparation and documentation.

These difficulties in the field of scientific research have not prevented the development of largely empirical criteria and methods of selection and teaching that have stood the test of time. The scope of this paper is to review some of these criteria and methods on the basis of some definitions and assumptions, and to point to areas where there is room for improvement and where scientific research might possibly lead to better understanding and to more scientific methods of evaluation and teaching.

DEFINITIONS AND ASSUMPTIONS

Students of conference interpretation enrol to become professional conference interpreters, not to be used primarily for teachers to experiment on with various untried methods. They are entitled to a type of teaching that familiarizes them as quickly and as closely as possible with the conditions they will encounter once they leave the school. We have mentioned the conditions which affect the quality of an interpreter's work. Other conditions, no less important, affect his chances of actually finding work as an interpreter. Here we have the market situation, competition, language combinations in demand or in over-supply. There has been a definite and no doubt lasting change in this respect. Whereas for many years conference interpreters for most of the usual language combinations of the main conference and congress circuits have been in demand, sometimes very much so, the demand curve is now levelling out, except for some relatively new languages in the international field. Of course, there will always be room for highly qualified recruits. But the time is gone when even mediocre or downright poor interpreters got all the work they wanted.

It is thus normal, and honest, vis-a-vis parents and would-be students, to be highly selective when it comes to admitting students into interpretation courses, and, once they are admitted, to put everything at their disposal, while making them work hard, to enable them to successfully pass their final examinations and to hold their own once they are out in the rough wind of competition. *This strict process and as-close-as-possible-to-the-real-thing training* is our first assumption. Interestingly enough, practice has shown that schools which have a reputation of living up to this assumption attract a large number of really talented students.

The *second assumption* for the training of conference interpreters in a relatively short period of time *is that of a sufficiently high level of previous education and training* at the moment of entry into the interpretation course. There are two reasons for that. One of the fundamental maxims of our profession stipulates that "to interpret is first and foremost to understand". To understand, the interpreter must be able to place himself at the intellectual level of the speaker he is to interpret. More often than not, these speakers will be scientists, university-trained people, who have acquired that typical approach to an intellectual problem. The interpreter should if at all possible possess the same frame of mind, master the same intellectual discipline. The second reason why interpreter students should be recruited at a rather high level lies in the very essence of the mental process of interpreting: once the message of the original speech has been understood, its rendering in the other language is not, must never be, a simple word-by-word translation, but the complete restitution, in the other language and at what is sometimes a very rapid rate of oral communication, of the original message with its contents and shades and emotions in such a way that the listener never realizes that there has been translation from one language into another. Experience has shown over and over again that to teach this, and to learn this, a certain maturity and a certain level of previous training is desirable, if not necessary. For these reasons the most advanced schools have placed their interpreter training courses at post-graduate level.

A word about *terminology*: when speaking about *schools*, we use this term irrespective of the level (university, etc) or institutional frame of the training. Special courses like those organized by the Commission of the European Communities or the course at the Polytechnic of Central London are included.

The *third assumption is that interpretation courses are not language courses*, in other words, that the would-be student must have mastered his language before entering into the course. Of course, he will improve his language proficiency during his studies, he will acquire the specific terminology of parliamentary procedure and "congressese", he will learn a lot of terms during the practical exercises, just as he will considerably improve his knowledge of the language of the host country if that language is different from his mother tongue. But he must have the required mastery of his active and passive languages before starting the interpretation course otherwise he will constantly stall and stumble under the tremendous pressure of interpretation *per se*. Insufficient criteria in respect of language proficiency, particularly the B-language (see definition below), has been one of the major stumbling blocks for students at the final exams in at least one of the major schools up to very recently.

The *fourth assumption is that conference interpretation should be taught by conference interpreters*. Strangely enough, while nobody would claim that medicine should be taught by somebody who has never seen an ill person, or music by somebody who has never been to a concert, there are, still now, quite a number of schools pretending to train interpreters where there is not one conference interpreter among the faculty, and where most if not all teachers have never been in an international conference let alone seen interpreters at work. They buy the well known texts by Herbert, Rozan and Van Hoof, and off they go happily training interpreters. They know languages, have an idea of translation, and that, for them, is enough. But it is not enough, alas, for the students, and what comes out of those schools (apart from the exceptionally gifted young man or woman who is a "natural" and who would have become an interpreter even without ever going to any school) are precisely those poor people we have seen being shot down in flames in the selection tests of international organizations – in spite of their super-note-taking-system and their pattern-drill training in simultaneous interpretation. When one bears in mind what makes a conference interpreter, the delicate interaction of all those elements that result in the overall quality of his performance, most of them the antithesis of theory and of anything that one could learn from a book or acquire through a "system", one understands why only one who has lived it all and seen it all, and often suffered under adverse conditions, can teach conference interpreting. It is granted that he should moreover have a gift for training and be familiarized with modern teaching methods.

One might argue that these four assumptions – or prerequisites – are too demanding and that it is possible to train interpreters at a lower level, that languages can still be learnt while getting training in interpreting, etc. Certainly, it is all a matter of how much one wants to invest in such training, of how long one can keep a student on a school bench, of how big a percentage of failures one is willing to accept. What has been said above about present and coming market trends and, consequently, the much bigger choice employers now have only to take the best, would seem to indicate that it would be rather irresponsible to enrol large numbers of students, raising hopes of promising careers, dragging them through classes for years, only to either have to eliminate them at the end of their studies, by failing them, or to see them eliminated by the inevitable forces of supply and demand despite their beautiful diploma. Significantly, enrolment numbers in interpretation classes have considerably, and consistently, gone down over the last few years in the most successful interpreters' schools (by successful we mean those whose graduates have had little or no trouble in getting employment as permanent or free-lance interpreters) and failure rates at the final examinations have gone down accordingly.

Definitions

The terms conference interpreting, conference interpreter, consecutive interpretation, simultaneous interpretation, A, B and C languages are used with the following meaning:

Conference interpreting differs from other forms of interpreting (in Courts of Law, in the Army, in Travel Agencies, etc) mostly by the techniques used: consecutive rendering of whole speeches and simultaneous rendering of all that is being said in the original (speaker's) language over a certain period of time, usually half an hour at least, whilst the traditional mode of other forms of interpreting – even far back in history – has been, and is, sentence-by-sentence translation.

Conference interpreter: The Seminar on "Interpreters and Interpreting" held by the European Forum at Alpbach, Austria, in 1968 agreed on the following definition: "A conference interpreter is one whose office it is to translate orally the speech of participants in meetings conducted in two or more languages. His office may be performed simultaneously or consecutively, in the participants presence". For the time being this definition corresponds to the way conference interpreters work. An extension may become necessary the day interpretation via satellite and video becomes routine professional practice.

Consecutive interpretation: The interpreter sits with participants in the conference room and takes notes of what is being said. At the end of each statement he gives an oral translation, with or without the help of his notes.

Simultaneous interpretation: The interpreter works in special booths and listens through earphones to the speaker in the conference room, watching at the same time what is going on in the meeting room (projections, etc) through the booth window. As the speaker's statement proceeds, it is translated simultaneously into the other language or languages of the conference and fed back through booth microphones to earphones in the meeting room. Delegates can listen in whichever language they wish by switching their earphones to the appropriate channel.

Whispered interpretation (the interpreter, sitting between delegates, whispers into their ears), and *Out-of-booth simultaneous interpretation* (the interpreter sits in the meeting room, whispers his interpretation into a microphone, with or without a two-way sound-link with earphones for the interpreter) are but sub-varieties of simultaneous interpretation. They are not in favor with professional interpreters since the quality of sound reception and working environment leave much to be desired.

For the *language categorization* we use the definitions of the International Association of Conference Interpreters (A.I.I.C.), i.e.: *A-language*: Mother tongue. When they are strictly equivalent to a mother tongue the main active languages (active: those languages into which one interprets) normally used both for simultaneous and consecutive interpretation.

B-language: Active language other than mother tongue, in which proficiency is fully adequate to the needs of understanding. Some interpreters work into their B-language(s) in both simultaneous and consecutive, others in only one of the two techniques.

C-language: Passive language(s). Those into which interpreters do not work, but of which they have a complete understanding and from which they interpret into their active language(s).

Language combination: The set of languages at an interpreter's command from, and into, which he interprets. A conference interpreter's language combination is of paramount importance for his chances of finding work in international conferences. Most interpreters schools make the mastery of at least three languages a prerequisite for admission to interpretation courses (somc make an exception for genuine bilinguals). Among these three languages there should be one A-language, one B-language and one C-language, since in professional practice teams are often made up in such a way as to require at least some of the team members to work into more than one language.

With reference to language classification, efforts are being made by some members of A.I.I.C. to obtain a change in the present definitions. For instance, the B-languages group often leads to uncertainty as to whether the interpreter concerned actually interprets simultaneously or consecutively in his B-language. The aim of one proposal is to formulate a classification that would group languages into S-languages (simultaneous interpretation), C-languages (consecutive only) and P-languages (passive languages). Such a change would have no bearing on the present discussion of language combinations.

Some schools regularly inform student-candidates about market demand in language combinations. They obtain information from employers and professional interpreters. The difficulty in this field is that trends can change very rapidly, new demands crop up rather suddenly, as was the case with Danish when Denmark joined the European Communities, or Arabic. And it suffices that the European Community "overrecruits" interpreters of a given language combination for the free-lance market for that combination to be seriously perturbed for a certain number of months. But again: highly qualified interpreters will eventually find their place in the sun, provided they have some of the main language combinations (combinations with rare or "exotic" languages will open the path for bilateral working relations only) and the more languages, active and passive, an interpreter commands, the better are his chances of finding work. Just for completeness' sake let us mention the two other factors that play an important role in an interpreter's attractiveness for potential employers: the choice of the professional domicile (in or as near as possible to headquarters of the employer using the interpreter's language combinations) and specialization in certain fields such as medicine, nuclear energy, computer science and applications, finance, law, etc.

SELECTION OF CANDIDATES – ENTRANCE EXAMINATIONS AND APTITUDE TESTS

When speaking about selection of candidates we mean selection at the moment of entry into the interpretation section of a school or course. If the interpretation section or department represents an important part of a school, some of the criteria valid for interpretation should already be checked with candidates entering the language or translation section that the school may have upstream in the teaching cycle. These are: language proficiency, language combinations, capacity for comprehension of oral information. If the interpretation courses are not connected with previous language or translation training, as is the case with some post-graduate schools and with students having studied in other faculties, but wanting to acquire the techniques of interpreting, the criteria of selection and the aptitude test or entrance examinations will not normally include any interpretation exercises *per se*. In some schools, students are allowed to participate in courses in consecutive interpretation, the final selection being at the moment of access to the course in simultaneous interpretation. In that case, the test will be a genuine test of consecutive interpretation.

Without going at length into the pros and cons of these various practices, it would appear, in the light of the assumptions mentioned in the previous section, that the most rational (time saving) and the most honest approach is that of selection taking place at a moment when the student has not had anything to do with conference interpreting, either at a post-graduate level, where students will have a graduate title as a translator or anything else, or, in translation and interpretation schools where interpretation courses start before the end of the under-graduate cycle, at a moment where translation and interpretation become different specializations. The author's preference for the post-graduate system has already been mentioned, and need not be repeated here.

Language proficiency tests for candidates not coming from a school for translators have been used by some post-graduate schools. The results, however, have so far been inconclusive since the results from the written language tests have hardly ever been different from the impressions about language proficiency gained at the moment of the actual interpretation aptitude test. Thus, it was felt that one might just as well save the time needed for the written test, and only base one's judgement on the oral aptitude test.

One word about translation: Although both belong to the family of language communicators, translators and interpreters are not often interchangeable. Their techniques are different in many respects, they differ often by their temperament (it has been said that the translator is an introvert, the interpreter an extravert), furthermore, the factors of speed and sheer physical stress in interpretation have prevented many otherwise gifted translators from becoming conference interpreters.

Still, there is no doubt that practice in translation prior to interpretation can be an excellent ground on which to build. And a return to translation, from time to time, is an excellent exercise in language discipline and correctness for an interpreter who knows how to translate. But translation should definitely not be part of the curriculum during the actual period of interpreter training, and written translation should not be part of an interpreter aptitude test, nor a prerequisite for admission to such a test.

Aptitude for interpretation

Much has been written about what it takes to become a conference interpreter. The qualities and knowledge which make a conference interpreter are not rare in themselves, but relatively rarely encountered in one and the same person. This explains the considerable failure rate at entrance examinations for interpretation courses. A short list of some of these personal qualities and elements of knowledge might read as follows:

Knowledge: Perfect mastery of the active language(s); fully adequate understanding of the passive language(s); solid general background – university training or equivalent professional experience.

Personal qualities: The faculty of "analysis and synthesis", together with the ability to intuit meaning; the capacity to adapt immediately to subject matter, speakers, public, and conference situations; the ability to concentrate; good short – and long-term memory; a gift for public speaking and a pleasant voice; intellectual curiosity and intellectual probity; tact and diplomacy; above average physical endurance and good "nerves".

The author does not intend to analyse these qualities and elements of knowledge in detail. This has been done excellently elsewhere. More new and interesting is the question of the very purpose of the interpreter aptitude test, the conclusions that may be drawn from various test-exercises and the matter of possible research and improvements. The first two aspects of the problem have been competently dealt with on the occasion of the Symposium on entrance examinations at interpreters schools that took place in Paris on October 19 - 20, 1974, under the auspices of L'Ecole Supérieure d'Interprètes et de Traducteurs de l'Université de Paris. Other schools represented were the Ecole de Traduction et d'Interprétation de l'Université de Genève, and the Dolmetscher-Institut der Universität Heidelberg. The Paris Symposium felt that the term Aptitude Test for Conference Interpreters was a misnomer since the candidate is not asked to prove that he can interpret, and that one should talk rather of an Entrance Examination giving access to courses in conference interpretation. On reflection, however, the author thinks that there may have been a misunderstanding of the term aptitude test at the Paris Symposium. In occupational psychology it appears that the term aptitude test implies a testing a potential for, or the quality of being fit for a particular position or job i.e. a person's suitability or capacity for carrying out certain tasks. Such a definition does not necessarily imply a direct test of the task or situation involved, and the exercises described below are precisely of this type.

One of the first questions debated was whether language proficiency was the main asset a candidate should have when entering an interpretation course or rather the other intellectual capacities such as faculty of comprehension, capacity of oral expression, etc. The symposium did not agree on a choice in respect of language proficiency at the entrance to interpretation courses. Too often interpretation classes degenerate into language courses. Too often candidates fail final exams because of insufficient active mastery of their B-language or passive knowledge of their C-language. Too often the author finds himself in a simultaneous booth with a graduate from this or that school supposed to know German as a C-language who is completely lost as soon as the German delegate uses colloquial expressions, or with another graduate who is supposed to work from English and throws in the towel as soon as an Irishman takes the floor.

The question arises as to whether this shortcoming is due to an excess of leniency of the part of the examiners or to the very nature of the tests. If the latter were the case, this would be a most appropriate field for research with a view to finding more certain methods of testing language proficiency of the kind needed in conference interpreting.

On the aptitude side, the Paris Symposium distinguished between two elements: *ability to comprehend* and *expressive ability*. Auditory comprehension ability, as distinct from language proficiency, is a very important element in evaluating the ability of a candidate to successfully follow a course in interpretation. For this, even an A into A-language test is revealing. (See exercise C, hereafter). The ability to express oneself orally is not tested in terms of eloquence, which might be misleading, but in terms of communication, i.e. clarity of ideas expressed, intonation, power of conviction, good voice. The art of public speaking can be learned, to a large extent, in the interpretation classes, but only if the capacity of expression as such is there, both in the A- and B-languages.

As to *general knowledge* ("culture générale", but bearing in mind that today's conception of "culture générale" is rather different from what it was twenty years ago) the interpreter-candidate should at least have good general knowledge of the major fields of daily human interest, be they political, economic, scientific or cultural. The Paris Symposium deemed that comprehension and self-expression are hardly conceivable without this minimum of general knowledge. The test, in this respect, is thus not a test for specialized knowledge in any specific field, but the ascertainment that the candidate has an open mind, the power of deduction, intellectual curiosity and flexibility. Here again, the older, more mature post-graduate student would normally have an advantage over younger candidates.

Which then are the tests or exercises used for this examination? They vary considerably in their form, little in the conclusions which they are to yield. Here is a short list of such exercises:

a) *The interviews*: in the candidate's languages, with frequent switching from one to the other. Personal questions about prior schooling, professional practice if any, interests in life, etc. Aim: to appreciate the personality of the candidate, his capacity for expression, his language proficiency.

b) *Improvised short speech*: about a subject chosen at random from several, all dealing with publicly debated questions of the moment (divorce, abortion, petrol, pollution, etc), in the A-language. Aim: to assess general knowledge, his ability to express himself, quality of A-language.

c) *A short exposé in the B-language or C-language*: non-technical, but in characteristic vernacular. Improvised by the speaker, or the oral version of a text. *The candidate renders this information in his A-language.* Some schools permit the candidate to take a few notes, others don't. Aim: to check auditory comprehension of oral information; quickness of mind; good nerves; richness of linguistic rendering. *The same test repeated, from A- or C-language into B-language.*

d) *Sight translation*: the only exercise where the candidate gets a text. The text is read to him once, followed by immediate off-the-cuff translation. Aim: to reveal whether the candidate knows how to translate; whether he knows the source language; whether, in spite of the stress inherent in this exercise, he is able to express himself coherently. Test from B- or C- into A-language and from A- or C- into B-language.

Not all schools use all of these exercises. Some use still other tests (including written translation to ascertain language proficiency). Some schools have made these tests competitive, others see them as important prerequisites for the would-be interpreter student. Practice has shown that if this test is taken seriously, i.e. if enough time is allowed per candidate (not less than one hour, more in case of doubt), if exercises are repeated, possibly in A- to A-language combination for exercise c), the number of wrong positive decisions is very limited. Wrong negative decisions are still possible. But there we come again into the field of assumption one (high selectivity) i.e. to know whether it is better to possibly thwart the start of "slow starters" ("vocations tardives") or to encourage people to embark upon this training only to have to eliminate them later if they should not be able to make the grade.

One condition is essential: that the board of examiners be composed of several (preferably three) members covering all the language combinations of the candidate and that they *be professional conference interpreters.* What is true for teaching is even more true for these entrance examinations. For very rare languages it may sometimes be necessary to add a non-interpreter language expert but even in these cases experience has shown that the professional senses at once whether he is in the presence of a potential conference interpreter or not.

Little progress has been made in devising methods for evaluating the physical and psychological stamina of candidates – either during selection or training. Some students who pass the entrance examinations brilliantly have to give up later because they cannot stand the stress of conference interpreting. Short of the case of a candidate actually stalling or losing his head during the tests, or that of nervous lability or physical deficiency having been noted during previous (translator) schooling, there is no way to-day for the examiners to get a clear idea in this respect during the test. Yet, such a test would be highly desirable, since the number of students who have to drop out for health reasons is not insignificant. Here is definitely a field where research would be welcomed by the schools, and by the profession.

Standardized Tests?

Research is being carried out in some countries, in Prague in particular, with a view to developing a standardized series of tests for potential conference interpreters. All candidates would have to pass the same exercises, based on the same texts, the same speeches, etc. Language proficiency would be assessed by measuring the candidates' ability to make correct use of homonyms, polysemic words and synonyms, by his ability to understand a spoken text and a written text, by a phonetic test, measuring phonetic resolution, i.e. decoding words with different degrees of clarity and deviation from standard pronunciation. To these would be added tests for intellectual qualities (reaction time, logical thinking, abstract thinking, concentration, etc), tests of general knowledge, plus a set of easy interpretation tests with and without notes.

In its essence, the method does nothing other than the present practice, but tries to divide the various operations into many separate sub-tests which would be standardized and applied to all candidates of a given language combination.

This might be another field of interesting research. The difficulties, as seen by the author, are twofold: The interpreters, as well as the interpreter candidates – have such widely different temperaments and come from such widely different backgrounds as regards their education and schooling (at least in the Western countries) that it seems very difficult to conceive of a test that would really do justice to their respective qualities and knowledge, and that could still be genuinely standardized. The second difficulty lies in the time factor. If one were to go through all these exercises and tests with all candidates this would take a very considerable time. If it were a matter of finding thousands of prospective interpreter candidates this might be justified, but this is simply not the case in our countries where there is at most room for but a few dozen additional conference interpreters a year.

TRAINING OF CONFERENCE INTERPRETERS

The reason that so much stress has been laid in this paper on assumptions one to four (you might call them prerequisites for selection and training of conference interpreters), and on proper selection, is that once these criteria and methods are systematically applied the actual training of candidates who have passed the entrance examinations becomes relatively easy and permits extreme flexibility.

To bear this out we take two examples: That of the considerable number of people who, coming from all sorts of other professions, have become highly qualified conference interpreters without ever setting foot in an interpreters school or course. They were just asked to do it and did it, and did it well after a very short time. Why? Because they had all the qualities and knowledge needed. They knew their languages perfectly. They had studied and had professional experience in various fields. They had travelled and knew about the World and its problems. They were quick-minded and quick-tongued and fascinated by this intellectual challenge we call conference interpreting. The second example is that of the Commission of the European Communities. Recruitment from interpreters schools not providing a sufficient number of candidates to satisfy the huge need of the Communities, the Commission started its own training program, but limited recruitment for such (remunerated) trainee posts to people who had completed their university training (not from interpreters schools), mastering at least three of the Communities' official languages and, of course, successfully passing the aptitude test. In six months and with the ideal training environment of the Communities (all teachers are professional interpreters, and students do not have to leave the premises to see it all happening) trainees are turned into interpreters with a very low failure rate and can start working in meetings together with recruits from the interpreters schools and experienced professionals.

Interpreter training: the curriculum

The curriculum of the typical post-graduate interpreter school looks roughly like this:

- Consecutive interpretation courses
- Simultaneous interpretation courses
- Public speaking courses, often combined with courses on Parliamentary Procedure and Conference Terminology and on International Organizations.
- Documentation courses (these are sometimes at the Translator curriculum level)
- Interpretation as a profession (rules of conduct, working conditions, etc). Sometimes not a course per se but included in other courses, sometimes completely neglected.

The duration of the curriculum is between one and two years, and translation courses are not included. Translation may be carried out in mock-conference exercises with translation of resolutions and drafting of meeting minutes by first year students. The special case of interpretation from texts will be dealt with later. Subject matter such as international law, economics, finance, nuclear energy, insurance, etc. is not specifically taught at this level. It may however, normally be included in the translator curriculum if the school includes a translation section, but these matters and many more are constantly dealt with during the interpretation classes.

Some discussion has taken place as to whether more specialized subject matter should be included and dealt with in depth during the interpretation course or not. Likewise, there seems to be some measure of disagreement among teachers as to whether descriptive speech should be used for interpretation exercises before more argumentative or downright rhetoric texts (always spoken texts or improvisations in these styles of speech) are used for interpretation. In the author's view this kind of debate becomes pointless as soon as the teacher applies the principle that his teaching should be as close to professional reality as possible, the only concession being that to begin with he chooses examples that are not too difficult, and does not introduce subjects that are too technical or too scientific. In specialized professional practice the interpreter, especially the free lance interpreter, encounters a large variety of fields and, even within any given conference, he can be confronted at any moment with all three styles of speech. It is but normal that students should get used to the same variety and the same mix of styles of speech. This does not mean that the example of those teachers is commendable who come to their class, pull a newspaper clipping out of their pocket, read it to the students and have them interpret it completely out of context. Nor should a funeral speech be made in the middle of a technical paper. With proper preparation by the teacher and by the pupils, however, the subject matter to be dealt with having been announced in advance and sources of documentation given, it is amazing how deep into technology and science, economics and finance, one can go without this becoming a problem for the students. Such sessions, organized as mock-conferences, can go through the whole range of conference procedure, with an opening speech to start with, a eulogy to continue, adoption of the agenda, report of the rapporteur, scientific contributions, discussion, drafting of resolutions, amendments thereto, closing of meeting, after-dinner speeches, etc. Likewise, there is tremendous pedagogic value in a well prepared multi-language seminar with pupils from several departments participating as well as their teachers, possibly with invited guest speakers, the pupils sometimes playing the part of delegates, sometimes of the interpreters.

Another debate in the field of methodology concerns the sequence in which consecutive and simultaneous interpretation should be taught. Should consecutive come first and, if yes, when should simultaneous start?

The Symposium organized by the Geneva University School of Translation and Interpretation on March 6 and 7, 1976 discussed this and several other problems in detail. The main argument of those considering that consecutive interpretation must necessarily come first is that this is the best way to make the student really understand the mental processes involved in conference interpreting, i.e.: phase I (listening and understanding of the original speech), phase II (abstraction, synthesis, discarding of redundant information, breaking away from the grammatical structures of the original) and phase III (re-creation and restitution in the target language). Others deem that, given a strict selection of students at the entrance examination and qualified professional teachers in charge, simultaneous exercises can start at a rather early stage, provided preparatory exercises, beneficial both for consecutive and simultaneous (technique of reporting, on-sight translation, "décalage", i.e. deliberate time-lag between original and interpretation, dissociation of attention), have been successfully completed. The author tends to the second school of thought, without denying that the supreme test of the conference interpreter is his qualification for consecutive interpreting.

Two other questions of method seem rather academic to the author, one concerning consecutive, the other simultaneous. Should notes be taken in the source language or in the target language? Should simultaneous interpretation be based on the practice of "décalage" or rather that of "anticipation"? Again, let us see what happens in professional practice: *In consecutive*, notes are taken by professionals in all imaginable ways: with or without symbols, plenty of notes or almost none, with or without system, in the language of departure, the target language or even a third language, but usually completely mixed all three. If only teachers would at last understand and accept that once the basic principles of consecutive note-taking (so masterfully defined by Rozan) have been understood by the students, the best service the teacher can render to the student is to let him develop his own way of taking notes, symbols or not, system or not. The "systemitis" and "symbolitis" as they exist in certain schools have done great harm to innumerable students. I have seen students who were able to faithfully reproduce quite long speeches without a single note, when asked to do so during an introduction course for consecutive. They were able to tell a story backwards, not missing one element, from memory. When I saw them again six months later, they were completely lost in notes and symbols and they never recovered and never became conference interpreters. Likewise, in simultaneous interpretation anticipation and décalage go hand in hand, constantly, possibly more so with certain language combinations, possibly more or less of this or that according to the interpreter's gifts and temperament. But they are complementary and not mutually exclusive. Students must understand this and not be made to believe that it is one *or* the other, but this does not mean that for teaching purposes topic exercises of décalage and of anticipation cannot be carried out separately, but the combination of the two should be introduced as soon as possible. There are two areas in the field of simultaneous interpretation where positions formerly adopted by teaching interpreters have changed. The 1965 Symposium on Teaching in Interpretation (Paris) had formally recommended not to use *written material* for teaching purposes and not to resort to *taped speeches* for exercises in simultaneous interpretation since this would run contrary to the eminently oral nature of conference interpreting.

While it is still true that for teaching purposes, especially in the first stages of consecutive interpretation, written matter should be avoided so as to force students to totally immerse themselves in this auditory comprehension-oral expression relationship with its three phases, the facts of professional life are that in certain conference circuits written speeches read sometimes at great speed and without emphasis are the interpreter's daily fare. Since the purpose of training is to produce interpreters who can hold their own as soon as they leave school, it is but normal that students should be taught how to handle this kind of situation which corresponds more to rapid on-sight translation, but becomes interpretation again when the speaker gets away from the prepared text, when he jumps a few paragraphs and the interpreter has to say something coherent while trying to pick up the thread or when the speed is such that it becomes impossible to follow the text, but the interpreter, knowing the subject and the delegate's position, may still be able to intelligently and obliquely give the essence of what is being said. Conversely, the student must also be taught where to draw the line and switch off the microphone rather than risk telescoping sentences and talking nonsense.

Recording technology has made such progress that it is possible to-day to obtain from international organizations or to produce for oneself recordings of speeches of outstanding quality that can be used for teaching purposes. Again, with the proviso that this is not the ideal situation since the visual bridge between the interpreter and the speaker is lost. What is lacking, in the author's experience, in several interpretation schools, are correspondingly good electronic equipment and interpretation booths on the reception side. When one thinks of the many hours a student spends in these school booths one can but pity him. One may argue that conditions are not always ideal in the conference field either, but for teaching, the technical conditions should be first class.

As to *correction of simultaneous work* by students, there are several methods: recording of the original (if improvised speech by teacher) and of the student's interpretation: parallel recording of several students' performances, and comparison of specific passages; relay taken by other students or by teacher, and comparison of this performance with the original; notes taken by the teacher while listening to the student and discussed afterwards. Discussion should occur preferably always in the presence of all students, but not criticism alone: evaluation should always lead to advice, sometimes with practical demonstration by the teacher. The latter is often the best way to make students understand techniques that are difficult to explain in theory, e.g. the case of anticipation or décalage. Needless to say such demonstrations must not be made with prepared texts, but with improvised speeches given by a student.

CONCLUSION

Interpreter training, once the first preparatory stages have been passed and the student has really understood and assimilated the phases of the mental processes involved and the techniques to master them, and in this respect excellent research has been done and teaching approaches and exercises are well known and proven, really boils down to systematically confronting the student with situations, types of speeches, subject matters he will encounter over and over again in professional practice.

The secret of interpreter training, provided the initial selection has been accurate, lies in practice, in the living example chosen from everyday work situations, explained, exercised, corrected, repeated. It is all rather simple, but takes a lot of preparation time for the teacher. It can only work however, if the teacher knows what he is talking about, if he has lived it himself, if he can convey to the student how imperative it is not to get locked into systems, clichés and stereotypes, but to practice maximum flexibility in adapting to changing language and changing conference situations.

While there seems relatively little room for radical change or improvement of the teaching process in conference interpreting, there is promising ground for research in the field of selection tests and occupational health.

Reflections on the Training of Simultaneous Interpreters

A metalinguistic approach

Claude Namy

University of Geneva

Geneva

According to Vinay and Darbelnet (1958), Cassirer wrote that differences between languages are less a matter of phonemes and signs than of differing conceptions of the universe. There is thus an interaction between the universe and language. Whorf sums it up by saying: "We dissect nature along lines laid down by our native languages" and "The study of the structural semantic categories . . . yields significant information concerning the "thought-world" of the speakers of the language" (Vinay and Darbelnet, 1958). Envisaged from the point of view of the interpreter, language is not an end in itself but the means to an end which is the communication of ideas, facts, experiences and emotions. But language being to a large extent the reflections of the speaker's "thought-world" the interpreter must transcend language in order to apprehend the message in its plenitude. Interpreting, therefore, is not merely transposing from one language to another. It is, rather, throwing a semantic bridge between two different cultures, two different "thought-worlds".

My purpose here is to show that good simultaneous interpreting cannot rely on words alone. A great deal more is involved: knowledge of the speaker's cultural background, intentions and motivations; knowledge of the subject matter of the conference; knowledge of the listeners' cultural background, intentions and motivations, to name but a few elements.

But perhaps one should start by trying to define what good simultaneous interpreting is. I use the adjective "good" because it is my contention that unless simultaneous interpreting is good – some would even say "very good" – it is well-nigh useless and, worse still, a considerable waste of money. One only has to think of the cost of simultaneous interpretation facilities (I open a short parenthesis here to say that although I am aware of the difference between "interpreting" and "interpretation", I shall use both words indifferently, for convenience's sake), and of the fees of an interpreter to appreciate the latter point.

Now why this insistence on "good *simultaneous* interpreting? Why not just say "good interpreting" and include thereby consecutive interpreting as well? The answer, I think, is obvious to anyone used to consecutive: a bad consecutive interpretation is sure to be denounced on the spot. Since the interpreter sits at the conference table, all in the room can hear him and even the most blasé of diplomats, if he understands the two or three languages spoken at the conference, will listen with one ear to the consecutive interpretation, if only out of curiosity, to see how the interpreter gets round certain difficulties in the original speech. Some delegations even make it a point of having a linguistically talented young aide in their midst to check on the interpretation. Since the interpretation takes place consecutively, that is to say after the original speech, our young aide has ample time to check the interpretation against the original.

Things are quite different with simultaneous interpreting. Those in the audience who understand the speaker's language are most unlikely to switch on to the interpreters' channel. Conversely, those who rely entirely on the interpreter have no way of knowing whether he or she is being accurate or not. As for our linguistically talented young aide, chances are he will find it extremely difficult to check on several interpreters at once – since presumably there will be several booths working at the same time – while listening to the original. The mere fact of having to put on several pairs of headphones at once is bad enough, but having to listen to both the original and the interpretation at the speed at which some speakers rattle on is a formidable challenge. I defy any but the most experienced interpreter to detect the occasional mistake. It has been our experience at ETI, the Geneva University School of Translators and Interpreters, that jury members at simultaneous interpretation exams find it very hard to judge on the basis of a single hearing. They usually ask for the tape recording of the interpretation to be played over again until they are quite satisfied thay have not missed out anything.

Because of these practical difficulties, inaccurate simultaneous interpreting can go undetected for a long time, the more so as an agreeable voice and pleasant delivery will easily lull delegates into a false sense of security. The result will be a dialogue of the deaf which can continue for hours on end until at last someone realizes the interpretation is at fault.

To get back to my original point: what is good simultaneous interpreting? I might venture to suggest the following definition: it is the art of re-expressing in one language a message delivered in another language at the same time as it is being delivered; the re-expression should be clear, unambiguous and immediately comprehensible, that is to say perfectly idiomatic, so that the listener does not have to mentally re-interpret what reaches him through the earphones.

The key word here, of course is "message". The language in which this message is delivered is merely a code, so that the message has to be mentally decoded by the interpreter and then re-phrased to suit the other code.

But these codes, as I suggested before, are more than a simple matter of vocabulary and syntax. They are the product and the expression of a culture which is itself a certain vision of the universe around us, in other words a certain way of thinking. Some cultures, and therefore languages, prefer to proceed from the abstract to the concrete, or the general to the particular, others prefer inductive reasoning and go from the particular to the general. Others yet favour a spiral form of reasoning, starting from one point, circling around it in wider and wider arcs only to come back to it in the end.

In consecutive interpretation, the interpreter can, to a large extent, reorganize the terms of a statement in a way that will make its message more immediately comprehensible to his audience. In simultaneous, he is condemned to follow the original statement semantic unit by semantic unit; he seldom has time to rearrange them in a different order. But he can and, I contend, must take as much liberty with the original as is necessary in order to convey to his audience the intended meaning – what Danica Seleskovitch calls "le vouloir dire" – (Seleskovitch, 1968) of the speaker. When a French Polytechnicien, addressing his American counterpart, says: "Quelle est la proportion de main d'oeuvre indirecte que vous appliquez à l'entretien du capital installé?" should the interpreter say "What is the proportion of indirect labour you apply to the maintenance of fixed capital?" or should he say "How many people do you employ to keep the place clean and maintain the equipment?" Similarly, I once heard a French historian whose lecture was being interpreted into English, say about the followers of the Comte de Chambord, pretender to the throne of France in 1875, "leurs ancêtres avaient fait la nuit du 4 août; eux ne rêvaient que d'un 18 Brumaire", and the interpreter, quite rightly, in my view, said: "Their ancestors had given up their privileges in 1789; *they* were dreaming of a Coup d'Etat". The interpreter should never hesitate to depart – even considerably – from the original if in doing so he makes the message more clear.

These few examples show the difficulty of good simultaneous interpreting. And yet, most students at the beginning tend to think that it is easier than consecutive. This is a dangerous fallacy. What is easier is *poor* simultaneous. *Good* simultaneous is infinitely more difficult. Earlier on I tried to define what good simultaneous is. Perhaps I should now try to give an example of what I consider poor simultaneous interpreting. I recently had to test a candidate for admission to the interpretation department of our school who said she had already done some simultaneous interpretation. I showed her into a booth and then read out the following passage of a Newsweek article to her:

> "Like all small nations living on the flanks of a major world power, Romania is extremely sensitive about the potential danger lying just beyond its borders. Accordingly, the country's leaders have tried to maintain an independent political line on the international level while avoiding the kind of domestic reforms that made the Soviet Union so nervous about conditions in Czechoslovakia prior to the 1968 invasion."

It came out as:

> "Comme toutes les petites nations vivant au bord d'une grande puissance mondiale, la Roumanie est extrêmement sensible aux dangers potentiels qui se trouvent juste au delà de ses frontières. Par conséquent, les dirigeants du pays ont essayé de maintenir une ligne politique indépendante au niveau international, pendant qu'ils évitaient les réformes domestiques (sic) qui rendaient l'Union Soviétique si nerveuse au sujet des conditions en Tchécoslovaquie avant l'invasion de 1968."

Now, this may be intelligible to those who, knowing English, have heard the original, but for the delegate who knows only French it is highly misleading. Nothing is wrong with the syntax, hardly anything is wrong with the vocabulary, and yet the message does not come through. This is because the interpreter did not bother to mentally analyze the content of the statement in order to bring out the message. Instead she merely transposed the words. The result is an ambiguous statement in French. ". . . vivant au bord d'une grande puissance mondiale" could be interpreted as "being about to become a great world power", by analogy with the cliche "vivant au bord de la faillite". Similarly, the unidiomatic use of "pendant" in the sixth line is likely to reduce the French speaking listener to perplexity. It is what I call two-dimensional interpretation, by anology with Danica Seleskovitch's famous analysis of the interpreting process as a triangular – or three-dimensional operation (Seleskovitch, 1968).

The question, therefore, for the "instructor" in simultaneous interpretation is how to bring students to work intelligently and conscientiously. I try to do it by deliberately playing down the language aspect of interpreting. As there are many ways to kill a cat, there are many ways to express an idea once you've grasped it. In my course I rely mostly on live recordings, that is to say recordings of actual meetings, interviews, lectures, etc. which I have patiently collected over the years. I know some of my colleagues object to using recordings and insist that the physical presence of the speaker is essential to good interpreting. I agree that it is in real interpreting conditions. But you cannot duplicate reality 100% in a school. Besides, enough of my colleagues at the School bring in outside speakers or read out themselves while listening to the interpretation (a feat, by the way of which I am quite incapable) for me to indulge in my controversial teaching method with a clear conscience.

Not only do I use recordings, but I tend to favour those by non-native English speakers. My purpose here is twofold.

1. In an age when most speakers at international conferences have to express themselves in a language which is not their own, usually English, it is important for future interpreters to get their ears attuned to all sorts of accents so as not to be put off by them.

2. More important still: a speech delivered in broken English simply *cannot* be transposed literally. Students must be made aware that clumsy though it may be, it made sense to those who were in the room when it was delivered, as is attested by the minutes of the meeting. It made sense because the other delegates took the trouble to analyze it as the speaker went along and to reconstruct the meaning on the basis of their own knowledge of the subject, the position of the speaker's country etc. This, I try to explain to students, is precisely what a good interpreter should do, for such a speech cannot be properly interpreted unless the interpreter reaches for the "vouloir-dire" behind the smoke screen of misstressed words and approximative syntax.

A key element in this "metalinguistic" approach to interpreting is a proper appreciation of the nature of the conference and of the kind of simultaneous interpretation it calls for. One could list dozens of different kinds of international gatherings where simultaneous interpretation is used. In any attempt at classifying them, however, the same broad categories will emerge: *didactic* – a lecturer addressing trainees, a professor giving a class; *rhetorical* – the U.N. General Assembly, the Inter-Parliamentary Union or the Council of Europe; *emotional* – a preacher addressing a religious gathering, a politician addressing a political rally; *technical* – an engineers' convention, a medical convention; *negotiating* – a GATT trade negotiation group; *legal* – the International Court of Justice or the Law of the Sea Conference; *diplomatic* – a Summit Conference. It is important for students to realize that each of these different types of meetings calls for a different interpreting approach.

In my course, I give a sample of each category. Time does not permit me here to deal with them all. I shall confine myself to discussing two extreme cases: that of a lecturer and that of a negotiator.

The lecturer is a Swedish economist giving a talk to a group of trainees from developing countries on UNCTAD. His English is none too good and he speaks with a heavy accent. Students are first asked to try and identify the accent. Then we play some of the most characteristic passages from the standpoint of accent several times over so that students get used to the typical Scandinavian lilt and syncopated pronunciation of two-syllable words: bet'//er, cheap'/per, mat'/ter. Then we analyze the situation. This man is here to present UNCTAD to a group of trainees. There should be no mystery about his message. His purpose is to describe as clearly and accurately as possible the objectives and activities of his organization. If at times he is not very clear it is because his English fails him. Students are made to reconstruct the meaning of obscure passages on the basis not only of the verbal context itself but also of their own knowledge of the subject and of the speaker. As regards the subject, students will have previously been given a list of books and documents as assigned reading on UNCTAD. They should therefore be fairly familiar with the subject. As regards the speaker, it should be pointed out to the students that the fact that he is a Swede is not entirely irrelevant. Sweden has traditionally adopted a very liberal attitude towards the problems of the less developed countries. The speaker is bound to be sympathetic to their cause, the more so as he is a member of the UNCTAD secretariat. The interpreter should be attentive to such clues as the speaker's cultural background and personal views. More than once, it is these clues that will help him decipher confusing statements in broken English.

That the interpreter should literally "interpret" what he hears can be best examplified by the following passage of the recording in question. The speaker is referring to the Santiago conference:

> "When we came there in April, we were more or less carried on their shoulders (*). They hoped so much that by some witch . . . (speaker hesitates) . . dom the whole situation for the developing countries would change because of this . . . conference that there could be achievements, and as the weeks went on without nothing, without anything . . . coming out of the conference, only big problems about . . . er . . . developing countries themselves having to . . . er . . . getting into agreement on the resolutions, resolutions

> were formulated very late . . . everything was done at the last minute, very few . . . er commitments, concessions were made on the part of . . (**) thus consequently, when we left Santiago, I felt I had to go through the back door in order to avoid to . . . to . . . er . . . be badly treated by the Chileans. Well, this is more . . . er . . . exaggerating, but that was the feeling you had, that you came like an emperor and you went like a prisoner or . . . er . . . a small man (***)".

(*) flags the first difficulty in this passage: the meaning of "we were more or less carried on their shoulders" becomes clear only after "they were hoping so much that by some witchdom . . .". This is a typical case of the interpreter having to wait for the semantic unit to be completed. Under (**) the interpreter must complete the unfinished sentencc: "on the part . . . of developed countries". The context ("concession") and his knowledge of the subject should enable him to do this. Finally, under (***) the metaphor need not be the same in the interpretation; any other image that brings out the meaning clearly will do just as well.

It will be realized from what precedes that my philosophy of interpreting – which I try to impart to my students – implies that in cases of doubt the interpreter should be prepared to take risks. An ambiguous statement may be interpreted in any one of several ways. For this reason the interpreter must constantly relate in his own mind the utterances of the speaker to the verbal context and to the known object of the meeting or conference. Clearly, no lecturer addressing a group of students would want deliberately to be fuzzy or obscure. If he should turn out to be fuzzy then it is the interpreter's job, to the best of his ability, to help him appear clear to his audience. When faced with an ambiguous statement, the interpreter has to make a split-second decision: the statement can only mean one of two things. Which is it? The answer lies in the interpreter's knowledge of the subject, of the speaker's background and approach to the subject. Hence the importance of good intelligence work before the meeting.

Things are quite different in a negotiation. Here the interpreter must exert the utmost caution. Not only does he have to contend with accents but also sometimes with statements which are willfully confusing. It is not infrequent for a negotiator to want to gain time either because he has not received his instructions or because he finds himself in an untenable position in the negotiation. He may then resort to the following expedient (this is an excerpt from a live recording):

> "Well . . . er . . . we, this delegation listen with great interest the various points, suggestions put forward by our colleagues, especially delegates from developing country. I – er – of course, I do not want to prejudge this discussion. These points are particularly welcome this juncture. We . . . er . . . reserve right to support some of them to the extent that some of them fit in quite good with past expressions this delegation. Some of course relate more closely to position of some colleagues in this room. These we can support with some reserve. But we shall see how discussion proceeds. Thank you."

Now, in a case like this, I suggest the only way for the interpreter not to betray the speaker is to find out in advance what the respective positions of the delegations in the negotiation are, or to put it simply; who is trying to get what and how?

Students, therefore, must have their attention drawn to the fact that whereas in our first example, that of the lecturer, it is the interpreter's duty to try to improve if necessary on the original, in this second example, that of the negotiator, the interpreter must be careful to distinguish between accidental obscurity, which may be due to faulty English, and deliberate obscurity inspired by tactical considerations. I try to further emphasize this point in my classes by playing two recordings of an obscure statement: one heavily accented, the other in perfect English. In any negotiation, the interpreter must make it his business to find out what the negotiation is all about. He must also observe the speaker closely. Facial expressions, nods, gestures, a glance across the room, are just as much part of the message as words themselves. This, incidentally, is why interpreters insist always on having a direct unobstructed view of the room.

It is not easy to obtain recordings of negotiating sessions, since negotiations are almost invariably secret. Still, I was able to lay my hands on some declassified material which, although fragmentary, helps me to prove the various points I try to make. It includes several lengthy statements by Japanese delegates. Here again, the first part of the exercise consists in analyzing the typical features of a Japanese accent: the confusion between "R's" and "L's", the recurrent "er . . . er. . ." etc. We also analyze the thought pattern as perceived in the presentation of ideas. Most Japanese speakers take a long time getting to the point. The interpreter should not be deluded into thinking that the speaker is just rambling on and allow his mind to wander, for after what is merely a polite if lengthy introduction, the punch line, that is to say the message proper is likely to pop up unexpectedly in a sudden spurt of sounds which the interpreter must be sure not to miss. Similarly, students must learn how to extract the "message" from what at first may appear to them a confused and illogical presentation. Cartesian logic is by no means universal. Here is an example:

> "Bliefly, thank you Mr. Chairman, as to . . . on the point of the next mitting well, we . . . having the next mitting in the week of May the 12, that proposal could be acceptable to this deregation . . . However, on the point of whether we should have one week mitting or two weeks mitting, we prefer . . initially we decide on the one week mitting. The leason is, as you know, the items we're discussing now are vely vely complicated and . . . er . . . in some fields these matters are vely technical, so maybe after we discuss in a one week mitting we need a little bit of cooling off peliod, therefore . . . and as some one pointed out, mebbe we lest and we lefrect on what will have been discussed at that time, so initially we plefer one week mitting and if it is possible to decide light now . . . er . . . we would have pleferred one week mitting. Then we lefrect, then decide when the next mitting, the following mitting will be held . . . er . . . it seems to me that kind of idea might be more attlactive to the deregration. Then, well, mebbe, let me stop here . . . er . . . I have something to say in the . . . as far as the agenda items are concerned but mebbe rater on. Thank you".

As a conclusion to this first part of my presentation here is a checklist which I give students at the beginning of the course:

– Who is the speaker?

– What is his nationality?

– What is his cultural background?

– What is his "thought-world"?

– What is he hoping to get out of the Conference?

– What is the position of his Government in the negotiation?

– What are his personal views?

When the speaker takes the floor:

– Does what he say make sense?

– Can the interpreter assume that what the speaker is saying faithfully reflects what he really wants to say?

– If not, why not?

– Is his command of the language inadequate? (often the case)

– Is he deliberately trying to fog the issue? (sometimes the case)

– If he uses offensive language, is it because he got carried away, or because he is deliberately trying to provoke his opponent?

Other important clues:

– Intonation

– Facial expressions

– Gestures

So far, we have been discussing the speaker only. Equally important, if not more, is the listener. Because they work in artificial conditions, students tend to forget that interpreters work for an audience. Interpreters themselves for that matter, confined as they are in their little glass bowls, sometimes two or three floors up above the room, find it very hard to realize that they are not working in a vacuum and that people are actually listening to them. And yet, if it were not for these people, they would be out of a job. It is essential for the interpreter always to have his "client" in mind. While working, he must constantly ask himself: "Am I being clear? Do I make sense? Is my delivery all right?" I try to impress my students with the idea that the interpreter is there to help delegates and that consequently he should spare no effort to be clear and accurate. No matter what, the message, like the post, must go through. Working in this frame of mind has its rewards.

There is always some feedback in the form of a word of praise or an expression of thanks. This is where the interpreter enjoys an immense advantage over his colleague the translator: he knows his audience and his audience knows him.

We are very fortunate in Geneva in having a large number of international organizations. It is comparitively easy therefore to put students in contact with delegates. In my opinion it is an essential part of their curriculum. Students must know from very early on what delegates expect of their interpreter, and delegates expect a great deal. For the more talented students this challenge is the best motivation. Most of the comments I made earlier on about the speaker apply, *mutatis mutandis* to the listener. For brevity's sake, I shall limit myself to listing out a number of questions future interpreters should keep in mind with respect to their audience:

- Who is the listener? Is he a student? A diplomat? A business man? A worker?

- What is his nationality?

- What is he hoping to get out of the Conference?

- What is his cultural background?

- What is his native tongue? Is the language in which he follows the proceedings his own? Should the interpreter adapt his own language to him, so as to be better understood?

- How much does he know about the subject at hand? Does he require explanatory comments? Should the interpreter, for instance, explain what AFL/CIO means?

- What is his social position? Should the interpreter be very formal, or can he indulge in a certain familiarity?

In this paper I have been able to skim over but some aspects of conference interpretation. I hope that the discussion will have provided some insights which others will pursue in research.

REFERENCES

Seleskovitch, D., *L'interprete dans les conférences internationales*. Paris. Lettres modernes. Minard, 1968.

Vinay, J. P. et Darbelnet, J. *Stylistique comparée du Français et de l'Anglais*, Paris: Didier, 1958, 259.

Intercultural Communication and the Training of Interpreters at the Monterey Institute of Foreign Studies

Etilvia Arjona

Monterey Institute of Foreign Studies

Monterey, California

The formal training of interpreters in the United States was started by the late Leon Dostert in 1951 at Georgetown University. However, it was not until 1967 that, at the Monterey Institute of Foreign Studies in California, the first integrated curriculum for the training of translators and interpreters within an academic structure of higher education was established. Two senior interpreters of the U.N. team in New York, as well as Mr. Walter Keiser, past president of AICC, acted as consultants during the developing stages of the curriculum. At present, the program offers training in English, French, German, Russian, and Spanish. All students have English as their A or B language and hold either a Bachelor of Arts or a Master of Arts degree prior to entrance into the program. They follow a two-year program of professional and multi-disciplinary studies which, after the defence of a thesis and professional comprehensive examinations, leads to an M.A. degree in Intercultural Communication and a Certificate in their chosen specialization.

In this paper, I shall present briefly the integrated "block method" into which the program has been divided and the relationship that has been established between the theory courses and the practical courses. In addition, I shall discuss examples of some of the principles that have been taken from other disciplines to develop theoretical models and tools that are used in the practical courses. I shall also discuss the structuring of the beginning exercises that are given to the students prior to bilingual interpretation. I have used this integrated approach over a three-year period, specifically with the Spanish group; but the theoretical models and core courses have been implemented with all language groups.

At the Monterey Institute of Foreign Studies, the underlying philosophy is that: (1) translation is the generic term for the inter-lingual, socio-linguistic, and cultural transfer of any message from one community to another through various modes of written, oral, or mechanical means, or combinations thereof; (2) translation is a specialized discipline of academic study within the field of international and intercultural communication; and (3) interpretation is the oral translation of a message across a cultural/linguistic barrier.

As such, the translation process is considered as taking place within a situational/cultural context that is, in itself, an integral part of the process and that must be considered in order to bridge, in a meaningful manner, the gap that separates both sender and receptor audiences. This transfer must encompass the unique linguistic, paralinguistic, and logic systems for interpersonal communication of both the sender and the receptor audiences. Consequently, our program first aims at sensitizing the student to the basic problems of intercultural/interpersonal communication; understanding, non-understanding, and mis-understanding. The extent of the likenesses and differences in frames of reference, value systems, or World Views of the cultures involved, in terms of both their cognitive and affective distances from each other, determines the dimension of the problem. Culture, then, is seen as the factor which calls for the exchange of ideas and messages, not merely of words, when people of differing linguistic communities attempt to communicate.

With this in mind, the professional program has been developed in order to: (a) sensitize the student to the communication process within the cultural and interpersonal communication scope; (b) familiarize him with the concepts and principles which are gleaned from different disciplines and serve as tools and techniques in the actual interpretation situation; (c) provide guided application of the theoretical principles and techniques learned; and (d) integrate theory and practice under simulated interpretation situations.

The implementation of this methodology is effected by a division of the professional program into core (described below) and practical courses. Subsequently these are sub-divided into different stages which are determined by the emphasis placed on the degree of assimilation and application of the principles learned. In synthesis the aim is to achieve an integrated approach in the training of the student. Core and practical courses complement each other and the courses in any given discipline supplement and complement those in all the other disciplines.

All core courses are taught in English and the exercises used in said courses are learned in English. Each core course serves as the theoretical introduction to the practical courses of its discipline. Practical courses, which are bilingual, are divided according to discipline and cover written translation, sight translation, and consecutive and simultaneous interpretation. As students advance in their work, they specialize by increasing the number of courses in the area of concentration. In addition, practical courses are classified according to the type of supervision received by the student: (a) supervised work in the language laboratory; (b) seminar or workshop-type work with supervised group discussion of exercises; (c) out-of-class practical or research assignments; and (d) actual experience in scheduled colloquia and symposia or in conferences.

Furthermore, the courses in each discipline are divided into four stages of progression with a given emphasis prevailing during each stage. The first stage aims at producing an awareness of the translator/interpreter's role as an intercultural communicator; providing theories and models that can facilitate analysis during the communication process, and presenting a preliminary taxonomy of the field. Since instruction during the first stage is in the student's A language, the main emphasis is not an expertise in translation per se, but rather on training the student to analyze the translation process as a whole. Bilingual practicals start during the second stage of instruction in which the ability to identify and to abstract the kernel of information in the source language is emphasized. The main thrust of the exercises during this stage is the correct identification of the problems involved and the practical reinforcement of the theory learned in the core courses. The third and fourth stages comprise advanced work in which the student is given graded exercises to improve his mastery of the techniques learned. During the third stage, specialization starts with the study of procedural matters, a growing emphasis on the study and research of terminology, improvisations, mock situations, and emphasis on stamina. The fourth stage focuses on the global assimilation of the translation process by the student, who must now show mastery of all the basic techniques learned and the ability to implement these when appropriate.

Five specific examples will illustrate the relationships which have been explained so far: (1) the extension of the speech chain into an interpersonal, intercultural communication model of the translation process; (2) the use of componential analysis of meaning for elaborating awareness exercises to cover the elements of time, semantic overlap, levels of language, and regionalisms; (3) the use of the role-playing technique for student awareness and analysis of the cultural, paralinguistic, and multi-disciplinary interplay in the interpersonal, intercultural communication process; (4) the use of folk taxonomies for use in linguistic flexibility, substitution, and paraphrasing; and (5) the use of the verbotonal system for elaborating beginning exercises in simultaneous interpretation.

THE SPEECH CHAIN AND THE TRANSLATION PROCESS

As an extension of the speech chain model in linguistics, I use a diagram of a translation chain to describe the complex interplay of cultural and linguistic factors in which the interpreter participates. In this diagram the different elements in the

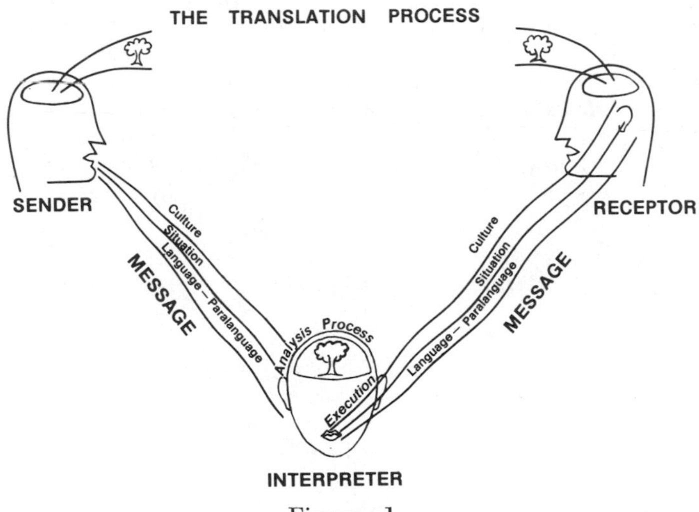

Figure 1

interpersonal communication process and the general factors that influence the sender (the speaker), the interpreter (the analyst/processor/executor), and the receptor (audience) are represented with the interpreter acting in three cultural/linguistic capacities: first, as a cultural and linguistic analyst, upon receipt of the message from the sender; second, as a processor of said information; and third, as an inter-cultural communicator (analyst/processor/executor), when, after processing the information received, the interpreter renders the original message into the necessary meaningful linguistic and paralinguistic symbols and codes of the receptor culture and language. The interpreter must first analyze the message which has been presented through the complex verbal, nonverbal, and psycho-cultural situational mold of the original sender culture and language.

All elements of the communication act influence each other. The culture mold structures the acceptable and meaningful forms for the communication act. The communication mode used for a given situational context is determined as well by what is called for by a given culture: if the act takes place between two people, many people; if it is formal or informal, or takes place at a given time and place, etc. The communication act starts with the sender and therefore, the interpreter, as analyst, must first determine what the resultant sender message really says. The interpreter, therefore, must go, in his analysis, beyond the mere summation of the words that he hears. He must, so to speak, listen in-between the lines and know how to grasp the deep structure of the message received. However, when the interpreter in turn assumes the function of a sender of a rendition, he must attempt to reproduce as closely as possible the original intent of the message and he must do so while treating the message as a communicative whole. Consequently, the problem then facing the interpreter is one of choice, of accuracy, of flexibility, and of adaptation. It follows as well that when acting as a sender, the interpreter in his processing role must avoid any choice which would make his rendition other than neutral. To the extent possible, the interpreter must attempt to be a neutral element in the tri-cultural process in which he participates.

I have developed some exercises in order to sensitize the student to this interplay of culture, language, and interpersonal communication. One type of exercise is based on some of the principles presented by Nida (1975) and others for the componential analysis of meaning. The objective of these is to increase not only the student's awareness of the role that value judgement plays in the matter of choice but also his knowledge of semantic areas of words and his ability to use words discriminately:

Exercise:

Choose the word which is most closely synonymous with the underlined word in the sentence-

The <u>deterioration</u> of moral standards in Roman society has been explained in many ways.

a) degeneration b) decadence c) lowering

d) decline e) decay

Example 1

In this particular example, the definite role which collocation and collative meaning can play is brought out since, for example, a student's own linking of the chain of words, "decay of the Roman Empire" may influence his choice of a synonym. Through such examples, the student is shocked (we hope) into accepting that personal value judgement does in effect influence the choice of words unless he exercises conscious, deliberate care in his choice and use of language.

Another type of exercise is used to study the emotional overtone of words as well as to compare their semantic areas in terms of language levels or regionalisms. This exercise points out semantic overlap, the role that time and regionalisms play, and the affective meaning that the choice of one word over another can carry; for example, backward versus Third World country.

A third type of exercise used for cultural awareness purposes is that of "role-playing". This is done in the intercultural communication and translation theory course. Students are grouped into presentation groups made up of at least one representative per language group who must have the language represented as an A language. Based on prior theoretical discussions, the students are given topics for further research, development, and presentation before the class. A very successful presentation has been one which contrasts the interplay of levels of language, forms of address, and the cues used to show respect or disrespect in the English, French, German, Russian, and Chinese languages. By presenting this interplay in a multi-language, multi-cultural, contrastive manner, the unique verbal ways used by each language community to express overt and covert messages in this particular topic become evident. Moreover, the fact that there is more to a communication act than the mere interplay of words becomes clearly evident.

Exercise:

Evaluate the following words according to:

a) positive, neutral or negative emotional overtones;

b) technical, formal or informal level of speech.

1) police officer, pig, policeman, cop, bobby, fuzz.

2) primitive, backward, underdeveloped, developing, emerging, under-equipped, affluent, non-affluent, Third World countries.

Example 2

Other dramatizations done at the M.I.F.S. for the presentation of cultural, non-verbal elements in the communication process include the repeated acting out of skits portraying given situations: say, the conversation ensuing between an employee and his boss, as it might take place in two different cultures (Pearson, 1977). In this manner paralanguage, proxemics, non-verbal cues, and other subtle cultural elements of the communication act are studied, analyzed, and experienced. According to Nida (1945), five types of cultural knowledge enter into the translation process: (1) ecology (flora, fauna, climate, exploitation techniques, etc.); (2) material culture and technology (food, housing, transportation, clothing, etc.); (3) social categories (kinship relations, sex roles, etc.); (4) mythic patterns (cosmology, taboos, etc.); and (5) linguistic structures (phonology, morphology, syntax, lexical semantics, etc.). To these, I have added two additional types needed for a more comprehensive scope; (6) legal-political categories and values; and (7) World View or logic system. Given this as a basis, a group of students may be asked to develop a cultural skit for a situation involving an American and a Russian in order to portray which elements are acceptable or un-acceptable to the Russian and/or the American. Such an exercise integrates the professional and the multi-disciplinary training of the student. It also serves to stress the interplay which exists when any communication takes place between two given cultures as seen through the manifestations expressed in their political values, status symbols, taboos, value systems, perception of self, and language.

The subsequent analysis of the skit provides the means for studying the exchange in terms of points at which understanding, mis-understanding, and non-understanding take place or in terms of what is acceptable, un-acceptable, or offensive to a given cultural/linguistic community. Although the use of such role-playing is still in its beginning stages in the program, its importance cannot be overlooked. It has been a key factor in enabling the students from all the language groups to awaken both to the complexity of the communication process involved in interpretation and, perhaps most important of all, to the fact that the abstraction of the idea and of the message prevails over the mere understanding of the string of words that hits the interpreter's ear or the translator's eye,

THE USE OF FOLK TAXONOMIES

Aside from having to cope with the problem of choice and adaptation, the interpreter must be able to increase his flexibility in the use of the terminology at his disposal. We use folk taxonomies or the inclusion hierarchy principle for introduction to the use of substitution and paraphrasing. Conklin (1967) developed the idea of folk taxonomies in the early 1960's in anthropology. To form such a taxonomy, a hierarchy is made in which the less numerous or larger items are placed at the top, and the smaller, more specific items are included below the larger items. A sort of pyramid of items results. Since each item or term is included in the more generic term above it, the resultant pyramid has been called an inclusion pyramid or an inclusion hierarchy. Such an inclusion hierarchy can be made for nouns or for verbs. For example, if we establish a pyramid for the English verb "to move", and we use it as a guideline for our choice in translating from Spanish, we get the inclusion hierarchy illustrated in Figure 2. If a person "pasea" in Spanish, and we choose from our pyramid, the word "amble" for our English translation, we are over-translating since by selecting from our hierarchy a term that is too specific, we are giving, in our rendition, more information than necessary. On the other hand, if we choose to say only that the person "moves", we are under-translating by using too generic a term. However, the translator may want to do just this; but if such is the case, it should be a conscious, deliberate choice. If not, the translator must just as consciously and deliberately know how to compensate and adapt in order to achieve a closer, more meaningful rendition.

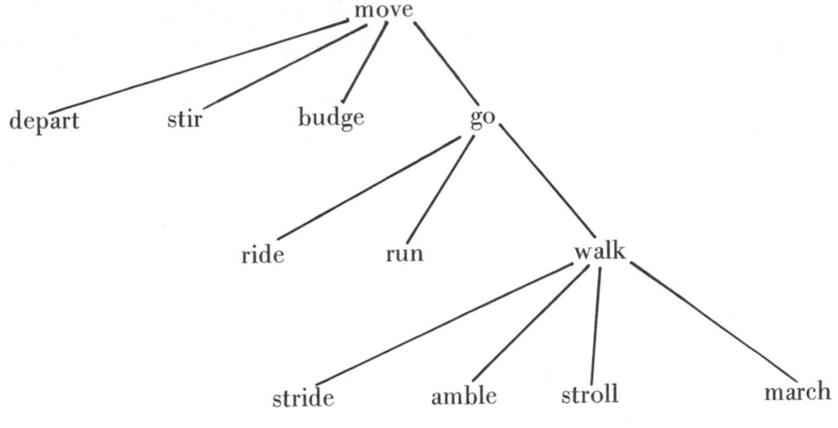

Inclusion hierarchy of "move"

Fig 2

The use of the inclusion hierarchy in the teaching of terminology is only too obvious. In this respect it also serves as an excellent theoretical explanation for the systematic study of terminology and it can easily be complemented by the study of terminology presented by Herbert (1975) and Paenson (1963) in their well known books on terminology.

SIMULTANEOUS INTERPRETATION EXERCISES

The student's introduction to simultaneous interpretation takes place in two distinct stages. The first stage aims at preparing the student to cope with the problems of hearing, listening, and vocalizing speech. The second stage provides the student with guided supervision in bilingual interpretation and with actual interpretation experience during scheduled colloquia and conferences. I have used some of the principles elaborated by Guberina (1972) in his verbotonal system and in the audio-visual global and structural methodology for teaching foreign languages as a conceptual basis for some of the exercises developed for the first stage of training in interpretation. Suggestions found in the writings of Herbert (1952), Ilg (1959), Paneth (1957), and others, for possible exercises for interpreters have also been incorporated in these beginning exercises.

Guberina (1972) elaborated the verbotonal system for the rehabilitation of persons with impaired hearing and speech; and in so doing, he also studied the close connection which exists between the perception of foreign sounds by the student of a foreign language and the perception of speech by persons with impaired hearing. In the early 1950's, Guberina and others applied the verbotonal system to foreign language teaching, and it became known as the Guberina-Rivenc audio-visual global and structural method of foreign language teaching. In developing the interpretation exercises, the following tenets of the verbotonal system were used: (1) the rhythm of speech is the basis for the articulation and the perception of speech;

(2) the whole body structure in movement produces the rhythm which influences pronunciation of speech; (3) the entire emission of speech is of a polysensoric character in which auditive, extra-auditive, and proprioceptive signals form a structure; and (4) listening to speech must be done through natural, contextual sentences, for "thought-wholeness" is the underlying linguistic principle. The aim is then, to stress both the perception of the acoustic structure of speech as such, and the acquisition of the normal articulation pattern of speech, in its broadest sense, through sounds, rhythm, and intonation.

In addition to the verbotonal system, two other objectives underlie the development of the exercises: (1) the student must learn how to perceive and hear sound. "Hearing" is taken to refer to the perception of sound by the ear, and the analysis and transmission of sound to the brain; and (2) the student must learn how to listen, which is considered to be the ability to pay attention to sound; that is, the ability to hear with thoughtful, discriminative attention.

With this in mind, the introductory exercises are taken in two stages. The first stage takes the student through a series of exercises in his A language. The second then takes the student through slightly different but similar exercises in his B language. These two stages serve as preparation for bilingual simultaneous interpretation. Each stage takes approximately ten weeks with the students meeting two hours a week in the language laboratory for the exercises. Students are issued different recordings and instructed to carry out specific exercises during class time. They may come to the laboratory at other times for extra practice or may request other exercises of the same type. At periodic intervals additional explanatory lectures are given covering principles of acoustics, memory retention, voice projection, and the interpretation act. The specific laboratory exercises are explained and the students are given the opportunity to discuss as a group the problems they may be encountering with the exercises.

The first exercises stress practice in learning how to hear in the A language. Consequently, the exercises start by having the student try to repeat what a native-speaker of English is saying. The recording, however, is of a speaker with an accent that is markedly regional: Australian, Indian, Texan. The student is instructed to repeat what he hears but using his own personal speech patterns. While so doing, the student is asked to write in descending order from 100, by one's, then by two's, and finally by three's. The student is told not to play back the recording when he cannot distinguish the sounds but rather to "keep on going" and attempt to continue the flow of speech by catching up with the first meaningful cluster of words that he can perceive and repeat. As his ability to do this increases, the student starts to shadow the speech and to attempt to increase the phase between the recording and his articulation. At this stage, the student is given copies of very well known texts in the same language of the recording; for example, in English, the texts used include the preamble of the U.S. Constitution and the Gettysburg Address. The student is asked to write out the text while doing shadowing exercises. Once the student can do all these exercises with some degree of ease, substitution and paraphrasing are introduced. The most advanced type of exercise that the student is given in his A language is reportage, for which short news broadcasts are used. During the final phases of the exercises in the A language, the emphasis is shifted towards coping with fast speech delivery as well as with foreign accents with correct syntax and foreign accents with awkward or unfamiliar syntax.

The main difference between the exercises done in the A language and those done in the B language is that when the student does the exercises in his A language, he is told to repeat the master recording. That is, the student, who has the same linguistic proficiency as the person who has been recorded, repeats what he is perceiving while using his own speech and intonation patterns. In the exercises done in the B language, however, the student is told to imitate or mimic the speech patterns of the master recordings. Consequently, whereas the A language exercises provide examples of regional characteristics which serve as one means to produce awareness and listening ability in the student, the exercises in the B language are carefully screened in order to provide him with patterns for imitation and for improvement of his own B language speech patterns and articulation. In the B language sequence, only at the advanced stage does the student deal with regional accents. Care is taken to provide recordings of accents which are in themselves good oratorical examples and which do not possess any possible negative elements that the student may then acquire. In synthesis, the goal of the B language exercises is for students to practice not only the listening, shadowing, reportage, and other exercises, but also to improve their performance in the B language through imitation of the intonation patterns, rhythm, and speech patterns of native speakers.

In addition to the exercises in the laboratory, the student is given a certain number of recordings which must be transcribed or subjected to terminology analysis. In these analyses, the speech is examined in terms of units of translation which are highly repetitive in nature, can be substituted by other units,and can be paraphrased. This final type of assignment serves as an introduction to the more intensive study of terminology emphasized during the second stage of interpretation exercises.

The integrated "block method" approach that has been described has provided for a flexible way of training the student on how to cope with some of the basic problems encountered in the actual bilingual situation. With these exercises, the student is first given an analytical tool that can be used discriminately to fascilitate reaction and flexibility and to reduce the stress of the interpretation situation. Thus, upon entering the bilingual training, the student can concentrate on learning how to cope with the more complex linguistic problems presented by actual bilingual interpretation.

REFERENCES

Conklin, H. C. Problems in Lexicography, in Householder and Saporta (Eds.). *Lexicographical Treatment of Folk Taxonomies.* The Hague: Mouton, 1967.

de Saussure, F. *Course in General Linguistics.* New York: McGraw-Hill, 1966.

Guberina, P. La méthode audio-visuelle structuro-globale. *Revue de Phonétique Appliquée No. 1,*1965, Mons: Université de l'état.

Guberina, P. Phonetic rhythms in the verbotonal system. *Revue de Phonétique Appliquée No. 16,*1970, Mons: Université de l'état.

Guberina, P. *Case studies in the use of Restricted Bands of Frequencies in Auditory Rehabilitation of the Deaf.* Zagreb: Institute of Phonetics, Faculty of Arts, 1972.

Herbert, J. *The Interpreter's Handbook.* Genève: Faculté des Lettres, Ecole d'Interprètes, 1952.

Herbert, J. (Ed.). *Conference Terminology.* Amsterdam: Elsevier Publishing Company, 1975.

Ilg, G-E. L'Enseignement de L'interpretation à l'Ecole d'Interpretes de l'Université de Genève. *L'Interprete*, 1959, *14*.

Nida, E. Linguistics and Ethnology in Translation Problems. *Word*, 1945, *I*, pp. 194 - 208.

Nida, E. *Componential Analysis of Meaning.* The Hague: Mouton, 1975.

Paenson, I. Systematic glossary of selected economic and social terms. Oxford: Pergamon Press, 1963.

Paneth, E. *An Investigation into Conference Interpreting.* Thesis, University of London, 1957.

Pearson, C. *Communication and Culture: Teaching Non-Verbal Behavior in the Language Class through Dramatization and Discussion.* Thesis, Monterey Institute of Foreign Studies, 1977.

An Integrated Programme for Training Interpreters

Patricia Longley

Polytechnic of Central London

London

The role of the conference interpreter is to be the medium and not the message, but as we all know now – the medium *is* the message! This statement is true, of course, of translators, but the performance parameters are so different that the executants must almost perforce be different and their training in the very specific techniques required should be different. The Conference interpreter is neither a freak nor a genius, but an individual who either instinctively, or through training, uses his or her knowledge of languages in a certain way, and whether he does so successfully or not depends on a number of personal characteristics – as is the case in most professions.

Whether conference interpreting is and should be a life-time career is a moot point. Most of my professional colleagues would not question the fact. But there is a view which considers that because of the somewhat limited scope for personal progression it might well be conceived as an incidental, additional skill to be practised at an early stage of a career in, for example, international administration, national politics, journalism or public health. The average interpreter with the right language combination is earning his top potential income approximately three years after he starts work and the top 'plum' jobs in the interpreting world are very few. Whether, however, the individual regards it as a life time career or an incidental skill, training is becoming more and more important. The current demand for conference interpreters, albeit limited, outruns any available supply of people who have acquired their knowledge of languages through force of circumstances, who have sometimes consecrated this knowledge with a University degree, and who find in interpreting a ready source of income.

The day of the bilingual interpreter, even in Africa, is almost over. Two or three so-called passive languages, with one or two active languages are now required, so any stereotype based on the old concept of a conference interpreter would not fit present requirements. These seemingly random considerations do have some bearing on the selection of candidates for training and on the subsequent motivation of students.

In general, these were the considerations which led to the establishment of the first systematic six-month post-graduate course in conference interpretation techniques in London in 1963. Some experience had already been gathered in short courses – training interpreters for specific field jobs with UNESCO, for the Arab League, for the Yugoslav Government – but all were ephemeral and designed to fill a purely immediate requirement. The conviction that the training of conference interpreters should be kept quite separate from the teaching of languages or from the training of translators – both of which should be left to the professionals concerned – was the *prime reason* why the course was designed as a short term one, based on a prior rigorous selection of students. It was originally to be confined solely to interpretation into English from other UN languages as the need for good interpreters with English mother tongue was beginning to create a serious problem within the UN family. This limited application for the first three years enabled the course to develop, through the experience gained on a small scale, into the integrated programme that exists today.

The examiners were all staff interpreters from UN agencies, and the final product aimed at was obviously the sort of interpreter who would be likely to be employed by the UN family: an interpreter capable of working in both consecutive and simultaneous methods, with at least one active language and two passive languages, with a broad background of general knowledge and an understanding of the international scene, but also with a mind sufficiently free from current prejudices and preconceptions really to understand and transmit the substance of a message, whatever the source might be. As the reputation of the course grew and as new language combinations were added to meet the demands of the market, the course grew more complex, but the addition of students from other countries added a new wealth of cross-cultural communication within the student group. We increased the number of students accepted, but have never exceeded 30 in any given year, covering the language combinations required by the market at any given time. If the course grew and expanded therefore, it was solely to try to meet a genuine need for more interpreters.

The choice of a Technical College rather than a University was deliberate. Intensive training of graduates for a specific profession is not an "academic" subject per se, it is an applied technique: although many of our students have told us that they have learned to think coherently, to analyse texts and lectures better during this course than at any previous stage in their education. We were given a completely free hand to accept or reject applicants and to design the course.

CANDIDATES

We were fortunate in being allowed to apply a *numerus clausus.* The number of disappointed applicants is far higher than the number of students who fail. Also we did not have to run a language combination in any given year if there was little chance of employment. Furthermore, since there is a scarcity of professional interpreters willing to spend six months of the year teaching, it would be impossible to attempt properly to train a large group of students. The greater number of applicants are University graduates. With rare exceptions they have not acquired a sufficient command of their foreign languages and frequently do not know how to use their own. Some of them could transmit a message of their own in another language, but could not, necessarily, thoroughly understand a native speaker. Unless we are faced with a genuine bilingual, and these are being described elsewhere, we discourage candidates with knowledge of less than three languages (including their own) with the exception of candidates from regions such as Africa, Asia etc. where there is a demand for bilingual interpreters.

In addition to young graduates, we receive applications from mature candidates, who either through marriage, previous jobs or some form of happenstance have acquired a real knowledge and understanding of the languages required (they may or may not have a language degree) and who wish to train for a different or a better job. The rare prize is the applicant between 23 and 35, with a degree in a subject other than languages, and who has acquired his knowledge of them through early exposure, either in schools abroad, through mixed parentage etc. We do not believe that any 'special' training at undergraduate level in either translation or interpreting is an especially good qualification, as the subsequent struggle to reduce the students reliance on the bad habits thus acquired makes teaching and learning all the more difficult.

SELECTION

Since a lot of interpreters of my generation were reluctant interpreters – usually enticed away from other jobs for which we had been trained because there were not enough professionals available – we might be excused if we believed that no special training was required and that it all depended on an innate special skill, plus the knowledge of one or two foreign languages. We might also, since this skill was apparently recognisable in our own case, believe that it can easily be discerned in others and on the basis of such an assumption we might today tend to select for training only those who were already able to interpret, and only needed a few special hints to prepare them to work at conference level. This approach has been a frequent one in the past, but it is one that largely ignores the potential skill and talent inherent in a lot of young language graduates.

Hans Jacob, an interpreter of the old school and with whom I worked for many years, used to claim that "for conference interpreters language ability is thrown in for free". This slight exaggeration contains a real grain of truth. If you ignore the language factor and consider the essence of the job, it consists in concentrated listening, absorbing information and reproducing it in a form which is comprehensible to others.

So when we select students, we are looking for individuals who can listen, and who can reproduce what they hear. In the booth test which we apply, candidates repeat a text in the same language as the speaker, and when they have become accustomed to listening and speaking at the same time, they proceed to the next stage and have to translate what they hear into their mother tongue. In order to see how they react to ideas which are strange to them, and to check that they are really listening, there are one or two sentences in every test piece which have an unusual twist. In addition, there are several sentences which cannot be rendered word for word in the other language. The phrases grow progressively more difficult, and the last two or three can only be translated by someone who really understands the source language. They are not technical, because no one can be expected to know technical jargon in their own language, outside their own speciality. We also try to assess short term memory, of the type which can follow a logical sequence and recall how one point leads to another.

In addition to a short interview at the end of the test, in which several languages may be spoken, a short written translation from B and C languages into A, or both ways if candidates claim to be bilingual, provides some evidence of their knowledge of their B and C languages, as well as of the way they express themselves in their A language. They are given a reasonable time for work, no dictionaries are allowed, and we insist on a single draft. If they wish to revise it, they must do so on the original version. These are checked not only for accuracy, clarity and style but for any misunderstandings which may appear due to imperfect grasp of grammar, e.g. foreign verb tenses, (the historic present in French, for example).

During the test, which lasts the best part of a day, and involves waiting while other candidates are interviewed and auditioned in the booth, we were able to see the effect of nervous pressure. The first excuse they gave, if they fail the test, or if they feel that they have not done well, is "I was nervous"! During the interview we also question the motivation of students and inform them of the work possibilities open to them, if they succeed, with their particular language combination. Students with language combinations which are not required on the market are not interviewed. On average, we have 120 applicants each year, from whom between 20 and 30 are selected for the course.

Since 1975, we have been carrying out research on student selection for the course. In collaboration with David Gerver and John Long, Sylvie Lambert and I have assembled a battery of personality tests, as well as tests of cognitive skills and performance under stress. We are also developing our own test instruments for assessment of ability to recall text. The test battery is administered to all candidates, as a part of the selection procedure. Performance in the final exams is then correlated with test scores and evaluation of performance on the other aspects of the selection procedure in order to try to determine the best predictors of success on the course. Not only are we trying to define the qualities needed for success on the course, but also in relation to student selection, and the criteria used by the examiners in evaluating students in their final exams. Since the research is still in progress, it would be premature to discuss results at this stage, but we are hopeful that the final outcome of the project will be of use to all concerned with the selection of students for courses in conference interpretation.

TRAINING

Our methods are pragmatic, practical and insofar as they can be adapted to any real individual needs that may be revealed during the course, they are empirical. *But* we *do* have a programme and a clear idea of our aims. If the glamour of the profession were to rest solely on the idea that 'it enables one to travel and meet interesting people', it would soon wear off in the day to day reality of interpreting. So from the very beginning, the student is involved in the hard grind of professional situations, but the substance of interpretation, the human and intellectual subject matter, which makes the job really interesting also becomes part of his daily routine. In other words, although there is no ex-cathedra lecturing, every practical exercise must feed in knowledge, open windows on the new concepts, new forms of language and expression. Most graduates have had a surfeit of literature, much of it ill absorbed – they will talk glibly of Sartre or Tolstoy, but if questioned about the political situation in France, or the Napoleonic Wars, they are lost.

Our program of subject matter is planned to interest students in the actions and reactions of people (which is what delegates are!), to encourage them to get under the skin or inside the mind of the delegate and understand his motivation. They are led to try to understand the mores and values, the political and religious attitudes of countries and areas about which they know little (including their own), and this in turn leads to the political, religious and cultural values within a Region and obviously, to the international distillation of all these, either at the Regional level (EEC, OAS, OAU, etc.) or at the Intercontinental level (the UN family). At the end of the first three months, they have acquired, through the subjects treated, and the material used for interpretation exercises, a broad perspective of the contemporary (and the immediate past) political world and of human beings who live in it.

Only then do we begin to deal with more esoteric subjects; with the language of experts wrapped in their different cocoons of jargon. If students have hitherto mainly been concerned with language studies, it is often because they find science, mathematics or law repugnant. So the barriers of alien language and ideas (alien even when expressed in their mother tongue) have to be broken down, and they must want to enter these ivory towers – otherwise when they interpret they will just learn the technical vocabulary and transmit the jargon of technical material — leaving the delegate (who is an expert in the subject) to reconstruct from this flow of words, the scientific message beneath (this, in fact, is what a listener has to do when a speaker at a conference reads a paper at full speed). It is hard for delegates who understand the original language, and the jargon to follow, let alone the interpreter, whose work then becomes analogous to machine translation. This may be adequate when in written form for the expert to cull enough information, but in the spoken ephemeral form it is irritating and almost useless.

If an interpreter is to work well in economic or legal subjects, he must have some knowledge of the concepts involved, as analogies and comparisons have to be made when interpreting them. Chemistry, Physics, Mathematics are the basis of industrial, scientific, engineering and similar meetings. Biology, as well as Chemistry, is essential to do medical meetings well. Obviously, the basic elements in all these fields cannot be absorbed in 3 months, but students learn to break down the barriers, to use the same language as the experts and above all not to be afraid of trying to understand. They learn to look for the background material before a meeting, and to seek expert help.

CONSECUTIVE INTERPRETATION

Many students think they can take notes, because they have done so during lectures. There is, however, an enormous difference between selective note taking for a specific purpose, and the notes required for total recall. When reading a journalists account of meetings or press conferences I have interpreted, I often wonder whether we have attended the same meeting. My notes tell me something quite different. Instead of attempting to wean them away from their habits, we let them try total recall on the basis of the system they know until they find that it does not work.

As a positive step, from the very beginning of the course, students have to prepare half-hour lectures, one or two a month each, within the program of subjects mentioned above. This implies reading two or three books, and then preparing notes on the basis of which they deliver their lecture. Fully written texts are not allowed. Some succeed at the first attempt, and most of them soon find how many or how few notes they require, and how to lay them out so that salient points stand out, to separate ideas clearly or indicate links between arguments. The important thing is for each individual to evolve his own system, one in which he can have full confidence and the assurance that when he turns to his notes and begins to interpret, they will contain all the elements he requires for total recall, laid out for easy and rapid reference. In giving their own lectures from notes, the students learn to what extent they can rely on symbols, just how much they need to write and how to lay it out so that the thread of logic, the connections between one idea and the next is clearly perceived by them. Of course, they are given guidance and examples, but the logical analysis of a speech will give them far more clues as to the pattern they individually need to follow, than any number of symbols and short cuts. Many students see a collection of symbols as a mnemonic crutch. Unless they have the sort of mind which revels and indeed almost thinks in symbols, lists of ideograms and abbreviations only form another barrier to speedy note-taking. Any symbols used must be spontaneous and spring from the subconscious response to a need, rather than acquired by rote. During the first few years of their professional life they will be under pressure every time they begin to interpret a new meeting in consecutive and if their system of note-taking is a reflection of their own personality, their own approach to analysis, it will stand the test of nervous pressure and will be so automatic that they can afford to concentrate on listening and understanding. We do exercises without taking notes at all, or notes may only be taken after short intervals of speech. This is only done in the early stages, but it helps to force the students to rely on analysis, on memory and to learn to summarise only the essential in note form.

When delivering their own lectures to the group, the students overcome their nervousness in facing a critical audience, learn the correct speed at which to speak to get the message over clearly, broaden their active vocabulary in their own language or any of their active languages, by deliberately using polysyllabic or new words. Voice projection, pronounciation, intonation are all commented on daily and are not the subject of special lessons; it is through constant practical examples that good habits become ingrained. We are lucky in having a group which often contains 10 to 12 different nationalities and several language combinations, so that the students become used to colleagues delivering lectures in a language other than their mother tongue, which often causes trouble at international meetings. Timidity has to be overcome at an early stage, but it must not develop into over-confidence or over-acting. Mock meetings on a subject for which the student-speakers have prepared their role are frequent. Strict conference procedure is followed, the speakers have prepared their own briefs and the interpreters feel that their work is necessary. They learn the courtesies due between delegates, the interaction within a meeting and the role and place of the interpreter. As they develop confidence and knowledge, the students speak with conviction and show an understanding of the point of view they are presenting.

We find that some African students have difficulty in speaking as substitutes for European or American speakers and vice versa. To cope with this, we have found it useful, as well as fun, to improvise plays. The students choose a subject (the introduction of birth control in an African village, for instance – or a political refugee being sought by the police in a friendly community), they write a brief outline of the action, distribute the roles among themselves and then rehearse by themselves. No dialogue is written, they spend a day or so thinking themselves into the part and improvise the dialogue during rehearsals. It's a relaxing way of understanding people who are different or alien and of representing them – in other words of interpreting them, with understanding.

In the course of six months, each student has contributed, through the lectures or speeches he has prepared, to the pool of knowledge and experience of the rest of the class. They have learned the essential part of team work and conference discipline. No student is allowed to lecture on a subject that they already know a lot about. They do not speak about their own countries, for example. We will ask a Latin American student to lecture on China, or an English student to talk about Lesotho. They are given a broad outline of the sort of information wanted in each case and that is all. As already stated, at the end of the first term the class has a fairly good general background knowledge of the political and economic state of the present world, as well as of the cultural, religious and other values which motivate speakers. When we tackle the technical subjects in the second term, it is not to give the students exhaustive vocabulary or a thorough understanding of these matters – the idea is ludicrous – but so that they may learn to differentiate between subjects such as the law or economics, where similar words in different countries cover very different concepts, and subjects such as Chemistry, atomic energy etc. where words, the jargon of the milieux concerned, are vital, and have to be learned almost afresh for every meeting.

We do not aim to produce students with a rag-bag collection of partial knowledge, we aim at enabling them to understand the basic interconnection between all the sciences, as well as the cultural man-made differences that have divided them into closed circles, each with their own jargon. It is no use closing the mind to mathematical concepts if one is expected to interpret at meetings on airworthiness or engineering, or refusing to study the second law of thermo-dynamics if required to interpret a meeting on insurance risks.

For their technical lectures, the speaker/students are asked to use the correct technical expressions, to prepare a terminology in their own language combination, which is distributed 24 hours before the lecture and which other students who have to interpret them, will learn before they come to class. They thus learn the importance of preparing for meetings (whether in consecutive or simultaneous). They are not told which books to read or where to go for information, not because of any sadistic tendencies amongst the lecturers, but because they thus learn for themselves to seek out sources of information and find pleasure in their self-reliance.

SIMULTANEOUS INTERPRETATION

Training in simultaneous interpretation begins at the same time as the consecutive. There is a real interaction between the two modes, they both fulfill the same functions – merely, in simultaneous, the immediacy is greater. But this need for translation (and here I refer to language rather than ideas) helps in consecutive note-taking. Young interpreters find it easier to take notes in the language of the speaker, but their task is already half completed if they begin taking notes in the language into which they are going to interpret, and the speed of translation required in simultaneous helps the note-taking process in the other mode of interpretation. The stress engendered by the public nature of consecutive interpretation is somewhat tempered by the aquarium effect of the booths. The anonymity, the pane of glass between the interpreter and the speaker soothes the inhibitions which some students find when working on consecutive. If they are good at simultaneous, some of the self-confidence they acquire in the booth is usually reflected in improved consecutive -- as they improve in consecutive, they understand more easily that careful but rapid analysis of an idea before putting it into words, can contribute to relaxation of the pace in simultaneous.

The first few exercises are intended to teach microphone discipline; how to overcome the initial difficulty of speaking and listening at the same time. Only when they are at home in a booth do we move on to actual translation. Students repeat a series of exercises, all based on conference terminology, in the same language as the speaker. The same texts are used for all languages. So they repeat the exercises until they can then anticipate the speaker. Next, the original will be read in English and they repeat in French and so on. They are not bothered by the language switch at this stage, because they *know* the translation, even though many of the expressions were unknown to them a few days before. It is only when they can comfortably do these exercises, that we give them speeches concerned with procedural matters with the same terminology that they have heard in their exercises, (questions concerning the agenda – the quorum – the method of voting etc.). Suddenly they realise that they are interpreting something new, without too much difficulty. Speeches in which procedure is being used for political ends are then introduced and the easy initiation to simultaneous interpretation has begun.

Through these exercises, they learn fairly painlessly to remember new words and new concepts, to listen and to speak, to use the microphone – it can be compared to an athlete running on the spot to limber up the muscles and to test endurance and breathing before learning the subtleties of long-distance running, pacing, conserving energy, outwitting competitors (in this case the speaker) etc. But in no way are they parrot-like interpretations, which they might be if students had not also heard the translations. When they proceed to speeches which use a terminology they know and have mastered, they get a feeling of accomplishment and it is at this stage that their individual weaknesses begin to show. They are taken in groups of up to 15 students and classes last two hours. Every student records the original speaker and his interpretation on two tracks of the same tape. During the speech no corrections are made by the speaker – but during the listening period, the lecturer can switch in to each individual booth, comment on mistakes, on speed etc. Students are not encouraged to repeat the interpretation immediately, they are told to listen to their own rendering, to switch off the speaker track and only to switch in to that track when their own rendering is incomprehensible. A critical assessment of one's own work is vital to an interpreter and from listening to the playback of their interpretation, students gradually begin to be self-critical at an earlier stage, i.e. during the interpretation itself.

Speeches are carefully chosen and gradually they learn to anticipate, to react to a surprising element in a speech correctly and in a relaxed manner, to improve their style of delivery, to choose alternative words in the other language which are more appropriate to the idea they have to transmit. To the English listener, a beautiful, literate and eloquent rendering of speech is a pleasure, but to the multinational audience who are listening to the English booth a clear, simple rendering may be much more useful.

One of our most serious lacunae in London is the lack of international organisations where students can go and listen to meetings and hear interpreters actually at work. The comments of students for whom we are able to arrange attendance at conferences are very revealing. They have a greater realisation of their role and of the necessity of doing the job well. They realise the importance of apparently tedious procedural rules. Above all, they assess critically the work of colleagues and apply this same criticism to their own.

TEACHING STAFF

Some 30 years ago I lectured for a short time, in the early evening, two or three times a week, always after a long days work as an interpreter. The students were a large group, selected on the basis of their knowledge of languages, but only about 3 of them had any real aptitude for interpreting. This brief experience taught me a triple lesson – 1) there are some things that only a professional can teach, but at the end of the days work in the booth, one is too tired to think a great deal about proper pedagogical methods, 2) in a group of 30, 27 inadequate students make it impossible to train 3 good ones properly, 3) although there are some things that are best taught by experienced professional interpreters, unless that interpreter also knows how to impart his knowledge, and develop skill and ability in others, his students will become but pale reflections of their teacher.

So, when we started the PCL course, I had to make a definite choice between full time teaching and full time interpreting. Fortunately, since the course only lasts six months each year I still have the time to practice my profession, which is essential. Provided we have one language in common, I have found it possible to train interpreters with all sorts of language combinations, with the help of a native speaker to check on accuracy. Each language combination has its own problems, but these can be pinpointed very rapidly. Since it proved impossible in the early stages to find working interpreters who were willing to undertake fixed hours of teaching during the day, we used the excellent services of language teacher colleagues and native speakers to feed material to the simultaneous and consecutive groups. They were all linguists, and therefore able to discuss terminology and meaning with the students, but all matters of actual interpreting techniques were always referred to the only professional on the course.

Last year, for the first time, AIIC interpreters in London formed panels in which one of their number assumed responsibility for ensuring that a member of the panel is available for a two hours lesson, at a fixed time, and we have thus been able to broaden the pool of professional expertise available.

Briefing meetings for lecturers at the beginning and during the course are held. Material on similar subjects are provided by all lecturers throughout the program, so that students do not jump from one subject to another every hour. It is essential that an interesting program, increasing in difficulty and subject matter be observed as students respond better to a logical progression. Our language teacher colleagues at first have a tendency to use texts of speeches that are far too easy, whereas I believe that speeches should always be just that little bit beyond the known skill of the student, they then make the extra effort required, and this gives them a sense of satisfaction and reward when they succeed. No formal language teaching is given during the course.

EXAMINATIONS

The Assessors are always professional interpreters, usually Chief interpreters from the organisations where the candidates' languages will be used. Lecturers on the course may attend, but are not members of the decision-making panel. The Assessors improvise speeches, both for consecutive and simultaneous tests, and in fact these speeches are often more difficult to interpret than those of professional politicians. The speakers have their individual quirks and fancies which they use to test the ability of the candidate to understand. They frequently include some political absurdity, to see the reaction of the student.

Once, when running a short postgraduate course for a particular Government, we were requested to allocate specific weighted marks for 'types of errors', for 'professional behaviour and characteristics', for 'eloquence' etc . . . We tried, but the resulting marking took so long that the time needed for assessment was doubled and the results which we all jotted down as our conclusion immediately after the student left the room, were found on comparison not to differ from the final marking which had been so painfully awarded. The marking was in fact, almost invariably a post factum justification. At PCL a general mark is given to each student after each test, and these serve as the basis for the final award of a diploma or the reverse.

Students have to do one test in each of their A and/or B languages from their B and C languages in consecutive. Failure to pass in consecutive is eliminatory, although we allow candidates to complete the examination without informing them of the preliminary results. The reason for this is to avoid engendering over-confidence or hyper-nervousness in other candidates. They do a double test in simultaneous; one based on improvised speeches by the examiners (there are always 2 speeches) and another based on technical papers in two subjects, which they have chosen from a list given to them about 3 weeks before the examination and for which they have prepared. The purpose is not so much to show that candidates have mastered a particular technical vocabulary, but to demonstrate that they know how to prepare for a technical meeting. One of the technical papers must be either in the field of law or economics.

RESULTS

About two-thirds of our students usually obtain the diploma at the end of the course. If someone has been failed because their third language was considered inadequate, but their technique was good, we recommend a course of work or further study to improve their knowledge of the language and they may attend part of the course again and re-sit. But these cases are rare. Generally the reasons for failure are lack of capacity for endurance, the inability of a student to master his nerves sufficiently to enable him to operate under examination conditions or, occasionally, a genuine inability to acquire the speed of transference required at this level. The inability to overcome nervousness is a decisive factor at this stage. If a candidate cannot do so under examination conditions, he will not be able to perform well in conference conditions.

We have some 146 past students working as professional interpreters. Many are permanent officials in international organizations, or governmental offices and many are free-lance. Some do not make the professional grade, but they are few and the reasons are usually personal – perhaps they do not like the cut and thrust of free-lance life or the routine of the international civil service. Some of the women leave to raise a family and a few find they have to live in countries where there is no demand for their language combination. Most of them stand the test of actual working experience well, but the occasional one appears to have reached a peak at the end of the course which they never succeed in surpassing in day to day conditions, and they are eliminated by the forces of competition.

RESEARCH

Current

I have always wanted to progress from pragmatic selection to proof that we were selecting the right people, or, perhaps an even more worrying thought, that we were not accepting some potentially good material. Our results tend to show that in a positive way our *empirical* selection methods were working reasonably well.

As I have already mentioned, we have been carrying out research on student selection for the past two years. Since the research is still in progress, we do not allow the data to influence our current selection of students in any way. We do, however, hope that eventually other schools will join us in research on selection techniques.

THE FUTURE

To test for language knowledge, rapidity of understanding, short term memory are all relatively easy, but we need to go a step further and to pinpoint those who will continue to work well when constantly under control of an outside will (the speaker) – but possess the large measure of self-control required for constant concentration.

Many students find it hard to do without some of the academic crutches they have been taught to use (the written word, a text, a certain way of expressing their own thoughts and reactions) or, even worse, they hesitate to commit themselves to a word or an idea for fear of criticism. We would need to know the psychological consequences for some students of having to make that extra and constant effort to do something which is just a bit too difficult, and for which their usual supports are lacking, or why others are thrown off course by their sudden realisation that they are capable of doing something really well. There are some individuals for whom, I believe, (but I cannot prove it as yet), interpretation is dangerous; it can emphasise and activate all sorts of personality problems, whereas there are other individuals whom it stabilises and enables them to work out their difficulties of adjustment to society. Any work done on actors might provide some material. There is also the problem of longer-term frustration in a job with little prospect of promotion or change, where you reach a high level at an early stage, but need other qualifications to transfer to another field at the same level. A serious program for the integration of newcomers into the profession is badly needed, especially in the free-lance field, where too many have to undergo traumatic experiences due to the fears and conceits of established colleagues which expresses itself in unwelcoming behavior or downright unpleasantness.

In the language teaching field, there is the desperate need to research how best to teach people the difference between speaking and understanding a language, whilst at the same time enabling them to speak the language well and without inhibitions. Some real research on the effects of many years of translation courses on future students of interpretation is also an area which could be covered. How much of it helps and at what stage does it become a hindrance?

CONCLUSION

To summarise – we believe and have acted on the belief – that to train interpreters is to train young people to open their minds not only to language but to jargon – not only to words, but to ideas, to be interested in the people who are expressing these ideas, to try to understand their motives and the probable consequences. Only then can they really hope to enjoy this profession and put up with the physical discomfort of sitting constantly in a confined booth, of never working at their own pace but at a rhythm dictated by the speakers, and with the intellectual disappointment of making a real effort to understand a subject at least superficially, and at the point one is beginning to get a grasp of it, the meeting is over.

I once interpreted Jean Louis Barrault who said, inter alia:

> "My ambition is to ensure that at the end of a performance of Hamlet the audience will say not 'I've just seen Barrault's Hamlet', but 'I have just understood Shakespeare's Hamlet'. The sort of interpreters we hope we train are the ones about whose performance delegates will say not "that was a wonderful interpretation" – but "that was a very good speech".

The Role of Oral Language in the Evolution of Manual Language

Harlan Lane and Robbin Battison

Northeastern University

Boston

An examination of various French and English documents of the 18th and 19th century, especially reports, articles and books written by instructors of the deaf in Europe and the U.S. throws light on the conditions under which and the ways in which manual language evolved over the last two hundred years. This inquiry has revealed the following: (1) Manual languages in the U.S., France, and Italy (among other countries) have been subject to systematic efforts at annihilation by the dominant (oral) language group. (2) In this, they are like other minority languages such as Basque, Catalan, Canadian French, etc. (3) Efforts at annihilation take two forms – dialectizing a language (Provençal in France) or outright replacement (American Indian Languages in the U.S.). With regard to manual communication in the U.S., the former approach is called "Signed English", the latter "oralism". (4) Both ways of annihilating sign have been attempted in the 18th and 19th centuries, generally in alternation, using the schools as a vehicle, and with little lasting effect. (5) Intrusions from oral language that remain in ASL can often be detected because of their lack of pictorial roots. It is hypothesized that all formational, morphological and syntactic processes in ASL that do not have a pictorial basis are either the result of extrinsic oral language forces or the intrinsic evolution from iconicity to encodedness.

LINGUISTIC SOLIPSISM AND THE REPRESSION OF SIGN LANGUAGE

There is no more fundamental truth, nor any more self-evident, concerning the deaf of the nations represented here today than this: they are a linguistic minority; their second language is that of the oral majority and their primary language is their sign language. From this fact, so often overlooked or denied, follow the major givens of the deaf condition: their cruel ostracism and oppression by the oral language majority, their low standing economically and socially, their effective exclusion from most higher education and their segregation in compulsory education; likewise, the concerted effort, for nearly a century, to annihilate their languages. No imperial power has as ruthlessly suppressed the language of its colonized peoples, no state has as systematically sought to undermine a linguistic minority within its borders, as the hearing people in our several nations have sought to deny, denigrate, and disbar the manual languages of the deaf.

How successful has this campaign proved? In the U.S. for example, eighty percent of the American deaf are engaged in manual or unskilled labor; thirty percent cannot read and write English. American Sign Language is prohibited in most schools for the deaf; it is rarely taught as a foreign language in our colleges and even more rarely does it satisfy the requirement to learn a second language; unlike Spanish, Russian, Latin, and Chinese, for example, it is never taught in our elementary or high schools. It is a remarkable fact, therefore, that American Sign Language and Italian vie for second place as the most populous minority languages in the U.S., with an estimated half-million Americans using each. Yet most Americans are ignorant of ASL and those who are not are, with rare exception, prejudiced against it.

How do we explain such linguistic bigotry? One might as well ask how to explain the resistance to French among English-speaking Canadians, to Basque among Spanish speakers, to Tamil among Hindi speakers, and so on. The natural state of man is linguistic solipsism: my language is the only true language; all others are impoverished and cumbersome – in fact, not true languages at all. Mark Twain held a mirror to this ignoble side of our character in an exchange between Huckleberry Finn and his pal Jim; Huck is defending the strange way of speaking of their French friend, Froggy:

> "Looky here, Jim; ain't it natural and right for a cat and a cow to talk different from us?"
>
> "Why, mos' sholy it is."
>
> "Well, then, why ain't it natural and right for a Frenchman to talk different from us? You answer me that".
>
> "Is a cat a man, Huck?"
>
> "No".
>
> "Well, den, dey ain't no sense in a cat talkin' like a man. Is a cow a man" – er is a cow a cat?"
>
> "No, she ain't either of them".
>
> "Well, den she ain't got no business to talk like either one er the yuther of em. Is a Frenchman a man?"
>
> "Yes".
>
> "Well, den! Dad blame it, why doan' he talk like a man? You answer me dat!"

Education alone is not a sure cure for linguistic solipsism. As distinguished a scholar as Diderot argued that the study of French structure could reveal principles of thought, because the order of words in French corresponds to the order in which they arise in the mind. Similarly, an instructor of the deaf at the New York Institute wrote: "(We must) change signs into the English order . . . I believe the adjective should come before the noun, that the substantive should come before the verb – just the same in the sign language as the written language . . . Let the signs be used as nearly as possible in the order in which we think" (Valentine, 1870, p. 58). Napoleon exclaimed to the Abbé Sicard, the great 19th century instructor of the French deaf, that sign language had only nouns and adjectives and Sicard's contemporary, the founder of otology and instructor of the Wild Boy of Aveyron, Jean-Marc Itard, villified signs as:

> "that barbaric language without pronouns, without conjunctions, without any of the words that permit us to express abstract ideas, which provides only a vague collection of adjectives, nouns, and a few verbs, without determinate time and always in the infinitive (Blanchet, 1850, p. 96). For example, instead of the sentence 'Would you like us to water your garden this evening', the signs say only 'We, this evening, to water garden you' (Itard, 1826, cited in Lane, 1976, p. 228)."

These examples make clear how misleading word-for-sign transliterations can be and remind us that the translator, in choosing between transliteration and translating, not only communicates information but shapes attitudes.

Linguistic solipsism will not explain, however, why sign languages are singled out for particular repression among minority languages. At least three other considerations come into play. First, if the language bigot is abetted by the mismatch between the structure of the foreign language and his own, how much greater is that mismatch, and how much more grievously will he be misled therefore, when the foreign language is in another mode – manual-visual, rather that oral-auditory? We propose to show that the structural mechanisms of sign language are appropriate to its singular mode: Itard and thousands of oral language users since him would have found their precious time markers, question markers, conjunctions, reference and co-reference markers and so on, if they had only known where to look. The long-delayed development of sign language interpreting as a profession allowed the illusion that there was nothing much to translate in this strange pantomime, or, worse, that a series of English glosses for the signs indeed constituted a translation.

If the language itself was too alien to be accorded equal status with our own, its speakers, on the other hand, were too like us to be accorded their own language. Only two kinds of people, after all, fail to use your language properly: foreigners and retardates. The deaf clearly were not the former. They did not come from some other land, like the French, nor visibly constitute a distinct community in our own, like the Cajuns. Therefore, they cannot have their own language and their failure to use ours properly, like that of a retarded person, can only be the result of faulty intellect. The errors that the deaf student makes in writing English were viewed not as a product of second-language learning – that is, as a result of interference from his first language and overextension of the rules of the language he is acquiring – but rather as a product of defective cognition (but see Charrow, 1974 and Charrow and Wilbur, 1975). In the U.S., the same federal agencies that support research on the English of retardates support research on the English of the American deaf, whereas those agencies that support research on the English language skills of Spanish, French, and other language minorities exclude the deaf. Government's tendency to view the deaf as dim-witted since they are not foreign has a long history. When President Monroe made his tour through the New England states in the summer of 1817, he stopped at Hartford to visit the institution for the deaf which had just been founded by Thomas Gallaudet and Laurent Clerc. Gallaudet had met Clerc at the Abbé Sicard's famous school for the deaf in Paris where Clerc was a professor; he was captivated as much by the deaf Frenchman's urbanity as by his fluency in the sign language and he contracted with him to return to the U.S. to disseminate sign language and to instruct the deaf. The newspaper *Portfolio* for January 1817 announces that Clerc has arrived in Boston:

> "and has excited a deep interest in all of our fellow citizens to which he has been introduced not only from his condition and the sauvity of his deportment, but for the eminent attainments of his mind – his knowledge of the sciences and acquaintance with the English language – exhibited in the various answers he instantly gives to all questions propounded to him (p. 85)."

Gallaudet and Clerc were seated beside President Monroe on a raised platform overlooking the institution. Spectators were on all sides. "If your excellency will be so kind as to ask some question", Gallaudet said, "I will repeat it to Mr Clerc on my hands and he will write an answer on the slate to show the manner and facility of conversation by signing". Gallaudet had astutely chosen interpreting as a way of convincing the President that sign language was indeed a language. Let our contemporary author report what happened:

> "Everybody expected something profound – equal to the occasion, and worthy of the chief magistrate of the greatest nation on the face of the globe. We waited a long time, every minute seeming an hour, through our impatience. At last it became awkward, and Mr Gallaudet [repeated his offer].
>
> The President again changed the position of his legs, and again meditated. We all supposed he was at the very bottom of the abyss of philosophy, hunting up some most profound and startling interrogation. Expectation was on tiptoe; every eye was levelled at the oracular lips, about to utter the amazing proposition. Still, he only meditated. A long time passed, and the impatience became agonizing. Again Mr Gallaudet, seeming to fear that the great man was going to sleep, roused him by repeating his request. The President at last seemed conscious; his eye twinkled, his lips moved, sounds issued from his mouth –"
>
> "Ask him – how old he is!" – was the profound suggestion. (Goodrich, 1857, p. 128).

This tendency to view the deaf as having no language rather than having one primary and one second language is abetted by the fact that, in varying degrees and at various stages of life, their hearing became impaired. Many deaf persons define the sensory privation as one of relatively small moment in itself. Their disastrous privation is their exclusion from society at large because of their language. In identifying the deaf as handicapped, a term we do not normally use for Spanish-speaking Americans for example, a problem in bilingualism is disguised as one in medicine and the failure of the oral majority to come to grips with a minority language is disguised as a constitutional flaw in that minority. The deaf are indeed handicapped, but it is a handicap entirely within our power to remove. It is born of an age old ignorance, linguistic solipsism, the mystical belief in the primacy of one's own language, which must be conquered throughout the world before any nation can be truly indivisible, before groups of nations can be truly allied. The interpreter has a critical role to play in this struggle.

In recent years, linguists and psychologists have pursued the systematic analysis of American Sign Language as a means of gaining insight into the nature of all language. They have studied its rules of lexical formation, of morphology, and of syntax, its stylistics, poetics and social interface to see in what ways the language bears the hallmarks of its particular modality and in what ways, on the contrary, it is like oral language, thus implicating processes more deeply rooted in the human mind. In the same way, we propose to show today that a careful examination of the evolution of manual language in the environment of the majority oral language can give us insight into more general phenomena of bilingualism, in particular the mechanisms of linguistic annihilation. Interpreters will need these insights if they are to combat linguistic solipsism effectively. For this historical examination, we must be equipped with a precis of the major structural features of American Sign Language.

AMERICAN SIGN LANGUAGE

What do linguists find in American Sign Language? ASL has a multilevelled grammar, and each part is to some extent interdependent with the other parts. Let us begin with the unfamiliar by discussing articulation of the signal itself. Instead of building a linguistic analysis on the articulatory aspects of glottal state, and position of the lips, velum, and tongue, or the frequencies, amplitudes, and durations of the resulting acoustic spectra, we are dealing with language in a manual-visual medium. The visual signal transmitted consists of spatial configurations of body parts (primarily hands and arms) changing through time. But charting such movements, as on a time-dependent graph, would be extremely cumbersome for discussions of grammatical properties. We need categories or units of activity which have some viability at different levels of the grammar. Here we are indebted to William Stokoe, who more than fifteen years ago outlined the major parameters needed to describe the essential qualities of signs in ASL (Stokoe, 1960). He developed a transcription system which coded the location of a sign (articulated in space or in contact with some part of the body), the handshapes or hand configurations of the sign, the movement made by the hands or arms, and the orientation of the hands with respect to each other or with respect to the body. Each sign must be specified for these four simultaneously occurring elements. (CHINESE[2] and SOUR contrast only in location, BLACK and SUMMER in handshape, FATHER and GRANDFATHER in movement, PREACH and PEPPER in orientation. [Figs 1 - 8]).

Stokoe's purposes were to provide a transcription system and the foundation

Figure 1.

SOUR. Extended index finger tip contacts chin and twists repeatedly.

Figure 2.

CHINESE. Same as SOUR, but location is the temple.

Figure 3.

I/ME. Index tip touches chest.

Figure 4.

COMPLAIN. Tip of all five bent and extended fingers contact the chest (the single sharp movement depicted here is emphatic; citation form is normally a repeated action).

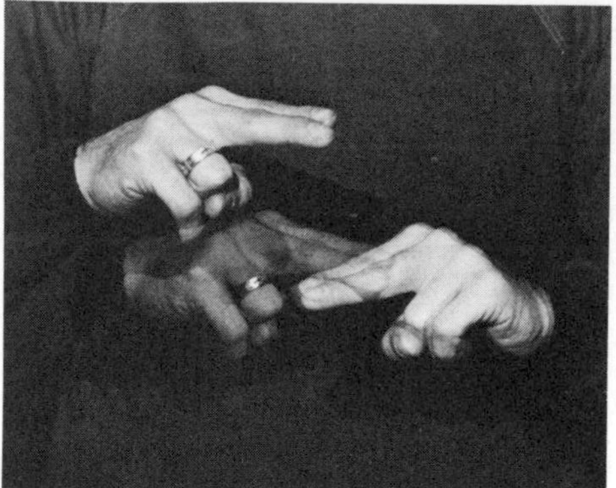

Figure 5.

SIT/CHAIR. Index and mid finger extended from each hand; one hand moves down to make contact along fingers.

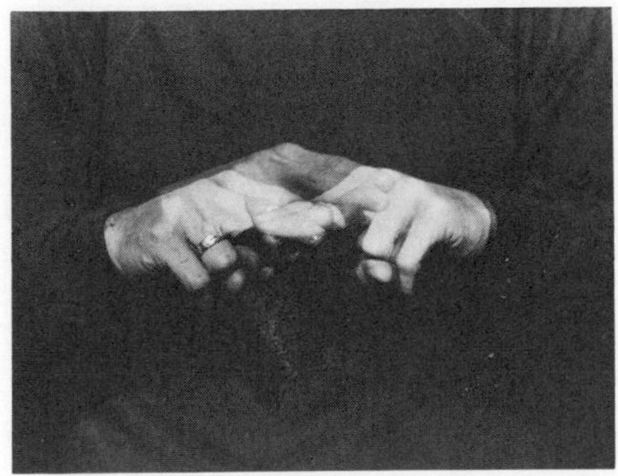

Figure 6.

TRAIN (railroad). Same as SIT/CHAIR, but repeated sliding contact along fingers.

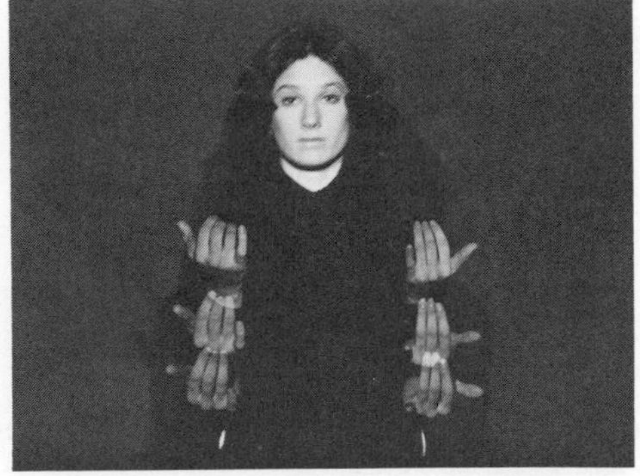

Figure 7.

NOW. Thumb and little finger extended from palm-up fists, the hands move downwards.

Figure 8.

STAY. Same as NOW, but palms face downward.

Figure 9.

DAY. Forearm makes one sweeping arc, ending horizontally.

Figure 10.

TWO-DAYS. Same as DAY, but with index and mid finger extended.

Figure 11.

HURT. Hands with extended index converge and diverge repeatedly.

Figure 12.

HEADACHE. Same as HURT, but location is in front of the forehead.

Figure 13.

I-SHOW-YOU. Hands move forward while index tip of one hand contacts palm of the other. YOU-SHOW-ME is identical but for the direction,which is towards the signer.

(Note: The model's somber expressions are not natural accompaniments to these signs, but are dictated by the photographic method employed.)

of a formational analysis of signs. Using this analysis as a point of departure, linguists have noted restrictions on the co-occurrence of combining elements and have sought to account for them with either morpheme structure constraints or structure-changing rules analogous to phonological rules. One such constraint, for example, the Dominance Condition, holds that simple sign morphemes made with two hands with different handshapes must have one hand static and one hand active, and the static hand must be specified for one of the six least marked handshapes, (e.g. FLATTER, PRINT, ENOUGH, GET-INTO-VEHICLE; Battison, 1974, in press). The thrust of this and similar morpheme structure conditions is that ASL (and undoubtedly other sign languages as well) has discrete inventories of formational units which can be assembled in restricted ways. One guiding principle of this restricting tendency is to limit both the articulatory and perceptual complexity of the signal. This is a principle familiar to linguists from treatments of spoken languages.

Turning from the formational or "phonological" aspects of signs to the morphology of ASL, we encounter a surprise: although individual signs in ASL take longer to articulate than individual words in English, information is conveyed at similar rates in the two languages (Bellugi and Fischer, 1972; Klima and Bellugi, in press). The explanation appears to lie in the contrast between the linear temporal nature of English and other spoken languages and the spatial and simultaneous nature of ASL and other sign languages. English distributes much grammatical information over time that ASL packs into each individual sign. Phonemes and morphemes of English are linearly concatenated as they form larger and larger meaning-bearing units; those of ASL occur more or less simultaneously. But the contrast between concatenation and modulation extends beyond phonology and morphology to syntax and discourse. In fact, much of the difference between speaking and signing a language and, ultimately, much of the cross-language interference and translation difficulty, owes itself to this difference in channel characteristics for encoding information. An examination of some of the more common morphological and syntactic properties of ASL should illustrate how it distributes information spatially instead of linearly.

1. *Conflation/incorporation.* There are many examples of concepts rendered in English as a string of separate lexical items, or as a lexicalized string of morphemes, that are represented in ASL as a single sign, albeit polymorphemic. Signs relating to (calendrical) units of time are particularly good examples, since they frequently incorporate a numeral by varying the handshapes. Thus the sign DAY (Fig. 9) can be made into TWO-DAY (Fig. 10), THREE-DAY, etc. MONTH becomes TWO-MONTH, WEEK becomes FOUR-WEEK. ASL also has classifiers marked with handshapes which, as part of a sign, represent conventionalized morphological and semantic information. For example, the person-classifier (G)[3] is used in many signs denoting personal encounters: MEET, the reduplicated MEET-MANY-PEOPLE, PERSON-COMES-UP-TO-ME, PERSON-GOES-AWAY-FROM-ME, FLATTER, etc. There are also classifiers for moving vehicles (3), stationary objects (A), and flat objects (B), all of which take a productive role in ASL morphology.

2. *Location.* The use of spatial dimensions also allows the signer to encode

concepts non-linearly. The signer may articulate signs in space in order to represent their spatial arrangement in the real world. Such concepts as relative distance, proximity to the signer, and the nature of the interaction of two objects may be shown by establishing a "map" of the real world with the hands. For example, one can sign HURT in space (Fig. 11), or one can inflect it spatially to make the signs HEADACHE (Fig. 12) or STOMACH–ACHE.

Likewise, pronominal reference and anaphora in general takc advantage of the space available for articulation. I and YOU are executed by pointing to the signer and receiver(s), respectively. Third persons are pointed to if present, and if not present are assigned a spatial locus which may be pointed whenever reference is desired. Thus, although ASL does not mark gender on its anaphora, it can distinguish several third-person referents.

"He gave it to him while he looked on", while ambiguous in English, is unambiguous in ASL, because each unique third person would have a separate spatial locus in signing the utterance.

3. *Directionality of movement and orientation.* Because objects and anaphora are articulated with spatial loci in ASL, predicate relationships (verbs and adjectives) can be spatially modified to agree with their arguments, or make specific the relationships of various noun phrases to the predicate. For example, by establishing "my brother" on the left and "my sister" on the right, one then attributes various qualities unambiguously to one or the other by making signs either to the left or to the right. The signer can also modify the orientation or direction of many verb signs to make explicit the subject and object of the verb. For example, I-SHOW-YOU is one sign, moving outward from the signer YOU-SHOW-ME moves inward toward the signer (Fig. 13). "My brother shows my sister" can be rendered as one sign which moves from left to right, in accordance with the spatial relationships and loci established for these referents within the discourse. Other verbs that may be spatially inflected for subject and object include: GIVE, NAME, PREACH, SAY-NO, ASK, HATE, MOCK, and many more.

4. *Movement modulation.* Perhaps an even richer (and as yet, largely unexplored) set of spatial inflections involves systematically changing the movement of a sign. Plurals, for example, are not denoted by a separate signing affix in ASL, but often by repetition of movement, and in other cases by indefinite or definite quantifiers. Nouns and verbs are also distinguished by repetition (e.g., NAME vs. TO NAME and CHAIR vs. TO SIT, Supalla and Newport, in press). Bellugi and Pedersen (in Klima and Bellugi, 1977) have found that temporal aspects of sign predicates are often encoded by a complex set of movement modifications internal to the sign itself – that is, without affixes. These investigators distinguish movements which encode inceptive, resultative, frequentative, habitual, durative, incessant and other aspects of predicates.

5. *Discourse markers.* While verb aspects may be complexly coded using movements, verb tense is handled in an entirely separate way, but still without

sign affixes. There do exist signs WILL/FUTURE, PAST/AGO, NOW/PRESENT, FINISH/PERFECTIVE, and UP-TILL-NOW/CONTINUOUS. Overt tense marking, however, rarely employs the signs PAST or FUTURE. Instead, separate or incorporated time adverbials (RECENTLY, NEXT-WEEK, LAST-YEAR) are often used to establish time reference at the beginning of a discourse, and thereafter time indicators are used largely to indicate changes of tense within a discourse. There simply is no need to mark every verb for tense. The receiver will also rely on context in determining temporal relationships of verb structures.

Question formation is dealt with primarily through specific question formatives such as WHAT, WHY, WHAT-FOR, and HOW, which may frequently appear copied to sentence-final position, and – especially for yes-no questions – by accompanying facial expressions, changes in eye-gaze, and prolongation of the sentence-final sign. There are no specific inversions or verbal auxiliaries, as in English.

The question of order is an important one for considering the relations between spoken and signed languages. Since it uses space to encode lexical units and the grammatical relations between them, ASL is less constrained to use sign order for the same purposes. For example, the three signs HORSE, COW, and KICK might be arranged in any order in an ASL sentence, and the subject-object relations specifying who was kicking whom would be unambiguously coded using spatial loci and directions. Order is relatively free, although there may be preferred orders. One such observed preference is the tendency to place nouns before their modifiers, rather than the reverse, as in English. This may be one specific case of a more general tendency to adhere to topic-comment ordering in constructing sign sentences.

Just as we have been at pains to distinguish sharply between the structural principles of American Sign Language and English, so we must equally distinguish ASL and pantomime. People often approach sign language for the first time with the belief that it is highly mimetic and hence universal. Neither is true. To dispel the impression that sign is for the most part transparently iconic, you need only watch a few minutes of signing, even at reduced speed, and compare your guess with an accurate translation. Likewise, historically unrelated sign languages, such as American and British sign language, are mutually unintelligible. Having dispelled these myths, we should hasten to restore a little of the true complexity of affairs by pointing out that sign has its roots in mimesis, that signers use mime interwoven with sign language in communication and that consequently, signers from different lands have somewhat more success in communicating than would be predicted purely from a comparison of their two languages.

WAYS OF ANNIHILATING A LANGUAGE
PART I: Dialectization

Speakers of a dominant language have two ways of attempting to annihilate a nondominant language: replacing it outright or dialectizing it. In the latter case, they lead the users of the nondominant language to believe that theirs is a substandard dialect of the dominant language, a "vernacular" which should not be employed for serious purposes such as education or government. It has generally been thought that the nondominant language could be dialectized only if it was related to the dominant language. Kloss contrasts the cases of Basque and Catalan:

> "So the Spanish government, in trying to establish and maintain the monopoly of Castilian Spanish must (and does) try to blot out the Basque language completely, for there is no possibility that the Basques will ever lose consciousness of the fact that their language is unrelated to Spanish. The position of Catalan is quite different, because both Catalan and Spanish are Romance Languages. There is a chance that speakers of Catalan can be induced to consider their mother tongue as a patois, with Castilian as its natural standard language. As a matter of fact this attitude to Catalan is already to be found not in Catalonia proper but in the province of Valencia and in the Balearic islands. In a similar manner, nearly all speakers of Low Saxon (Low German) and the overwhelming majority of Occitan (Provencal) speakers have lost consciousness of their linguistic identity and consider their folk speech as naturally subordinated to German and French respectively, though linguists continue to group these folk languages with other Gothic and Romance Languages. The spiritual subjugation of speakers of Sardinian, and of Haitan Creole is no less complete. (1967, p 46)"

At first it might seem improbable that people whose native language is American Sign Language could be induced to consider their mother tongue as a patois, with English as their natural standard language; the two are as unrelated as any two languages could be. From time to time the oral majority has, however, waged such a campaign, using deaf educational institutions as the vehicle for indoctrination. The fact that such efforts have never had longlasting effects has not prevented renewed attempts at long intervals: what we learn from history, as Shaw pointed out, is that we do not learn from history. Unhappily, we are currently witnessing such a program of dialectization in which one or another version of Manual English is taught in the schools. All versions have in common that they utilize some signs from American Sign Language as root morphemes and then inflect them in accord with English morphology by adding invented sign suffixes for tense, number, etc. It is doubtful that any deaf student ever objected that this was unnecessary as he understood time, number, and so on perfectly well in the unaltered language. Manual English goes on to invent signs for pronouns, prepositions, conjunctions -- all of the appurtenances of the well-equipped language; never mind that the time to sign a message has been doubled; that there was no need for all this apparatus, sign language having its own genius to conduct its grammatical housekeeping: utilizing space, direction of movement, handshapes, and facial expression among other means. Manual English goes on to declare that the order of the signs shall be in the order of English and that sign shall also adopt the semantics of English; no matter that often one word in English subserves several concepts for which there are several signs, so that whichever one sign is adopted it is generally incongruous. Can speakers of a visual language ever be induced to believe that such a contortion of their native tongue, annihilating its basic principles, is in fact a language of which they speak a substandard dialect? Yes indeed. Some deaf people refer to their sign language as "low verbal", "broken language" or as "slang." A deaf friend of ours referred to her signing in ASL as "low sign"; for her, "high sign" was Manual English. Other informants have referred to ASL as "broken English", or "bad English", or "broken language".

The following are instructions to a language bigot intent on dialectizing American Sign Language. Equally, they are the inverse of instructions to a good translator. All versions of Manual English attempt to linearize signing and make it correspond as closely as possible to English structures, despite the overwhelming evidence that ASL (and other sign languages) has evolved in particular directions because of the gestural-spatial medium in which it is articulated.

1. Place the signs in the order of English words, not in the order appropriate to ASL. As order doesn't seem to matter to ASL signers, they won't complain.

2. Inflate the number of separate signs used in a sentence by lexicalizing what would be conflated in ASL; use the uninflected citation forms of the signs. (If the ASL sign incorporates an intensifier, perhaps by modifying movement, lexicalize it to a sign like VERY, MANY, etc. followed by the original sign. Likewise, lexicalize the ASL if it incorporates numerical or aspectual information; the single sign THREE-ENTIRE-WEEK, "for three entire weeks", becomes in Sign English the four separate signs FOR THREE FULL WEEK, which matches the lexical content and order of the English phrase. Or if content is specified by non-manual components, such as eye gaze or postural body shifts, lexicalize it to an appropriate sign. For example, the conjunctions "and", "or", "but", and "if-then" are often encoded in ASL using spatial loci, specific facial expressions, and/or postural shifts. That is all too complicated, just lexicalize each case with separate signs for "but", "or", etc. Pronouns like YOU, I/ME should be lexicalized separately, even when they are encoded by the direction or orientation of the verb. When there is no uninflected form of the verb, settle on the form which normally incorporates "I" as subject and "you" as object, however confusing.)

3. Do not use ASL signs that are hard to translate into English, or that strictly depend upon an ASL grammatical context for translation.

4. Use only signs that correspond to English words in the range of their meaning; ASL has no semantics of its own. A lack of correspondence calls on your inventiveness. On the one hand, English may make valuable distinctions that ASL is too impoverished to capture. You are free to make up additional signs *de novo* but a common remedy is to "initialize" an existing sign – add a fingerspelling handshape to it that corresponds to the first letter of the English word you have in mind. Replace the handshape of HABIT, for example, with that for spelling U and let that mean "used-to" (i.e., "accustomed"); or with that for T and let that mean "traditional". Initializing is fun and can only help reveal correspondences with English so you may wish to use it even when you are satisfied with the ASL sign. On the other hand, there are cases where English captures a generalization in a single word that ASL obscures by needlessly proliferating signs. For example, ASL has quite distinct signs for "look for", "look up", and "look like". Select one and use it in all cases, adding the appropriate sign in each case for "for", "up", "like", etc.

5. Invent signs for functors and derivational and inflectional morphemes.

ASL doesn't inflect *anything*, and is in desparate need of articles, tense and aspect markings, form class markers, plurals, gender-differentiated pronouns, etc. Invent separate signs for "-ing", "-ly", "-ment", "-tion", etc.

6. Translate idioms and compounds directly into sign literally, sign-for-word. "I can't stand it", "fire away!", "drive me crazy", and "all washed up" are particularly good and confusing.

7. When all else fails, fingerspell English words.

The first attempt by the oral majority to dialectize sign language occurred, interestingly enough at the same time that the essential conditions for the propagation of the language were created. The name of Charles Michel, Abbé de l'Epée is associated with both developments in mid-18th century France. On the one hand, Epée was impressed by the medium of communication that had grown up between two deaf sisters he was asked to instruct and he undertook to learn from them. He offered them bread and obtained the sign for eat; water, and obtained that for drink; pointing to objects nearby he learned the names they applied to each. Soon, he could hold a conversation with them. As the class of his pupils grew, what were originally "home signs" became the signs used by a small community. On the other hand, Epée's goal was to teach his pupils to read and write French. To accomplish this, he invented what we can term "Signed French". "we chose first", he explains "the signs of the three persons singular and plural because that is easiest. Then we go on to the tenses and moods and we gave to each of them signs which connoisseurs find simple and natural, hence easy to remember" (Epée, 1784). The connoisseurs, significantly, are his deaf pupils, as his description of how he chose tense-markers makes clear:

> "The pupil, though Deaf and Dumb, had like us, an idea of the past, the present, and the future, before he was placed under our tuition, and was at no loss for signs to manifest the difference.
>
> Did he mean to express a present action? He made a sign prompted by nature, which we all make in the same case without being conscious of it, and which consists in appealing to the eyes of the spectators to witness the presence of our operation; but if the action did not take place in his sight, he laid his two hands flat upon the table, bearing upon it gently, as we are all apt to do on similar occasions: and these are the signs he learns again in our lessons, by which to indicate the Present of a verb.
>
> Did he design to signify that an action is past? He tossed his hand carelessly two or three times over his shoulder: these signs we adopt to characterize the past tenses of a verb.
>
> And lastly, when it was intent to announce a future action, he projected his right hand: here again is a sign we give to him to represent the Future of a verb (Epée, 1784, p. 22 of the 1860 translation).

In addition to requiring signs for affixes, articles, prepositions, conjunctions and so on, Epée found his little community short of signs for various root morphemes in French. In this case he used one of two strategies: if the meaning of the word immediately suggested a sign to his pupils, he seized upon it. If it did not then he analyzed the word as a combination of simpler concepts each of which was associated with a sign. Thus, for example, the word "believe" was analyzed as the sum of "know" plus "feel" plus "say" plus "not see" and it was signed by executing the corresponding four signs and that for "verb" – all, as the good abbot puts it, "in the twinking of an eye". Once his deaf pupils learned the written word that corresponded to each sign, they had no difficulty in signing a written text or in transcribing such signs into writing. Indeed, it was a matter of little importance what the written language was – Italian, Latin, Spanish, French (as long as it was a Romance language) – since it was not a question of translating but merely of transliterating. This was too fine a distinction to make out at the dawn of the education of the deaf and Epée's annual demonstrations drew hordes of laymen, scholars, and royalty alike; the last, in 1774, was attended by eight hundred people in two sittings, including a score of disciples who mastered the signed French and returned to their cities scattered over Western Europe – from Copenhagen to Rome, from Amsterdam to Zurich – to found similar schools.

Epée's school grew to 68 pupils by 1783 (Peet, 1857, p. 295) and when, on his death in 1789, it was declared a National Institution for Deaf-Mutes, it numbered over one hundred. With the founding of a veritable deaf society in the midst of Paris, the sign language grew by accretion. Epée's successor, Sicard, promises us a dictionary but notes that the particular signs are not critical to his method of instruction and, in any event, were not invented by him.

> "It is not I who am to invent these signs. I have only to set forth the theory of them under the dictation of their true inventors, those whose language consists of these signs. It is for the deaf-and-dumb to make them, and for me to tell how they are made. They must be drawn from the nature of the objects they are to represent. It is only the signs given by the mute himself to express the actions which he witnesses, and the objects which are brought before him, which can replace articulate language. (1803, p. xiv)"

Speaking of his celebrated deaf-and-dumb pupil, Massieu, he says:

> "Thus, by a happy exchange, as I taught him the written signs of our language, Massieu taught me the mimic signs of his . . . So it must be said that it is neither I nor my admirable master (the Abbé de l'Epée) who is the inventor of the deaf-and-dumb language. And as a foreigner is not fit to teach a Frenchman French, so the speaking man has no business to meddle with the invention of signs, giving them abstract values. (1803, pp. 18 - 19)"

Although Sicard, as Epée before him, turned to his deaf pupils for aid in elaborating Signed French, the fact remains that his central purpose was to create a signed variety of French, to dialectize the evolving sign language of the deaf community (let us call it FSL) by imposing the grammar of spoken French and the ideology that signing unmodified – without "method" as they called it – was not a language at all. It was Signed French that Clerc taught to Gallaudet during their nearly two month's voyage to the U.S. – although they "reformed certain signs which we thought would not well suit American manners and customs" (Clerc cited in Barnard, 1852, p 106). Gallaudet and Clerc must also have introduced reforms to suit the different grammar of English. For a little more than a decade, while Signed French was taught in Paris, Bordeaux, Rouen and so on, Signed English was taught in Hartford – and then New York, Kentucky, Pennsylvania and so on. Clerc taught this language not only to the seven deaf pupils with whom the Hartford Asylum opened, and to the rapidly growing numbers of pupils who came in their wake, but also to the hearing professors who left to found one school after another throughout the United States and to disseminate Signed English. In an early report of the Hartford Asylum, Gallaudet writes that:

> "The instructors, by a constant familiar intercourse with the deaf and dumb, and still more by means of the daily lectures on the language of signs which have been given by their ingenious and experienced associate, Mr Clerc, have made such attainments in the acquisition of the principles of this science, that they hope very soon to become masters of their profession and thus to secure its advantages beyond the danger of loss. (1819b, p 5)"

While the rules of English grammar were respected in the classroom, we can be sure that they were not respected outside. Two years after the founding of the Asylum, Gallaudet wrote:

> "A successful teacher of the deaf and dumb should be thoroughly acquainted both with their own peculiar mode of expressing their ideas by signs and also with that of expressing the same ideas by those methodical signs which in their arrangement correspond to the structure of written language. For the natural language of this singular class of beings has its appropriate style and structure. They use it in their unrestrained communication with each other, [it is marked by] great abruptness, ellipses, and inversion of expression. . . . To take a familiar example . . . "You must not eat that fruit, it will make you feel unwell". . . . In [the deaf's] own language of signs, literally translated, it would be thus "Fruit that you eat, you unwell, you eat no". (1819a, p 785).

It gradually became clear, on both sides of the Atlantic, that the effort to dialectize sign language was unsuccessful and that precious class time was lost in attempting to teach Signed English and Signed French. In Paris, Sicard had learned from Epée's attempts that merely translating a French sentence into Signed French did not assist its understanding; therefore the meaning of each sentence was first explained in FSL. It remained only for Sicard's intellectual successor, Bebian, to propose dropping the intermediate step and using FSL as the language of the school as well as of everyday life. When, in 1830, the New York Institution sent their director to Paris to return with a Clerc of their own, they obtained Leon Vaisse, a hearing professor, who proceeded to introduce Bebian methods. Their Fifteenth Annual Report in 1834 described methodical signs as "wholly discarded".

> "The method of Sicard in constructing his system of methodical signs, was, first, to define or illustrate each new word, by means of a group of colloquial or *natural* signs, (as they are, not very properly, called) constituting something like a circumlocution in speech; and from a consideration of this group, to devise some brief sign, named a *sign of reduction*, to stand as the

representative of the whole. His published dictionary, denominated by him the "*theory of sign*", is composed wholly of such definitions, unaccompanied however, by corresponding signs of reduction; and is, therefore, as we are informed by M. Degerando, far from conveying a correct idea of his practice.

Our American schools have hitherto pursued the system of Sicard, making methodical signs the great dependence in instruction. But it has been only for words of most frequent occurrence, that signs, strictly methodical, have been instituted. Beyond this limit the complex sign, the circumlocution has been retained without reduction, while the plan of *verbatim* translation or dictation having been still pursued, the system has failed of that lightness, simplicity, and that adaptation to the purposes of rapid execution, which its theory presumes: it has become unwieldy in its material, and burdensome in its use; retarding the labors of the instructor, and seriously impeding the progress of the pupil.

As an instrument of instruction, therefore, methodical signs have been abandoned in the New York Institution. The means, on which the principal reliance is now placed, are the language of action, so far as it is in familiar use, writing, symbolic grammar, design, and the manual alphabet. The employment of words themselves, is considered preferable to that of signs, instituted for the sole purpose of recalling the same word. (1834, p. 29 - 30)"

Back in the United States, instructors were protesting similarly that:

" . . . instead of presenting the idea vividly in brief natural signs, and then turning at once to written language, the idea was first given in natural sign, then in word sign in the order of the words, and lastly by signs in the order of the words with each word accompanied by other signs indicating the part of speech and giving its grammatical construction. After all this preparation came the written language for the idea. (cited in Williams, 1893, p. 22 - 23)"

"The purpose of the school is not to teach signs but words", a Hartford instructor (later President of Columbia University) wrote. "And the labor thus spent in defining a [methodical] sign is the very labor, and no other, required to teach a word . . . Truly the system of methodical signs is an unwieldy and cumbrous machine, and a dead weight upon the system of instruction in which it is recognized". (Barnard, 1835, p. 389).

By 1835, Signed English was thus abandoned, not only in New York and Hartford, but in most if not all schools throughout the U.S. (Peet, 1857, p. 339). Strategy I for annihilating the minority language had failed – not because the oral majority lacked the prestige, power and access, but for a linguistic reason: the structural principles of the two languages were so radically different that their bizarre superposition would not be transmitted from parent to child. This should make clear that Signed English is not properly considered a pidgin since it can never be a creole. Although the failure of Signed English was definitive, a hardy group of latterday Sicards is trying again in the U.S. In historical perspective, we will not be misled by their stated goals.

RESIDUAL INFLUENCE OF DIALECTIZING: AN HYPOTHESIS AND COROLLARIES

Although the effort by the English speaking majority to dialectize ASL was unsuccessful in the sense that deaf people persist in using ASL, it is interesting to ask in what ways their language has been shaped by that effort. It is not easy to discern what is indigenous to ASL and what was an intrusion mediated by Signed English for several reasons. First, although we have some descriptions of Signed English in the early 1800's, we have very little by way of useful description of the concurrent ASL. Second, as we have seen, inventors of methodical signs often drew their inspiration from their pupils, even to the point of appropriating an already existing sign; therefore, formationally deviant signs are probably intrusions but not all intrusions are formationally deviant. Pursuing such historical records as we have been able to find, however, we are struck by the considerable purchase on the problem that a single hypothesis provides, one based on a difference in the central organizing principles of the two languages. We take as a point of departure the profusion of pictorial "explanations", or *ad hoc* etymologies with which deaf people bombard others interested in their language: MAN is signed here because of the hat, WOMAN like this because of the bonnet string, etc. Consider the hypothesis that all indigenous signs were originally pictorial – all else began as an intrusion from oral language. Six corollaries follow with regard to specific features of ASL. First, initialized handshapes are not pictorial, therefore they began as intrusions. Second, the use of "function words" – conjunctions, prepositions, and the like – is not pictorial and they are therefore intrusions. For example, OR is clearly an intrusion but UNDER may also be because the indigenous solution would simply be to position A under B without the preposition. Third, the less the ease of pictorial representation, the more open the field for oral intrusion. Note that BLUE and YELLOW are initialized but BLACK (location: eyebrow) and RED (location: lips) are not. Concepts like "vehicle" and "fruit" are represented pictorially by giving an ostensive definition; the ASL sign for "fruit" contains the four morphemes APPLE ORANGE BANANA ETC. (Klima and Bellugi, in press). Fourth, order is indigenously pictorial and all other orders (stylistic variants aside) are intrusions. The object precedes the action and the agent, the attribution; the objects precede their relational signs. Likewise, in compounds, the focal noun is first and other orders are intrusions. Fifth, affixing is not pictorial and is an intrusion. Sixth, fingerspelled words and loan words derived from fingerspelled words are, of course, intrusions. These empirical hypotheses are strongly worded to focus the issue; they are probably wrong in detail but the general thrust is clear; sign language drew its original shape from mime, an avenue utterly blocked to oral language. All that we find in sign that is not pictorial, then, is either due to the intrinsic evolution of the language from iconicity to encodedness (Frishberg, 1975) or to the influence of the non-pictorial oral language that has engulfed it, in the United States, for one hundred and fifty years.

WAYS OF ANNIHILATING A LANGUAGE PART 2: Replacing it

When a single language is the national language of the great majority, the dominant language group can aspire to impose that language on all the people. In the period between the two World Wars, so many European Governments pursued this policy of replacement, that it would appear to be a necessary consequence of linguistic solipsism (often abetted by other motives) were it not for a few enlightened states that demonstrate true linguistic broad mindedness. Kloss (1967) points out that successor states to the Turkish, Hapsburg and Russian empires ruthlessly pursued linguistic annihilation. A crucial method was, of course, to substitute the majority for minority languages in the schools. In 1918, there were 147 Lithuanian schools in Poland; in 1941 there were two. The number of German schools in Lithuania fell to one third in the same period. There were 2600 Ukranian schools in East Galatia in 1918 and 400 in 1928. There were 26 American institutions for the education of the deaf in 1867 and ASL was the language of instruction in all 26; by 1907, there were 139 schools for the deaf and ASL was allowed in none. The French figures provide a comparable glimpse of ruthless linguistic imperialism. In 1845, 160 schools for the deaf with FSL the accepted language; by the turn of the century, it was not allowed in a single French school. The crucial event in the linguistic revolution that concerns us here took place in 1880 in this very country, in Milan; it was the Second International Congress for the Welfare of Deaf Mutes.

As with most revolutions, it was a long time coming. At first, there were only sporadic and half-hearted efforts to include straightforward communication in the dominant oral language in schools for the deaf. Epée and Sicard saw no insurmountable problems in teaching articulation and lipreading, so they said, but they preferred Signed French. The New York School toyed with spoken English as a supplement to Signed English, beginning in 1818, but considered the experiment a failure and dropped it in 1821. The director of the Paris school in 1834, Ordinaire, made a brief attempt to supplant FSL with spoken French but the corps of professors, some of them deaf, opposed him so resolutely he abandoned the project. Hartford would have none of it and in one report gave these ten reasons:

1. too much time is lost in teaching sound, which is to no benefit in mental culture;

2. under this system a large number of deaf-mutes must be left without instruction;

3. the intonations of the voice and the distortion of the countenance in teaching and practicing articulation are disagreeable;

4. success in articulation teaching has come principally to pupils who retained their speech after becoming deaf;

5. the ability to converse in general society is not secured by this method of instruction;

6. more teachers are required, resulting in more expense;

7. religious instruction must be deferred, and religious worship is almost impossible;

8. in teaching articulation, signs are still indispensable;

9. lip reading must be taught also;

10. the results of instruction by signs are beyond those attained by articulation. (Cited in Wheeler, 1920, p. 372)

Interestingly, the first serious inroads of the majority oral language in American schools for the deaf coincides roughly with the abandonment of Signed English, as if the forces of linguistic imperialism, blocked on one route, took an alternate and more ambitious path. In 1843 two leading American educators, Howe and Mann, returned from Europe with great praise for the oral schools for the deaf in Germany. The New York and Hartford schools dispatched their own scouts who returned steadfastly in favor of sign but advocating some oral training as a supplement for those with partial hearing loss, especially when deafened postlingually. By 1845, 30 out of 182 pupils were receiving this training at Hartford and 40 out of 192 in New York. The next major developments awaited the late 1860's when, at Howe's instigation, an oral school for the deaf was organized in Massachusetts. Shortly thereafter another was founded in New York, one in London, and one in Paris. In the 1870's, Alexander Graham Bell added considerable prestige, and his fortune derived from the invention of the telephone, to the oralist movement. He was the recognized leader of those in the U.S. who not only opposed the use of sign language, but opposed intramarriage among deaf people, as well (Mitchell, 1971)! Note the tenet was not that the American deaf must be bilingual but, on the contrary, that they must be monolingual – in spoken English. Bell's chief adversary, the leader of the bilingual camp, was a son of Thomas Gallaudet–Edward, president from 1857 to 1910 of what is now Gallaudet College for the deaf in Washington, D.C.

During the French Universal Exhibition of 1878 a meeting of instructors of the deaf was hastily convened. Only 54 people enrolled, 27 of them instructors, and of these 23 were from France. Léon Vaisse, honorary director of the Paris Institution and long a champion of the oral instruction of the deaf, was president of the meeting rather grandiosely called the First International Congress. The Congress claimed that only oral instruction could fully restore the deaf to society and hence was the educational method of choice, although signing is a useful auxiliary. The Paris Congress appointed a committee of twelve of its own members to make arrangements for a second Congress. Eleven members of the committee were, as it happened, from France and most were advocates of oralism. Milan was selected as the site; in this city were to be found two institutions for the deaf, formerly conducted in sign language, which for the ten years prior had been predominantly oralist. The head of one of the school, the Abbé Tarra, was made President of the Congress, and the leading instructor of the other was made Secretary. Two days before the opening of the convention and every afternoon of the convention were devoted to public examinations of the Milan schools which the delegates were urged to attend. The demonstrations were so impressive, a delegate from England wrote to her American colleague, that "the victory for the cause of pure speech was in great measure gained, as many were heard to say afterwards, before the actual work of the congress began" (Hull, 1881, p. 286). Yet there were reasons to fear that the delegates were taken in. One observer reports that:

"There was evidence of long previous preparation, of severe drilling and

> personal management to produce the most striking effect. There was an apparently studied absence of definite and all-important special information as each case came up for exhibition . . . My neighbors, themselves Italian and articulation teachers informed me that [the best pupils] were not congenitally deaf and had probably mastered speech before entering the institution (Denison, 1881, p. 45)."

Another adds that the deaf pupils' answers:

> "were in many instances begun before the examiner had completed his question. That no real examination was made by outside persons; that many pupils were asked very few questions while certain others were examined at great length; that these discriminations were made by the teachers in every instance; that no information was given as to the history of any pupil – that is to say, as to whether deafness was congenital or acquired, and whether speech had been developed before hearing was lost or not. That the impression was thus sought to be conveyed that all the speech possessed by all the pupils had been imparted to them by their teachers, which was certainly not the case. (Gallaudet, 1881, p. 4)"

These reserves were not shared by most of the 164 delegates, all of them hearing, seven-eighths of whom were from Italy and France. All but the Americans voted for a resolution exhalting the dominant oral language, and disbarring the minority language in whatever nation:

1. the Convention, considering the incontestable superiority of speech over signs, for restoring deaf-mutes to social life [and], for giving them greater facility of language, declare that the method of articulation should have preference over that of signs in the instruction and education of the deaf and dumb;

2. considering that the simultaneous use of signs and speech has the disadvantage of injuring speech and lip-reading and precision of ideas, the convention declares that the pure oral method ought to be preferred (Gordon, 1892, xxxv).

In the closing moments of the Congress, the special French representative cried from the podium "Vive la parole!"

Oh day of ignominy, when linguistic solipsism, one of man's basest traits, was elevated to a guiding principle of instruction! But how effective was the oral majority in its efforts to annihilate sign by replacing it with spoken language in the schools? In some ways devastatingly effective. First, as we have seen, following the Milan Congress most schools in America and Europe became, and remain to this day, oralist, prohibiting sign. As a result, the education of most deaf children is conducted in a language that is not their primary language. As with minority users throughout the world whose education is conducted in some language other than their primary language, deaf people suffer the consequences – social, economic, political – of an inferior education. But we bring good news: in America, as elsewhere, the tide is turning. The deaf have witnessed too many other minorities reclaim their rights, notably their right to their own language, to continue to tolerate linguistic oppression. They are rising up. They are lobbying. They are appealing to hearing people of good judgement and goodwill. As we appeal to you. Let us undo in Venice what was done in Milan. Let us set right in 1977 what was set wrong in 1880. Let us, in this international symposium on language interpretation, affirm that no language is incontestably superior to any other, that every language is equally the priceless heritage of all mankind, and that we particularly cherish the free use and development of minority languages precisely because they are subject to repression at the hands of the majority.

REFERENCES

Anonymous. Arrival of L. Clerc in the United States. *Portifolio,* 1817, *3*, 84 - 89.

Barnard, F. A. P. Existing state of the art of instructing the deaf and dumb. *Literary and Theological Review*, 1835, *2*, 367 - 398.

Barnard, H. *Tribute to Gallaudet.* Hartford: Brockett and Hutchinson, 1852.

Battison, Robbin . Phonological deletion in American Sign Language. *Sign Language Studies*, 1974, *5*, 1 - 19.

Battison, Robbin. *Lexical Borrowing in American Sign Language: Phonological and Morphological Restructuring.* Silver Spring, Md.: Linstok Press, in press.

Bellugi, Ursula and Susan Fischer. A comparison of sign language and spoken language. *Cognition*, 1972, *1*, 173 - 200.

Blanchet, A. L. *La Surdi-Mutite*, Paris: Labé, 1850.

Charrow, V. *Deaf English – An investigation of the written English competence of deaf students. Report 236.* Institute for Mathematical Studies in the social sciences, Stanford, California, 1974.

Charrow, V. and Wilbur, R. "The Deaf Child as a Linguistic Minority", *Theory into Practice*, 1975, *14*, 353 - 359.

Denison, J. Impressions of the Milan Convention. *American Annals of the Deaf*, 1881, *26*, 41 - 50.

Epée, Abbé de l'. La Véritable Manière d'Instruire les Sourds-Muets, Confirmée par Une Longue Experience. Paris, 1784. Nyon. English translation: *American Annals of the Deaf,* 1860, *12,* 1 - 132.

Frishberg, N. Arbitrariness and iconicity: historical change in American Sign Language. *Language*, 1976, *51*, 696 - 719.

Gallaudet, E. M. The Milan Convention. *American Annals of the Deaf*, 1881, *26*, 1 - 16.

Gallaudet, T. H. Letter to the Editor. *Christian Observer*, 1819, *18*, 784 - 787.

Gallaudet, T. H. *Third Report of the Directors of the Connecticut Asylum for the Education and Instruction of Deaf and Dumb Persons.* Hartford: Hudson, 1819.

Goodrich, S. *Recollection of a lifetime.* New York: Miller, Ortan, and Mulligan, 1857.

Gordon, J. C. Progress of speech teaching. In: J. C. Gordon *Notes and Observations upon the Education of the Deaf.* Washington, D.C.: Volta Bureau, 1892, Pp. xxvi - 1.

Hull, S. E. Instruction of deaf Mutes. *Education*, 1881, *1*, 286 - 293.

Klima, E. and U. Bellugi. *The Signs of Language.* Cambridge: Harvard Press, in press.

Kloss, H. Bilingualism and nationalism. *Journal of Social Issues* 1967, *23*, 39 -47.

Lane, H. L. The Wild Boy of Aveyron. Cambridge, Mass.: Harvard University Press, 1976.

Mitchell, S. The haunting influence of Alexander Graham Bell. *American Annals of the Deaf.* June 1971, 349 - 356.

Peet, H. P. *Fifteenth Report of the New York Institution for the Instruction of the Deaf and Dumb.9* New York, 1834.

Peet, H. P. Memoir on the art of instructing the deaf and dumb – second period. In: *Proceedings of the Fifth Convention of American Instructors of the Deaf and Dumb.* Richmond: Wynne, 1857.

Sicard, R. A. *Cours d'Instruction d'un Sourd-Muet de Naissance.* Paris: Le Clère, 1803.

Stokoe, William C. Sign language structure: An outline of the visual communication system of the American deaf. *Studies in Linguistics, Occasional Papers 8*, University of Buffalo, 1960.

Stokoe, W., Casterline, D., and Croneberg, C. *A Dictionary of American Sign Language on linguistic principles.* Gallaudet College Press: Washington, D.C. 1965. (Reprinted: Linstok Press, Silver Spring, Md.: 1976).

Supalla, R. and Newport, E. How many seats in a chair? The derivation of nouns and verbs in American Sign Language. To appear in P. Siple (Ed.). *Understanding Language through Sign Langauge Research.* Academic Press: New York, in press.

Valentine, E. G. The Proper order of signs. In: *Proceedings of the Seventh Convention of American Instructors of the Deaf and Dumb.* Indianapolis: Sentinel, 1870.

Wheeler, F. R. Growth of American schools for the deaf. *American Annals of the Deaf*, 1920, *65*, 367 - 378.

Williams, J. A brief history of the American Asylum at Hartford. In E. A. Fay. *Histories of American School for the Deaf (1817 - 1893).* Washington: Volta Bureau, 1893, 1 - 30.

NOTES

1. An address presented to the NATO Symposium: Language Interpretation and Communication, Venice, September, 1977. Preparation of this manuscript was supported in part by a grant from the National Science Foundation.

2. Signs of ASL are represented by their glosses printed in all capitals.

3. Handshapes of ASL are designated by symbols listed in Stokoe, Casterline and Croneberg (1965).

Sign Language Interpretation:

The State of the Art

Rita L. Domingue
Gallaudet College, Washington D.C.

Betty L. Ingram
New York University, New York, N.Y.

The field of sign language interpretation has existed for many years as has the field of spoken language interpretation, but only became a profession as recently as 1964. The profession of sign language interpreters is unique due to the fact that a manual means is used to transmit language. Although the term interpreter is used, a clarification of terms is in order. Sign languages are genetically and structurally independent of spoken languages even within the same language community. There are, however, numerous artificial sign languages which have been developed in various countries to code the spoken language of the community. Where a message in a *natural* sign language is recreated in a spoken language, or vice versa, the process is known as *interpretation.* Where the conversion involves an *artificial* sign language, the process is called *transliteration.* Therefore, the re-creation of messages between Manual English and English (two forms of the same language) is transliteration. The definitions of transliteration and interpretation are after Fant (1972).

Interpretation of sign languages began in the area of religious work, and these interpreters assumed the role of "Saviors of the Deaf". Their task arose from, and focused on, the "handicap of deafness". This focus has been maintained by educators of the deaf, rehabilitation workers (which are comparable to the European Social Workers) and family members of deaf persons. In recent years, however, some interpreters have begun to realize that their tasks arise, instead, from the fact that two or more people cannot communicate with one another. The "handicap" they deal with is not deafness, but the absence of a common system of communication.

WORLDWIDE VIEW OF SIGN LANGUAGE INTERPRETERS

In June 1964 a workshop on interpreting for the deaf was held at Ball State Teachers College with support from the Vocational Rehabilitation Administration. That meeting was undoubtedly an historic event in the advancement of the welfare of deaf people (Huff, 1965). The profession of sign language interpretation in America has come a long way since that first meeting, for no longer do we function under the theory "that interpreters are born, not made" (Smith, 1964). In 1964 the United States formed the National Registry of Professional Interpreters and Translators for the Deaf stating, "Presently we have two basic sources on which we draw for interpreting when needed. These are: our children, and the educators of the deaf who are familiar with the language of signs. Neither of the two, however, has a full concept of the function of an interpreter and as a consequence, the full value and benefit of a competent interpreter is yet to be appreciated". (Smith, 1964). However, the National Registry of Interpreters for the Deaf, as it is presently called, saw the need to change its views as the field of interpreting expanded. The expansion came as a result of people wanting to become interpreters out of a sheer interest in the profession, and not due to family affiliations or backgrounds. Thus the growth came in size, in numbers, and in needs. The demands are great – but so are the resources. The Registry of Interpreters for the Deaf began with 42 charter members, and now has 2,864 members.

With the National Registry of Interpreters for the Deaf, the United States is not the only country with a National Organization. There are 4 other countries which also have organizations of sign language interpreters: Denmark, Japan, the United Kingdom and Sweden. The Japanese organization being the oldest of these. In most European countries, interpretation is a service which has been provided by government employed Social Workers. A few Social Workers in Denmark and the United Kingdom have begun to realize the obvious role conflicts in this system of service and delivery, as well as the compounded problems of training dual specialists in Social Work and interpretation. They have, therefore, begun to advocate a separation of the two positions. In some countries such as Puerto Rico and Canada there is an added problem in the fact that there is more than one spoken language, and there is, therefore, a need for people who can interpret the sign language, or sign languages, of the country as well as the various spoken languages. For example, at the recent Fifth World Conference on Deafness in Copenhagen quite a number of interpreters had to interpret from English into their respective national sign languages. Now, these interpreters were, for the most part, trained in the interpretation of sign language, but not trained in the interpretation of English which was for them a foreign language. What is needed, then, is training for those who can interpret various spoken languages as well as various sign languages.

Consider, for example, a situation that arose at the Seventh World Congress for the Deaf in 1975 in Washington, D.C. A delegate from Japan arose to address the Congress. Being deaf, he made his remarks in Japanese Sign Language which was interpreted into spoken Japanese, and subsequently from Japanese to English, by a second interpreter. From this English output official interpretations were then rendered into manual English, spoken German, French, and Spanish. The persons providing the interpretation were members of TAALS – The American Association of Language Specialists. At the same time, other interpreters were interpreting into various sign languages from the various spoken languages, and another interpreter, a deaf people, worked from Manual English to Gestuno, the international auxiliary sign language. Consider how matters would have been greatly simplified if there had been interpreters who could have interpreted directly from Japanese or English rather than from other interpretations two or three times removed from the original message.

THE EDUCATION OF INTERPRETERS AND THEIR CLIENTS

To adequately meet the needs of all those presently interpreting and those wanting to interpret, local, state and federal funds are being utilized to develop training programs. At present the largest training program is the National Interpreter Training Consortium and consists of six member institutions: California State University at Northridge, Northridge, California; St. Paul Technical – Vocational Institute, St. Paul, Minnesota; The University of Arizona in Tuscon; Gallaudet College, Washington, D.C.; New York University, New York City; and the University of Tennessee in Knoxville, Tennessee. This program was conceived in February, 1974 at the National Rehabilitation Association's Congress on Deafness Rehabilitation in Tuscon, Arizona, and is funded by The Rehabilitation Service Administration (RSA) of the Department of Health, Education and Welfare. The government granted funding because deaf clients going through the Vocational Rehabilitation process were not receiving adequate interpreting services. The NITC has five major goals to be reached by the termination of the grant in 1980: to improve the skills of those who are presently interpreting but not as yet certified; to train beginners who want to learn how to become an interpreter; prepare trainers to provide training activities to interpreters in their home states; to teach the deaf how to use interpreting services; to train interpreters to work with people having limited language skills.

On a national basis the six member institutions are providing materials in the form of curricula, video tapes, audio tapes, role play situations, etc. to provide the necessary tools for interpreter training. The NITC can provide two-day to ten-week training programs. The length of a workshop relates strictly to personal needs as some may desire a refresher type program while others seek a more extensive program. There are, however, additional programs which are offered as extensive training leading to a degree in interpreting. Although university degrees in sign language interpreting are obtainable only in the United States, university courses are offered in Sweden, Iran, and the Soviet Union. In addition, there is non-university training in Denmark and Norway, and this is presently beginning in the United Kingdom.

In addition to the training of hearing interpreters, the training of deaf people to serve as interpreters is also of paramount importance. The deaf person can serve as an intermediary interpreter. This occurs most often when an interpreter cannot adequately interpret for a deaf person who possesses minimal language skills. Thus, a deaf person, skilled in communicating with those having minimal language skills, can serve as an intermediary interpreter. Deaf people can also serve as interpreters for the deaf-blind. There is thus a need for workshops for the deaf in order to enable them to expand their knowledge of interpreting.

It should be borne in mind, however, that education also relates to deaf people as clients. Since, in the past, interpreters were volunteers and worked without remuneration, their clients had an easy time. The deaf person did not have to worry about communication with the hearing since the interpreter could take control of the situation. Today, however, when a client enters into a contract with an interpreter he is purchasing a communication service. The purchase is for a "communicator" – not a "mother", "counselor", or "teacher". The consumer should not expect or allow the interpreter to do anything for him that he can do for himself. The interpreter's role is not to do things for the deaf client, but allow the deaf client the opportunity to do things for himself, (Ingram, 1977). Since educational necessities far exceed a simple role clarification, the education of interpreters and consumers becomes one of the major responsibilities at this point in the development of the profession.

In addition, there is a tremendous need to collaborate with psychologists in the development of tests for screening purposes in order to select applicants before they are trained. An evaluation system has been developed in order to assess the qualifications of interpreters. The evaluation team used for sign language interpreters consists of a five-member evaluation panel three of whom are hearing impaired. The entire evaluation process takes approximately two hours. One hour is used for a preparation period. The members score the candidates on the basis of their knowledge of the interpreters' ethical code and their expressive and receptive skills. Both expressive and receptive skills are scored on the basis of interpretation and transliteration. The scores are then sent to the National Office, which in turn sends them to the scoring center in Wisconsin. The scores are computed on a percentile basis and returned to the National Office with either permission for, or denial of, certification. The National Office informs the candidate as to the evaluation results. The reliability of this particular procedure of evaluation has recently been brought into question, and the procedure is now in the process of modification.

Attempts to develop education procedures have been made in the United Kingdom, Sweden, and Denmark, but these do not approach the comprehensiveness of the American system.

EMPLOYMENT OPPORTUNITIES AND LEGISLATION

The increase in educational opportunities for interpreters has led to a corresponding increase in employment opportunities. Although the majority of interpreters today are interpreting as an extension of their primary roles, as for example; social workers, educators, religious workers, etc., there are also increasing numbers functioning exclusively as interpreters. Some full-time and part-time jobs have begun to open up in government agencies, educational institutions, and private community service centers, depending, of course, on the extent of enlightenment and legislative action which has occurred in a given community, (Ingram, 1977).

The United States has responded to the need for updated and revised legislation. The term "deaf-mute" in antiquated state laws indicates the need for revision. Today 40 states have either revised or completely re-written interpreter laws to meet the needs of the deaf. These laws naturally have a direct effect on the need for interpreters, but more so the need for *qualified* interpreters. The National Center for the Law and the Deaf at Gallaudet College in Washington, D.C. has written a model law which can be adopted, or adapted, to meet the needs of individual states.

In conclusion, sign language interpreters have begun to collaborate with one another by establishing an international committee charged with investigating the possible organization of an International Federation of Sign Language Interpreters. This committee also has the responsibility of promoting collaborative research on sign language interpretation as well as research on issues common to the interpretation of both sign languages and spoken languages.

REFERENCES

Fant, L. J. Jr., *Ameslan: An Introduction to American Sign Language.* Silver Spring, Md.: National Association of the Deaf, 1972.

Huff, Kenneth, Interpreting for Deaf People, *U.S. Department of Health Education. Vocational Rehabilitation. Administration.* Washington, D.C., 1965, p.vii.

Ingram, Robert, Teaching Deaf Students How to Purchase and Use Interpretation Services. *Deaf American*, May, 1977.

Smith, J. M. (Ed.), *Workshop on Interpreting for the Deaf.* Ball State Taylor College, 1964.

Research in Sign Language Interpreting at California State University, Northridge

Harry J. Murphy

California State University

Northridge, California

INTRODUCTION

The nature of communication through the use of sign language is of growing interest to educators, psychologists, and linguists. For example:

1. in California, Nevada, and Oklahoma, psychologists are exploring the ways and means by which primates communicate with each other, and with humans, after they have been taught sign language;

2. in Washington, D.C., and La Jolla, California, linguists are in the process of describing the grammar of a unique language, American Sign Language;

3. at California State University, Northridge (CSUN) the use of a sign language interpreter in regular classes offers an exciting alternative model of educating deaf college students.

Still, not much is known about sign language or a particular use of it which we call interpreting. One reason for the relative lack of knowledge is that the use of sign language has been discouraged in the education of deaf children. At the first International Congress of Educators of the Deaf, held in Milan, Italy, in 1880, a resolution was passed which declared the superiority of speech over signs and which stated that the preferred method of teaching deaf children was to be the oral method (Meadow, 1972). From 1880 until just the past ten years or so, most educators of the deaf assumed that the use of sign language by young deaf children would result in inhibited reading, writing, speaking, and speechreading skills. The Milan Conference held that sign language had the disadvantage of injuring the "precision of ideas". A small number of educators felt that the use of sign language would facilitate and accelerate the development of these same skills. Their model was a deaf child of deaf parents who learned sign language in the home, and who seemed to do as well, if not better, in language skills, academic achievement, and psychological growth.

The difference of opinion remained just that until some recent research brought some objectivity to what had previously been an emotional argument. Through the late 1960's and early 1970's, two developments paralleled each other. First, research was reported on the educational, psychological, and social gains of children who used, and did not use, sign language. Studies by Mindel and Vernon (1971), and Schlesinger and Meadow (1972) showed superiority of early users of sign language over non-users or late users of sign language. Deaf children of deaf parents – users of sign language from birth – achieved at greater academic levels and had fewer psychological or social problems than non-users, or late users. None of these studies showed negative effects in any phase of language development among the early users. Secondly, linguists (Stokoe, 1976; Bellugi, 1972) were coming to the conclusion that sign language, as used by most deaf adults and thought for so long to be "poor English" was not English at all, but a distinct language. The name, American Sign Language, was given to a symbol system which was ordered in a unique way; so unique, in fact, that it was concluded that it had the integrity of a distinct language, one that is not English. In other words, American Sign Language (sometimes called ASL or Ameslan), is *not* English.

Fant (1974) writes: "Ameslan is a legitimate language in and of itself. That is to say, it is not based on English, but stands by itself, on its own feet. If English did not exist, Ameslan could still exist, just as French or Spanish exist independently of English." The conclusion that American Sign Language is not English becomes more understandable when one realizes that the sign language used by most deaf people in the United States was imported from France in 1917. There appears to be a higher correlation between American Sign Language and French Sign Language than between American Sign Language and a system used in England. The system used in England has a different syntax and there is less mutual agreement upon the symbols used. While investigating the uniqueness of American Sign Language, it was found that not *all* manual expressions in that language are independent of English. In fact, it is possible to sign in one language (American Sign Language), or the other (English), or indeed, in a combination of both.

I feel the obligation to interject at this point that it is not the purpose of this paper to fully defend or explain these various systems. For those with a special interest in the distinct properties of the manual languages,let me refer them to the literature, and let me now say that the purpose of this paper is to describe how deaf students and sign language interpreters function at CSUN.

DEAF STUDENTS AT CSUN

During the Spring semester of 1977, 169 deaf students shared the college experience at CSUN with approximately 27,000 non-handicapped students. Deaf students attend regular classes. The faculty has no special knowledge or training to deal with the problems of deafness. A unit known as Campus Services for the Deaf provides "support services" to these deaf students to insure their academic success. The major support service is interpreting. Other services include note-taking, tutoring, and counselling. Approximately 80 part-time interpreters, most of whom are themselves students at CSUN, are available to serve these 169 deaf students. Deaf students registered in 485 classes, of which 268 classes, meeting on the average of three times per week, were served by interpreters. The typical classroom situation has these components: a regular professor, an interpreter, a deaf student or two, and 20-25 non-handicapped students. The interpreter hears the spoken remarks of the professor and translates the remarks into sign language for the benefit of the deaf student. When a deaf student wishes to ask a question or make a comment, he does so in sign language and the interpreter translates this into spoken language for the benefit of the professor and the other students.

This form of "integrated" education is an alternative model to the more traditional form of "segregated" education, where deaf students are educated only in the company of other deaf students and are taught by instructors who simultaneously transmit lectures in spoken language and sign language. The integrated model is thought to have these benefits (Jones and Murphy 1972, 1974; Carter, 1976):

1. There are considerably more curriculum offerings at CSUN from which deaf students may choose than at a smaller segregated institution.

2. Non-handicapped students come to understand the special talents of deaf people.

3. The normal working and social patterns of life bring handicapped and non-handicapped individuals together; therefore, it is felt that educational models should approximate the experience one will face upon leaving college.

4. Contact with deaf students influences the career choices of non-handicapped people. Hearing students who have had classes with deaf students are more likely to learn sign language and serve as interpreters while in college, and to consider careers in areas of service to deaf people.

Because the model of integrated education is relatively new and because our knowledge of sign language and sign language interpreting is relatively sparse, the Campus Services for the Deaf unit, in addition to delivering interpreting services, is also responsible for research and evaluation studies that deal with the effectiveness of the services.

SIGN LANGUAGE AND INTERPRETING STUDIES

The remainder of this paper is divided into two parts. The first part deals with brief reviews of studies of: the attending behavior of deaf people to the interpreter, the onset of fatigue on the part of the interpreter, and the ways in which deaf people respond to information transmitted in two different ways (American Sign Language, and Signed English). The second part of the paper deals with a series of current research studies designed to document the relative efficiency of sign language in the transmission and reception of messages.

PART I: REVIEW OF PREVIOUS RESEARCH

Attending Behavior

The deaf students at CSUN must *see* language. They must *actively* attend to the linguistic stimuli which they receive through an interpreter. The need to attend visually requires constant activation of the voluntary neuro-muscular mechanism and leads to fatigue. Information may be missed and misinterpreted if an attendee blinks or momentarily turns away. Imagine the ensuing confusion if one missed the word, NOT, in this sentence: There will not be a test tomorrow. Imagine also an environment in which there is dust, or smoke, or in which there is visual "noise" i.e. two or more people in the visual field, background movements, bright lights, clashing colors, etc. These things lead us to conclude that deaf people cannot attend, visually, 100% of the time to such things as a college lecture which could go on for an hour or more. This raises the question of interest: what is a reasonable estimate of attending behavior on the part of deaf college students at CSUN?

Rudy (1976) attempted to determine the rate of attending behavior of CSUN deaf students to their interpreters. The procedures were unsophisticated: he observed deaf graduate students and attempted to determine when they were, and when they were not, attending to an interpreter. He used a cumulative stopwatch as he observed 14 deaf students in 14 different graduate education-class situations. He observed attending behavior in five minute segments. He recorded attending behavior during the first, third, and fifth five minutes of each class period. In other words he recorded for five minutes, did *not* record for five minutes, recorded the next five minutes, did *not* record the next five minutes, recorded the next five minutes. Over a 25 minute period he recorded for 15 minutes of that time. Rudy found that the overall attending rate was 88%. In other words, these deaf students watched the interpreter 88% of the time and did not watch the interpreter 12% of the time. He also found attending behavior to be greater in the earlier periods of time. Attending rates tended then to drop as time went on. The attending rate of 88% is almost certainly an overestimate of attending behavior. This is so because Rudy used the *most* academically capable deaf students, i.e., graduate students at CSUN. Also, the subjects knew they were being observed and the measures were estimated only over the first 25 minutes of a class period whereas most class sessions go on for an hour or more. Nonetheless, Rudy's contribution is twofold: (1) documentation of the basic rate of attending behavior, and (2) documentation of the attrition of attending behavior over time. These two considerations are critical to the efficient use of interpreters and also suggest training strategies to increase attending behavior. Clearly the need for more research in this area, using more precise methodologies, is apparent.

Fatigue on the Part of the Interpreter

A deaf person may experience fatigue in attending to an interpreter. The interpreter may also experience fatigue in delivering sign language. Sign language is delivered with considerable physical effort. CSUN interpreters are asked to mouth what they hear as well as to deliver the message manually. The fingers and arms are mostly used in delivering signs and fingerspelling, but the whole body comes into play as well. Consequently, fatigue on the part of the interpreter is a predictable factor. Brasel (1976) examined the error rate of information delivered by interpreters over time. It was found that interpreting skills remained at their highest levels during the first 30 minutes. After 30 minutes there was a slow but steady increase in errors, and after 60 minutes, the error rate became statistically significant. Brasel concluded that interpreting skills begin to deteriorate after 30 minutes of interpreting, and begin to deteriorate significantly after 60 minutes. Obviously, interpreters should be rotated or a single interpreter should have a rest period after about 30 minutes of interpreting, wherever possible.

American Sign Language and Signed English

As noted earlier in this paper, it is possible to sign in American Sign Language, which is not English, or an English form of manual communication, Signed English, or a combination of both. College-level deaf students, who have mastered 12 years or more in a school system which emphasizes success in the use of English, obviously have high English skills, even though they may be most comfortable with American Sign Language. In a study by Murphy and Fleischer (1976), CSUN deaf students were asked to state their preference for either American Sign Language (ASL) or Signed English (Siglish). The ASL group was broken into two subgroups. Half received treatment in ASL; half received treatment in Siglish. The Siglish preference group was also divided into two subgroups, of whom half received treatment in Siglish whereas the other half received treatment in Ameslan. It was found that there were no statistically significant differences regardless of preference and no statistically significant difference regardless of treatment received. Those who preferred Ameslan and received Siglish did as well as those who preferred Ameslan and received Ameslan. Those who preferred Siglish and received Ameslan did as well as those who preferred Siglish and received Siglish. It is clear from this study that CSUN deaf students have bilingual skills as evidenced by equal facility in two languages, regardless of their stated preference for one language over the other. Since CSUN interpreters receive training in both languages, it would appear that they are appropriately prepared to deal with the CSUN population of deaf students.

PART II: REVIEW OF CURRENT RESEARCH

Information processing models have been identified to test the efficiency of sign language in the transmission and reception of messages. These models approximate usual classroom practices in that they parallel (A) the transmitting mode of delivering sign language, and (B) the receiving mode of understanding sign language. In the first instance (see Figure 1) a spoken verbal message originates with a lecturer, is processed through an interpreter, and is received by a deaf person. The dependent measure is test scores of deaf subjects based on information processed.

The second processing model has two components (see Figures 2 and 3). In Processing Model B, a message has a manual origin, and is received by an interpreter. The dependent measure is test scores of material received by the interpreter. In Processing Model C, a message has a verbal origin and is received by an interpreter. The interpreter must now verbalize the message in spoken English to a third party. The dependent measure here is test scores of material received by a third person. With the above in mind, we may now talk about three behaviors of interpreters: transmitting (Model A), receiving (Model B), and reversing (Model C).

The following explanation for these terms seem to meet general agreement among interpreters:

1. To transmit: the interpreter listens to the spoken word and transforms the spoken message into sign language.

2. To receive: the interpreter attends to and understands the sign language of another person. He is not required to verbalize what he receives. This might also be thought of as "reading" the signs of another. One who is skilled at this is said to evidence "reading comprehension".

Verbal
Origin
Interpreter
Manual
Reception
Test

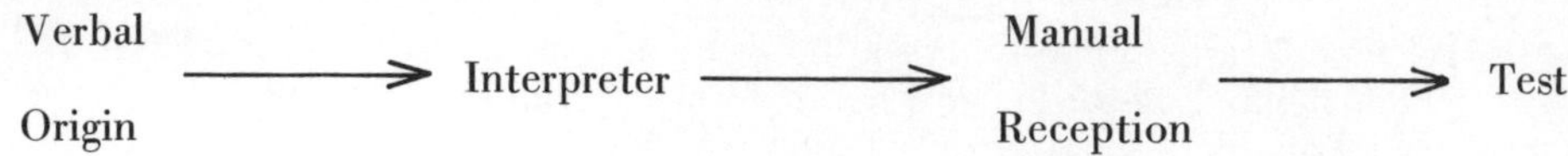

Figure 1. Processing Model A

Transmitting Behavior

Manual
Origin
Interpreter
Test

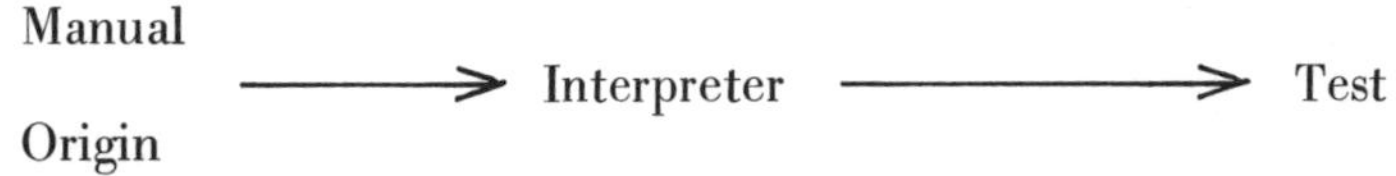

Figure 2. Processing Model B

Receiving Behavior

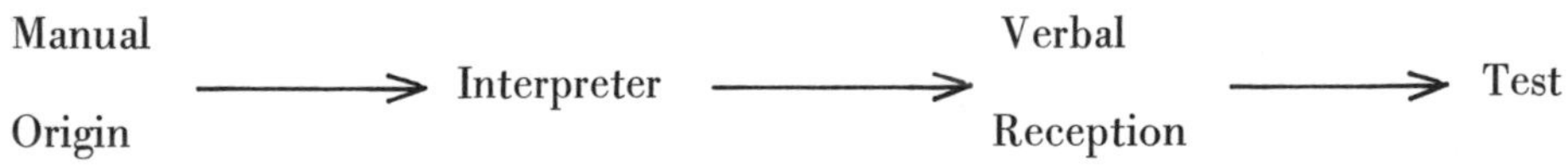

Manual
Origin
Interpreter
Verbal
Reception
Test

Figure 3. Processing Model C

Reversing Behavior

3. To reverse: in addition to being able to "read" the original signer, the interpreter must also vocalize the message. He follows the incoming signs and as he reads, he also verbalizes what he sees. Both are done at nearly the same time, with the verbalizing slightly behind the reading. This is considered the most difficult task for the interpreter because the initiator of the message may be transmitting in one language (American Sign Language) while the vocal translation may be in another language (English), and the reading and the translation must be done at almost the same time.

One of our research interests deals with the experience of the interpreter. CSUN is a major training center for interpreters and also the world's largest employer of sign language interpreters. We offer a certain sequence of training courses and assign and pay interpreters according to their experience. Hence, it would seem reasonable that we would explore this variable closely to see how efficient our training has been, and to suggest other ways to manipulate the quantity and/or quality of the experience in order to improve the entire interpreting situation.

In one study it was found that the transmitting skills of interpreters at different levels of experience were essentially equal. In other words, interpreters with Minimum experience transmitted about as well as interpreters with Maximum experience. This first study was limited to transmitting and did not deal at all with receptive (receiving) or reversing skills, which are generally considered by interpreters to be higher order functions of somewhat greater difficulty than simply transmitting. The practical application of the finding of this first study to postsecondary education is limited to specific situations where material needs only to be transmitted. This assumes a passive receiver. It is clear, however, that college students best acquire knowledge in an interactive environment, i.e. one in which information is received and where a student may question a lecturer and comment on the lecture material. It seems reasonable therefore, to examine the receptive skills of the interpreter, as well as the transmitting skills. Consequently, a second study was designed to gather evidence on the "receiving" or "reading comprehension" skills of interpreters at different levels of experience. Studies on the "reversing" skills of the interpreter are planned in the future.

Methodology

Reading comprehension of the interpreter was tested through a series of videotaped lectures. Typical college lectures originally devised by Jacobs (1976), were signed on camera and a master black and white tape, without sound, was made for research purposes. The material consisted of one practice lecture, and five research lectures. Each lecture averaged about five minutes in length. After each lecture, the interpreter-subject received a 10-item test. The on-camera signer held a Comprehensive Skills Certificate (CSC) from the Registry of Interpreters for the Deaf. He carefully rehearsed each lecture and played a verbatim audiotape in the studio to cue his signing. The audiotrack was erased in the master tape used in the study. The signer rarely used lip movements. He rendered the lectures in American Sign Language vocabulary, yet followed an English syntax.

Results

It was found that interpreters with a greater amount of experience outscored interpreters with less experience. More specifically, interpreters with 1,200+

hours of classroom interpreting experience at CSUN (N=7) significantly outscored those who had less than 300 hours of classroom interpreting experience at CSUN (N=24). Those with between 600 - 900 hours of classroom interpreting experience also significantly outscored the lesser experienced group, but were the approximate equals of the group with the most experience (N=7). From these data it was concluded that reading comprehension appears to be a function of experience. It may also be concluded that interpreters of Moderate experience appear to "read" about as well as those with Maximum experience. One further conclusion is that interpreters with Moderate and Maximum experience appear to "read" somewhat better than interpreters with Minimum experience.

Data were analyzed in still another way. In the earlier cited Jacobs study, hearing students with no knowledge of sign language, and deaf students who normally use an interpreter in CSUN classes were subject to the same lecture. These were delivered orally in a live situation, and were interpreted at the same time in a single room in which there were hearing and deaf individuals. A comparison of their scores with the scores of interpreters with various levels of experience leads to some interesting conclusions:

Group I -- Hearing subjects in Jacob's Study with no knowledge of sign language.

Group II -- Deaf subjects in Jacob's study who depend on an interpreter at CSUN.

Group III – Minimal level interpreters.

Group IV – Moderate level interpreters.

Group V – Maximum level interpreters.

Post hoc comparisons showed no significant differences between scores of Minimum level interpreters and Deaf subjects on most tests. Therefore, it is concluded that Minimum level interpreters evidence reading comprehension skills at least equal to, and perhaps a little better than, CSUN deaf students. Further comparisons showed that Moderate level interpreters outscored the Deaf group, and that Maximum level interpreters outscored the Deaf group. It is concluded that the Moderate and Maximum level interpreters show greater reading comprehension skills than CSUN deaf students.

Additional comparisons were made between the three interpreting groups and the Hearing group from the Jacobs study. It was found that the Hearing group outscored the Minimum level interpreters. No significant differences were found between the Moderate and Maximum level interpreters and the Hearing group. It is concluded that scores obtained by Minimum level interpreters after reading sign language messages are inferior to scores of a Hearing group receiving information through audition. It is further concluded that Moderate and Maximum level interpreters "read" as much information through signs as CSUN hearing students do through normal audition. More will be said about this later in this paper.

Discussion

This research followed small group research models and the usual cautions govern interpretation of the following findings. It has been found that reading comprehension appears to be a function of the experience of the interpreter whereas transmitting skills apparently are not related to experience (as "experience" has been defined herein). It would seem that CSUN interpreters develop adequate transmitting skills after training and within the first 300 hours of paid experience whereas reading comprehension becomes most efficient after training and at least 600 hours of paid experience. This being the case, a clear recommendation to those who are responsible for the basic training of new interpreters, and in-service training of experienced interpreters, is to emphasize reading and reversing skills over transmitting skills. This assumes that transmitting skills are developing along predictable lines and meet minimum proficiency levels. The comparison of data between the Jacobs study and the present study leads to some interesting conclusions.

1. Jacobs found significant differences in favor of a hearing group receiving information through audition over a deaf group receiving information through an interpreter. The scores of deaf subjects averaged 16% below those obtained by hearing persons.

2. No significant differences were found on five of six measures between Minimum level interpreters in this study and deaf subjects in the Jacobs study.

3. Significant differences were found in favor of scores of Moderate and Maximum level interpreters in this study, over scores obtained by the deaf group in the Jacobs study.

4. No significant differences were found between Moderate and Maximum level interpreters in this study, and hearing subjects in the Jacobs study.

These data must be interpreted with care. The immediate temptation is to conclude that sign language is 16% less efficient than spoken language, that Minimum level interpreters "read" about as well as deaf subjects, and Moderate and Maximum level interpreter "readers" are superior to deaf "readers" of sign language. But the finding of no significant differences between Moderate and Maximum level interpreters and Jacobs' hearing subjects suggests a different explanation and this chain of thought: If Moderate and Maximum level interpreters acquire as much information through sign language as hearing counterparts do through normal auditory channels, then it must be concluded that sign language apparently equals spoken language as an efficient channel for the communication of information. If sign language is the equal of spoken language, then the 16% gap in scores between deaf and hearing subjects, as found by Jacobs, is not attributable to deficiencies in sign language itself. If the 16% score gap between deaf and hearing subjects cannot be attributable to deficiencies in sign language, then the gap must be explained by other factors, most likely the basic language and educational deficit of deaf people. If deaf people score lower because of linguistic and educational deficits, then Minimum level interpreters may obtain equal "reading" scores, not necessarily because they read as well, but because they have superior language skills. Further support for this possibility comes from the fact that Minimum level interpreters have had only about three years experience with sign language whereas the deaf subjects have had considerably more years of experience, some from birth. If reading comprehension is a function of experience, as this study concludes, then we would expect the most experienced group of readers, i.e., deaf people, to score highest. They do not. This is probably so, not necessarily because they are poor at reading sign language, but because a basic language and educational deficit penalizes them as they process information through to the final measure of a formal paper and pencil test.

It appears, therefore, that the problem is neither with the ability of sign language to transmit information accurately, nor with the "reading" ability of the deaf person, but with unfamiliar words, or the multiple meaning of words, or other factors inherent in the basic problems associated with deafness. Some previous doubts about the efficiency of sign language in our field come from observations of deaf subjects. Research using hearing subjects with normal language skills *and* a knowledge of sign language is recommended in future studies of the efficiency of sign language, particularly in that it frees the researchers from the confounding variable of the language limitation of deaf subjects.

REFERENCES

Bellugi, U., and Klima, E. S. The roots of language in the sign talk of the deaf. *Psychology Today*, June 1972, *76*, 61 - 64.

Brasel, B. B. The effects of fatigue on the competence of interpreters for the deaf. In H. J. Murphy (Ed.), *Selected readings in the integration of deaf students at CSUN*. Center on Deafness Publication Series (No. 1). Northridge: California State University, Northridge, 1976.

Carter, S. H. Some effects of association with hearing-impaired students upon hearing students at CSUN. In H. J. Murphy (Ed.), *Selected readings in the integration of deaf students at CSUN*. Center on Deafness Publication Series (No. 1). Northridge: California State University, Northridge, 1976.

Fant, L. J. Jr., Ameslan. *Gallaudet Today*, 1974 - 75, *5* (2), 1 - 3.

Jacobs, L. R. *The efficiency of sign language interpretation to convey lecture information to deaf students*. Unpublished doctoral dissertation, University of Arizona, 1976.

Jones, R. L. and Murphy, H. J. The Northridge plan for higher education of the deaf. *American Annals of the Deaf*, 1972, *117*, 612 - 616.

Jones, R. L. and Murphy, H. J. Integrated education for deaf college students. *Phi Delta Kappan*, 1974, *55*, 542.

Meadow, K. P. Sociolinguistics, sign language, and the deaf sub-culture. In T. E. O'Rourke (Ed.), *Psycholinguistics and total communication: The state of the art*. Washington, D.C.: American Annals of the Deaf, 1972.

Mindel, E. D. and Vernon, M. *They grow in silence*. Silver Spring, Md.: National Association for the Deaf, 1971.

Murphy, H. J. and Fleischer, L. The effects of Ameslan versus Siglish upon test scores. In H. J. Murphy (Ed.), *Selected readings in the integration of deaf students at CSUN*. Center on Deafness Publication Series (No. 1). Northridge: California State University, Northridge, 1976.

Rudy, L. H. A survey of attending behavior of deaf graduate students to interpreters. In H. J. Murphy (Ed.), *Selected readings in the integration of deaf students at CSUN.* Center on Deafness Publication Series (No. 1). Northridge: California State University, Northridge, 1976.

Schlesinger, H. and Meadow , K. P. *Sound and Sign. Deafness and Mental Health.* Berkeley, University of California Press, 1972.

Stokoe, W. C. The study and use of sign language. *Sign Language Studies,* 1976, *10,* 1 - 36.

Sign Language and Psycholinguistic Process: Fact, Hypotheses, and Implications for Interpretation

Ryan D. Tweney

Bowling Green State University

Bowling Green, Ohio

It is true, as some of the papers in this conference have recognized, that laboratory studies of language cannot directly be carried over and used as models of naturally occurring language processes. Yet, even if laboratory experiments do represent artificial situations, the people in those experiments are very real. Thus, we cannot uncritically reject laboratory results any more than we can uncritically accept them. Instead, we should ask *empirically* just how relevant lab results are, and carry out the studies needed to find out. My work is based on long-standing psychological laboratory paradigms, but I hope that you will agree that it has much broader implications. Each of its implications will, of course, require separate test.

Nearly all published works on the nature of translation and interpretation have been concerned solely with the transformation of messages in one spoken language (or its orthographic code) into another. Yet, as Jakobson (1959) has argued, consideration of interpretation to and from other linguistic modalities may contribute greatly to complete understanding of the language process. Some of the known facts about sign languages indicate the correctness of Jakobson's claim and point toward areas in need of further research.

It is first necessary to ask whether interpretation in which either source language or target language is signed actually involves interpretation from one language to another. As you will see, I think there is abundant reason to believe that sign languages are *linguistic* systems in every meaningful sense, and that we must direct full attention to their linguistic properties if we are to properly understand them as psycholinguistic systems. But the old idea that sign represents a universal language, perhaps of a primitive, pre-linguistic sort, is still with us. Mallery (1881), in the most extensive studies of North American Indian Sign Language ever conducted, believed this was so. More recently, Hewes (1974) presented an argument based on the widespread uses of gestures in cross-cultural contact when no common linguistic system is available. Because such gestural communication can incorporate a wide variety of semantic relationships, Hewes concluded that there must be a "pan-human, cognitive deep structure" which supported such communication.

Whether or not informal gesture systems are linguistic systems is not a question I am prepared to answer. They may be better understood if they are regarded as pantomimes, not sign *languages*. In any case, there definitely is at least one sign language, American Sign Language (ASL), that *is* fully linguistic, a claim that can be supported with a good deal of empirical evidence. At the same time, ASL does possess unique properties which undoubtedly have an effect on the processes of translation and interpretation. I will review studies which are relevant to both sides of this question and attempt to relate what we know to directions for further research on translation and interpretation.

THE NATURE OF SIGN LANGUAGE

A significant fraction of the world's population is deaf and does not possess a speech-based first language. Many who are either born deaf or become profoundly deaf prior to acquiring a spoken language, lip-reading, or reading and writing in the spoken language, learn some form of sign language as their first linguistic system. Because of the dominance of oral ways of teaching the deaf, until fairly recently almost no research had been conducted on these languages. Nevertheless, because of the greater utilization of sign languages in educational settings in recent years, a number of investigators in psychology, sociology, and linguistics have begun to examine the properties of sign language.

A sign language is a linguistically structured communication system in which meanings are mapped primarily onto gestures made by the arms, hands, and face of the communicator. Such systems differ markedly from fingerspelled encodings of vocal languages (Stokoe, 1974), in which an alphabet is represented by hand gestures. Thus, a particular hand configuration stands for the letter "*A*" and another for "*B*", and so on. Such systems are not sign languages but, rather, manual encodings of vocal languages. In a true sign language, particular gestures stand for concepts in the same sense that words in a vocal system stand for concepts. There is no necessary correspondence between the form of the gesture and the concept, and no necessity that a particular sign be translated by a single English word. Exact translation may, in fact, be exceedingly difficult or impossible (Tweney and Hoemann, 1976). Finally, it has to be emphasized that there is no inherent correspondence between the grammatical rules of ASL and those of any spoken language.

The difference between the types of codes can be clarified by an example. The ASL sign that corresponds to the English word "again" is made by striking the outstretched palm, fingertips together, of one hand by the fingertips of the other hand held in the same configuration. The moving hand may touch the base hand twice in short succession without change of meaning. Repeated striking, however, with the location changing slightly from the wrist toward the tip of the base hand changes the meaning and results in the sign for "often". The English word "again" can be fingerspelled by successively forming the five hand configurations that correspond to the letters A–G–A–I–N. The ASL gesture is in no sense a pantomime or acting out of the concept but is, rather, a purely symbolic encoding. Most signs in ASL are abstract gestures having no discernible iconic or pantomime component.

LINGUISTIC STRUCTURE OF ASL

Stokoe (1960) first described the structure of ASL signs using contrastive categories derived from structural linguistics. Following extensive distributional analyses, Stokoe isolated combinational units that were analogous to phonemes in spoken languages. Three types of linguistic primes were described: a place marker, a hand-configuration marker, and a movement marker. The sign for "girl", for example, consists of moving the ball of the thumb along the signers' cheek. If a different hand configuration were used, say the outstretched palm instead of the ball of the thumb, then the meaning of the sign would differ (in this case, the result would be the sign for "brown"). Stokoe's three primes are not exactly equivalent to the phonemic system of spoken languages since the three formatives occur more or less simultaneously rather than sequentially (Klima, 1975). The three formative dimensions do not exhaust the set of characteristics which can alter the meaning of a pair of signs. In particular, hand orientation (whether a particular hand is turned toward or away from the receiver, for example) is a significant dimension which has only recently received attention by linguists.

How do we know that Stokoe's description is a meaningful one? The validity of the system was confirmed by the results of short-term memory studies. Bellugi, Klima, and Siple (1975) found that errors in memory for ASL signs occurred along dimensions that corresponded to the linguistic primes isolated by Stokoe. Thus, the sign for "noon" was mistakenly recalled as "tree", a sign that differs only in the type of movement. Other errors occurred along hand configuration or place dimensions or along some combination of more than one dimension. A similar process occurs in the perception or memory of speech sounds. Miller and Nicely (1955) found that acoustic confusions among speech sounds could be related to the linguistically derived distinctive features for speech. Conrad (1972) and others (e.g. Sales, Cole, and Haber, 1974) have shown that short-term memory errors for words reflect acoustic interference along distinctive feature lines. The reality of the three formative dimensions for ASL is further supported by the occurrence of "slips of the hand", which occur along dimensions predictable from the formatives (Bellugi and Klima, 1975a), just as errors in speech correspond to formatives in words (Fromkin, 1971).

While ASL phonology is thus beginning to be understood, little formal description of ASL syntax is available, although some have described particular grammatical devices in ASL. For example, reference to agents and objects in ongoing discourse is often provided by manual indication, with the pointing index finger, of either the sender or the receiver (for the first person and second person pronoun, respectively). Third person pronoun functions are often subsumed by pointing to either side between the sender and receiver. Of special interest, a kind of imaginary "stage" is sometimes positioned in the space in front of the signer's body. Particular actors, objects, and indirect objects can be placed at specific locations on this stage by pointing. Later pronominal reference to any of the persons or objects can then be achieved simply by pointing to the appropriate stage location (Hoemann, 1976). This device all but eliminates the need for pronouns of the type commonly found in spoken language.

Liddell (1975) described a number of complex cues that signal relative clauses in ASL. Consider the sentence which can be glossed in English as "RECENTLY DOG CHASE CAT COME HOME". Liddell showed that a sentence of this type is accompanied by a specific conventionalized facial expression while the signs DOG CHASE CAT are being articulated. The facial expression indicates that the phrase is a restricted relative clause. Thus, an English translation of this sentence would be "Recently, the dog which chased the cat came home". Aside from an indication of clausal boundary, other mechanisms are, of course, needed to disambiguate the signed sentence. Is it the cat that came home or the dog? A particular, distinctively intense facial expression can be added to either DOG or CAT. Alternatively, a sign can be preposed to the subject noun of the clause – "RECENTLY THAT DOG CHASE CAT COME HOME". Many spoken languages use inflections, function words, or word order to achieve these purposes. ASL, however, is able to use simultaneously occurring facial expressions to signal one kind of grammatical information, and a set of inflection signs, akin to what is possible in spoken language, to disambiguate structures within clauses. It is not yet known how general these processes are in ASL or in other sign languages. Liddell has argued, however, that similar disambiguating devices and similar clausal structures are found in Diegueno, an American Indian language spoken in the Southwestern United States.

Investigation has also been initiated into the morphological process of ASL (Bellugi and Klima, 1975b). Thus, new signs in ASL can be formed by compounding single signs in regular ways. Such processes appear to be productive in ASL and result in the formation of new signs. As an example, the sign for AMBULANCE is a compound and can be analyzed into two single signs, HOSPITAL and CAR. Furthermore, articulation of the compound sign is different from articulation of the two signs in isolation, suggesting the operation of a morphologically generative process. Similar phenomena occur in English. Thus, "blackbird" is a compound, the pronunciation of which differs from the ordinary pronunciation of either of the words in isolation. Battison (1974) has provided striking description of similar morphological processes operating historically to change finger-spelled words into true signs. Ironically, this process seems to defeat the many schemes for reforming ASL by adding English-like inflection signs. Such signs have a strong tendency to become assimilated to other signs in a kind of analogical change process.

Modulation of the meaning of specific signs has been found in ASL (Bellugi and Klima, 1975b). The sign for SICK, for instance, can be modified to indicate a process of slowly becoming sick or a tendency to get sick easily or the fact that everyone is sick. Such modulations are achieved by changing the movement articulation of the sign in regular productive ways. Similar processes occur in spoken language using inflections, the addition of -ly to "recent", for example. The process is generative in sign, just as it is in speech.

PSYCHOLINGUISTIC PROPERTIES OF ASL

Several lines of research have been initiated by psychologists interested in the functional properties of ASL. It is clearly of central importance to determine if the linguistic properties of ASL constitute "psychological realities" which are utilized in the processing of ASL, just as linguistic structure in spoken language is known to be used in the processing of spoken language (Fodor, Bever, and Garret, 1974; Clark and Clark, 1977). For example, Stokoe's analysis of signs into linguistic primes was based on contrastive analysis of lexical items in ASL. That the primes constituted psychological realities, however, was not shown until the memory studies of Bellugi, *et al.* Thus, one task for psycholinguistic research is to determine which of the linguistic structures in ASL can be psychologically real in this sense.

At the present time, relatively little is known about which aspects of sign are psychologically real, though our knowledge is accumulating quickly. It is clear from the results of Bellugi *et al.* that handshape, location, and movement are important. Yet, this is clearly not a complete account, since little is yet known about the particular distinctions within each of the three parameters. In particular, no systematic description of ASL in terms of distinctive features is yet available (though attempts have been made, e.g., Lane, Boyes-Braem, & Bellugi, 1976). Since sequential organization is less important in sign than in speech, Klima (1975) suggested that analysis in terms of contrastive features may be less relevant than an analysis akin to that of Gestalt wholes. In whatever fashion this issue is ultimately resolved by linguistic analysis, it will be necessary to separately determine the psychological reality of the units of the linguistic analysis.

Several studies have been conducted in our laboratory which suggest that in spite of the differences between visual and auditory modes, sign language structure provides the user with the same gain in communicative and cognitive efficiency enjoyed by speech users. In addition to memory tasks (Tweney &Heiman, 1977), we used the simple expedient of visually distorting video-taped signed messages by introducing various sorts of disruptive video "noise" (Tweney, Heiman, & Hoemann, 1977; Tweney, Liddell, & Bellugi, 1977). This reduces the ability of an observer to determine just what has been seen and, more importantly, allows us to determine what variables make the observer's task easier or more difficult. The results of these studies showed clearly that grammatical sentence structure in ASL contributes "redundancy" (Miller & Isard, 1963) which makes processing easier. As in speech, the syntax of an ASL sentence is a kind of matrix around which a user can construct a meaning. For this reason, sentences in ASL are more resistant to video disruption than are unorganized lists of signs. The specific mechanisms by which this facilitation is achieved are not yet entirely clear. By presenting very complex ASL sentences with relative clauses (of the type described by Liddell), we were able to show that elements within clauses are more inter-dependent than are two elements separated by a clause boundary (Tweney, Liddell, & Bellugi, 1977). If a subject perceived one element within a clause, then there was a very high probability that he or she would get other items in the clause also. No such interdependency was observed across clause boundaries, however. The result supports Liddel's linguistic analysis of relative clause structure by confirming its effects in a performance task. This study represents a start, though I suspect that a complete process-oriented account of the way in which ASL sentences are perceived will prove to be as difficult and complex an undertaking as it has proved to be for speech.

INTERPRETATION AND SIGN LANGUAGE

What does all this have to do with interpretation? Ordinarily, interpretation has not had to concern itself with the question of whether or not source languages or target languages constitute fully developed linguistic systems. The question does, however, arise when sign languages are involved, because of the claim that sign languages are not true languages. I think this possibility can be dismissed, both because extensive, complex, linguistic structure *does* characterize sign, and because psycholinguistic studies confirm the utility of that structure for the user.

Other issues do, nonetheless, require analysis. It is entirely possible that certain characteristics of sign languages render untranslatable some very central meanings. To see this point, consider how one might approach the problem of "interpreting" a pantomime into spoken sentences. Presumably, one could relate components of the total physical action to specific words and phrases. This is clearly not a true linguistic interpretation problem (unless we wish to argue that all description is interpretation – a position that so enlarges the concept as to make it trivial). Of course, some aspects of pantomime may be quite indescribable verbally – imagine describing Charlie Chaplin's walk! Now consider another case. Suppose we have a description of the pantomime in, say, French, which we wish to have interpreted into English. The problem now is very different. It will not be difficult to preserve the referential fidelity of the French sentences, especially if the pantomime has been observed by the interpreter. The hard part will come in the attempt to capture in English the precise shades of meaning which the French description incorporates. The difficulty with "shades of meaning", as Steiner (1975) has recently argued so well, is that they are mapped onto words in different languages in vastly different configurations. The more of the connotative meaning we wish to incorporate, the longer will be the English text – and the greater the interference caused by the surplus connotations of the English sentences!

We may have a similar problem in translating sign languages. Insofar as the grammatical structure of sign is unique, and insofar as the mapping of signs to conceptual structures which they represent is unique, then the problem is of course the same as for any pair of languages. There may be additional difficulties in sign, however, arising from the occurrence of sign iconicity: the partial visual resemblence of some signs to the object represented. The sign for *tree*, for example, is iconic insofar as parts of the arm and hand configuration can be related, by analogy, to parts of a real tree. It is important here not to confuse iconicity with pantomime. An iconic sign does not amount to a *picture* of the thing represented. That this is so was clearly shown by Hoemann (1975) and by Bellugi and Klima (1975b). They presented samples of ASL signs to hearing subjects who had no knowledge of ASL and required that they guess the meanings of the presented signs. Performance in both studies was exceptionally poor, even though the iconic character of many of the signs was easily recognizable when subjects were told the meaning. In fact, many signs proved "falsely iconic" in suggesting a commonly agreed-upon, but erroneous, meaning.

It seems clear that iconicity could create translation difficulty, especially if the iconic aspect of the signs is deliberately used in the signal message to carry a joke, a pun, or a kind of suprasegmental "editorial" by the signer. The interpreter may then be in the difficult position of trying to describe one of those indescribable visual events. How much of this goes on in actual sign language use? We do not fully know the answer to that question. Recently, Eastman (1974) published an English gloss, with stage directions, of a play, *Sign Me Alice*, composed in ASL. The published English version was not a true translation – and it certainly did miss a substantial fraction of the allusions, jokes, and images that were a fundamental part of the dramatic work. Do such problems find their way into more prosaic situations which require translation or interpretation? I suspect they do. Most deaf ASL users are adept at switching codes, from relatively pure ASL to a sign much closer to English grammatical order. There is, in fact, very great variation in sign structure as a function of sociolinguistic variables – relative status of sender and receiver, geographical locus, and whether one of the participants is non-deaf (Woodward, 1974). Stokoe (1972) has, in fact, argued that sign usage in America represents a true instance of diglossia, with alternation of style between a high-status and low-status variant. Because of the social bias against use of sign language created by a century of oral education, English-like word order corresponds most closely to the H or High variant. That does, however, seem to be changing, and we may now be in a period of inversion, with pure ASL – the previous L or Low variant, becoming the H variant in some communities! In any case, switching to a more English-like grammatical structure is quite usual when deaf individuals sign with non-deaf users of sign.

Mention of diglossia brings up another question relevant to translation. Is the sign language translator or interpreter truly a bilingual individual? Perhaps this question will sound less strange if one considers the possibility that the sign interpreter may be doing something very much like what a skilled typist is doing, namely, recoding from a visual representation to an articulated representation which is digital for the typist and vocal for the interpreter. Something like this occurs when "transliterating" versions of sign which are very close to English grammatical structure. There are, in fact, several sign systems which are lexically highly similar to ASL, but which have been deliberately designed to mirror English structure (e.g., Anthony's, 1971, SEE system). Such languages can be recoded without true interpretation. Is this possible with pure ASL? Probably not, and it is for this reason that we need a distinction between trans-literation and interpretation.

One way to show that a person possesses two language systems is to show that long-term memory for lexical items is organized separately for items from each language. Siple, Fischer, and Bellugi (1977) tested this by presenting mixed lists of signs and printed words to ASL users and testing recognition after 30 minutes. Whenever subjects indicated that they recalled a specific item, they also had to indicate whether it had been signed or printed. It is this second judgement that is critical. Following correct recognition, subjects were nearly always able to specify what the mode of presentation had been. This argues strongly that the two kinds of items are coded into two separate lexical systems (Seagert, Hamayan, & Ahmar, 1975). No comparable difference was found for hearing subjects presented with spoken or printed words – their judgements of modality were close to chance levels, as one would expect if both kinds of stimulus items are parts of the same language system. The evidence thus supports the claim that ASL-English users are truly bilingual. We can deduce from this that true translation and interpretation (not just recoding) is possible.

There is an especially fascinating issue involving ASL translation that I would like to discuss. Jakobson (1971) first suggested that speech, unlike visual symbols, possessed sequential structure which permitted a super-imposed hierarchial structure. Since a visual symbol contains all relevant elements in a simultaneous array, there is no need for hierarchical structure. Jakobson did not have sign languages in mind when he wrote that. It is now clear that, at least at the inter-sign level, ASL does possess hierarchical linguistic structure which serves to structure a sequence of signs – just as in speech. It is, however, still an open question whether signs as such possess simultaneous structure unlike that found in speech. Klima (1975) raised this possibility when he referred to the possible need for analysis of signs as Gestalt wholes. I think we were up against the same problem in our temporal disruption studies (Tweney, Heiman, & Hoemann, 1977). We were unable to determine whether the redundancy of single signs derived from linguistic structure (i.e., the linguistic primes or distinctive features) or from the redundancy which would derive from any dynamic gestural display (i.e., from the Gestalt properties of gestures). The problem was especially intriguing because single signs proved to be extremely resistant to disruption in the temporal domain – rapid on-and-off switching of the presented image. In many conditions, speech was far more fragile than sign when subjected to such distortion. The resistance to disruption manifested by signs may stem from several sources: (1) intrinsic resistance to disruption possessed by any moving visual image, or (2) resistance possessed by signs which is a function of its linguistic structure. The second possibility is especially intriguing – it would be remarkable if the Gestalt properties of signs made them more coherent, more intelligible under adverse conditions than words!

There are interesting implications for translation theory here. It is known (Barik, 1973; Gerver, 1976; Goldman-Eisler & Cohen, 1974) that simultaneous interpretation involves a curious start/stop property in which bursts of translated material are preceded and followed by long silent pauses. Insofar as the interpreter's task requires both comprehension and production, then clearly some mechanisms must be used to "buy time" for one activity, without hindering the other. Might different strategies be possible when one of the languages is a sign language? Experienced sign interpreters claim that they often will sign and comprehend at the same time, but such introspective accounts are not sufficient to resolve the issue. Gerver (1976) discussed the possibility that interpreters may be able to utilize redundancy to make predictions about what a speaker will say. Such predictions could ease the task of the interpreter enormously, though, as Gerver also noted, such predictions are likely to be useable only sporadically during the course of interpretation. For sign interpretation, however, the redundancy of signs may be useable in two ways: as an aid in the prediction of forthcoming signs and as a kind of built-in mnemonic aid, to reduce the cognitive short-term memory load. If so, then sign interpreters may show very different start/stop patterns than speech interpreters. It is a possibility that deserves serious study.

In closing, I hope you have become convinced that we know a good deal now about the nature of sign language as language but still have much to learn about its specific, unique properties. Further, we have a great deal to learn about the process of interpretation and translation when sign language is involved. It is my firm conviction that research on the latter set of issues will prove to be immensely valuable for our knowledge of translation in general, as well as for our knowledge of the unique properties of sign language.

REFERENCES

Anthony, D. A. *Seeing Essential English. Vol. I and II.* Anaheim, California: Educational Services Division, Anaheim Union High School District, 1971.

Barik, H. C. Simultaneous interpretation: Temporal and quantitative data. *Language and Speech*, 1973, *16*, 237 - 270.

Battison, R. Phonological deletion in American Sign Language. *Sign Language Studies,* 1974, *5*, 1 - 19.

Bellugi, U., and Klima, E. S. Aspects of sign language and its structure. In J. F. Kavanagh and J. E. Cutting (Eds.)., *The Role of Speech in Language*. Cambridge, Massachusetts: The MIT Press, 1975a.

Bellugi, U., and Klima, E. S. Two faces of sign: Iconic and abstract. In S. Harnad (Ed.)., *Origins and Evolution of Language and Speech*. New York: New York Academy of Sciences, 1975b.

Bellugi, U., Klima, E. S., and Siple, P. Remembering in signs. *Cognition: International Journal of Cognitive Psychology*, 1975, *3*, 93 - 125.

Clark, H. H., and Clark., E. V.. *Psychology and Language: An Introduction to Psycholinguistics*. New York: Harcourt Brace Jovanovich, 1977.

Conrad, R. Speech and reading. In J. F. Kavanagh, and I. G. Mattingly (Eds.). *Language by Ear and by Eye: The Relationships between Speech and Reading*. Cambridge, Massachusetts: MIT Press, 1972.

Eastman, G. C. *Sign Me Alice: A Play in Sign Language*. Washington, D.C.: Gallaudet College Bookstore, 1974.

Fodor, J. A., Bever, T. G. and Garrett, M. F. *The Psychology of Language: An Introduction to Psycholinguistics and Generative Grammar* New York: McGraw-Hill, 1974.

Fromkin, V. A. The non-anomalous nature of anomalous utterances. *Language*, 1971, *47*, 27 - 52.

Gerver, D. Empirical studies of simultaneous interpretation: A review and a model In R. W. Brislin (Ed.). *Translation: Applications and Research*. New York: Gardner Press, Inc., 1976.

Goldman-Eisler, F., and Cohen, M. An experimental study of interference between receptive and productive processes relating to simultaneous translation. *Language and Speech*, 1974, *17*, 1 - 10.

Hewes, G. W. Gesture language in cultural contact. *Sign Language Studies*, 1974, *4*, 1 - 34.

Hoemann, H. W. *The American Sign Language: Lexical and Grammatical Notes with Translation Exercises*. Silver Spring, Maryland: National Association of the Deaf, 1976.

Hoemann, H. W., The transparency of meaning of Sign Language gestures. *Sign Language Studies*, 1975, 7, 151 - 161.

Jakobson, R. About the relation between visual and auditory signs. In R. Jakobson, *Selected Writings II: Word and Language*. The Hague: Mouton, 1971.

Jakobson, R. On linguistic aspects of translation. In R. A. Brower (Ed.)., *On Translation*. Cambridge, Massachusetts: Harvard University Press, 1959.

Klima, E. S. Sound and its absence in the linguistic symbol. In J. Kavanagh and J. Cutting (Eds.). *The Role of Speech in Language*. Cambridge, Massachusetts: The MIT Press, 1975.

Lane, H., Boyes-Braem, P., and Bellugi, U. Preliminaries to a distinctive feature analysis of American Sign Language. *Cognitive Psychology*, 1975, *8*, 263 - 289.

Liddell, S. K. *Restrictive Relative Clauses in American Sign Language*. Unpublished manuscript. The Salk Institute, La Jolla, California, 1975.

Mallery, G. Sign Language Among North American Indians, Compared with that Among Other Peoples and Deaf-Mutes. *First Annual Report of the Bureau of American Ethnology*. J. W. Powell (Ed.)., 1881, 263 - 552. (Reprinted 1972, The Hague: Mouton & Co.).

Miller, G. A. and Isard, S. Some perceptual consequences of linguistic rules. *Journal of Verbal Learning and Verbal Behavior*, 1963, *2*, 217 - 228.

Miller, G. A., and Nicely, P. E. An analysis of perceptual confusions among some English consonants. *Journal of the Acoustical Society of America*, 1955, *27*, 338 - 352.

Saegert, J., Hamayan, E., and Ahmar, H. Memory for language of input in polyglots. *Journal of Experimental Psychology: Human Learning and Memory*, 1975, *1*, 607 - 613.

Sales, B. D., Cole, R. A., and Haber, R. N. Mechanisms of aural encoding: VIII. Phonetic interfercnce and context-sensitive coding in short-term memory. *Memory and Cognition*, 1974, *2*, 596 - 600.

Siple, P., Fischer, S. D., and Bellugi, U. Memory for non-semantic attributes of American Sign Language signs and English words. *Journal of Verbal Learning and Verbal Behavior*, 1977, *16*, 561 - 574.

Steiner, G. *After Babel: Aspects of Language and Translation*. London: Oxford University Press, 1975.

Stokoe, W. C., Jr. *Semiotics and Human Sign Languages*.The Hague, Mouton, 1972.

Stokoe, W. C., Jr. Classification and description of sign languages. In T. A. Sebeok (Ed.)., *Current Trends in Linguistics, Vol. 12: Linguistics and Adjacent Arts and Sciences*. The Hague, Mouton, 1974.

Stokoe, W. C., Jr. Sign Language structure, an outline of the visual communications systems of the American deaf. *Studies in Linguistics, Occasional Paper # 8*, 1960, Buffalo, New York.

Tweney, R. D., and Heiman, G. W. The effect of sign language grammatical structural on recall. *Bulletin of the Psychonomic Society*, 1977, *10,* 331 - 334.

Tweney, R. D., Heiman, G. W. and Hoemann, H. W. Psychological processing of sign language: Effect of visual disruption on sign intelligibility. *Journal of Experimental Psychology: General,* 1977, *106,* 225 - 268.

Tweney, R. D., and Hoemann, H. W. Translation and sign language. In R. W. Brislin (Ed.), *Translation: Applications and Research*. New York: Gardner Press, Inc. 1976.

Tweney, R. D., Liddell, S. K., and Bellugi, U. *The perception of grammatical boundaries in ASL*. Unpublished manuscript. Bowling Green State University, Bowling Green, Ohio, 1977.

Woodward, J. C., Jr., A report on Montana-Washington implicational research. *Sign Language Studies*, 1974, *4*, 77 - 101.

Sign Language Interpretation and General Theories of Language, Interpretation and Communication

Robert M. Ingram

Brown University

Providence, Rhode Island

The practice of interpretation of sign languages dates back many, many years, though the practice is just now struggling to achieve the status of a profession – shifting from a more-or-less clinical focus to a more-or-less linguistic one. Research on sign languages, which is itself very recent, has convincingly demonstrated that at least some sign languages are indeed languages in the linguistic sense, thereby forcing us to expand our conceptions of the nature of language and to re-examine our approaches to the study of language. Experiments on the simultaneous interpretation of sign languages are contributing to our knowledge and understanding of language and communication in general as well as to the resolution of problems dealing specifically with sign language interpretation. These are the major points that we have gained from the presentations by Domingue and Ingram, Tweney, and Murphy. The relevance of their discussions of sign language interpretation to the general subject areas of language, interpretation, and communication is largely self-evident. Essentially, we are all saying that the interpretation of sign languages is an integral part of the general study of interpretation and that no description (practical or theoretical) of interpretation which fails to take account of sign language interpretation can be regarded as complete. I have set myself the task of demonstrating this point beyond any doubt. The papers by Domingue and Ingram, Tweney, and Murphy have called attention to a number of problems in interpretation of sign languages. My approach will be to explore some of these problems further in relation to language, interpretation and communication in general.

LINGUISTIC VERSUS SEMIOTIC TRANSLATION

In his opening remarks, Tweney alludes to Jakobson's (1959) distinction between linguistic translation and semiotic translation (or transmutation), and, in an earlier paper with Hoemann, he refers to sign languages as 'semiotic systems' (after Stokoe, 1972) and to sign language interpretation as a type of 'intersemiotic translation' (Tweney and Hoemann, 1976, p. 138). But when Jakobson speaks of semiotic translation, he is speaking of the translation of one non-linguistic code to another, such as the translation of painting to music, or of a linguistic code to a non-linguistic code, as in the translation of a verse to a series of drawings. If we regard sign languages as 'the drawing of pictures in the air', then we might conclude that sign language interpretation does belong to Jakobson's category of semiotic translation. However, Tweney cites considerable evidence to support the conclusion that sign languages are not 'pictures in the air' but are, in fact, linguistic systems, thus establishing sign language interpretation under the category of linguistic translation rather than semiotic translation. What appears to be a dilemma here is, in fact, no different from the problem that we face in characterizing the interpretation of spoken languages. That sign languages are indeed languages in the linguistic sense is a point which has been well established. Lest there be any equivocation on this point, consider the conclusion of Klima and Bellugi (1976, p. 46).

"When we refer to sign languages as "languages", we mean that they have sentential units which have a strict semantic-propositional interpretation (providing among other things for the possibility of paraphrase); that they also have a hierarchically organized syntax – open-ended in terms of possible messages – and furthermore, that at the formational level of the individual lexical units (the individual signs) as well as the syntactic level, there are specific constraints as to well-formedness. What is more, there is a definite sense among those with a sign language as a native language (for example, the offspring, deaf and hearing, of deaf parents – offspring who learned sign language as their first language) that the sign decidedly has a citation form – a form which exists out of any specific real-life context. That is, the sign is not situation-bound as are some affective units of communication. (We presume, for example, that a scream does not have a citation form in this sense; nor presumably would an element of free pantomime). Thus, an ASL sign as such is no more bound to a particular context than is a word of spoken language."

Given this view of sign languages as linguistic systems, we can only conclude that sign languages belong with spoken languages within the category which Jakobson calls linguistic translation.

There is, on the other hand, a sense in which sign language interpretation can be regarded as semiotic, but that is a sense in which all simultaneous interpretation – indeed all use of language – is semiotic. Rather than establishing language in opposition to other semiotic systems, Jakobson (1975) has more recently argued for a view of language as a type of semiotic system, a position also taken by Eco (1976). From this perspective, we see linguistic translation, including the simultaneous interpretation of sign languages as well as of spoken languages, not as distinct from semiotic translation but as a subset of the more general category of semiotic translation.

LIMITATIONS TO A LINGUISTIC POINT OF VIEW

Recent findings about sign languages are but one entry in a growing list of factors pointing to the inadequacy of contemporary linguistics to describe human languages. Says one prominent anthropological linguist (Hymes, 1973, p. 60): 'Thus, one of the problems to be overcome with regard to language is the linguist's usual conception of it. A broader, differently based notion of the form in which we encounter and use language in the world . . . is needed.' To Hymes, this broader view is representated by the term 'ways of speaking', or 'the ethnography of communication'. To others, the answer lies in the study of speech acts, ethnomethodology, or the intersection of linguistics with other disciplines, e.g. sociolinguistics, psycholinguistics, or neurolinguistics. Semiotics incorporates contributions from all of these approaches and others besides and, in my view, represents the most productive platform from which to study language in general and simultaneous interpretation in particular.

Seleskovitch (1976) takes a similar view of the insufficiency of linguistics to describe simultaneous interpretation. Interpretation, she says (1976, p. 94), 'is so unconcerned with language (as a linguistic system) that it denies words or sentences any claim to translatability as long as they fail to merge into a meaningful whole: the discourse'. Compare this statement with the following one by a leading semiotician (Eco, 1976, p. 57): 'I am saying that usually a single sign-vehicle conveys many intertwined contents and therefore what is commonly called a "message" is in fact a *text* whose content is a multilevelled *discourse*.' Referring to the work of another semiotician (Metz, 1970), Eco (1976, p. 57) claims that 'in every case of communication (except maybe some rare cases of a very elementary and univocal type) we are not dealing with a message but with a text' and he defines a text as 'the result of the co-existence of many codes (or, at least, of many subcodes)'. Now, again, compare Seleskovitch (1976, p. 99):

"An interpreter receiving a speech never receives linguistic units entirely devoid of context (verbal and situational) but rather receives utterances spoken by a person whose position, nationality, and interests are known to him, speaking with a purpose in mind, trying to convince his listeners. Thus an utterance bearing a message differs absolutely from a sequence of words chosen at random, for the former evokes not only their intrinsic linguistic meaning but facts known to all those for whom the message is intended".

What Seleskovitch is saying, in essence, is that the interpreter must decode, transfer, and re-encode not single, linguistic messages and codes at a time but a multiplicity of messages in a multiplicity of interwoven codes with every single act of interpretation.

Treatments of interpretation in general tend to play down the significance of all codes except the linguistic ones, but interpreters of sign languages cannot afford this luxury. We have to interpret every act of communication – intentional or unintentional, human or non-human – that a receptor would normally perceive except for his hearing loss. For example, if a telephone rings during the course of an interview, that ringing must be interpreted. When static comes through the sound system in a conference room, interpreters of spoken language try to ignore the noise, but interpreters of sign languages have to interpret that noise. We interpret airplane noises, sneezes, falling chairs; anything and everything that the receptor would otherwise perceive if he were not deaf. The reverse principle applies as well. If the deaf person signs haltingly, our spoken rendition is halting. Paralinguistic manipulations of the hands, face, and body are interpreted as speech suprasegmentals. We do not filter out ambiguities, either in content or form. Rather, we try to match those ambiguities as best we can in the corresponding codes of the receptor. The primary codes with which we deal are linguistic codes, but we are also concerned to a considerable extent with non-linguistic codes, and, in this sense, sign language interpretation serves to remind us that only a semiotic view of interpretation can be sufficient to describe this complex process.

POSSIBLE CONTRIBUTIONS OF LINGUISTICS

A major problem we face in sign language interpretation is the lack of data to describe the linguistic codes, i.e. the sign languages, we use. Of course, there have been linguistic studies of American Sign Language (ASL), much of which has been reviewed by Tweney in his paper, and there have also been studies of the sign languages of Denmark (Hansen, 1975; Lieth, 1976; Sorensen and Hansen, 1976), Sweden (Ahlgren, 1976; Bergman, 1976), Israel (Schlesinger, 1969), Japan (Tanokani et al, 1976), the South Sea island of Rennel (Kuschel, 1974), and elsewhere. Still, what we know of the linguistic structures of various sign languages, including ASL, is very meagre and very tentative.

A central issue in second language teaching concerns whether one should teach about the language or simply teach the language. With sign languages, unless we know about the language, we cannot at all be certain that we know the language. Sign languages have for so long been regarded as mere surrogates of speech, as noted by Murphy, that interpretations of sign languages all too often appear as transliterations rather than as interpretations. Not until we have adequate linguistic descriptions of sign languages will we be able to deal with this problem effectively. We need descriptions that will tell us not only how a given sign language differs from a given spoken language, e.g. how ASL differs from English, but also how various sign languages differ from one another. In recent years, we have seen a new kind of interpretation developing at international conferences– interpretation from one sign language to another, with or without the use of an intervening spoken language. Personally, I suspect that these sign-to-sign renderings are more like glossings than like interpretations, but we cannot be sure of this assumption, nor can we correct it if it proves to be true, so long as we lack accurate linguistic data.

There is another way that linguistics can help us, and that is in the development of approaches to the teaching of sign languages. In the United States alone, thousands of persons receive education in some form of American Sign Language every year. Yet, few, if any, of these courses are based on viable principles of linguistics or second-language learning (Ingram, 1977). It is possible to pursue a Bachelors degree with a major in sign language interpretation, but it is not possible to get a major in sign language per se. We pretend to offer training in the interpretation of sign languages, while at the same time we admit that we do not know enough about the sign languages involved and about methods of teaching those languages. 'The learning of a natural sign language . . . requires not only the acquisition of new lexical items in new syntactic structures in a new frame of (semantic) reference but also the adjustment to perceiving language through the eyes rather than through the ears and to producing language through the manipulation of the hands, face, and upper body rather than through the vocal apparatus' (Ingram, 1977, p. 29). Exactly how this adjustment can best be effected is a task for psycholinguists and learning theorists. Brault (1963) has argued that the teaching of cultural gestures should be an integral part of second-language teaching, but by what methods should these gestures be taught? Perhaps studies of the teaching of sign languages can provide answers to this question. And what part do these gestures play in the interpretation of spoken languages? Here again, perhaps studies of sign language interpretation can provide the answers.

DEAFNESS AS A CULTURAL DISTINCTION

In the study of sign language interpretation, we must combat the assumption that sign languages are not only grammatical surrogates of spoken languages, but also that they overlap spoken languages semantically. Eco (1976) defines meanings as 'cultural units', and a number of researchers (Boese, 1964; Lieth, 1977; Meadow, 1972; Padden and Markowicz, 1976; Reich and Reich, 1974; Schein, 1968; Schlesinger and Meadow, 1972; Vernon and Makowsky, 1969) have clearly established that deaf people constitute at least a subculture if not a separate culture. The emerging attitude among sign language interpreters, as discussed by Domingue and Ingram, is that sign languages are distinct forms of representing cultural experiences that are peculiar to deaf people. In other words, deafness is, for the interpreter at least, not a clinical condition but a cultural one. If, as Tweney says, meanings 'are mapped onto words in different languages in different configurations' and if there is no one-to-one correspondence of these mappings, then how do the cultural meanings of deaf persons (as reflected in their sign languages) differ from the cultural meanings of the hearing cultures around them? Here we have a challenge for ethnographic semanticists.

SIGN LANGUAGE AS A SOURCE LANGUAGE

Among interpreters of spoken languages it is considered axiomatic that one can interpret more easily into one's own native language than into a second or later-learned language. This axiom, however, does not hold true in the interpretation of sign languages. If it did, then we would expect to find that interpretation from a sign language into a spoken language would be easier for persons who have acquired a sign language as a second language, but what we find, in fact, is that almost all interpreters regard interpretation into the spoken language as more difficult than interpretation into the sign language. In a few rare cases, an interpreter will report that it is easier for him to interpret from the sign language into the spoken language, but these persons are invariably children of deaf parents who have acquired their sign language before they acquired a spoken language – a situation revealing the opposite of what we would normally expect in interpretation. Why should interpretation from a sign language to a spoken language be considered a more difficult process than interpretation from a spoken language to a sign language?

In the first place, that interpreters regard interpretation from a spoken language to a sign language as an easier task is no assurance that that process is more effective in terms of communication than the reverse process. A sign language output may seem easier to facilitate than a spoken language output simply because the former is easier to fake. The interpreter can always shift into a sign language form that is easier for him, but not necessarily more comprehensible to the deaf person receiving the message. Unfortunately, deaf persons receiving such interpretations frequently just shrug, 'Oh, well, he (the interpreter) signs like a hearing person', and let it go at that. A spoken language output, though, is not so easy to fake; its flaws become readily apparent to the hearing receptor, and the interpreter's only recourse is to complain that interpretation from a sign language to a spoken language is a more difficult task.

But suppose we give the interpreters the benefit of the doubt and assume that there is, in fact, a viable reason why interpretation should be more difficult when the source language is a sign language. What might this reason be? One possible reason might be the very high incidence in sign languages of what Eco (1976) calls *undercoding*, which he defines as 'the operation by means of which in the absence of reliable pre-established rules, certain macroscopic portions of certain texts are provisionally assumed to be pertinent units of a code in formation, even though the combinational rules governing the more basic compositional items of the expressions, along with the corresponding content-units, remain unknown' (pp. 135-36). In other words, 'undercoding is an assumption that signs are pertinent units of a code in absence of any pre-established rules, that is, it is an imprecise, and still rough coding' (Sherzer, 1977, p. 81). This is not to say that sign languages are, in general, imprecise and rough codes. Rather, what I am saying is that sign languages may frequently become imprecise in those moments when their users attempt to expand them beyond their current limits. Murphy has reported about the suppression of sign languages that has existed throughout the ages. But now deaf people are beginning to share in events and experiences that were once closed to them, and they are finding their sign languages much too inadequate to represent these new experiences. They are constantly borrowing new lexical items in the form of fingerspelled words and initialized signs, and they are developing their own new signs. When this linquistic creativity takes place across a single deaf culture, there is the opportunity for cultural criticism and standardization, but many signs developed at a given moment to express a given concept fall by the wayside as nonce signs, perhaps never to appear again. It is these signs which constitute the bulk of the undercoding in a sign language and which present perhaps the greatest difficulty in interpreting from a sign language to a spoken language. The problem of undercoding is particularly strong in sign languages, but it is not a problem that is restricted to sign languages. I suspect that the same phenomenon exists in the languages of all cultures that are undergoing technological development or languages that are struggling to break free of suppression. No, the problem is not unique to sign languages, but, here again, we see a problem that should be of concern to all of us most clearly represented in sign languages.

In sign languages, we also find a kind of *overcoding*, meaning that there 'is either an over-analysis from within the system, or a mis-analysis from outside the system' (Sherzer, 1977, p. 81). Sign languages code in ways quite different from spoken languages, as Tweney has demonstrated, not just in that they symbolize meanings through the manipulation of the hands but also in their extensive use of the face and upper body to signal grammatical functions. Fischer (1975) has shown that certain word orders can be deemed grammatical, ungrammatical, or anomalous by the raising of an eyebrow or the tilting of the head ever so slightly. Pro-nominalization takes place through the manipulation of space rather that through the ordering of lexical items (Friedman, 1975). These overcoded linguistic rules are known subconsciously to every native user of a sign language, but where many interpreters falter is in determining how a lift of an eyebrow or a twitch of a shoulder is to be expressed in a vocal interpretation.

CHARACTERISTICS OF SIGN LANGUAGE INTERPRETERS

As anyone who has ever attempted to work with interpreters (of spoken languages or sign languages) knows, we are a strange breed. Schein (1974) attempted to find out just how strange we really are. He administered the Edwards Personality Preference Schedule to 34 interpreters in three Northeastern United States cities. Analyzing the scores of the 20 interpreters who completed the tests, Schein concluded that the successful interpreter 'desires to be the center of attention and to be independent, is not overly anxious, does not seek sympathy for self, and is not rigid' (Schein, 1974, p.42). Anderson (1976) discusses the interpreter and his role in terms of 1) the interpreter as bilingual, 2) ambiguities and conflicts, and 3) power. Each of these topics is applicable to the study of sign language interpreters.

Children of deaf parents usually learn their sign language before they acquire a spoken language (Cicourel, 1973; Cicourel and Boese, 1972; Klima and Bellugi, 1976; Mindel and Vernon, 1971; Schlesinger and Meadow, 1972). The sign language should, therefore, be the child's dominant language. But, societal pressures being what they are, it is likely that the spoken language eventually becomes established as the dominant language, at least most of the time. This reversal of dominant languages might help to explain why interpreters, even those for whom a sign language is their first language, consider interpretation from a sign language to be a more difficult task than interpretation into a sign language.

Anderson also observes that 'in general, it is expected that the greater the linguistic dominance the more likely an interpreter will identify with the speakers of the dominant language, rather than with clients speaking his "other" language' (1976, p. 213). Certainly, the problem of client identification is a major one for sign language interpreters, as we have heard from Domingue and Ingram. Some interpreters tend to identify with their signing clients in a paternalistic way; they feel they have to take a dominant role in 'straightening out' the deaf person. Some other interpreters tend to be maternalistic, to try to speak for the deaf person when he is perfectly capable of handling his own affairs. Clearly, the best interpreter and the one who is, in the long run, the most effective is the one who remains neutral in his role between two communicators.

The interpreter, whether of sign languages or spoken languages, is unquestionably a person in a position of power. Some children of deaf parents in particular, and some other people as well, become interpreters for this very reason. The child of deaf parents, says Lieth (1976, p. 318), 'is in an exceptional position; he will usually have sign language as his maternal language, but at the same time he will have to form a link to the hearing world; this gives him a special position within the family which may later cause him difficulties in adjusting himself to social situations where he has neither the responsibility nor the power he used to have in his home'. Rather than give up that power, many of these children of deaf parents assume the role of interpreter for other deaf people, a role which allows them to continue to exert power and influence.

Sociological and social psychological studies of interpreters and their roles are greatly needed to help us understand why people become interpreters and how they behave as interpreters. The added factor of deafness makes this line of inquiry all the more interesting, but the basic questions are essentially the same as those raised by the interpretation of spoken language.

NEUROLINGUISTIC AND PSYCHOLINGUISTIC STUDIES

There are many more ways in which the relevance of sign language interpretation to the general areas of language, interpretation, and communication can be demonstrated. Not the least of these are the intriguing mechanisms by which the brain is able to process two languages simultaneously, particularly where one of those languages is perceived visually rather than auditorily. Kimura (1976) cites the five known cases of deaf aphasics, and other neurological evidence, to support her claim that 'the left parietal region is an important part of a system controlling certain motor sequences, both vocal and manual', and that 'the symbolic-language functions of the left hemisphere are assumed to be a secondary consequence of specialization for motor function' (1976, p. 154). The implications here for a theory of simultaneous interpretation are significant indeed, but just how that significance can be applied must await further evidence.

CONCLUSION

I believe I have made my point. Just as no theory of language is complete unless it accounts for the total linguistic competence of human beings, i.e. the ability of people to acquire and use language in *all* its forms, likewise no theory of interpretation is complete unless it accounts for interpretation of language in all forms. A theory of interpretation based solely on languages which are orally produced and aurally perceived is an incomplete theory. Research into interpretation of sign language serves two main purposes: 1) to develop models and explanations that will contribute to the practice of sign language interpretation, and 2) to develop models and explanations that will contribute to our general understanding of the nature of language and communication. Certainly, there is value in asking 'What can research contribute to the theory and practice of sign language interpretation?' but there is perhaps even greater value in asking 'What can research on sign language interpretation contribute to general theories of language, interpretation, and communication?' or, to put it another way, 'How can the general study of language, interpretation, and communication be advanced by the application of data from research on sign language interpretation?' I hope that some of the answers I have tried to provide to this question will stimulate collaborative research.

REFERENCES

Ahlgren, I. *Rapport om planering och förarbete i projektet 'Tidig Språklig Kognitiv Utveckling Hos Döva och Gravt Hörselskadade' (Forsikning om Teckenspråk I).* Stockholm: Stockholms Universitet, 1976.

Anderson, R. B. W. Perspectives on the role of interpreter, in R. W. Brislin (Ed.). *Translation: Applications and Research*, New York: Gardner Press, 1976.

Bergman, B. *Teckenspråkets lingvistiska status: Rapport Nr. V (So-projekt LiS 237).* Stockholm: Stockholms Universitet, 1976.

Boese, R. J. *Differentiations in the deaf community.* Unpublished study submitted to the Department of Sociology, University of British Columbia, 1964.

Brault, G. J. Kinesics in the classroom: Some typical French gestures. *French Review*, 1963, 374 - 382.

Cicourel, A. *Cognitive Sociology*. Harmondsworth: Penguin Books, 1973.

Cicourel, A., and Boese, R. The acquisition of manual sign language and generative semantics. *Semiotica*, 1972, *3*, 225 - 56.

Eco, U. *A Theory of Semiotics*. Bloomington: Indiana University Press, 1976.

Fischer, S. Influence on word order change in American Sign Language, in C. Li (Ed.). *Word Order and Word Order Change*, Austin: University of Texas Press, 1975.

Friedman, L. A. Space, time and person reference in American Sign Language. *Language*, 1975, *51: 4*, 940 - 61.

Hansen, B. Varieties in Danish Sign Language and grammatical features of the Original Sign Language. *Sign Language Studies*, 1975, *8*, 249 - 56.

Hymes, D. On the origins and foundations of inequality among speakers. *Daedalus*, 1973, *102 : 3*, 59 - 86.

Ingram, R. M. *Principles and Procedures of Teaching Sign Languages*. Carlisle: British Deaf Association, 1977.

Jakobson, R. On Linguistic aspects of translation, in R. A. Brower (Ed.). *On Translation*, Cambridge: Harvard University Press, 1959.

Jakobson, R. *Coup d'Oeil sur le Développement de la Sémiotique. (Studies in Semiotics, 3)*. Bloomington: Indiana University Press, 1975.

Kimura, D. The neural basis of language qua gesture, in H. Whitaker and H. A. Whitaker, (Eds.). *Studies in Neurolinguistics, 2 (Perspectives in Neurolinguistics and Psycholinguistics)*, New York: Academic Press, 1976.

Klima, E. S., and Bellugi, U. Poetry and song in a language without sound. *Cognition*, 1976, *4*, 45 - 97.

Kuschel, R. *Lexicon of Signs from a Polynesian Outlier Island (Psykologisk Skriftserie Nr. 8)*. Kobenhavn: Kobenhavns Universitet, 1974.

Lieth, L. v. d. *Dansk Dove-tegnsprog*. Kobenhavn: Akademisk Forlag, 1976.

Lieth, L. v. d. The use of deaf sign language, in F. B. Crammatte and A. B. Crammatte (Eds). *Proceedings of the VIIth World Congress of the World Federation of the Deaf*. 1976.

Lieth, L. v.d. *Dov i Dag 3*. Kobenhavn: Danske Doves Landsforbund, 1977.

Meadow, K. P. Sociolinguistics, sign language and the deaf sub-culture, in T. J. O'Rourke (Ed.). *Psycholinguistics and Total Communication: The State of the Art*. Washington, D.C.: American Annals of the Deaf, 1972.

Metz, C. *Language et Cinéma*, Paris: Larousse, 1970.

Mindel, E., and Vernon, M. Psychological and psychiatric aspects of profound hearing loss, in D. E. Rose (Ed.). *Audiological Assessment*, Englewood Cliffs, N.J.: Prentice Hall, 1971.

Padden, C. and Markowicz, H. Cultural conflicts between hearing and deaf communities, in F. B. Crammatte and A. B. Crammatte (Eds.). *Proceedings of the VIIth World Congress of the World Federation of the Deaf*. 1976.

Reich, P. A., and Reich, C. M. *A follow-up study of the deaf*. Toronto: Research Service, Board of Education, No. 120, 1974.

Schein, J. *The Deaf Community: Studies in the Social Psychology of Deafness*. Washington, D.C.: Gallaudet College Press, 1968.

Schein, J. Personality characteristics associated with interpreter proficiency. *Journal of the Rehabilitation of the Deaf*, 1974, *7 : 3*, 33 - 43.

Schlesinger, H. S., and Meadow, K. P. *Sound and Sign: Childhood Deafness and Mental Health*, Berkeley: University of California Press, 1972.

Schlesinger, I. M. *The grammar of sign language and the problem of language universals*. Hebrew University and Israel Institute of Applied Social Research (mimeo), 1969.

Seleskovitch, D. Interpretation, a psychological approach to translating, in R. W. Brislin (Ed.). *Translation: Applications and Research*, New York: Gardner Press, 1976.

Sherzer, D. Review of a Theory of Semiotics, by U. Eco, and Coup d'Oeil sur le Développement de la Sémiotique, by R. Jacobson. *Language in Society*, 1977, *6 : 1*, 78 - 82.

Stokoe, W. C. *Semiotics and Human Sign Languages*. The Hague: Mouton, 1972.

Sorensen, R. K., and Hansen, B. *Tegnsprog: En Undersogelse af 44 Dove Borns Tegnsprogskommunikation*. Kobenhavn: Statens Skole for Dove, 1976.

Tanokami, T. *et. al.* *On the Nature of Sign Language*. Hiroshima: Bunka Hyoron Publishing Co., 1976.

Tweney, R., and Hoemann, H. Translation and sign languages, in R. W. Brislin (Ed.). *Translation: Applications and Research*, New York: Gardner Press, 1976.

Vernon, M., and Makowsky, B. Deafness and minority group dynamics. *The Deaf American*, 1969, *21* 3 - 6.

Linguistic Abilities in Translators and Interpreters

John B. Carroll

University of North Carolina at Chapel Hill

Chapel Hill, North Carolina

My purpose is not to report any results of empirical research on linguistic abilities in translators and interpreters, for I have never had the opportunity to do any such research, but to review research in the general area of linguistic abilities that might have relevance to the selection and training of translators and interpreters. As I understand the purpose of the symposium, it is to bring research workers in psycholinguistics together with practitioners in language translation and interpretation, with the hope that new research directions can be defined.

I cannot claim any great familiarity with problems of translation and conference interpretation, except that I, like many scientists who attend international meetings, have observed conference interpreters at work and have been impressed with their efforts, although in the nature of things it is usually difficult for a conference participant, even if he knows the language being translated, to know just how well they perform that work. This raises one of the first issues that would occur in any empirical work on the selection and training of translators and interpreters: what is the criterion of success, that is, how can success in translation and interpretation be measured? In the case of translation (i.e., written translation), what kinds of measures of accuracy and effectiveness could be obtained? In the case of conference interpretation, could conference participants (not being able to understand the language from which the interpretation is made) provide any reliable and valid judgements of the success of the performance? Or could success be measured only by a detailed comparative analysis of the input and output messages?

I suppose that this problem of defining the criterion has been faced, in one form or another, both by practitioners and by research workers in the field, but I am unaware of any thoroughgoing study of the matter. It may, however, be pertinent for me to mention a small contribution that I have made to evaluating the quality of translations. This was in connection with a policy committee (the Automatic Language Processing Advisory Committee) of the National Academy of Sciences that sought to evaluate whether machine translation algorithms available in the middle 1960s were capable of producing useful translations of Russian scientific writings. My procedures involved a sentence-by-sentence analysis of (Russian) input and (English or quasi-English) output messages. Two measures were employed: first, output sentences were evaluated by a panel of judges on a 9-point scale for "intelligibility"; next, a very carefully-made translation of the input message was presented to the subjects, who then made a judgment of the degree to which the careful translation was "informative", i.e., reduced any uncertainty inherent in the output sentence. The judges did not know Russian. Output sentences came from three different machine translation algorithms, but also from three human translators. These measures differentiated the quality of the three machine translations, but they also differentiated the quality of the three human translations, which were done under the normal conditions under which human translators work (Carroll, 1965-66, 1966). No one of the three "normal" human translations was quite as good as the "careful" translation. I would think that procedures similar to these might serve to provide measures of the quality of conference interpretations, although they do have the disadvantage of requiring a sentence-by-sentence analysis, the availability of a very careful translation, and a panel of judges. Actually, it is moot whether it is necessary to have the careful translation as a basis for the judgments of "informativeness", since the ratings of "intelligibility" were highly correlated (negatively) with the ratings of "informativeness". This finding encourages me to think that judgments of the output of conference interpreters might be highly reliable and valid even without any consideration of the accuracy of that output as translation of the input.

It is not within the scope of this paper, however, to consider the problem of defining and measuring success in translation and interpretation, but I do not see any paper specifically devoted to that topic on the conference program. Probably it is a topic that will come up in various connections, however; certainly it is one that merits careful and thorough investigation, since any empirical research in the selection and training of translators or interpreters will require the availability of a criterion of success.

I made some effort to inquire into methods of selecting persons for training in translation and interpretation, but my resources were somewhat limited since there are few schools of translation and interpretation in the United States. In April 1977 I spent a day at the Division of Interpretation and Translation in the School of Languages and Linguistics at Georgetown University, Washington, D.C., observing procedures in examining candidates for study in that division. The Division offers two distinct certificate programs, one in translation and one in interpretation. The interpretation program is a full-time two semester course. Entrance examinations are given six times a year, and I was privileged to observe these examinations on one occasion.

The entrance examination consists of several procedures, depending partly on what the candidate is applying for. Written translation exercises are given in both directions over the candidate's two languages (or several languages, in some cases), the candidate not being allowed to use a dictionary in at least some of these exercises. I did not directly observe the translation examinations, but believe I can make fair inferences about the nature of those examinations. The oral examination is conducted individually in the presence of several examiners. The standard procedure is to start by giving the applicant a text in his passive language, to be translated orally at sight. Texts are passages of moderate difficulty from magazine articles, speeches given at international conferences, etc. Next, the applicant is asked to render in his or her own words, in the active language, the content of what has just been translated. Then the applicant (if indeed he or she has done well enough to get this far) is asked to listen to a spontaneous, "live" discourse (of 3 to 5 minutes duration) given by one of the examiners, in the passive language. The applicant is encouraged to take notes on this discourse while it is being delivered; then the applicant is asked to give an oral consecutive translation. Finally, the applicant is asked to deliver, in a language of his choice, an oral discourse or argument on some topic, usually a rebuttal of the discourse that has just been heard. (Frequently, applicants are in effect asked to deliver speeches supporting views that they are probably in disagreement with, e.g., a speech supporting colonialism, in rebuttal to a speech that is critical of colonialism).

The whole interview is conducted in a highly informal manner, to put the applicant at ease. The examiners may intersperse the examination procedure with conversation concerning the applicant's educational background, foreign language training, expectations regarding training and employment as a conference interpreter, etc.

Over a period of about 6 hours, I observed the oral examinations of 11 candidates (about a half-hour per candidate, but the duration varied widely since some candidates with obviously poor qualifications were dismissed after only a few minutes, and other candidates were kept under examination for nearly an hour). It was evident that the major purpose of the oral examination was to assess the applicant's knowledge of the respective languages, his fluency in speaking the active language, his demeanor in speaking (voice quality, directness of gaze, tempo, freedom from hesitation), his ability to comprehend and remember the content of a discourse, and the agility of his mind in shaping an elegant rendering of a discourse in another language.

What surprised me was the poor qualifications of many of the applicants. (Since I have at least reasonable competence in several of the languages involved, I was able in most cases to judge the candidates' expertise in giving accurate sight translations of written materials, and to judge the quality of their consecutive translations of spoken discourses). Many of the applicants seemed to have only a relatively elementary knowledge of their passive language, with large gaps in their knowledge of both vocabulary and grammar. Even those who were able to exhibit good knowledge of the language from which they had to translate seemed to have much trouble in expressing themselves competently and gracefully in their language. On the whole I got the impression that most of the applicants not only had poor knowledge of the second language or languages they claimed to know, but also had immature knowledge of their native language and inadequate skill in expressing themselves in it.

Perhaps I should not have been as surprised as I was about the poor foreign language qualifications of most of the applicants who presented themselves at the Georgetown University examinations. I should have remembered that in an extensive survey of foreign-language attainments of senior college students majoring in a foreign language in U. S. colleges and universities (Carroll, 1967a, 1967b), relatively small proportions of these students were found to have attained the levels of foreign language knowledge that I would think would be required for training as translators and interpreters. I do not know how matters stand in countries outside the United States, but I gather from at least one survey of attainment in German in the United Kingdom, paralleling my US study (Gomes da Costa, Smith & Whiteley, 1975), that the foreign language attainments of foreign language specialists emerging from universities are not always impressive. It would appear that the pool of individuals with sufficient qualifications in foreign languages to merit training as translators and interpreters is relatively small in many countries. The smallness of this pool will present a practical difficulty in the conduct of any empirical research that might be done on the selection and training of translators and interpreters.

The interviews I observed at Georgetown University permitted some assessment of applicants' characteristics besides their knowledge of foreign languages – their mastery of their native language, their general level of educational background, their fluency and readiness to express themselves, and their speech mannerisms. Since very few of the applicants I observed had adequate foreign language knowledge, however, it was impossible for me to judge whether any assessments that might have been made of applicants' characteristics other than their foreign language skills could have been either accurate or relevant to training in translation and interpretation. In talking with the directors of the Georgetown University training program, David and Margareta Bowen, I got the impression that they felt that there would be differences among candidates, even if well qualified in linguistic knowledge, in amenability to, and success in, training. In the remainder of this paper, I want to offer speculations on what the dimensions of these differences might be, based on the considerable amount of research that is now available about verbal abilities and other traits that might have relevance to performance in foreign language translation and interpretation.

It will be necessary to consider various aspects of performance in translation and interpretation. I assume that the situations that might have to be considered would include the following more or less distinct types:

(1) *Careful written translation.* This would involve the preparation of appropriate translations of any of a wide variety of genres of materials: fiction and non-fiction, newspaper and magazine writing, official documents, scientific articles, manufacturer's guides and instruction books, etc., up to the point of formal publication. The translator would take his time and use whatever materials (dictionaries, reference works, specialized publications, etc.) he might deem necessary.

(2) *Quick, informal written translation.* Here, the translator works under at least a moderate time pressure and has limited opportunity to perfect his translation through use of reference materials; the purpose of the translation is mainly to give the user an approximate idea of the content of the original material, and it is usually assumed that the user already has any specialized background that is necessary to comprehend that content. Frequently, in this case, the translator dictates a "sight" translation into a recording machine, with limited editing of the transcription.

(3) *Consecutive conference interpretation.* The interpreter listens to, and (optionally) takes written notes on, short segments of a discourse, and gives a rendering in another language after each segment.

(4) *Simultaneous conference interpretation.* Usually this occurs in a specially designed booth in which the interpreter listens to a discourse through earphones and renders his translation by speaking into a microphone as the input discourse proceeds. Sometimes the interpreter has available an approximate text in the source language, and may have an opportunity to review it before the discourse is actually delivered.

Different patterns of aptitudes and skills would, I suppose, be relevant for these four types of situations, but all require a high degree of verbal intelligence and general culture. Mere knowledge of a foreign language, and skill in understanding, speaking, reading, and writing it, does not ensure that the individual has the degree of verbal intelligence that is required for translation and interpretation. It would likewise not ensure that the individual has the educational background, and general culture, that would be demanded.

If I were asked to propose a battery of formal tests for selection of personnel for translation and interpretation training, the battery would certainly include, besides tests of foreign language skills, tests of verbal intelligence and culture in the native language.

Psychologists have proposed various models and theories of intelligence. Up until about 1935, the dominant model was that proposed by Charles Spearman, the British psychologist, who emphasized the importance of what he called "g" or general intelligence (Spearman, 1927). With the advent of more sophisticated mathematical models for analyzing cognitive ability tests, Thurstone (1938) proposed analyzing cognitive abilities into a series of "primary factors", including several that had relevance to verbal performance. Of these, the factor usually identified as "V", or "verbal intelligence", is probably most relevant to performance as an interpreter or translator. In a more detailed study of the V factor, I (Carroll, 1941) identified it as representing "differences in the stock of linguistic responses possessed by the individual – the wealth of the individual's past experience and training in the English language". But for "English language", one may equally well read, "native language". The tests appearing on the V factor in the author's study were such as to suggest that the verbal factor involves not only the individual's knowledge of advanced vocabulary, but also his sensitivity to established word usages, to the nuances of idiomatic phrases, and even his ability to predict the transitional probabilities of words in phrases, as in a test called Phrase Completion, wherein the subject was required to complete phrases like "As for . . . .", with the responses scored in terms of the frequency with which they were used by other respondents. The verbal factor is one of the best and most easily established factors of intelligence. It is involved not only in tests of vocabulary knowledge, but also tests of reading comprehension, ability and facility (speed) in detecting semantic and syntactic ambiguities, and ability in writing effective, highly rated themes. It would be my assumption that effective translators and interpreters should be high on this "verbal factor." The verbal factor would be particularly demanded in written translation, where exact verbal expression in the target language would be required, but it could be important in oral interpretation because it would reflect or predict more adequate comprehension of the content of the source message. For practical testing purposes, the verbal intelligence factor is best measured by a wide-range vocabulary test, with emphasis on the exact meanings of the more difficult and rarer words of a language. It may be expected that scores on such a test will be correlated with scores on tests of other aspects of verbal intelligence, such as reading comprehension tests.

Scores on verbal intelligence tests are highly correlated with amount of education, although it cannot be assumed that a diploma from an institution of higher learning will necessarily be accompanied by high scores on verbal intelligence tests. A test of advanced vocabulary knowledge can be challenging and taxing even for advanced university students, and it is likely to reveal the extent to which the student can accurately comprehend a variety of verbal materials, because students do not ordinarily acquire advanced vocabulary knowledge without extensive and critical reading. From a practical standpoint in using selection tests for translators and interpreters, the issue of whether verbal intelligence has genetic sources is completely irrelevant; the issue is whether the individual has attained the required level, through education and experience.

I would suppose that verbal intelligence would be particularly critical in the selection of personnel for training in careful, written translation, because this type of work makes great demands on the individual's sensitivity to words and their meanings, to appropriate ways of expressing ideas, and to the nuances of verbal argumentation. At the same time, high levels of verbal intelligence would be required in all forms of translation and interpretation work.

Closely related to verbal intelligence, although not ordinarily considered as a factor of mental ability, is general culture and education. Because of the wide variety of subject matter contexts in which translators and interpreters are required to work I would think that general culture and diverse educational background would be of importance. Breadth of information and culture can be assessed by tests of general educational development. Even if the tests assess nothing more than the level of factual information that the individual has acquired, they are likely to be predictive of the success of a translator/interpreter in meeting the demands of a wide variety of contexts in humanities, natural and social sciences, commerce and industry, governmental foreign affairs, etc. (No firm recommendations can be made as to tests and examinations currently available. The Co-operative General Culture Test, with scores in social studies, literature, science, fine arts, and mathematics, once available from the Co-operative Test Division of Educational Testing Service, is out of print, but similar tests with pertinent current content could be devised).

While these tests of verbal intelligence and general culture would be useful in selecting individuals with qualifications for either translation or conference interpreting, the particular kinds of verbal facilities required in either consecutive or simultaneous conference interpreting, particularly the latter, would provide the most fascination for the psycholinguist interested in linguistic abilities.

Thurstone's model of "primary mental abilities" provides little scope for the study of *productive* verbal abilities. His studies disclosed what he called a W or "word fluency" factor, measured by various tests designed to explore the individual's ability to manipulate orthographic materials to create lists of words, for example to think of words that begin with a certain letter and end with another letter, or that begin with a certain prefix (like *pre-*) or end with a certain suffix (like *-ness*). Psychologists have been unsuccessful in showing, however, that this type of test has anything to do with fluency in *speaking*, and the relevance of whatever ability is measured by such tests to any kind of creative activity has always been in doubt. Later studies (e.g. by Taylor, 1947; Taylor, Ghiselin, & Yagi, 1967) have disclosed, besides the "Word Fluency" factor, three other factors of individual differences in verbal fluency: Ideational Fluency, Expressional Fluency, and Associative Fluency. All these factors involve speed in producing a variety of verbal responses under particular constraints, and in this light one might consider that they would possibly be involved in the kind of rapid-fire verbal production required in simultaneous conference interpreting. In the manual for a kit of factor tests published by Educational Testing Service in 1963 (French, Ekstrom & Price, 1963) the following information about these factors was given:

Ideational Fluency: defined as "the facility to call up ideas wherein quantity and quality of idea is emphasized", this factor was measured by a Topics test requiring the subject to write as many ideas as possible on a given subject (e.g. "a man climbing up a ladder"), Theme, which asks the subject to write as long a composition as possible on a topic, and Things Category, which asks the subject to list as many items as possible that are alike in some way, e.g. things that are round.

Expressional Fluency: defined as "the ability to think rapidly of appropriate wording for ideas", this factor was measured by various tests in which the subject was asked to rephrase certain ideas in as many ways as possible or to invent sentences in which the syntax is in some way constrained.

Associational Fluency: defined as "the ability to produce words from a restricted area of meaning", this factor was measured by tests requiring subjects to write, in a brief period of time, as many synonyms or antonyms as possible for given words.

It should be noted, however, that existing tests of these fluency factors are practically all written tests in which sheer writing speed may play a part. There has been relatively little investigation of these fluency factors in situations involving oral production. Taylor et al. (1967) studied various fluency tests, some requiring oral production, and found their scores related to success in such activities as instructing others, conducting conferences and interviews, and writing reports. Cattell (1971) and others have claimed that the fluency factors are also related to certain personality traits, such as "extraversion" and "exuberance". I understand that simultaneous conference interpreters often have the reputation of being out-going, extraverted, exuberant people. Thus it would appear that investigations of the linguistic abilities and personalities of interpreters might well employ tests of the various fluency factors, both in oral and written modes. Performance on fluency tests, incidentally, is relatively independent of verbal intelligence; even when individuals are asked to give large numbers of synonyms to given words, their productions do not depend upon large vocabularies, but rather on speed and facility in retrieving the many relatively common words that meet the requirements of this task.

Interestingly, Ekstrom, in a review of recent literature on factors of cognitive ability, remarked, with regard to the associational fluency factor:

> "There appears to be no evidence to suggest that this factor is confined to the English language. It would be interesting to determine if the ability to produce an appropriate word when translating a well-known foreign language would involve associational fluency." (1973, p 25).

One other factor, possibly related to the above-described fluency factors, that is possibly relevant to rapid word-retrieval in a conference-interpreting situation is the Naming Facility factor, identified by Carroll (1941)and Thurstone and Thurstone (1941, factor X3) and later studied by Carroll (1967b). The Naming factor is tested by tasks in which individuals are asked to retrieve the names for pictured objects as rapidly as possible; the test can be given either in written form (in which the subject is asked to write the first letter of each name, for a long series of pictures) or in oral form, in which reaction time of naming is measured in a specially designed experimental situation in which pictures are presented tachistoscopically. Carroll and White (1973) and Lachman, Shaffer & Hennrikus (1974) have shown that speed of naming is influenced both by the frequency and the age-of-acquisition of the name, but after adjusting data for name frequency and age-of-acquisition, strong and consistent individual differences remain as determinants of speed of naming. It is entirely possible that properly controlled measurements of naming time, in a given language, would show an important relationship with success in conference interpreting, since conference interpreting would seem to demand that the performer be able to retrieve words very readily and rapidly.

The research work in the investigation of fluency and naming factors reflects an increasingly emphasized direction in the study of cognitive abilities, namely an emphasis on an "information processing" approach (Carroll, 1967a; Hunt and Lansman, 1975). It is assumed that individuals vary not only in the extent of their cognitive information (in "lexical memory stores") but also in the speed and facility with which they can store, retrieve and manipulate elements of information. Rapid rendering of a message in one language into a message in another language represents what would appear to be a tremendous feat in information processing. One component of that feat seems similar to what has been called "speech shadowing" (Cherry, 1953), i.e., repeating an auditory message aloud, word for word, while listening to it. Speech shadowing with a competing message has been extensively used in various studies of speech perception and selective listening. While shadowing appears to be a task that can be performed fairly easily by most speakers, there are apparently individual differences in the ability to shadow at very short distances. Marslen-Wilson (1973, 1975) was able to identify people who could shadow continuous speech, in the absence of a competing message, at a distance of only a quarter of a second. Tests of ability to shadow at short distances, with increasing speed and complexity of the input message, might be predictive of a person's ability to become an efficient simultaneous interpreter, even though the average time between input in a given language and output in another language, in simultaneous translating, is probably much longer than one quarter of a second. I know of no studies in which individual differences in shadowing ability have been studied in relation to other types of verbal abilities.

The shadowing task would involve the input and immediate output of continuous discourse material. With a longer delay of the output, i.e. only at the end of a segment of discourse, the task would resemble the sentence and paragraph recall tasks that have been much studied in experimental psycholinguistics. It would also resemble the task of the consecutive interpreter. Usually, ability to give an accurate immediate verbatim recall of a sentence has been found to correlate with general verbal intelligence; in fact, sentence recall tasks are to be found in such standard intelligence tests as the Stanford-Binet. Ability to give an acceptable rendering, in one's own words, of the gist of a longer passage is also related to general verbal intelligence, but it may also call on special abilities to organize the memory structure, to notice particular types of details in the input message, and to formulate the linguistic structure of the output. There has been little study of individual differences in the *oral* recall of sentence and paragraph material; most of the studies have involved written recall, or written recognition tests, for example using multiple-choice comprehension questions, and even in these cases the evidence for any kind of special "meaningful memory factor" is unclear (Ekstrom, 1973, pp. 78 - 79). Cattell (1971) has suggested that meaningful memory ability represents only a projection of intelligence into memorizing performance. Nevertheless, there are promising possibilities for research into the kinds of meaningful memory abilities that might be required by a consecutive conference interpreter, or that might be trained.

In this review of linguistic abilities that might be relevant in translation and interpretation, I have not mentioned the special kinds of abilities included under what is called foreign language aptitude. In my continuing research in foreign language aptitude (Carroll, 1962, 1973) I have identified certain abilities that seem to make for rapid learning of foreign languages – abilities that I have called "phonetic coding" and "grammatical sensitivity", for example. I doubt, however, that these abilities would be relevant to the prediction of success in translation and interpretation, given that the individuals selected for training in such work would have *already* attained a high level of competence in one or more languages other than their native language. To the extent that foreign language aptitudes are relevant in learning foreign languages, such individuals would be found to possess whatever level of aptitude that would have been required for their learning. Furthermore, foreign language aptitudes appear to be predictive only of the *rate* of learning under the kinds of conditions that usually obtain in formal language training; people who learn a foreign language in a bilingual milieu, for example, would not necessarily possess high degrees of foreign language aptitide as measured by aptitude tests.

While research in the aptitudes and abilities required in translation and interpretation work might have considerable practical value in providing means whereby candidates for training could be counselled and guided into particular kinds of work appropriate to their abilities, or discouraged from attempting training at all, my real interest in this type of research would center in what it might reveal about the mental processes of translators and interpreters in performing their tasks. Research in the underlying abilities is, of course, only one way of studying these mental processes, alongside other approaches that rely more on studying the effects of various experimental treatments. Even experimental psychologists, however, have come to recognize the possible value of the psychometric approach to the study of cognitive processes (e.g., Underwood, 1975; Estes, 1974; Hunt and Lansman, 1975).

REFERENCES

Carroll, J. B. A factor analysis of verbal abilities. *Psychometrika*, 1941, *6*, 279 - 307.

Carroll, J. B. The prediction of success in intensive foreign language training. In Robert Glaser (Ed.), *Training Research and Education*. Pittsburgh: Univ. of Pittsburgh press, 1962, 87 - 136.

Carroll, J. B. Quelques mesures subjectives en psycholinguistique: Frequence de mots, significativité et qualité de traduction. *Bulletin de Psychologie*, 1965-66, *19*, 580-591.

Carroll, J. B. An experiment in evaluating the quality of translations. *Mechanical Translation*, 1966, *9*, 55 - 66.

Carroll, J. B. The Foreign Language Attainments of Language Majors in the Senior Year: A Survey Conducted in U.S. Colleges and Universities. Cambridge, Mass.: Laboratory for Research in Instruction, Harvard Graduate School of Education. (ERIC Document Reproduction Service, ED 013 - 343), 1967a.

Carroll, J. B. Foreign language proficiency levels attained by language majors near graduation from college. *Foreign Language Annals*, 1967b, *1*, 131 - 151.

Carroll, J. B. Implications of aptitude test research and psycholinguistic theory for foreign language teaching. *International Journal of Psycholinguistics*, 1973, *2*, 5 - 14.

Carroll, J. B. Psychometric tests as cognitive tasks: A new "structure of intellect". In Lauren Resnick (Ed.), *The Nature of Intelligence*. Hillsdale, N.J.: Erlbaum, 1976a, 27 - 56.

Carroll, J. B. Word retrieval latencies as a function of frequency and age-of-acquisition priming, repeated trials, and individual differences. Princeton, N.J.: *Educational Testing Service Research Bulletin RB-76-7*, 1976b.

Carroll, J. B., and White, M. N. Word frequency and age of acquisition as determiners of picture-naming latency. *Quarterly Journal of Experimental Psychology*, 1973, *25*, 85 - 95.

Cattell, R. B. *Abilities: Their Structure, Growth, and Action*. Boston: Houghton Mifflin, 1971.

Cherry, E. C. Some experiments on the recognition of speech with one and two ears. *Journal of the Acoustical Society of America*, 1953, *25*, 975-979.

Ekstrom, R. B. Cognitive Factors: Some Recent Literature. Princeton, N.J.: *Educational Testing Service, Project Report PR-73-30*, 1973.

Estes, W. K. Learning theory and intelligence. *American Psychologist*, 1974, *29*, 740 - 749.

French, J. W., Ekstrom, R. B., and Price, L. A. Kit of Reference Tests for Cognitive Factors. Princeton, N.J.: *Educational Testing Service*, 1963.

Gomes da Costa, B., Smith, T. M. F., and Whiteley, D. *German Language Attainment: A Sample Survey of Universities and Colleges in the U.K.* Heidelberg: Julius Gross Verlag, 1975.

Hunt, E., and Lansman, M. Cognitive theory applied to individual differences. In W. K. Estes (Ed.)., *Handbook of Learning and Cognitive Processes. Vol. 1: Introduction to Concepts and Issues*. Hillsdale, N.J.: Erlbaum, 1975, 81 - 110.

Lachman, R., Shaffer, J. F., and Hennrikus, D. Language and Cognition: Effects of stimulus codability, name-word frequency, and age of acquisition on lexical reaction time. *Journal of Verbal Learning and Verbal Behavior* 1974, *13*, 613- 625.

Marslen-Wilson, W. D. Linguistic structure and speech shadowing at very short latencies. *Nature*, 1973, *244*, 522 - 523.

Marslen-Wilson, W. D. Sentence perception as an interactive parallel process. *Science*, 1975, *189*, 226 - 228.

Spearman, C. *The Abilities of Man*. London: Macmillan, 1927.

Taylor, C. W. A factorial study of fluency in writing. *Psychometrika*, 1947, *12*, 239 - 262.

Taylor, C. W., Ghiselin, B., and Yagi, K. *Exploratory Research on Communication Abilities and Creative Abilities*. Salt Lake City: University of Utah, 1967.

Thurstone, L. L. Primary mental abilities. *Psychometric Monographs*, 1938, *1*.

Thurstone, L. L., and Thurstone, T. G. Factorial studies of intelligence. *Psychometric Monographs*, 1941, *2*.

Underwood, B. J. Individual differences as a crucible in theory construction. *American Psychologist*, 1975, *30*, 128 - 134.

Psychological Approaches to Bilingualism, Translation and Interpretation

W. E. Lambert

McGill University

Montreal, Quebec

In my opinion, the translator, whether professional or not, could be a very special person because he or she, compared to other humans, is more likely to become a serious listener. In most aspects of life, inter-personal communication is mainly a system of reacting wherein one person listens to another only long enough to prepare an appropriate response, presumably with the aim of keeping the exchange flowing. Few people, I find, listen selflessly to others; rather we take what was said, interpret it, and prepare what we believe to be an appropriate reply. This is even so in situations where it is vital that we – as friends, loved-ones or counsellors – really listen. What could be special about interpreters is that they are expected to listen and dwell on what is being said and implied, to find meaning in talk and gestures, to search out root meanings, and to store this information so as to relay it with as much fidelity as possible through another language. The demands on the interpreter are enormous: we psychologists know from our own research that witnesses to the most simple situations are embarrassingly unreliable and personal in what they think they saw and heard. And yet we expect exactitude across languages from the interpreter. My hunch is that certain interpreters do stand out as special because they become out-of-the-ordinary listeners and witnesses and thus out-of-the-ordinary people.

Rarely in life does anyone stop the exchange process and accord a speaker's message the compliment that it is worth repeating. Interpreters thus pay the speaker the compliment – whether deserved or not – that his message is worth a replay or worth the processing time. The preoccupations of the interpreter should induce speakers to monitor carefully what they say. In some cases it should shut them up, although in my experience it is those speakers in particular who do anything but shut up. Either they try to "snow" the translator-interpreter through speed or verbiage, or, by slipping into jargon, cut the interpreter out, or use him as an excuse, implying that, because of translation, they can only present a simplified outline of what they really want to say. These ploys are part of the weaknesses of mankind. We are all conditioned to expect interlocutors to take off on what we say rather than listen to us, and we all know about that for we do the same with others with whom we interact. To have someone really listen to us is a worrisome prospect.

All I mean here is that the profession of translation and interpretation intrigues me, and I have a deep suspicion that we cognitive psychologists have much to learn from those in this profession. It could be that they form a subclass of humans who, either as a consequence of their occupation or because they have been so selected, have special skills at ferreting out meanings. It may be that their bilinguality, a prerequisite for membership in the profession, has the effect of providing them with special forms of intelligence, sensitivity, and skills at teasing out what is meant and what is left half said. Our own research suggests that bilingualism does have these types of effect (Lambert, 1977).

At the same time, there are many unanswered questions about interpreters and the translation process. For instance, interpreters often give the impression of doing their work without becoming preoccupied with messages *per se*; some I'm told interpret while knitting or even while reading a mystery story, and their memory for what was translated is said to be ephemeral. What might this mean? It sounds much like the typist who speedily and accurately recasts information from copy to final form in an automatic fashion and also with little recall of the information that was processed. What is meant by "automatic" in this sense? Perhaps interpreters are not serious listeners at all. At what level of consciousness is the translation done? Is the processing compartmentalized so that the interpreter's own cognitions go on quite independently? How does the interpreter divide his/her attention; does attention alternate from knitting to message or are the two processed simultaneously? But surely there are individual differences in attentiveness and profundity of analysis. Those of us who know two languages have all encountered some professional interpreters who work to the roots of meaning and others who are approximative and superficial. It would be especially instructive to have research information on individual differences of this sort.

It is also true that at times interpreters have to bluff and fill in, and thus they can be as anxious as speakers are that someone might find out that they have missed the main points or glossed over essentials. Interpreters in fact learn stock phrases that help smooth out their renditions. But how much filling in is permissible? This is an important question because the user of the interpreter's services rarely knows if the replay is a good one since he is usually ignorant of the source language. What is done within the profession to check on or improve the accuracy and truthfulness of the re-rendition, smooth-sounding fill-ins aside? Could the behavioral scientist be of help in this delicate matter? Finally, why is it that professional translators often have their suspicions about simultaneous interpretation, as though it has to be at best an approximation, and thus not to be taken seriously. Does this mean that translators and interpreters are two different breeds? And what do we know about the differences, if in fact they exist?

What I mean to say is that there is much to be learned about this fascinating profession and about those who practice it. Because this is so, I feel we are fortunate to be together here. A group of professionals in the fields of translation and interpretation, and a group of behavioral scientists, with the opportunity to explore the phenomena involved in translation and interpretation. Although fortunate, we have to be careful with one another, because we can get on one another's nerves. In the early 60's, I was at a seminar on translation and interpretation in Washington and there we missed in our attempts to communicate. The psycholinguist moves too quickly into jargon, and this is insulting and threatening to the outsider. Then, too, the professional translators at that meeting put psychologists off because they showed their irritation by demanding practical answers that were not available or by asking embarrassing questions that were obviously beyond the state of the art of cognitive psychology.

My hope then is that here we will be able to communicate and to explore issues and topics we have in common and both enjoy and profit from the interaction.

With this in mind, I have chosen to open a communication pathway by reviewing some attempts psychologists have made to explore and elucidate the distinctive styles of perceiving and thinking of bilinguals. In doing so, I will select examples that are relevant to the multi-disciplinary make-up of this conference and will highlight the *questions* we as psychologists are prone to ask; the sometimes complicated and elaborate *methodologies* we develop to provide what we consider to be credible answers to these questions; and some of the tentative conclusions we feel confident in drawing at this stage of our research. The *conclusions* can be profitable if the non-psychologists here can stay attentive enough to understand why we are so worried about our methodologies and testing, and then perhaps they can suggest ways for us to move more swiftly and directly to what they consider to be the central issues of bilingualism and its relevance to interpretation and translation.

THE MEASUREMENT OF LANGUAGE DOMINANCE

In the early 1950's I was intent on devising behavioral tests of the relative degree of dominance of one of a bilingual's two languages over the other. The central idea here was that a good definition of bilingualism has to include degrees of relative dominance, where one language is more pervasive and pivotal than the other as well as the rare instances where the two languages are equally pivotal or equally pervasive. To map this domain out in some objective fashion, bilingual adults were given tests to assess their relative speed of responding to simple directions presented alternatively in languages A and B. For example, they were instructed to "Push the yellow button", or "Poussez le button jaune", and so forth for a number of differently colored buttons. Care was taken that the frequency of usage of the color names was similar in the two languages, and all combinations of directions and languages were used. In this fashion, it was possible to distinguish subgroups of bilinguals who, in terms of speed of reaction, were relatively sluggish in language B versus A or vice versa, or who were apparently balanced in their swiftness of processing via A and B. The next step was to make sure that these differences in reaction times had a more general significance. So a battery of tests was developed including a) the time taken to recognize words in each of the bilingual's langauges, b) the relative fluency of giving free associations to stimulus words in each of the languages, and c) the relative speed of reading words and translating words from one language to the other, and so forth (Lambert, 1955; Lambert, Havelka and Crosby, 1958; Lambert, Havelka and Gardner, 1959). Interestingly, most measures of relative dominance clustered together in consistent ways, suggesting that the relative dominance of language A versus B, or the balance of the two, manifests itself in a variety of fashions. In other words, a bilingual who was balanced in his speed of pushing buttons on command was also balanced in his fluency of associating in the two languages, in perceiving words in the two languages, or in reading. The same relationships held for bilinguals who were relatively dominant in one of their two languages. With this as a base, we were then able to search for all sorts of correlates of bilingual balance and linguistic dominance, and to follow changes from dominance to balance among serious students of a foreign or second language.

Translation speed, however, did not fit in that well with the various other measures, and this was apparently so because one can have a bias for translating one way or the other even though the bilingual in question would be otherwise balanced. For example, an Anglo-Canadian studying law at a French-Canadian university could be faster at translating from English into French than the reverse, as though he had developed the habit of using the English to French half of a bilingual dictionary because he had found it valuable to anticipate how things are said in French.

A particularly exciting finding was that several bilinguals showed dominance in their recently acquired language over their native, mother tongue. That is, certain young American graduate students who spoke English only until college were in several cases revealing a relative dominance of French or Italian over English on the test battery, and doing so consistently. What followed was in-depth interviews to determine why this was so and it became clear that these young people, specializing in a foreign language academically, had so immersed themselves in French readings, in social and language contacts with the few French people available to them that little waking time was given over to the English speaking world around them. And just one layer below the daily usage level, they revealed why they were so ardent in their foreign language ventures: two I recall were Jewish and they were so plagued by the anti-semitic world they felt that they were in in the U.S.A., that they had made full plans to escape to France or Italy and restart their lives there. Two others revealed that they were homosexuals and were escaping from non-tolerant puritan America to what they thought was a more understanding and tolerant Europe.

The main point, though, is that by focusing on a simple surface matter like dominance, a route was opened to deep motivational forces that play a crucial role in determining one's linguistic and cultural worlds of experience, and motives of this sort might even determine the success one would have in trying to acquire a second or foreign language. Since then, several graduate students and I have explored the roles that motivation and attitude can play in language learning, in particular how an "integrative" outlook – wherein one has a positive attitude toward the cultural group whose language he is studying, coupled with a strong desire to be accepted as a member of that cultural group – in contrast to an "instrumental" or practical outlook toward language learning can effect one's progress in language study (Gardner and Lambert, 1971). Our current work follows from these ideas. Thus we find that an integrative outlook is helpful for those learners who enjoy the security of a major world language base, such as Anglo-Americans learning any foreign language, whereas for members of linguistic minority groups, such as Filipinos learning English, or French-Canadians learning English, an integrative orientation can lead to assimilation and thus the subtraction or loss of their own cultural-linguistic identity (see Lambert, 1973; Clement, Major, Gardner and Smythe, 1977). As a consequence, much of our current work has to do with developing school programs wherein linguistic minority groups in Canada and the U.S.A. can be given opportunities to develop full-fledged language strengths in their home languages before the major national or international language is given its free reign as a medium or learning (Lambert, 1973; Lambert, Giles and Picard, 1975). In sum, we started here with a simple question and as we proceeded we encountered a series of deep and complex issues.

THE TIME TAKEN TO TRANSLATE

In this example, we again ask a simple question and although the answer also seems simple enough, there are many complexities working just below the surface. Here we wanted to explore the mental time it takes to translate, and for this purpose we asked numbers of balanced bilinguals to take part in a sentence translation and/or transformation experiment. For example, in a thesis by Reynolds (1970), subjects were presented with simple active-affirmative (AA) sentences like "The old man tied up the boat", and they were trained in advance to transform each sentence to the passive (P), the negative (N) or the passive-negative form (NP), etc. In training, each form had been associated with a distinctive signal, one for P, another for N, etc. One signal indicated that the sentence was also to be translated; French and English were the languages involved. This procedure, using voice-operated time switches, permits one to determine the time added by the requirement of translation. We have not yet gone far into the complications of this investigation, but several conclusions are clear already. For example, on the average, translation takes up extra time, which should be no earth-shaking surprise to anyone, but this is not always the case: certain translations, when coupled with certain transforms, are consistently *faster* than the transforms without translation. Furthermore, the time taken to go from French to English was equivalent to going from English to French, except for certain forms like the French passive which was particularly difficult to restructure into its English active form. As this research proceeds, we hope to be able to map out those forms that cost extra time in translation and those that cost little extra or even save processing time when translation is involved. We will, of course, have to consider other language pairs than English and French.

This study also throws light on the way bilinguals hold the base sentence in temporary memory before they start translating and/or transforming it. The base sentence is apparently not kept in its original form in memory, but rather in some rudimentary state. For example, the bilingual subject cannot repeat the original, when asked to do so, any faster than he can when the direction signals lead him back to the original. In fact, the indirect route back to the original sentence using signals is in several cases faster than attempts to repeat the original from memory. It is not yet clear whether some form of Chomsky's deep level kernel sentence replaces the original sentence or whether, as some of us have argued (Hebb, Lambert, and Tucker, 1971), higher order neural representations of meaning are automatically brought into play. It does seem though that the more concrete elements of the original sentence are held in the form of images whereas the more abstract elements are held in the form of a key word or two or a truncated phrase.

THE BILINGUAL'S "ASSOCIATIONAL MEANING" SYSTEMS

Psychologists have proposed a number of different ways of thinking about meaning. One that is especially interesting to me is that of "associative meaning" described by Deese (1962) and Carroll (1964). When a native-speaker of English, for example, is presented with a "stimulus" word like TABLE and is asked to give the first verbal associate that comes to mind, chances are extremely high that "chair" will be ellicited. In fact, when large samples of subjects are surveyed, some 80% or more give "chair" as the *primary* response, and the *secondary* and *tertiary* responses for large groups of native-speakers are also highly predictable, even though much smaller proportions of common responses are involved (e.g., TABLE-chair; TABLE-wood; TABLE-top). What is more, these highly common associations hold up within a language community for generations; Jenkins and Russell (1960) studied changes over a 50 year span in the U.S.A. and found not only that the same common associates held up over time, but also that there was an increase in the use of the more popular associates in 1950 than 1910.

Lambert and Moore (1966) wondered how similar these common associates would be from language to language. Thus, if we asked English and French speakers to give their first associates to a long series of words, translated across languages, how much overlap would there be? Would French people give as many common associates as Americans, and would their common associates match those of the Americans? We also wondered how bilingual persons would manage with their associative meanings in two languages, especially in cases where it was clear from group data that the first three associates differed from one language community to another. Our investigation was Quebec-based and it involved developing association norms for sizeable samples of English-Canadian and French-Canadian monolingual subjects as well as Canadian-based bilinguals. Our norm would then be compared with those already published for monolingual English-speaking Americans, French-speaking people from France, or whatever.

What we found is that there is much variability in degree of associational meaning overlap from one ethno-linguistic group to another, ranging from a near 88% overlap between American (A) and English Canadian (EC) norms to a low of some 40% between the French-French (FF) norms and those of North Americans, be they EC, A, or FC. In other words, FF people have substantially different associative meanings for concepts so that the French word TABLE might be more likely to evoke *manger* rather than *chaise*. But the data also show that EC and FC norms are quite different (overlap around 50%) and that the norms for E-F Canadian bilinguals are very similar to the separate EC and FC monolingual norms. Apparently these bilinguals are tuned into the separate linguistic norms around them, helping them to maintain their bilinguality and equipping them to serve as mediators between the two monolingual communities. In fact, the data show that the bilinguals have the potential of lifting the EC-FC figure of 50% overlap up to 60% if they are asked to relay messages between EC and FC speakers. That's some improvement, but we are still left with a good deal of associational mismatch between these two groups. For example, BIBLE evokes God as the primary associate for ECs while BIBLE (French) evokes *livre* among FCs! If one views these as connotative meaning networks, then ECs and FCs can pass one another pathetically when they try to share the nuances of meaning. For example, the string of stimuli CHILD, SICKNESS and DOCTOR evokes two different sets of primaries; for ECs: *mother*, *health*, *nurse*, while for FCs: *bébé*, *hôpital* and *maladie*!

One other point. These Canadian-based bilinguals might be helpful mediators between Canada's two major groups, but this does not mean they will be able to help mediate between FF and either FC or EC subgroups. In fact, what we found in our study might even add to the meaning gap. Thus, the overlap in meanings between EC and FF monolingual norms was 46% while the overlap between our Canadian-based bilinguals and the FF monolingual was only 30% which suggests that they added distortion in this instance. They were apparently out of their realm of connotative experience in this task. Perhaps European-based bilinguals would be better communicational aids, but we weren't able to test that possibility in our study. In any case, the findings suggest that the cultural and linguistic background of a person's bilinguality is more specific than one might have expected: Canadian-based French experience is not synonymous with France-based French experiences.

BILINGUAL LANGUAGE PROCESSING

The associative networks example led us into the complexities of meaning. Meaning, in fact, has been the focus of the bulk of our research on bilingualism, starting back in the early 50's. One distinguishing feature of this line of research, as you will see, is the abstract level we retreat to when we start interpreting our findings, even when we try our best to ask simple, straight-forward questions.

Psycholinguistic research on bilinguals is rather limited, in spite of the long-standing interest linguists and psychologists have had in the topic (see, for example, Weinreich, 1953; Ervin and Osgood, 1954; Lambert, 1955, 1969; Kolers, 1963; Macnamara, 1967; and Preston and Lambert, 1969). Much of the research so far available has been concerned with two matters: (a) the fascinating way most bilinguals keep their two languages functionally separate – when one is active, the other appears to be dormant; and (b) the possible role that the language acquisition histories of bilinguals play in this ability to keep the two languages functionally independent. Different positions have been taken on this matter. Kolers (1963), for example, saw no need to complicate matters by looking into acquisition histories and he conducted important studies that were designed to determine whether bilinguals as a group (without regard to how or when they learned their two languages) have separate semantic systems for each of their languages or a common system covering both languages.

Others, and I am among them, are of the opinion that we must give full attention to the particularities of language acquisition histories if we want to really understand the different strategies bilinguals use to control the interplay of their two languages. As I see it, acquisition histories reflect a range of distinctive learning experiences and these should be reflected in a bilingual's style of coding, storing and retrieving experiences tied to each of their languages. One valuable suggestion came from Uriel Weinreich (1953) and Charles Osgood (Ervin and Osgood, 1954), namely, to consider a range of possible bilingual background experiences that would produce various approximations to either a "compound" or a "co-ordinate" bilingual type. The theoretically pure "compound" bilingual would be one who learned his two languages simultaneously (e.g., from infancy on) and with interlocutors who used the two languages equally often and interchangeably; the compound bilingual would develop a common system of meaning subserving concepts in both languages. The pure "co-ordinate" bilingual would be one who had distinctive acquisition settings for each language, distinctive as to time of acquisition (the second language learned after infancy), socio-cultural context (one language at home, the other from outside), or usage settings (see Ervin and Osgood, 1954; and Lambert, 1955, 1969). The pure co-ordinate experiences would tend to make the two language systems relatively independent and thus more functionally autonomous.

Although vague and abstract, the theory of compound-co-ordinate forms of bilingualism is of interest to me because it provides a research objective for psychologists and because it holds out the promise of explaining how bilingual skills are developed and how bilingual processing of language takes place. With this goal in view, numerous studies have been conducted to test the theory which lend a good deal of support to the psychological validity of the compound-co-ordinate distinction (see Lambert, 1969, for a review of the early studies). There are, nonetheless, many reasons to question the adequacy of the original statement of the theory (see, for example, Reynolds and Flagg, 1977), and in time it may be put aside for better models. To illustrate, in one study we examined the similarity of the semantic profiles of translation equivalents (such as *church* and *église* or *friend* and *ami*) to see whether those with more compound acquisition experiences would have more similar connotative interpretations of concepts in both languages than would those with more co-ordinate experiences who might well have different networks of meaning for concepts that were originally developed in different context or at different ages in the person's life span. Thus, because the two language systems may have been kept more independent in their usage, the connotative meaning of translating equivalents like *church* and *église* might be different for the more co-ordinate bilingual than for the more compound. This is essentially what we found in our early studies, using the "semantic differential" of Osgood as the measuring instrument (Lambert, 1955).

Next, we argued that if the two language versions of a concept are more inextricably linked for compound than for co-ordinate bilinguals, then if we were to deplete the meaning of one version of a concept, say *church*, the effect of the reduction in meaning should more strongly affect the other language equivalent, *église* for compound than for co-ordinate bilinguals. Our procedure for depleting meaning is known as verbal or semantic "satiation": the subject is asked to repeat continuously a word say *church*, for about a minute and then to give semantic ratings of the meaning of the other-language equivalent at that very moment. Of course, controls were run wherein the satiated word itself was equally often rated, and in both instances, comparisons were made with semantic ratings taken in normal, no-satiation conditions. Furthermore, only balanced bilinguals were included in our pool of bilingual subjects. The results were clear enough: there were, as expected, co-satiation of the other-language equivalents for those with compound acquisition histories but not for those with co-ordinate histories; for the co-ordinate histories; for the co-ordinates, in fact, the depletion of *church*, for example, tended to *increase* rather than deplete the semantic clarity of the other-language equivalent (Lambert and Jakobovits, 1961). Apparently there were different forms of processing going on somewhere in our bilinguals' brains, and the differences were traceable to their language acquisition backgrounds.

The same difference turned up when we collected a large number of cases of aphasics who were bilingual before they had some type of "cerebral accident", such as a serious blow on the head, a cerebral-vascular accident, or a tumor of the brain. We interviewed patients and their families in order to discover when and how these bilinguals originally learned their second languages, and then we collected as much information as possible about the state of each language after the accident. We also studied various cases of bilingual aphasia reported in the neurological journals. The results show that those with more compound-type acquisition histories were more likely to have both languages equally affected by the accident, whereas those with more co-ordinate histories were more likely to have one of their languages more intact after the accident, that is, their aphasia was more reflected in one of their languages than the other.

In these early studies, various criteria were used to differentiate degrees of compounded and co-ordinated language systems, and the least ambiguous criterion turned out to be age of acquisition – the case of being bilingual from infancy on versus learning the second language at school age or later with the proviso of ultimately achieving a balance or equivalence of skills in the use of the two languages. When age of acquisition is used as the criterion, it is more appropriate to refer to a distinction between "early" and "late" bilingualism, and here we start to modify the older compound-co-ordinate idea.

The more recent studies suggest that the "early" bilingual is more inclined to have functionally interdependent linguistic systems, that is, systems less functionally distinctive or segregated than in the case of "late" bilinguals. For instance, early bilinguals were found to be better able to utilize mixed-language associational clues such as *chaise*, *food*, *desk*, *bois, manger*, to arrive at a unifying concept like TABLE (Lambert and Rawlings, 1969). Also in tests of free recall, early bilinguals were also better able than late bilinguals to cluster and remember mixed-language strings or words, such as *apple*, *pamplemousse, pear*, *citron*, (Lambert, 1969). In other words, the late bilinguals were more disrupted with the mixture of languages, much as we would predict because we presume their languages were learned in a more segregated fashion. Thus, the late bilinguals were more comfortable when they were asked to remember lists of words where one semantic category (pomme, orange, poire) came in one language while another category (maple, oak, elm) came in another language. The early bilinguals were more able to cope with language mixtures within a category (apple, citron, etc.).

However, early bilinguals were *less* able than late bilinguals to ignore or set aside the meaning of the potentially distracting words appearing in a bilingual version of the Stroop Color Word Test (Lambert, 1969). In the Stroop Test a subject is presented with this task: the word *red* is printed in a green ink, followed by the word *yellow* printed in blue ink, the word *green* in red ink, and so on for a 100-word display on a large card. The subject merely has to say aloud the colors of the *inks* as fast as possible, trying to ignore the printed color names. It is a difficult task, taking much more time than to simply say aloud the names of patches of color, distributed in a 100-item display. The subjects, being bilingual, can be required to sometimes say aloud the names of the inks in English and sometimes in French. Thus, we arrange it so that we can compare their speeds when the distracting color words are in the same language as the language of report and when the background and report languages are different. As we predicted, the early bilinguals were less able than the late bilinguals to set aside the other-language distractors. In other words, the late bilinguals had a better ability to gate out the distracting other language, whereas the early bilinguals showed signs of having their two languages more inextricably linked.

These studies, taken as a set, suggest that those who develop their bilingual skills early or in a more compound fashion have a stronger inclination to process the deeper meaning of linguistic information, especially those aspects of meaning that cut across language demarcations. For them, the two languages are no less autonomous linguistic systems, for they do no more language mixing or show no more surface signs of inter-language interplay, but it may be that they have developed relatively general, super-ordinate meaning systems that subserve both languages. Or at least this is my view of the state of our knowledge, limited as that is. In contrast, late bilinguals may have relatively more compartmentalized semantic systems and their two language systems may be more functionally segregated. This difference in degree of semantic distinctiveness attributable to acquisition histories has been the focus of several of our most recent studies, which I will now review.

The first example is titled "Language processing strategies of bilinguals: A neurophysiological study" (Genesee, Hamers, Lambert, Mononen, Seitz and Starck, 1977); here we compared three groups of young adult bilinguals: *infant bilinguals* whose bilingual skills dated from early infancy, *childhood bilinguals* who became bilingual at about 5 years of age, and *adolescent bilinguals* who became bilingual at secondary school age only. At the time of testing, all subjects were in their early twenties and all were perfectly balanced in their skills with English and French. The experimental procedure was a simple language recognition task in which the subject had merely to press a reaction time button to indicate whether each word in a series, presented monaurally through earphones, was French or English. At the same time, EEG activity in the left and right hemispheres of the brain was monitored. Measures were taken of the latencies of EEG reactions: Averaged Evoked Reactions were measured and latencies to N_1, to P_2, and $N_1 - P_2$ peak to peak amplitudes were calculated. These are commonly accepted indices of the neural activities that accompany the early stages of perceptual processing or incoming information. They are extremely rapid, occuring within 75 to 100 ms. after the presentation of a stimulus, much in advance of the button push which takes from 800 - 1000 ms. Briefly, these processing latencies were much faster in the left than in the right hemisphere for the "early" bilinguals (the infant and childhood subgroups), but faster in the right than in the left hemisphere for the adolescent bilinguals. Statistically this was a very clear difference, indicating a left hemisphere preference for early bilinguals and a right hemisphere preference for later bilinguals, and it held up regardless of the ear of input of the stimulus material and regardless of the language of input. It was also true that the adolescent bilinguals were much faster in their neurological processing than were the early bilinguals. We are inclined to interpret these findings in terms of strategy differences: the early bilinguals seem to have a proclivity for a left hemisphere-based strategy, one that draws on what we believe to be a more semantic or analytic form of processing while the adolescent subgroup seems to have a proclivity for a right-hemisphere-based strategy, one relying more on a gestalt-like or melodic form of processing. To explore one implication of this interpretation, subjects were recalled and presented with a somewhat more demanding task: to repeat aloud each word as it appeared monaurally through the earphones. It was felt that this task would require a deeper level of processing, one closer to a semantic analysis, and thus more likely to involve the left hemisphere. If this were true, the early bilinguals should react more rapidly because of their left hemisphere proclivity whereas the adolescent subgroup should be at a disadvantage because the stimulus information would have to be transferred from the favored right hemisphere to the left for final processing. Using a voice key to register reaction times, these expectations were supported: the vocal reaction times were significantly shorter for the early bilingual subgroups. All told, these findings help us to relate language learning experience to cerebral processing styles and they fit well with other behavioral distinctions already found between early and late bilinguals.

Another ongoing study, very much in the pilot stage, starts out by examining bilinguals as a group, but then ends up with fascinating subgroups. The paper is titled: "Visual field and cerebral hemisphere preferences of bilinguals" (Hamers and Lambert, 1977) and it addresses itself to the question of whether the bilingual's two languages are both "controlled" by the same cerebral hemisphere. Fifteen "balanced" French-English bilinguals, all right-handed, were asked to identify each of a series of words, presented in a random order, as being French or English. The words were presented equally often through the left and the right *visual fields*, and reaction times were recorded. It was found that twelve of the fifteen bilinguals identified the language of verbal material faster when it was presented in the right rather than the left visual field as one would expect, because the right visual field is believed to have stronger neural connections with the left hemisphere of the brain, the hemisphere supposedly more involved with language processing. Still, three subjects identified more rapidly via the left visual field. All told, thirteen subjects supported a "both languages on the same side" principle, but two interesting cases turned up: they demonstrated a greater facility in processing one language on one side of the brain and a greater facility with the other language on the other side of the brain. We have found, then, one subgroup providing support for Penfield's belief that one hemisphere only (usually the left hemisphere) is dominant for both languages of the bilingual person, but also a fascinating subgroup, albeit small, that goes counter to that belief. Needless to say we will be following both these subgroups in much more detail.

I would like to conclude by mentioning a pilot study being carried out by Sylvie Lambert (1977). Her approach was based on some observations made by Parsons (1973) who found that some interpreters might slip off one of their pair of headphones while working in the booth. Not all interpreters do this, but those who do will be receiving the source language message predominantly in the hemisphere of the brain contralateral to the headphone kept on. Remember that the right ear is predominantly linked neurologically with the left hemisphere, and the left ear with the right hemisphere.

Since many people have ear preferences when, for instance, listening to the telephone (even right-handers place the receiver on the right ear, and cradle it there or cross over to hold it there with the left hand while taking notes), Lambert wondered whether interpreters would have ear (and hence, cerebral) preferences for interpreting in the same way as they might for telephone conversations.

So far there is information from some 40 professional interpreters only, and though these trends may not be reliable ones, they are extremely interesting. For instance, there seems to be a consistency in ear-hemisphere preference for interpreting and phoning. In other words, those who process messages through the right ear to the left hemisphere tend to do so both in the interpretation booth and on the phone; another subgroup shows no such preference, either on the phone or in the booth. (Keep in mind here that the left hemisphere is said to be more involved in verbal and semantic processing.) It turns out that male interpreters are more likely to use the right-ear to left-hemisphere route for incoming messages than are female interpreters who are more likely to involve the right hemisphere in the processing. Furthermore, although much more data are needed on this point, age of acquisition seems to play a role in that those who were bilingual from infancy on are more likely to involve both left and right hemispheres in their processing while those few interpreters who learned their second language in adolescence only are more likely to process exclusively via the right hemisphere. Finally, there are trends suggesting that interpreters who consider themselves to be fluently bilingual are much less likely to depend on a particular ear-to-hemisphere route. They appear, in other words, more inclined to involve both hemispheres in the process. Interestingly, these "bilingual" interpreters also show more signs of ambidexterity than do the non-bilinguals.

All this, of course, is at the pilot-study stage only: the sample sizes must be increased and more details of age of acquisition included. Still it is a happy note to end on for it suggests that the mysteries of how the two hemispheres are involved in the process of conference interpretation may be more easily solved than we at first thought.

REFERENCES

Carroll, J. B., *Language and thought*. Engelwood Cliffs, New Jersey: Prentice-Hall, 1964.

Clement, R., Major, L. J., Gardner, R. C., and Smythe, P. C., Attitudes and motivation in second language acquisition: An investigation of Ontario Francophones. In *Working Papers on Bilingualism* January, 1977, *No. 12.*

Deese, J. On the structure of associative meaning. *Psychological Review*, 1962, *69,* 161 - 175.

Ervin, S. M., and Osgood, C. E. Second language learning and bilingualism. *Journal of Abnormal and Social Psychology Supplement*, 1954, *14*, 139 - 146.

Gardner, R. C., and Lambert, W. E. *Attitudes and motivation in second language learning*. Rowley, Massachusetts: Newbury House, 1971.

Genesee, F., Hamers, J., Lambert, W. E., Mononen, L., Seitz, M., and Starck, R. Language processing strategies of bilinguals: A neurophysiological study. *Brain and Language*, in press.

Hamers, J., and Lambert, W. E. Visual field and cerebral hemisphere preferences in bilinguals. In S. J. Segalowitz and F. A. Gruber (Eds.), *Language Development and Neurological Theory*. New York: Academic Press, 1977.

Hebb, D. O., Lambert, W. E., and Tucker, G. R. Language, thought and experience. *Modern Language Journal*, 1971, *55*, 212 - 222.

Jenkins, J. J., and Russell, W. A. Systematic changes in word association norms: 1910 - 1952. *Journal of Abnormal and Social Psychology*, 1960, *60*, 293 - 304.

Kolers, P. A., Interlingual word associations. *Journal of Verbal Learning and Verbal Behavior*, 1963, *2*, 291 - 300.

Lambert, S. M., Personal communication, 1977.

Lambert, W. E., Measurement of the linguistic dominance of bilinguals. *Journal of Abnormal and Social Psychology*, 1955, *59*, 197 - 200.

Lambert, W. E., Psychological studies of interdependencies of the bilingual's two languages. In J. Puhvel (Ed.), *Substance and Structure of Language.* Los Angeles: University of California Press, 1969, 99 - 126.

Lambert, W. E., Culture and language as factors in learning and education. In F. E. Aboud and R. D. Meade, (Eds.), *Cultural Factors in Learning and Education. The fifth Western Symposium of Learning,* Bellingham, Washington: Western Washington State College, 1973.

Lambert, W. E., Giles, H., and Picard, O. Language attitudes in a French American community. *International Journal on the Sociology of Language*, 1975, 127 - 152.

Lambert, W. E., Havelka, J., and Crosby, C. The influence of language acquisition contexts on bilingualism. *Journal of Abnormal and Social Psychology*, 1958, *56*, 239 - 44.

Lambert, W. E., Havelka, J., and Gardner, R. C., *Linguistic manifestations of bilingualism.* American Journal of Psychology, 1959, *72*, 77 - 82.

Lambert, W. E., and Rawlings, C. Bilingual processing of mixed-language associative networks. *Journal of Verbal Learning and Verbal Behavior*, 1969, *8(5)*, 604 - 609.

Lambert, W. E., and Moore, N. Word-association responses: Comparison of American and French monolinguals with Canadian monolinguals and bilinguals. *Journal of Personality and Social Psychology*, 1966, *3*, 313 - 320.

Lambert, W. E., and Jakobovits, L. A. Semantic satiation among bilinguals. *Journal of Experimental Psychology*, 1961, *62*, 576 - 82.

Macnamara, J. The bilingual's linguistic performance: The psychological overview. *Journal of Social Issues*, 1967, *23*, 58 - 77.

Parsons, H.M., Unpublished research report. Institute for Behavioral Research Inc. Silver Springs, Md. 1973.

Preston, M. W., and Lambert, W. E. Interlingual interference in a bilingual version of the Stroop color-word task. *Journal of Verbal Learning and Verbal Behavior*, 1969, *8*, 295 - 301.

Reynolds, A. G. *Information processing when translating or transforming sentences.* Ph.D. dissertation, McGill University, 1970.

Reynolds, A. G., and Flagg, P. W. *Cognitive Psychology.* Cambridge, Mass.: Winthrop Publishers, 1977.

Weinreich, U. *Language in contact.* New York: Linguistic Circle of New York, 1953.

True Bilingualism and Second-language Learning

Christopher Thiery

Université Paris III – Sorbonne Nouvelle

Paris

INTRODUCTION

"Bilingual: Having, speaking, spoken or written in, two languages". (Concise Oxford Dictionary).

With such a definition it is hardly surprising that the word is used to cover a multitude of very different things. Even in scientific literature it is often used without being properly defined. The many adjectives which often adorn it do not dispel the general confusion: expressions like preschool, cultural, social bilingualism tell us something about *who* is bilingual, or the discipline the writer belongs to, but nothing about what bilingualism really is. Does bilingualism mean knowing two languages or speaking two languages? What is meant by "knowing" or "speaking" a language? At what level of performance? Is writing included? How have the languages been acquired? The answers to these questions are by no means academic. Both the linguist and the psychologist will get very different results from the study of "bilingual" subjects depending on what kind of bilinguals they are. The purpose of this paper is to attempt to define and describe an extreme form of bilingualism, which is fairly common among children but very rare in adults, and which we have called "true bilingualism".

TRUE BILINGUALISM : A DEFINITION

In common parlance when someone is referred to as being "perfectly bilingual" two things are implied: a) the subject speaks both languages equally well; b) the subject has two mother tongues. The first condition, equality between the two linguistic performances, is unfortunately of no help in defining bilingualism, because there is no means of determining if someone speaks two languages equally well. No one speaks any language "perfectly" and linguistic performance cannot be measured. Even a vocabulary count would be meaningless, because who knows what treasures a long forgotten word association will unearth? And what cannot be measured cannot be compared. It is obvious, furthermore, that no individual can have gone through every single linguistic experience twice. Suppose someone has done a lot of sailing in England, but not in France. The lack of sailing vocabulary in French does not mean that he (or she) does not speak "perfect" French, because the vast majority of the French population shares his (or her) ignorance. Direct comparison between two linguistic performances in the same subject is therefore both meaningless and impossible. The notion of equality between the two linguistic performances, which is definitely present in the common use of the term "perfectly bilingual", will have to be approached in a different way.

The second condition, having two mother tongues, is of greater interest in that it introduces the question of the manner in which the languages were acquired. To start with, however, it is necessary to define the term "mother-tongue". For the purpose of this exercise, we will consider the mother-tongue(s) to be the language (or languages) which the child has acquired by "immersion", by natural reaction to the sounds made by its environment in order to communicate with it. It is the language (or languages) in which the child learns to speak. It may or may not be the actual language spoken by the mother – it usually is, of course. The important thing is that it is *not* learned via another language, by tuition. The mechanism by which a young Anglo-Saxon American "absorbs" his native language is very different from the way he will learn French in later life. It is true that English as a subject is taught at school. But what the child is taught is how to read and write, not how to speak. He may also be taught (with varying degrees of success) how to speak the oral version of written English, which may be very different from the "English" he speaks at home, and which he acquired without any tuition whatsoever.

What is not always realized is that a child can have several mother tongues in succession if it is moved to different linguistic environments. For instance, a boy born in Indonesia can go from Indonesian to Dutch, and then to French by the age of 6 as he is moved from country to country. He may end up without a trace of Indonesian. There having been no second language tuition in Dutch or French, the child must have "picked-up" Dutch and French by more or less the same process as the original Indonesian. It is in this that he can be said to have "learned to speak" three times: the basic speech-learning mechanism (whatever it is) will have come into play three times, albeit more smoothly and faster the second two times. Now if the new linguistic environment is added to the first without taking its place, such as in the case of a child of British diplomats in Italy who first spoke Italian with the maid, and then English with the family, then the child will have two mother tongues at the same time. Such cases are numerous.

The second condition, then, having two mother tongues is meaningful although not in itself sufficient for there to be bilingualism: it would apply to a New York lawyer of Italian origin who still speaks 6-year old Italian to his mother. He would not pass as "perfectly bilingual" in Italian and English, because in Italy he would be considered illiterate. There is clearly no "equality" between his two linguistic performances. The concept of equality can only be approached, as we have seen, indirectly. Hence the following definition that we propose:

"True Bilingualism: a true bilingual is someone who is taken to be one of themselves by the members of two different linguistic communities, at roughly the same social and cultural level".

The test of true bilingualism is purely empirical. The subject is placed in his two linguistic environments, which either reject him as a foreign body, or accept him as one of themselves. The immersion must be a prolonged one. Many people can pass as a native speaker for limited conversations with hotel porters, thanks to a good ear for accents and a large fund of colloquialisms. Sooner or later, however, a strange intonation, or a lack of instinctive linguistic creativity will reveal them to be one of those wonders "who speak the language beautifully for a foreigner . . ."

Having defined true bilingualism by an indirect approach to the "equality" condition, the next step is to demonstrate that, ipso facto, the "mother tongue" condition is fulfilled, i.e. that in a true bilingual both languages have been acquired by immersion, and not via another language by tuition; this is another way of saying that second-language learning cannot lead to true bilingualism. This was part of the object of the following enquiry.

TRUE BILINGUALISM: AN ENQUIRY

As defined above there are many truly bilingual children, but very few adult true bilinguals – so few that some writers dispute their very existence (Braine, 1971; Christopherson, 1973). Mastery of language being to such a high degree dependent on motivation and opportunity, this is hardly surprising: there are many callings in which it is necessary to have a good command of a foreign language, but very few in which one has to be considered as one of themselves by the members of two different linguistic communities.

Conference interpreting is, to some extent, the exception. It is certainly not necessary to be a true bilingual to be a successful conference interpreter, but only a true bilingual is entitled to the A-A language classification in the AIIC Yearbook (International Association of Conference Interpreters). The AIIC language classification consists of 3 categories:

A: mother tongue
B: 2nd active language
C: passive language.

A complicated system of individual sponsors ensures that anyone with an A-A classification in French and English, for instance, is considered by delegates and interpreters alike to be French when in the French booth, and English (or American) in the English booth. For all intents and purposes an A-A classification corresponds to our definition of true bilingualism. As conference interpreters have motivation *and* opportunity for being true bilinguals, they appeared to offer an excellent field of investigation. In the 1973-74 AIIC Yearbook out of 955 members there were 176 A-A interpreters of whom 48 were A-A in English and French.

THE QUESTIONNAIRE

An 11 page questionnaire was sent to the 48 conference interpreters with an A-A classification in English and French. There were 34 replies. The main headings were as follows:

- Personal particulars
- Definitions

- Linguistic environment in childhood and adolescence for every two year period from 2 to 18, including the language spoken by and to the parents, in the home, in the street, at school, etc.
- Schooling
- Language and nationality
- Degree of bilingualism over the years
- How bilingualism is maintained in the adult (radio, reading-material, etc)
- Description of adult bilingualism (in what language docs one count, swear, etc)
- Linguistic performance
- Transition from one language to the other
- Bilingualism and conference interpreting

The detailed analysis of the replies can be read elsewhere (Thiery, 1975).

MAIN CONCLUSIONS

I – The true bilingual has two mother tongues

All the replies indicate that the subject acquired both languages by "immersion". In 29 cases out of 34 both English and French were spoken in the home (not necessarily by the parents) up to the age of 18. In 1 case up to the age of 16, and 1 up to the age of 14. A mixed home environment, however, is not enough. The vast majority of subjects indicated that the family had moved, during schooling years, from one language community to another. A minority stayed in the same place, but went to a "foreign" school (e.g. French Lycee in London).

In pre-school years the child is subjected to two linguistic forces: the home and the street (including radio, television, advertising, etc). Once schooling begins, there are three forces: school, street and home. The first two become more and more powerful as the child gets older, and there were only two cases where monolingual parents were able to hold out against the combined forces of street and school. In the majority of cases, however, the parents made no special effort to make their child a "true" bilingual.

This finding is consistent with the fact that it appears to be impossible to produce true bilingualism artificially, deliberately. Children react negatively to any artificial situation. Very few of the true bilinguals questioned were even attempting to make their own children bilingual. In our series it is perfectly clear that true bilingualism in the child is the fruit of circumstance, not of deliberate effort. In most cases the following conditions are met: a bilingual environment in the home; a move from one language community to another during schooling; a change in school language.

II – True bilingualism is acquired before or at puberty

29 subjects answered specific questions relating to the age at which they became true bilinguals. The age given was 14 or under in 26 cases, 16 in one case, and between 20 and 30 in one case.

Subjects were asked to indicate for each age column (there were 9 columns from 2 to 18 and one column for 20 to 30):

- the language(s) they *spoke* so as to be indistinguishable from a native speaker of the same age
- the language(s) they *understood* perfectly for their age without however being taken for a native speaker when using it (or them)
- the language(s) in which their father/mother/brothers and sisters/servants addressed them
- the language(s) in which they answered.

They were also asked:

-3.1.1 Were you a true bilingual as a child?
-3.1.2. If so, did you remain one?
-3.1.3 Did you cease to be a true bilingual at any time?
-3.1.4 If you were not a true bilingual as a child, when did you become one? In what circumstances?"

Without going into a detailed consideration of the exceptions analysis of the results suggested that as a rule true bilingualism is acquired by puberty or not at all. This is another way of saying that the ability to acquire a language by immersion, without tuition via a "first" language, is lost at about the age of puberty. This finding is consistent with work by Sperry (1951), Penfield and Roberts (1959), Guttman (1942), Lenneberg (1967), Piaget (1972), Vygotsky (1962) and many others. It may be wrong, however, to conclude (as Penfield and Roberts do) that foreign languages should necessarily be taught at a very early age. Immersion, even for limited periods, will certainly be more beneficial in younger children, but it is unlikely that the very different mental processes involved in learning a second language via a first one, by tuition, *will* be effective much before the onset of Piaget's "formal operations" stage or Vygotsky's "concept formation" stage, which both are around puberty.

III - True bilingualism does not have an adverse effect on school performance

Out of 34 replies, school progress was normal in 16 cases, advanced in 14 cases, retarded in 4 cases. Retarded progress was only temporary, and was due to a change of school from one country (and language) to another. In other words, in the few cases where there were school problems they were caused not by bilingualism, but by the *lack* of bilingualism. This finding is consistent with the observation that school problems in so-called bilingual frontier areas (like Alsace) are not due to the children's being bilingual, but to the fact that they are not bilingual.

Having been brought up in the home to speak one language, or dialect, they are then sent to a school where everything is taught in what to them is a foreign language. Little wonder that they should need a little time to catch up. (cf. work by Lambert, 1976; Gaarder, 1965; Fishman, 1965).

IV – True bilingualism in adults is the result of a conscious effort

The combination of circumstances that produces true bilingualism in children is somewhat exceptional, but occurs sufficiently frequently for there to be a fair number of truly bilingual children, particularly in diplomatic circles. Very few of these children retain their true bilingualism in adult life. The reason is that in most cases there is neither reason nor opportunity to do so.

Our enquiry has shown:

a) that none of the subjects had been required to be true bilinguals in any profession (many had belonged to several) other than conference interpreting;
b) that all took deliberate steps to create and maintain a bilingual environment (radio, reading, etc);
c) that all showed a degree of awareness of language problems that is unusual among monolinguals.

The importance attached to poetry is of interest: a third of the subjects still learn poems by heart in both languages, which is remarkable in view of the mean age of the series (48. 2 years), and two thirds actually write poetry (half in one language only, half in both). It appears clearly that our true bilinguals make a deliberate effort to maintain their bilingualism; that such an effort is based on the professional motivation of conference interpreting with the A-A classification; that conference interpreting provides ample opportunity for such efforts to be successful.

It is therefore understandable that true bilinguals are few and far between outside conference interpreting, at any rate in the author's experience – which seems to be borne out by the very small number of actual cases of true bilingualism described in the literature. It would be interesting to find out, in Canada for instance, if there are many adult true bilinguals, and if so what kind of professional motivation they have.

V – True bilingualism does not imply written bilingualism, and vice versa

The replies to the questionnaire do not reflect any particular aptitudes as far as writing is concerned, in either language. All subjects belong to a sociocultural category in which everyone can read and write in their mother tongue, and having two they can read and write in both languages, but without showing any particular talent, and not without spelling mistakes in a fair number of cases (12 for French, 5 for English).

This is to be expected, since language in the oral sense, in which it has been used all along in this enquiry is innate in human beings, like walking. Reading and writing are not, and have to be learned. And what has to be learned, can be inadequately learned. There is no particular reason that a true bilingual should have any particular mastery over either or both of his written languages, anymore than anyone else. The mental processes that come into play when pen is put to paper are certainly not identical to those which produce speech. The two forms of communication are very different. The writer has *time*, time to search for the best way of expressing his thought. And that is why it is by no means necessary to be a true bilingual to achieve complete mastery of a second *written* language. Joseph Conrad is an obvious example. True bilingualism is an *oral* phenomenon, and fundamentally has nothing to do with how well a completely different medium – the written language – is mastered.

VI – True bilingualism, linguistic relativity and non-verbal thought

Several questions concern the degree to which the same idea can be expressed in different languages. Here we should recall that all the subjects are conference interpreters whose activity is geared not to words, but to meaning. A language is not a mere code; conference interpreting is not transcoding. The interpreter's role is to receive a message, adapt it and then utter it as if it were his own. The fact that the utterance is in another language is incidental and in no way affects the basic mental processes involved. In training interpreters much stress is placed on the need to get away from the words used in order to extract the essence of the message. This doubtless explains why the gist of the replies is that everything can be expressed in all languages (at least in the two we are dealing with) but not necessarily with the same (or corresponding) words, nor even with the same number of words.

It is axiomatic that all communities develop ways of expressing every meaning they want to express. Some things they choose to express in a particularly concise manner. Such things differ from country to country: when the English say that someone is "considerate", or the French use the word "net" (of a person) they are using a concise form for an idea that needs a fairly lengthy explanation in the other language, with quite different words. The message can be got across, but the effect on the person one is talking to will be different, thereby altering the communication relationship.

The difficulty that all those who use two languages are aware of, but that true bilinguals feel particularly keenly as a dilemma, is that while one is talking in one language ideas come into one's mind that have found concise expression in the *other* language. As the choice of what to express concisely reflects the way the language is used as a medium for all the person to person relationships which make up society, one can say that the true bilingual, in attempting to convey an idea which has *not* found concise formulation in the language he is using will in fact be giving his audience some insight into the structure of the other society. Much can be learned by observing how people ask each other for the time in the street in London, Paris, or Dublin. Everything is different: choice of words, voice, posture, distance between speakers and so on.

The true bilingual's dilemma leads us to another interesting point: the fact that an idea comes to mind in a language other than the one one is speaking indicates the presence of a non-verbal stage in speech. In the middle of the constant shuttle between the non-verbal meaning seeking expression and the innumerable forms offered for use another idea intrudes. The curious point is that it is able to intrude precisely because it is highly verbalized, having been given concise formulation in another language. All conference interpreters have at least once had the experience of giving a consecutive interpretation in the same language as the original, which again points to the fact that the message is stored in a non-verbal form. This point is developed at length by Seleskovitch (1975).

VII – True bilingualism and second-language learning

It has been seen that the true bilinguals in our series all have two mother tongues, acquired before puberty, by immersion. The acquisition of both languages is direct, not via a "first" language. Indeed the very notion of "first", or "dominant" languages is alien to the concept of true bilingualism. As the replies indicate, there are certain areas of knowledge which our subjects are more familiar with in one language than in the other, but that does not make one language dominant in relation to the other. Nor is there any distinct pattern as far as counting, swearing, or answering the telephone is concerned. The adult second-language learner, however proficient he may become, may well have an impressive vocabulary, clever syntax and careful phonology, but the process he has gone through in learning a second language is so different from the way a child absorbs language that it is hardly surprising that the result can never be quite the same.

Linguistic competence, we are told is innate, and is the foundation on which is built the acquisition of the mother tongue(s) (i.e. linguistic performance). It is in the mother tongue(s) that the child produces phrases that he has never heard and complies with syntactic rules that no one ever taught him. It is in the mother tongue that any speaker can detect a phrase that is wrong, even if it is apparently grammatically correct. It is in one's mother tongue that one can recognize garbled phrases over a faulty loud-speaker, merely by their outline, just like a face can be recognized by a glimpse even from an unusual angle. The adult second-language learner never achieves such an instructive, creative relationship with his second language, and the reason may be that his painstaking performance has not been built on the appropriate linguistic competence, but on cognitive structures established for another language, his mother tongue.

Linguistic interference

This study bears on people, not on language. Interference between the two languages, transfers, switching, etc. have not been analyzed in detail, and indeed the method of enquiry chosen would not have permitted such an exercise. It is clear, however, that our true bilinguals *can* mix their languages and sometimes do so for fun, but in the normal way make a deliberate effort not to. The effort is generally successful.

This short paper attempts to summarize the main conclusions of a more detailed study which was designed to draw attention to the need to define "bilingualism". What we term "true bilingualism" is an extreme form of bilingualism, but which has the merit of being identifiable pragmatically.

REFERENCES

Braine, M.D. S., The acquisition of language in infant and child. In C. E. Reed (Ed.), *The Learning of Language*. New York: Appleton – Century – Crofts, 1971.

Christopherson, P. *Second-language learning*. London: Penguin, 1973.

Fishman, J. A., The status and prospects of bilingualism in the United States. *Modern Language Journal*, 1965, *XLIV/3,* 143 - 155.

Gaarder, A. Bruce, Teaching the bilingual child; Research, Development and Policy. *Modern Language Journal*, 1965, *XLIV/3*, 165 - 175.

Guttman, E., Aphasia in children. *Brain*, 1942, *65*, 205-19.

Lambert, W., *Contribution to XXIst International Congress of Psychology*. Paris, 1976.

Lenneberg, E. H. *Biological foundations of language*. New York: Wiley, 1967.

Penfield, W. and Roberts, L., *Speech and Brain Mechanisms*. Princeton: Princeton University Press, 1959.

Piaget, J. *Problèmes de psychologie génétique.* Paris: Gonthier, 1972.
Seleskovitch, D., *Language, langues et memoire.* Paris: Lettres Modernes, 1975.
Sperry, R. W, Mechanisms of Neural Maturation in S. S. Stevens, (Ed.)., *Handbook of Experimental Psychology.* New York: Wiley, 1951.
Thiery, C. A. J., *Le Bilinguisme chez les Interprètes de Conference Professionels.* Unpublished Doctoral Thesis, Universite de la Sorbonne Nouvelle (Paris III), 1975.
Vygotsky, L. S., *Thought and Language.* Cambridge: M.I.T. Press, 1962.

Translating as an Innate Skill

Brian Harris and Bianca Sherwood

University of Ottawa

Ottawa, Ontario

1.1 GENERAL THEORY OF NATURAL TRANSLATION (NT)

Two previous articles, Harris (1973) and Harris (1977), have argued that the data for *translatology* (the scientific study of translating) should come primarily from *natural* translation rather than from literary, technical and other professional or semi-professional branches of translation as in the past. Natural translation was defined as: "The translating done in everyday circumstances by people who have had no special training for it."

Furthermore it was postulated that *all* bilinguals are able to translate, within the limits of their mastery of the two languages; therefore translating is coextensive with bilingualism.

1.2 Purpose of the paper. Hypothesis

The postulate that all bilinguals can translate may be expanded in several ways: (i) culturally (i.e. in all cultures); (ii) linguistically (in all languages and all registers); (iii) historically (throughout history); or (iv) ontogenetically and linguo-developmentally (from the moment that an individual starts to acquire a second language). This paper is mainly about the last aspect, and secondarily about (ii). If all bilinguals, even nascent ones, can translate, and since the onset of bilingualism often occurs in infancy, we ought, so our postulate predicts, to find young children translating. The previous articles brought forward evidence that it is so: young children do translate. However, that evidence, though significant, was fragmentary. This paper will furnish more, and in greater detail. In addition, one does not expect a natural skill to develop fully overnight. An attempt will be made to trace the stages that the young natural translator goes through. Our hypothesis is that the basic ability to translate is an innate verbal skill. Just what is meant by 'innate' will be taken up in our Discussion.

2.1 METHOD

Most of the data consists of individual case histories collected in North America. However, the study of LR comes from France. Some of the cases are new ones of our own, viz. AA, BS, GS, HB, PW and RW. Cases mentioned in our previous articles are not included in this one. Most of the data was observed at the time by investigators, but an important part of it, notably BS, is due to *S*'s own recall.

2.2 Data range

The age range in the cases goes from birth (HL, KL, LR) to 18 years (BS). Some of the studies of individuals are longitudinal: approximately 4 years of LR, 6 years of HL and VRE, 8 years of KL, 18 years of BS. All other studies cover a period of less than 3 months or are momentary. The language pairs involved are English and French (AA, BS), English and German (HL, KL), English and Greek (GS), English and Italian (BS, VRE), French and Bulgarian (HB), French and German (LR), Italian and Spanish (BS), Standard Italian and Abruzzi Dialect (BS); also the trio of English, German and mathematical symbolism (PW, RW).

2.3 Presentation of the data

The data has been extracted from the case histories in reverse age order, i.e. from oldest to youngest, and grouped into age bands. The reason for doing it in this order is that the youngest examples are the most pertinent to our Discussion. The bands are not discrete.

3.1 RESULTS

3.1.1 7 – 18 years

BS immigrated to Canada with her family at 8;4. (To avoid confusion with the numbering of the sections of this paper, we use a semicolon to divide years from months). She was already trilingual. Within three months of her *obligatory submersion* in the Anglophone school and town of Welland, she was active in English and nearly a true quadrilingual. Nevertheless she continued to speak Italian at home and with family friends, most of whom were members of the sizeable community of Italian immigrants in Welland. *Language switching* caused her no hardship; perhaps her previous trilingualism helped. On the other hand she found the move to a different culture a trying experience that left her feeling sensitive and insecure. In her relations with her family and the extra-family world she remained more conscious of *culture switching* than of language switching.

We mentioned in Harris (1973) that Montreal Italophone children in similar circumstances to BS's saw themselves in the role of interpreters between older family members who spoke little or no French or English and the community at large. BS's experience replicated theirs. Her fluent English and her understanding of Canadian attitudes and mores bestowed on her important *expert power* as an interpreter. She was expecially valuable to her mother, who did not learn much English. Decidedly her translating was *socially functional.* For ten years, until she left to go to University, BS translated, orally or in writing, phone calls, messages, conversations with visitors, mail, newspaper articles, etc. Indeed, she undertook almost all the written work that the family had to have carried out in English: filling out forms, composing business letters, etc. This broad range of NT – certainly as everyday as it was untrained – may be characterized sociologically as *intra/extra-family, interpersonal, pragmatic* and *documentary.* Linguistically the usual modes were *semi-consecutive interpreting* and *sight translation*, both of them *two way.* This kind of childhood experience must be common in immigrant communities: it is therefore disappointing that a recent book-length sociolinguistic study of Italian immigrant children in Boston, Massachusetts, makes no reference to it (Biondi, 1975).

When BS was 12 years, the clientele for her translating expanded because her uncle and his family also immigrated to Welland. Italian language and culture were preserved within the joint family and remained socially important in its relations with fellow immigrants. BS held a privileged position of esteem in it as the eldest of the 'Canadian' generation and because she obtained good marks at school. From 12 to 18 years BS performed the same functions for her uncle's family as for her own. She accompanied them to government offices to perform *liaison interpretations*. They turned to her for translations and explanations of words and idioms as they themselves learned English. Sometimes they argued amongst themselves over language problems, and then they would call on BS to arbitrate. Thus she served as their *bilingual informant*, to use a term familiar to linguists and anthropologists; and she was drawn into assisting their second-language acquisition, another function of immigrant child translators.

Part of BS's role as informant was indeed as much ethnic as linguistic. As an intercultural 'mediating man' (Brislin, 1976, citing Bochner), she tried to explain why things were done the way their were, both to her relatives from the viewpoint of the 'Canadians' and to her native Canadian friends from the viewpoint of Italians. Although from about 12 years she felt more at ease in her bicultural society and found culture switching easier, she was continually conscious of translation difficulties caused by cultural differences.

Discussing the professional interpreter, Anderson (1976) remarks on:

> "role conflict resulting from his pivotal position in the interaction network . . . the relative ambiguity of the interpreter's role [which] allows him considerable latitude in defining his own behavior vis-a-vis his clients . . . considerable manipulation of communicative content in the direction of moderation and rationality. Hidden losses in fidelity would blunt angered words and soften rigid stances."

BS provides us with an NT example of this. Hard bargaining, as readers may well know, is one of the 'games people play' in Italy. An admissible tactic in it there is to call one's adversary a fool. Not so in Welland. BS's father would use her to liaison interpret for him at bargaining sessions with non-Italians. Father would get worked up in the Italian style and become angry and upset. BS would attenuate his outbursts in her interpretations, even at the risk of drawing some of her father's anger on herself. It led to exchanges like this one:

Father to BS: "Digli che è un imbecille!" (Tell him he's a nitwit).
BS to 3rd party: "My father won't accept your offer".
Father angrily in Italian: "Why didn't you tell him what I told you?

BS's strategy, or strategem, of cultural adaptation strongly suggests that the professional behavior described by Anderson has its origin in the natural translator's way out of uncomfortable intercessions!

A more surprising link between NT and professional practice is suggested by another of BS's regular functions: interpreting TV programs at home and films at the cinema from English into Italian. Sometimes the interpretation was in *sum-*

mary consecutive and would then be very *free*, preserving only the rough story outline. Sometimes it was a relative who interpreted, and then BS's task was to check from the translation whether the relative had understood correctly (*comprehension-by-translation*). At other times while watching TV, BS was required to interpret while the program was still on. In that set-up she was doing a kind of *simultaneous interpretation*, however rudimentary it may have been. No doubt simultaneous interpretation is the least natural mode of interpretation: few people are gifted with the talent to do it professionally (cf. Thiery, 1976). The experimental psychologists who conducted the first empirical studies of it in the 1960's were really more interested in problems like single-channel versus multi-channel processing than in translatology: see Gerver (1976). Yet, when we marvel at the mental agility of professional simultaneous interpreters in their electronically equipped booths, we also ask ourselves how the pioneers ever thought such a demanding task would be feasible in the first place. In fact it evolved from an earlier professional technique called *whispering*. And now we observe that it is not entirely beyond the powers of a child natural translator. Contrary to other modes of interpreting, which she enjoyed, BS disliked having to interpret TV programs in this way. But then simultaneous interpretation is stressful and tiring, even for professionals.

3.1.2

HB, 7 years, could also interpret a TV program. He lived near Ottawa, and was bilingual in French and Bulgarian with French dominant. His mother took him to visit a Bulgarian family recently arrived in Canada. During the visit HB was left alone with a child of the new family to watch the French version of the children's program "Sesame Street" on TV. The other child, 11 years, did not speak French. Afterwards HB told his mother he was tired because he had translated all the program into Bulgarian for his playmate. Unfortunately we do not know in what mode the interpreting was performed. As in BS's case, it was socially functional, an exercise of expert power; but it was done from a dominant language into a weaker one.

3.2.1 5;3 – 8 years

The cases in this section differ from the others by being based on elicited translation. Elicited translation, because it is done under the conditions of an experiment and uses specially prepared texts, violates the "everyday circumstances" stipulated in our definition of NT (see 1.1). Nevertheless the translators were certainly capable of NT proper outside the experiments.

GS at 5;4 was a nearly *balanced bilingual* in Greek and English. Greek was his *true mother language*; he had learned English since coming to Canada from Greece at 4;1. At our suggestion his mother tried the following two experiments in *narrative translation* with him.

i) Prior to the first experiment she herself translated a children's story, "1001 Dalmatians", into Greek. She then read her Greek translation to GS sentence by sentence, stopping after each sentence while he *back-translated* it orally into English. She wrote down at his dictation. We then compared the back-translation with the original English text, consulting her to make sure differences were not due to her Greek translation.

ii) She read an English version of the story of "Peter and the Wolf" to GS sentence by sentence, stopping after each sentence while he translated it orally into Greek. She wrote down at his dictation. Subsequently she back-translated it into English for us and we compared the back-translation with the original English text. We questioned her to make sure that the divergences really occurred in GS's translation and not in her back-translation. (c.f. Brislin, 1976, where he describes the use of the back-translation test in a professional environment).

GS had heard both stories already, but not for several weeks before the test; he could not repeat them by rote. Unfortunately he was not pretested for recall of the content and vocabulary. He declined to go on translating after 29 sentences of (i), having started to tire around the eighteenth. He gave up after 16 sentences of (ii). His translation contained scattered examples of the following phenomena: *idiomatic translation*, e.g. The conventional Greek opening "Mia fora kai ena kairo." → "Once upon a time,"; *syntactic translation*, e.g. Greek noun + genitive noun (literally, 'thief of dogs') → "dog thief"; *lexical approximation*, e.g. "andres" → "people" instead of 'men'; lexical interference, e.g. "today night" instead of 'tonight'; *elaborated translation*, e.g. "skulakja" → "Dalmatian puppies" ("Dalmatian" added); *reduced translation*, e.g. "tous eipe ê Kroulla" → "said Cruella" ('to them' omitted).

So far as he went with them, both translations make good sense as individual sentences and maintain the story line. We may conclude that GS was good at this kind of translation, even though he was doing it for the first time. He grew tired of it after a while, but then we do not know what his attention span was like at other tasks.

3.2.2

Two brothers, PW and RW, came from Germany to spend six months at Madison, Wisconsin. On arrival they spoke only German. During the stay PW attended first-grade classes in a local Anglophone primary school; both brothers made numerous Anglophone friends; their parents continued to speak German with them. At the end of their brief English submersion, we spent several days in their company and took the opportunity to play games with them that would test their translating. They were then 6;6 and 5;3 respectively. Both had learned sufficient English to converse with us in it; indeed the *person identification* usual in child bilinguals made them reluctant to talk German with us.

One of our games was numerical and arithmetical. We first established that both brothers could count from one to ten in English. Then we tested exhaustively their ability to translate these numbers into German. They were always able to translate the numbers individually, i.e. without having to run through the list; which would indicate, according to von Raffler Engel (see 3.2.3) that they were advanced in the Piagetan operation 'conservation of amount'. We went on to make them do simple sums and subtractions in English and in German, not mixing the two languages. We also had them make magnitude comparisons: "Which is bigger . . .?", "Which is smaller . . .?" We next played the same games, but mixing English and German numbers, for example, "What's eight minus eins?", or "Welcher ist grösser, six oder vier?" No writing or other physical support to the mental arithmetic was used, not even fingers.

There were very few errors in their replies, even RW's. Indeed RW sometimes replied faster than his elder brother; but their relative latency was surely independent of their translating ability, since their mother had already observed that RW was faster at arithmetic. We did not observe any differences in latency according to language, but we did not have measuring apparatus. Their accuracy and speed surprised us at the time; but Leopold observed of HL (see 3.4.2) that she could do subtraction in her second language at 5;4 and adding at 5;8, and he remarks: "I marvelled at the unexpected revelation of elementary mathematical proficiency."

The significance we see in this experiment lies not so much in the translation of the individual digits as in the mathematical operations. Mathematics, even elementary arithmetic, is a semiotic system in its own right, with its own syntax and its own writing system. In a sense, even monolingual schoolchildren are bilingual in their spoken language and in mathematics; and to perform an operation which is stated to them in ordinary-language words they have to 'translate' it into mathematical symbolism either on paper or only mentally: cf. Ljudskanov (1972). Of course the semantics of mathematics is much more limited, though more precisely defined, than that of natural language. Nevertheless, to arrive at a correct answer in mathematics, the 'lexical' meaning of the digits as well as the syntactic meaning of the operators must be correctly understood. Moreover, mathematics is 'international' and pasigraphic, i.e. autonomous in respect of specific natural languages. It therefore offers a potentially useful instrument to translatology: a formally defined, graphically represented, meaningful 'interlanguage', into and out of which a very large population can translate whatever their natural languages may be. The fact that our two young *S*s performed equally accurately and with little if any difference of latency in the three modes we tried, viz. English and mathematics, German and mathematics, and (English and German) and mathematics, suggests that their internalized mathematical symbolism may indeed have been an *interlingua*.

Our other popular verbal game together was English children's crossword puzzles. As the answer words were found we would ask one or other of the brothers to give us the corresponding German words, which they did with ease. Translation of individual words is nothing remarkable for children of their age. What amused us unexpectedly was that when RW got bored he would start to give us deliberate nonsense translations, e.g. "tooth" → "Mutti" (Mom). On such occasions PW, who never did that himself, would warn us that his brother was "lying". PW's competence (in Chomsky's sense of 'competence') included judgement of his brother's translations and the ability to distinguish between correct translations and mistranslations. He verbalized his 'mistranslation' judgement as "lying". As for RW, he knew what he was doing and his 'lying' was part of the game. Sometimes both brothers would turn the tables by asking the investigators for a translation. PW and RW's translating was *conscious* and *ludic* (playful).

3.2.3

Von Raffler-Engel (1970) has made the only attempt so far to link translating ability with Piaget's model of cognitive development. Her subject, a boy we call VRE, 5 years, had been a natural bilingual in Italian and English from infancy. At this later age, after a move from Italy to USA, VRE's entourage often elicited translations from him. The experiment was designed to compare VRE's facility at translating (A) member words of a conventionally listed set, with (B) member words of sets he had built up himself. 'Conventionally listed sets' are ones like the names of the days of the week, which children usually learn as a list. An example of (B) is the pair of ad hoc sets in: "Three houses are large and two are small".

VRE had no difficulty translating (B)-type sentences. Yet he was unable to translate elements of a conventionally listed set which he had learned en bloc. For example, in order to translate a single day of the week, "he would switch to the other language and, quietly to himself, run through the corresponding series . . . until he reached the correct correspondence . . . and repeat the word aloud". By 6;4 VRE no longer suffered from the cumbersome way of translating (A). On the other hand he exhibited lexical approximation when translating the names of the seasons, e.g. "March" → "Oh yes that's Spring: primavera."

3.3 3;6 to 6 years

We return to non-elicited NT.

3.3.1

In this age band BS (cf. 3.1.1) was trilingual in Spanish and two varieties of Italian. Her mother spoke only the Abruzzi dialect of Italian. Her father spoke the dialect and Standard Italian. Like Professor Higgins, and like many Italians, he saw mastery of the standard language as a way of breaking out of the lower 'peasant' classes of society. He therefore made it a private tabu for BS to converse with him in dialect, or indeed for her to speak dialect with anybody except relatives. Her Italian *diglossia* began at 2;6 and has continued ever since. Diglossia led to *diglossic translation.* In order to convey messages between her father and her mother or other relatives, she had to translate between dialects. She recalls becoming aware of two different 'languages' and of doing diglossic translation before 4 years.

By that time the family had emigrated to Venezeula, where BS promptly learned Spanish from her new peer group before going to a Hispanophone school at 4 years. In Venezeula her translating, which had hitherto been *intrafamily*, now became intra/extra-family for the first time. Her mother kept a grocery store. BS would greet customers in the store if her mother was busy in the house, and transmit messages from them to either parent. She translated both ways between Spanish and Abruzzi for her mother, between Spanish and Standard Italian for her father. Certainly her translating was socially functional, and probably it was stimulated by the environment of the store: a young trilingual consecutive liaison interpreter at work.

3.3.2

At about 5 years a child may not only be conscious of translation, he or she may even form a rudimentary theory to explain it. AA was a monolingual Francophone who, at about 5 years, played with bilingual Anglophones. She believed that they could understand her French because their ears were different from hers. Their ears changed the French sounds into English for them. An analogous displacement has been discussed by Piaget and is quoted in Leopold (1949):

> "Piaget reports numerous cases in which children seven years of age designate the mouth as the organ of thinking, with astonishing agreement. He

draws the conclusion that for children of this age . . . thinking and speaking are identical."

3.4 Infant translators

We shall deal in this section with children whose translating was observed by investigators from its beginning.

3.4.1

VRE (cf. 3.2.3) lived in Italy until 5 years. He learnt English from his Anglophone father, Italian from his Italophone mother and the rest of his entourage. He distinguished his two languages from about 3;0. His parents wished him to speak both languages without interference, so "as a matter of pedagogical principle, no one in the household had ever asked him to translate" before the following incident occurred.

VRE was 3;6. The family was at table. Father tasted the soup and said in English that it was well flavoured but slightly oversalted. VRE ran to the kitchen and told their Italian cook, in Italian: "Father says even though the soup is too salty it tastes good, or rather, has good ingredients." Then, with reference to his translation "well flavoured" → "has good ingredients", he added: 'È una cosa che somiglia, ma non è uguale" (It's something similar, but not the same). Von Raffler Engel comments: "The point is, he had translated his father's phrase as a conceptual unit and had noticed the diversity in verbal expression in the two languages". We would add that not only did he *notice* his own lexical approximation, he could *describe* it by "È una cosa che somiglia . . ."

Besides lexical approximation there are several other interesting features to this example. The naturalness of the translation was ensured by the parents' pedagogical principle. The translation act, VRE's first so far as was recorded, was *spontaneous*: nobody asked, nor even wanted, VRE to translate the father's remark. The utterance translated was a brief but complete piece of discourse. VRE was concerned to translate its *content* accurately. On the plane of expression, he transformed his father's direct speech to the indirect speech mode in his translation (*direct/indirect speech switching*). Socially the incident was intrafamily, and no example is given of *extrafamily* translation.

3.4.2

Leopold's diary (1949) describes his two daughters' speech development meticulously throughout their early childhood.

3.4.2.1

Leopold spoke with HL only in German, her mother to her only in English, and she was brought up in the USA. By 3;6, Leopold records that she "usually translates my messages to her mother into English without effort; but sometimes she delivers them in their German wording".

At 4;4 – 4;5, he records: "I am teaching her a little Christmas rhyme in German . . . At first she replaced a few words here and there by English ones related to them in form and meaning. She is so used to translating automatically in English that she pays as much attention to the meaning as to the form." Whereas her translation of the messages between her parents was socially functional and *stimulated*, this kind was spontaneous and *socially redundant*. By contrast, since her English was dominant, she had much more difficulty translating into German. At 4;2 – 4;4, he records, she often made requests to him in English first and then had to translate. She "does so with an effort, rarely quite correctly, but not always literally. She often needs help." Perhaps in the direction of her weaker language she was still in the *autotranslation* stage (cf. 3.5.1). Nevertheless, Leopold stimulated her to persist by pretending not to understand her English. As a result, her translation towards German by 5;3 contained more *transduction* (c.f. 3.5) and although still slow it became more idiomatic. Example:

Mother to HL: "Tell him I like it."
HL to father, after pause: "Mutti mag das gerne."

Leopold comments: "Thus she translated the statement as a whole, not translating word for word." About that time HL went to Germany for seven months. The result, for a while after her return to the USA, was that her bilingualism became more balanced. At 5;7 Leopold remarks: "She often translates freely with remarkable feeling for idiom, sometimes after a false start." About the same time, HL came to realize that her father did really understand her English. Yet he went on pretending since "she usually enjoys that as a game." Consequently "she is often compelled to translate and does so freely" – but her translating was henceforth only ludic and redundant.

Finally Leopold juxtaposes her translating and paraphrasing at 5;11: "She speaks both English and German fluently. Both languages are fully formed . . . no significant gaps in the grammar . . . Vocabulary is large in both languages . . . Memory of content instead of form: In the well-known song . . . she replaced the words 'dann ich kann dich nicht begleiten' by the words 'weil ich . . .', which mean the same thing but call for a different word order. She gives explanations of considerable length in German readily, even when she has just given them in English to her mother. Anglicisms are less numerous on such occasions than otherwise." Probably HL the translator had progressed as far as she could in an environment in which only one person spoke her second language with her often, and then only in play.

3.4.2.2

The German of KL, HL's younger sister, always remained passive. Nevertheless she translated *one way*, from German to English. At 3;11 Leopold records: "When she turns communications of mine into English for the benefit of other members of the household, she uses a free translation, with correct reproduction of the sense." At the same age she tried to exploit comprehension-by-translation: "Whenever I use a word which is not familiar to her she translates it into English and says it with an interrogative intonation asking for confirmation. Usually the equivalent is correct, completely or approximately."

Like her sister, KL eventually realized that her father understood his children's English, but she too continued to translate as part of a family game: "She takes it as a joke." At 7;10 Leopold records the following incident: "K just played at translating her former evening prayer, 'Ich bin klein', into English. She was trying to remember it in German. Half of it was forgotten, and in spots the English equivalent intruded. That gave her the idea to translate the whole four lines. She started: 'I am small. My heart is in.' She misinterpreted the last word of 'Mein Herz ist rein' (pure) as 'rein' from 'hierin', has probably misunderstood it during all the years that she said the prayer!" Leopold comments on this example of documentary translation: "This . . . was the first case of formal translation which I have ever observed."

In spite of the ludic context, some at least of KL's translations were still functional in some way. In the example just cited, translation enabled her to reconstruct a text that was beyond recall for her in the original language. Leopold says himself: "Functionally she translates often . . . She translates often when she reports my words in English to another person or repeats them in English to me for confirmation of her comprehension." KL's NT development was virtually the same as her sister's, except that her passive bilingualism kept it one-way. Beyond 5 years both of them continued translating because it was fun.

3.4.3

LR seems to have been precocious as a translator. He was conscious of his bilingualism at 1;8. At 2;2 he could already translate single words and very simple sentences without difficulty, and was into transduction. Indeed he could do it well enough for him to act as liaison interpreter between his Francophone grandparents and the Germanophone family cook, asking the latter to fetch milk, light the lamp, etc., for the former. We see no reason to doubt our source: Ronjat was as careful an observer of his son as Leopold was of his daughters. There are examples, from LR's third year, of 'translation' at several levels:

i) *Phonological translation* (cf. Catford, 1965), e.g. father to mother, in German: ". . . Approbation" (German pronunciation)/LR to father: "Qu'est-ce que c'est approbation?" (French pronunciation).

ii) *Morphological translation*, e.g. he invented a German verb "müschen" from the French "moucher".

iii) Direct/indirect speech switching (cf. 3.4.1), e.g. at 2;6 father to LR: "Non, ne reste pas ici, il fait trop froid, va voir Deda [the housemaid]." /LR to Deda: "Papas Zimmer ist zu kalt."

Although his parents observed the person identification rule strictly, LR realized by 3;0 that they were bilingual and so could understand one another without his help. Yet like the Leopold girls (3.4.2) he went on translating redundantly; he would translate between them at table even if they were addressing one another directly. Meanwhile LR's translating remained functional with other members of the household. An example from 3;8 illustrates both the extent and one of the limits of his translating ability:

LR to Germanophone mother: "Clotilde [their French cook] will einen Phonographen kaufen."(Clotilde wants to buy a phonograph.)
Mother to LR: "Einen Phonographen! es ist zu teuer." (A phonograph! That's too dear.)
LR to Cook: "Clothilde, maman a dit que c'était trop cher." (Clothilde, Mama said it's too dear).

> Cook to LP: "Mais je ne crois pas, ce n'est pas si cher que ça, on peut en avoir pour . . ." (But I don't think it's all that dear. You can get one for . .)
> LR brings message to mother in German.
> Mother to LR: "Das erstaunt mich sehr."

LR rushes towards the door to tell the cook, but suddenly stops short of it, comes back to his mother and says: "Aber das kann ich der Clotilde nicht sagen: sag mir mal das auf français." (But I can't say that to Clotilde: tell it to me in français.) Ronjat explains this setback by saying that LR is sometimes unable to translate abstract expressions. LR does not give up, however, until his mother provides him with the French translation, which he repeats to the cook, so completing the exchange of messages. Since he knew so quickly that he would be unable to do the translation himself, it would seem that he already attempted to rehearse it during his brief rush across his mother's room. We notice in the above illustration that to ask for a translation LR does not use the word for 'translate' , but says, "tell it to me in . . ." This is common to all the subjects in this section, despite their consciousness of the relationship between utterances in different languages which their elders call 'translation'. The relationship is a metalinguistic concept, at a higher level of abstraction than bilingual stimulus and response. The following socially redundant autotranslation illustrates that LR, at 3;7, apprehended the concept:

> LR to Francophone housemaid: "Maria, apporte-moi mon fusil." (Maria bring me my rifle.)
> LR to mother in German: "Maria, bring mir mein Gewehr, hab ich gesagt." (Maria, bring me my rifle, I've said.)

This conscious *linguistic translation* accompanies what Ronjat calls 'full consciousness of bilingualism', which he dates from the end of the third year. At that period, he says, the bilingual progresses from the concrete ideas of 'speak like Papa' or 'speak like Mama' to the abstract motion of 'language'. Indeed by the time he is 4;2, adults turn to LR to act as *their* language informant (cf. 3.1.1). "Was bedeutet tiens?" (What does 'tiens' mean?) a Germanophone housemaid asks him, perplexed by the French word. He replies without hesitation, "Tiens, das heisst Ach!" ('Tiens', that's called 'ach'.) Ronjat's evaluation of his translating at that age is as follows: "He shows remarkable skill as a translator when it comes to finding equivalents for idioms . . . it is more than everyday lexicography, it is excellent intuitive stylistics."

3.5. 1;9 – 3;11. Autotranslation

Translation is usually (A) communication in which the translator acts as an intermediary between two other people. Sometimes, however, (B) a translator translates to others what he has said or written himself; and sometimes (C) he translates *to* himself. We call (B) 'autotranslation'. What then to call (A)? Usually the word 'translation' itself is good enough; but as a technical contrasting term to 'autotranslation', we propose 'transduction'. Infant bilinguals autotranslate as well as transduce.

3.5.1

The following exchange between HL and her father at 3;3– Father, in German: "Ich hab dich lieb." (I like you). HL: "I love you too."– wastranslation for herself only, socially redundant since she still believed her father could not understand her English (see 3.4.2.1). Her socially functional autotranslation had appeared earlier. At 2;5 she asked her father for a pencil. When he pretended not to understand, she said in German, "Bleistift" (pencil). The beginnings of her redundant autotranslation might be traced to as young as 1;11: Father, in German: "Alle kleine Kinder sind jetzt im Bett." (All little children are now in bed). HL: "All babies Bett." But in this example we seem to be back to the threshold of an earlier stage of development which will be described shortly (3.6). Leopold himself comments: "The point was not translation, but replacement of a passively familiar form by the active current one."

3.5.2

Precocious LR started autotranslation at 1;9. Ronjat states that his son "began to transpose messages from one of his languages to the other." For example he said something to their Germanophone cook (Ronjat does not specify what) and repeated it in French to other servants.

3.6 From 1;2 Pretranslation

3.6.1

We have already hinted (3.5.1) that there is an earlier stage than autotranslation. Let us exemplify it first by extracts from Ronjat. (The English translations of Ronjat throughout this paper are ours.)

i) At 1;2:
Father to LR, in French: "Dis merci." (Say thank you.)
LR, in German: "Danke." (Thank you.)

ii) At 1;8:
Mother to LR, in German: "Was hat Papa im Mund?" (What's Papa got in his mouth?)
LR, in German: "Pfeife." (Pipe.)
Father to LR, in French: "Qu'est-ce que c'est que ça?" (What is it?)
LR, in French: "Pipe." (Pipe.)

Ronjat comments on (i) that LR's response is a reflex because he is more often asked to do the same thing in German. We call this reflex *bilingual response.* About (ii) he is categoric: "Of course this has no resemblence to *translation.* The monolingual child makes a connection between the visual percept of an object, the mental representation of an attribute, etc . . . and the mental image of a word to designate that object, etc . . . Our child makes a twofold connection between the visual percept, etc . . . and the mental images of *two* words. Which of the elements of the double connection is in operation depends on what person the child is speaking to."

Pretranslations are mostly single words, which is hardly surprising since the monolingual child too may still be in the 'one-word sentence' stage at that age. They may be interpersonal, as in the examples just given, or the child may be observed doing autotranslation on his own (*intrapersonal*), LR was so observed at 1;8: he found it amusing to say word pairs like "oeil/Auge" (respectively French and German for 'eye'), 'Schiff/Bateau" (German and French for 'boat').

3.6.3

Leopold agrees with Ronjat about bilingual response. On examples like: Someone to HL at 1;4, in German: "Aufstehen!" (Get up!) / HL: "Up!" Leopold comments: "Passively she realized that she was faced with two languages which contained interchangeable words of identical reference. This must be considered a preparatory stage for the active bilingualism of a later time . . . To call this a translation would be rash. She understood the German word, at least its stressed prefix, performed the action of standing up, and the motion conjured up the English word which had just become associated with an upward motion. This is not conscious translation, but it is transposition from one language medium to another via an act which was linked by association with words in both. It differs from translation in the ordinary sense merely by the unconscious character of the process and by the need for the bridge to action. The path did not yet lead from the word of one language to the corresponding word of the other directly, without an intermediary."

DISCUSSION

4.1

In the presentation of our data we have sustained a developmental model of NT extending from pretranslation at 1;2 (see 3.6) to semi-professional translation at 18 years (3.1.1). We have also shown that child NT occurs in many combinations of languages. The succession of stages in development seems to be as follows:

i) Pretranslation (3.6) before interpersonal autotranslation (3.5) and transduction (3.1 – 3.4).

ii) Intrapersonal autotranslation concurrent with the late part of pre-translation (3.6.1). The data for this is likely to be scantier because the presence of an observer stimulates inter-personal communication.

iii) Autotranslation before transduction.

iv) Intrafamily translation before extrafamily.

How far is this succession due to causes inherent in translation? It is possible that all the stages have their analogues in monolingual language development from infant one-word sentences to semi-professional compositions and authorship. For (i) through (iii), perhaps further analysis of Leopold (1949) and Ronjat (1913) or a comparison with Halliday (1976) would help to establish such a parallel; while (iv) is probably due to general conditions of family and social life. Natural translation has many natural connections. On the other hand, it may be that (i) through (iii) are *necessary* predecessors to socially functional transduction, at least in infants. In pretranslation the child seems to be building up and exercising a co-ordinated bilingual lexicon and not two autonomous monolingual ones: consider LR's rehearsal of pairs of words (3.6.1). Autotranslation provides plenty of practice irrespective of the degree of adult co-operation. 'Socially redundant' does not mean developmentally redundant.

4.2

Investigators of elicited NT (Swain, Dumas and Naiman, 1974) have raised the question of whether all natural translators translate alike; and if not, whether the differences are due to how well the translator knows the two languages or to other factors. Ronjat and Leopold both note with satisfaction that their children's NT becomes freer, more idiomatic and stylistically correct with time and with exposure to their languages.

4.3

In none of the data, in none of the comments by subjects, parents or investigators do we find anything to suggest that NT hinders successful acquisition of a second language or language development in general. Nor is there anything to suggest that it improves it. It just seems to be a concomitant.

4.4

Finally, we draw attention to the features in the data which we believe support our hypothesis that NT is an innate skill:

i) The early age at which translation may start: 1;9 is the youngest so far recorded (LR).

ii) The even younger pre-translation.

iii) The prevalence of spontaneous translation.

iv) The small amount of exposure to a second language that older children need before translating (e.g. GS in 3.2.1).

v) The prevalence of socially redundant translation.

vi) The prevalence of ludic translation.

vii) The lack of positive correlation between subject's translation performance and instruction in translation. Amongst the *infant* translators we have described (those under 5 years), none was given direct requests to translate. Quite the contrary, the parents of several (HL, KL, LR, VRE) deliberately abstained from eliciting translations or translating *for* the child.

'Innate' has a double meaning these days in developmental psycholinguistics. In its 'weak' sense it means a specialized predisposition in children to learn how to speak from the language they hear in their environment; in the 'strong' sense it means an inherited 'theory' of language ('universal grammar') which enables the child to speak sooner and more grammatically than can be accounted for by its contact with the environment. If temporarily we adapt the weak sense to translatology, what are the 'design features' we might require in the special disposition for learning NT? Features, that is to say, additional to those needed for acquisition of the bilingual's two languages without NT. An adequate reply must await much more research on the translation process, but we will close with a few of the points that have struck us in the course of our study:

i) The *pleasure* that translating may give the young translator. Prior to our study, we believed that NT arose from urgent needs in interpersonal communication. It still seems so, especially if we imagine a child's view of urgency and necessity. But now we also have to seek motivation for intrapersonal, spontaneous, auto- and ludic translation. This leads us to posit that the young NT translator experiences pleasure in translating, irrespective of the interpersonal communicative function of the translation.

ii) The functioning, from the second year, of an *associative memory* which is capable of storing an *NT lexicon*, i.e. one in which pairs of words from different languages are linked pair by pair, and from which there is rapid recall. It is true that a bilingual lexicon is only sufficient for a rudimentary kind of translation, viz. *word-for-word transcoding*; none the less it appears to facilitate all translating.

iii) The ability to recall the content of utterances from memory irrespective of the language through which it was entered. KL's reproduction of the German prayer in English (3.4.2.2) presents an illustration involving long-term memory. The arithmetic operations in 3.2.2 perhaps involve the same ability in short-term memory. Both would support a model of language-independent semantic storage.

iv) An operation of *conservation of meaning across languages* (COMAL). Ljudskanov (1975) puts forward the very general concept of *semiotic transformation* (ST), meaning "a transformation of symbols that preserves information". In translatology one is usually concerned with a specific type of ST, where the symbols are those of two natural languages and two cultures. COMAL, we propose, is the *discriminatory judgement* needed to monitor a bilingual ST. PW exhibited it, at 6;6 in the "lying" episode (3.2.2). VRE and LR exhibited it at 3;6 and 3;7 respectively: the one certainly, in his "somiglia ma non uguale" comment (3.4.1); the other very probably, in his "Bring mir mein Gewehr, hab ich gesagt" (3.4.3). Ljudskanov's semiotic taxonomy of translation (*ibid*) would predict for us that COMAL is a special case of a more general operation 'conservation of meaning within and across semiotic systems', e.g. in paraphrasing or between the verbal description of an object and a drawing of it. Be that as it may, perhaps COMAL is the psychological operation most vital to advanced NT, and hence to all socially useful translation.

REFERENCES

Anderson, R. B. W., Perspectives on the role of interpreter. In R. W. Brislin (Ed.), *Translation: Applications and Research*, New York: Gardner Press, 1976.

Biondi, L. *The Italian-American child, his sociolinguistic acculturation*. Washington: Georgetown U.P., 1975.

Brislin, R. W. Introduction. In R. W. Brislin (Ed.)., *Translation: Applications and Research*, New York: Gardner Press, 1976.

Catford, J. C., *A Linguistic Theory of Translation. An Essay in Applied Linguistics*. London: Oxford U.P., 1965.

Gerver, D. Empirical studies of simultaneous interpretation: a review and a model. In R. W. Brislin, (Ed.), *Translation: Applications and Research*, New York: Gardner Press, 1976.

Halliday, M. A. K. *Learning How to Mean: Explorations in the Development of Language*. London: Edward Arnold, 1976.

Harris, B. La traductologie, la traduction naturelle, la traduction automatique et la sémantique. In J. McNulty *et al* (Eds.), *Problèmes de sémantique* (Cahiers de Linguistique 3), Montreal: Presses de l'Univ. du Québec, 1973.

Harris, B. The importance of natural translation. *Working Papers on Bilingualism* 1977, *12*, 96 - 114.

Leopold, W. F. *Speech Development of a Bilingual Child. A Linguist's Record*. Evanston, Il: Northwestern U.P., 1949.

Ljudskanov, A. K. *Mensch und Maschine als Übersetzer*. Halle, GDR: Niemeyer, 1972.

Ljudskanov, A. K. A semiotic approach to the theory of translation. Trans. B. Harris. *Language Sciences*, 1975, *35* : 5 - 8.

Ronjat, J. *Le développement du langage observé chez un enfant bilingue*. Supplementary thesis for Doctorat ès-Lettres. Paris: H. Champion, 1913.

Swain, M., Dumas, G., and Naiman, N. Alternatives to spontaneous speech: elicited translation and imitation as indicators of second language competence. *Working Papers on Bilingualism*, 1974, *3* : 68 - 79.

Thiery, C. *Le bilinguisme chez les interprètes de conférence*. Doctoral Thesis: Univ. of Paris - III, 1975.

Von Raffler-Engel, W. The concept of sets in a bilingual child. In *Actes du Xe Congrès International des Linguistes*. Vol. III. Bucharest: Romanian Academy Press, 1970.

Four Generations of Machine Translation Research and Prospects for the Future

Yorick Wilks

University of Essex

Colchester, Essex

INTRODUCTION

There is an ancient Chinese curse that dooms recipients to live in an interesting age, and by those standards Machine Translation (MT) workers are at present having a bad time. The reason things are interesting at the moment is that there is a number of *conflicting* claims in the air about how to do MT, and whether it can, or indeed has already, been done. Such a situation is unstable, and we may confidently expect some kind of outcome – always cheering for the empiricist – in the near future.

What has happened is threefold. First, the "brute force" methods for MT, that were thought to have been brought to an end by the ALPAC (1966) Report have surfaced again, like some Coelacanth from the deep, long believed extinct. Such systems are now being sold under such trade names as LOGOS, XYZYX, SMART and SYSTRAN; and the last, and best known, is now undergoing extensive testing in Paris (Van Slype, 1976) and Luxembourg.

Secondly, some large-scale, more theoretically based, MT projects continued – usually based in Universities – and are now being tested in use, though sometimes on a scale smaller than that originally envisaged. METEO, for example, in Montreal (Chandioux, 1976), which was to have translated official documents from English to French, is now in use for the translation of the more limited world of TV Weather reports.

Thirdly, workers in natural language in the field known as Artificial Intelligence (AI) have begun to make distinct claims about the need for their approach if there is to be general and high quality MT (Wilks, 1973; Charniak, 1973; Schank, 1975a). Small pilot systems illustrating their claims have been programmed, but their role in contemporary discussion is mainly of a theoretical nature.

However, these are not merely three complementary approaches, for they seem to be making different claims, and, unless we take the easy way out and simply *define* some level of MT appropriate to each of the enterprises, it seems they cannot all be right, and that we may hope for some resolution before too long.

What I shall do in this brief paper is to sketch the recent background from the AI point of view, and then outline very briefly a development within the overall AI approach that should have some bearing on the possibility of high quality MT.

SOME BACKGROUND NOTES

As the title hints and the introduction sets out, we now have, in my view, four generations of MT research: the original efforts of 1957-65 plus the three types of project now surviving, and indeed competing. The key to their relation can be found in their different responses to Bar-Hillel's critique of MT, which he updated at intervals, but which came down to one essential point: MT is not only practically, but theoretically, impossible.

"Expert human translators use their *background knowledge*, mostly subconsciously, in order to resolve syntactical and semantical ambiguities which machines will either have to leave unresolved, or resolve by some "mechanical" rule which will every so often result in a wrong translation. The perhaps simplest illustration of a syntactical ambiguity which is unresolvable by a machine except by arbitrary or ad hoc rules is provided by a sentence, say ". . . slow neutrons and protons . . .", where an expert will have no difficulty in resolving the ambiguity through utilization of his background knowledge, no counterpart of which could possible stand at the disposal of computers". (Bar-Hillel, 1962)

The immediate context of Bar-Hillel's argument was the performance of early syntax analysers which, according to legend, were capable of producing upwards of ten parsings of sentences like "Time flies like an arrow", where, with respect to standard dictionary information, any of the first three words could be taken as a possible verb.

The standard reaction to such syntactic results was to argue that this simply showed the need for linguistic semantics, so as to reduce the "readings" in such cases to the appropriate one. Bar-Hillel's addition to this was to argue that it was not a matter of semantic additions at all but of the, for him unformalizable, world of human knowledge.

It is interesting to notice that the reactions of Bar-Hillel and AI workers like Minsky were in part the same: Minsky (1968) argued that MT clearly required the formalization of human knowledge for a system that could be said to *understand*, or as Bar-Hillel reviewed the situation in 1971 (Lehmann and Stachowitz, 1971, p. 72):

"It is now almost generally agreed upon that high-quality MT is possible only when the text to be translated has been understood, in an appropriate sense, by the translating mechanism".

What Minsky and Bar-Hillel *dis*agreed about, of course, was what followed: Bar-Hillel thought that the impossibility of MT followed, whereas Minsky believed that the task had now been defined, and the job of AI was to get on with it.

The contrast is clear between these two and the views of linguists: Chomsky's generative theories are also, in a clear sense, a reaction to the failure of early MT, in that they state with great force the case for a solid theory of natural languages as a precondition for any advance with machines and language. Fodor and Katz's semantics, adjoined to a generative grammar, represent, as it were, the linguistic analogue to those who thought that semantic information would resolve the multiple parsings of the notorious "Time flies like an arrow". Later linguists broke from the Chomskyan paradigm by arguing that Fodor and Katz's rigid exclusion of human knowledge from a linguistic system was inadequate, and that many forms of pragmatic knowledge would be required in a full linguistic system. Lehmann-Stachowitz (1971) contains contributions along these lines from Ross and Fillmore, specifically in relation to MT.

The attempt by AI research to respond to Bar-Hillel's challenge is of a different sort. It is an attempt not only to admit ab initio the need for "knowledge structures" in an understanding system, but also to formulate theories and systems containing *processes for the manipulation* of that knowledge. "Processes" here is not to be taken to mean merely programming a computer to carry out a task, for many AI systems of interest have either not been programmed at all or made to do only partial demonstrations. The word "process" means that a theory of understanding should be stated in a symbol processing manner, one in which most linguistic theories are *not* information processing. This is a contentious position, in that generative grammar has been in some sense a description of a process since the earliest descriptions of transformational theory. The AI case is that it never quite comes up to scratch in processing terms. The nature of this dispute can be seen from such work as Bresnan (1976) where an attempt is made to present transformational grammar at the highest level in an unfamiliar (to linguists) and process-orientated manner.

The METEO system represents what one might call the linguistic tradition in MT work: with the claim that an MT system based on a linguistic theory is sufficient and that whatever knowledge is required for MT can be assimilated to the structure of a grammar-based system with a semantic component.

The work of Ross and Fillmore referred to (as well by Lakoff and McCawley among others) represents a breakdown of the paradigm that has dominated linguistics since 1957, and in their search for more general notions of process to express knowledge computations it is no longer clear that anything fundamental separates them from what we have here called the AI approach to MT.

The additional contrast with the resurrected "brute force" methods should now be clearer. These approaches have in essence *ignored* the challenge of Bar-Hillel as well as the earlier one from linguistics for a theoretically motivated syntax and semantics. The assumption behind work like SYSTRAN is that the main fault of the early MT period was inadequate machines and software, *not theory*. The striking demonstrations [1] given of that system are not yet conclusive, and detailed descriptions of its methods are not available because of understandable commercial considerations, but there can be no doubt that it does pose a considerable challenge to both linguists and AI theorists, who claim, in their different ways that some higher level theory is essential for MT.

WHAT THEN IS AN AI THEORY?

Apart from their common emphasis on knowledge structures and process form, AI theories can only be illustrated by example, since they differ so much among themselves on a wide range of issues (see Wilks, 1976a). Moreover, MT is not usually the implementation environment of a typical AI program (though see Wilks, 1973; 1975) which is normally dialogue, question-answering or paraphrase. But no issue of principle arises here, especially if one accepts Steiner's (1975) claim that every act of understanding is, in essence, one of translation.

Winograd's well-known program (1972) was perhaps the first AI language understander not directed to what one could call the classic residual problems of MT: word sense ambiguity, pronoun reference ambiguity etc. He was concerned to show the role of knowledge of a microworld of blocks as a tool for resolving syntactic ambiguities in input to a dialogue system. So, for example, when his system saw the sentence "Put the pyramid on the block in the box", it would immediately resolve the surface syntactic ambiguity of that command according to whether there *was* a block either under a pyramid or already in the box in the blocks scene that it understood.

More typical of an implicit response to MT problems were the systems of Schank, 1975a; Charniak, 1973; and Wilks, 1975, which, in their different ways, were concerned with the semantic representations, real world knowledge and inference rules needed to understand various aspects of every-day story-like sentences, and to produce deep representations for them, from which translations in another language could in principle be produced.

In the last few years the paradigm in AI and language understanding has itself shifted, largely in response to an argument of Minsky's (1975) that more complex knowledge structures were required than had been contained in any of the systems mentioned so far. He called these more complex structures *frames*, and argued that without the more specific knowledge of concepts that they expressed, language understanding would not be possible.

So far, as in Schank (1975b) and Charniak (1975) frames have been taken to be representations of stereotypical situations, such as the normal sequence of events in shopping in a supermarket. He argues that we can easily construct stories that will not be understood without such knowledge: "John put some bacon in the basket in the supermarket, but then slipped a bar of chocolate off the shelf and into his pocket. When he got to the checkout his face went red and he said I didn't mean to take it". He might argue that one cannot refer the "it" correctly in that sentence, and so understand it or translate it into a suitably gendered language, without the sequential knowledge of what is and is not normal in a supermarket. There is still some unclarity about what precisely are the claims implied by the use of such frames (see Wilks, 1977b), but there is no doubt that they do represent a real form of language-related knowledge and can be seen as a new attempt to tackle the old MT problem of topic. So, for example, Schank has a program for using restaurant frames such that when it sees, say, the word "order" it will know that it is the word "order food", because it is encountered in a restaurant frame, and not the more general "order an object".

Schank has also supervised the construction of a program that reads stories into a frame format and then translates out the whole frame (including the stereotypical parts not actually mentioned in the original story) in a number of different languages.

In what remains of this paper I would like to sketch a proposal for the relevance of a rather different type of frame to MT: a static and not a dynamic frame to do with normal sequences of actions. It is directed towards another intractable problem of MT: of what to do when the input does not fit our semantic expectations. I will now turn to this, and then finally make some remarks about how far such AI proposals may take us in MT even when they eventually work as programs.

MEANING BOUNDARIES AND KNOWLEDGE STRUCTURES

The remainder of the paper sketches how one might deal with *extensions of word sense* in a natural language understanding system (NLUS): that is to say, normal utterances that break preassigned selection, or preference, restrictions. The proposals here extend the knowledge representation of the preference semantics NLUS (Wilks 1967,,1973, 1975) with *pseudo-texts* (PT) which are frame structures in the sense of Minsky, (1975), but which are also consistent with the general assumptions of this NLUS.

It is essential to see that extended use, in the sense of *preference-violating* use is the *norm* in ordinary language use, and so cannot be relegated in an NLUS to some special realm of treatment, as "performance" is in generative linguistics, nor neglected in a general consideration of MT. The following sentence is chosen, I promise you, at random from the front page of a daily newspaper: (*The Times*, 5 - 2 - 76):

1) Mr Wilson said that the *line* taken by the Shadow Cabinet, that an Assembly should be given no executive *powers* would lead to the *break-up* of the *United Kingdom.*

The sentence presents no understanding problems whatever to an informed reader, yet each of the four italicised entities violates the normal preference restrictions of an associated verb: "line", for example, would violate thc normal physical object restriction on "take", and so on.

The process to be described in this paper is called *projection*; we shall show how sense descriptions for words can be rewritten, in preference-violating texts (as in 1), *with the aid of the specific knowledge in PTs*: part of the PT will be *projected into* the sense description for a word. So, for example, in (1) some detailed political knowledge in a PT for "United Kingdom" could show that a breaking of that entity could be caused, and we would then replace the sense description of "lead to" by one equivalent to "cause", thus overcoming the preference violation in "lead to the break-up" and providing a *more appropriate* sense description of "lead to" for analysis of the rest of this text.

BRIEF RECAP OF REFERENCE SEMANTICS

In previous papers I have described an NLUS in which rules operate on semantic word-sense descriptions to build up text descriptions. The rules that insert sense descriptions into text descriptions are what I have called "preferential": they seek preferred entities, but will accept the less preferred if necessary. A sense description for the action "drink" might be the *formula*:

2)

A SEMANTIC FORMULA FOR THE ACTION OF DRINKING.

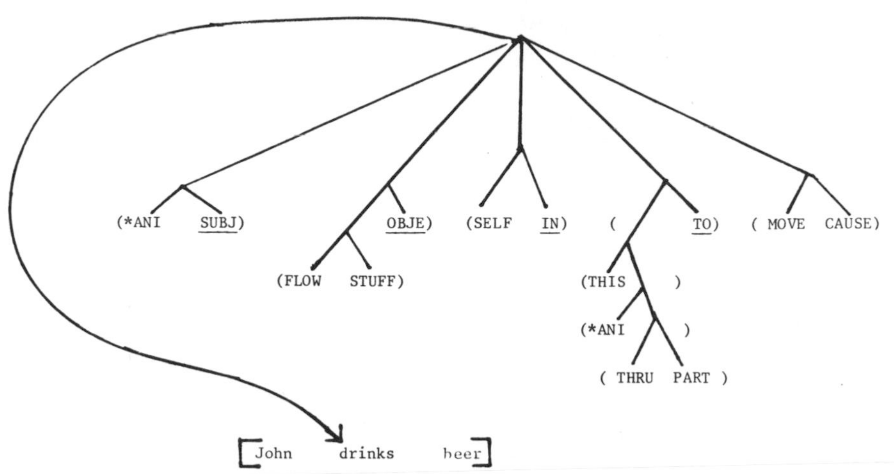

THE ACTION FORMULA FOR DRINKING INSTALLED AT THE (CENTRAL) ACTION NODE OF A SEMANTIC TEMPLATE OF FORMULAS FOR "John drinks beer".

This is a formal structure of semantic *primitives* expressing the meaning of the action (see King and Wilks, 1977): that drinking is a CAUSing to MOVE, preferably done by an ANImate SUBJect (=agent) and to a liquid (FLOW STUFF), TO a particular ANImate aperture (THRU PART), and INto the SELF (=the animate agent). For short we will write (2) and [drink]. The text structures in the system are semantic templates (together with semantic ties between them): a *template* is a network of formulas, containing at least an agent, action and object formula. Thus the template for "The adder drinks water" will be written the+adder drinks water for short where the whole of (2) is in fact at the central (action) node.

The process of setting up the template allows the formulas to compete to fill nodes in templates. Thus the formula for the (snake-)adder goes to the agent node in the template above in preference to the (machine-)adder because (2) specifies, by (*ANI SUBJ), that it prefers to be accompanied in a template by an *animate* agent formula. However, in the sentence:

3) My car drinks gasoline

the available formula for the first template node, namely [car], is not for an animate entity, yet it is accepted because there is no competitor for the position. The purpose of this paper is to sketch how the system might not merely accept such a preference-violating structure for (3) but might also *interpret* it.

An important later process is called *extraction*: template-like structures are inferred and added to the text representation even though they match nothing in the surface text. They are "deeper" inferences from the case structures of formulas in some actual templates -- where the *case* primitives are those italicised in (2). Thus, to the template for (3), we would add an extraction (in double square parentheses in abbreviated form):

4) [[gasoline in car]]

which is an inference extracted from the *containment* subformula of (2), (SELF IN). Analogous extractions could be made for each case primitive in each formula in the template for (3).

Since the programed version of the system, reported in Wilks, (1975), a structural change (Wilks, 1976a) has allowed a wider, and more specific, form of expression in formulas by allowing *thesaurus items*, as well as primitives, to function in them. No problems are introduced by doing this, provided that the thesaurus items are also themselves words in the dictionary, and so have *their* formulas defined elsewhere in their turn. One advantage of this extension is to impose a thesaurus structure of the *whole vocabulary*, and so render its semantic expression more consistent.

A thesaurus, like *Roget*, is simply an organisation of a vocabulary into semi-synonymous rows, which are themselves, classified hierarchically under *heads*, and even more generally, *sections*. Thus under some very general section name MOVE (= motion) we would find heads, two of which might be ≠ engine and ≠ vehicle. The former might be the name of a row of actual types of engine:

5) ≠ 525 engine: turbine, internal combustion, steam . . .

where the number simply indicates the sequence position of ≠ engine in the thesaurus. It is no accident that the most general section names like MOVE can be identified with the semantic primitives of the present system.

The organization is imposed by requiring inclusion relations, between the formulas for word senses, corresponding to the thesaurus relations of the words. Thus, all the words in the row (5) would have a common subpart to their formulas, and *that common subpart* would be the dictionary formula for "engine", probably expressing in primitives no more that "a thing used by humans to perform some task and self-moving in some way". If now thesaurus items can be inserted in formulas we may expect a formula for "car" at least as specific as:

6)

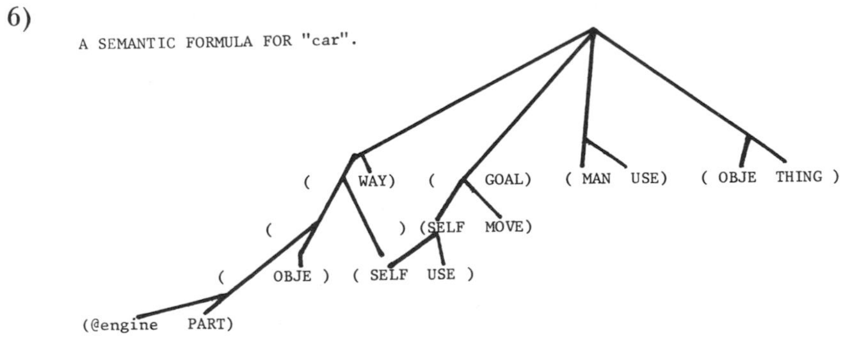

LANGUAGE BOUNDARIES AND PROJECTION

Let us return to examples like (3) for which the system constructs a template even though it contains a violated preference, and ask what should an intelligent system infer in such a situation?[2] I would suggest that cars can be said to drink in virtue of something a system might already know about them, namely that they have a fluid (gas/petrol) injected into them, and they use that in order to run. That is to say, the program should have access to a sufficiently rich knowledge structure to express the fact that cars stand in a relation to a particular fluid, a relation that is of the "same semantic structure" as the relation in which a drinker normally stands to the thing drunk. All that may sound obvious, but how else are we to account for the naturalness of (3), but the relative unnaturalness (and uninterpretability) of "My car *chews* gasoline", and, the more distant, "My car carves the Sunday roast". One upshot of these proposals is to distinguish plausible (with respect to a knowledge base) preference violation from the implausible.[3]

The procedural upshot of the above would be to replace *at least one* formula in the template for (3) with another, either constructed by rule [4] or drawn from the knowledge structure itself, to be called a *pseudo-text* (PT). Let us now postulate that "car" points not only to (6), i.e. [car] but that [car] in turn points to:

7)

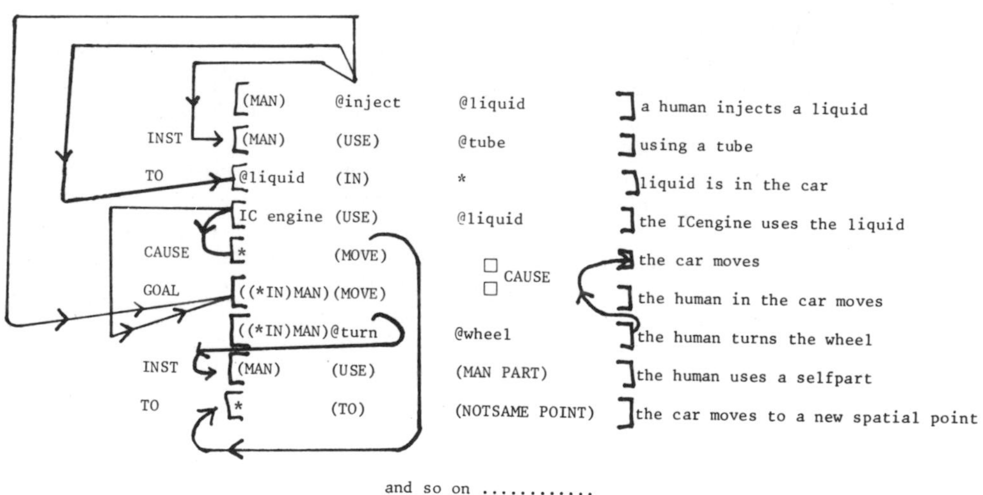

This structure is called a *pseudo-text* because it is of just the same format as the text representations produced by the present NLUS. It can be extended to taste to express as much specific information about cars as is thought appropriate – given the parser for the present NLUS, it could even be *input as a real text* about cars. The representation consists of the templates (explained loosely at the right), together with the (self-explanatory) case and cause ties between them. In the templates, □ dummy and *denotes the formula [car] that points *to* this object (7). The ≠ prefixed items are thesaurus items, though "IC engine" is simply a specific dictionary word pointing to its own formula – specificity is thus a matter of taste. So, for example, the thesaurus head ≠ liquid could be replaced by the more explicit "gasoline". Items in round parentheses remain in primitive form. It will be clear that the same information can be expressed in a number of different ways, and at different levels of generality; though the spirit of Minsky (1975) suggests that they should be as specific as possible. The intention here is that THE PROCESSES THAT OPERATE ON SUCH ENTITIES AS (7) SHALL BE IDENTICAL WITH THOSE THAT MANIPULATE REPRESENTATIONS DERIVED FROM INPUT TEXTS. The approach is thus the reverse of the conventional one: we seek to assimilate knowledge structures to text structures, rather than the reverse, on the grounds that the representation of language is the difficult task, and that the representation of *knowledge as such* makes no sense apart from that.

We should note, too, that just as the thesaurus structure imposes a containment relation on the *formulas* of co-row-member words, so it also imposes a hierarchical relationship on PTs: that for vehicle, for example, will be a less specific version of (7). Further up the thesaurus would be PTs for high-level *sections*: that for MAN would be highly complex, for example. But note there is no "inheritance of property" problem in this system: the formula for "amputee" would have head MAN and would specify the loss of limbs. Any inherited pseudo-text from MAN – asserting "two legs" – would be modified by [amputee].

The system now uses (7) to make a *projection*, so as to derive an interpretation for (4), by seeking, in (7) templates matching the source template [my+car drinks gasoline]: namely the first and fourth lines of (7). The first match is in virtue of the similarity of [drink] and [≠ inject] – based on the expression in primitives, as in (2), of causing a liquid to be in an entity of the same type as the agent. This would allow us to confirm by projection, the "humanness of the drinker", that has already been noted by earlier extraction[5] routines, extracting out from the drink formula (2) independently of the PT (7). However, no projection is made at this stage onto [car]. (Though it might be later in the face of a sentence after (4) like "His thirst is never slaked", that confirms the humanness projection) because in the case of violations of the preferences of actions, like "drink" in (4), the system ALWAYS PREFERS TO MAKE A PROJECTION ONTO THE ACTION ITSELF IF IT CAN. The strong match detected is between the above template for (3) and the *fourth* line of (7) in virtue of the containment of [≠ engine] in [car], and by [≠ liquid] of [gasoline], which is evident in the formulas themselves. This results in the projection of the action node of the fourth line of (7), namely [use], onto [drink] in the template for (3). This projection is taken to be strongly confirmed by the match with the first line of (7), and is considered to carry over more sense than any alternative projection. The confirmation (of the match of the fourth line of (7) by the first line) is necessary here, because [my+car leaks gasoline] would also match the *fourth* line, but no such projection would be appropriate. Conversely, no projection could be made for "My car drinks mud" from the fourth line, even with the confirmation of the first. The general rule of *action projections* then is: SEEK A PSEUDO-TEXT, FOR AGENT OR OBJECT, WITH A TEMPLATE MATCHING ON AGENT AND OBJECT NODES. PROJECT THIS *GENERALLY* IF THERE IS ALSO A PSEUDO-TEXT TEMPLATE MATCH TO THE ACTION ITSELF, FOR ANOTHER TEMPLATE IN THE SAME PSEUDO-TEXT.

We may note in passing three interesting developments of the above suggestion. First consider the more complex example presented by a recent headline:

8) Britain tries to escape Common Market.

Clearly, some projection would be appropriate here, of humanness onto the country, and perhaps even "prisonlikeness" onto the formula for the Common Market. These might be drawn from the formula for "escape" alone, by extraction and without recourse to the pseudo-texts for either of the entities. Even if we did consult those entities, we would find a historical account of Britain *joining*, but not of leaving. In such circumstances mere facts are not enough, even when highly structured. We might conceivably be able to project some notion [disassociate] onto [escape], from the "Britain pseudo-text", given some new matching criterion that placed relevance *above negation* in such cases (i.e. would match [escape] with [associate] or [join].).

Secondly, we might consider the problems presented by an example like:

9) I see what you mean.

Here the last clause breaks the preference expressed in [see] for a physical object. A system procedure will present the *actual* object of (9) to the top-level template simply as the primitive SIGN (the primitive for symbols and intensional representations of them) which has been obtained, by extraction, from the preferred object in [mean]. Thus the system is effectively dealing with the template sequence [I see (SIGN)] [you mean (SIGN)]. But what could we expect as a pseudo-text for something as general as SIGN, so as to use the above procedures to project on to [see]? If we take advantage of the hierarchical nature of the thesaurus, we might expect pseudo-texts at the very top level, associated with the section names – pure primitives like SIGN – just as specific pseudo-texts are associated with the lowest level items in the thesaurus – row members like "car". The psuedotext for a primitive like SIGN would be wholly "core structural": it would consist of no more than primitive concatenations, in template form, like MAN THINK SIGN,[6] the most general thing that can be said about what is normally done in signs. However, even something as general as this might suffice to project THINK correctly onto [see]. The interesting generality would come from using *exactly the same projection procedures* on the most general pseudo-texts like this, as on the most specific, like (7).

Thirdly, and this is treated at length in (Wilks, 1977a), we can consider a quite different type of projection for phrases like:

10) a toy lion.

This comes from a much discussed class of examples ("plastic flower", "stone horse" etc.), where an obvious projection mechanism is to replace the head of the formula for the noun (BEAST in [lion] in (10)) by the preferred object of prediction in the qualifier – here *PHYSOB in [toy]. This would be a very limited and general class of projections, not requiring access to PT's, but which might still provide a "projected formula" appropriate for examples like:

11) The cat walked round the toy lion.
Then he came back and sniffed it.

where we might be helped to refer "he" and "it" correctly by the new, projected, formula [lion] whose head was no longer BEAST, and which could therefore no longer be the reference of "he" as a real lion would be.

A more radical and interesting development would be construction of "PT repacking functions" specific to certain qualifiers. Thus, for example, such a function for "toy", if faced with the phrase "toy car" might repack (7) using a general rule to delete all constituent templates based on the action USE, as well as all those that are at end of a GOAL tie, since toy cars cannot, normally, serve human needs, uses and purposes.

POSTSCRIPT

The above suggestions are, as should be clear, only in the pre-program stage, but they will be implemented. What I have tried to suggest in this paper is that AI language programs do bear upon the traditional difficulties of MT, and often do so more directly than conventional linguistic theories, with their preoccupation with well-formedness, and with delimiting the class of all utterances of a language.

I have given the impression perhaps that all AI programs are concerned with what could be called stratospheric considerations: the solution of the most general problems of language and understanding. That would be unfair: there is a number of more task-oriented projects under construction, attempting to limit vocabulary and world knowledge to very limited domains, such as plumbing repair, say, so as to produce concrete results while at the same time appealing to very general philosophical principles (see Levin and Moore, 1976).

What all the AI projects, of whatever level, have in common is an appeal to very general knowledge and principles, coupled to the claim that MT work must take account of these if it is ever to achieve generality and reliability. The reply to this claim, from experience with projects like SYSTRAN, is that the AI examples that make these points are artificial and/or rare, and they can be ignored for practical purposes. This is clearly an empirical dispute and open to test, which is what makes the present situation interesting as I remarked at the beginning.

That much does depend on one's choice of examples can be seen by returning to those of the beginning: Bar-Hillel's "slow neutrons and protons" should be amenable to treatment by an expert "atomic physics frame", one no more open to the charge of "ad hocness" than is human knowledge of physics itself. But with the old favourite "Time flies like an arrow", things are not so clear. In terms of what I called preferences, it may well be that the desired reading (where time does the flying) satisfies no more semantic preferences than, say, the reading where the flies like certain objects. Moreover, it is hard to imagine that *any* topic-determining frame could help here – one would hardly expect this slogan in any frame about time, except as an arbitrary addition. Nothing that has come from recent "speech act" theorists in linguistics and philosophy seems likely to help either. Perhaps, the only explanation of our competence with this sentence is that we read it off a list of cliches for which we have the assigned readings: a sad conclusion for all theoretically-motivated work, and an awful fate for a long cherished example.

REFERENCES

ALPAC: Automatic Language Processing Advisory Committee. *Language and Machine*. Washington, D.C. National Academy of Sciences, 1966, *1416*. Sciences.

Bar-Hillel, Y. The future of machine translation. *Times Literary Supplement*. London: Times Newspapers. April 20th 1962.

Bobrow, D. and Winograd, T. KRL – an overview of a knowledge representation language. *Cognitive Science*, 1977, *1*, 3 - 46.

Bresnan, J. Towards a realistic model of transformational grammar. Unpublished mss., 1976.

Bruderer, H. *Handbook of Machine Translation and Machine-Aided Translation*. Amsterdam: North Holland, in press.

Chandioux, J. METEO, In Hays and Mathias (Eds.). F.B.I.S. Seminar on Machine Translation. *American Journal of Computational Linguistics*. 1976.

Charniak, E., Jack and Jane in search of a theory of knowledge. In: *Proceedings of the Third International Joint Conference on Artificial Intelligence*. Menlo Park, California: Stanford Research Institute, 1973, 115 - 124.

Charniak, E. Organization and Inference. In: *Proc. Theoretical Issues in Natural Language Processing*. Cambridge, Mass.: M.I.T., 1975, 105 - 114.

Fillmore, C. On a fully developed system of linguistic description. In Lehmann and Stachowitz (Eds.). *Feasibility study on fully Automatic High Quality Translation*. Rome Air Development Center, N.Y., 1971.

Givon, T. *The structure of ellipsis*. Mimeo. Santa Monica. California: Systems Development Corp., 1967.

Grice, H. Logic and Conversation. Unpublished mss., 1967.

Hays, D., and Mathias, J. (Eds.). Proc. FBIS Seminar on Machine Translation. *American Journal of Computational Linguistics*, 1976, *46*.

King, H. and Wilks, Y. *Semantics, Preference and Inference*. Geneva: Institute for Semantic and Cognitive Studies, 1977.

Levin, J., and Moore, J., Dialogue Games. In: *Proc. A.I.S.B. Conference*, 1976, Edinburgh: Department of Artificial Intelligence.

Lehmann, W., and Stachowitz, R., (Eds.). *Feasibility study on fully automatic high-quality translation, Report RADC-TR-71-295*. Rome, N.Y.: Rome A. F. Development Center, 1971.

Minsky, M. (Ed.). *Semantic Information Processing*. Cambridge, Mass.: M.I.T. Press, 1968.

Minsky, M. A framework for representing knowledge. In P. Winston (Ed.). *The Psychology of Computer Vision.* New York: McGraw Hill, 1975, 211 - 277.
Schank, R. (Ed.) *Conceptual Information Processing.* Amsterdam: North Holland 1975a.
Schank, R. Using knowledge to understand. In: *Proc. Theoretical Issues in Natural Language Processing.* Cambridge, Mass.: M.I.T. Press 1975b, 67 - 77.
Steiner, G. *After Babel: Aspects of Language and Translation.* London: Oxford U.P., 1975.
Van Slype, *Etat des activites multilinques en matiere d'information scientifique et technique: Vol. 1., Rapport Final.* Bureau Van Dijk, Brussels, 1976.
Wilks, Y. *Computable Semantic Derivations.* S.P. 2758. Systems Development Corporation, Santa Monica, 1967.
Wilks, Y. An artificial intelligence approach to machine translation. In Schank and Colby (Eds.). *Computer Models of Thought and Language.* San Francisco: Freeman, 1973, 101 - 129.
Wilks, Y. A preferential, pattern-matching, semantics for natural language understanding. *Artificial Intelligence*, 1975, *6*, 55 - 67.
Wilks, Y. De Minimis: the archaeology of frames. In: *Proc. AISB Conference, Edinburgh Department of A.I.,* 1976a, 133 - 142.
Wilks, Y. Processing Case. *American Journal of Computing Language*, 1976b *56.*
Wilks, Y. Making Preferences more active. Mimeo Edinburgh: Department of A.I., 1977a *memo No. 32.*
Wilks, Y. Frames, scripts, stories and fantasies. *Pragmatics Microfiche*, 1977b, *3.*
Winograd, T. *Understanding Natural Language.* Edinburgh: Edinburgh U.P., 1972.

NOTES

1 One at the University of Zurich, before Swiss academics and military on 12th June, 1975 successfully translated 30,000 lines of unknown text.

2 The system already deals with certain preference violations, such as those constituting the ergative case paradigm ("The hammer broke the window" see Wilks, 1976b) and certain examples like "John got a shock", a class central to Reisbeck's thesis (see Schank (Ed.) 1975a).

3 An important aspect of the interpretation of (3) is *idiomatic*, namely that the car uses a lot of gas/petrol. This aspect of the meaning is beyond this, or I suspect any, general inference procedure.

4 In a fuller version of this paper (Wilks, 1977b) I describe the relation of this work to attempts, such as Givon (1967), to give general rules for projection: rules operating on the dictionary and independent of contexts of use.

5 Extractions it will be seen, differ from projections in that they produce new template-like entities, rather than, as here, replacing formulas inside existing templates.

6 Those familiar with the system of Wilks (1967, 1975, etc.) will remember that these are the "bare template" structures actually used to obtain the initial template match. The suggestion here is that the "Knowledge-aspect" of these highly general structures is to be found as the pseudo-texts of primitives — as the latter function right at the top of the conceptual hierarchy imposed by the thesaurus.

On the Distinction between Linguistics and Pragmatics

E. M. Uhlenbeck

University of Leiden

Leiden, Netherlands

Since about 1970 Morris' tripartite division of the study of signs – seemingly fallen into oblivion during the Chomskyan era of linguistics – is again attracting the attention of linguists, philosophers, psychologists and in general of all those who share an interest in language and linguistic theory. Especially Morris' third branch, pragmatics, defined by him as the study of the origin, the uses and the effects of signs (Morris 1946: 352) is seen rapidly moving into the center of current linguistic interests. This is not to say that there is general agreement as to what kinds of phenomena this term actually covers, nor is there at present much clarity about the validity or usefulness of Morris' trichotomy. At the International Symposium on Pragmatics held in 1970 in Jerusalem and attended by some 30 scholars from 7 countries, very little was accomplished on this point, and the papers subsequently published offer a rather confusing tableau of different positions and approaches. However, one important conclusion was reached. As Bar-Hillel, the convenor of the Symposium reported, there was consensus among the participants that "the pragmatic aspects, or at least some of them, of communication through natural languages have to be treated by linguistic theory proper, just like its syntactic and semantic aspects, and that this treatment can only be delegated to some other field with a considerable loss to linguistics itself" (Bar-Hillel 1971: v-vi).

Unfortunately this conclusion has not yet found general acceptance. To the contrary. In many quarters there remains a strong tendency to consider pragmatics -- now taken by many as referring to the study of actual language use, and as covering nearly the same ground as Saussure's *parole* and Chomsky's *performance* – not only as a discipline of its own, but also as a discipline of a completely different nature than linguistics. As Stephen Anderson in his recent handbook of phonology puts it: "The linguist is interested in studying *langue; parole,* on the other hand, is some different sort of empirical science, a branch of psychology, physiology, neurology, physics. If the system of *langue* can be isolated from the facts of *parole*, an important step will have been taken toward isolating the sort of properties that make a linguistic system what it is" (Anderson 1974: 12).

It is against this conception, which strongly reminds one of Joos' earlier restrictive dictum that the study of meaning does not belong to linguistics, but rather to sociology, that my paper is directed. In fact, it is in the first place my intention to show why the narrow view of linguistics as primarily concerned with the study of language systems in abstraction from actual language use, introduced twenty years ago by Chomsky, had to be abandoned. My paper has also a more positive purpose. I will try, as far as is possible within the limits of a short presentation, to present a theoretical conception worked out over the years, which takes a broader view of linguistics, which rejects any division of labour over two disciplines and which accepts as a legitimate concern the study of actual language use. Some features of this conception will be illustrated with a few English sentences discussed in recent publications.

The artificiality of the distinction between linguistics and pragmatics, and the inseparability of the study of language from the study of language use, can be appreciated best by taking a brief look at the development of transformational-generative grammar during the last two decades, a development which can be seen – I will try to show – as a perhaps exciting, but unsuccessful experiment in reduction.

By the end of the Fifties when the Neo-Bloomfieldian approach began to lose its impetus, because of a nearly total absence of imaginative proposals for the study of syntax and semantics, Chomsky's *Syntactic Structures* had a nearly instantaneous appeal not only because of its apparent newness and originality, but also because of its promise to put linguistics on the road to becoming a real science, an old ideal which had haunted American linguistics since Bloomfield's *Language*.

In retrospect and upon closer inspection, however, it becomes clear that there was much more continuity (Uhlenbeck 1978). Some basic views underlying *Syntactic Structures* may be seen as a remarkable blend of Saussurean and Bloomfieldian doctrine. On the other hand it is an undeniable fact that the early Chomsky made a number of decisive moves on crucial points of linguistic theory, on which Saussure and Bloomfield had remained hesitating or non-committal. And it is these moves which are highly relevant for my present purpose.

Chomsky began with accepting the Saussurean *langue: parole* dichotomy and with it took over the Saussurean view that *la langue* constituted the main descriptive goal of linguistics. But Chomsky went further by completely severing, at least in theory, all ties between *langue* and *parole* while Saussure had laid emphasis on the close relationship between the two (Saussure 1916: 38).

Secondly, Chomsky took equally firm decisions as to the content of *la langue* and especially as regards the position of syntax in it. It is sometimes forgotten that at the time when Saussure delivered his courses on general linguistics which formed the materials for the *Cours*, syntax was not a prominent field of linguistic activity. It had been defined since Ries (1894) as the study of the grouping of words into larger constructions (Saussure 1916: 194). Saussure remained uncertain about the place of syntax vis-a-vis the *langue: parole* distinction and, as we know from Godel's volume, was of the opinion that as far as syntax was concerned the distinction between *langue* and *parole* lost its validity (Godel 1957: 82). Chomsky made two decisive moves. In the first place he put syntax squarely in the center of *la langue*. Secondly he assumed that syntax meant first of all the study of sentences, a conclusion which Saussure never reached. *La langue* could now be viewed as a set of sentences, entities, of course sharply to be distinguished from (actual) utterances, a natural consequence of the separation of *langue* from *parole*. By these moves the concept of *langue* was given greater clarity, simplicity and homogeneity. However, Chomsky took further reductive measures. From Harris he had inherited the a-semantic conception of language. Semantics was viewed in *Syntactic Structures* as something perhaps largely parallel with language, but in any case outside of it. A second, extremely complicated sentential dimension, which might have blurred the *langue:parole* distinction, was silently thrown out or at least disregarded in actual practice: the intonational dimension. And in this way language and its constituents, the sentences, were reduced to rather simple objects of study. Sentences were thought to consist of nothing else than sequences of soundshapes of which it was not of great importance whether they could be identified with morphemes or words, sequences each finite in length and of course sharing the property that they belonged to the language under investigation.

By these severe measures of reduction and simplification the *langue* was made fit to be subjected to algorithmic treatment. Such a treatment would be eminently suitable as there seemed to be no reason whatsoever for assuming, as Chomsky himself had done in 1965, that there would be an unbridgeable gulf between artificial and natural languages. The quest for an adequate set of generative rules could begin, further facilitated by the assumption explicitly made in Chomsky's *Aspects of the theory of syntax* that all the information provided by traditional linguistic analysis was basically correct. Moreover, a simple but far-reaching hypothesis was made as to the relation of *la langue* to the adult native speaker, which helped to keep the attention of all who followed in Chomsky's tracks, turned away from the study of actual linguistic performance. It was assumed that every adult native speaker had "internalized a structure which is isomorphic with a grammar in the sense envisaged by linguistics" (Matthews, 1967: 123). This assumption formed the basis for the further hypothesis that the linguist *qua* native speaker has direct access to his own language by means of some sort of introspection.

Although Putnam was right in observing that nowhere in *Syntactic Structures* is it assumed that the sentences studied by the linguist are produced by a conscious organism (Putnam 1967), yet language as reductively defined by Chomsky remained connected with the human user of the language by means of a kind of double umbilical cord: the linguist still had to know whether a sentence belonged to the language or not. Somewhat later, when the grammar was meant to give an explicit account of the tacit knowledge of the native speaker, he was obliged to consult his intuitions in his capacity of native speaker.

It is precisely at these two points that serious trouble arose. Everybody who has attended international linguistic meetings has witnessed the inconclusive and for outsiders boring disputes about the acceptability of certain sentences, seemingly resolved by appeals to differences in idiolect. Or, if he was conversant with the linguistic literature, he would have been amused, or irritated as the case may be, by the arbitrariness with which the sentence-starring game is being played. Even more serious was the realization that the native speakers' intuitions did not prove to be similar and consistent. The expectation that they would be so – an expectation not founded on any research – turned out to be merely a pious hope. Still worse: experiments showed that the admission of data and judgements of grammaticality were influenced by or even dependent on the theory adopted or the particular hypothesis put forward (Levelt 1973).

These were perennial problems for which no solution could be found, but for our purpose it is more relevant to point out that there were other developments which made it necessary to enrich the so drastically impoverished concept of *langue* of *Syntactic Structures.* In 1963 Katz-Fodor showed their transformational colleagues that the asemantic stance could no longer be taken. This conclusion necessitated a transition from the linear to the familiar triangular descriptive models. For a short while it seemed as if the strategy of simply adding a new component to an otherwise not fundamentally revised descriptive apparatus was successful. However, it soon appeared that this new semantic component, although still in its infancy, was a troublesome newcomer, as it began to affect the rest of the descriptive edifice and to threaten the dominant place of syntax in the descriptive model. Generative semantics was born and began to develop unorthodox ideas about the relation between the semantic and the syntactic components and one might say that from about 1970 onwards the Chomsky concept of deep structure, once hailed as one of the greatest recent discoveries of linguistics, came increasingly under attack.

The inclusion of semantics in *la langue* led to the inclusion of further lingual territory. At the end of the Sixties it was no longer a secret, even among transformationalists, that to pass judgement on the grammaticality of sentences required information about the situation and context in which they are used (G. Lakoff 1969) and information about the social relationship between the speechpartners (R. Lakoff 1972). This awareness was a first, but important, step towards recognizing that abstraction from pragmatic factors would prove difficult, if not impossible. Already on earlier occasions linguistic phenomena were encountered, such as pronouns of various kinds and imperative sentences, which seemed to require that one takes into account the fundamental features of the situation of actual language use: the presence of a speaker and a hearer, the utterance itself within the situation in which it was spoken and the things referred to. However, the transformational-generative theory, tied to its concept of competence, could not accept this and had to follow another course, attempting to get rid of these factors by the setting up of more or less abstract and complicated deep structures, subsequently deleted and transformed in various ways. For the one-word sentence *Go! I order you to go* had to serve as deep structure, and pronouns were viewed – following an old, but antiquated traditional view – as literally pro-nouns, derived elements which took the place of nouns: *John washed himself* had to be derived from a deep *John washed John.* Also those who became interested in the study of speech acts, and consequently began to pay attention to the work of ordinary language philosophers such as Austin, kept pursuing the same line. Ross for instance presented arguments – proven by Matthews to be invalid – that all declarative sentences should be derived from a structure with a subsequently deleted clause with a verb of saying. For a simple sentence such as *Prices slumped,* a deep structure such as *I tell you that prices slumped* was to be posited (Ross 1970; Matthews 1972), and more recent studies (for instance by Sadock 1974 and by Gordon and Lakoff 1975) still follow essentially the same strategy of trying to set up intra-sentential structures to account for extra-sentential factors, a strategy which led to increasingly abstract and complicated deep structures, quite rightly criticized by Siertsema (1972).

The general line of development is clear. We see a gradual crumbling of the theoretical basis of transformational generative grammar accompanied by an equally gradual, inevitable expansion of the object of study. First Chomsky linguistics tried to concern itself only with strings of sound shapes, then it was recognized that the semantic aspect could not be omitted from consideration. Once let in, the semantic phenomena forced the linguists to turn to the study of actual language use. The main reason for this is that any serious study of linguistic meaning brings us into contact with the problem of inference and interpretation. One can also put things in a different perspective. There was at first – in the asemantic period – the hypothesis that an algorithmic approach would be feasible, then after 1963 language was considered to be a purely psychological phenomenon to be studied and described by the linguist sitting in his study, consulting if necessary his own intuition and confident that what he intuited was what all native speakers intuited. As Labov said: "The culmination of this puristic program is the generative view of linguistics as the study of an ideal homogeneous structure, revealed in the intuitions of the most highly sophisticated members of the community who create through introspection both the theory and the data" (Labov 1974: 825). Now it is realized that this view is one-sided and unrealistic. Now one begins to understand that in language psychological and social factors combine in a unique way. Much ingenuity has been spent on attempts to devise deep structures which could keep out the monster of performance. But all this effort has been of little avail. It is clear that an inquiry into the general conditions of language use is definitely on the agenda, and recent work like that of Grice (1975) deserves the attention of all linguists who see the need to develop a new, more realistic linguistic theory. It does therefore not come as a surprise that linguists in different parts of the world begin to converge in the opinion that it is their first task "to achieve a scientific understanding of how people communicate in speech" (Schank and Wilks 1974: 318 - 323; Yngve 1975: 544). The founders of the new journal *Pragmatics,* Haberland and Mey, take a similar attitude when they declare that "the pragmatic aspect can neither be separated from linguistics proper, or even postponed, or added on as a new component" (Haberland and Mey 1977: 9). The study of language finds its natural starting point not in *la langue* as de Saussure thought, but in cases of language use. If this is correct, it makes sense then – as I wrote ten years ago – to study "the actual act of speech and guided by a carefully selected set of general principles to examine what actually happens when speakers speak and hearers apparently manage to grasp what the speakers want to convey to them" (Uhlenbeck 1967: 282). I will now proceed with a sketch of my own theoretical conception based on this point of view.

There are three central notions underlying our approach to the study of the lingual phenomena:

1. The Saussurean view that linguistics is a science concerned with phenomena which owe their existence to the simultaneous presence of a perceptible and a cognitive aspect, that is: with bipartite entities of sound and meaning, or if you like, with more or less complex sign structures.

2. The Saussurean terms *langue* and *parole* are not to be taken as referring to

two different and separable domains, but rather as two sides of one and the same object: the study of speech implies the study of language and vice versa. For grammatical analysis this means that the linguist takes his point of departure in the study of instances of speech – actual or elicited – in order to discover and to describe its regular recurrent features.

3. In the study of *le langage,* the useful broader term which the French have for *langue* and *parole* together, one has always to do with *words* and sentences, correlative units irreducible to each other and undefinable in terms of each other.

In our linguistic conception it is required that all further distinctions to be made should be brought into a precisely determined relation with these two polar and universal entities. The sentence is in all languages characterized by the presence of two differently structured components, each serving different functions: the intonational or melodic component and a so-called phatic component, minimally containing one word but in most cases a shorter or longer sequence of words or word-like elements. This dual structure of the sentence is already firmly established and has found strong support in recent research on the various linguistic functions of the left and right cerebral hemisphere (Balonov and Deglin 1976).

Words are linguistic signs which by grammatical as well as semantic criteria can be distinguished on the one hand from morphemes, on the other from word-groups. Words have the property of valence, that is they can combine into larger constructions according to language-specific rules. Grouping itself is a universal phenomenon which finds its ultimate raison d'être in the nature of word meaning. This means that in our view syntax, or at least a large area of it, is a servant of semantics, and not vice versa.

As to speech three principles hold: First of all there is the principle which, for lack of a better term, I will call the "makes-sense" principle. It says that the hearer always takes the view that what the speaker is saying to him somehow makes sense. It is this certitude which makes him try to infer – on the basis of the lingual and extra-lingual evidence available to him – what the speaker is actually conveying to him. This formulation implies that on occasion the hearer may be unable to do so or that he may make the wrong inferences. It is difficult to exaggerate the importance of this very general attitude. Awareness of its always being operative may keep us from entering into linguistically irrelevant discussions on the truth-value of sentences, or from participating in sterile debates about establishing a distinction between deviant and normal sentences.

A second principle functioning in speech is the principle that the attention of the participants in the speech-event is largely directed and focussed on the things spoken about and not on speech itself. Accordingly, what is normally retained in memory is the content of what is said, only very rarely the exact wording. This attitude reveals the essentially instrumental character of non-literary language use, and offers a partial explanation of the striking difference between the data of actual language use and data which are the result of reflection on the part of the native speaker. What the native speaker says is far from identical with what he says that he does say.

In the third place all speech is used by human beings and is spatially and temporally determined. Speech always takes place in a certain situation. I will not try to analyze this complicated notion of situation here, but only emphasize the fact that the lingual phenomena and especially their semantic aspect count on the fact that they take place in a situation, and that the human beings who participate in speech have other than linguistic knowledge i.e. knowledge of the environment in which they live, of the situation in which speech is used, and of each other.

The process of interpretation, or if you prefer, of inference, always consists in combining the information inherent in what is spoken with extra-lingual information from various sources. It is one of the most serious problems of linguistic semantics to find out the mechanism behind this "combining". In other words, language is not at all a self-contained system; it is built in such a way that interaction of knowledge *outside* language with information *from* language is possible.

After these short introductory remarks which serve no other function than to give a general idea of the theoretical climate in which we view language and speech, it is time to leave general principles aside and to turn to some concrete lingual material in order to clarify some further aspects of my approach.

The first sentence which I have selected for discussion is taken from a recent article by the social-psychologist Rommetveit whose linguistic views are closely parallel to my own.

1. My spinster aunt is an infant. (Rommetveit, 1977).

Sentences such as this one are often considered to be anomalous. With Rommetveit I am of the opinion that there are no valid linguistic arguments for such a qualification. No linguistic rule has been violated and the suggestion of anomaly is caused by a fundamental error on the part of the linguistic observer, namely that he has looked at sentences in isolation. Rommetveit's analysis convincingly shows how the hearer – acting according to the makes-sense-principle – will try to interpret the sentence, relying on the conversational context and the situation in which the sentence has been spoken. In all probability the sentence has not to be taken in the sense that the aunt of the speaker literally is a child not yet capable of speech, but only that she is immature or is acting childishly in financial, political or social matters or in whatever aspect the aunt is being discussed at the moment. Although the exact interpretational mechanisms involved are not yet describable in detail, one may say that the extra-lingual information has a sort of directional or selective function. The word *infant,* for instance, provides the hearer with no more than a general cognitive orientation, open to further elaboration in different directions. It is the particular conversational situation which indicates what is relevant and what is the specific direction in which this cognitive orientation has to be elaborated. There is one factor not mentioned by Rommetveit which makes the process of inference even more complicated, namely the intonational component. It is largely from this multifunctional component that the hearer derives information about the emotional attitude of the speaker concerning the hearer, but also concerning the matter spoken about. Is the speaker well disposed towards his aunt or is he hostile, indignant? Is the sentence a sober, objective appraisal or simply an emotional outburst? Is he singling out his spinster aunt as the one who is acting childishly, in contrast to other possible candidates? The final interpretation of the sentence by the hearer turns out to be the outcome of weighing and integrating a variety of cognitive data: factual and emotional information inherent in the sentence itself, together with extralingual information about the speaker, about the situation including the topic under discussion and about the culture in which speaker and hearer are living. Analysis of all these factors is needed for understanding how the semantic aspect of language functions. Sentence 2 is taken from McCawley (1976).

2. Kissinger conjectures poached.

He gives it as an example of a sentence which makes no sense in isolation, but is perfectly normal when used as the answer to questions such as:

2.a Does anyone know how President Ford likes his eggs?

McCawley then concludes from his example "that the question whether (2) is grammatical has no substance and that the closest one can come to answering that non-question is to reply that (2) is a possible way to say that Kissinger conjectures that Ford likes his eggs poached when it is used in a context that allows for the ellipsis of *President Ford likes his eggs*". Although I am sympathetic towards the general tenor of McCawley's recent paper, I believe that McCawley's comment is objectionable on two counts. First of all I would like to remark that since McCawley does not provide us with any information about the intonational component of (2), one cannot even identify the sentence so long as we do not know that sentence (2a) has preceded (2). If spoken with the intonation pattern of listing unconnected words:

2.b Kissinger, conjectures, poached.

the sentence could easily have been an answer to a request to enumerate words in a crossword puzzle. It also may be that there is the intonation pattern with a short pause after *conjectures* which sets off the group *Kissinger conjectures* against *poached.* It is of course this pattern that McCawley is assuming when he considers the sentence an answer to (2a), although the sentence could be spoken without such an intonation pattern if (2a) indeed had preceded. The point I want to make is simply this: as soon as we know the intonation pattern (and as we have seen also the situation) there is no problem either about sentence identification or about the question of grammaticality as well. If we have found a use for a sentence, we are certain of its grammaticality.

There is a second objection. McCawley suggests that a sentence such as (2a) must have preceded in order to make (2) perfectly normal. I believe that this is too restrictive a formulation. It might very well be that no such sentence as (2a) has been spoken at all, but that the situation itself could have contained sufficient elements to make (2) a quite normal first sentence. It is enough to imagine a situation in which somebody, after examining a dead hare found in a forest near Washington, informs his companion about Kissinger's guess about what had happened to the poor animal. And with some ingenuity an egg-situation could be constructed in which *Kissinger conjectures poached* could have been said, with *poached* in the sense of *cooked in a liquid.*

The sentences which come up for comment next are taken from an article by Kirsner and Thompson which I value highly as one of the best discussions on semantic problems recently written (Kirsner and Thompson, 1976):

3. a The farmer fed the sheep.
   b The sheep fed the farmer.
   c The recipe fed eight.

The authors follow the approach known as form-content-analysis as developed at Columbia University by Diver and Garcia, an approach which in many respects is similar to my own. Kirsner and Thompson use these three sentences to explain the distinction between meaning and message. They do this in the following terms:

All the verb *feed* communicates in each case, i.e. its meaning, is simply 'supply food for'. The particular way in which we understand food to be provided in each sentence referred to is not signaled overtly by three different homophonous verbs, but is rather an inference from (a) our knowledge of the different cultural (biological) properties of the referents of the noun phrases and (b) the differences in role (on the event of providing food) assigned to each. Accordingly, given that, in our culture, farmers raise sheep to use and sell their wool and meat, the difference in interpretation in (3a, b) is due to the differences in the conclusions that are likely to be reached when it is claimed, in the one instance, that the farmer is the provider and the sheep the recipient and in the other that the sheep is the provider and the farmer the recipient. We would agree that how the food is provided is not specified by the language, but is rather inferred or guessed at, intelligently, from cultural knowledge. The way food is provided in (3c) is different from (3a) and (3b). This difference in interpretation depends not on the verb *feed* but rather on our knowledge of what a recipe is. The point, then, is that in all three sentences, the message communicated with the verb *feed* is richer, more specific than the imprecise meaning 'provide food for' which this verb signals. Language users infer how food is provided from their knowledge of the properties of the participants in the event of feeding and the relative responsibilities in that event assigned to each by virtue of their occurrence as "subject" or "object". In the following figure:

DETAILED MESSAGE 1
"to obtain food for from elsewhere"

SIGNAL – IMPRECISE MEANING – "inferential gap" — DETAILED MESSAGE 2
"to constitute food for in itself",

Feed – 'provide food for' — DETAILED MESSAGE 3
"to guide in the preparation of food for"

they summarize the relationship between the *meaning* of feed and the *message* it is used to communicate in the three sentences.

What is important in their perspicacious discussion of the three *fed* sentences, is (1) that Kirsner and Thompson clearly realize the crucial role played by inference, (2) that they fully understand that there is a difference between the inherent meaning of linguistic signs and the result of the process of inference, and (3) that they are aware that one and the same word *fed* with the same meaning is used in all three sentences.

These are important virtues of their analysis, but there are also serious gaps. By pointing them out I hope to clarify my own position especially about semantics and about the relations between semantics and syntax.

I have five critical comments to make:

1. The account given by Kirsner and Thompson suffers from the fact that the inferential process is brought into a direct relationship with word meaning. However, inference is an activity performed by the hearer on the semantic content of the *sentence*. Therefore discussion of inference would always call for a description of the inherent overall semantic content of the sentence. It is not enough to discuss *fed*, one has to take into account (1) the semantic contributions made by the other words in the sentence, that is also *the farmer, the sheep, the recipe,* and *eight,* and (2) the information supplied by the intonational component of the sentences.

2. The semantic terminology employed by Kirsner and Thompson is not rich enough even to discuss the semantics of these relatively simple sentences. The semantic content of a sentence has to be distinguished from the semantic content of word groups, and words too are semantically not on a par. For instance, deictic words, appellatives and proper names are semantically quite different elements. Most important of all is to realize the difference between the inherent semantic content of the sentence and the result of the process of inference in which lingual information is interpreted against the extra-lingual information available to the hearer.

3. The definition of meaning as "what a linguistic signal explicitly asserts" is perhaps suitable for the semantic content of sentences, but not for word meaning. The word *fed* does not assert anything.

4. Kirsner and Thompson apparently do not give enough attention to the role of syntax and especially to the interaction of the meanings of words brought together in a certain construction. The basic point is that this interaction of word meanings does not lead to a complete semantic determination. There is underspecification. This is another way of saying that the semantic organization of language reckons with the presence of supplementary information coming from extra-lingual sources. It is not necessary that in the sentences (3a) and (3b) there always will be a difference "in the particular way in which we understand food to be provided in each scene" (Kirsner-Thompson 202). This depends on the situation in which the sentences are used. We can easily imagine a situation in which farmer and sheep feed each other in exactly the same way. This proves again that in semantic analysis one simply has to take the possible semantic contribution of situation and context into account.

5. Finally there is a small terminological point. Kirsner and Thompson speak

about pragmatic inference in semantics. I believe that the word pragmatic is superfluous. Inference is a concept which has a central role to play in understanding the semantics of natural language. It does not belong to any other domain than semantic theory.

The principled discussion by Schank and Wilks of the requirements of a linguistic theory contains some material which again permits me to explain some other theoretical points in our conception.

Their *Grand Canyon*-sentence – perfectly grammatical and acceptable of course:

4. I saw the Grand Canyon flying to New York.

is considered by the authors to be an example of an ambiguous sentence with two meanings (Schank and Wilks 1974: 319). This view is acceptable only if one is willing to assume that a sentence is basically a (linear) string of sound shapes. However, from my point of view – explained in the previous section of this paper – the conclusion can only be that we are faced with two homophonous sentences, each with its own syntactic structure – or as I would say – with its own relational structure, and of course each with its own semantic content. The difference in syntactic structure is easy to perceive and has to do with the group *flying to New York*.

In the one sentence this group is connected with *The Grand Canyon* in a more complex word group, in the other, *flying to New York* is directly connected with *I*. In the latter case *flying to New York* may also be put in initial position:

4.a Flying to New York I saw the Grand Canyon.

This movement results in a perfectly acceptable sentence. However, if *flying to New York* is to belong to *the Grand Canyon,* its position is fixed, and movement to initial position is out of the question. It is clear then that in our conception an ambiguous sentence can only be a semantically ambiguous sentence; the concept of syntactic ambiguity as found for instance in transformational-generative accounts would be translated in our theory as the concept of syntactic homophony. It is perhaps not superfluous to add that our analysis does not force us to deny that in actual speech it may happen that homophonous sentences are incorrectly identified by the hearer, as may also happen to different, but homophonous words.

A beautiful example of such a semantically ambiguous sentence is also provided by Schank and Wilks:

5. Have you started the chicken yet?

It is true – as the authors state – that the action referred to in this sentence has in all probability to do with cooking, or as I would prefer to say, that the sentence will have been used in a "cooking" situation. However, as Schank and Wilks again quite rightly observe, it is not at all necessary to assume this. Here again we are faced with the fundamental fact that language is so organized that the presence of supplementary information is taken for granted. It is this principle which also makes it understandable that the inferential process may go wrong, as it may happen that the hearer for some reason or other is not able to make the inferential jump which the speaker expects him to make.

Finally some attention has to be given to the door-locking sentences discussed by Schank and Wilks:

6.a John prevented Mary from leaving the room by locking the door.
6.b Mary couldn't leave the room because John locked the door.

Of these two sentences the authors say that they basically mean the same thing in spite of their being largely composed of different words. Schank and Wilks require of a good linguistic theory, that it explains how the concept of prevention can be conveyed even in the absence of the word *prevent,* or else how the word *prevent* embodied a combination of more basic concepts. I have strong doubts about this requirement and I do not believe that it is quite correct to say that the sentences (6a) and (6b) basically mean the same thing.

The danger of this last statement lies in the word *basically*. It cannot be denied that the meanings of the two sentences are fairly close, but they are by no means identical, and this is just because the sentences contain different meaning-bearing elements, combined into different syntactic structures. One could easily say for instance: *Mary couldn't leave the room because John locked the door, but this does not mean that John prevented Mary from leaving the room.* I firmly believe that it is likely that we are faced here with a general principle to be embodied in a good linguistic theory: if the word-composition and/or the syntactic structure of two sentences differ, their inherent meaning is never identical.

It is now time to conclude. I believe that it is possible to present four interrelated conclusions:

(1) The recent history of transformational generative grammar contains an important lesson. It shows that the object of linguistics cannot be fruitfully restricted in the way attempted by this theory and inevitably forces us to pay attention to actual language use.

(2) The pragmatics/linguistics distinction is artificial and superfluous. The study of the semantic aspect of language, if pursued along the lines indicated in the preceding sections, will necessarily include the study of all factors operative in and relevant to the use of language.

(3) In the analysis of the speech event it is necessary to investigate the general conditions of language use and the extra-lingual factors operative in it.

(4) Analysis of these conditions should not follow the approach of Ross, Sadock and others, but should be more along the lines of the recent work of Grice on the strategies followed by speaker and hearer in the act of verbal communication.

REFERENCES

Anderson, S. *The Organization of Phonology.* New York: Academic Press, 1974.

Balonov, L. J. and Deglin, V. L. *Hearing and Speech of Dominant and Non-Dominant Hemispheres*, (In Russian). Leningrad: Publishing house Nauka, 1976.

Bar-Hillel, Y. (ed.), *Pragmatics of Natural Languages.* Dordrecht: D. Reidel, 1971.

Chomsky, N. *Syntactic Structures.* The Hague: Mouton, 1957.

Chomsky, N. Formal Properties of Grammars. In: R. Duncan Luce, R. R. Bush, E. Galanter (eds.), *Handbook of Mathematical Psychology 2.12.* New York: J. Wiley, 1963, 324 - 418.

Chomsky, N. *Aspects of the Theory of Syntax.* Cambridge Mass.: M.I.T. Press, 1965.

Godel, R. *Les sources manuscrites du Cours de linguistique générale de F. de Saussure.* Genève-Paris: Droz-Minard, 1957.

Gordon, D. and Lakoff, G. Conversational Postulates. In: P. Cole and J. L. Morgan (eds.), *Speech Acts, Syntax and Semantics*, 1975, *3*, 83 - 106.

Grice, H. P. Utterer's Meaning, Sentence Meaning and Word-Meaning. *Foundations of Language*, 1968, *4*, 225 - 242.

Grice, H. P. Logic and Conversation. In: P. Cole and J. L. Morgan (eds.), *Speech Acts, Syntax and Semantics*, 1975, *3*, 41 - 58.

Haberland, H. and Mey, J. L. Editorial: Linguistics and Pragmatics. *Journal of Pragmatics*, 1977, *1*, 1 - 12.

Kirsner, R. S. and Thompson, S. A. The Role of Pragmatic Inference in Semantics: A Study of Sensory Verb Complements in English. *Glossa*, 1976, *10*, 200 - 240.

Labov, W. The Study of Language in its Social Context. *Studium Generale*, 1970, *23*, 30 - 87.

Labov, W. On the Use of the Present to Explain the Past. *Proceedings of the 11th International Congress of Linguistics vol. 2*, 1974, 825 - 851.

Lakoff, G. Presuppositions and Relative Grammaticality. In: W. Todd (ed.), *Studies in Philosophical Linguistics*, 1969, *1*, 103 - 116.

Lakoff, R. Language in context. *Language*, 1972, *48*, 907 - 927.

Levelt, W. J. M. *Formele grammatica's in linguistiek en taalpsychologie*, 3 vols. Deventeer: Van Loghum Slaterus, 1973.

Matthews, P. H. Review of N. Chomsky, Aspects of Theory of Syntax 1965. In: *Journal of Linguistics*, 1967, *3*, 119 - 152.

Matthews, P. H. Review of R. A. Jacobs and P. S. Rosenbaum (eds.), Readings in English Transformational Grammar. *Journal of Linguistics*, 1972, *8*, 125 - 136.

McCawley, J. D. Some Ideas not to Live by. *Die neueren Sprachen*, 1976, *75*, 152 - 163.

Morris, Ch. *Signs, Language and Behavior.* New York: Prentice Hall Inc., 1946.

Putnam, H. The Innateness Hypothesis and Explanatory Models in Linguistics. *Synthese*, 1967, *17*, 12 - 22.

Reichling, A. *Het Woord, Een studie van taal en taalgebruik.* Den Bosch: Berkhout, 1935.

Reichling, A. *Over essentiële en toevallige grammatica-regels.* Groningen-Batavia: J. B. Wolters, 1939.

Ries, J. *Was ist Syntax.* Prag: Taussig und Taussig, 1894.

Rommetveit, R. *On Message Structure, A Framework for the Study of Language and Communication*. New York: John Wiley, 1974.
Rommetveit, R. On the Architecture of Intersubjectivity. In: L. Strickland et al. (eds.), *Social Psychology in Transition*. New York: Plenum Press, 1977.
Ross, J. R. On Declarative Sentences. In: R. A. Jacobs and P. S. Rosenbaum (eds.), *Reading in English Transformational Grammar*. Waltham Mass.: Ginn and Co., 1970.
Sadock, J. *Toward a Linguistic Theory of Speech Acts*. New York: Academic Press, 1974.
Saussure, F. de. *Cours de linguistique générale*. Lausanne-Paris: Payot, 1916.
Schank, R. C. and Wilks, Y. The Goals of Linguistic Theory Revisited. *Lingua*, 1974, *34*, 301 - 326.
Siertsema, B. De linguistische status van J. L. Austin's "performatives" en hun verwanten. *Forum der Letteren*, 1972, *13*, 11 - 31.
Uhlenbeck, E. M. Some Further Remarks on Transformational Grammar. *Lingua* 1976, *17*, 263 - 316.
Uhlenbeck, E. M. *Critical Comments on Transformational Generative Grammar 1962 - 1972*. The Hague: Smits, 1973.
Uhlenbeck, E. M. *Taalwetenschap, een eerste inleiding*. The Hague: Smits, 1978.
Uhlenbeck, E. M. Linguistics in America 1924 - 1974, A Detached View. To appear, *Papers Third Golden Anniversary Symposium of the Linguistic Society of America*, 1978.
Verhaar, J. W. M. Philosophy and Linguistic Theory. *Language Sciences,* 1974, *14*, 1 - 11.
Wunderlich, D. Die Rolle des Pragmatik in der Linguistik. *Der Deutschunterricht*, 1970, *22*, 5 - 41.
Yngve, V. H. Toward a Human Linguistics. In: R. E. Grossman, L. James San, T. J. Vance (eds.), *Papers from the Parasession on Functionalism*. Chicago Linguistic Society, 1975, 540 - 555.

Language-Meaning and Message-Meaning : Towards a Sociolinguistic Approach to Translation

Maurice Pergnier

University of Paris Val de Marne

Paris

The history of the relationship between linguistics and translation is a long and rich one. Many books have been written on the subject by linguists, and the study of translation has enriched theories of language in many ways. Roman Jakobson's article "On linguistic aspects of translation" (1966) for instance, is very well-known among translators as well as linguists.

Translation occupies a central position in linguistics since it entails all the fundamental issues the science of language has to tackle, from the nature of linguistic meaning to the process of communication by language, through the pivotal problem which Jakobson calls "equivalence in difference", i.e. the possibility of reformulating the *same* sense units into *different* linguistic units. All these questions that occupy a central position in the practice and theory of translation are also paramount for general linguistic theory.

CONFERENCE INTERPRETATION AND GENERAL TRANSLATION THEORY

Until very recently however the attention of linguists working on translation has been focussed almost exclusively on written translation, leaving aside the specific problems raised by oral practice. Conference interpretation has seldom served as a basis of observation and study, although it would seem that simultaneous and consecutive interpretation should provide a very fertile field of observation from which to formulate and investigate theoretical issues in language and translation as a whole.

The emphasis laid on the study of written translation has had consequences for the way problems have been formulated. In the first place, as a consequence of the prevalence of the written word, translation has tended to be considered by many linguists as a case of contrastive linguistics; that is, they have tended to give preference to an approach to translation based on the comparison of linguistic structures to assess their potential use as translation equivalents.

However rich for the comparative study of languages, an approach to translation along these lines obscures the central issue which should be borne in mind whenever theoretical explanations of translation are attempted, namely: it is messages, not languages, that are translated. Taking oral translation in its most elaborate form – consecutive and simultaneous interpretation – as a basis for observation helps to formulate or reformulate the main axes along which theoretical issues of translation are to be organised. In particular, as a consequence of the very specific conditions in which interpreters operate, interpretation makes it necessary to break with the too familiar association: Source Language ⟶ Target Language that serves as a common explanatory model to posit the way in which translation is supposed to operate. Observation of consecutive (and to a lesser degree simultaneous) interpretation shows that this pattern does not apply to it, since at no moment in its process can the two languages be considered as being in contact (Seleskovitch, 1968). Like many apparently obvious assumptions this simple and well-known pattern blurs and conceals the real operation that takes place. Everybody here knows that the interpreter forgets the words he has heard in one language immediately after he has heard them and that he cannot be said to translate these words as such into the "target language". Yet he translates, that is he says in a different language what he has heard in another language. He transfers not the words but the meaning of the message, thus demonstrating that to translate a message and to find equivalences between words of two languages are not one and the same thing.

The postulate according to which to translate the language is to translate the message is but an assumption that must be carefully reconsidered, and so is the opposite assumption that untranslatability in words leads to untranslatability in messages. There is no tangible evidence of such a possibility to reduce message-meanings to word-meanings. The fact that interpretation "translates" messages without establishing comparative equivalences between words of two languages as such provides arguments to separate the translation process proper from the comparative operation between language units and helps to give a special status to the branch of linguistics concerned more specially with translation.

Indeed, it can and will be objected that conference interpretation is carried out on languages and on informational data of comparable, and often identical, cultural levels. It cannot, as such, be considered as a model for all translation, since it ignores many aspects that are of primary importance in other types of translation, such as the translatability of cultural, religious or technical data between cultures separated by time or space (for instance translating a scientific text on lasers into an African language, or translating the Odyssey into modern French or English). These types of translation raise specific problems without however modifying the central issue. Neither has interpretation to take into account the special issues involved in the poetic use of language, in which the importance of word form and word rhythm is prevalent. Within these limits, however, interpretation serves as a very good means of differentiating translation mechanisms proper from contrastive aspects of language pairs.

The measure of adequacy in translation is the degree of equivalence between the meaning of the original message and the meaning of the translated (or interpreted) one, whereas the measure of adequacy in contrastive linguistics is the degree of equivalence between pairs of words or phrases. Saussurean linguistics distinguishes as between *signifié* (meaning pertaining to the words of the language) and *sens* (meaning pertaining to the words in a given message). In the rest of this paper we shall call them language-meaning and message-meaning respectively, in order to avoid ambiguity.

LANGUAGE MEANING

Language-meaning – that is the meaning conveyed by each structural unit or group of structural units – is the result of a conventional association between phonological and semantic items and implies that the convention be identical between members of the same linguistic community. Comprehension of linguistic signals, from this point of view, means recognition of semantic units memorized prior to the communication act. If one compares semantic units taken from two different languages one finds that, except for a very restricted number of units in each language, every item of a given language corresponds not to a single concept but to a series of concepts (a sum of different meanings), and that the sum of meanings attached to one of these units does not correspond to the sum of meanings attached to the unit of the other language (Pergnier, 1977).

For instance, the French word *glace* will correspond to the English words ice, glass, mirror, window, etc . . without, in fact corresponding to any of them; and each one of the English terms will in its turn manifest a number of meanings not included in the meaning of the French word *glace.* This non-coincidence of items taken from different languages has very few exceptions, and can be observed for any pair of languages whatever their origin, and affects all types of units (lexical or grammatical) of all languages compared. One could summarize these considerations in the following way: in itself a linguistic unit of a given language is ambiguous, and its ambiguity is not equivalent to the ambiguity of a linguistic unit in another language. Let us emphasize that this range of virtual meanings does not depend on any situational context, but only on a convention within the linguistic community based on speech habits.

MESSAGE MEANING

Let us now examine the characteristics of message-meaning in contrast to the characteristics of language-meaning briefly sketched above. Message-meaning, i.e. the meaning of any utterance or fragment of an utterance as it is intended by the speaker or writer is normally unambiguous, not-agreed upon (original), and predominantly dependent on situational context.

Every individual uses speech in order to communicate new original information that has not been encoded and memorized previously (otherwise human speech would only be a reiteration of what has already been said many times before). The words used, be they adequate or inadequate to express the experience or thought conveyed, are chosen not for their own sake, but in relation to the goal that is to be attained, and it is this choice that constitutes their meaning on any given occasion. The French person who asks for "une glace" in a restaurant will get his ice-cream without being, ever so transiently, conscious of the fact that, at the level of language-meaning, he has simultaneously asked for (and the waiter might in theory have understood that he has asked for) a looking-glass, a piece of ice, a window-pane, and many other things apart from an ice-cream. Neither does the one who says, in given circumstances, "j'attends mon frère", realise that, in his language, his utterance can be interpreted as meaning many different things such as: I am waiting for my brother (every day, all my life . .); I am expecting my brother (any minute); I can't decide without my brother; I have been waiting for my brother (for several hours, days, years . . .); I look forward to seeing my brother; and so on. Whatever the French phrase may mean, the Frenchman who uses it in a given situation intends to convey one particular and unambiguous meaning. The problem for any individual who "receives" a message is not knowing what the *words* mean, but knowing what the *speaker* means. Such is the translator's and interpreter's problem.

Post-Saussurean linguistics have demonstrated that languages are autonomous structures at every level, and that neither lexical nor grammatical units of a language can be directly converted into another language and why that is so. This does not mean that translation is impossible or only partly and imperfectly possible. It only means that the equivalences that translation creates are established on the level of message-meaning, not on the level of language-meaning, and that if linguistics wants to promote explanatory models of translation, it must explore in the first place the relationship between the message and each of the two languages involved rather than the degree of equivalence between structures of the two languages.

Words as such cannot be translated, i.e. have no exact and constant equivalents in another language (one might add that even within the same language there are no real synonyms). Translation equivalence is not primarily a problem of "languages in contact" but a problem of communication. This is why, in our opinion, a linguistic approach to translation (in the restricted sense) is not sufficient to explain and formalise the processes involved in translation and why it must be complemented by other approaches. The necessity of a psycholinguistic approach is obvious enough, but a sociolinguistic approach is of equal importance.

SOCIOLINGUISTICS AND TRANSLATION THEORY

While linguistics in the restricted sense studies natural languages as autonomous, self-regulated structures in relation to thought and reality, the aim of sociolinguistics is the study of language as a medium of communication between individuals and communities.

In this respect, the first reality to be taken into consideration is the fact that language is not only a means of communication in the usual sense of the word, but also the reverse. Non-communication, language opacity and resistance to communication, must be taken into consideration if one wants to account for human communication. Throughout the world there is actually more non-communication than communication between human beings, because of language. The multitude of languages that exists throughout the planet create a situation of non-communication between the majority of its inhabitants, and each of these languages (even English) raises a barrier between a much greater number of individuals than the number of those who communicate through its medium. Babel is the primary reality of language.

Even if one leaves aside the multiplicity of languages, it is a commonplace to say that, within what is considered to be the same language, non-communication due to language prevails. There are two reasons for this: on the one hand because of the internal variety of dialects, slangs, specialised jargons, etc. that constitute a language, and on the other hand because – as previously mentioned – the function of language is to express new, personal, individual, situational, meanings with a limited (however large) number of elements. The same phrase or word may express an infinite variety of different individual meanings, and the same individual meaning may be expressed by a variety of words or phrases according to the idiolect of the speaker.

Misunderstanding, partial understanding, are inherent in language. Whereas communication theory may consider non-communication as "noise" that must be eliminated from the circuit, in language theory non-communication is a factor inherent in the circuit itself, due to the fact that speech is a creative process which generates its own codes as well as the messages transmitted. This is why communication theory provides very poor models of human language. It may not be a paradox to say that we will probably learn more about communication through language by studying non-communication than by studying communication itself.

The operation usually known as communication (i.e. the fact that a message received by a human "decoder" is identical in meaning – and not only in "code" – to the message emmitted by the "encoder") is only the successful result of a series of unconscious dynamic processes aimed at getting through different layers of opacity. Translation is an extreme case of this general situation, owing to the fact that the message is not only received by the receiver, but also re-emitted in an entirely different "code".

A type of translation based only on the attempt to translate the code (i.e. the meanings of the language) is not only impossible on account of the fact that the range of meanings and "value" of a word in one language do not correspond to the range of meanings of a word in a different language, but also because the range of meanings of a word (or phrase, or structural unit of any sort) varies from one individual to another, and from one field of interest to another. The translation of language-meanings does result not in translation of the message, but in interferences between languages. Interfering systems never produce a translation in the true sense of the word, they only give birth to intermediate forms that are neither the original nor the "target" language. One might say, without being paradoxical, that the more one translates the message, the less one translates one language into another. On the other hand, the more one attempts to translate (convert) lexical and grammatical structures of one language into those of another language, the less one translates the message.

Translation is an interplay between a message and two linguistic systems (in this respect it is an subject for psycholinguistic study). The translator, however, is not only a mediator between the languages as such; he is also, and perhaps in the first place, a mediator between two individuals or communities. In this respect, translation is a sociolinguistic problem, and must be studied along all the parameters that determine sociolinguistic entities, whether it be from the point of view of languages or from the point of view of the processes at play in the adaptation of a message to a receiver with a different linguistic and cultural background (Pergnier, 1977).

REFERENCES

Jakobson, R., On linguistic aspects of translation. In: *On Translation*, R.Brower (Ed.)., New York: O.U.P., 1966, 232 - 239.

Pergnier, M., "L'envers des mots". *Etudes de Linguistique Appliquée*, 24. Paris: Didier, 1977, 92 - 126.

Pergnier, M., *Les Fondements Sociolinguistiques de la Traduction* Paris: Honore Champion, p.491 (forthcoming).

Seleskovitch, D., *L'interprete dans les conférences internationales, Problèmes de language et de communication*, Paris: Minard, 1968, p. 261.

Contributions of Cross-Cultural Orientation Programs and Power Analysis to Translation/Interpretation

Richard W. Brislin

East-West Center

Honolulu

At a meeting held recently in Japan, an American was discussing two alternative proposals with his colleagues, all of whom were native speakers of Japanese. The American was well schooled in the Japanese language and was, indeed, often called "fluent" by those around him. At this meeting, proposal A was contrasted to proposal B, and a consensus was reached about future action, and the meeting then dismissed. Upon leaving the room the American commented, "I think the group made a wise choice in accepting proposal A." A Japanese colleague, however, noted, "But proposal B was the group's choice." The American continued: "But I heard people say that proposal A was better." The Japanese colleague concluded, "Ah, you listened to the words but not to the pauses between the words."

This (true) cross-cultural misunderstanding is just one example of the difficulties in communicating with people from other cultures. Communication is not based solely on verbalizations. There are non-verbal cues, styles, routines, acceptable and unacceptable techniques for confrontation and disagreement, and so forth, that are rarely found in language-instruction courses and materials but which play a tremendous role in communication among people. Using Japan again as an example, the Japanese do *not* increase the intensity of their voice or use hand/arm gestures to indicate anger to the degree that French or English speakers do. How, then, can people learn about the communication skills in other cultures that will allow them to express a wide range of feelings and emotions *in a manner acceptable to natives of those cultures*? Long-term travel abroad is sometimes cited as the best method, but such an approach is too expensive and too inefficient for a large-scale solution. Another alternative is the establishment of cross-cultural orientation programs. My goal in this chapter is (1) to discuss these programs, (2) to indicate their potential for the training of interpreters and translators, and (3) to indicate two content areas of possible use for such training: power analysis and the relationship between language, culture, and translation.

CROSS-CULTURAL ORIENTATION PROGRAMS

Cross-cultural orientation programs (Brislin and Pedersen, 1976) are designed to prepare people from one culture in methods of adjusting and interacting (with minimum stress) in a culture other than the one(s) with which they are familiar. The clearest examples are programs for students about to study in a foreign country, businessmen about to be given an overseas assignment, or members of the American Peace Corps about to live in a third-world country. Because they are not a well established entity, some of the descriptions of cross-cultural orientation programs are not complimentary. Such programs are usually of short-term duration, and staffed by people for whom cross-cultural training is not a full-time job, are only modestly budgeted, and are aimed at people who are not always sure that the program is necessary for them. Elaborating on this last point, many potential participants feel that adjusting to another culture is not difficult and that the time necessary for the orientation program will not be well spent. In my experience, this feeling is more common on the part of people who have not experienced another culture than for people who *have* encountered a culture different from their own.

There are five basic techniques which an administrator might consider in setting up a program. Most programs use more than one of the following, based on the administrator's preferences, resources, and predictions about acceptability to the program participants:

1. *Cognitive training.* This approach is concerned with beliefs and facts about other cultures as seen by outsiders who have lived in those cultures. Topics such as food, clothing, entertainment, methods for making decisions, and etiquette might be covered. This approach is usually staff-centered, meaning that the staff prepares material and presents it to participants in lectures or guided group discussions. This approach is the most common of the five to be considered, is probably the easiest to administer, and is the "safest" since it is difficult to have a completely unsuccessful program if materials are well prepared. The common complaint of participants, however, is that the number of facts presented can become overwhelming, and that the accumulation of facts does not necessarily add up to a meaningful whole.

2. *Attribution training.* The key to this approach is that beliefs and facts are presented as seen by members of the host culture. For instance, a personal question may be seen as nosiness by an outsider, but it may be seen as friendliness by members of the host culture. The behavior (a personal question) is *attributed* to different qualities dependent upon the culture from which the individual comes. The most well-developed materials for this type of training are culture assimilators (Friedler, Mitchell, and Triandis, 1971), which consist of over 100 incidents which might be encountered by people who live in another culture. Different culture assimilators are prepared for each culture to which participants will be assigned, an obvious disadvantage if the budget is finite. After reading the incident, participants choose which of several attributions is the best explanation as seen by host nationals.

3. *Self-awareness training.* The foci of this approach are the qualities that participants bring to another culture. Participants might learn about traits

typically shared by members of their own culture or perhaps about their own personal traits. Americans, for instance, might learn about their typical "rugged individualism", a trait that can cause misunderstanding in cultures where ties to groups are very important. The advantage of the technique is that a large group can be trained in one place regardless of the number of countries to which the individuals will be assigned. The disadvantage is that there is no established relationship between self awareness and successful adaptation to another culture.

4. *Behavior modification*. Rarely used, possibly because of the specialized and technical nature of the concepts employed, this approach is based on well established principles of learning. Participants study such concepts as stimulus transfer, response, and modification of present reinforcing systems. They then apply these concepts to their behavior in relation to the culture in which they will live. For instance, they might list rewards they like and punishers they avoid in their own culture, and examine how they might find the rewards and avoid the punishers in the other cultures. The advantage of this approach is that it forces a specific examination of the other culture in terms of people's preferences. The disadvantage is that the concepts are foreign and/or distasteful to many.

5. *Experiential training*. The goal of this approach is realism, with exercises designed to involve the participants in behaving as if they were in another culture. For instance, Peace Corps trainees about to be assigned to remote islands in the Pacific were introduced, during training, to life on these islands (Trifonovitch, 1977). Participants lived in a training village in rural Oahu, Hawaii, and had to gather their own food, find their own fresh water, dig their own latrines, and so on. Role-playing is also an experiential technique, and it has been used in interpreter training (Arjona, this volume). The advantages of the technique are realism and the active involvement of participants. Disadvantages are its cost (as in simulations of a Pacific village), and the danger of participants reaching an emotional level which an administrator is not prepared to handle. I personally am most interested in the experiential technique and am constantly collecting techniques that seem involving to participants and yet not outrageous (as in some so-called sensitivity or T-groups) and dangerous (Weeks, Pedersen, and Brislin, 1977).

I realise that much of what is called cross-cultural orientation is now part of interpreter training, although the terms used in this chapter may not be used in such training. For instance, interpreter trainees are often warned that they are entering a profession of ambiguous status. They will be respected for their skills by some, considered parrots by others, and ignored socially by many of the people for whom they interpret. These aspects of the profession could be communicated through a lecture ("cognitive training"), from the point of view of conference speakers ("attribution"), or through role-play exercises with some people acting as interpreters, some as speakers, at an after-hours dinner. Other training might be much more other-culture specific. Interpreter trainees could learn about cultural differences in vocal intensity during disagreements by studying, for instance, interpretation between Japanese and English. Other examples are the handling of aggressive and humorous material in English vs. the Pilipino language, as will be reviewed in the last section of this chapter. Again, such material could be presented through several of the five cross-cultural orientation methods already reviewed.

ANALYSIS OF POWER

Assuming that the desirability of cross-cultural orientation programs has been accepted by administrators in charge of interpreter training, the next obvious step is to decide on the content for these programs. Two examples will be put forth here: power analysis and the relation between language, culture, and translation.

Power is a word that has a number of negative connotations, but its use in social psychology simply refers to the influence one person has over another. In everyday language, if a person A can get person B to do what A wants to do, then A has power over B. There are five types of social power as defined by French (1956), and they were applied to the role of translator/interpreter by Brislin (1976). The reason for repeating them here is to indicate how they may form the basis for the content of cross-cultural orientation programs.

1. Attraction power: This form of power is based on a strong affective feeling ("liking") between people. There are cases on record in which a certain high-level communicator chose a certain interpreter largely because of this type of relationship. Interpreters (just as members of every other profession) have to learn that competence alone rarely leads to job success. People have to be liked (or at least not disliked) by their co-workers and potential employees. Cross-cultural programs can instruct people on behaviors likely to lead to good relations with people in other cultures.

2. Expert power: In cases where one person is perceived to have superior knowledge in a relevant area, that person is said to have expert power. Such power is probably the most common for interpreters since communicators know that interpreters are the experts in the various other languages into which a message must be conveyed. But in addition to language per se, message conveyance involves styles and conventions that differ among speakers of different languages. Cross-cultural orientation programs can provide instruction in these non-language aspects of communication and so can increase the basis of interpreters' expert power.

3. Reward power: When a communicator feels that an interpreter can help mediate rewards during a conference or meeting, the interpreter has reward power. Such power is common since the goal of many meetings is to decide upon courses of action that will benefit communicators in one way or another. Wise communicators sometimes ask interpreters for guidance on the best way of presenting a certain message so that the best results will be obtained. In addition to interpreters providing rewards for communicators, the flow of rewards can also be in the opposite direction. The ambiguous status of interpreters, with consequent feelings of low self-concept, has been mentioned earlier in this chapter and in other chapters in this volume. If communicators are more conscientious about rewarding their interpreters by praise, invitations to socials, and so forth, the interpreter is more likely to do an even better job in the future. I would like to see short orientation programs established for *communicators* who frequently have the need for interpreters. In addition to the obvious content like number of words/minute and the danger of colloquialisms, such programs would include guidance on communicator-to-interpreter rewards.

4. Coercive power: When a communicator perceives that the interpreter can mediate punishments, then the interpreter is said to have coercive power. Such power thus leads to fear on the part of the communicator. Coercive power should not be dismissed completely since it is based on the communicator's realization that misunderstandings can arise in negotiations carried out in more than one language. Communicators might then be careful to prepare materials that can be interpreted with less probability of misunderstanding. Of course, too much coercive power based on fear will debilitate communication and cause unfavourable communicator-interpreter relations.

5. Legitimate power: When the communicator feels that the interpreter has the *right* to prescribe certain behaviors, the interpreter is said to have legitimate power. Such situations can be quite common when there are cultural differences involved since communicators may not know that a misunderstanding has arisen, whereas the interpreter might see the cause of the misunderstanding. Does an interpreter have the *right* to interrupt a meeting to indicate that a misunderstanding may have arisen? This question was discussed at the conference at which the chapters in this volume were presented, and there was disagreement as to the answer. I feel that the answer is "yes". This additional input by interpreters should make meetings more productive. In addition, the added responsibility should increase the status and visibility of the interpreter. It would also make cross-cultural orientation more salient because training could partially center around situations in which communication across cultures is impeded to the extent that the interpreter has to take the drastic and emotion-arousing step of stopping a meeting.

THE RELATION BETWEEN LANGUAGE, CULTURE, AND TRANSLATION

Another content area for cross-cultural orientation programs is based on the observation, made by interpreters and translators, that some types of material are more easily conveyed in one language than another. This observation has also been put forth by researchers interested in the "Sapir-Whorf" hypothesis (reviewed by Miller and McNeill, 1968). In its strongest version, the Sapir-Whorf hypothesis states that the language people speak shapes their perceptions of the world and ultimately their behavior. The causal link is proposed to be language→behavior. Empirical research has not supported this strong version of the hypothesis.

I am taking a modest view of the hypothesis that is more in line with that accepted by a number of people who have done research on translation/interpretation (e.g., chapters in Brislin, 1976). People in a given culture place a high value on certain behaviors, ideas, or material possessions. Examples are snow for Eskimos, horses for Arabs, the automobile for Americans, and kinship for tribes in New Guinea. These concerns are then reflected in the culture's language and the language develops so that the concerns can be easily communicated among a culture's members. Examples are the number of vocabulary items related to snow, horses, cars, and kin in the four cultures mentioned above. Vocabulary includes nouns and verbs that describe action associated with the nouns (e.g. what is done with a car; obligations to kin). But the development of a language to match a culture's concerns leads to a situation in which translation out of that language is difficult. It is likely that most potential target languages do not have the same development (to communicate the same concerns) as the source language. Thus it will be difficult (not necessarily impossible) to depict certain concerns in one language as compared to another.

If such concerns can be documented, and training exercises developed, the materials can be incorporated into orientation programs. The materials should be of great interest to translator-and interpreter-trainees since the issues are so similar to problems they will face in their actual work.

Since few differences in translation across different domains have been documented, Dr Virgilio Enriquez (of the University of the Philippines) and I designed an experiment to discover if such differences could be measured. The languages we investigated were American, English and Pilipino, the national language of the Philippines. Since we did not have facilities for the analysis of oral interpretation, we depended upon gaining our inferences from a study of written translations. We feel that the basic measuring process and type of demonstration, however, may be of interest to both translators and interpreters. The material with which we worked consisted of literary passages available to readers in the United States and/or the Philippines. A more complete description of the experiment is available (Enriquez and Brislin, 1977). Space restrictions permit treatment of only a few aspects in this chapter.

The reasoning behind the experiment is that almost all literature is written for people other than the author alone, and translators also work so as to communicate to a large number of people. One general criterion of translation quality is that the source and target versions "produce a similar response" (Nida, 1964, p. 164) on the part of readers. It is assumed that such a response can be measured, and so a determination of respondents' feelings to translated as compared to original language versions should be of use both to translators and to researchers interested in translation.

THE EXPERIMENT: THE MEASUREMENT OF AFFECTIVE CONTENT IN ENGLISH AND PILIPINO

In designing techniques for the measurement of affect in translation, Enriquez and I began with these assumptions.

1. Respondents can indicate their feelings about either original language or translated passages by marking specific points on rating scales.

2. Responses will differ according to obvious content differences in the passages. We chose four types of material for this investigation: humorous, violent, factual, and passages depicting positive affect in interpersonal relationships (hereinafter called "interpersonal"). Space restrictions permit us to report here only on the humorous and violent materials.

3. Given assurances of translators doing the best work of which they are capable, affective differences in original vs. target language versions of a passage will not be large. Rather, there may be nuances that can lead to slight differences in interpretation on the part of respondents who read the original vs. translated versions. In other words, a violent passage will not be rated

"humorous", but it may be consistently rated somewhat less violent in one language as compared to another.

4. If responses are gathered from a large number of raters, the average ratings for the different passages (in their original and source language versions) can easily be determined through basic statistical calculations. These statistics will then give an indication of how the passage is seen by a large number of people. Averaging over a large number of raters eliminates the idiosyncracies of any one person so that the overall rating is more similar to the response of a large audience (the eventual target of most translations).

More complex predictions are based on previous cultural studies of the Philippines and the United States. All predictions have as an assumption that competent translators have put forth their best efforts.

5. Humorous passages would be rated as more humorous in Pilipino than in English versions. This prediction is based upon the observations that the Filipino people greatly value a sense of humor and that they use humor a great deal in their verbal play (Morales-Goulet, n.d.). Double meanings are common in their verbal play, perhaps more so than in the United States. Enriquez has observed that people often engage in a teasing sort of verbal play with each other, and that there is a negative term ("pikon") applied to the few who cannot "take" being the occasional target of such play (Enriquez, 1976).

6. Violent passages would be rated as more violent when presented in English than when presented in Pilipino. This prediction is based upon the fact that violence is strongly discouraged in the Philippines (Jocano, 1969). Even among children, parents frown upon fighting back whereas in other societies (including the USA) fighting back would be seen in the light of defending oneself against an enemy. The avoidance is related to the very positive value placed on "pakikisama" or "smooth interpersonal relations", as documented by Guthrie and Azores (1968). "Pakikisama" involves good feelings and pleasant relations among people, which of course are impossible with any sort of violence. Critics of this view make the counter claim that Filipinos have a predisposition to violence, as shown by reports of political assassinations and careless logging operations in rain forests for economic gain at the expense of indigenous villagers. But others would argue that these are atypical examples that have been sensationalized. In contrast, the American system of interpersonal behavior seems to include violence as a common staple, the evidence of which can be seen in books, movies, magazines, television, and so forth. Loud, hostile arguments in public are much more common in the U.S.A. than in the Philippines, leading to the prediction that language befitting such interpersonal hostility is more easily available in American English. A related sociolinguistic observation is that, among married couples composed of Pilipino-English bilinguals, arguments at home are held more often in English than in Pilipino (Cariño, 1975).

SPECIFIC METHODOLOGY OF THE EXPERIMENT

Raters: Thirty-two college students from the University of the Philippines, fluent in both English and Pilipino, were asked to participate in the study. They were told that they would read some English language and/or Pilipino language passages and would then make ratings. Among the 32 raters, 18 were females and 14 were males, their ages ranging from 16-22 years. While English is the language of instruction at the University of the Phillipines, a number of elective courses are available in Pilipino. All raters had chosen to take at least one college course in which Pilipino was the language of instruction.

The raters were randomly assigned to two major groups. One group was given materials containing solely English or solely Pilipino passages while another group was given materials containing both English and Pilipino passages. This latter group was further sub-divided to control for order of presentation in either language in the different domains.

Materials: Passages in Pilipino translated into English, and vice-versa, were used. For each domain, two passages were given. In the case of the passages given in Pilipino, one was originally written in Pilipino while the other was a translation from English. The same was true for English, i.e. one was originally written in English while the other was a translation from Pilipino. Shown below are the passages used for the experiment and indicated also are their respective sources. Only the English versions are presented here: Pilipino versions can be obtained by writing to the authors. All of the passages originally written in either English or Pilipino are from published sources that are available to a wide audience: none were written solely for this study.

1a *Humorous* (originally written in English)
A serpent attacked Tarzan and Jane while they were up on a tree. Tarzan panicked and grabbed a nearby vine. He directed Jane to do the same, "Hold mine." So she did and quickly grabbed it. Tarzan emitted a painful shriek and his famous "aaah, aaah" cry started from then on.

Green Jokes in Cebuano Folklore: An Analysis of their Socio-Cultural Context. Lillian Garcia. Cebu City: University of San Carlos, 1972, Appendix III, p. 16.

1b *Humorous* (originally written in Pilipino)
"Do you love me?"
"With my whole heart and soul"
"Are you ready to die just for me?"
"Oh no . . . my love knows no death!"

Liwayway. Liwayway Publishing House. (Jan. 24, 1977) p. 70. (Translated for this study by Rogelio V. Tangco, University of the Phillipines).

2a *Violent* (originally written in English: a sample reproduced below)
Then Brasi took an axe from its place against the wall and started hacking at one of the Capone men. He chopped the man's feet off, then the legs to the knees, then the thighs where they joined the torso . . . The second Capone gunman out of sheer terror had, impossibly, swallowed the bath towel in his mouth and suffocated.

The Godfather. Mario Puzo. Pan Books, Ltd., London, 1970, p. 222. The translation into Pilipino is available in book form: Ang Harahasan sa Nobela at Pelikulang *The Godfather* at ang Epekto nito sa Madla. *Tao at Lipunan.* Violet Lagmay, p. 189.

2b *Violent* (originally written in Pilipino: sample reproduced below)
He was lashed with a belt and a rope,
    and was forced to repeat dictated testimony;
    like a crossword puzzle
Were the lashes on his back, breast and arms,
    but he didn't "confess"
Until he dropped on the floor like a log.

Bayang Malaya. Amado V. Hernandez. Manila: Ateneo University Press, 1969, pp. 68, 82. Translated by Eduardo Deveza.

Rating Scales: We designed the rating scales with several considerations in mind. First, complete sentences were used to label the ends of each scale in contrast to single words often used in social psychological research. This decision follows the principle that sentences are easier to translate than single words, (Longacre, 1958; Werner and Campbell, 1970), and so we used the former since we prepared rating scales in both English and Pilipino. Second, we used 5-point scales since they can be explained graphically as follows:

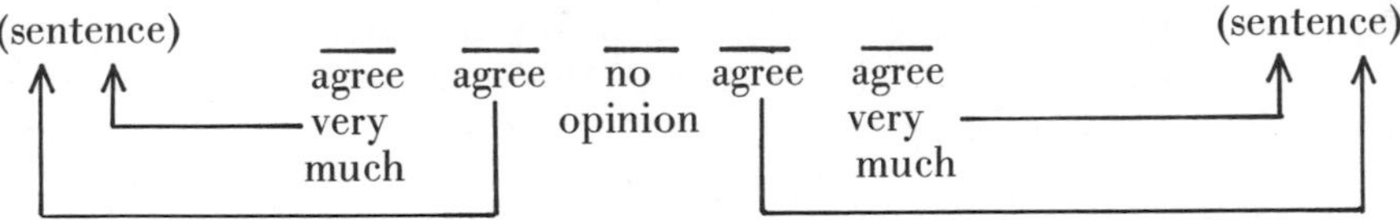

Third, we used sentences that would measure the affective content of the passages as discussed in the presentation of hypotheses.

The scales in English are presented below. These were also available in a Pilipino version. After reading a passage, raters indicated their feelings on the scales. The scales they rated were in the same language as the passage. On the scales below, the numbering system we used in analyzing the ratings is also presented; the raters did not see this numbering system.

a	I liked reading this passage	1	2	3	4	5	I did not like reading this passage
b	I learned some things by reading this passage	1	2	3	4	5	I did not learn anything by reading this passage
c	I understand what the author wanted to explain	1	2	3	4	5	I did not understand what the author wanted to explain

d I feel that the content of the passage is humorous	1	2	3	4	5	I feel that the content of the passage is not humorous
e I feel that the content of the passage is violent	1	2	3	4	5	I feel that the content of the passage is not violent
f I feel that the author understands the subject matter that is presented	1	2	3	4	5	I feel that the author does not understand the subject matter that is presented
g I feel that the author was sensitive to relations between people	1	2	3	4	5	I feel that the author was not sensitive to relations between people
h I feel that the author was sensitive to how people express emotions	1	2	3	4	5	I feel that the author was not sensitive to how people express emotions

RESULTS

"Statistical significance" or "significant" in the following description of the results refers to the .05 level, t-tests, with 30df. The results are based on specific scales that correspond to each passage, e.g., the humorous scale (letter "d") for the humorous passage, the violence scale (letter "e") for the violent passage.

Humorous passages were rated more so in Pilipino than in English, as predicted, *if* the passage was originally written in Pilipino. The mean for the Pilipino version of passage 1b is 1.9 (sd = 1.2); for the English version, the mean is 2.8 (sd = 1.5). This is a statistically significant difference. The humorous passage (1a) originally written in English was rated as slightly more humorous in its Pilipino version, but the difference did not reach statistical significance. Other scales showed no differences between the two versions (e.g., violence, learn new things). This is a positive finding in favor of the technique since concepts unrelated to the affective content of a passage *should* be rated as similar across different-language versions.

Violent passages were rated more so in English than in Pilipino, as predicted, regardless of the passage's language of origin. Passage 2a, originally written in English, had a mean rating of 1.5 (sd = .9) in that version and a mean rating of 2.2 (sd = 0.8) in the Pilipino translation, a difference that reaches statistical significance. For passage 2b, originally written in Pilipino, the English translation had a mean rating of 1.8 (sd = 1.3) and the Pilipino original had a mean rating of 2.9 (sd = 1.1), a difference that reaches statistical significance. Other scales not explicitly related to the passages (e.g., sensitivity to relations between people and to how people express emotions) were rated the same for the different-language versions.

DISCUSSION

Results of the study demonstrate that violent and humorous passages can be translated between English and Pilipino, but not with exactly the same intensity. As predicted, passages were rated more humorous in Pilipino versions, and more violent in English versions. The point must be made that the issue of non-translatability is not under discussion. The findings indicate that certain qualities are easier to depict in *written* original and target language passages.

These findings have application to the training of translators and interpreters. Trainees could have their work analyzed in experiential-orientated sessions, according to the method outlined above, to determine the amount of affect contained in their translation in contrast to the original language version. They could then adjust their efforts to produce a translation more like the original version. Various types of changes might be tried. For instance, interpreters might concentrate on vocal inflection and emphasis if they are convinced that they have done as much as possible in their choice of vocabulary.

An important point to consider is who decides what is the affective content in a passage that should be translated. Often, the translator/interpreter is the person who makes this decision. Mistakes sometimes arise at this step, not in subsequent transformation to another language. Interpreters often have to make decisions quickly during fast-moving discussions between communicators. In analyzing literary works, on the other hand, translators have more time to search out authors' views about their work and to read the opinions of respected critics. If other demonstrations like that in the present study show differences in affect across translations, perhaps more attention will be given to a conscious decision about exactly what affect should be conveyed. This is ultimately the communicator's decision, not the translator's. For instance, a communicator could write down exactly what affect is to be conveyed as part of a message to another person (e.g., firmness presented in a diplomatic way; willingness to negotiate in the future; anger, but implicitly rather than explicitly expressed). This set of notes would be an addition to the actual message. Perhaps another method would be inclusion of the translator/interpreter in all discussions that preceded the actual meeting at which the multi-language communication takes place. By sitting in on planning meetings, the interpreter is more likely to understand the various aspects of what is to be communicated and so should be more effective in the actual communication situation.

The techniques described here may be applicable to the broader field of the relation between culture, language, and behavior. If various types of material are examined to determine what can and cannot be easily described in a certain language the results may give insights into important aspects of various cultures. Likewise, such results may lead to predictions about what aspects of behavior are likely to be especially sensitive during cross-cultural encounters. For instance, the results of this study suggest that Americans living in the Phillipines should be careful about hostile arguments in public and should cultivate a sense of humor. These techniques are also practical in their application since (1) they are not expensive, being based only on paper-and-pencil instruments; and (2), they can be used with college-level students (who are bilingual in most parts of the world, in contrast to the USA) who will probably enjoy the active involvement in research which the techniques encourage.

REFERENCES

Brislin, R., Ed. *Translation: Applications and Research.* New York: Gardner Press, 1976.

Brislin, R., and Pederson, P. *Cross-Cultural Orientation Programs.* New York: Wiley/Halsted Division, 1976.

Cariño, L. Theory of language and language acquisition: its sociololinguistic aspect. *Philippine journal for Language Teaching.* 1975, *8 (7 & 8)*, 58 - 66.

Enriquez, V. Sikolohiyang Pilipino: Perspektibo at Direksyon. *Proceedings of the First National Conference of Filipino Psychology.* Lunsod Quenzon: Pambansang Samahan as Sikolohiyang Pilipino, 1976, 221 - 243.

Enriquez, V., and Brislin, R. The measurement of affective content in translation: American English and Pilipino, 1977. *Philippine Journal of Psychology*, 1978, in press. Also available from Dr Brislin at East-West Center, CLI, Honolulu, Hawaii, 96848, USA.

Fiedler, F., Mitchell, T., and Triandis, H. The culture assimilator: an approach to cross-cultural training. *Journal of Applied Psychology*, 1971, *55*, 95 - 102.

French, J. A formal theory of social power. *Psychological Review*, 1956, *63*, 181 - 194.

Guthrie, G., and Azores, F. Philippine interpersonal behavior patterns. In W. Bello and A. de Guzman (Eds.), *Modernization: Its Impact in the Phillipines* (IPC Papers #7). Manila: Ateneo de Manila University Press, 1968.

Jacano, F. *Growing up in a Phillipine Barrio.* New York: Holt, Rinehart, and Winston, 1969.

Longacre, R. Items in context — their bearings on translation theory. *Language*, 1958, 482 - 491.

Miller, G., and McNeil, D. Psycholinguistics. In G. Lindzey and E. Aronson (Eds.), *Handbook of Social Psychology*, 2nd ed., vol. 3. Reading, Mass.: Addison-Wesley, 1968, 666-794.

Morales-Goulet, R. *Bilingualism in the Philippine Setting.* Quezon City: Souvenir Publications, (n.d.).

Nida, E. *Toward a Science of Translating.* Leiden, Netherlands: E. J. Brill, 1964.

Trifonovitch, G. On cross-cultural orientation techniques. In R. Brislin (Ed.), *Culture Learning: Concepts, Applications, and Research.* Honolulu, Hawaii: University Press of Hawaii, 1977, 213 - 222.

Weeks, W., Pedersen, P., and Brislin, R., (Eds.). *A Manual of Structural Experiences for Cross-Cultural Learning.* Georgetown University, Washington, D.C.: Society for Intercultural Education, Training, and Research, 1977.

Werner, O., and Campbell, D. Translating, working through interpreters, and the problem of decentering. In R. Naroll and R. Cohen (Eds.). *A Handbook of Method in Cultural Anthropology.* New York: Natural History Press, 1970, 398 - 420.

Interpreter Roles and Interpretation Situations: Cross-Cutting Typologies [1]

R. Bruce W. Anderson

University of Texas

Arlington, Texas

At the outset it is essential that the use to which several important and recurring terms will be put be made explicit. The first of these is "interpreter". Probably the most common understanding of this term is as a somewhat shortened version of the phrase "conference interpreter". Seleskovitch (1976: 97) places the number of conference interpreters in the Western world at a maximum of a few thousand, of whom something over one thousand are members of the International Association of Conference Interpreters AIIC.

Seleskovitch argues both directly and by example that the act of interpreting is engaged in by others who could not be considered conference interpreters, and that this broader activity is the basis for 'universal interest' in the phenomenon.

One of my informants, an AIIC member and teacher of interpreters, agreed that only a small portion of interpretation is conference interpretation, and extended the concept of interpretation to include monolingual activity. As an example of monolingual interpretation this informant described the retelling of a film, lecture, or television program by someone who had been present to another who had missed the event. He also suggested that the parent commonly engages in monolingual interpretation in talking to his or her children; reformulating adult conceptions into a speech act comprehensible to the youngsters. Each of these acts begins with a message, or meaning, available to one party in the interaction but to which the other party is, in his phrase, "temporarily deaf". But the original message is not merely replayed, as with a tape recorder. Rather it is reformulated and retransmitted (accurately, if the interpreter is a good one), but in a manner that is different from the original precisely in those ways which make it understandable to the listener. These interpretive acts differ from those engaged in by conference interpreters, in this informant's view, largely because they do not "accidentally pass through another language".

We conclude, therefore, that the act of interpreting occurs both within and between languages. In what follows, however, we shall limit our attention to interpretation only as it occurs between languages. We shall then say that interpretation occurs whenever a message originating orally in one language is reformulated and retransmitted orally in a second language. This definition of interpretation is satisfied in many situations where no conference interpreter is present, and leads us to a broad definition of "an interpreter" which includes, but is not limited to conference interpreters. For our purposes any individual who is able to receive a message in one language and reformulate and retransmit it orally in a second language is an interpreter when he does so.

The remainder of this paper is devoted to the development of two cross-cutting typologies based on these definitions. The first is a typology of situations in which interpretation, as defined above, occurs. The second is a typology of interpreter roles which emphasizes both the characteristics of individuals who meet the above definition of "an interpreter", and the expectations that others have of them as they engage in interpretation. The data from which these typologies are developed are derived from in-depth interviews with 17 interpreters. These 17 interviews ranged in length from one to three hours, and provide the major source of materials used in the discussion which follows. The discussion is also informed by insights gained in informal conversations with about a dozen other interpreters with whom more detailed interviews were recorded. Finally, the writer has had the opportunity to observe conference interpreters in action, from within the glass booth and to personally simulate the process of conference interpreting from that setting. This paper can only begin to discuss the data from these several sources, which it is hoped provide some depth of insight as well as a basis for further research.

THE INTERPRETER

Among the 17 individuals interviewed:

1. nine were conference interpreters located through the directory listing in yearbooks kindly provided by AIIC. Each was, of course, an AIIC member, and each spoke English, the language in which interviews were conducted. Three of these interviewees were male, and six female. Among them they had sufficient command of five languages to engage in interpretation involving combinations of those languages. Two of them had two languages which they spoke as "mother tongues", while the remainder had only one mother tongue. French was the most common language other than English, and was the mother tongue of five respondents including one of those with dual mother tongues;

2. six respondents were pursuing advanced degrees in Russian at the University of Texas at Austin. These four females and two males had in common the fact that they had all served as interpreters for a group of Soviet athletes who were visiting the Austin campus. The most experienced among them included a lady who had served as a tour guide and interpreter in the Soviet Union for two years and was currently employed as a documents translator for N.A.S.A. and a man who had previously been employed in the Soviet Union by the U.S.I.A. as an interpreter associated with one of their travel-

ing exhibitions. The least experienced among them was a young lady who had just completed a Bachelors' degree in Russian and had spent a total of three months travelling in the Soviet Union.

3. two Spanish-English interpreters, one of whom was a native Spanish speaking Central American who had interpreted in court while employed as a probation officer, and who had subsequently interpreted in other settings while employed by Berlitz and as owner of a language school. The other was a female social worker, for whom Spanish was a second language, and who routinely found herself interpreting for Spanish speaking clients who had reason to interact with English monolingual members of the medical, and other professions.

In addition to the seventeen interpreters described briefly above, interpretation has been informally discussed with about a dozen other "interpreters". Notable among these were three members of a team of Russians who were touring the United States with the Scientific Siberia exhibit. One of these was a linguist by training, and another an editor of *Soviet Life*. Others included several members of the Summer Institute of Linguistics who had had experience as interpreters, and also previous experience working through interpreters in Southeast Asia and Latin America with "exotic" languages. Finally, a number of University faculty members with experience in interpreting for visiting scholars from Japan, China, Russia, and Germany have provided informal insights into their experiences. The languages, other than English, which have been employed in interpretation by our informant-interviewees, include the following: French, German, Spanish, Russian, Japanese, Chinese, several dialects of Vietnamese, Danish, Polish, and several languages spoken by Indian peoples of North, Central, and South America.

INTERPRETATION SITUATIONS

Interpretation situations appear, on the basis of our data, to differ in two respects: attributes of the physical environment, and attributes of the social environment. In the first instance we refer to such things as whether or not the interpreter is physically isolated from those from and to whom he is interpreting, the noise level, and the like. In the latter instance we refer to the number, and relational aspects, of the interpreter's position relative to his clients (a client is either the originator of material interpreted or the recipient of such material [c.f. Anderson, 1976]). The question of social situation is conditioned, in part, by the physical constraints and serves as a bridge to the interpreter role in the sense that different social situational configurations have different role-expectational dimensions. Thus, for example, the conference interpreters said that the differences in their experiences when interpreting in physical situations where they are relatively isolated (e.g. in a glass booth *a la* United Nations), or in face-to-face confrontation around a negotiating table, influence their role relations *vis-a-vis* those to, and for, whom they are interpreting. In such comparisons the social relationship varies according to whether the physical relationship is face-to-face or isolated, and this will in turn create differences in role relations among the participants in the interaction. More will be said regarding interpreter reactions to these differences in the following section, which deals explicitly with interpreter roles.

Anderson (1976) dealt explicitly with the matter of the social environment as it related to the power structure of the interpretation situation. At that time he attempted to set forth arguments, based upon a literature review, in which the power of the interpreter was associated with his identification with one or the other of his clients. It was argued there that social constraints might influence the interpreter to adopt one of several roles as a result of the social structure of the interactive network. It was suggested that the interpreter could either act as a nonpartisan as a result of neutrality based upon some sort of equal attachments to the arguments of both parties (hence serving as a 'mediator' seeking justice), as a detached party who 'let the chips fall where they may', or finally he could take a partisan role which served to enhance his own position with respect to the client or clients who employed him. The impact of the social situation upon the behavior of the interpreter was judged to result from similarities and differences in the social characteristics of the interpreter in relation to those of other participants in the interaction.

The matter of interpreter identification with a client is important *if* it influences the quality of interpretation, and thereby the outcome of the interaction. This premise was the basis for the previous argument regarding power in interpretation situations. This issue was raised with each of the interpreters interviewed, and *all 17 gave virtually identical responses*. All of them said essentially "Of course I never take sides, it is unethical". Generally, they went on to explain that the interpreter's job was to convey the meaning received to their listeners as faithfully as possible. It was not surprising to find that the respondents shared this ethical orientation and took pains to stress that *they* were good interpreters. As the interviews progressed each respondent was asked to reflect upon one or several actual interpreting experiences which they had had. As they did so, some interesting fragments of information about their identification with one or another client came to light, and in two instances admissions of misinterpretation were elicited. Among the AIIC interpreters, one stated that he had left a permanent position because he did not like the people for whom he worked and found the material he was asked to interpret banal. Another was observed to cup off the microphone during a pause and remark to another interpreter in the booth that the speaker was a pompous fool. We have no evidence that these instances of "taking sides" influenced the quality of interpretation to any significant degree, though it would seem likely that such negative sentiments might dull the interpreter's enthusiasm and lower the creativity of his effort. Both of these situations involved potential monitoring by other interpreters, a factor judged significant as a check upon misinterpretation since any systematic departure from the professional ethic of neutrality would leave the transgressor open to censure both by his employer and by AIIC.

One important aspect of the social situation appears to be the presence of actual or potential monitoring of the interpretation. It appears to be the case that in most situations in which AIIC interpreters are employed, whether in permanent positions with international organizations such as the various branches of the United Nations or on a free-lance basis with multinational conferences, monitoring is at least possible. In most situations there are several interpreters with overlapping language competancies who may, at any time, decide to listen to a colleague's interpretation. It is also quite common that the listeners to such proceedings include among their numbers some who are able to follow both the original and the interpretation. Not only is monitoring possible in many situations where AIIC interpreters work, but a number of our informants told us about the skills of other interpreters with whom they had worked, giving clear evidence that interpreters do listen to each other at work. It would appear that the potential for monitoring will have a salutory influence upon the quality of interpretation, and will reduce the likelihood of distortion resulting from the interpreter's identification with clients. The presence of potential monitoring would not be expected to influence the interpreter's identification with clients.

As noted previously, only a small portion of the world's interpreting qualifies as conference interpreting. A great deal of interpreting is done in settings in which monitoring is unlikely or even impossible, and people who work in these situations are often recruited for their jobs in just the same way as were those whom we interviewed. Unlike AIIC members, the majority of these interpreters (and all whom we interviewed) are not members of organizations which publish directories. Rather, they are contacted through informal networks, contacts with language schools and university departments of foreign languages. Without a formal organization, these members have no possibility of censure, except by their clients, and the settings in which they work generally do not involve the presence of clients who could monitor the interpretations. It is suspected that in most instances the interpreters would not have been engaged if either client was sufficiently versed in the other's language to conduct the necessary interaction without his services. As the non-AIIC interpreters recounted their experiences in these settings the fact that they were not only subject to identification with one or another client, but also that this taking of sides at least occasionally influences the quality of the interpretation, could be appreciated.

For example, the Central American informant said that, while working as a probation officer, he was frequently asked to interpret both to and from Spanish in courtroom situations where the accused was the only other person present who spoke Spanish. This was one of several team interviews, and both interviewers came away with the clear impression that by and large he was very unfavorably disposed toward most of the Spanish monolinguals for whom he had interpreted in such situations. He repeatedly remarked that they often lied while on the witness stand and he felt uncomfortable in translating these lies as he interpreted. Other remarks indicated that, in general, negative responses to those for whom he was interpreting were triggered by social class differences between himself and his clients. Such comments as "Their Espanish was really bad, you know, mostly slang", as well as comments about the educational level and general appearance of the persons for whom he was interpreting led both interviewers to wonder how it would be possible for such strong negative feeling not to affect interpretation quality.

Among the student interpreters who worked with the young (high school age) Soviet athletes the oldest and most experienced of the females had an interesting response to questions about her experience. She indicated that she had no difficulty maintaining neutrality when interpreting either into English or into Russian when the subject matter related to the track and field events. Neither situations in which the interpretation revolved around a dispute between officials or coaches, nor more amicable interaction in which the competitors were announced before an event or the winners presented afterwards, caused her difficulty. On the other hand, she was often called upon to interpret for an interview by a member of the press or an interested spectator who wanted to ask a few question of one of the young Soviets. She reported, quite candidly, that she became irritated at the repetitious asking of questions which she thought silly. Finally, she admitted, that she began interjecting her own replies without bothering to interpret the question or wait for a reply. For example if the question was "What do you think of American girls ?" she would tell the Russian youth "They are asking about girls again, I'll tell them you think they are pretty" and then proceed to answer the question herself.

Yet another aspect of the social characteristics of interpretation situations came out in an interview with one of the AIIC informants who told of his experiences in relay interpretation. In this instance he was interpreting materials which originated in Japanese, were interpreted into English by another interpreter, and then he reinterpreted them from English into French. The tapes of this interview do not indicate the effects of this additional complication upon the behavior of the interpreter in any direct manner. It appears, however, that such a situation may induce the interpreter to concentrate more upon the meanings to be transmitted than would normally be the case. The same interpreter commented upon the relationship of noise to interpretation quality, remarking that (to a certain point) increases in noise increase the fidelity (quality) of interpretation. It seems plausible, from his remarks at different times during the 3 hour interview, that the added complication of relay interpretation serves a similar function, namely increasing the attentiveness of the interpreter to the listening aspect of his task (c.f. Seleskovitch, 1976) to, or towards, an optimal level and thereby resulting in improved interpretive fidelity.

Taking the above discussion into account, interpretation situations would appear to differ from each other in terms of social-interactive characteristics in the following ways. First, situations differ in the extent to which direct, face-to-face interaction occurs. This aspect of variability is related to the physical constraints of the situation, and will be discussed in greater detail below. For the present it is enough to say that interpreters whom we have interviewed are in agreement that these differences are important, though they differ in their preferences for situations which can be characterized by interpreter isolation as contrasted with interpreter integration with clients. We may then differentiate situations in which the interpreter is relatively isolated from his or her clients, from those in which he or she is relatively integrated. At the extreme of isolation we find the situation in which the interpreter is situated in a glass booth, connected electronically to speakers and listeners, whereas at the other end of the continuum we find interpreters who are in face-to-face contact with both speakers and listeners.

Social characteristics of interpretation situations can also be differentiated with respect to the matter of monitoring. At one extreme we find those situations in which the interpreter knows that he is being monitored by another interpreter. Such situations were mentioned by Ekvall (1960) and are especially common in major international organization meetings, such as the United Nations, where each delegation brings its own interpreters even though "official" interpretations are provided. An intermediate type of situation, in which monitoring is possible appears to be common in other conference situations. Finally, there are many cases in which interpretation occurs, and in which interpreters are employed, in which monitering is unlikely if not impossible due to the fact that there are no other bilinguals present. Anderson (1976) discussed the possible effect of monitoring upon interpretation if a client happened to be bilingual.

The third, and last, area in which social aspects of the interpretation situation seem of particular relevance concerns the existence of a combination of languages requiring relay interpretation. Data in this respect are fragmentary, but we can speculate that interpretation through relays which involves interpretation and reinterpretation, and processing from a language of origin through an intermediary language to a final language *may* introduce potential added sources of error. The logic involved here is extendable to cases of multiple relays where more than one intermediate language is required in order to convey a particular meaning from its originator to its ultimate listener. Parallels are to be found in the studies of Bavelas (1951) on communication networks, and Allport and Postman (1945) on the diffusion of rumor in social psychology. On the other hand, the presence of a single relay *may*, as noted above, serve to provide near optimal tension levels under which the interpreters are better able to perform their tasks than they would be in the absence of relays. Gerver's (1976) discussion of the effects of stress and personality implies that interpreter performance under varying noise-stress conditions exhibits the well known inverted U relationship between anxiety and performance under stress. It seems to this writer that the effects of various numbers of relays also merit investigation in somewhat parallel fashion to his study of noise-stress, Indeed, when the interpretation through relays is simultaneous, the presence of relays may generate noise with which the interpreters have to contend.

The non-AIIC informants earned their livelihood by some means other than interpreting. Without exception they indicated that they enjoyed what interpreting they had done, and would welcome the opportunity for more regular employment as interpreters. While they collectively described a wide variety of physical situations in which they had worked, they seemed rather unconcerned with the physical characteristics of their working environment. It appeared that these people had resigned themselves to working under any and all sorts of adverse conditions, considering that preferable to reducing still further their opportunities to engage in interpreting. In contrast, informants who were AIIC members were all quite willing and able to comment upon the characteristics of physical situations and their impact upon interpretation quality. This, in part, reflects the concerns of AIIC which include detailed specifications of the physical requirements of conference, especially simultancous, interpreters in their *Practical Guide for Users of Conference Interpreting Services* (AIIC, 1966) , and encourages its members to refuse employment under inadequate working conditions.

Thiery (1974) describes a number of aspects of the physical situation which will increase the likelihood of unsatisfactory interpreting:

> " . . . if the interpreters cannot hear properly; if they cannot see the speakers and the audience properly, and of course the screen if slides are to be shown; . . . if they are expected to squat for a full working day in ill-ventilated rabbit-hutches; . . . if the participants cannot hear the interpreters properly over the head phones; or if they hear the interpreters only too well because of bad sound-proofing of the booths; if there is interference between the simultaneous interpreting system and the loudspeaker system."

None of these situations will obtain if conference organizers follow the guidelines suggested by AIIC in arranging physical facilities – and have sufficient resources to implement them completely. Unfortunately many important international conferences are held at places which are not fully equipped for simultaneous interpretation and it is impossible to install the best equipment for an occasional conference. The result is that interpreters will probably have to deal with some of the problems which Thiery describes – at least occasionally – for a long time in the future.

Thiery's list of problems of the physical situation is organized around the assumption that each will reduce the quality of interpretation. The most thoroughly investigated of these appears to be the first. Gerver (1976) reviews a number of studies which assessed the effects of poor listening conditions upon the interpreter's performance and the results clearly indicate that accuracy of interpretation suffers with increasing noise levels. The other problems which Thiery discusses appear to be relatively unstudied to date. AIIC interpreters, including those interviewed, seem to be virtually unanimous that each is important. It would seem useful to mount a series of experiments which explore the effects of varying degrees of each of these other problems upon the quality of interpretation. In designing such studies one should be clear that Thiery's list is something of a mixed bag. Obviously the extent to which the interpreter is unable to hear what is being said is related to his ability to translate it. If he cannot hear he cannot interpret. Similarly, the visual cues will affect his ability to interpret because they typically carry a part of the meaning. The visual cues, however, are probably somewhat less important than the auditory in many instances. The creature comforts, or lack thereof, which the interpreter encounters in his working environment will likely also influence his ability to interpret. If the physical setting in which he works is oppressive he will probably tire faster than if it is agreeable, and his performance will decline accordingly.

The remaining items on Thiery's list are of an entirely different sort. They do not have to do with how well the interpreter is able to perform, but rather with how well his audience is able to receive his performance. To be sure, the most elegant interpretation is useless if those for whom it is intended are unable to hear it due to faulty equipment. The studies of noise discussed by Gerver (1976) indicate that people engaged in non-interpreting behavior (specifically shadowing) are less affected by a given noise level than interpreters. It stands to reason that the quality of sound transmitted to the audience is less important, since they may concentrate their attention upon the single task of listening, than is the audio quality reaching the interpreter. Exactly what the differential here is deserves careful investigation.

The AIIC interviewers were quite concerned about the quality of the sound transmitted to their listeners. Several commented to the effect that, if the sound system is poor the ordinary conference delegate is likely to blame the interpreters, or at least to phrase his complaint in terms of poor interpretation. This reaction was usually tied in with a comparison between the physical situation commonly encountered during consecutive interpretation and that experienced more frequently during simultaneous interpretation. Consecutive interpretation usually occurs in face-to-face settings where the interpreter is seated near the chairman of the meeting. Seating arrangements are usually such that the interpreter can establish direct eye contact with any member of the conference and interpreters directly, without electronic equipment. Input and output systems from within a soundproof booth led many conference participants to view them as "part of the equipment". Several remarked at the frustration of not being recognized or appreciated for the efforts that they had expended in trying to make a conference successful.

INTERPRETER ROLES

Anderson (1976) considered interpreter roles in terms of the literature pertaining to bilingualism, role conflict, and the power structure in small groups. The present interviews with interpreters have not led to the abandonment of the earlier analysis, though they have led to the modification of some considerations about aspects of interpreter roles. It has for example, been found that the earlier definition of bilingualism is not acceptable to AIIC informants. They count bilinguals as a very rare species consisting of a few individuals whom we would earlier have called "completely bilingual and bicultural". Such people not only are able to function as native adult speakers of two languages, they grew up doing so, and as a consequence have full command of the cultures to which the languages are native. This definition is so strict that it is virtually impossible for one to acquire the requisite abilities except by growing from childhood in, and of, a two language environment. Thus an adult whose speech was such that he was readily accepted as a native speaker by native speakers of two languages would not meet this definition of bilingualism unless he also had native command of other aspects of culture,such as children's games and folk tales. We are sympathetic with the AIIC interpreters' concerns here, as the extremely bilingual and bicultural individual (to return to the less strict usage of the 1976 paper) has a clear advantage over his bilingual but not bicultural colleague. Nearly every interpreter encountered who had worked in simultaneous conference situations had a favorite story about an instance in which some bilingual and bicultural acquaintance produced some obscure phrase from the folk-lore that conveyed the meaning carried by an equally obscure and otherwise wholly untranslatable phrase in the source language. For scientific purposes, however, we consider it preferable to maintain the distinction between bilingualism and biculturalism and to consider both as continua.

Thus a monolingual is defined as a person who speaks one language with native fluency and has no familiarity with any other language. At the other end of the linguistic continuum a multilingual is defined as a person who speaks more than two languages with native fluency. A bilingual then is similar to a multilingual except that his command is of two, rather than more than two, languages. The terms mono-, bi-, and multi-cultural have similar meanings except that they refer to native command of the full range of a culture including, but not limited to, its language. Thus, the present informants would all qualify as reasonably bilingual, though even some of the AIIC interpreters interviewed would not qualify as completely bilingual since their English bore traces of some other mother tongue. Among our informants we are only qualified to guess at the bilingualism of those for whom the language of the interview (English) was a second language, since no data was obtained which would permit assessment of the degree to which their speech approximated native fluency in other languages. It can be stated with confidence that the AIIC interpreters interviewed were the most bilingual, while those who were not members of AIIC but for whom English was a second language were somewhat less bilingual. None of the informants, however, had difficulty expressing or understanding complex sociological or linguistic concepts which were introduced into the interviews. Varying degrees of bilingualism could be assessed from the tapes of interviews only in terms of relative degree of "accent" in spoken English and in the rate of production which, for one non-AIIC interpreter at least, was occasionally markedly slower and more hesitating than would be expected for a native speaker.

Interviews with 17 interpreters having different backgrounds and interpreting experiences have suggested two additional dimensions along which the role of interpreter seems to vary. The first of these is inextricably linked to the definition of an interpreter. It was asserted, above, that the term "interpreter" applies to one who has the requisite skills to receive messages aurally in one language and retransmit them orally in a second language. Such an individual is "an interpreter" when he uses these skills. The interpreter's skills may, however, be used in many different ways which are largely coincident with the situations in which interpretation occurs. He may, for example, interpret simultaneously, listening and speaking at the same time. Alternatively, he may alternate listening and speaking consecutively. He may also limit his interpretation performances to relatively every-day situations, or he may engage in interpretation of technical and/or specialized materials. Among the non-AIIC interpreters it is interesting to note that both the Central American and the Russian students had some experience with specialized materials, whereas the social workers and the bulk of the Central American's experiences were limited to materials which touch upon the daily experiences of their clients. Interpreter roles may then also be classified as being more or less specialized as to content and style.

By content we mean the topics dealt with in the materials interpreted (c.f. Hymes, 1968 and Ervin-Tripp, 1969). Though it is practically impossible to recruit interpreters who are expertly familiar with particular topics for each and every instance in which one would like to engage interpretation services, interpreters are, in fact differentially able to deal with different topics. AIIC recognizes this fact and makes much of the importance of providing interpreters with briefings, glossaries, and source materials in advance so that they may "bone up" on the vocabulary relevant to specialized conference topics.

By specialization with respect to style is meant the fact that interpreters differ in their willingness to undertake either simultaneous or consecutive interpretation assignments. One of the more experienced non-AIIC interpreters described in detail his procedures for controlling the situation so that he never was expected to render simultaneous interpretations, which he described as very difficult. He reported that he often interrupted speakers and insisted that they pause while he interpreted what they had just said, thus maintaining manageable units for consecutive interpretation. Among the AIIC interpreters, one made a point of saying that she really preferred consecutive interpretation, and would like to specialize in that form if sufficient opportunities arose for her to earn her livelihood from such activities. She was particularly frustrated by the anonymity of the simultaneous arrangements in which she was forced by economic exigencies to work most of the time. Another reported that she preferred the anonymous surroundings of the sound-proof booth. She was more comfortable being able to take off her shoes and relax in the relative privacy of the booth than in situations in which she was "on display".

Finally, the interviews suggest that interpreters differ in the extent to which they identify themselves with the role of interpreter, and this dimension may be of paramount importance. All the AIIC respondents thought of themselves as professional interpreters, as a dominant identification. In contrast the other interpreters, whom we can call "casual interpreters" had more varied self images. Several thought of themselves as primarily "language experts" whose roles included, but were not dominated by the role of interpreters. These included several, but not all of the Russian students (notably the most experienced among them) and the language-teacher/interpreter. Others, including this writer, the social worker as well as several of the Russian students and all but one of the people interviewed informally thought of themselves as primarily occupied with other activities and only occasionally as interpreters. There is, thus, a dimension of analysis which involves a continuum ranging from professionalism to extreme casualness with at least one intermediate category of linguists who are quasi-professionals. It is clear that most of the world's interpreting is done by quasi- or non-professional interpreters. What is not clear is how well they succeed or how, if at all, their skill as interpreters is associated with their self identification. We suspect that there may be non-conference interpreters who are equally skillful at the art as are many AIIC members. It would be of interest to learn whether the salience of the interpreter role was similar to that observed in the AIIC interviewees.

Of equal interest is the question of how the clients perceive interpreters having different self-images and different experiential backgrounds. As noted, the AIIC respondents reported that they thought their clients appreciated them more when they worked in the consecutive rather than the simultaneous mode. If the phrasing of these remarks has been correctly interpreted, and similar phrases were employed in independent interviews by seven of the nine AIIC members, the other two were present when one of the seven was interviewed, and agreed with their colleague's statement, then the concepts of respect and deference seem appropriate here. By their actions delegates to conferences employing consecutive interpretation convey to interpreters, through behavior which is somewhat deferential, that they respect the interpreter's skills and efforts. They seem to legitimate the power associated with control over the communicative channels, and value the work, and the interpreter doing that work. In contrast, delegates to conferences employing simultaneous interpretation generally are thought to lack proper respect. It is quite discouraging for an interpreter, who has done his best, to hear negative comments about the interpretation when mingling with delegates in a lobby after a session. This experience is not uncommon, since the interpreter is generally not recognized except by his voice.

The only information we have from the non-AIIC interpreters regarding the views of their clients comes from two of the Russian student interpreters and the former probation officer. The latter commented upon the impatience of American clients who continually urged him to speed up the process in his courtroom encounters. He attributed this to a general cultural trait that contrasted strongly with the more leisurely approach of the "Latins". He also suggested that some of the lawyers with whom he had worked knew a little Spanish and occasionally attempted to "play language expert", catching a particular phrase that they recognized and arguing about the interpretation without having a proper understanding of the context and therefore of the meaning. Thus we get the impression that at least some of his clients, in the consecutive courtroom situation, had as little respect for him and his skills as the AIIC informants felt delegates had for them under simultaneous conditions. On the other hand, he reported that his subsequent experiences interpreting for industrial and governmental groups (also in a consecutive mode) were more satisfying, in part because his role was accorded "proper" respect.

On the matter of clients' perception of the interpreter, the Russian student informants were both favorably impressed. These two informants were the most experienced of the group, and they both reported that in the context of the track and field competition and also in their previous interpreting experience in the United States and in the Soviet Union they had frequently had clients express interest in their work, and comment upon its apparent difficulty. We infer from the fact that our other non-AIIC interpreters enjoyed their limited interpreting experiences and generally would welcome the opportunity to do more, that these experiences have been rewarding. Had they felt themselves under-appreciated or ill-used it is doubtful that they would have desired more interpreting work since each of them had some other means of earning a livelihood. Of course the rewards apparently outweighed the frustrations for the AIIC members, otherwise these highly skilled individuals would probably direct their talents elsewhere in search of employment. We wonder, however, if the interpersonal rewards derived from the respect of clients might be somewhat greater for the casual and quasi-professional interpreters than for the professionals.

LOOKING AHEAD

The primary function of exploratory research such as that reported here is to uncover variables and possible relationships among variables for subsequent, more systematic investigation. Thus, it is appropriate to conclude this paper with a brief sketch of some of the possible directions for future research into interpretation as a social process.

Among the phenomena to be probed by application of survey techniques are the interpreters' experiences regarding the influence of varying degrees of bilingualism and biculturalism upon the quality of interpretation. The necessity for complete biculturalism in interpreters is probably rare, and we should like to document or disprove this assertion with more comprehensive and systematic data. We should also like to learn the extent to which interpreters do, or would like to, specialize both with respect to content and style, and to explore their reasons for doing so. This will also lead to the study of matters of self-identification and client perceptions as seen from the interpreter's perspective. It is hoped that it will be possible to develop another survey to be administered to clients in an effort to gather "better" data regarding their actual perceptions of interpreters working under different conditions and in different physical and social situations. It will be interesting to compare the client and interpreter reports of clients perceptions of the interpreters. Finally the surveys proposed will include background data regarding the language skills, national origins, and socioeconomic characteristics of client as well as interpreter respondents.

We do intend to develop experiments to assess the influence of visual clues upon the quality of interpretation, and if possible on the variations in quality which obtains, if any, under diverse working conditions. The quality of interpretation should also be assessed under experimentally controlled conditions in which the interpreters are and are not monitored, face-to-face interactive situations and electronically mediated situations, and when one or more relays are involved. We are particularly interested in investigating the extent to which interpreters identify (whether positively or negatively) with clients in monitored and unmonitored interpretation, and would like to discover whether the presence of monitoring has any effect upon the quality of interpretation when identification does occur. Finally, it should be possible to devise an experimental situation in which the limits of output quality can be investigated. Such an experiment would also be an appropriate setting in which to gather controlled data regarding the relationship, if any, between output quality and the client's perceptions of the interpreter.

Clearly the future research suggested above is an ambitious agenda. It is our hope that this conference will provide information that will aid us in establishing priorities, and perhaps also bring us together with potential collaborators.

REFERENCES

AIIC (International Association of Conference Interpreters). *Practical Guide for Users of Conference Interpreting Services.* Brussels: Union of International Associations, 1966.

Allport, Gordon, W., and Postman, L. The basic psychology of rumor. *Transactions of the New York Academy of Sciences*, Series II, VIII, 1945, 61 - 81.

Anderson, R. Bruce W. Perspectives on the role of interpreter. In Richard W. Brislin (Ed.)., *Translation: Applications and Research.* New York: Gardner Press, 1976.

Bavelas, Alex. Communication patterns in task-oriented groups. In D. Lerner and H. D. Lasswell (Eds.). *The Policy Sciences: Recent Developments in Scope and Method.* Stanford, California: Stanford University Press, 1951.

Ekvall, Robert, *Faithful Echo.* New York: Twayne, 1960.

Ervin, Susan, and Osgood, G. E., Second language learning and bilingualism. In C. Osgood and T. Sebeok (Eds.). Psycholinguistics, *Journal of Abnormal and Social Psychology*, 1954, *49*, 126 - 146.

Ervin-Tripp, Susan M. Sociolinguistics. In L. Berkowitz (Ed.). *Advances in Experimental Social Psychology.* New York: Academic Press, 1969.

Gerver, David. Empirical studies of simultaneous interpretation: A review and a model. In Richard W. Brislin (Ed.). *Translation: Applications and Research.* New York: Gardner Press, 1976.

Hymes, Dell. The ethnography of speaking. In Joshua A. Fishman (Ed.)., *Readings in the Sociology of Language.* The Hague: Mouton, 1968.

Lambert, W. E., Just, M. and Segalowitz, N. Some cognitive consequences of following the curricula of grades one and two in a foreign language. *Georgetown Monograph Series on Language and Linguistics*, 1970, *23*, 229 - 279.

Lambert, W. E. and Tucker, G. R. *Bilingualism sans larmes: An Experiment in the Bilingual Education of Children.* Rowley, Mass.: Newbury House, 1972.

Seleskovitch, Danica. Interpretation, a psychological approach to translation. In Richard W. Brislin (Ed.). *Translation: Applications and Research.* New York: Gardner Press, 1976.

Thiery Christopher. Can simultaneous interpreting work? *AIIC Bulletin*, 1974,*2*, (May), 3 - 7.

NOTES

1. Support for the research reported here was provided by the Organized Research Fund of the University of Texas at Arlington. The "we" employed in this paper refers to the author and Mrs. Deb Grant who served as research assistant and colleague during a significant portion of the data collection process. I should also like to express my appreciation to AIIC for providing various published materials and my special thanks to all of the interpreters who gave so generously of their time and hospitality.

Behavioral Aspects of Liaison Interpreters in Papua New Guinea: Some Preliminary Observations

Ranier Lang

Australian National University

Canberra

INTRODUCTION

For the past decade there has been a steadily increasing interest in the analysis of everyday conversation. Researchers have focused on how we open conversations, how we close them, how we interrupt, and recently, how we effect repairs in discourse. The research has been carried out on a corpus of tape-recorded American English (Schegloff, 1968; Schegloff and Sacks, 1973; Sacks et al, 1974; Schegloff et al., 1977), although Moerman's studies on Thai natural discourse confirm these findings (Moerman, 1972, 1977). Researchers have also begun the analysis of video-taped or filmed occurrences of natural conversation (Kendon, 1967, 1970; Goodwin, 1977a and b), and attempts are now being made to correlate the findings from the analysis of audio-tapes with those from video-tapes and films. It is clear that filmed instances (whether by video or sound film) of natural conversation provide a more complete record of the total interaction taking place as the researcher now has access to the same behavior the participants to the conversation had in the first place, and which they used to facilitate their understanding. Very often the only clue we give when we have finished talking, or are ready to begin, is a postural or gestural one, and without visual contact such clues will be missed, resulting in impaired communication.

In this paper I will examine in detail some postural and gestural clues, and how an interpreter does or does not react to them. There are several limitations to this, especially as my data derive from a non-Western environment: (a) as yet no complete model exists of normal conversational practice for English speakers (and by implication none exists for normal interpretational practice and how it might differ from conversational practice without interpreters); (b) as yet no model at all exists for normal conversational practice among the Papua New Guinea society from which my data derive. This has two important seemingly contradictory consequences: my paper is (1) heavily data-oriented, and (2) speculative through the interpretation of these data.

DATA AND METHOD

The data for this paper were collected in December 1975 in Laiagam in the Enga Province in the Highlands of Papua New Guinea.[1] There my colleague[2] and I filmed instances of Enga natural behavior, including approximately 2½ hours of Enga interpreters at work. In this paper I describe some of the behavioral mechanisms that operate in an interpreting situation, and the discussion is based on a small filmed segment of approximately five minutes duration of a court case conducted by a police sergeant. The languages involved are Enga, the local vernacular, and Tok Pisin, one of Papua New Guinea's three national languages. The actual filming was done by my colleague who endeavoured not to make a movie but to obtain a record (as complete and uninterrupted as possible) of what was actually happening: this entailed having all the participants to the court session on the film at all times and to have the camera stationary so as to allow us to observe changes in behavior by reference to previous behavior. Sound was recorded independently and later put on film with the help of synch marks. Each frame of the film was numbered consecutively by the developing laboratory, allowing frame by frame analysis of the data. I transcribed the tape recording with the aid of two Enga assistants, providing both a literal interlinear translation and a free one. Then I did detailed frame-by-frame analysis of each person's behavior on a moviola (a viewer with both sound and variable speed), correlating the behavior of each person with that of the others and what they said.[3]

THE SETTING

The court session took place out-of-doors; this was done at our request since the police station where it would normally have taken place proved too small and dark for us to record the event on film. This did not substantially alter the arrangement of the participants in relation to each other, as can be seen from the following two diagrams:

Interpreter (IP) Sergeant (S)

[counter]

Litigants

Normal arrangement inside police station

Interpreter (IP) Sergeant (S)

[bench

Litigants (D, K, C)]

Arrangement outside the police station

Inside all parties to the event would have been standing, outside they were all sitting down, IP and S in folding chairs, the litigants on a bench. Inside there would have been a distinct physical boundary (the counter) to separate the litigants from S and IP, whereas outside there was merely an empty space between them (which was partially filled by our soundman with the tape-recorder). Inside the number of spectators would have been nil, outside there was a substantial number of onlookers; the latter did not seem to influence the participants' actions significantly. The interpreter, being in the employ of the police, was not a neutral party, and this was communicated by his positioning himself: normally behind the counter with S; outside by his sitting next to S and across from the litigants. Thus, his primary orientation posturally was in the direction of the litigants, which was also S's primary orientation. He was an extension of S rather than a neutral intermediary which could have been signalled via a triangular arrangement. (The latter would have created certain difficulties since there were at least two litigants and he, therefore, would have always been closer to one than the other of the two). This meant that whenever either S or IP looked straight ahead they were looking at the litigants, while if they wanted to establish eye contact with each other they had to turn either their heads and/or their bodies.

TURN-TAKING

Taking of turns could be accomplished by auditory devices alone; e.g. speakers could arbitrarily agree that whenever speaker A pauses for two seconds or more, he has effectively relinquished his turn to B, or they could agree that each give a verbal signal at the end of his utterances such as "I am finished now" or "It is your turn now" and these are used, especially the latter when there has been a breach in the established order of taking turns. Similarly, the taking of turns with an interpreter could be accomplished along these lines as well, such that we ask the interpreter to talk now, or that the interpreter tells us that he is finished interpreting for the moment. I have documented such linguistic turn-taking devices for the Enga interpreters elsewhere (Lang 1975, 1976, 1977). When such strictly linguistic clues are absent, however, the participants, and especially the interpreter, whose presence is supposed to be felt as little as possible, must rely on visual clues and they do so extensively. It becomes encumbent for the interpreter, therefore, to maintain visual contact with all of his clients, but especially with the one who is talking.

Normally in a conversation we train our eyes on the speaker, or we do so periodically so as to make sure the party that is being addressed by the speaker (be it ourselves or someone else) is still the intended recipient; for it is through eye contact that we very often and exclusively signal who we pay attention to and who we are addressing ourselves to. In a court, e.g. without interpreters, the attention of the participants is usually on the party that is doing the addressing or that is being addressed, especially if it is a court where there are no lawyers involved. The judge secures the attention of the defendant by talking to him, and this talking-to-him involves considerably more than the mere act of talking. It involves his orienting his entire body in the direction of the defendant, sometimes literally talking down to him by bending forward, looking at him ("fixing him with his eyes") and other more subtle and still little understood features. The defendant in turn will orient his body towards the judge, keep a low profile by often keeping his head down, but nevertheless glancing periodically at the judge to let him know he has his attention; if he failed to periodically acknowledge that he is the recipient of the judge's message, he might well find himself confronted with a question like "Are you listening?" As regards the taking of turns, both judge and defendant, speaking the same language, would be thoroughly conversant with the clues each gives in regard to when he is coming to a close or when he is ready to talk, the clues being both linguistic and more narrowly behavioral; there is no doubt though, that they would heavily rely on the linguistic clues and interpret the others as ancillary ones against which they would check their strictly linguistic institutions.

But if we find ourselves confronted with a situation in which the linguistic clues are reduced to a minimum, and maybe not even a reliable one, non-linguistic behavioral clues assume a salience not previously noticed. If we assume, for the moment, that none of the parties to the conversation understands what the other is saying, how is it communicated to the other that the first party has finished and that it is the second party's turn? How is a pause to be distinguished from a finished utterance? Very often these matters are signalled via shifts in posture and gaze direction, a matter significantly attested to in my data.

THE COMPLAINANT'S BEHAVIOR

One of the participants, C, the complainant, exhibited two basic postures throughout the proceedings: one, an expository posture, the other a listening posture. The former involved sitting bent forward with his hands with outstretched fingers held together, almost as if he were trying to come closer physically to the person he was talking to. This posture he took whenever he had to say something which he considered of importance, and which he felt he had to elaborate on. He held this posture during the entire period he was pleading his case, whenever he felt persuasive arguments needed to be brought forth. This posture he maintained even through IP's interpretation of his talk, except after he had finished arguing and IP was interpreting the closing stretch of his speech. This posture he also took up when it was his turn to speak, but while he had yet to wait for IP to officially communicate this to him; this, incidentally, is one indication that he understood, at least in part, matters communicated to him in Tok Pisin, which officially needed to be interpreted for him into his native Enga.

In one example C went into the expository posture before S, the sergeant, had finished speaking, and before IP had had a chance to interpret. He stayed in that posture for 61.4 seconds when he began to go into his listening posture. With that he effectively signalled that what he had to say was finished and that he was relinquishing his turn to S. What is striking in this regard is the fact that C retained his expository posture when he relinquished his turn to IP, but that he regarded that as a different kind of relinquishing from the one he exercised when he let S take his turn (when he was in his listening posture); furthermore, when he relinquished his turn after 61.4 seconds it was not to IP, but to S, even though it occurred at a C/IP rather than a C/S junction. This is corroborated by another example (immediately following the first) where C again went into his expository posture as soon as the interpretation started, the latter preceding the former by .2 seconds. He remained in this posture somewhat into the beginning of IP's interpretation of his final utterance, but he went into his listening posture well before IP had finished interpreting.

C assumed his listening posture, sitting upright with legs crossed at the knees, and looking in the direction of IP/S, whenever he or one of the other litigants was addressed by S, whether it was by S directly or through IP. He also maintained this posture when asked a question which demanded a brief factual answer rather than an explanation. Thus, when S was questioning C's wife through IP, C remained in his listening posture during the entire exchange. When S was briefly questioning C after C's last utterance in his expository posture and after he had relinquished his turn to S by going into his listening posture, C remained in the latter posture and answered only briefly. Until then S had, for the most part, restricted himself to listening to C, very often looking down or at C or occasionally IP, but 3 minutes 44.3 seconds into the film he changed his posture, his movements became more decisive, and after another 12.8 seconds he had taken command of the situation and it was now he who was informing C rather than the other way around (as it had been until then). C, in turn, several times nodded in agreement during S's speech, indicating thereby that he understood at least the gist of what S was saying. C remained in his listening posture until 4 minutes 43 seconds into the film when he went into his expository posture again. That was at a point where S had announced his decision, IP had interpreted it, and C concurred with it, but apparently only half-heartedly for he now tried to plead his case once more. The fact that he could assume that it was his turn was brought about by a series of behavioral changes in both IP and S which signalled to him that S had finished.

THE SERGEANT'S BEHAVIOR

While S had still been holding the floor he had been using his arms extensively, pointing and gesturing, and after 4 minutes 8.9 seconds into the film he frequently tried to establish eye contact with C, looking at him and looking down again at his notepad. The frequency of such alternating behaviors, looking at C and looking down, decreased as IP came to the end of his turn, and the stretches of looking at or in the direction of C (⩚) and looking down or away from C (⩛) became progressively longer especially those where he was looking at or in the direction of C. When he was looking at C at one point for 6.3 seconds (a prolonged look in comparison to others which lasted as little as .2 seconds) C could rightly interpret this as an invitation to take his turn again, especially since it occurred towards the end of IP's interpretation. When IP had finished interpreting and S did not continue after that, C could go into his expository posture and begin to talk 1.1 seconds later. It should also be noted in this context that opening speech behavior is usually accompanied by a downward glance, a behavior which has been documented extensively for native speakers of English (Scheflen, 1973). When S did not exhibit such a downward glance (when IP's interpretation of his speech came to an end), C could legitimately interpret this as S relinquishing his turn and turning it over to C.

THE INTERPRETER'S BEHAVIOR I: AN OVERVIEW

IP acted markedly different from C and S when it came to taking turns and it seems he thereby signalled his status as a neutral rather than an active initiating party to the proceedings. IP looked mostly down and/or away from either C or S; he busied himself with his hands or arms, inspecting himself in detail. When he focused on either S or C it was not to acknowledge that he was an active listener to their speech, but rather to either let them know that they had been talking for too long and that therefore he would find it difficult to interpret their talk adequately if they did not stop, or to check whether the other party was concluding their speech so that he would be ready to interpret. 4 minutes and 13.8 seconds into the film IP was looking down at his hands, beginning to bend down as if to pick something up. S was coming to the end of his talk (he was finished 9.3 seconds later) and IP, as he was bending back up again, turned his head in the direction of S, looking at him for .9 seconds (1.2 seconds before S finished) after which he turned his head back to center and looked down again, having ascertained that S was indeed coming to a close and knowing that it would be his turn to interpret. But, rather than lowering his gaze and then turning it towards the intended recipient of his interpretation as he would have done if he were not interpreting, he left his gaze lowered, thereby signalling that he was interpreting; interestingly, as S began to lower his gaze, IP began to talk. S, in other words, behaved as if he was talking to C, by lowering his gaze (when IP began to talk), thereafter raising it and looking at C. C, on the other hand, responded to IP by looking at him, a behavior IP only responded to when he came to the end of his interpretation. During the main course of his interpretation, when he interpreted in the first person what S had said he would do, and through C's affirmative reply and through part of his final interpretation he kept his gaze down. He raised it to look at C at a point where he interpreted S's instructions to C which involved addressing C in the second person ("I sense he says: 'You come early tomorrow morning!' "), and it was at that point that S again behaved as if he himself had been talking to C, for while he had been looking at C through the main part of IP's interpretation he now lowered his gaze to look at C again after his (C's) reply and with the beginning of IP's interpretation of the reply. With C's last utterance (which was an affirmative reply) and its interpretation by IP, the latter began to turn his head to his left towards S, so that while he was not directly looking at him he could nevertheless observe him completely while at the same time observing some other event. Yet what he achieved with this turn was an orientation away from C and towards S, thus signalling that C had finished and it was now S's turn. IP began to orient himself away from S and towards the center again .7 seconds after S had begun to speak (S finished speaking 2.3 seconds later). IP's interpretation of S's instructions was accompanied by his looking down at his hand, and, as he came to the end of his interpretation, an upward movement of his head and eyes with his gaze focusing on C (beginning 1.6 seconds into his interpretation and lasting almost through C's entire reply), while IP's interpretation was finished .8 seconds after he had focused his gaze on C. This pattern was repeated again in the subsequent turn, along with that described for S above. S's gaze at C then served as the signal for C to go into his expository posture as described above.

THE NEED FOR VISUAL MONITORING BY THE INTERPRETER

The participants, when not directly involved in the proceedings, showed a disinterest in the proceedings by not "paying attention" (by looking at the ground or away from the other participants), while those who were actively involved maintained eye contact or tried to re-establish it periodically. Thus, when S was talking to D, the defendant, at the beginning of the proceedings, C was looking down, maintaining neither his expository nor his listening posture, but instead sitting motionless or busying himself with his hands, but in either case, not looking at the other participants. D, likewise for the remainder of the proceedings when the focus was on C, maintained a stance of non-involvement which was signalled via her looking down or away from the other participants.

IP's preferred mode, posturally, gesturally, and gaze-wise, was also one of non-involvement: he looked down or away from the other participants most of the time, he did not bend forward (as if to make a case), and he busied himself in a rather self-centered manner mostly by inspecting his left forearm and bringing his right arm over so as to be able to better focus on parts of his left forearm. He focused only on the other participants when he was not sure of the intentions of a speaker, especially whether he was coming to a close which would have involved his having to interpret. On three occasions IP's non-involvement backfired: once at 15.7 seconds into the proceedings (referred to hereafter as A^1); once at 2 minutes 7.2 seconds into the proceedings (referred to hereafter as A^2); once at 2 minutes 55.6 seconds into the proceedings (referred to hereafter as A^3). In each case he missed important behavioral clues which would have alerted him to the fact that the speaker was not finished yet, and in each case he had to interrupt his just-begun interpretation in order to let the previous speaker finish what he had to say. All three interruptions involved instances where the auditory clues might have led one to assume that the speaker had finished: two involved afterthoughts, while the other involved the speaker gathering his thoughts in order to bring his utterance to a close.

Let us deal with the interruption at A^3 first, as it differs behaviorally from the other two. 7.1 seconds before A^3 IP began to turn his head slightly to his left to focus his attention on S who, .8 seconds later began a series of postural changes which may have functioned as a preliminary to the shift referred to in the last paragraph of the discussion of the Complainant's Behavior above (which itself started 55.1 seconds later, 3 minutes 44.3 seconds into the film), especially since during this series of shifts (beginning 7.1 seconds before A^3 and lasting 18.1 seconds) S repeatedly looked at his notepad, bringing it into writing position, and at his watch. IP once having focused his attention on S held it there and remained oriented to S .1 seconds into his interpretation, when C also continued with his explanation, so that IP's shifting his attention away from S after he began interpreting must be seen as a response to C's continuing. C's linguistic behavior makes IP's beginning to interpret when he should not have, perfectly intelligible. C had in fact given IP all the linguistic clues that ordinarily go with someone relinquishing his turn: C had ended his utterance with ". . . he says you say!", thus effectively instructing IP to begin interpreting. He then added as an afterthought "I want it to be taken care of at home," with a comma intonation which he did not follow up for 1.1 seconds until IP began interpreting. Thus the instruction to interpret, followed by the afterthought, followed by the long pause, linguistically communicated to IP that he could now begin his interpretation. C's behavior, on the other hand, was not the turn relinquishing kind, for he remained in his expository posture, with his gaze fixed on IP, thus indicating that he was not yet finished, and quite possibly expecting IP to acknowledge that he was listening. IP did just that .1 seconds after he began interpreting, when he oriented himself away from S and towards the center again. He interrupted his interpretation .3 seconds after he had started to wait for C to finish 1.4 seconds later, and he continued with his interpretation after another .9 seconds with C finally relinquishing his turn behaviorally as well by gazing down and going into his listening posture (1.6 seconds later). IP made no attempt to repair his interpretation, but instead continued where he had been interrupted by C, probably because he had got no further than "He says:" when C had continued.

In the other instances of interruption caused by IP, he was both times self-oriented, looking at the back of his hands (at A^1) or inspecting his fingernails (at A^2). The linguistic and behavioral circumstances of the other participants were analogous, however, to the episode described above. In the IP-caused interruption beginning with A^1 there had been linguistic clues that S was coming to an end, both syntactically and intonationally: S had been lecturing to D, recounting what she had done and he had finished with the recounting 13.4 seconds into the film. He then made a moral judgement on what she had done ("that won't do,") with a comma intonation, followed by a nominal reference back to what she had done ("this sort of thing"). The linguistic cues indicated that he had finished his exposition .6 seconds before the interruption, and his initial behavior indicated that he intended to close his utterance, for while he had been steadily looking at D, beginning with the end of his recounting to when he finished saying "that won't do,", he looked down (i.e., away from D), but then he immediately looked at her again, indicating that he had changed his mind and wished to continue. His linguistic behavior, however, was so strong that both D and C interpreted his coming to a close .6 seconds before the interruption as his coming to a final close, for D lowered her gaze .4 seconds before then (she had kept it on S until then) and C continued his already lowered gaze (also .6 seconds before the interruption). S continued after 1.2 seconds, but not before IP had begun to interpret after .7 seconds at A1 , a project he immediately abandoned after S continued (.5 seconds later). Had IP been focusing on S, the speaker, he no doubt would have been alerted to the fact that S intended to continue. The continuation was sufficiently long for IP to start over again with his interpretation rather than to continue where he had left off when he was interrupted, even though he began again identically with his abandoned attempt.

The IP-caused interruption at A 2 was also caused by an afterthought on the part of S. S had been listening to IP, looking at him until 9.8 seconds before the interruption when IP started coming to a close and S lowered his gaze. IP stopped talking 1.6 seconds later and S then looked at C 2 seconds later for .7 seconds when he lowered his eyes and head; he began to talk .3 seconds after that. After 1.7 seconds he began to raise his head and eyes so that after a further .6 seconds he was looking at C again. He stopped talking just before the interruption and linguistically that appeared to be the end of his utterance, while behaviorally he remained in the continuation posture. IP had been looking down at his hands and a second before the interruption had bent the fingers of his left hand back into the palm to inspect his fingernails. He could not see, therefore, that S might be continuing, and since S's linguistic clues appeared to signal unambiguously the close of S's turn, IP began to interpret at A 2 , almost at the same moment as S came to a close. S, however, by then had come to realize that part of his question to C needed some further elaboration and began to talk again, but with such little force and apparent inconsequence that IP once more interrupted .9 seconds later and partly overlapped now with another attempt by S to complete his question .3 seconds after that. IP in fact stopped in mid-word this time to let S finish, and then waited for nearly a second before continuing with his interpretation. During the entire episode neither S nor IP turned to each other for visual signals that would have resolved the problem of whether S was finished and whether IP could proceed with his interpretation. IP steadfastly looked down at his hands, and S looked at C. As a result, both S and IP had to repeat parts of their message in order to obliterate the effects of each others' interruptions. IP's repair is especially instructive as he began with the first word of his interpretation, found himself interrupted, repeated the first word and began to utter the second, an attempt which he abandoned mid-way because of the renewed interruption, and then continued his interpretation by omitting the first word, but repeating the beginning part of the second and going on from there as if there had been no interruption:

Mena/interruption/Mena pa-ta-/interruption/pa-ta-p-u-mo-pa . . . . .
pig pig go-COM go-COM-PAST-3SG-DEC-TEM

When the pig disappeared . . . .

(COM = completive, 3SG = third person singular, DEC = declarative, TEM = temporal)

THE INTERPRETER'S BEHAVIOR II: DATA ON CLIENT-DIRECTED GAZES

Let us now look in more detail at where IP was turning his attention. Percentagewise he looked 55.4% of the time at his hands or arms, 23.1% at either S, C, or D (10% at S, 9.2% at C, and 3.8% at D), 5.8% at or in the direction of the camera, and 12.8% elsewhere; the elsewhere category comprises IP's watching spectators and/or events beyond and unrelated to the immediate circle in which the court case took place.[4] In particular, I would like to examine those instances where IP was turning his attention to his clients. There are two main classes, (i) when IP was talking, and (ii) when someone else was talking or was due to talk.

(i) When IP himself was talking it was usually towards the end of his interpretation that he turned his attention towards the person to whom he was interpreting, a behavior typical of turn-taking during normal conversation. IP conformed to this mode of behavior with but one partial exception where, instead of maintaining his attention on the other person through at least part of the other person's turn, he averted his gaze before he finished interpreting. Such focusing one's gaze on one's partner at the close of one's turn is exemplified nowhere better than at turns involving questions and orders or, in the context of our corpus, interpreted questions and orders. I will describe one such example in more detail[5] before turning to other determinants which influenced IP to focus his gaze on his clients while he was talking: (a) possible turns and (b) long stretches of interpreting.

IP finished interpreting a question to D 29.5 seconds into the film and as he finished began to focus his gaze on her for 2.7 seconds to wait for the answer. When the answer was not forthcoming, he repeated his question .2 seconds before he averted his gaze, and when this produced no answer, he once more tried to establish eye contact 3.8 seconds after he had averted his gaze by looking at D for 1.9 seconds; S in the meantime verbally asked for an answer which IP interpreted, followed by a tag expressing impatience which was also accompanied by IP's focussing his gaze on D:

Frame No. 48921 ⟵ .6 seconds ⟶ Frame No. 48935 ⟵ .4 seconds ⟶ Frame No. 48944

Si-l-i-pi   la-l-u-mu   ongo aki!

hear-PRES-2SG-Q   utter-PAST-3SG-SENS   DET   what

'Do you understand' is what I sense he says, what's the matter?

IP glances downward ⟶ IP begins to look at D ⟶

(PRES = present, 2SG = 2nd person singular, Q = question, SENS = sensed mode, DET = determiner)

Possible turns: When IP was turning to his client to whom he was interpreting at the end of his interpretation and his interpretation did not involve a question or order, it was at possible turn-taking junctures which involved an S/C turn. Thus he was interpreting for C and 1.3 seconds before he finished he looked at S for 2.2 seconds. His interpretation had involved interpreting to S C's answer to a question of S's and it would have been S's turn if he had wished to make use of this option. But C had maintained his expository posture which S interpreted correctly as C's wishing to continue; S let C continue, but not before IP had oriented himself towards C 1.5 seconds after he had finished looking at S since C was slow in taking up his turn (he finally continued after another second). Similarly, in another example, IP was interpreting C's answer to S. When it would have been S's turn, he looked at S, but S was looking at his hands, giving no indication whether he wished to take up his turn or let C continue. When IP checked again he found S looking at C, with C continuing with his argument .3 seconds later and IP began to orient himself away from S towards C .9 seconds later.[6]

Length of utterance: Aside from these occasions IP almost never looked at his clients when he was interpreting, except when he had a long stretch of speech to interpret to S. In one piece of interpretation lasting 11.1 seconds he looked at S for .7 seconds, 3.5 seconds after he began interpreting, a gaze which occurred between two gazes at the camera, the first lasting .8 seconds, the other .6 seconds; he again looked at S for .2 seconds after 5 seconds of interpretation and for 1 second after 6.1 seconds of interpretation, the latter two interrupted by a gaze away from S, but in such a way that he could keep S in view. The first gaze 3.5 seconds into his interpretation appears to be related to its being sandwiched between two gazes at the camera (it found a repetition when S was talking for 22.2 seconds, when IP looked at S for .7 seconds 10.4 seconds into S's speech, also between two camera gazes; notice that the gaze came at about the midway mark of S's speech). The second one (5 seconds into his interpretation) appears to be related to the length of the utterance. IP's interpretation lasted just over 11 seconds (266 frames) and his gaze focused on S after exactly 5 seconds (120 frames), about mid-way through his interpretation. In another instance during an interpretation which lasted 20 seconds (480 frames) the beginning of his gaze came after 10.2 seconds (246 frames): he looked at S, the addressee of his interpretation, when he had finished interpreting one segment of C's exposition and before he began interpreting the second; during his interpretation he paused several times. These midway gazes are probably attempts to secure the addressee's attention during longer stretches of interpretation.

Finally, a gaze to a person other than the addressee of IP's interpretation is likely to take place when the interpretation is about the person to whom the gaze is directed, such as when IP was focusing his gaze on D when he was talking to C; he did so while talking to C about what D had done.

(ii) When one of his clients was talking, IP looked at them (a) when they appeared to have answered a question and (b) when they appeared to have finished. In one example, 51.1 seconds into the film, IP looked at C 2.3 seconds after C had started talking. That was at a point when in terms of criteria for what constitutes an answer C had answered S's question. However, C went on, elaborating on his answer, with IP looking at him once more 9 seconds after the first gaze, again at a point which one might consider a possible closure to an answer.[7]

Instances of IP focusing his gaze on his clients when they appeared to be coming to a close occurred 1 minute 44 seconds into the film, .1 seconds before C finished his speech which had lasted 20.2 seconds, and 4 minutes 16.6 seconds into the film, when IP glanced for 1.2 seconds at S who had been talking for 19.8 seconds and continued to talk for another 1.2 seconds after IP had already averted his gaze again.

There were three examples of IP focusing his gaze on the client who was not being addressed. One occurred 2 minutes 48.4 seconds into the film when C was talking. He paused 2 minutes 54.4 seconds into the film by which time he had wandered considerably off the topic of immediate concern at that point of the proceedings. IP had cast a puzzled look at C and, when C did not respond, turned his gaze to S, .1 seconds beyond the point when C continued to talk; the continuation coincided with IP's beginning his interpretation which he abandoned .3 seconds later. During a short break in S's instructions to C (which lasted 22.2 seconds, with the break lasting nearly 2 seconds) IP cast a brief glance at C lasting .2 seconds which occurred towards the end of one of C's nods to S's instructions, possibly an acknowledgment of the fact that he recognized C's comprehension of what S was saying. He also cast a glance at C .1 seconds after C began to talk at a point where the proceedings had appeared to be over while C's manner indicated he wished to continue, a move which came unexpectedly and prompted IP to check with a glance.

Finally, there were two occasions which involved IP's looking at S when S was formulating questions, once when S was asking a question, and once when S finished asking a question with IP looking at S half-way into his interpretation.

DISCUSSION

From the foregoing it is evident that the interpreter cannot stand in isolation, but must fit himself into the total interactional pattern obtaining between himself and his clients. Although his official role is that of a passive participant as far as the origination of primary conversation is concerned, the realization of that role depends on the active co-operation of his clients and the extent to which they wish to include him as an active participant not only linguistically but also gesturally, posturally, and gaze-wise. Likewise it is the interpreter who can by these means actively involve himself, or abstain from such involvement.

More importantly, however, the interpreter can greatly improve his performance by careful monitoring of his clients' behavior which is often a more accurate indicator of their intentions than their speech alone. While my observations have dealt with only the grossest manifestations of non-speech behavior, that behavior has turned out to be rich and complex; a corresponding micro-analysis will no doubt reveal further complexities. In particular, I have shown that constant visual monitoring by the interpreter of his clients, especially at turns or possible turns is an absolute necessity. Such visual monitoring has to be balanced by a corresponding behavior of passive involvement which can be achieved most readily by postural means.

The need for visual monitoring by the interpreter of his clients is sometimes alluded to in the German and English interpreter training schools; however, the students are not made acquainted with the systematic nature of clients' behavioral clues nor with a method of how they can utilize such clues best in the performance of their duty. While I have dealt only with liaison interpretation, it should be clear that the simultaneous and consecutive interpreter faces similar problems. Nevertheless, it is in the area of liaison interpretation, and especially the training of liaison interpreters that the greatest benefits could be derived from a greater awareness of the total interactional pattern of which the interpreter is a part. Only at one institute for training conference interpreters did students receive a thorough training in liaison interpreting. The range and depth of interactional problems that surfaced during that training was impressive, even though the problems tackled and officially perceived were only of a linguistic nature. As most translators are called upon to interpret occasionally by their employer, a grounding in liaison interpretation, both in its linguistic and other behavioural manifestations should be an integral part of the training program of any reputable school for translators and interpreters.

REFERENCES

Goodwin, C., *Some Aspects of the Interaction of Speaker and Hearer in the Construction of the Turn at Talk in Natural Conversation.* Ph.D. Dissertation. Philadelphia: Annenberg School of Communications, University of Pennsylvania, 1977a.

Goodwin, C., *The Interactive Construction of a Sentence in Natural Conversation.* Manuscript, 1977b.

Kendon, A., Some functions of gaze-direction in social interaction. *Acta Psychologica*, 1967, *26*, 22 - 63.

Kendon, A., Some relationships between body motion and speech. An analysis of an example. In Siegman and Pope (Eds.), *Studies in Dyadic Communication*, Elmsford, N.Y.: Pergamon, 1970.

Lang, R., Orderlies as interpreters in Papua New Guinea. *Papua New Guinea Medical Journal*, 1975, *18*, 172 - 177.

Lang, R., Interpreters in local courts in Papua New Guinea. In O'Barr and O'Barr (Eds.)., *Language and Politics.* The Hague: Mouton, 1976.

Lang, R., Technical aspects of oral interpretation. In Wurm (Ed.), *New Guinea Area Language Study Vol. 3. Language, Culture, Society and the Modern World. Pacific Linguistics C40.* Canberra: The Australian National University, 1977.

Moerman, M., Analysis of Lue conversation: providing accounts, finding breaches, taking sides. In Sudnow (Ed.)., *Studies in Social Interaction.* New York: The Free Press, 1972.

Moerman, M., The preference for self-correction in a Tai conversational corpus. *Language*, 1977, *53*, 872 - 882.

O'Barr, W. M. and J. F., (Eds.)., *Language and Politics..* The Hague: Mouton, 1976.

Sacks, H., Schegloff, E. A., and Jefferson, G., A simplest systematics for the organization of turn-taking for conversation. *Language*, 1974, *50*, 696-735.

Scheflen, A. E., *How Behavior Means.* New York: Gordon and Breach, 1973.

Schegloff, E. A., Sequencing in conversational openings. *American Anthropologists* 1968, *70*, 1075 - 1095.

Schegloff, E. A., and Sacks, H. Opening up closings. *Semiotica* 1973, *8*, 289 - 327.
Schegloff, E. A., Jefferson, G., and Sacks, H., The preference for self-correction in the organization of repair in conversation. *Language*, 1977, *53*, 361 - 382.
Siegman, A., and Pope, B. (Eds.). *Studies in Dyadic Communication*. Elmsford, N.Y.: Pergamon, 1970.
Sudnow, D. (Ed.)., *Studies in Social Interaction*. New York: The Free Press, 1972.
Wurm, S. A. (Ed.). *New Guinea Area Language Study Vol. 3. Language, Culture, Society and the Modern World. Pacific Linguistics C40.* Canberra: The Australian National University, 1977.

NOTES

1. Funds for the research and much of the analysis were provided by the Australian National University. Harold Garfinkel kindly provided me with office space at the University of California at Los Angeles, and through the good offices of Michael Moerman I was able to obtain access to suitable viewing equipment at UCLA's Film and TV Archives.

2. Adam Kendon, director of the Human Ethology Laboratory at the Australian National University.

3. The film was shot at 24 frames/second and all time references in the body of the paper are based on a prior identification of the segment in question in terms of frames. At the suggestion of the editors I have converted most references to frame numbers into time segments. Similarly, in the interests of intelligibility I have omitted from the paper for publication most of the precise frame numbers (or their time equivalents) necessary to identify a given behavioral segment on the film. However, a few of the footnotes still maintain the style and preciseness of the paper as originally written for the Conference. Any 5 digit number between 48000 and 55000 in the paper is to be understood as referring to a particular frame on the film which has that number printed on it.

4. The direction of 2.9% of the gazes could not be determined from the film.

5. Three other examples of IP focusing his gaze on the recipient of an interpreted question occurred at (1) 49186 to 49265 when he was interpreting towards C from 49109 to 49203, (2) at 51177 to 51269, also towards C when he was interpreting from 51120 to 51177, and (3) at 53142 to 53172, again towards C, when he was interpreting from 53040 to 53139. There is one example of IP looking a C (from 54391 to 54431) when he interpreted an order to C from 54391 to 54431, with C responding from 54431 to 54461.

6. Other examples of IP focusing his gaze on his client at possible turns are the following: When IP was interpreting C's answer to S's question from 53290 to 53430, he looked at S (beginning with 53429 to 53538), again because it was S's turn. This was also true of his interpretation of C's response from 54461 to 54490 when he looked at S from 54485 to 55431, expecting it

to be S's turn. The same phenomenon could be observed when IP was interpreting S's informing C from 54590 to 54648 and looking at C from 54629 to 54669; again when he was coming to the close of his interpretation from 54680 to 54779 of S's informing C when he briefly glanced at C from 54768 to 54770, a glance to which D did not respond, and which prompted IP to again look at C from 54810 to 54824, when C had moved into his expository and began talking (at 54827). And when IP came to the end of his interpretation from 52283 to 52763 (with S being the addressee), and it was S's turn, IP looked at S from 52733 to 52784, with S beginning to ask a question of C at 52868.

7. The same phenomenon occurred once more when C was talking from 51188 to 51459, with IP looking at him from 51314 to 51345, and when C was talking from 51824 to 52193, with IP looking at him from 51846 to 51881.

On the Representations of Experience

Paul A. Kolers

University of Toronto

Toronto, Ontario

A key question for students of cognitive psychology concerns the representation of experience and of behavior. The question underlies work on memory, perception, psycholinguistics, and all other activities in which response to stimulation requires something other than "conditioning" as an explanation; in which, that is, there is some selection from, transformation of, or other processing directed at the stimulus. The phenonemon of bilingualism affords a particularly powerful way of approaching aspects of this question, insofar as it permits the investigator to present information in one of a bilingual person's languages and test for it in the other. Careful observation and judicious inference can then permit the investigator to make some assumptions about the nature of representation; in the course of things, he may also learn a good deal about bilingualism and the cognitive functions of the bilingual individual.

In my own work the question of representation – its adjunct is the structure and operation of the mind – has been as compelling as questions regarding the nature of bilingualism and the functioning of the bilingual individual; I have used one to illuminate the other. Here I will review some experiments of a few years ago, and some issues they bear on in respect both to bilingualism and to the nature of representation. My paper is addressed to the topic of bilingualism in a general sense, but not in a practical sense important to translating and interpreting; it is in the context of a theory of knowledge and of the operation of mind. The particular issues concern encoding and representing linguistic and pictorial stimuli, and the substance of my remarks is that representations are means-dependent, not general; that is, that what we know depends in some measure upon the means we used to acquire our knowledge.

Suppose that we use words to make sentences such as: *The boy kicked the ball; The ball was kicked by the boy; Der Knabe hat den Ball angestossen;* or *Il ragazzo ha calciato la palla.* All of these sentences make the same statement denotatively, and many psycholinguists would claim that they are equivalent and can be represented in the mind by a single abstracted form, for example Anderson (1976), Kintsch (1974), or Norman, Rumelhart and their colleagues (1975). In their view the abstracted representation is typically taken as independent of the means of acquisition of the information described.

Their assumption seems to be that on presentation of a sentence, say, the mind sees through the surface features of the sentence to an underlying relation, abstracts this relation and stores it, usually in some propositional form. Hence perception or encoding is at least a two-stage process of initial acquisition and assessment of the superficial features, followed by abstraction and storage of a propositional extract. (Parenthetically, it has been alleged that the superficial features, once assessed, are rapidly forgotten or discarded and only the semantic content retained. This claim has recently been shown to be quite wrong (Kolers, 1976).) Extended to the case of bilingualism, the argument predicts some form of generalized semantic store of information in the bilingual's mind, which his languages tap. Alterations or transformations of experience such as are commonly reported by bilingual persons, or failures of perfect translation across languages, are then laid at the door of structural limitation of the languages – availability of words, syntactic structures, and related linguistic properties – whereas the information abstracted from or projected into the linguistic forms is said to be in some abstract (hence language-free or metalinguistic) form, and the knowledge in the person's mind is common to them all. An alternative view is that knowledge is encoded in a means-dependent way, that what we know depends in part upon how we acquired the information and our skill in using it. The former takes an absolute view of the representation of information; the latter asserts that our knowledge is situational and relativistic. I shall describe some experiments directed at these issues.

LANGUAGE AS A SORTING DEVICE

Two studies were relevant to this question by showing how some properties of language affected perception and categorization of stimuli. Does one know the words of a language as words of a language, or does one know them as words plus language? If one has a common abstract store derived from presentation of a stimulus, seeing *pear* or *poire* should produce the same abstract representation of the fruit for a French-English bilingual, while remembering the language it appeared in should require an additional "unit" of memory, or altogether two units for the abstract representation plus the language. In one test French-English bilinguals were presented with long lists of words, one word per second, some lists wholly in English, some wholly in French, and some mixed, half English and half French, as one condition of the study, the language condition. In a second, color, condition they were again presented long lists of English words, but some lists wholly in black ink, some in red ink, and some mixed, half in red and half in black (Kolers, 1965). In both cases the people were to write down as many words as they could remember immediately after termination of each list. In the language condition the words in English were of course written in English, the words in French were written down in French; and for the color condition the words printed in black ink were written down with a black pen, the words in red ink with a red pen. The subjects recalled 9.1 words from the English list, 13.8 words from the French, average of single-language lists, 11.5; and they recalled 11.0 words in black and 11.5 words in red, average of single-color lists, 11.3. Hence they could recall about equal numbers of words from all the lists when the lists were homogeneous. Contrasting with these numbers are the numbers of words recalled from the mixed lists: 12.6 from the mixed-language lists, but only 5.7 from the mixed-color lists. The subjects recalled as many words from a linguistically mixed list as from single language lists, but when they were obliged to remember the color a word was printed in, they could recall only about half as many words as they could when color was not a required property of the response. The conclusion seems to be obvious that language of a stimulus is not encoded as a footnote or feature remembered along with or tied to the abstract representation. When the person sees *table* in black and *shirt* in red, the color of the print must be encoded as a separate feature of the stimulus; but when he sees *poire* or *pear*, the language of the words is given to a person who knows the language by the words themselves, and he does not have to recall some abstraction "particular fruit" plus a footnote for language. Hence, the language does not require treatment as a feature of the superficial representation, but operates as part of the coding scheme. Some properties of the coding scheme were studied in another test.

SEPARATE VERSUS COMMON REFERENCE

The question under test was whether we should regard the mind as an abstracting device, and information-processing as requiring at least two discrete steps or stages; or whether the means of acquisition are part of the information stored. This storage, moreover, might be of at least two forms, as a feature or footnote encoded along with the information, or as a categorizing or separating device.

One experiment used word association in an effort to tap into the bilingual's representation of experience (Kolers, 1963). In a word-association test the person is required to give as rapidly as he can the first word that comes in response to a stimulus word provided by the experimenter; the stimulus can be presented either in spoken or written form. In my tests the bilingual subjects were presented with stimulus words half the time in their native language, the other half in English, and they responded half the time in one language and half in the other. Tests were carried out with all four of the possible combinations: native stimulus-native response, English stimulus-English response, native stimulus-English response, and English stimulus-native response. There were four kinds of words, moreover: nouns naming every-day objects *(man, table, pencil, bicycle)*; imagery-eliciting words *(lamb, thorn, butterfly, smoke)*; words that named abstractions *(freedom, justice, wisdom, materialism)*; and words that named emotional states or feelings *(hate, jealousy, joy, love)*.

If information were abstracted into some common form that word associations tapped, then the response that a bilingual person made in his native language to some word in his native language should be a translation of the response he made in English to the English translation of that word. In the case of a Spanish-English bilingual person, for example, the word *table* as an English stimulus might elicit *chair* as response; and the word *mesa* ('table') as a Spanish stimulus would elicit *silla* ('chair') as a Spanish response. Here translation of stimuli would be associated with translations of response, and we could infer that information as represented by associations to stimulus words was encoded in some metalinguistic or abstract form that was a common source for which the two languages were expressive devices. If a large number of responses were of this kind, in which the responses shared their reference, we would have very strong evidence for some sort of two-stage process in representation.

As it turned out, however, only a small number of responses conformed to this sharing of reference, between 20% and 35%, depending upon the class of word and the criterion of similarity that was used, lexical or thematic. (A lexical criterion took as "same" only words that were dictionary translations, for example, only *leaf* as similar to *hoja* ('leaf'), whereas a thematic criterion accepted words more broadly, as *flower, blossom, bloom, plant, tree* were all thematically similar to *leaf*). On the other hand, between one-quarter and one-third of the responses were linguistically specific, the person giving one response in English to an English stimulus, a different response in the native language to the translation of the stimulus, and one or the other of these responses in the combined conditions, as *table-dish, mesa-silla* for the English stimulus-English response and native stimulus-native response conditions, respectively, and *table-silla* or *mesa-chair* for the combined conditions, for example. The remaining third of the responses were not scorable in either of these ways.

In this breakdown of the data, therefore, two-thirds of the responses were inconsistent with the hypothesis of a common storage of information, the one-third that conformed to linguistically-specific associations (the second example above) plus the third that were not scorable, and only one-third conformed to that hypothesis. That one-third is too large a number to make acceptable the notion of wholly separate linguistic encodings, of course. Hence, to the degree that the test is appropriate to the question under investigation, the data suggest that the shared hypothesis of a common abstract representation is not itself correct; but the alternative of wholly independent systems is too severe. This conclusion is supported by an analysis of responses according to the kind of word. Words that referred to objects that people manipulated in similar ways independently of language – words such as *desk, book, scissors* – were more likely to have similar expressions across languages than were abstractions – *materialism, duty, liberty* – and these were more frequently similar than were the associations to words that referred to or named emotions.

In terms of the logic of the theory, however, the shared or common storage hypothesis is the conventional wisdom or common assumption, and people who wish to challenge that view and argue for linguistic specificity of encoding operations need only show how the common storage hypothesis is inadequate. This I believe I have done. In other experiments I studied other ways in which different languages, different encoding systems, served to create means-dependent representations rather than abstract or common ones, and the psychological requirements for them.

MEMORY FOR DETAILS

One concern was to evaluate empirically the accuracy of the allegation that people do not remember the language of the stimulus but only its semantic content. For the purpose, French-English bilinguals read 56 sentences of connected text of which one-quarter were in English, one-quarter in French, and half were in "Franglais", preserving either French or English syntax (Kolers, 1974). After reading the passage with intent to comprehend or understand it, the subjects were presented with 56 pages, one sentence of the story per page, the pages ordered as in the story. On each of the 56 pages each sentence from the story was accompanied by five alternatives. If the story's: 1) sentence had been in French, the alternatives were:

2) its translation into English; 3) Franglais that preserved French syntax; 4) Franglais that preserved English syntax; 5) the same order of words as 3) but French words translated to English and English to French; and 6) the same order of words as 4) with its words similarly translated. Following are some examples:

1. Court et carré dans son chandail épais, il les regardait monter.
2. Short and square in his thick sweater, he watched them climb.
3. Short et carré dans son chandail thick, he them regardait climb.
4. Court et square in his épais chandail, il regardait them climb.
5. Court and square in his sweater épais, il les watched climb.
6. Short and carré dans son thick sweater he watched les monter.

The same treatment was applied to all of the other sentences of the story, so that each page contained six semantically equivalent versions of each sentence of the story. The subject's task was, on each page, to pick out the one version that had appeared in the story. If all that the subject remembered of each sentence was its gist or meaning, coded in some abstract form, he should not be able to choose accurately among the alternative expressions of that meaning, so each of the six alternatives should be chosen about 17% of the time. In fact, however, subjects remembered the superficial appearance with better than chance frequency, about 28% of the time. Although this is not a large number, we may wonder that appearance was remembered at all. Did subjects retain for a longer interval than was previously thought possible some pictorial representation ("snapshot" or "icon") which they could scan at the time of the test? To evaluate this possibility, the experiment was repeated with a slight variation.

Sentences were taken from a Sanskrit reader and were printed in the Devanagari alphabet (Figure 1), but the subjects were unfamiliar with both Sanskrit and the Devanagari alphabet. They were in other ways similar to the first group, however, so that if some pictorial memory of the stimulus had underlain the first group's performance, that should be expressed in the performance of the second group as well. In this test the subjects scanned 56 sentences in Devanagari script under instruction to "examine the text as if they were reading it", and then were presented with 56 pages on each of which appeared a sentence from the passage plus three others from other parts of the reader, four in all. If a "photographic memory" – in whatever psychological guise that notion is expressed, icon, image, or whatever – were the basis of the first group's above-chance performance, the second group should perform equivalently. To the contrary, they performed at the chance level, 24.9% correct. Moreover, when the test was repeated, the subjects now knowing exactly what to look for, performance improved only about 10%.

The experiment was carried out in another way on another group of subjects. The same sentences were transliterated and presented in the English alphabet (Figure 2), other conditions remaining the same. Required to indicate which of four sentences per page had appeared in the original passage, these subjects perform-

इतश्चास्ति तस्यामेव मनुजगतौ नगर्यामगृहीतसङ्केता नाम ब्राह्मणी । सा जन-
वादेन नरपतिपुत्रजन्मनामकरणवृत्तान्तमवगम्य सखीं प्रत्याह । प्रियसखि प्रज्ञाविशाले
पश्य यच्छ्रूयते महाश्चर्यं लोके यथा कालपरिणतिर्महादेवी भव्यपुरुषनामानं दारकं
प्रसूतेति । ततः प्रज्ञाविशालयोक्तं । प्रियसखि किमत्राश्चर्यम् । अन्यद्भूमेरुद्भूतम् ।

(A)

1. प्रियसखि प्रज्ञाविशाले पश्य यच्छ्रूयते महाश्चर्यं लोके यथा कालपरिणतिर्महादेवी भव्यपुरुषनामानं दारकं प्रसूतेति ।
2. समाकर्णय ।
3. भद्राः शृणुत ।
4. समस्तगुणभारभाजनमेष वर्धमानः कालक्रमेण भविष्यतीति ।

(B)

Figure 1. Part of a Sanskrit passage written with the Devanagari alphabet (A). The task was to identify which of four sentences had actually appeared in the passage (B).

Itascasti tasyameva manujagatau nagaryamagrhitasamketa nama brahmani. Sa janavadena narapati putrajanmanama-karanavr-ttantamavagamya sakhim pratyaha. Priyasakhi prajnavisale pasya yacchruyate mahascaryam loke yatha kalaparinatirmahadevi bhavyapurusanamanam darakam prasuteti. Tatah prajnavisalayoktam.

(A)

1. Priyasakhi prajnavisale pasya yacchruyate mahascaryam loke yatha kalaparinatirmahadevi bhavyapurusanamanam darakam prasuteti.
2. Samakarnaya.
3. Bhadrah srnuta.
4. Samastagunabharbhajanamesa vardhamanah kalakramena bhavisyatiti.

(B)

Figure 2. The same text as Figure 1 but transliterated approximately to the English alphabet.

ed at better than the chance level; moreover, their performance improved notably with repeated trials. The first group of subjects was able to evaluate the Devanagari alphabet only as so many marks on a page, and there were far too many to encode; performance was at chance level. When the second group of subjects examined the same sentence but in the English alphabet, their performance was better. These subjects were familiar with the graphic pattern – the letters of the alphabet, albeit strung out into meaningless sequences – and recognized more of the sentences composed of them. Best performance occurred when the graphic pattern could be interpreted, as by the bilingual subjects reading sentences in French and English. Figure 3 shows the consequences of the progression in the perceived properties of the stimulus, from mark to letter to word, in a corresponding progression in recognition. (In the figure the six-alternative French test and the four-alternative Sanskrit have been adjusted to a common baseline that discounts chance performance).

Neither the stimulus scale nor the response scale is composed of equal intervals, so it is difficult to say whether the advantage created by the semantic component (the French stories) is greater, compared to the literal (English alphabet), than the advantage of the literal is to the graphemic (Devanagari alphabet). On inspection the advantages seem about equal. Moreover, the performance of the students who remembered the appearance of sentences cannot be attributed to an iconic or other pictorial memory; that same memory would have operated in the second group of students to enhance recall of the Devanagari script. Rather, skill in operating on graphemic objects in a familiar symbol system seems to provide a better account of performance, and suggests once again that encoding and memory of sentences is a means-dependent process.

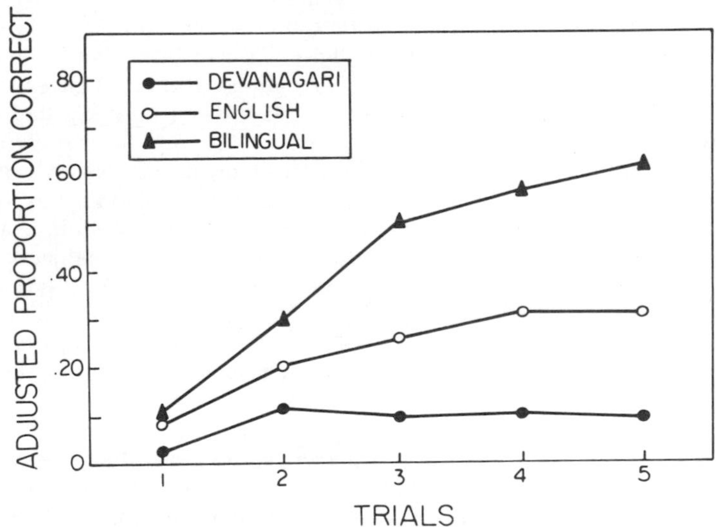

Figure 3. Performance on the Sanskrit passages and on a French-English passage, normalized to a common baseline.

The value of knowledge of the elements of the symbol system is shown in still another study, which took advantage of a well-known finding in education, that repetition tends to enhance recall, and applied it to the study of bilingualism and the nature of the representation of language and experience (Kolers, 1966). In terms of learning lists or words, the finding is that if some word in a list is repeated, the likelihood of its recall increases proportionately with an increase in the frequency of its repetition: a word that appears four times in a list is twice as likely to be recalled as a word that appears twice, other things remaining unchanged. The question under test was whether it mattered that the repetition was in one or the other of a bilingual's languages. Suppose, to illustrate the matter, that the words in a single list were as follows:

shoe	book	snow	
hat	book	neige	etcetera

The question concerns the recall of *snow* [or *neige* ('snow')]: As a graphemic pattern, *snow* appears only once in the list; will it be remembered with the frequency that characterizes recall of *shoe* or *hat,* or with the frequency that characterizes *book*? If words were perceived and stored only as graphemic objects, the frequency of recall would be that of *shoe* or *hat*; but if the semantic features were also perceived and coded, then *neige* could influence the recall of *snow* by the French-English bilingual who knows that the words translate each other. With a number of long lists of words, just the latter outcome was obtained: two presentations of a word in English and two presentations of its translation in French produced the same likelihood of recall as four presentations in one or the other of the French-English bilingual's languages.

At the time of their initial report I tended to emphasize in the data the semantic aspect of the encoding of the words, perhaps even to the neglect of the graphemic. An important aspect of the data was therefore under-represented in the report – the fact that there were remarkably few 'false alarms', false translations, or substitutions. By 'false alarm' I mean subjects "recalling" in one language words that appeared only in the other, "recalling" *chapeau*, say, when only *hat* had been presented in the list, or "recalling" *door* when only *porte* had been presented. By 'false translation' I mean that subjects "recalled" in Language 2 also a word that had appeared in the lists only in Language 1; and by 'substitutions' I mean subjects recalling *star* and *étoile*, say, when *star* and *astre* had been the stimuli. Altogether more than 7,000 words were recalled by the several groups of subjects from the many lists that were presented, but only 23 were false alarms, 27 false translations, and 9 were synonym substitution. In other words, not only did the semantic aspect of the words facilitate their recall across languages – the main effect described above – in addition, the subjects were remarkably accurate in recalling the words in respect to their surface features.

Of course one could argue that in perceiving and encoding a word the subjects encoded its semantic properties plus a footnote or tag to indicate the language of appearance. The subjects doing so would have yielded lower overall recall, however, for this would have meant encoding "concept" or "meaning" plus language or two units of memory. In the experiment, some subjects recalled lists of words none of which were translated or all of which were translated; and other subjects recalled words from mixed lists, that is lists made up of words some of which were and some of which were not translated. The subjects could readily see the kinds of lists they were responding to. Thus, if none of the words in a list were translated, or all were, the subjects could encode that fact once for a list, in a general way; whereas if some words in a single list were and others were not translated, the subjects would have to encode the fact of translation separately for each word. Predicting from the experiment on single-color and single-language lists described above, one would expect that the latter strategy would lead to *fewer* recalls from the mixed lists than from the homogeneous lists. No such diminution was found in the data, however; no additional "unit" of memory was required to maintain the surface features of the words in memory. Hence a better interpretation of the data is this: the subjects perceived and encoded the semantic features of the words; but that is only one of many features whose encoding forms the internal representation of the stimulus. In addition to the semantic features the subjects encoded the language, the spelling, and perhaps even the typography, along with the time of day, place, identity of the experimenter, and everything else that they could encode. To put it another way, the subjects did not extract a semantic core from the stimulus to which they added footnotes about language, time, place, and the rest; rather, the encoding of the physical event included the meaning of the word, the language of its appearance in the list, the occasion, and much else besides. The event itself was encoded, and its physical features form it and are part and parcel of its representation.

Any object in the environment has an infinite number of features; from this infinitude, those are encoded according to the skills available and appropriate to the task at hand. Our representation of that stimulus is then in terms of the skills we apply. As our skills and purposes may vary, so too will our encodings. Rather than in some common, abstract form to which footnotes are added as details, our representations are specific and situational. Moreover, mental skills and operations place even further constraints upon the notion of commonness of representation, as I shall now show.

SPECIFICITY OF OPERATIONS

I have written so far only about translation and equivalence of words; I turn now to operations. It is very well known in the literature on bilingualism that translation is a chancy business, and that perfect translations simply do not exist, if for no other reason than that the reference of translated words is often different in the two languages (Catford, 1965). These sorts of observation might be sufficient to argue against the notion of commonness of representation, but I have carried the matter further with the experiments I described above. Still another aspect of language use, however, and of the representation of experience, concerns the *operations* we perform upon our received worlds. Many mental operations characterize our encoding of experience; a few of them are listing, ordering, counting, inferring, translating.

The notion of common representation must assume that the person can always operate on a stimulus in the same way independently of the language he is using, that neither the acquisitive nor the combinatorial nor the expressive operations affect the abstract representation. Suppose however that mental operations were not general. Then, the encoding in one language would produce a different representation from that in another, and the notion of commonness of representation would again be questioned. Just this was the outcome of some other tests I carried out.

As a matter of convenience I chose for study the operations of listing and inverting lists (ordering). Bilingual students at American universities were the subjects; their native language was French, German, Arabic, Korean, or Thai (Kolers, 1964). Their task was first to say the alphabet in English and in their native language, and then to say one or the other of those alphabets backwards. Saying the alphabet forwards is a simple matter of listing items, usually well-practised; saying the alphabet backwards requires subjects to invert or reorder the list. Doing so produces unfamiliar sequences, and we studied the acquisition of skill at the task. Half the subjects in each group inverted the alphabet in English and the other half did so in their native language; after 60 trials the subjects were tested for their ability to invert the other: those who had practised in English, were tested in their native language, and those who had practised in their native language were tested in English.

If the mental operation of inverting a list were a general cognitive skill, then practice on one list should readily transfer to performance on others. If, on the other hand, the skill were specific to the items on which it was practised, the degree of transfer would depend on similarity of items in the lists. The more similar the items of the test list to the items of the practice list, the greater the degree of transfer from practice to test. The data supported the latter view, for practice on French or German and English yielded high degrees of transfer to the other (their alphabet are very similar); transfer between Arabic and English was poorer but marked (the Arabic alphabet has the same origin as the English, and some letter sequences are similar, as in the initial *alif, bey, say,* and a mid-list *kef, lam, mim, nun*); and transfer between Korean or Thai and English, if it existed at all, was negligible. Hence, the finding was that the task trained not a general operation of inverting lists, but a specific one of inverting a sequence of symbols, perhaps better, of sounds; and the degree of transfer between training and test was greater the closer the sounds were in any two sequences.

To guard against the possibility that some hidden feature of bilingualism irrelevant to the question of interest was responsible for this result, the experiment was carried out unilingually also. In one test half of a group of American university students learned to say the alphabet backwards, the same task of list inversion as before, and then said a familiar nursery rhyme backwards; the other half of the group inverted the nursery rhyme and then were tested with the alphabet. The sequence of sounds in the two cases is almost wholly different, and transfer was similarly slight, about 10%. To show that the transfer was specific to surface features rather than was a general property of mind, another group of subjects learned to say one nursery rhyme backwards and then were tested with another, both having similar metrical structures. ("Mary had a little lamb" and "Twinkle, twinkle, little star"). Transfer of skill across the tasks reached about 30%. Rhyme or meter aided the reorganization of the words of the nursery rhymes but not to a very great degree; the subjects ordered (or reordered) a set of words, they did not learn a general mental operation that could be applied to any of many stimuli. Means-dependent and object-dependent learning seem to be the processes occurring here.

Many other operations are language-specific. Bilingual subjects I have studied or interviewed tended to do their mathematics in the language of acquisition; arithmetic in one language, algebra in another, calculus in a third is not uncommon. Indeed, most kinds of computation (using the word broadly) seem to be means-dependent and situation-dependent skills rather than general ones. And to the degree that our encoding and evaluation of experience depend upon particular mental operations, then the qualities the bilingual person encoded must differ according to the skills he has practiced in each language. Hence, on this view both the representation of terms and the skills appropriate to encoding aspects of experience will reflect specific practice in a person's history, not general properties of mind.

KINDS OF SYMBOL SYSTEMS

Another point to raise against the hypothesis of common representation is the contrast that can be drawn between different kinds of symbol systems all of which are correlated with expressions in a *single* language. The particular contrast of interest here is between words or linguistic symbol systems and pictures or pictorial systems. In a well-known experiment that I use as an example only, Clark and Chase (1972) argued for commonness of representation, albeit in the context of a verification experiment. In their view the marks "*" and "+" combined as "$\overset{*}{+}$" have the same representation as the sentence "The star is above the plus sign." By extension, the argument is that, mentally, pictorial and linguistic representations are in a common form. I believe that their argument is wrong, and that, moreover, their example is not appropriate to their claim.

One point to note is that the term "pictorial" used in the present context is ambiguous. Any mark on a surface is a pictorial object. Some marks that are endowed with meanings exist both as marks on a surface and as semantic objects; marks such as +, &, %, 8, p, OK are examples insofar as they represent terms such as addition, summation, percentage, the quantity eight, probability, and agreement. Other kinds of mark that function in this same way are electronic symbols, such as a zigzag line to represent resistance, two parallels to represent capacitance, and the like. When marks can be ordered according to rule, we may write sentences with them. For example, "3 + 2 = 5" is a sentence, and an engineering drawing that shows a zigzag line beneath two parallels, their ends connected, is a sentence. (It is translated as saying "Connect one side of the resistor to one side of the capacitor and connect the second side of the resistor to the second side of the capacitor" or, alternatively, "Connect the resistor and the capacitor in parallel.") The letters of the alphabet, when ordered according to the orthographic rules of a language, function in a related way. Hence one aspect of the term pictorial is merely "mark on a surface" which may be interpretable within a symbol system.

A second meaning of the term refers to pictorial qualities – color, spatial position, size, texture, medium (water, oil, print) and the like. In an engineering drawing that shows a number of elements such as resistors, capacitors, transistors, or even integrated circuits – all of the elements represented by particular marks – the interest is usually in the connections illustrated, and it does not matter what size or color of ink they are printed in. Similarly, in the sentence "Beauty is truth, truth beauty", it usually does not matter in what typeface or color of paper the line appears; we are interested in what Keats might have meant by the sentence. The engineering drawing and the words function in the same way, for the marks in the engineering drawing are interpreted in respect to their syntactic and semantic relations, not their "pictorial" ones. But suppose that we look at an example of calligraphy (Figure 4) or at a painting by Rothko, say. Nothing can be ignored or altered in either without changing the objects; there is no way to specify exactly which aspects of the marks are important to or constitutive of the work and which aspects are accidents of construction. The marks in the sentence and in the engineering drawing serve as elements in a linguistic symbol system, but the marks in the calligraphy or painting cannot be characterized in terms of units or elements; as Goodman (1968) has shown, linguistic symbol systems are made of discrete elements, whereas pictorial symbol systems are dense and continuous. Only by imposing a linguistic sectioning upon a picture can we identify "objects" or "elements" in a painting or other set of marks that we are examining pictorially.

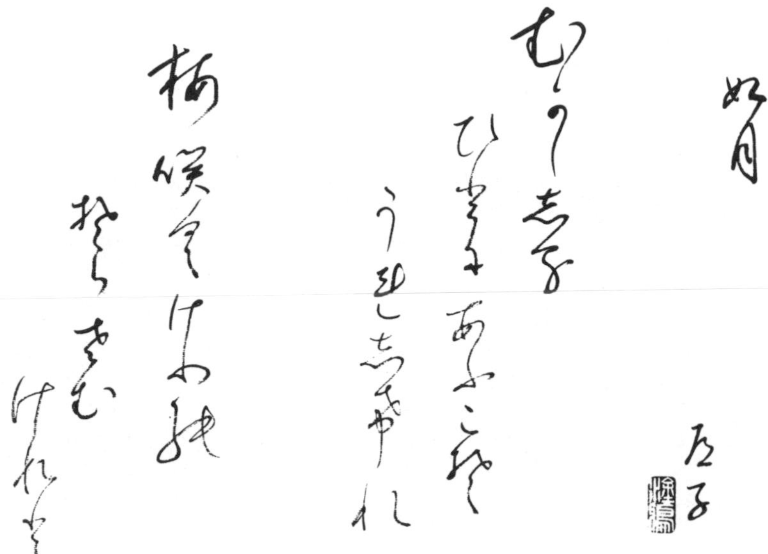

Figure 4. The poem *Kisaragi* ('February'), in a form of grasswriting, by the modern Japanese poet Michiko Toda. It can be translated as "Though the light of the sky is cold today over a cherry tree in blossom, My heart is warm in greeting a friend from old times." (Collection of the author.)

A confusion here characterizes the assertion of Clark and Chase (1972). They use spatial position in a semantic way ("above, left, right, below") and make sentences which actually translate each other in two different symbol systems. Positioning a star above a plus is exactly analogous in a linguistic symbol system to writing "star is above plus sign", but the two statements are wholly indifferent to the "pictorial" features of size, shape, color, texture, exact position, and so on, both in the marks of plus sign and star, and in the words themselves (type style, kind of paper, size of letters, etcetera). In sum, then, Clark and Chase have written the same sentence in two different writing systems; they have not compared a picture to a sentence. One could do fundamentally the same study if the two sentences were written in the English alphabet and the Cyrillic or the Hebrew, say. Just as one can transliterate many languages into the English alphabet – Russian, Hebrew, Japanese – so too one can write sentences with letters that stand for words or with other marks interpreted linguistically. Doing so is a far cry from demonstrating that words and pictures have a common cognitive representation.

Of course we may also note that the neural operations that encode words and pictorial events must needs be different. The pictorial objects of yellow light and blue light, when combined, yield a perception of gray or, as pigments, a perception of green. But the words *yellow* and *blue* do not combine similarly to yield *gray* or *green.* Hence the nervous system responds to the colors differently from the way it responds to the words that name the colors, and combines the colors differently from the way it combines the words. If then within a single mind different kinds of symbol systems operate differently, some digital and others analog, is it not possible, indeed, is it not likely, that across language symbol systems may be sources of differential partitioning of the experienced world?

A final word concerns the term "representation". I have argued above that a person's knowledge depends upon the symbol system he used for encoding the information of interest, and his skill in carrying out the cognitive operations that the encoding required. The conclusion I draw from this review is that we do not propositionalize our worlds so that what we know is abstracted across all acquisitive instances; our means of acquisition are part of our representation. Our knowledge has an operational basis to it – what we know is what we know how to do – although it need not be wholly operational. If we have learned to carry out different operations in different contexts with different symbol systems or different media, then our representations of the world will vary with, or at least depend upon, the symbol system or medium in which we are operating. The implication of the arguments I have made is that our world is not single but is multiple; we encode its aspects according to our skills in operating with different symbol systems. Moreover, we are not "single" either, but express ourselves with different operations in different contexts.

REFERENCES

Anderson, J. R., *Language, Memory and Thought*. Hillsdale, N.J.: Erlbaum, 1976.

Catford, J. C., *A Linguistic Theory of Translation*. London: Oxford University Press, 1965.

Clark, H. H., and Chase, W. G., On the process of comparing sentences against pictures. *Cognitive Psychology* 1972, *3*, 472 - 517.

Goodman, N., *Languages of Art*. Indianapolis: Bobbs-Merrill, 1968.

Kintsch, W. *The Representation of Meaning in Memory*. Hillsdale, N.J.: Erlbaum, 1974.

Kolers, P. A., Interlingual word associations. *Journal of Verbal Learning and Verbal Behavior*, 1963, *2*, 291 - 300.

Kolers, P. A., Specificity of a cognitive operation. *Journal of Verbal Learning and Verbal Behavior*, 1964, *3* 244 - 248.

Kolers, P. A. Bilingualism and bicodalism. *Language and Speech*, 1965, *8*, 122 - 126.

Kolers, P. A., Interlingual facilitation of short-term memory. *Journal of Verbal Learning and Verbal Behavior*, 1966, *5*, 314 - 319.

Kolers, P. A., Remembering trivia. *Language and Speech,* 1974, *17*, 324 - 336.

Kolers, P. A., Reading a year later. *Journal of Experimental Psychology: Human Learning and Memory*, 1976, *2*, 554 - 565.

Norman, D. A., and Rumelhart, D. E. *Explorations in Cognition*. San Francisco: W. H. Freeman and Company, 1975.

The Bilingual's Performance : Language Dominance,

Stress, and Individual Differences

Stanislav Dornic

University of Stockholm

Stockholm

I INTRODUCTION

The nonbalanced bilingual is much more typical of the present world than the balanced one. This is however by far not evident at first sight. The *apparent* balance of a bilingual's language systems is often due to strategies and compensatory processes which he has learned to employ when using his subordinate language. If his pronunciation is good and his lexicon reasonable, a mere simplification of speech will hide his slower functioning in the weaker language, less automaticity as well as inferiority in grammar and syntax. These shortcomings may well remain hidden until some stress is added. Information overload, environmental, emotional or social stresses, fatigue, all these factors may unveil the hidden imbalance between the dominant and subordinate languages. Stress enhances latent differences and renders them apparent: language dominance which under normal circumstances would not appear becomes evident under stress.

The difference between the dominant and subordinate language systems of a bilingual can be studied in many different ways, and analyzed on various levels. The present contribution deals with language dominance on an elementary level: it is concerned with the parameter of speed, and focusses mainly on decoding (comprehension) and encoding (production) of spoken language. Focussing on speed i.e. "automaticity" of the bilingual's linguistic performance, we will unavoidably be concerned with functions of short-term and long-term memory, mainly with rehearsal and memory search.

Simple processes and elementary operations that we will deal with seem sometimes to "get lost" when more complex processes are observed. However, it is those simple processes that most often cause a "chain reaction" – a considerable deterioration in more complex operations. If you are slower in an extremely simple task performed in your second language, you will also comprehend less when listening to a lecture in that language. The same applies to language production.

The first part of this paper will deal with differences between the dominant and subordinate languages under normal conditions. The second part will be concerned with those differences under stress, and the last part will focus on individual differences which may be at least indirectly relevant to interpreting skills.

II SPEED FACTORS IN LANGUAGE DOMINANCE

It is generally known that patterns of learned behavior – patterns of habits – become more automatic as time proceeds and as the behavior is repeated again and again. The index of increasing "automaticity" of behavior is speed. In language behavior, speed can be analyzed mainly with respect to the decoding of word meaning (comprehension) and encoding the meaning into words (production).

A. Input or Decoding

Although research reported in recent years does not yield unambiguous results, most of the work indicates that comprehension speed i.e. the decoding efficiency (and, consequently, speed of responding to verbal stimuli) in a nondominant language may generally be slower than in the dominant language even after many years of using it. This phenomenon is even found with high-frequency words where one would expect complete "automaticity" of decoding. The semantic content of words tends to be decoded more slowly, even at very elementary levels: the process of decoding words belonging to a subordinate language system seems to require more time.

A number of techniques have been devised to measure decoding time for verbal material in bilingual tasks. One common and simple method requires subjects to follow verbal instructions. In Lambert's study (1955) bilinguals had to press one of eight keys defined by position and color according to verbal instructions presented in one of their languages. Lambert obtained a clear-cut effect of language dominance on responding speed. On the basis of similar experiments, we designed a test that measures overall time necessary to follow short directions instructing subjects in one or the other of their languages, to check off a series of items defined by position, value, shape, or color. Even with the simplest form of the test, speed of responding has repeatedly been shown to be a reliable index of language dominance. Rao (1964) designed a test consisting of simple directions requiring relatively simple forms of response. This test has also successfully been used for measuring language dominance.

In another of our studies, the subject's task was to detect sequences or combinations of digits according to certain rules (e.g. odd, even, odd in increasing order). As can be seen in Fig. 1, longer detection times for stimuli presented in the subject's nondominant language indicated that the decoding process was slower than in their dominant language although they rated themselves to be "fully balanced" on such a task.

Other researchers have used different measures of comprehension, and more complex tasks. Macnamara (1967 b) found matching words with pictures to be much faster in the dominant language. Similarly, Scherer and Wertheimer (1964) as well as Kolers (1966) could state that bilinguals comprehended material in their native (dominant) language better than in the subordinate language.

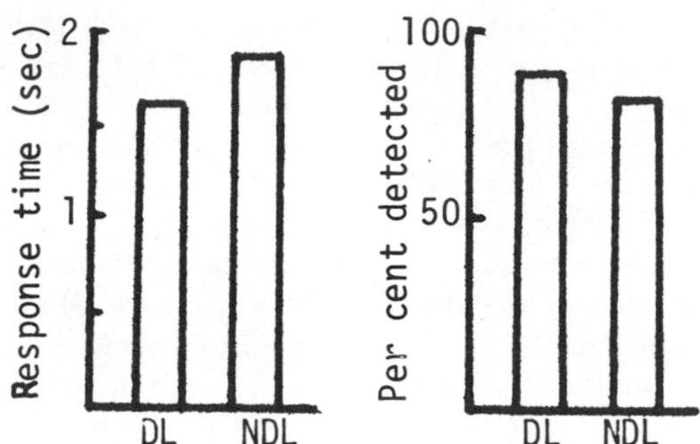

Fig. 1 Performance on an auditory detection task. Digits were presented in the Ss dominant language (DL) or in the non-dominant language (NDL).

B. Output of Encoding: Accessibility of Information in Long-term Store

Under this heading, findings can be listed ranging from verbal reaction time (naming latencies) to complex memory search. The reaction time experiments (or tests) include techniques like naming of colors, digits, or pictures of common objects. Variables are used such as number of alternatives (stimulus uncertainty) and word frequency in the given language. All these techniques are designed to measure encoding efficiency. The basic mechanism involved here is retrieval of the appropriate verbal label for a linguistically neutral stimulus from the long-term store.

As should be expected, naming latencies increase with decreasing frequency of words and, to a certain extent, with the number of alternatives. The magnitude of this increase is a function of the subject's command of the language: there is an interaction between this increase and language dominance.

The differences in naming latencies have often been found to be a sensitive index for very slight differences in language dominance, even with high-frequency stimuli occuring with high probability. Those differences may become especially clear under various kinds of stress. While verbal labels for colors or digits are usually deeply rooted and overlearned in both of the bilingual's languages, most of the reaction-time measurements reported in the literature show those verbal labels in the dominant language to be more overlearned, or more accessible than in a subordinate language.

Again, the research results in this area are sometimes contradictory. Most results point nevertheless in the above direction. Preston and Lambert's (1969) bilingual subjects performed a simple color-naming task. Longer naming latencies in the subordinate language were found for one group of subjects although they had had at least 6 years of training in that language. Similarly Hamers and Lambert

(1972) found simple naming of tones in a two-choice task (high and low tones) to depend on language dominance. In Ervin's test (1961), the subject has to name common objects in pictures. Naming latencies in this test have repeatedly been shown to be a sensitive index of language dominance: bilingual persons exhibit greater facility in naming common objects in their stronger language. Guttiérrez-Marsh and Hipple Maki (1976) employed a simple number naming task and found naming to be slower for their subject's nondominant language. It should be noted, however, that Macnamara, Krauthammer and Bolgar (1968) did not find any difference between bilinguals with "some knowledge" of a second language, and "equally competent" ones in a simple number-naming task. Similarly, in one of our earlier studies, no significant difference could be stated in a three-choice position-naming task between our subjects' dominant and subordinate languages. In later investigations however, in which we used simple pictures, colors, numbers, and again positions, naming latencies seemed to reflect language dominance in a reliable way. The above discrepancies may above all have to do with the lack of an independent, unambiguous and general measure of language dominance.

Translation, i.e. verbal response in one language to a stimulus word in another language, can be thought of as another measure related to "automaticity" of language habits and thus to reflect language dominance. The picture is, however, somewhat obscured since the speed of translation from or to the dominant language often depends on such factors as the way in which the bilingual has acquired his second language (cf. Lambert, Havelka and Gardner, 1959); moreover, the process of translation includes decoding so that it cannot be regarded as pure a measure of encoding efficiency as naming.

C. Covert Pronounceability of Words in Dominant and Subordinate Languages

There is a number of situations in which we use verbal labels in order better to perceive, rehearse, understand, organize, or encode information, or to transmit it for further processing. Even certain forms of thinking and reasoning use verbal forms. The material employed in these subvocal operations does not have the character of full words used in overt speech. Rather, it consists of simplified abbreviations. The more condensed, differentiated and economical these abbreviations are, the more effectively the operations can be carried out. As will be illustrated in this section, it appears that in a weaker language, those processes are less effective even with very deeply rooted, high-frequency verbal labels.

Due to the lower covert pronounceability in a weaker language, the use of these subvocal verbal labels is less rapid, less exact, or both. It turns out that under certain circumstances, a person with a nondominant "language set" may *perceive* less than when using his dominant "language set".

Some experimental examples will be given here. In these studies, our subjects' weaker language was rated both by themselves and by the experimenter (on the basis of a series of language dominance tests) to be at least 80 per cent of their dominant language.

In a rapid-counting experiment (Dornic, 1969) bilinguals counted silently sequences of light flashes, short tones, and vibratory pulses, either in their dominant or in their subordinate language. There was a clear tendency to underestimate the actual number when trying to count in the weaker language: the subject appeared to simply *perceive* less. (See Fig. 2).

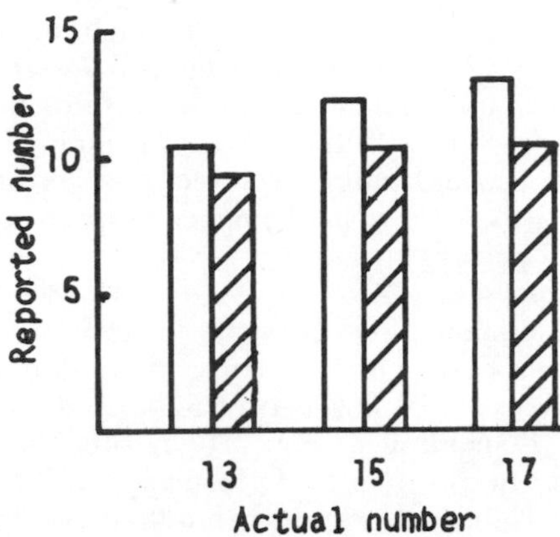

Fig. 2 Reported number as a function of actual number. The values are averaged over modalities. Blank columns = dominant language, shaded columns = subordinate language.

The results were interpreted as being due to a lower internal (covert) pronounceability and coding capacity in the subordinate language. As a result, the process of rapid silent counting was slower and less effective than in the dominant language. Similar data were obtained in a later study on rapid covert naming (and subsequently recall) of briefly presented pictures of common objects.

Differences of this kind can easily be demonstrated in experiments involving rehearsal. While short-term memory experiments without rehearsal load often do not show any difference due to language dominance, clear differences can be found as soon as rehearsal load is added, which seems again to be due to the lower pronounceability of words in the weaker language. We will come back to this topic in the section on stress.

III LANGUAGE DOMINANCE AND STRESS

The relationship between a person's dominant and subordinate languages may change under the influence of various stresses. This change can sometimes be quite dramatic, and if there is a deterioration of language behavior under heavy stress, it is typically more pronounced for the weaker language. Stress tends to enhance the differences that normally exist between the bilingual's language systems.

Different stresses can obviously affect the relationship between the bilingual's language systems in a different way, and the interaction of stresses is also an interesting problem in this connection. In real-life situations, a bilingual may have to act under the influence of various stresses at the same time (high information load, environmental as well as emotional stresses) and it is often virtually impossible to distinguish their respective effects. Simplified laboratory situations make such a distinction at least partly possible.

A. Task Stress

Very high information load, the so-called task stress, can have various forms. Regardless of whether the load is characterized by high input rate, or by task complexity, performance for a nondominant language will deteriorate more than for the dominant one, sometimes quite dramatically. In spite of the usual strategies with which the man will try to cope with the overload (ommissions, delayed responses, less exact or selective processing, failure to correct one's errors) a further increase in the load will lead to a breakdown of performance in the weaker language at a much earlier stage than in the dominant language.

We performed a number of experiments to study the influence of high mental load on information processing in dominant and nondominant languages in bilinguals with different degrees of balance between their language systems. Some of these studies will be briefly mentioned here. The results illustrate that it is *rehearsal load* which is particularly detrimental to performance in a weaker language even in rather simple tasks and in bilinguals whose skill in their two languages would be considered (at least for such a type of task) as virtually equal. Swedish - English bilinguals were used with very good knowledge of English; only a slight, nonsignificant dominance in Swedish could be found in tests of decoding and encoding involving moderate information load.

In one study (Dornic, Deneberg & Hägglund, 1975) a visual search task was employed. In one condition, search displays consisted of two-digit numbers. In another condition, the display consisted of either Swedish or English words meaning two-digit numbers. The subjects looked for one, two or three such targets at the same time. While searching, they were to keep in mind the target names as they heard them from the experimenter i.e. either in Swedish or in English. Thus, the subjects had to do two things at the same time: to rehearse (silently), and to search. The rehearsal load increased with the number of targets.

The results (Fig. 3) can be interpreted as being mainly due to a less effective process of rehearsal in the weaker language. A more laborious and time-consuming process of rehearsal, which is due to a lower covert pronounceability of words in a weaker language, obviously left less "spare capacity" for the search itself.

Another finding seen in the figure was that although search times for digits were shorter than for words, the interaction between load and language was more pronounced for digits. This tendency which, as we found later, is still more conspicuous when emotional stress is applied at the same time, seems to indicate that linguistically neutral symbols such as digits tend to automatically activate their names in the dominant language i.e. verbal responses which are more deeply rooted in the bilingual's past experience. Thus the process of matching the rehearsed target names to the corresponding visual symbols becomes more difficult when rehearsal is carried out in a weaker language.

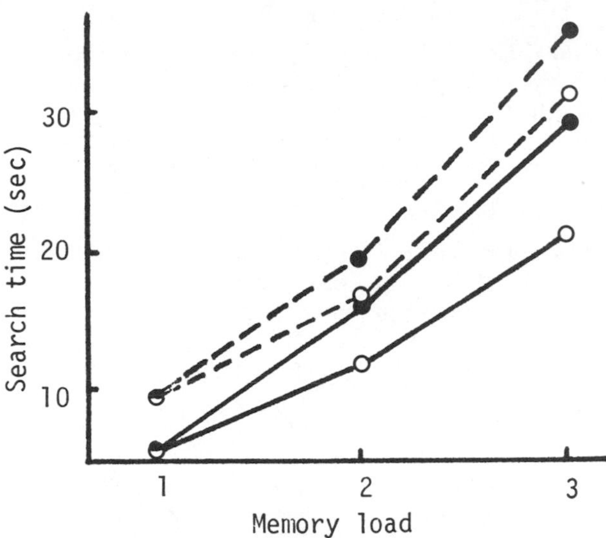

Fig. 3 Search time as a function of memory load (number of targets searched for at the same time). Open circles = dominant language, closed circles = subordinate language. Solid lines = search for numbers, dashed lines = search for words.

In another study, we used so-called closed-system-thinking tasks in which output is obtained by a series of transformations of the input. Counting backwards by threes can serve as an example. This was used at three different levels of difficulty. The difficulty depended on simple additional operations such as adding digits, categorizing numbers (odd/even) etc., which increases short-term memory load. Increasing difficulty led to a much more pronounced deterioration of performance when this type of task was performed in a nondominant language.

Following simple instructions like pressing one of a series of buttons, sometimes does not reveal any significant difference between the bilingual's languages but it may do so if we increase load on short-term memory. For instance, instead of instructing the subject to push the "left, two" button, we may instruct him to press the buttons "left, three; right, two; left, four". Such a load typically prolongs reaction time for the weaker language more than for the dominant language. This effect is still more pronounced if the instruction requires rehearsal before it can be responded to.

Similar mechanisms are involved in many situations requiring the subject to perform on a task (e.g. memory search) while some information must be kept in "working memory" by means of rehearsal. There is simply less "spare capacity" left for the task if rehearsal is performed in a subordinate language.

B. Other Stresses

Of *environmental* stresses, noise is probably the most relevant. Both nonverbal noise and "real-life", partly or fully verbal, distracting noise tend to have a more detrimental effect on performance in a weaker language, especially if the environmental stress is added to high information load. On many tasks, noise-induced arousal in our experiments influenced the relationship between the dominant and subordinate language in such a way that the former became more dominant.

A task, if performed in a weaker language, can be thought of as possessing a higher degree of complexity than a corresponding task performed in the dominant language. Thus, it appears to require lower arousal level for optimum performance. Increasing arousal may adversely affect performance on a subordinate-language task while the same degree of arousal may still be beneficial for the dominant-language task.

The main effects of environmental stresses seem to be on the encoding side (selection of response) of the bilingual's performance in the nondominant language although high-intensity noises may also cause difficulties in the decoding operations. (This indirectly concerns the often discussed question of whether an interpreter in a noisy environment should interprete *from* or *to* his dominant language. With respect to the elementary processes with which this paper is concerned, there is probably no difference. If the source language is the interpreter's dominant language, he will have less difficulty in perceiving it under poor listening conditions; consequently, more "channel capacity" will be available for memory search, translation and monitoring of output; this obvious advantage may nevertheless be outweighed by the fact that the encoding efficiency in the weaker language may be markedly reduced with noise especially if the noise involves a distracting verbal component. The opposite should be expected if the translation process is reversed. Thus there does not seem to be any general solution to this problem.)

Various sorts of *emotional stress* resulting from causes such as incentive, fear, risk-taking etc. that increase arousal tend to affect the relation between a person's dominant and nondominant languages in a way similar to environmental noise except that they do not raise the threshold for perceiving the subordinate language as noise may do.

There is one factor which strongly affects language dominance and that may also be placed under the heading of stress since it involves elements from both task stress and emotional stress. This factor may cause sudden shifts in language dominance and may be quite detrimental to a nondominant language. This factor results from *unexpected events,* often emotionally loaded, requiring prompt response.

In these situations, a person with an overt nondominant language set (e.g. an interpreter who is just using his second language, or a man having a conversation in that language) may revert to his dominant language, or be slowed down, or rendered less precise, or his speech may entirely be blocked. Under such circumstances, the strongest language system seems to behave according to what Uchtomski (1945) called a "dominant": being a well-established focus of activity in the cortex, the "dominant" has a tendency to absorb and sum excitation from other, weaker centers of activity in the brain.

Thus, even if a nondominant language system is activated, the dominant one is always "ready to take over" if an extremely prompt reaction is required. Even though the nondominant language is activated, it may still be more economical (prompter, or more precise) to switch to the other (dominant) language rather than to stay within the activated weaker language system. It looks as though in addition to the overt language set (in the bilingual's nondominant language he is just using) there exists another, covert language set in the stronger language. Besides, since at least part of our thinking is linguistic in character, using abbreviations of sentences or words, there is a permanent covert language set even in absence of an overt set. This covert set is, of course, always in the dominant language unless intentionally changed. Unexpected stimuli requiring prompt verbal response, or linguistically neutral symbols requiring prompt naming, will therefore always tend to elicit a response in that language. This permanent "background set" is obviously strengthened in stress.

One very common factor that contributes either to a selective deterioration or to a greater relative decrease of the bilingual's performance in his nondominant language, is mental fatigue. Anecdotal evidence (i.e. common experience), informal observations, as well as our own experiments carried out on bilinguals, indicates that the following conclusions can be made.

Mental fatigue caused by prolonged verbal and intellectual activity often leads to such effects as increased latencies, more time-consuming and less effective memory search, impaired short-term memory and lowered capacity of the buffer store, all the above symptoms being more pronounced for a weaker language than for the dominant one. Thus mental fatigue enhances again the latent inferiority of a weaker language. While output i.e. encoding efficiency appears to be affected in the first place, decoding can suffer as well, as has been shown in our experiments on auditory detection of digit sequences mentioned in the previous section: the effects of language dominance shown in Fig. 1 became more evident.

Mental fatigue reduces the bilingual's ability to keep his language systems distinct. Uncontrollable intrusions from the dominant language into the weaker language become more frequent. The threshold for mutual intrusions appears to be especially lowered for two (or more) subordinate languages: memory search for a word in one language often automatically yields an equivalent from the other language system. It is as if search for a word occurred across language borders: memory search often results in a spontaneous retrieval of a word which is simply more accessible regardless of the language to which it belongs. In a simplified form, this phenomenon can easily be demonstrated by a test of naming common objects.

Occasional spontaneous switching from one language to the other frequently goes unnoticed by the subject. It looks as though the bilingual partly loses control over his "output switch" whose functioning tends to be affected by the accessibility of words in the long-term store or by other random factors. Intentional switching between languages becomes more difficult. This is particularly conspicuous if two or more nondominant languages are involved.

As for the interaction with other stresses, fatigue clearly reduces tolerance for information overload but may occasionally increase tolerance for emotional stress. In combinations with low signal probability (unexpected events) fatigue greatly enhances the superiority of the dominant language over the subordinate language.

In conclusion, it can be said that stress tends to reduce the balance between the bilingual's language systems, and enhance the dominance of his stronger language. This indicates that for applied purposes, tests of language dominance (and even tests of bilingual proficiency at all) should include high information load at the very least; if possible, conditions involving other stresses should also be involved.

While a relatively greater deterioration of performance in a subordinate language under the influence of stress can be demonstrated in any bilingual who is not fully balanced, clear-cut individual differences exist. They will be briefly dealt with in the last section.

IV INDIVIDUAL DIFFERENCES

The existence of individual differences with regard to various aspects of bilingualism is well known. There are people with a "talent for languages", and others with poor abilities both for acquiring and for using bilingual skills. Most of these abilities are not specific to bilingualism: they form a part of general linguistic abilities. This holds also for basic processes which are the topic of this discussion.

Individual differences in the speed of decoding (comprehension) and encoding (production) are often enormous both in native language and in a secondary, weaker language. Bilinguals also differ considerably in their ability to keep their languages distinct, and to withstand uncontrolled interference from the other language system. The same applies to interlingual switching and to ability to translate which, incidentally, does not seem directly to depend on the degree of bilingualism (cf. Lambert, Havelka and Gardner, 1959; Macnamara, 1967a).

All the above individual differences will no doubt be a strong factor in determining an interpreter's performance. There is, however, another factor which is probably more important: tolerance for the type of stress which may be involved in using more than one language system in general, and in simultaneous interpretation in particular.

A first thing that may cross one's mind in this connection is the concept of arousal, and the personality dimensions of extraversion and neuroticism. Extraverts are supposed to have lower chronic levels of arousal than introverts, and neuroticism is sometimes thought of as reflecting a person's arousability when stress is applied. A neurotic introvert should be least stress-resistant while a stable (non-neurotic) extravert should possess high tolerance for stress. This should apply to task stress (a stable extravert should withstand high information load better than a neurotic introvert) as well as to environmental, emotional and social stresses. On the other hand, a person with low chronic arousal and with low arousability (a stable extravert) should perform worse on simple tasks with low stimulation value and with no other stresses involved.

Since the interpreter's job is no doubt to be regarded as stressful and arousing, one would expect extraverts to perform better than introverts, and stable persons better than neurotics. Data reported in the literature sometimes confirm the above assumptions, sometimes not. Most of these data were collected in experiments using tasks other than interpreting. However, recently Gerver (1976) looked into the relationship between the neuroticism score of a group of interpreters (as measured by Eysenck Personality Inventory) and their performance in noise. He found that neuroticism correlated positively with performance in a condition involving slight noise, while the opposite was true for high noise. This would be in line with the assumed relation between arousability and performance under stress.

We performed a series of pilot studies on extraversion and neuroticism as related to performance on a series of tasks in the subjects' subordinate language. The subjects varied in degree of language dominance. The tasks varied in difficulty, and were performed either in quiet or in loud verbal noise (distraction). Although no unambiguous picture of the multiple relationships between the variables used was found, there was a clear-cut difference in the performance of subjects belonging to extreme groups on difficult tasks. In a task performed in a subordinate language, involving heavy load on short-term memory, and under constant verbal distracting noise, subjects who scored high on extraversion and low on neuroticism tended to perform best while an opposite trend was observed with those who scored low on extraversion and high on neuroticism. There was an interaction with the degree of language dominance: the above-mentioned trend was more pronounced in subjects with lower degree of "automaticity" in the subordinate language used in the task (see Fig. 4). There was no significant difference between the two groups when the task was performed in the dominant language.

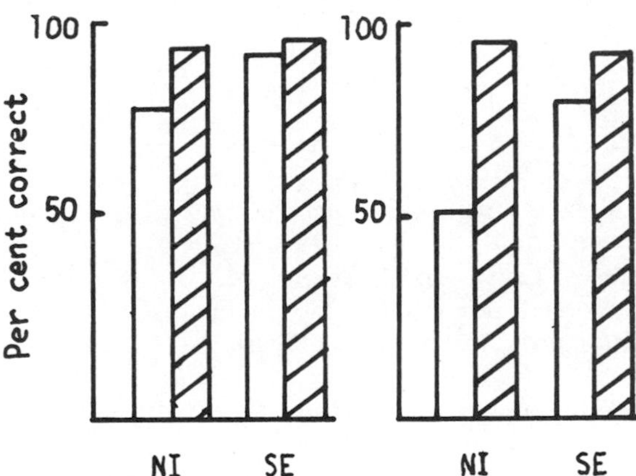

Fig. 4 Performance on a task involving load on concentration and short-term memory under the influence of loud distracting noise. NI = neurotic introverts, SE = stable extroverts. Blank columns = subordinate language, shaded columns = dominant language. Left-hand diagram: Ss with high degree of language balance; right-hand diagram: Ss with low degree of language balance.

(No unambiguous trend was found, however at the opposite end i.e. with easy tasks and no environmental stress, but this is less important in the present context since simultaneous interpretation is clearly a stressful situation).

For several years, we have been concerned with individual differences in tasks involving mental effort, particularly those posing high demands on short-term memory and switching of attention. Some of our results may be of interest here. With regard to concentration, mental effort and load on short-term memory, simultaneous interpretation may be described as "doing several things at the same time". This is where we found the most conspicuous individual differences. A typical example is a visual search task described earlier in this paper (Fig. 3): individual differences increased enormously with increasing rehearsal load (search and rehearsal at the same time).

Likewise, great individual differences have been found in a somewhat similar situation involving language switching: it is a situation that can be briefly described as "memory search under rehearsal load". Our bilinguals were told a series of unrelated words in one language and to translate them into the other language, but hold the output in store until the whole series was translated. With a high task difficulty (which did not only depend on rehearsal load but also on the difficulty of memory search), some people had response times as much as three times longer than other subjects with comparable language dominance levels. These differences become manifest in many similar situations and can be said to reflect a person's ability and/or preference for simultaneous or successive information processing. In a pilot study, this ability tended to correlate with performance on a simultaneous translation task in which bilingual subjects entirely unexperienced in translation technique were used. How that ability/preference for simultaneous vs. successive processing may be related to other variables, e.g. to the dimensions of extraversion and neuroticism, is the objective of a further study.

REFERENCES

Dornic, S., Verbal factor in number perception. *Acta Psychologica*, 1969, *29*, 393 - 399.

Dornic, S., Deneberg, C. B., and Hägglund, M. La exploración visual cuando se emplea una lengua dominante o no dominante. (Visual search in dominant and nondominant languages). *Revista de psicologia general y aplicada*, 1975, *30*, 1123 - 1134.

Ervin, S. M. Learning and recall in bilinguals. *American Journal of Psychology*, 1961, *74*, 446 - 451.

Gerver, D. Empirical studies of simultaneous interpretation: a review and a model. In R. W. Brislin (Ed.)., *Translation: Applications and research*, New York: Gardner Press, 1976.

Gutiérrez-Marsh, L., and Hipple Maki, R. Efficiency of arithmetic operations in bilinguals as a function of language. *Memory and Cognition*, 1976, *4*, 459 - 464.

Hamers, J. F., and Lambert, W. E. Bilingual interdependencies in auditory perception. *Journal of Verbal Learning and Verbal Behavior*, 1972, *11*, 303 - 310.
Kolers, P. A. Reading and talking bilingually. *American Journal of Psychology*, 1966, *79*, 357 - 376.
Lambert, W. E. Measurement of the linguistic dominance in bilinguals. *Journal of Abnormal and Social Psychology* 1955, *50*, 197 - 200.
Lambert, W. E., Havelka, J., and Gardner, R. C., Linguistic manifestations of bilingualism. *American Journal of Psychology*, 1959, *72*, 77 - 82.
Macnamara, J. The bilingual's linguistic performance – A psychological overview. *Journal of Social Issues*, 1967a, *23*, 58 - 77.
Macnamara, J. The effect of instruction in a weaker language. *Journal of Social Issues*, 1967b, *23*, 121 - 135.
Macnamara, J., Krauthammer, M., and Bolgar, M. Language switching in bilinguals as a function of stimulus and response uncertainty. *Journal of Experimental Psychology*, 1968, *78*, 208 - 215.
Preston, M. S., and Lambert, W. E. Interlingual interference in a bilingual version of the Stroop color-word task. *Journal of Verbal Learning and Verbal Behavior*, 1969, *8*, 259 - 301.
Rao, R. S. Development and use of Directions Test for measuring degree of bilingualism. *Journal of Psychological Researches*, 1964, *8*, 114 - 119.
Scherer, G. A. C., and Wertheimer, M. *A psycholinguistic experiment in foreign-language teaching.* New York: McGraw-Hill, 1964.
Uchtomski, A. A. *Sobranie sotchinenii.* Leningrad, 1945.

Summary and Recall of Text in First and Second Languages:

Some Factors Contributing to Performance Differences

John Long
M.R.C. Applied Psychology Unit, Cambridge

Edith Harding-Esch
Cambridge University, Cambridge

Research has shown that people generally perform the same task less well in a second language than in a first. 'First' is used in the sense of 'native' or 'dominant'. The phenomenon is referred to as the second language deficit. It has been demonstrated in simple tasks such as naming numbers, performing mental arithmetic (Marsh and Maki, 1976), remembering lists of nouns (McCormack and Novell, 1975) and counting rapid signals silently (Dornic, 1969). It has also been shown in more complex tasks, such as the reading aloud of text and its comprehension (Kolers, 1966).

The size of the deficit depends on at least three factors: a speaker's proficiency in the second language; the linguistic difficulty of the test material; and the psychological difficulty of the task. For example, a deficit in shadowing text obtained with speakers 'having a good knowledge of the second language' disappeared with those having 'no preference for one language over the other', that is with higher proficiency (Treisman, 1965). Elsewhere, in a comprehension test involving subject and object relations in sentences, the deficit increased as a function of linguistic difficulty, as reflected by changes in the relative pronoun and in the location of the verb specifying the relations (Cook, 1975). Similarly, in a task involving a visual search for digits in a matrix of squares, the deficit increased with psychological difficulty, as reflected by the memory load imposed by the number of possible targets (Dornic, 1973). The relationship between the deficit and the three factors is illustrated in Figure 1. The effect of proficiency and linguistic difficulty is shown at low, medium and high levels of psychological difficulty. The diagram illustrates how the deficit increases at a fixed level of proficiency with an increase in the other two factors. It also shows how at the highest level of proficiency little or no deficit may occur even at high levels of linguistic and psychological difficulty.

The concern of this paper is with the deficit, particularly with the pattern of deficit, which characterizes the summary and recall of text at high levels of all three variables. The approximate area identifying the levels is shown on Figure 1. Initial interest arose from informal observations at a laboratory class designed to practice English students' oral skills in their second language, which was French. The students seemed to experience more difficulty in summarising and recalling auditorily presented text than would have been supposed on the basis of their good command of French, as demonstrated in social communication. Was the difficulty real and hence demonstrable? What were the contributing factors?

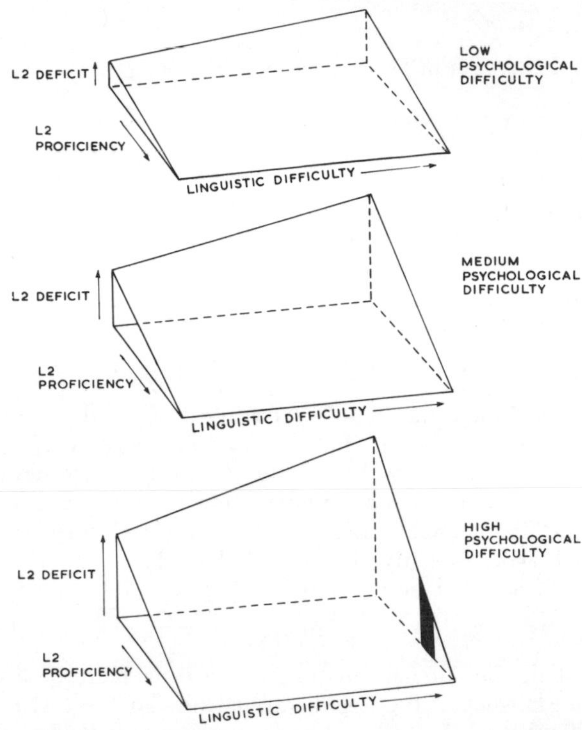

Figure 1 The relationship between the second language deficit, second language proficiency and linguistic difficulty at low, medium and high levels of psychological difficulty. The deficit is the difference in performance between first and second languages. The black area identifies the approximate levels of these variables used in the experiment reported (L2 = second language).

There is a considerable applied interest in the answers to these questions. Summary and recall tests are often used to assess second language skills of students (James and Rouve, 1973), especially those involving spoken language (Perren, 1968). Further, the tests are a likely choice for measuring the aptitude of candidates applying for training as interpreters, since summary and recall constitute the critical features of the consecutive interpreter's task (Paneth, 1957). Answers to the questions are also of theoretical interest. They should add to the hypotheses, mainly derived from simpler tasks, concerning the kinds of limitation, which govern the processing of information in a second language (Lambert, Ignatow and Krauthammer, 1968; Dornic, 1975). They should also aid understanding of summary and recall performance in a first language by clarifying the role of language in such tasks (Kintsch, 1974).

It was thus decided to evaluate the pattern of deficit associated with the summary and recall of text. First and second language performance was compared for subjects having either English as a first language and French as a second or the reverse. The experiment was preceded by tests designed to establish the subjects' second language proficiency and first language dominance. The research was not designed to decide between any specific explanations of the deficit. It was carried out, however, with two general notions in mind. The first supposed any deficit to be due to a failure to use those summary and recall skills which normally operate in a first language. The second supposed that the skills operate as well in both languages, but that the second language is processed less efficiently than the first. The two hypotheses emphasized respectively the cognitive and the linguistic aspects of the task.

LANGUAGE PROFICIENCY AND DOMINANCE

The function of the tests was to establish the subjects' high level of second language lexical, syntactic and semantic proficiency yet first language dominance. A questionnaire on language learning background was also administered. The results are reported in full, since the tests and questionnaire represent one solution to the problem of assessing second language proficiency for experimental purposes (see Dornic, 1975, for a review of the problem).

METHOD

Tests

1) *Reading* aloud was used to establish first language dominance. It is known to produce a reliable second language deficit (Kolers, 1966). Subjects read aloud two texts 150 words long, one in English, the other in French. They were taken from General Certificate of Education, Ordinary Level French examination papers. The subjects were instructed to read as quickly as possible without making more than the occasional error. The time taken was recorded and obvious errors noted, for example hesitations and repetitions.

2) *Vocabulary* was tested by means of the last 25 items of the Peabody Picture Vocabulary Test to establish lexical proficiency (Dunn, 1965). A French translation of both versions of the test was made. Subjects matched a typed word to its meaning as exemplified by one of four pictures. Examples of English and French words used are: 'obese', 'predatory' and 'pensile'; 'lavalliere', 'outrecuidant' and 'lucarne'. There was no time limit. For analysis, items were scored as correct or incorrect.

3) *Cloze* was used to assess syntactic and semantic proficiency, although vocabulary was inevitably involved. The test is a good index of general language proficiency (Stubbs and Tucker, 1974). An English and a French text 125 words long were taken from the same source as the reading texts. Each was translated into the other language (Oller, Bowen, Dien and Mason, 1972). Every fifth word was replaced by a gap fifteen spaces long. Subjects read the tests and filled in the gaps with a single word. There was no time limit. Only words identical with the original were scored as correct.

DESIGN

The tests were administered in the above order and followed by the questionnaire. Each subject performed each test first in one language, then in the other – the order of the languages remaining fixed for any subject. Written instructions were always in the language of the test. Subjects were assigned to a language group on the basis of their first language and to one of two groups within each first language having either the English or the French version of each test first. The English and French versions of the tests were balanced over groups within languages. They were administered at a single session.

Subjects

Twenty subjects were tested. Ten were native speakers of English and ten of French.

RESULTS AND DISCUSSION

Questionnaire

The background information provided by the questionnaire is shown in Table 1. Formal learning means at school or at an establishment of higher education. Free learning means having the opportunity to speak the second language outside any formal learning context.

Table 1 Background information provided by subjects' responses to the questionnaire.

Background information	Subjects' first language	
	English	French
1 *Sex*:		
male	2	1
female	8	9
2 *Parents' first language*:		
English	20	1
French	0	18
Others	0	1
3 *Second language learning*: (mean number of years per subject)		
formal	8.5	9.6
free (L2 country)	3.1	5.8
free (L1 country)	2.3	5.5
Total	13.9	20.9
4 *Subjects' self-rating of L2 on 7 point scale:*		
good or better	7	9
medium or worse	3	1

L1 = first language L2 = second language

Tests

The results of the tests are shown in Figure 2. A separate analysis of variance was applied to each, with language group as a between-subject factor (English versus French) and language dominance as a within-subject factor (first versus second language). For both factors and their interaction d.f. = 1,18. Nonsignificant means $P > 0.05$.

The vocabulary test showed no significant effects of any kind (English group = 84%; French = 82%; first language = 84%, second = 81%). Further, all subjects obtained a score indicating a mental age of at least 18 years in both languages. The outcome for the cloze test was the same (English group = 65%, French - 67%), except for a small but significant second language deficit (first = 69%, second = 63%; $F = 6.43$, $P < 0.025$).

Although the reading test likewise showed no effect of language group (English = 159 words per minute, French = 160), there was a significant second language deficit (first = 176 words per minute, second = 142; $F = 90.63$, $P < 0.001$) and a significant group x language interaction, indicating a larger deficit for the English speakers (English deficit = 45 words per minute, French = 23; $F = 9.43$, $P < 0.01$). The same outcome obtained for an analysis of the reading errors (English = 2.6, French = 2.5; and first = 1.6, second = 3.5, $F = 17.44$, $P < 0.001$) but with no significant interaction.

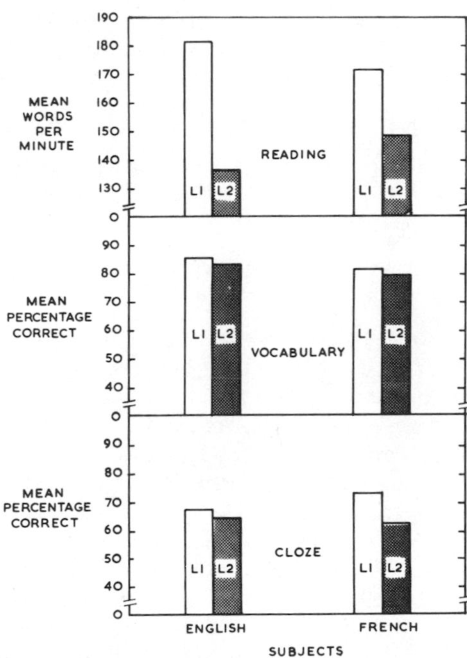

Figure 2 Tests. Language proficiency and dominance – results of reading, vocabulary and cloze tests. Mean scores per subject (L1 = first language, L2 = second language).

The test and questionnaire data taken together indicated that subjects were highly proficient in their second language. The vocabulary test showed no difference between languages and the cloze test only a six percent deficit. Their proficiency was thus lexical, syntactic and semantic. The high level of proficiency was consistent with the comparatively long time spent learning a second language and with self-rating scores.

Although proficient in their second language, the reading test showed subjects to be dominant in their first (all twenty on the basis of speed). Dominance was also consistent with first language superiority in the cloze test. The subjects' dominant language was also the first language of their parents, suggesting their second language was neither learnt at home nor when they were very young. These assumptions are consistent with the length of time spent in a free-learning situation. The time would have been longer in the case of very early acquisition of the second language.

The larger deficit shown by the English speakers on the reading test was unexpected. It might be that the particular motor patterns required to speak French (position of the tongue, tone of the facial muscles etc.) more easily accommodate speaking English than the reverse. Or, a sampling bias resulted in more proficient French speakers. The latter explanation seems more likely. Overall time spent learning a second language was longer by seven years for French speakers. Further, more of the French speakers currently lived in the country of their second language (5 versus 1) or taught it in the country of their first (4 versus 0). Lastly, there was evidence that French speakers were better at some aspects of the summary task, although this was written. On this basis, therefore, the French speakers are assumed to have been more proficient at English, than the English speakers at French.

EXPERIMENT: SUMMARY AND RECALL OF TEXT

The aim of the summary task was to evaluate the second language deficit. To this end, performance in the subjects' second language was compared with that in their first.

METHOD

Text

The subjects listened to a speech lasting about ten minutes. They were then allowed five minutes to write an informative summary in the same language. A time check was given after 2.5 and again after 4.5 minutes. No note-taking was permitted. Two recorded speeches were used, both in French delivered by the same person at the European Parliament. One assessed progress towards a European community; the other concerned legal procedures necessary for association agreements between the community and other countries. The speeches were about 1000 words long. They were of high psychological difficulty because of their length, the large number of points made and the complexity of the arguments. They were of high linguistic difficulty because they included a full range of syntactic construction. Their content, however, was not technical and their vocabulary and syntax were within the range used in the proficiency tests. Two faithful translations of the speeches were produced in English and recorded by a male speaker. Thus, the same male native speaker recorded both versions in a given language.

Design

Half the English speakers were tested on the English version of one speech and the French version of the other and vice versa for the remainder. The French speakers were tested similarly. The speeches were thus balanced over first and second languages for content. The test followed the questionnaire. A further five performance tests were also administered. The results will be reported elsewhere.

RESULTS

Analysis

A model summary of each text was constructed by the authors. It contained the most important points (termed gist or macrostructure – van Dijk, 1972), expressed in seven sentences for each text. For example, the fourth sentence for the 'association' speech was as follows: "About consultation: the parliament should be consulted before agreements are signed by the Council of Ministers". Each model summary was about 100 words long, that is one tenth of the original.

For scoring purposes, the subjects' written summaries were divided into clauses and typed. The clauses were then divided into 'claims' – the basic unit of analysis, and matched against i) the model summaries and ii) the original text excluded from the summaries. A claim supposed an explicit or implicit contrast and could be true or false depending on what was asserted in the speeches. The notion of claim was analogous to that of proposition (Kintsch, 1974). However, it was less detailed and involved only two levels of importance – 'main' and 'subsidiary'. It thus simplified the problem of matching the protocols to the text – never an easy task (van Dijk, 1975).

Although it is difficult to guarantee the absence of all inconsistencies in the application of the scoring procedure, the design of the experiment with dominance balanced over languages, and subjects tested on each language ensured that evaluation of the second language deficit was not affected.

In order to evaluate the pattern of deficit, four types of claim were identified by the analysis:

1) *Main claims.* These corresponded to what was asserted in the model summaries of the text. They were thus true. For example, one protocol began: "(1. A speaker) (2. addressing) (3. the European) (4. parliament) . . .". Four claims were identified – possible contrasts being: 1. An observer, 2. attending, 3. the international, 4. court. Each model summary contained about 50 possible main claims – or one for every two words.

2) *Subsidiary claims.* These were true claims involving points from the original texts not important enough to be included in the model summaries (compare the notion of microstructure – van Dijk, 1972). For example, the response " . . (1. America) (2. and potentially) (3. Russia) (4. are taking over) (5. European) (6. firms)" was counted as having six subsidiary claims. No formal estimate of the number of possible claims was attempted. On the basis of the ratio of words to main claims, however, a figure of 450 explicit subsidiary claims would seem likely.

3) *False claims.* These were claims inconsistent with assertions in the speech. For example, the response "(1. A chairman) (2. addressed) (3. a socialist) (4. meeting) was scored as having four claims of which three were false (numbers 1, 3 and 4). Note that the score is context-sensitive at the level of the clause, since all the claims in the response "(1. A socialist) (2. meeting) (3. addressed) (4. a Chairman)" would have been scored as false.

4) *Redundant claims.* These were claims which added no new information. They often involved the repetition of claims for which a score had already been given. For example, the response "(1. A speaker) . . . . . .(2. the speaker) (3. raises) (4. certain) (5. matters) . . . . ." was considered to involve five claims, two of which were redundant (numbers 2 and 4).

The protocols were scored for main, subsidiary, false and redundant claims independently by the two authors, one of whom was a native English speaker, the other French. Any disagreement was resolved by discussion. Subjects were not penalised either for spelling, grammatical or stylistic errors.

In order to validate the claim analysis and in particular the main claim measure, a maximum global score of 4 was separately awarded for all the claims in a protocol associated with each of the seven sentences in a model summary, making a possible 28 for each text. The number of words per protocol was also counted.

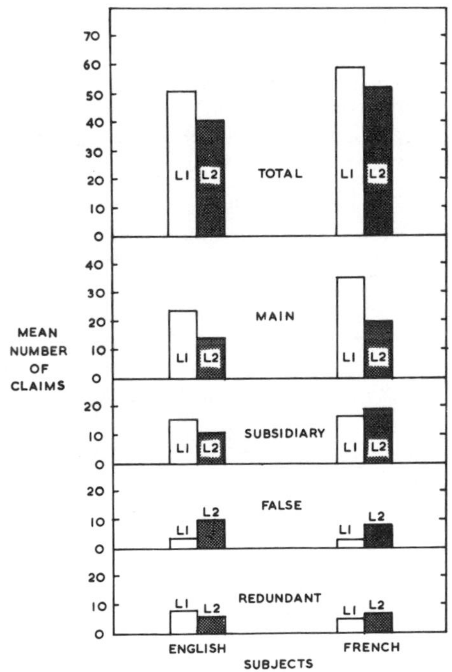

Figure 3. Experiment. Summary and recall of text. Mean number of claims per subject (L1 = first language, L2= second language).

Data

The mean number of claims made by each subject is shown in Figure 3 by type of claim and total. A separate analysis of variance was applied to the claim data with language group and dominance as factors. The effects of dominance have been summarised in Table 2. As for the earlier tests, d.f. = 1,18 and nonsignificant means $P > 0.05$.

Table 2 Experiment. Summary and recall of text: results of analyses of variance applied to claim data (1 and 18 d.f. in all cases; NS means nonsignificant $P > 0.05$).

Measure	First language	Second language	F ratio	Significance (P)
Main claims	29.7	17.2	17.56	< 0.001
Global score	12.6	7.8	16.65	< 0.001
Subsidiary claims	16.2	17.8	< 1.0	NS
False claims	3.0	9.0	4.74	< 0.05
Redundant claims	6.3	6.1	< 1.0	NS
Total claims	55.2	46.9	9.17	< 0.01
Total words	101.0	88.0	6.10	< 0.025

These results can be summarized as follows:

1. There was a second language deficit characterized by a significant decrease in main claims. The deficit was also shown by the global score, thus validating the claim measure. In addition, the language group factor was also significant for the global score (English = 7.9, French = 12.5; F = 5.15, $P < 0.05$). The deficit did not extend to subsidiary claims.

2. The deficit was further characterized by a significant increase in false claims. It did not, however, include redundant claims.

3. A significant decrease in the total number of claims and in the number of words per protocol also indicated a deficit.

No other effects or interactions were significant.

Correlations

The preceding analysis demonstrated a decrease in main claims and an increase in false claims. The outcome raised the question of whether they were related. The question is relevant to an interpretation of the language deficit. A close relationship would be consistent with a high correlation both within and between languages. To evaluate the relationship, the claims for each subject were correlated within and between languages by means of the Pearson product-moment correlation coefficient r. The results are shown in Table 3.

Table 3. Experiment. Summary and recall of text: Pearson product-moment corrclation coefficients within and between languages for types of claim.

Types of Claim	Correlation coefficient (r) Within first language	Within second language
main and subsidiary	+ 0.53 xx	+ 0.61 xx
main and false	– 0.59 xx	– 0.45 xx
main and redundant	+ 0.28 NS	+ 0.39 x
subsidiary and false	– 0.59 xx	– 0.51 xx
subsidiary and redundant	+ 0.28 NS	+ 0.05 NS
false and redundant	– 0.04 NS	– 0.13 NS
	Between first and second language	Between second and first language
main and subsidiary	+ 0.69 xxx	+ 0.49 x
main and false	+ 0.07 NS	– 0.54 xx
main and redundant	+ 0.26 NS	+ 0.39 x
subsidiary and false	+ 0.06 NS	– 0.24 NS
subsidiary and redundant	+ 0.15 NS	+ 0.05 NS
false and redundant	– 0.34 NS	– 0.13 NS
	Between languages	
main and main	+ 0.50 x	
subsidiary and subsidiary	+ 0.27 NS	
false and false	– 0.06 NS	
redundant and redundant	+ 0.32 NS	
	xxx P<0.001 x P<0.05	xx P<0.01 NS = nonsignificant

The results can be summarized as follows:

1. Measures of efficient summary performance were significantly correlated within both first and second languages (upper panel).

2. In general, correlations *between* languages were lower than *within* (middle panel).

3. There was a significant correlation between main claims between languages, but no relationship between false claims (lower panel).

These results suggested the decrease in main claims and the increase in false claims characterizing the language deficit were not closely related. The decrease in main claims seemed to be related to first language performance; the increase in false claims appeared to be unrelated.

The preceding results suggested a final observation – that the pattern of performance in the second language, although at a lower level was similar within the limits of this analysis to that in the first. The observation was consistent with the ratios between the ten best subjects and the ten worst in the two languages (first and second respectively: main claims – 2.26, 3.30; subsidiary claims – 1.95, 1.84; false claims – 0.02, 0.37; redundant claims – 1.29, 1.03). The best ten subjects were separately defined for each language on the basis of the number of main claims.

DISCUSSION AND CONCLUSIONS

Subjects highly proficient in their second language nevertheless exhibited a second language deficit on a task of high linguistic and psychological difficulty. The summaries were poorer in that they were less selective. They included *less* of the important information but as *much* of the unimportant. They also included less correct information and less information overall.

Note that the absence of a deficit for unimportant information may have been an artifact of the short response-time, all subjects being able to recall as much as could be written in five minutes. The deficit for main claims and its absence for subsidiary ones are thus best interpreted together as a 'summary' deficit.

The deficit suggests that important information is less well selected and organized for recall in a second language. This 'selection and organization' hypothesis supposes that subjects: listen to a speech; attempt to understand what is being said in terms of the text and of their own knowledge; identify and select the important points and relate them within the framework of the overall theme. The psychological processes may be conceived in terms of the listener either recoding the semantic representation of the separate sentences into a single structure (by means of mapping rules involving deletion, generalization and construction – van Dijk, 1972) or building up a representation of a domain of objects, their properties and their relations (Stenning, 1976). The hypothesis assumes that in a second language subjects fail to identify and select important information and to establish the relations between individual pieces of information and the theme. Recall is thus hampered because pieces of important information are either not in memory or are inaccessible. The result is a decrease in main claims with no change in subsidiary ones. Decreasing text structure has been shown elsewhere to produce a similar outcome (Barnard, 1974). The implication of text and language manipulations producing an analogous effect is taken up later.

Examination of the protocols suggested that the decrease in main claims resulted from false claims (see below), omissions and substitutions. Important information was either left out altogether or recalled only in part. For example, "The third point is of a political kind", instead of "About the political issue, the parliament should give its opinion when asked to do so". Substitutions consisted of false information or of subsidiary information. For example, instead of the preceding quotation, one subject wrote: "The third is of a political kind; he mentions the problem of Nigeria and the Treaty of Rome." All the information is correct, but the important point concerning the parliament and its opinion is missing. Failure to select and recall this information may have resulted from the frequent references to Nigeria whose political difficulties were used to illustrate the speaker's argument. Frequent reference seems to have been wrongly interpreted in this case as a cue for importance. Whether poorer selection also depends on less efficient use of prosodic and communicative cues in a second language remains to be established.

The 'selection and organization' hypothesis can also explain the increase in false information in the second language, if false claims resulted from attempts to relate and make consistent poorly integrated information. Internal evidence suggests this to be unlikely. Firstly, many false substitutions appeared to play no role in relating other information, for example, ". . . speaking in the name of the socialist party" instead of ". . . speaking in the name of the socialist group". Secondly, false claims tended to be related to main claims rather than to subsidiary ones (second language: 6.0 and 3.0 respectively). The opposite trend might have been expected with poorer summary and recall. Main points are better organized and hence better recalled than subsidiary ones (van Dijk, 1975; Thorndyke, 1977) and subjects recalled as many of each (17.2 versus 17.8). Thirdly, correlation analysis suggested that false claims were not related across languages, whereas main claims were. If poorer selection and organization accounts for the reduction in main claims, then a separate factor is required to explain false claims. Note that since false claims were not more associated with subsidiary claims than main ones, their increase must be assumed to have contributed to the second language deficit. If true, they would have helped offset the decrease in main claims.

An alternative hypothesis to account for the increase in false claims would be to suppose that the original texts were less well understood in the second language. Hence false substitutions unrelated to the integration of other information and a low correlation between languages for false claims. Note that since there was no evidence to suggest that main points were more difficult to comprehend than subsidiary ones, the hypothesis is not able to account for the summary deficit. The comprehension hypothesis is thus only to be preferred as an explanation of the increase in incorrect information.

There is evidence that decreasing the structure of verbal material decreases the amount recalled (Epstein, 1967; Barnard, 1974). Hence the 'selection and organization' hypothesis might explain the reduction in overall information, which occurred in the second language. However, examination of the protocols revealed difficulties of expression not required by the hypothesis. Although there were few spelling mistakes, the number of protocols without any grammatical errors was higher in the first language than the second (18 versus 11). For example, "That it (the subject) had to be dealt very cautiously". Likewise, there were more protocols free from errors of idiom in the first language than in the second (19 versus 8). For example, "He criticises the transport . . . apart may be the agricultural policy . . ." There were some stylistic differences too between languages. The number of subjects with at least one switch between direct and indirect speech was smaller in the first language than in the second (4 versus 10). For example, "The speaker mentioned three points . . . that is alright". Switching may be a strategy for coping with difficulties of expression – direct speech requiring less transformation of the original information.

Grammatical, idiomatic and stylistic differences between languages thus may be more easily accounted for by an additional 'production' hypothesis. It supposes that the information from the original text is stored in memory in a propositional code, which is not language specific (Kintsch, 1974). At the time of recall, subjects are less able to express this information in their second language. They do so more slowly and hence recall less overall – both in terms of words and claims. Since there was no evidence to suggest that main points were more difficult to express than subsidiary ones, the hypothesis is not able to account for the summary deficit.

In conclusion, therefore, three working hypotheses are proposed to account for the data: selection and organization for the summary deficit, comprehension for the increase in false claims and production for the decrease in overall claims and words. Subsequent research is now being directed at evaluating their individual contributions to the deficit.

Three implications are suggested by this interpretation of the results. They concern the dependence of the a priori notions preceding the research; the relative contributions of the language components to the deficit; and the relationship between cognition and language.

The first implication is that summary and recall skills and language processing are *both* less efficient in a second language. They may, therefore, interact, a possibility not reflected in the a priori notions described in the introduction. Failure to understand what is said may lead to the poorer selection and relating of main points. Alternatively, failure to select a main point may lead to subsequent poorer understanding. Thus, any attempt to evaluate independently the contribution of summary skills and language processing to the deficit must control for the possible interaction. Since decreasing the structure of a text produces an effect similar to performance in a second language (Barnard, 1974), control is required for both types of manipulation.

The second implication is that the contribution to the deficit made by less efficient language processing appears to involve both failures of comprehension and of production. Further, the two seem to go together (see Table 3). Whether they contribute equally to the second language deficit remains to be established experimentally. An imbalance is suggested by the preference of a number of international agencies for simultaneous interpretation into a first rather than into a second language. Further, it has been argued that frozen competence – the advanced speaker's poorer knowledge of a second language – is primarily due to a limited knowledge of the rules of lexical co-occurrence (Marton, 1977). The limitation constitutes a more serious difficulty for production than comprehension. Thus, although the two components go together here, their contribution to the second language deficit may not be equal.

The third implication concerns the role of language in such tasks as the summary and recall of text. The data and the conclusions all point to the crucial role of language. This view contrasts in part with the notion, derived from developmental work with children within a Piagetian framework, that whenever there is a relationship between cognition and language development, language depends on cognition (Cromer, 1974). Children learn the operation of 'seriation' or ordering before they learn the language of 'comparison'. Teaching them the language has relatively little effect on seriation performance (Sinclair-de-Zwart, 1969). When, however, as in the summary task the materials are themselves coded in language and further, language is the medium of response, it is more likely that cognition depends on language development. Part of the second language deficit demonstrated here, in line with two of the working hypotheses proposed, can be interpreted as a failure in development (of production and of comprehension), as indeed can part of the difference which distinguishes good and bad performers in a first language. The contrast is only partial for two reasons. Firstly, although the cognitive operations involved in summary and recall are likely to depend on language development, the evolution of the cognitive operations themselves may be dependent on the earlier development of analogous perceptual processes of selection and organization (for similar arguments see Bruner, 1975). Secondly, cognitive development cannot await full language development, since children are able to recall story texts, although not as well as adults (Mandler and Johnson, 1977).

The final conclusions concern the application of these findings to the testing of students and potential consecutive interpreters. The implications are not the same in the two cases. The difference is based on the assumption that summary and recall involves an important task or cognitive component as well as a language one. The assumption is based on the differential results for main and subsidiary claims and on the correlation of main claims across languages. For students undergoing proficiency testing, the language component is primary. The summary task should thus be simple, facilitating the selection and organization of important information yet requiring full use of comprehension and production skills. In contrast, for the potential consecutive interpreters, the task component is primary, since language proficiency is in any case a pre-requisite for training. The summary task should thus be complex in order to bring out the complete range of selection and organization skills. Comprehension and production can be minimized by administering the test in an applicant's first language — second language proficiency being evaluated by other tests. This would emphasise the cognitive aspect of the task. Indeed, it may be precisely this task-specific component involving complex selection and summary skills which is the crucial feature distinguishing simultaneous from consecutive interpreters — who presumably do not differ in terms of language proficiency. It may thus be the basis for the belief that a good consecutive interpreter is able to function as a simultaneous interpreter, but not necessarily the reverse (Paneth, 1957).

REFERENCES

Barnard, P. J. *Structure and Content in the Retention of Prose.* Unpublished Ph.D. Thesis, University College, London, 1974.

Bruner, J. S. The ontogenesis of speech acts. *Journal of Child Language*, 1975, *2*, 1 - 19.

Cook, V. J. Strategies in the comprehension of relative clauses. *Language and Speech*, 1975, *18*, 204 - 212.

Cromer, R. The development of language and cognition: the cognition hypothesis. In Foss, B. (Ed.). *New Perspectives in Child Development*. Great Britain: Penguin, 1974.

Dornic, S. Verbal factor in number perception. *Acta Psychologica*, 1969, *29*, 393 - 399.

Dornic, S., Deneberg, G., and Hägglund, M. Visual search in dominant and non-dominant languages. *Reports from the Institute of Applied Psychology*, University of Stockholm, 1973, *37*.

Dornic, S. Human information processing and bilingualism. *Reports from the Institute of Applied Psychology*, University of Stockholm, 1975,*67*.

Epstein, W. Some conditions of the influence of syntactical structure on learning: grammatical transformation, learning constructions and "chunking". *Journal of Verbal Learning and Verbal Behavior*, 1967, *6*, 415 - 519.

Dunn, L. M. *Expanded manual: Peabody Picture Vocabulary Test.* Minneapolis: American Guidance Service, 1965.

James, C. V., and Rouve, S. *Survey of Curricula and Performance in Modern Languages.* London: Hanbury, Tomsett and Co., Ltd., 1973.

Kintsch, W. *Representation of Meaning in Memory.* Hillsdale, N. J.: Lawrence Erlbaum Associates, 1974.

Kolers, P. A. Reading and talking bilingually. *American Journal of Psychology*, 1966, *79*, 357 - 376.

Lambert, W. E., Ignatow, M., and Krauthammer, M. Bilingual organization in free recall. *Journal of Verbal Learning and Verbal Behavior*, 1968, 7, 207 - 214.

Mandler, J. M., and Johnson, N. S. Remembrance of things parsed: story structure and recall. *Cognitive Psychology*, 1977, *9*, 111-151.

Marsh, L. G., and Maki, R. H. Efficiency of arithmetic operations in bilinguals as a function of language. *Memory and Cognition*, 1976, *4*, 459 - 464.

Marton, W. Foreign vocabulary learning as problem number one of language teaching at the advanced level. *Interlang. Stud. Bull. Utrecht* 1977, *2*, 33 - 57.

McCormack, P. D., and Novell, J. A. Free recall from unilingual and trilingual lists. *Bulletin of the Psychonomic Society*, 1975, *6*, 173 - 174.

Oller, J. W., Bowen, J. D., Dien, T. A., and Mason, V. W. Cloze tests in English, Thai and Vietnamese: native and non-native performance. *Language and Learning*, 1972, *22*, 1 - 15.

Paneth, E. *An investigation into conference interpreting, with special reference to training interpreters.* Unpublished thesis for the M.A. degree in Education of London University, 1957.

Perren, G. E. Testing spoken language: some unsolved problems. In A. Davies (Ed.). *Language Testing Symposium: a Psycholinguistic Approach*, 1968.

Sinclair-de-Zwart, H. Developmental psycholinguistics. In Elkind, D. and Flavell, J. H. (Eds.). *Studies in Cognitive Development: Essays in Honour of Jean Piaget*. London: Oxford University Press, 1969.

Stenning, K. Articles, quantifiers and their encoding in textual comprehension. In Freedle, R. O., (Ed.). *Discourse, Production and Comprehension*. Hillsdale N.J.: Lawrence Erlbaum, 1976.

Stubbs, J. B., and Tucker, G. R. The cloze test as a measure of English proficiency. *Modern Language Journal,* 1974, *58*, 239 - 241.

Thorndyke, P. W. Cognitive structures in comprehension and memory of narrative discourse. *Cognitive Psychology*, 1977, *9*, 77 - 110.

Treisman, A. M. The effects of redundancy and familiarity on translating and repeating back a foreign and a native language. *British Journal of Psychology*, 1965, *56*, 369-379.

van Dijk, T. A. *Some Aspects of Text Grammars*, The Hague: Mouton, 1972.

van Dijk, T. A. *Recalling and summarizing complex discourse*. University of Amsterdam mimeo, 1975.

Psychosemantics and Simultaneous Interpretation

Jean-François Le Ny

University of Paris VIII

Paris

INTRODUCTION

A psychosemantic analysis of simultaneous interpretation must account for several related types of problem; their solutions are also, at least partially, interdependent. They will first be stated here, from the most specific to the most general, but will be discussed in the text in reverse order, from the general to the specific. There are thus three types of problem:

1) those problems which are related to *simultaneous* interpretation. It seems that they are related to a certain extent to the oral character of the communication which is thus established, and to a much greater extent to the *information flow* which the interpreter must process under these conditions;

2) those problems which are proper to translation *in general.* It is generally admitted today that this process is not a simple transformation of a text from source language to target language, but is rather a double transformation. The translator first transforms the input text into a certain type of representation of its sense, followed by a second transformation of this semantic representation into a new text in the output language;

3) if these issues are viewed from the point of view of psychosemantics the nature of semantic information processing must be discussed. Thus, in order to solve these problems we need a model which is capable of telling us what this semantic information is, i.e. how it is constituted and how it is organized; in the absence of this model we would not be able to construct a clear idea of what simultaneous interpretation involves. Perhaps such an idea is a bit premature, at least on the present level, but in addition, without this model we would not be able to formulate psychologically meaningful hypotheses or pose pertinent questions which would enable us to progress towards this knowledge of simultaneous interpretation by analysis and experimentation.

I shall thus discuss these problems in reverse order and expose certain considerations concerning them.

A psychological semantic theory is inevitably one of semantic *memory* and presupposes the existence of a certain number of invariants, or entities, in the long-term memory of the speaker and which are related or organized according to certain structures. This approach is perfectly compatible, at least under certain conditions, with various linguistic, logical, philosophical or information processing concepts of semantics. In order for a theory to be comprehensive it must of course be compatible with the facts emerging from these different disciplines.

Our starting point will be a concept of the semantic structure of memory, which may be characterized as being of the componential-predicative type. This concept involves the idea that the lexical units, the lexemes, which are stored in an individual's memory may be psychologically decomposed into smaller-format units which may be called "semes", semantic features, components, primitives, markers, etc. The primary characteristic of these units is that they are based on differentiations – or on oppositions, in structuralist terms – which a member of a given society is capable of forming within his world. We may note in this context that certain facts related to translation, especially related to certain non-translatable utterances, are among the strongest arguments in favor of a componential theory. Within the framework of the concept adopted here, the structure of features within a lexeme is not different from the structure of words within a sentence or, more precisely, from elements (predicates and arguments), within a proposition: this is thus a predicative structure. The name I adopted for this theory is thus componential-predicative, but this will not be stressed here (see Le Ny, in Press).

It should nevertheless be added that the componential structure of the lexical unit must be considered as including a *flexible* feature hierarchy *i.e.* features have a varying degree of salience, adhering more or less to the central nucleus of the lexeme.

This idea of feature salience enables us to explain two very important types of effect in any utilization or comprehension of speech. One type involves effects related to polysemia and to the elimination of the ambiguities which normally occur as a result of the presence of polysemic words in speech. It is accepted that polysemic words arising in a given context in the native language rarely result in false comprehension. There is, moreover, very often even a lack of awareness of the occurence of polysemia, on the part of the speaker as well as the listener. As a result of conversations with interpreters, I presume that they have a greater immediate awareness of polysemia than do ordinary listeners.

The second category of effect involves the metaphoric use of words and the varying degree of acceptability of metaphors. This is especially true when one passes from one language to another. If we suppose that two corresponding lexemes of two languages are theoretically composed of the same set of features (which is not so frequently the case) nevertheless a metaphoric use in the first language may be impossible to translate word for word. This is apparently an indication of the fact that their features, even in this favorable case, may have a different hierarchical value. This obviously results in difficulties in translation.

This approach to the psychological aspects of lexical structure of course implies a series of theoretical options. They are different from the neo-associationist type of hypotheses advanced by other authors and also are different from those based, much too exclusively in my belief, on syntactical organization as described by recent theories of grammar.

The cognitive abilities of the speaker also include higher order structures, especially sentence structures. They must be conceived of as sets of places or slots used by the speaker to arrange, within syntactical and semantic restrictions, the units of semantic information, the features which are expressed in an utterance. The ordinary speaker selects the words he pronounces as a function of these pre-existing schemata. The "natural" listener also usually interprets the words he hears as a function of them, and during the discourse he anticipates the words to come as a function of these schemata. A simple example of such a schema is that of an event, which may be approximately verbalized as follows: "Something happened to something – or to somebody – under some circumstances (of time, of place, of manner, . . .)". The predicative writing of propositions furnishes a fairly good formalization of this kind of analysis. It leads to a better understanding of three types of facts: how even grammatically incorrect sentences can be interpreted, how people make inferences concerning missing information during discourse and also how "ideological" effects function, as a result of which the listener imposes his own prejudices on the sentences he hears.

Taking the above into account, we may attempt a more precise representation of the processes occurring during simultaneous interpretation. As I stated above, simultaneous interpretation will be considered in the same context as translation in general, *i.e.* both obligatorily involving an initial phase of psychological transformation of the input text into an immediate semantic mental representation. This representation may be qualified as "basic", "abstract", even (which is less adequate) as "logical" or as "conceptual". Clearly, in a large number of cases, this representation also contains emotional components, which may form a large part of it; however, this latter factor will not be considered here in order to remain within the context of the informative content of the message. Thus this semantic mental representation is the result of the processes involved in the psychological transformation of form into sense.

In the case of an interpreter who, by definition, is master of the input language, there is no reason to suppose *a priori* that the processes of comprehension used during simultaneous interpretation are any different from those underlying the ordinary comprehension of speech by a unilingual subject. We will discuss the other differences below.

MEMORIZING AND FORGETTING DURING SIMULTANEOUS INTERPRETATION

Before this, however, it is convenient to discuss a phenomenon which is particular but very important. In unilingual understanding of speech, the whole process may also be represented as involving two phases, the second of which seems to be different from that occurring during translation. The first phase indeed is composed of true comprehensional activity and its time scale is relatively short, of the order of fractions of a second or several seconds. After that, however, a second phenomenon develops with time, involving memory processes and which we may characterize as forgetting and integration.

First the essential idea is that a listener begins to forget a sentence as soon as he hears it. It is, however, well established that this forgetting differentially and unequally affects the semantic and non-semantic characteristics of the text. The term non-semantic here refers to the phonemic characteristics, (or grapho-phonemic in the case of a written text), as well as to the surface syntactic characteristics to the extent that they do not have a directly semantic value. If we consider memory over comparatively long intervals (e.g. several hours or several days), it is well known that the speaker or listener forgets the *manner* in which things were spoken more rapidly than *that* which was spoken.

We recently studied this differential decay, but during short intervals *i.e.* of the order of five seconds. In one of these experiments (Verstiggel and Le Ny, 1977) subjects were asked to compare two sentences which were successively presented to them and to state, by pressing one or another button, whether these sentences "said the same thing" or not. The second sentence was presented either immediately after the first or after a lapse of 5 seconds. In the latter case, the subjects were prevented from thinking of the first sentence by asking them to loudly count backwards. There were three kinds of second sentences: a) completely identical to the first; b) very different from the first; c) lexically different but semantically identical *i.e.* having the same meaning as the first. The main conclusions from this experiment are that the decay of non-semantic components begins very quickly. On the other hand, semantic mental representation of the sentence is *not* degraded during the initial seconds following sentence understanding, and in fact may even continue to evolve positively, even though the subject is occupied in processing other information.

In the case of a continuous text the situation is obviously different in that the information contained in successive sentences is normally related, which was not the case in the experiment previously cited. But this must strengthen the previous conclusions rather than change them.

An interesting question may then be posed. Does memory for semantic information decay differently than memory for non-semantic information? Such a difference would have important implications for simultaneous interpretation. In order to clarify this point, I will present three hypotheses, which of course must be tested experimentally.

1. The forgetting of the non-semantic information of the input text is more rapid in an expert interpreter than in the normal unilingual subject during the phase of comprehension;

2. this rapid decline of the non-semantic information is essential to carry out the task of simultaneous interpretation, because it facilitates better processing of semantic information;

3. if so, the training of simultaneous interpreters might involve exercises which will increase this difference between the two types of retention.

I personally do not believe that there are two distinct types of memory involved in this phenomenon, but rather that retention involves two types of features, formal (or "superficial") and semantic, depending on the manner in which processing occurs at the moment of understanding.

If events indeed occur as I have outlined, it may be understood that retention of the sense of a text in the memory of an interpreter is surprisingly good. It seems it might even be better than that of ordinary unilingual listeners.

Outside observations which have been made in real situations provide experimental evidence of this fact. Gerver (1974) has compared retention by interpreters of the content of texts they had previously listened to, interpreted or shadowed, *i.e.* repeated as they had heard them. The results showed that impairment of retention caused by interpretation relative to listening is rather weak – of the order of 12%, whereas the impairment caused by shadowing is stronger – of the order of 25%. If we consider that memorization depends more on the depth and extent of information processing than on anything else – and particularly on intention to memorize – we can understand these results; they contribute in an interesting manner to the psychological analysis of incidental learning, and, more generally, to that of the relationship between learning and the mechanisms of information processing.

UNDERSTANDING

These mechanisms will now be considered more directly in the context of their role in the activity of understanding. They may be represented as follows:

1. during the development of the temporal sequence constituting the spoken sentence, the words and their syntactic cues, including of course their place in the sequence, are successively *identified*. I will dwell neither on the true perceptual aspect of this activity, nor on the heuristic processes which lead to its success. This point is dealt with by Massaro elsewhere in this volume;

2. the identification of a word gives access to the corresponding meaning, which is conceived of as a flexible set of features, as we have stated above. It may be admitted that there then occurs a more or less comprehensive *semantic analysis* of the meanings. This analysis involves an exploration of the set of features which belong, or could belong to the meanings in question, as well as a selection of the pertinent features for the construction of the semantic mental representation of the sentence;

3. this exploration and selection depend directly on the context. They are prepared by the expectations which previously modified the contour of the features, and thus the conditions of selection of the pertinent features. We may thus explain, as already stated, resolution of the ambiguity of polysemic terms, comprehension of metaphors, etc.;

4. the features thus selected are simultaneously *recomposed* in order to produce the *semantic representation* of the sentence with its different portions;

5. this recomposition occurs according to the *semantic schemata* of propositions or sentences at the subject's disposition;

6. if there is a match between the content of the sentence and pre-existing schemata, it creates a subjective feeling of understanding. The listener then continues to actively gather information from that which follows, and to process it;

7. if such a match does not occur, the listener receives internal information leading to a subjective signal of *incomprehension.* He then implements various heuristic devices to correct the situation. The most often used is the re-exploration of the meanings; but this may be accompanied by a decrease of the standards of adequacy and, more generally, by a relaxation of semantic restrictions in order to assure the entry of at least a part of the feature content into the pre-existing schemata.

In the context of simultaneous interpretation, we might also represent the production of an output statement according to a symmetrical model. It should nevertheless be appreciated that there is even less evidence concerning the nature of sense transformation operations leading from a semantic representation to an adequate phonic chain. In fact, simultaneous interpretation offers an exceptionally interesting research situation in this regard. In comparison to other situations, it includes a much better understanding of "what the subject wants to say" before speaking and the possibility to compare this to what he actually says; I will, however, leave this subject here.

THE ROLE OF THE ANTICIPATION OF MEANING IN THE COURSE OF UNDERSTANDING AND INTERPRETATION

A very interesting question to be explored in simultaneous interpretation is: does the interpreter's preparation of the output in the target language modify his semantic mental representation of the input sentence and if so, how? This problem may be approached on a lexical level, or on that of sentence structure in general; it appears to me that both levels must yield a positive response. It may be expected that the existence of important differences in a given syntactic or semantic component of two languages will force the interpreter to impose the second language structure on the first structure. Thus, the translation from German to French or to English inevitably modifies, as a result of obligatory word order changes, *e.g.* in subordinate clauses, the quantity of information which must be stored in the interpreter's working memory, and forces him to restructure these clauses. The same types of example, but less obligatory, may be found in English-French and French-English translation, concerning the different use frequencies of active and passive voices. A similar situation exists between Russian and English or French concerning the handling of verb aspect, or in the different use of verbs or nominalizations of verbs. Similarly, for these three languages, the distribution of new and old information regarding articles (definite or indefinite) or the absence of articles, modifies the way in which the listener structures and comprehends what he hears.

This point gives rise to an important idea, which is related to that previously developed concerning semantic and non-semantic forms of recollection. Since the principal problem posed in any translation is actually the non-concordance between the semantic structures of two given languages, the good simultaneous interpreter seems to be one who directly transforms the *organization* of information, simultaneously with comprehension. This results in the information being immediately entered into the grammatical and semantic schemata of the output language. Except in the case of a perfect bilingual, where the native language is the interpreter's output language. The situation of interpretation in this regard is not fundamentally different from that of unilingual paraphrase, for example in the science writer, who must "translate" the content of a specialized text into a language which is comprehensible to a large general audience.

Thus the following parallel activities might occur during interpretation:

1. contemporaneous with the perception and semantic analysis of the input text, a second mental activity occurs, that of anticipation in the output language, composed of successive expectations of meanings organized according to the output language;

2. as the words of the input text are perceived, their meaning is compared to these anticipations, and if the two match, the sentence, clause or syntagm is uttered. This process might, in addition to pure motor anticipation or lapses, explain some of the self-corrections interpreters make in their speech (see Gerver, 1975).

I will illustrate this hypothetical mechanism of comparison by describing an experimental situation recently used. It involved the presentation on a screen of an isolated word; after it had been read it was followed by the presentation of a sentence; the subjects were asked to retain the isolated, or target word, in their memory and to press a button as quickly as possible if the same meaning appeared in the sentence. Of course there was an equal number of sentences in which nothing did appear corresponding to the word; these latter sentences normally led to a "no" response given by pressing another button. The "yes" responses were of two kinds: the first was found in sentences which contained textually the word previously presented; the other involved sentences in which no word corresponded textually to the one previously presented, but this latter could serve as a *title* for the sentence. The subjects were informed of this fact and knew that they had to answer "yes" as soon as they had all the semantic information at their disposal which would enable them to match the significance of the sentence and that of the title word.

This type of activity clearly demands the analysis of the semantic information contained in the elements of the sentence, as well as its recomposition into a unit which may be compared to the potential title word. The results show that this activity may be performed very rapidly, even, as in the present case, when formal and semantic identification are in competition. The majority of the native francophone subjects were able to correctly identify the title well before having processed the entire sentence and also without discontinuing the processing. In fact, since the title corresponded to the information contained in subject + verb or in verb + object, its identification was hardly longer than the identification of the second word of the units. On the other hand, for bilingual subjects whose second language was French, title identification time was longer than that of the last word of the sentence. In this case, semantic processing clearly did not operate in parallel with formal (word for word) processing.

Without going into detail here, and although this experiment was performed unilingually in a reading and not conversational situation, it suggests a processing model which may be applied to simultaneous interpretation. It illustrates a trained subject's capacity to analyse semantic content and to rapidly compare the result of this analysis, and of subsequent recomposition to pre-existing semantic content in order to emit an adequate response.

I believe this capacity to be inherent in simultaneous interpretation, the content to be compared being generated by the interpreter in the course of his continuous anticipation. Thus the comprehension of input information aims at the construction of a semantic mental representation which may be immediately consistent with syntactic and lexical schemata of the output language. Actual emission under these conditions would then be merely a behavior subordinated to this mental representation which is already interpreted.

TEMPORAL REGULATION IN SIMULTANEOUS INTERPRETATION

The last point I will briefly consider is the problem of *temporal regulation* which is an important aspect of simultaneous interpretation. In the present context, "simultaneous" is obviously inexact, since the interpreter must divide his work between two types of principal activity which in reality are slightly separated in time. In this respect we are in a situation that it would be interesting to compare with shadowing, or with reading out loud; we have seen that Gerver's (1974) results argue against too simple a view of that problem.

We have referred to "short term memory", but this concept in the literature rather involves ideas concerning rehearsal, limited capacity of phonemic storage and retention. However, the existence and the importance of a "working memory" cannot be seriously questioned here. It encompasses three closely related problems.

The first is the rate of the interpreter's work and his adaptation to the rate of the speech to be translated. The second is the partitioning of the speech into operating segments, and the third involves the limitations of the capacity of the interpreter's working memory and its eventual overload. It seems that these three problems have a common solution, based on the notion of the *flow of semantic information.*

It is known that good empirical evidence exists supporting the thesis that the processing of a unilingual oral conversation occurs in units, generally corresponding to the clause, (or the sentoid). In simultaneous interpretation it appears that shorter units are actually used when the clauses are long. These units may be prepositional syntagms or even separated words. In this case, the interpreter utilizes the anticipatory capacity of his listener; he opens points of suspension, in a manner of speaking, and has confidence that the listener will himself reconstruct larger sense units. It is undoubtedly useless to say that it is not a good idea to pursue this approach too far, but this aspect of the interpreter's behavior is a function of the characteristics of the input dialogue, especially its formal rate.

There are nevertheless good reasons for thinking that information flow should be defined not so much by these formal characteristics (for instance the number of words per unit time) related to the speaker's loquaciousness, but, once again, by the semantic properties of the speech. Apparently the pertinent variable in this situation is the *quantity of semantic information* produced by the speaker.

A series of experiments we have carried out yielded results which, here again, we believe can be applied to simultaneous interpretation. The main conclusion reached is as follows: it is the *quantity of features* carried by the sentences that determines the time required for their processing. Thus, for sentences of equal lengths (in terms of numbers of words), and which also are otherwise comparable, subjects require more processing time when the lexical content of the sentence is more specific *i.e.* when the terms of the sentence are more precise. The model advanced above justifies our being able to analyze this in terms of greater semantic richness (Le Ny, Denhiere and Le Taillanter, 1973). More exactly, it appears that the processing time for a sentence depends on the *new* semantic information it contains *i.e.* the quantity of features appearing *in addition* to those already encountered in the discourse (Cordier and Le Ny, 1975; Le Ny, 1977). These results could be related to those of Kintsch and Keenan (1973), who showed, that, for sentences of equal lengths processing times are a function of the number of propositions they contain.

All of this evidence is consistent with the model presented: in self-paced conditions the subject admits a quantity of semantic information into his working memory which corresponds to its capacity, and then processes it. When this operation is terminated, he transfers this information to another "place" and only at that moment can he admit another block of information. In the experiments presented, this second place was the long term memory of the subject, since its task was to memorize the text. It is not quite the same thing in the case of simultaneous interpretation since the interpreter seems to "empty" his working memory by emitting a portion of the speech. We have seen that this in fact does not in the least prevent this information from being stored in long term memory.

This processing mechanism may, however, occasionally become overloaded. The experience of interpreters concerning this question is, however, consistent with what we have just said: the determining factor is not so much the formal rate of the speech, the loquaciousness of the speaker, but rather the rate at which *new* semantic information arrives, formal rate merely being an annoyance factor. The professional training of the interpreter undoubtedly helps greatly to progressively reduce the extent of this rate by decreasing the novelty of that which is heard. Prior familiarity with a text obviously aids the interpreter to reduce the flow of oral semantic information on a given subject.

CONCLUDING REMARKS

Several considerations have thus been presented concerning a psychosemantic analysis of simultaneous interpretation. As we have seen, a fair number of them are conjectural and are based on generalizations drawn from psychological analyses of other situations. They are nevertheless consistent with empirical observations of the interpreter at work. It is certain that a more systematic psychological study of simultaneous interpretation would contribute knowledge useful for the practice, and particularly for the training, of this profession. In addition, because of the rather exceptional cognitive skills utilized by the interpreter, such a study would also lead to a deeper understanding of the processes involved in the comprehension and functioning of speech, as well as of the psychological structures upon which it is based.

REFERENCES

Cordier, F., and Le Ny, J-F., L'influence de la difference de composition sémantique de phrases sur le temps d'étude dans une situation de transfert sémantique, *Journal de Psychologie normale et pathologique*, 1975, *1*, 33 - 50.

Gerver, D., Simultaneous listening and speaking and retention of prose, *Quarterly Journal of Experimental Psychology*, 1974, *26*, 337 - 341.

Gerver, D., A psychological approach to simultaneous interpretation, *META*, 1975, *20*, 119 - 128.

Kintsch, W., and Keenan, J. M., Reading rate as a function of the number of proprsitions in the base structure of sentences, *Cognitive Psychology*, 1973, *5*, 257 - 274.

Le Ny, J-F., *Appredimento e semantica*, 1977, to appear in Italian.

Le Ny, J-F., *Notions de sémantique psychologique*. Paris, Presses Universitaires de France, in Press.

Le Ny, J-F., Denhiere, G., and Le Taillanter, D., Study-time of sentences as a function of their specificity and of semantic exploration, *Acta Psychologica* 1973, *37*, 43 - 53.

Verstiggel, J. C., and Le Ny, J-F., Information sémantique et mémoire à court terme: l'activité de comparison de phrases, *Année psychologique*, 1977, *77*, 63 - 78.

An Information-processing Model of Understanding Speech

Dominic W. Massaro

University of Wisconsin

Madison, Wisconsin

INTRODUCTION

Simultaneous interpretation provides an ideal situation for a logical analysis of an information-processing model. To the external observer, the interpreter listens to a speech in one language, while simultaneously (or at least within a few seconds or so) articulating the same message in a second language. In terms of an information-processing description, the simultaneous interpreter must decode the surface structure of the original message, map it into some abstract representation, take this same abstract representation and map it into a new surface structure, and finally articulate the translated message.

Almost every aspect of information-processing research and theory is relevant to language interpretation. The initial decoding and analysis of the spoken message by the listener is a pattern-recognition problem. Work in speech perception research should contribute to our description of this initial stage of language interpretation. Understanding the decoded message goes hand in hand with its perception, but additional processes are critical. If the listener did not "know" the language being spoken, many of the patterns of syllables might be recognized, but very little meaning could be imposed. To know the language means to have knowledge of the correspondences between the perceptual representations of the language and the conceptual ones. Psychologists and psycholinguists have recently developed a plethora of descriptions of the representation and utilization of conceptual knowledge. It is at this stage that language appears magical, but probably not unique, since one could argue for similar underlying representations in music experience (for example, Bernstein, 1976). Once the interpreter obtains meaning at some level, he can actually translate the message by mapping the meaning onto the new surface structure. This skill would seem to reduce to one that even the unilingual has; for example, he/she might be asked to describe a recent book that was read, or what did John say at the party last night.

Our analysis of the language interpretation and communication situation would seem to imply that no unique or novel skills are required, as long as the interpreter knows the two relevant languages as well as the person on the street knows one. This analysis must be wrong, however, or else why would this august group be assembled on the island of San Giorgio? The interpreter is clearly more than the simple sum of the component skills that we have discussed. Time-sharing between processes and simultaneous processing are necessary for language interpretation. Deriving the deep structure message and selecting the appropriate surface form must go on simultaneously with decoding the speech currently being heard. But our person communicating in San Marco must also time-share and parallel-process in the unbroken chain of political discussion, although he/she operates in terms of just one surface form whereas our interpreter must work in two. The apparent similarities in language interpretation and everyday language usage would seem to imply that what we know about normal language usage would be relevant to understanding simultaneous translation. This paper reviews the current state of the art in understanding spoken language, in terms of a general information-processing model. It is hoped that the researcher interested in simultaneous interpretation will be able to encode the surface message into something of value in this regard.

The present paper describes some of the processing stages involved in language performance along with relevant research questions. We use an information-processing model as a heuristic device to analyze theory and data from a variety of approaches. Language performance begins with the language stimulus and involves a sequence of internal processing stages before communication occurs. The processing stages are logically successive although they do overlap in time. Each stage of information processing operates on the information that is available to it and makes this transformed information available to the next stage of processing.

The speech stimulus consists of changes in the atmospheric pressure at the ear of the listener. The listener is able to experience the continuous changes in pressure as a set of discrete percepts and meanings. Our goal is to analyze the series of processing stages that allow this impressive transformation to take place. Figure 1 presents a flow diagram of the temporal course of perception of a language pattern such as speech. At each stage the system contains structural and functional components. The structural component represents the information available at a particular stage of processing. The functional component specifies the procedures and processes that operate on the information held in the corresponding structural component. The model distinguishes four functional components; feature detection, primary recognition, secondary recognition, and rehearsal-recoding. The corresponding structural components represent the information available to each of these stages of processing. The stages will now be described in more detail, along with some theoretical issues and relevant research.

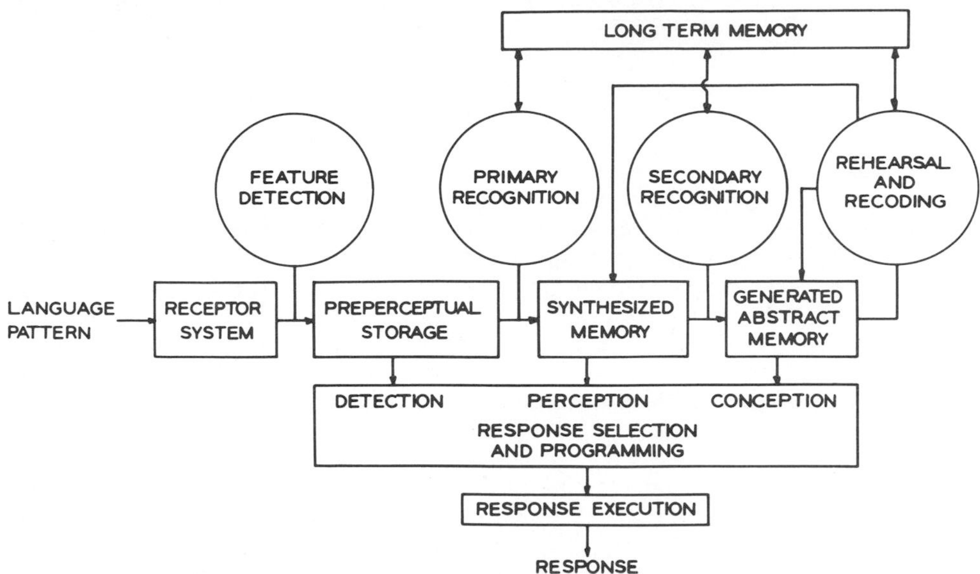

Figure 1 Flow diagram of temporal course of understanding a language pattern.

FEATURE DETECTION

The changes in sound pressure set the eardrums in motion and these mechanical vibrations are transduced into a set of neural impulses. The neural impulses have a direct relationship to the changes in mechanical vibrations. We call the transformation from mechanical to neural information feature detection and evaluation. The signal in the form of continuous changes in vibration pattern is transformed into a set of relatively discrete features. Features do not have to be relatively primitive such as the amount of energy in a particular frequency band, but they may include information about the duration or rate of intensity and frequency change. It would be possible, for example, to have a feature detector that responds to the rising first formant transition that is characteristic of the class of stop consonants.

a. Acoustic features

One traditional concern in speech research has been to determine the acoustic features that are utilized in perception. In terms of our model, the feature detection process places features in a brief temporary storage called preperceptual auditory storage (PAS), which holds information from the feature detection process for about 250 msec. The primary recognition process integrates these features into a synthesized percept which is placed in synthesized auditory memory. One question is what features are utilized, and a second important question is how are all of the features integrated together? Does the listener only process the least ambiguous feature and ignore all others, or are the features given equal weight, and so on? Despite the overwhelming amount of research on acoustic features, very little is known about how the listener puts together the multitude of acoustic features in the signal in order to arrive at a synthesized percept.

The integration of acoustic features has not been extensively studied for two apparent reasons. The first is that research in this area was highly influenced by linguistic descriptions of binary all-or-none distinctive features (Jakobson, Fant, and Halle, 1961). One of the goals of distinctive feature theory was to minimize the number of distinctive features of the language. Therefore, distinctive features were designed to be general and not stimulus-specific. If a distinctive-feature difference distinguished two phonemes in the language, that same distinction was assumed to distinguish several other phoneme pairs. Given the distinctive feature of voicing, then, the distinction of voiced versus voiceless can account for the differences between /z/ and /s/, /v/ and /f/, and so on. Given the assumption of a binary representation of distinctive features the integration of information from two or more dimensions would be a trivial problem. Integrating binary features from voicing and place of articulation, for example, could be carried out by simple logical conjunction. If the consonant /b/ were represented as voiced and labial and /p/ were represented as voiceless and labial, the identification of voiced labial sound would be /b/ whereas the identification of a voiceless labial sound would be /p/.

A second reason for the neglect of the integration problem is methodological. The primary method of study involved experiments in which the speech sound was varied along a single relevant dimension. For example, in a study of voicing all voicing cues were made neutral except one, such as voice onset time and then this dimension was varied through the relevant values. Similarly, place of articulation was studied by neutralizing all cues but one, and then varying the remaining dimension through the appropriate values. Very few experiments independently varied both voicing cues and place cues within a particular experiment. Therefore, little information was available about how these cues were integrated into a synthesized percept.

More recently, we have initiated a series of experiments that are aimed more directly at the study of the integration of acoustic features in speech perception (Massaro and Cohen, 1976; Oden and Massaro, 1977). In contrast to the traditional linguistic description, we assume that the acoustic features held in preperceptual auditory storage (PAS) are continuous, so that a feature indicates the degree to which the quality is present in the speech sound. Rather than assuming that a feature is present or absent in PAS, it is necessary to describe a feature as a function of its degree of presence in PAS. This assumption is similar to Chomsky and Halle's (1968) distinction between the classificatory and phonetic function of distinctive features. The features are assumed to be binary in their classificatory function, but not in their phonetic or descriptive function. In the latter, features are multivalued representations that describe aspects of the speech sounds in the perceptual representation. Similarly, Ladefoged (1975) has also distinguished between the phonetic and phonemic level of feature description. A feature describing the phonetic quality of a sound has a value along a continuous scale whereas a feature classifying the phonemic composition is given a discrete value. In our framework, the continuous features in PAS are transformed into discrete percepts in synthesized auditory memory (SAM) by the primary recognition process.

Given this theoretical description, acoustic features in PAS must be expressed as continuous values. That is to say, the listener will be able to hear the degree of presence or absence of a particular feature, even though his judgement in a forced choice task will be discrete. Oden and Massaro (1977) have used this description to describe acoustic features as fuzzy; that is to say, varying continuously from one speech sound to another. In this representation features are represented as fuzzy predicates which may be more or less true rather than only absolutely true or false (Zadeh, 1971). In terms of the model, fuzzy predicates represent the feature detection and evaluation process; each predicate is applied to the speech sound and specifies the degree to which it is true that the sound has a relevant acoustic feature. For example, rather than assuming that a sound is voiced or voiceless, the voicing feature of a sound is expressed as a fuzzy predicate.

$$P(\text{voiced}(S_{ij})) = .65 \tag{1}$$

The predicate given by Equation 1 represents the fact that it is .65 true that speech sound S_{ij} is perceived to be voiced. In terms of our model, then, the feature detection process makes available a set of fuzzy predicates at the level of PAS. In addition to being concerned with the acoustic features in preperceptual storage this analysis of the feature evaluation process makes apparent that an important question in speech perception research is how the various continuous features are integrated into a synthesized percept.

As an example of the study of acoustic features, consider the dimension of voicing of speech sounds. In English, the stops, fricatives, and affricates can be grouped into cognate pairs that have the same place and manner of articulation but contrast in voicing. The question of interest is what acoustic features are responsible for this distinction and how the various features are integrated together in order to provide the perceptual distinction. The integration question has not been extensively studied, however, since the common procedure in these experiments is to study just a single acoustic feature at a time. Consider two possible cues to the voicing distinction in stop consonant syllables: voice onset time (VOT), the time between the onset of the syllable and the onset of vocal cord vibration, and the fundamental frequency (F_o) of vocal cord vibration at its onset. Each of these cues has been shown to be functional in psychophysical experiments when all other cues have been held constant at neutral values. But it is difficult to generalize these results to the perception of real speech, since no information is provided about the weight that these features will carry when other features are also present in the signal. To overcome this problem, it is necessary to independently vary two or more acoustic features in the signal. The results of this type of experiment will not only provide information about the cue value of one feature when other features are present in the signal, but will also allow the investigator to evaluate how the various acoustic features are combined into an integrated percept. (For a further discussion see Massaro and Cohen, 1976, in press; Oden and Massaro, 1977).

b. Acoustic features in fluent speech

The success of finding acoustic features in perception of isolated speech sounds might lead one to expect that perception of fluent speech is a straightforward process. Sound segments could be recognized on the basis of their features and the successive segments could be combined into higher-order units of words, phrases, and sentences. However, the acoustic structure of words in fluent speech differ significantly from the same words spoken in isolation. Two sources contribute to the large variation of the words in fluent speech: coarticulation and psychological parsimony (Cole and Jakimik, 1977; Ross, 1975).

In fluent speech, the speech articulators must assume an ordered series of postures corresponding to the intended sounds, and the articulators cannot always reach their intended targets because of influence of adjacent movements. Coarticulation refers to altering the articulation of one sound because of neighboring sounds. The words *did* and *you* spoken as/dId/ and /ju/ in isolation will be articulated as /dIdʒu/ in combination because of palatalization. The alveolar stop followed by a front glide when combined produce the front-palatal affricate /dʒ/, even though a word boundary intervenes. Psychological parsimony, sometimes called laziness (Ross, 1975), refers to the minimization of effort when we speak (Lieberman, 1967; Ross, 1975). Extending our example, *did you* can be further modified to give /dIdʒu/ or just /dzu/ in the utterance *Did you want to go?* Therefore, we get the message when a close friend asks /dʒəwanəgo/or even/jəwanəgo/?

Luckily, the speaker is not only lazy but also intelligent. He anticipates the linguistic competence of his audience and the contextual constraints in the message (Lieberman, 1967). For example, a speaker will usually tend to give the listener a better acoustic signal for words that have high information content. Lieberman (1963) asked listeners to identify words excised from continuous speech. Identification was good to the degree that the excised word was unpredictable in the original utterance. The word "nine" was recognized about twice as often when it was excised from the sentence, "The number you will hear is nine", than when it was taken from "A stitch in time saves nine." If a word is not highly predictable from context, the speaker compensates by providing the listener with a better acoustic signal. In a heroic study, Umeda (1977) measured the temporal properties of consonant sounds in 20 minutes of speech. Content words had longer durations than function words, and she interprets these results in terms of the high information value of content relative to function words.

PRIMARY RECOGNITION

The primary recognition process evaluates the acoustic features in PAS and compares or matches these features against those defining perceptual units in long-term memory (LTM). Every perceptual unit has a representation in long-term memory, which is called a sign or prototype. The prototype of a perceptual unit is specified in terms of the acoustic features that define the ideal acoustic information as it would be represented in PAS. The recognition process operates to find the prototype in LTM which best matches the acoustic features in PAS. The outcome of this process is the phenomenological experience of hearing a particular sound at some location in space. This synthesized percept is held in synthesized auditory memory (SAM). In contrast to the feature detection process, the outcome of the primary recognition process is influenced by the listener's knowledge and expectations and can be modified by learning experience. Two issues are critical for understanding the nature of the primary recognition process. The first issue is the properties of preperceptual auditory storage (PAS) and the second is the nature of perceptual units.

a. Preperceptual auditory storage

Preperceptual auditory storage holds the features passed on by the detection process for a short time after a sound is presented. Given that a speech sound is temporally extended, its acoustic features can be detected at varying times during or after the speech sound. Furthermore, different features might require different amounts of time for feature detection. Given that the features do not enter preperceptual storage simultaneously, they must be integrated across some short period. In speech perception, preperceptual auditory storage accumulates the acoustic features of a speech stimulus until the sound pattern is complete. Primary recognition occurs during and possibly after this time in order to arrive at a synthesized auditory percept. A second pattern does not usually occur until the first pattern has been perceived. However, if the second pattern is presented soon enough, it should interfere with recognition of the first pattern. By varying the delay of the second pattern, we can determine the duration of preperceptual auditory storage and the temporal course of the recognition process. The experimental task is referred to as a backward recognition masking paradigm (Massaro, 1972).

In one study (Massaro, 1974) the consonant-word (CV) syllables /ba/, /da/, and /ga/ were used as test and masking stimuli. Only enough of each syllable was presented to make it sound speech-like. The 42-msec syllables had 30 msec of CV transition plus 12 msec of steady state vowel. On each trial, 1 of the 3 syllables was presented followed by a variable silent interval before presentation of a second syllable chosen from the same set of 3 syllables. The subject's task was to identify the first syllable as one of the 3 alternatives, and to ignore the second syllable, if possible. The speech sounds were presented at a normal listening intensity.

Figure 2 plots the observed results in terms of discriminability (d')values for each of the three test alternatives. The d' measure of signal detection theory

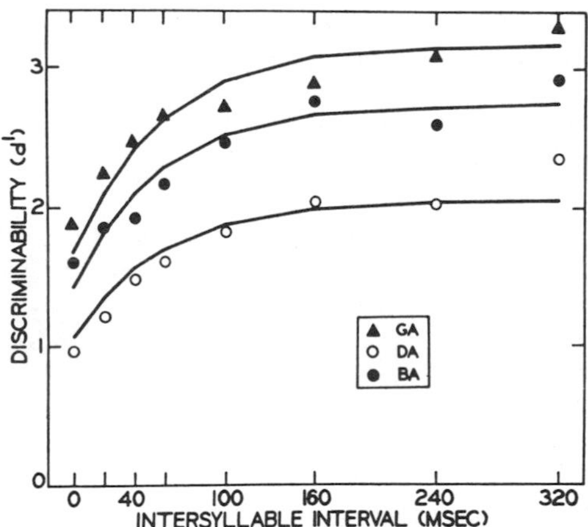

Figure 2 Accuracy of recognition of the three voiced stop-consonants (measured in d' values) as a function of the silent interval between the offset of the test syllable and the onset of the masking syllable. The points give the observed results and the lines give the predictions of a quantification of the primary recognition process.

provides an index of how well the subject discriminates a given test alternative from the other test alternatives in the task. This measure allows the experimenter to correct for any decision bias the subject may have under a particular experimental condition. The d' values are computed from the hit and false alarm probabilities. The probability of identifying a syllable correctly is designated as a hit, and responding with that syllable to any other syllable alternative is designated a false alarm. For example, the probability of responding /ba/ given the test alternative /ba/, P(ba | ba), would be a hit, whereas the probability of responding /ba/ to /da/ or /ga/, P(ba| da or ga) would be a false alarm. The d' value given by these two independent probabilities indexes the discriminability of the syllable /ba/.

Figure 2 shows that correct identification of the first speech sound increased with increases in the silent interval between the two sounds. These results show that recognition of the consonant phoneme was not complete at the end of the CV transition or even at the end of the short vowel segment of the sound. Syllable recognition required perceptual processing after the speech sound was terminated. The second speech sound interfered with perception if it was presented before recognition was complete. These results support the idea that the speech sound is held in preperceptual auditory storage while processing takes place. A second sound interferes with any further resolution of the first sound.

What do these results imply about the on-line processing of continuous speech? We will argue below that V, CV, and VC syllables function as perceptual units in speech processing. The backward masking experiment with CV syllables shows that the consonant is not recognized before the vowel, but rather the CV syllable is recognized as a unit. In our model, accurate recognition requires sufficient processing time after the information of the sound pattern is placed in PAS. Massaro (1972, 1974) has presented some evidence that V and CV syllables are processed during the steady-state vowel period. In this view, the extended vowel periods in continuous speech are redundant in terms of providing additional segmental information, but could serve the important function of allowing for sufficient processing time before new information is presented. Silent periods also allow time for processing and it has been shown that silent time after a VC syllable is critical for accurate recognition (Abbs, 1971). (For a further discussion of processing time in continuous speech, see Massaro, 1975b).

b. Perceptual units in speech

In the framework of the information processing model, the primary recognition process integrates the featural information held in preperceptual storage into a percept in synthesized memory. One question relevant to the model is the functional units at this stage of processing. The functional units are called perceptual units which correspond to units that are described in long-term memory. The primary recognition process finds the best match between the featural information in PAS and the descriptions of perceptual units in long-term memory. The recognition process, then, involves the transformation of the featural information into a synthesized percept.

We have argued that perceptual units correspond to sound patterns of V, CV, or VC size since these units can be described by relatively invariant acoustic features (Massaro, 1975b). Smaller units such as phonemes lack invariance, and in fact, this lack of invariance has been one of the central foci of speech perception theory (cf. Liberman, Cooper, Shankweiler and Studdert-Kennedy, 1967). Perceptual units of larger size have also been proposed. However, the results in backward recognition masking shows that preperceptual auditory storage cannot maintain featural information for a period of time greater than roughly one quarter of a second. Therefore, some transformation must take place on the order of every syllable; phrases, clauses, or even words are inappropriate perceptual units at the primary recognition stage of processing. (For further discussion, see Massaro, 1975b, Chapter 4).

SECONDARY RECOGNITION

Secondary recognition transforms synthesized percepts into meaningful forms in generated abstract memory. In speech perception, it is assumed that the input is analyzed syllable by syllable for meaning. The secondary recognition process makes the transformation from percept to meaning by finding the best match between the perceptual information in SAM and the lexicon in long-term memory. Each word in the lexicon contains both perceptual and conceptual information. The concept recognized is a function of two independent sources of information: the perceptual information in synthesized memory and the syntactic/semantic context in the message. It should be noted that the latter source of information does not have to be in the message per se but could result from the situational context and the knowledge of the listener.

a. Perceptual and contextual contributions

We assume that the secondary recognition process operates syllable by syllable on the output of primary recognition. In this sense, our conceptualization of speech processing is one that is perceptually, and, therefore, acoustically driven. However, contextual constraints also exert a strong influence at this stage of processing, so that both contributions must be accounted for in describing how meaning is imposed on the spoken message. A series of recent studies have shown that abstracting meaning is a joint function of the perceptual and contextual information. In one experiment, Cole (1973) asked subjects to push a button every time they heard a mispronunciation in a spoken rendering of Lewis Carrol's *Through the Looking Glass*. A mispronunciation involved changing a phoneme by 1, 2, or 4 distinctive features (for example, *confusion* mispronounced as *gunfusion, bunfusion*, and *sunfusion*, respectively). The probability of recognizing a one-feature mispronunciation was .3 whereas a four-feature change was recognized with probability .75. This result makes apparent the contribution of the perceptual information passed on by the primary recognition process. Some of the mispronunciations went unnoticed because in our view the contribution of contextual information worked against the recognition of a mispronunciation. The syntactic/semantic context of the story would support a correct rendering of the mispronounced word, outweighing the perceptual information. In support of this idea, all mispronunciations were correctly recognized when the syllables were isolated and removed from the passage.

A second paradigm that has been used to study speech processing is the shadowing task, in which the listener repeats back the message as it is heard. It is well-known that shadowing performance improves with increases in the syntactic/semantic constraints in the message (Rosenberg and Lambert, 1974; Treisman,

1965). Recent research has been directed at how these higher-order constraints are integrated with the ongoing perceptual analyses in order to arrive at the meaning of the message. Marslen-Wilson (1973) asked subjects to shadow prose as quickly as they heard it. Some individuals were able to shadow the speech at extremely close delays with lags of 250 msec, about the duration of a syllable or so. When subjects made errors in shadowing, the errors were syntactically and semantically appropriate given the preceding context. For example, given the sentence "He had heard at the Brigade", some subjects repeated "He had heard that the Brigade". In this example, *that* shares acoustic information with *at* and is also syntactically/semantically appropriate in the same position in the sentence.

In another experiment (Marslen-Wilson, 1975), subjects shadowed sentences that had one of the syllables mispronounced in a three-syllable word. Subjects never restored the word, that is, repeated back what should have been said when the mispronunciations occurred in the first syllable. With mispronunciations in the second and third syllables, however, a significant proportion of restorations occurred. If the mispronounced word was syntactically and semantically anomalous, however, restorations did not occur for any mispronounced syllable. These results indicate that restorations will not occur if the shadower does not have sufficient acoustic information and syntactic/semantic context to make the restoration appropriate. If context were the exclusive and overriding factor, we might expect subjects to replace the syntactically-semantically anomalous word with the appropriate word. This did not occur, however, showing that both context and acoustic information influenced speech processing.

Marslen-Wilson and Tyler (1975) had subjects monitor sentences for a target item in three types of target monitoring tasks. The target item was either a particular word, any word that rhymed with the target, or a member of a superordinate category. Three types of sentences were used: (1) normal, (2) syntactically corect but semantically anomalous by randomization of the content words, and (3) a completely random ordering of the words in the sentence. The mean reaction time for detecting the target was a function of both the monitoring task and the sentence structure. The reaction times were shortest for detecting a specific target, next shortest for a rhyme, and longest for a member of a superordinate category. Sentence structure facilitated monitoring in all three tasks, however, showing that higher-order constraints were functional, regardless of the nature of the target analyses that were required.

Marslen-Wilson and Welsh (in press) asked observers to shadow (repeat back) spoken passages from a popular novel. The words of the passage were read to the subjects at a rate of 160 words per minute. The subjects were told to repeat back exactly what they heard. At random throughout the passage, common three-syllable words were mispronounced. When the words were mispronounced, only a single consonant phoneme was changed to a new consonant phoneme. The new phoneme differed from the original by one or three phonemic distinctive features, based on Keyser and Halle's (1968) classification system. Independently of the degree of feature change the changes could occur in the first or third syllable of the three-syllable word. Finally, the mispronounced words were either highly predictable or unpredictable given the preceding portion of the passage. Subjects were not told that words could be mispronounced although they probably became aware of this early in the experiment. All subjects shadowed at relatively long delays greater than 600 msec. The primary dependent measure in the task was the percentage of fluent restorations, that is, the proportion of times the shadowers repeated what should have been said rather than what was said. About half of the mispronounced words were restored and the restorations were made on-line with an average latency, and the shadowing was not disrupted. (When the mispronunciation was repeated exactly, i.e., not restored, shadowing was disrupted and response times increased).

The change in the percentage of restorations as a function of the 3 independent variables in Marslen-Wilson and Welsh's study can illuminate how acoustic information and high-order context are integrated by the listener in language processing. Figure 3 presents the observed results in terms of the percentage of fluent restorations. All three variables influenced the likelihood of a restoration: shadowers were more likely to restore a one-feature than a three-feature change, a change in the third then in the first syllable, and a change in a highly predictable than in an unpredictable word.

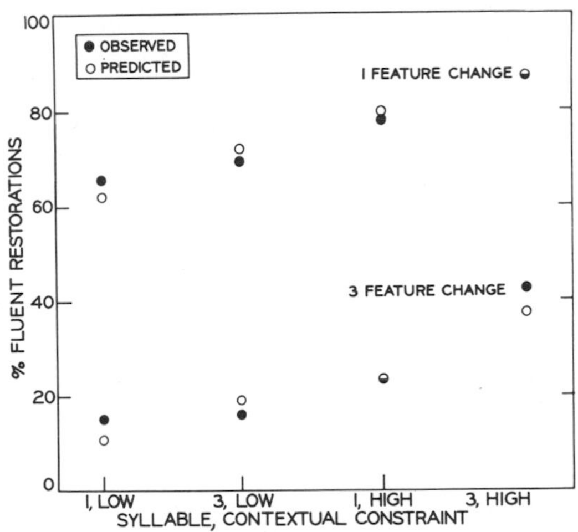

Figure 3 The percentage of fluent restorations of mispronunciations in a shadowing task as a function of the degree of feature change of the mispronounced sounds, whether the mispronunciation occurred in the first or third syllable of the word, and whether the mispronounced word was highly or lowly predictable given the preceding context. (Observed results from Marslen-Wilson and Welsh, in press).

Marslen-Wilson and his colleagues interpret this series of experiments as evidence against serial theories of language processing, which assume that "varying degrees of delay before information at any one level of analysis can interact with information at a higher level" (Marslen-Wilson and Tyler, 1975, p. 784). However, the results do show exactly such a delay. Restorations seldom occur when the first syllable is mispronounced by 3 features even though the word is relatively probable given the preceding context. This means that some low-level perceptual analyses of the word occurred regardless of the high-order constraints available and then thc outcome of these analyses was combined with the higher-order constraints. The fact that higher-order constraints in the passage influence shadowing does not mean that some analyses do not begin before others. More importantly, their view might be interpreted to mean that higher-order analyses modify the output of lower-level analyses. However, a quantitative model that assumes that both levels of analyses are functionally independent can accurately describe the results of their experiments. Figure 3 presents the predictions of a quantitative formulation of the independent model. The model assumes that the information passed on by the feature detection and evaluation process is equivalent regardless of the higher order constraints in the message. Therefore, it is not necessary to assume that higher-order constraints allow the subject to selectively attend to or selectively process certain acoustic properties of the speech input. In this sense, we argue that higher-order constraints do not modify the nature of the low-level perceptual analyses performed on the input data.

REHEARSAL AND RECODING

In the present model, the same abstract structure stores the meaning of both listening and reading. Generated abstract memory (GAM) in our model corresponds to the working memory of contemporary information processing theory. Rehearsal and recoding processes operate at this stage to maintain and build semantic/syntactic structures. There is good evidence that this memory has a limited capacity, holding about 5 ± 2 chunks of information. For a more detailed discussion of processing at this stage, see Massaro (1975a, Chapter 27). Rehearsal and Recoding operations are the workhorses of the simultaneous translation task and it is at this stage the task becomes unique relative to normal language processing.

a. Generated abstract memory

Although GAM is assumed to be abstract relative to SAM and SVM, the nature of the information appears to be tied to the surface structure of the language rather than in terms of underlying meaning that is language independent. Relevant research comes from work experiments carried out with bilingual subjects (Dornic, 1975, provides an excellent review). Recall from immediate memory (supposedly tapping GAM) does not differ from unilingual and bilingual lists, whereas recall of items assumed to be no longer in GAM was poorer in bilingual than unilingual lists (Tulving and Colotla, 1970). Similarly, Kintsch and Kintsch (1969) showed that the semantic relationship between the words in different languages did not influence immediate memory, but did affect recall of items no longer active in GAM. Saegert, Hamayan and Ahmar (1975) showed that multilingual subjects remembered the specific language of words in a mixed language list of unrelated words, but this information was forgotten when the words were presented in sentence contexts. Dornic (1975) points out that surface structure and item information are integrally related in immediate memory; subjects seldom report translations for the words. If the items are remembered, so are the appropriate surface structure forms.

b. Rehearsal

Although some work has been carried out on rehearsal and recoding operations, it is not clear how relevant it is to the simultaneous translation situation. In our model, GAM has a "limited capacity" and the learning and memory for information is a direct function of rehearsal and recoding processes. Memory of an item will increase with the time spent operating on that item, and will decrease with the time spent operating on the "unrelated" items. This "limited capacity" rule has provided a reasonable description of the acquisition and forgetting of information in GAM (cf. Massaro, 1975a, Chapter 27).

c. Recoding

The simultaneous translator must recode the surface code of the source language to that of the target language. A critical question at this stage of processing centers around the size of the units that are recoded. It seems unlikely that recoding occurs word by word given that many words are ambiguous until later context disambiguates their meaning. It might be assumed, therefore, that the translator builds syntactic/semantic structures in the source language and then translates these structures into abstract forms and finally recodes the abstract structures into the target language.

The success of the simultaneous translator depends, in part, on how quickly the recognition of the original units of the message can be recoded into their appropriate transformations. The degree of stimulus-response compatibility may be important in this regard. Consider an experiment carried out by Alluisi, Strain, and Thurmond (1964). Subjects were visually presented with a single digit under three different levels of stimulus uncertainty. Subjects had to either name the digit, name the digit that was one larger than the test digit, or name another number that had been previously assigned to the digit at random. Reaction times increased with increases in stimulus uncertainty on all response conditions, but at a much faster rate for incompatibile than for compatible responses. Responding with a low-compatible response will require much more time than with a high-compatible response, especially when there is high stimulus uncertainty.

Theios (1975) has formulated a model in which each name code in a stimulus is associated with a hierarchy of responses. Selecting a response high in the hierarchy is fast and relatively independent of stimulus uncertainty. To the extent the appropriate response is low in the hierarchy, response selection time will be slow and will depend on stimulus uncertainty. In this view, the simultaneous interpreter must organize his response hierarchy so that the surface forms of the target message are high and other forms are low.

LONG-TERM MEMORY

The structure of long-term memory in terms of the representation of meaning has been a central concern of "cognitive scientists" during the last decade. Lexical storage is usually assumed to be a necessary and central component of the representation of meaning. We view the subjective lexicon as a multidimensional representation with both perceptual and conceptual attributes. The perceptual codes of *wind* consist of the sound of the spoken word *wind*, the look of the letters that spell *wind*, a picture of a windy scene, and the sound of the wind blowing, and so on. The conceptual code consists of the relatively abstract (but fuzzy) properties that define the meaning of *wind*, such as air movement. Language understanding involves going from perceptual codes to conceptual ones, whereas production goes in the reverse direction. Secondary recognition performs this function in understanding, whereas recoding must be involved in production.

The translator must have perceptual codes of both languages stored with the conceptual codes. Also, the two sets of perceptual codes must be differentiated at some level, so that memory access and retrieval will be limited to the appropriate surface form. One central issue in discussion of the memory structures of multilinguals is whether the two languages share the same memory or whether each language has a unique and separate memory (cf. Dornic, 1975). In terms of lexical representations, would there be additional codes for *wind* in the second language or would there be another unique entry for *wind* in the second language? In the former case, additional perceptual codes are added to the same conceptual codes, whereas in the latter, new conceptual codes would be established along with the new perceptual codes of the second language. As Dornic (1975) points out, however, neither of these extremes may be correct with the truth lying somewhere in-between.

If bilinguals have a single conceptual code, then accessing this code makes available more perceptual codes than would be available for the unilingual. Traditional results and theory in reaction-time research would then lead to the conclusion that response times should be longer for bilinguals; reaction-time usually increases with increases in the number of response alternatives (Ervin, 1961). Given that bilinguals do not seem to show this deficit, they must be able to filter out one language and switch in the other with very little decrement in performance. Dornic (1975) has provided some evidence for this capability by showing that a set and expectation for one language interferes with processing a second language. Many of the issues in bilingual research seem to be basic to understanding simultaneous interpretation.

CONCLUSION

It is hoped that analyzing simultaneous interpretation in terms of an information-processing framework is more than an academic exercise. Many of the skills required in translation are currently being studied in language-processing research. Knowledge acquired in this work should be directly applicable to understanding and training interpreters. Gerver (1976) has admirably reviewed empirical studies of simultaneous interpretation and has outlined a model similar to the one proposed here. The permanent structural features and control processes in his model are similar to the structural and functional components in the present model. Finally, it should be mentioned that Moser (this volume) has had some success in extending and exploiting these models in the development of training programs for interpreters. I look forward to further developments that will provide the critical question for information-processing theory: how well does it work in the real world?

REFERENCES

Abbs, M. H., A study of cues for the identification of voiced stop consonants in intervocalic contexts. Unpublished dissertation, University of Wisconsin, 1971.

Alluisi, E. A., Strain, G. S., and Thurmond, J. B. Stimulus response compatibility and the rate of gain of information. *Psychonomic Science*, 1964, *1*, 111 - 112.

Bernstein, L. The unanswered question. *The 1973 Norton Lectures at Harvard.* Cambridge, Mass.: Harvard Univ. Press, 1976.

Chomsky, N., and Halle, M. *The sound pattern of English.* New York: Harper and Row, 1968.

Cole, R. A. Listening for mispronunciations: A measure of what we hear during speech. *Perception and Psychophysics,* 1973, *13*, 153 - 156.

Cole, R. A., and Jakimik, J. *Understanding speech: How words are heard.* Technical Report, Department of Psychology, Carnegie-Mellon University, 1977.

Dornic, S. Human information processing and bilingualism. *Report from the Institute of Applied Psychology*. The University of Stockholm, *No. 67*. 1975.

Ervin, S. M. Semantic shift in bilingualism. *American Journal of Psychology*, 1961, *74*, 233 - 241.

Gerver, D. Empirical studies of simultaneous interpretation: A review and a model. In R. Brislin (Ed.) *Translation: Applications and research.* New York: Gardner Press, 1976.

Jakobson, R., Fant, C. G. M., and Halle, M. *Preliminaries to speech analysis: The distinctive features and their correlates.* Cambridge, Mass.: MIT Press, 1961.

Keyser, S. J., and Halle, M. What we do when we speak. In P. A. Kolers and M. Eden (Eds.), *Recognizing patterns.* Cambridge, Mass.: MIT Press, 1968.

Kintsch, W., and Kintsch, E. Interlingual inference and memory processes. *Journal of Verbal Learning and Verbal Behavior*, 1969, *8*, 16 - 19.

Ladefoged, P. *A course in phonetics.* New York: Harcourt, Brace, and Jovanovich, 1975.

Liberman, A. M., Cooper, F. S., Shankweiler, D. P., and Studdert-Kennedy, M. Perception of the speech code. *Psychological Review,* 1967, *74*, 431-461.

Lieberman, P. Some effects of semantic and grammatical context on the production and perception of speech. *Language and Speech*, 1963, *6*, 172 - 187.

Lieberman, P. *Intonation, perception, and language.* Cambridge, Mass.: MIT Press, 1967.

Marslen-Wilson, W. Linguistic structure and speech shadowing at very short latencies. *Nature*, 1973, *244*, 522 - 523.

Marslen-Wilson, W. D. Sentence perception as an interactive parallel process. *Science*, 1975, *189*, 226 - 228.

Marslen-Wilson, W., and Tyler, L. K. Processing structure of sentence perception. *Nature*, 1975, *257*, 784 - 786.

Marslen-Wilson, W., and Welsh, A. Processing interactions and lexical access during word recognition in continuous speech. *Cognitive Psychology*, in press.

Massaro, D. W. Perceptual images, processing time, and perceptual units in auditory perception. *Psychological Review,* 1972, *79*, 124 - 145.

Massaro, D. W., Perceptual units in speech recognition. *Journal of Experimental Psychology*, 1974, *102*, 199 - 208.

Massaro, D. W. *Experimental psychology and information processing.* Chicago: Rand-McNally, 1975 (a).

Massaro, D. W. *Understanding language: An information-processing model of speech perception, reading, and psycholinguistics.* New York: Academic Press, 1975 (b).

Massaro, D. W., and Cohen, M. M. The contribution of fundamental frequency and voice onset time to the /zi/ and /si/ distinction. *Journal of the Acoustical Society of America*, 1976, *60*, 704 - 717.

Massaro, D. W., and Cohen, M. M. Voice-onset time and fundamental frequency as cues to the /zi/ — /si/ distinction. *Perception & Psychophysics*, in press.

Oden, G. C., and Massaro, D. W. Integration of place and voicing information in identifying synthetic stop-consonant syllables. *WHIPP Report No. 1, Wisconsin Human Information Processing Program,* July, 1977.

Rosenberg, S., and Lambert, W. E. Contextual constraints and the perception of speech. *Journal of Experimental Psychology*. 1974, *102*, 178 - 180.

Ross, J. R. Parallels in phonological and semantic organization. In J. F. Kavanagh and J. E. Cutting (Eds.), *The role of speech in language*. Cambridge, Mass.: MIT Press, 1975.

Saegert, J., Hamayam, E., and Amhar, H. Memory for language of input in polyglots. *Journal of Experimental Psychology: Human Learning and Memory*, 1975, *1*, 607 - 613.

Theios, J. The components of response latency in human information processing. In S. Dornic and P. M. A. Rabbitt (Eds.)., *Attention and Performance V*, New York: Academic Press, 1975.

Treisman, A. M. Verbal responses and contextual constraints in language. *Journal of Verbal Learning and Verbal Behavior*. 1965, *4*, 118 - 128.

Tulving, E., and Colotla, V. A. Free recall of trilingual lists. *Cognitive Psychology*, 1970, *1*, 86 - 98.

Umeda, N. Consonant duration in American English. *Journal of the Acoustical Society of America*, 1977, *61*, 846 - 858.

Zadeh, L. A. Quantitative fuzzy semantics. *Information Sciences*, 1971, *3*, 159 - 176.

Human Factors Approach to Simultaneous Interpretation

H. McIlvaine Parsons

Institute for Behavioral Research

Silver Spring, Maryland

This paper, based on the author's consultation for the United Nations in 1975, describes a human factors (or ergonomic) approach to simultaneous interpretation in an international organization. A human factors intervention in a human information processing system seeks to solve some real-life problem, such as increasing the effectiveness of individual or system performance, or, as in the United Nations instance, resolving the problems of stress and tension that the system and its processes impose on participants.

Whichever the aim, in a human factors investigation the first step is to describe and analyze the tasks and procedures in which the participants engage and the environments in which they work, including their equipment. A task analysis of simultaneous interpretation calls for considering all task characteristics that contribute to input load on the interpreter, including speakers' speed, tempo, accent, vocal characteristics, and use (or misuse) of microphone; availability of advance text, speakers' reading from text, changes from text, provision of background material, and novel content or terminology; differences between languages, and relaying; background noise in meeting room and reactions of audiences; and such temporal factors as number of preceding meetings interpreted, recovery time, length of meeting, on-air time, and durations of speakers' utterances.

Environmental and equipment analysis of the interpretation booth should cover illumination, ventilation, temperature, noise interference, dimensions, writing surfaces and storage spaces, seating, visual access between booths, cueing and control panels, and earphones. Attention should also be given to such motivational factors as feedback from speakers and fellow interpreters and to such social factors as intrabooth relationships between interpreters and overall relationships between interpreters and speakers.

If the investigation's aim is to improve interpretation, it would be necessary to obtain objective data for effectiveness measures such as accuracy, quality, and completeness of interpreters' output relative to input from speakers. Such measures could also reflect the effects of stress and tension, as would physiological data such as heart rate and urinary excretion of noradrenaline and adrenaline. In the absence of these measures, the best one can do is get subjective reports from the interpreters themselves in interviews and through rating scales. Ideally, task, procedural, environmental, equipment, and motivational variables would be manipulated experimentally in simulations of meetings. Alternatively, data about such variables could be collected at actual meetings and correlated with output and physiological data. The United Nations study had to depend on retrospective verbal reports by sixteen interpreters.

First, eleven of these provided information through interviews, some in their interpretation booths. From these interviews and by observing the interpretation process itself it was possible to specify an array of process variables, time variables, and environmental (booth) variables that might contribute to the stress and tension that the interpreters said they experienced and wished to keep from becoming too debilitating. Indeed, a year earlier most of them had stayed away from their jobs for one day and the UN ground to a halt. It was this job action and a resulting change in interpreter scheduling that led to the investigation of which my consultation was a part.

These process, time, and environmental variables were the task, environmental, and equipment characteristics to which I referred as contributing to the input load on the interpreter, the "difficulty factors." It seemed important to me to bring these to the attention of the UN Secretariat and, perhaps, the delegations, so there would be a wider understanding than there seemed to be of the interpretation process. If some of these factors could be ameliorated, the interpreters might experience less stress and tension and they might be less likely to avoid that stress and tension by failing to come to work. In this sense, my study was a motivational one, and I tried to suggest other motivational factors as well. But I hoped that my brief survey and analysis would also benefit the interpreters themselves and would be helpful to the UN management by examining items that might be making simultaneous interpretation at the UN less effective than it should be. As I noted earlier, it was not possible to get any effectiveness data, though such data are most characteristic of human factors investigations.

Instead of seeking such objective data, I administered a questionnaire to five experienced UN interpreters. Each came from a different language section: Chinese, Russian, Spanish, French, and English. There were 62 items. Other than 14 that concerned the use of earphones, all the items requested a rating on a scale of 1 to 5 for the "stress and tension" that a process variable or booth condition occasioned in the interpreter. Of course, I realize the difficulty of providing a satisfactory objective or behavioral definition of either tension or stress. But these are words that people do use to describe how they feel, and the interpreters seemed to have no difficulty in supplying the ratings, although there were individual differences among them, as one might expect. A rating of 1 meant no or slight stress and tension, whereas 5 meant an extreme amount.

Although with such a small sample I don't consider this little inquiry more than exploratory and suggestive, you might be interested in some of the results.

With regard to process variables, the interpreters indicated little or no stress (1) when the speaker was of a different sex (my sample included both men and women), (2) when they lacked previous experience with the speaker, or (3) when they had to switch between languages. The process variable that occasioned the most tension and stress, they said, unanimously giving it a 5, was relaying from poor interpretation. (Relaying consists of interpreting into one's native language what another interpreter has said in his or her own (and different) language in interpreting from the source language – a practice used when the two-person team in a UN booth lacks mastery in the speaker's language.) Four interpreters said they were extremely stressed (1) when the speaker talked very fast (which occurs frequently when a speaker reads from text) and (2) when they had to spend more than three hours in a booth. Other factors almost as stressful included (1) a speaker's vocal idiosyncracies or lack of clarity or coherence, (2) the awareness of making interpretation errors (but others' errors were not especially troubling), (3) awareness of verbatim reporting at the same time as interpretation, (4) need for intense concentration, (5) inexperience with subject matter, (6) changes by a speaker from his or her text, (7) a speaker's accent (the mother tongues of many delegates are not among the UN meeting languages), (8) long speaker utterances (between pauses), (9) background noise in the meeting room, and (10) mispositioning of the speaker's microphone relative to the speaker.

There were mixed reactions to such variables as unusual content or terminology in a speech (e.g., technical terms), failure to get an advance text, failure to get advance background material, awareness of being monitored by delegates for interpretation accuracy, uncertainty as to when a meeting will end, and having an incompatible colleague in the booth. But in every case at least two of the interpreters in the sample gave these items a rating of 4. The interpreters themselves suggested some of the items at the start of the questionnaire session – at which, incidentally, they were assured of anonymity – and one of these was a concern expressed that an interpreter was "a conduit rather than an agent." Though this kind of self-image might have been more strongly associated with other feelings or behavior, it occasioned subjective stress and tension above the 2 level in only one interpreter. The same might be said of lack of feedback from delegates and non-identification of interpreters to the speakers they interpreted.

I heard considerable complaining from some of the interpreters about environmental conditions at work. They all reported much tension and stress arising from noise interference in their booths, and two were much concerned that because of the in-line arrangement of booths, those in one booth could not see those in the others. Though reactions among them differed, at least two gave stress and tension ratings of 3 or more to illumination, ventilation, temperature, booth dimensions, chair design, writing surfaces, and storage facilities. At the outset it was explained to the five interpreters that stress/tension was not the only or necessarily the best criterion for environmental design. Subjective assessment of comfort and convenience and objective criteria such as ambient recordings and measurement of interpretation effectiveness might have been preferable. Had they been feasible, such recordings would have determined to what extent illumination, ventilation, temperature, noise interference, and dimensions of the UN booths matched the requirements of International Standard ISO 2603: Booths for Simultaneous Interpretation – General Characteristics and Equipment, developed by the ISO

Central Secretariat in collaboration with the International Association of Conference Interpreters and published in 1974.

Had I been more expert in psychoacoustics, I would have given more attention to the equipment and circuitry that bring a speaker's output as input to the interpreter and the interpreter's output as input to the delegates. I did query the five interpreters about their earphones, an important part of that equipment. Three said they disliked them. Reflecting what I had discovered in the booths, some said they used the earphones that were provided, others said they used their own. All said they were disturbed by the electronic noise in their earphones, at least to some extent, and all reported they regulated the earphones' volume. Three gave discomfort ratings of 4 or 5 to their earphones, where 5 represented extreme discomfort.

Four said they normally kept an earphone off of one ear, either completely or a little. Two said it was the right ear, one specified the left ear, one reported alternating, and one did not respond. All said they heard their own voices when they spoke; four said they heard them through an ear, and one of these added it was resonance in the head. Three reported closing their eyes at times when they were interpreting. (This might be an index of concentration.)

Although I did not ask these five interpreters much about temporal variables, these did figure importantly in my analysis of stress effects on the interpretation task. I distinguished between salaried time (the hours per week for which an interpreter is paid), on-call time (availability for duty), in-house time (at the UN), booth time (in the booth), meeting time (actual duration of a UN meeting), on-air time (composed of attending time and processing time), and recovery time. I tried to make the point that a few arduous minutes of processing time (a peak load), especially towards the end of two or three hours of booth time during a meeting, might result in considerable tension and stress but would not show up in statistical data about in-house time and weekly booth time. As noted earlier, the interpreters were emphatic that more than three hours in a booth resulted in excessive stress and tension, especially compared with a shorter time.

I was rather proud of developing the concept of recovery time. This term means uncompensated or compensated non-booth or non-in-house time to recuperate from previous work. Some recovery time (as in weekends and vacations) is implicit in some jobs, including those with a standard 40-hour or other weekly extent, and explicit in others, such as airline pilots. It implies the accumulation of stress and tension either over time or from relatively brief but intense experiences (or both) and the need to dissolve such stress and tension. What a person does during recovery time is presumably important and varies between individuals. Some UN interpreters played games such as bridge or chess. One exercised. Another went camping. Sleeping and meditation could be other "unwinding" techniques among those that may occur to you. Difficult to resolve in a practical context are such questions as how to relate special very short-term recovery time (e.g., a half-day off) to customery recovery times, such as a weekend, and the durations of these kinds of recovery time to those of longer ones, such as vacations. For example, it was suggested to me that free-lance interpreters were less concerned about short-term recovery times than were regular UN interpreters because they took longer vacations.

The question of short-term recovery time went to the heart of the UN interpreters' protest about working hours and the stress and tension they said resulted from working more than seven half-day sessions per week, the limitation they achieved through their work action in 1974. My recommendation to the UN Secretariat was to place more emphasis on enforcing another, earlier convention, that a simultaneous interpreter should not be required to work more than three half-day sessions in succession.

In examining the motivational aspects of simultaneous interpretation at the United Nations, I drew on some concepts from operant conditioning rather than human factors. I suggested that if some unfavorable or aversive aspects of the job were diminished and some favorable or positive aspects were enhanced, there might be a better relationship between job disincentives and incentives, that is, the negative and positive consequences of coming to work. Among the unfavorable consequences or disincentives I listed the stress and tension I have already reviewed, the discomfort of the physical environment of the booths, and uncertainties as to whether and how long an interpreter might have to work on a particular day. This last factor seems to have become significant to younger interpreters, whose personal lives off the job have acquired increased importance relative to their lives on the job. As favorable consequences or incentives I mentioned recognition and vicarious reinforcement through modeling. Favorable consequences can include feedback from fellow interpreters or feedback from delegates stating or implying a praiseworthy performance. The first type is limited, as implied earlier, by the linear design of the UN booths. The anonymity traditionally assigned to interpreters has precluded the second, especially if interpreters and delegates do not associate with each other socially – and apparently they do so less than in the past. Let me quote from my consultant's report some further observations about recognition and vicarious reinforcement:

1. *Recognition.* I've already noted that the UN interpreters are anonymous, as far as their principal audience is concerned, the delegates. It was suggested to me that individually, and perhaps collectively, they also receive little recognition from higher UN management. Recognition that someone is performing a job is a powerful incentive to spend time on the job. Further, since it destroys anonymity, it makes it easier for consequences to affect performance *within* the job and thereby to improve job performance. How might recognition be accorded UN interpreters? A simple method would be to install lighted name plates on the inside of the booth window, clearly visible to the people in the chamber. The name plates would identify the interpreters in the booth and would be changed as these changed, or even as they alternated in interpretation. To be sure, the objection might be raised that this innovation would be too distracting to the delegates. If the identification displays attracted no attention at all, they would serve no purpose. But would they attract so much that they would interfere with the business of the meeting? Perhaps this would best be decided through an empirical test, a try-out. In any case, the concept is not entirely novel. Nilski (1969) had the following to say:

   ". . . it is sheer anachronism to maintain the disembodied trappings of anonymity . . . AIIC has passed resolutions

> urging its members to make sure, during each assignment, that their individual names are known not only to the conference organizers but can also be readily checked by the conference participants. In some cases, this is done by having the interpreters' names printed in the conference programme. However, since this is just one of the many details crammed into such a programme, here in Canada the practice of placing each interpreter's name on the booth in front of him has been gaining a foothold and seems to have much to recommend it. It is a powerful incentive to interpreters to do a good job, with the built-in reward of recognition; it is a protection to them against unqualified competition; and is one of the best ways a conference can safeguard itself against incompetence in a field of work whose fleeting nature makes merit hard to assess."

2. *Modeling.* People imitate each other. Notably, interpreters model delegates. In fact, that's just what they are supposed to do in interpreting. If they model their speeches, they are also likely to model their other behavior. What other behavior? That of spending time on the job. If the delegates show up on the job and keep long or late hours, the interpreters are more likely to do the same. Indeed, such modeling may account for the traditional job involvement of interpreters in diplomatic gatherings. However, how much someone will imitate another person's behavior depends on a number of factors.

   a. The model must exhibit the behavior to be copied. If delegates are frequently absent from meetings – and UN records could presumably show whether this is true – there will be less delegate behavior to model. If they show up, there will be more.

   b. Imitation becomes more likely if the model has prestige or status for the modeler. If UN delegates have lost prestige in the eyes of the interpreters (possibly for reasons beyond the control of the delegates), interpreters will model them less. Conversely, greater delegate prestige will increase modeling.

   c. To this point the discussion of modeling hasn't been tied to the discussion of positive motivation. But modeling and positive motivation are closely linked. Person A imitates Person B if either A or B receives consequences. Person A may receive consequences for the behavior involved in his or her modeling. But if B receives consequences, Person A gets them vicariously – indirectly. They affect A's behavior as well as B's. A will imitate the behavior of B according to the consequences of that behavior for B. UN interpreters will model the job attendance of delegates if the latter visibly achieve satisfactions, accomplishments, peer approvals, and enjoyment in their jobs. If they don't, the interpreters are less likely to model them, even if the delegates show up on the job and have prestige. Thus, positive motivation *about* their jobs can be brought to the interpreters in the degree it characterizes the delegates about *their* jobs.

Such, then, was a rather short-lived human factors investigation of simultaneous interpretation in an operational setting, with supplementation from operant psychology. If in this talk I have omitted references to the experimental research on simultaneous interpretation, I did include a review of this research in my report, with help from H. W. Sinaiko, in part because I got the impression that no one I encountered at the UN, at that time, was particularly aware of that research. Although I also referenced investigations of the effects of noise (Gerver, 1974) in my report in discussing process and environmental variables, most of these factors seemed to have lacked emphasis in the experimental literature. That may have been one reason why individuals in an operational setting were unfamiliar with that literature. Reciprocally, it may be useful for those who conduct laboratory research to know about operational variables, either to control them to increase the internal validity of their experiments, or to manipulate them to augment their external validity. I hope that this paper will help relate the two worlds of operations and research to each other.

I also hope that research and applications in human factors or ergonomics will grow in this fascinating area of human information processing, simultaneous interpretation. Outcomes of a human factors investigation could include changes in procedures, improvements in booth and equipment design, and provision of incentives or reduction of disincentives. More broadly, such investigation could lead to better specification of personnel requirements and more effective training. But before all this can come to pass, diplomats and administrators of international secretariats may need to learn more about simultaneous interpretation and to support research which can benefit their own organizations.

REFERENCES

Gerver, D., The effects of noise on the performance of simultaneous interpreters: Accuracy of performance. *Acta Psychologica*, 1974, *28*, 159 - 167.

Nilski, Therese, *Conference interpretation in Canada.* Documents of the Royal Commission on Bilingualism and Biculturalism. Ottawa: Queen's Printer for Canada, 1969.

Simultaneous Interpretation –

Units of Meaning and other Features

Marianne Lederer

Université Paris III – Sorbonne Nouvelle

Paris

It is certainly fit and no coincidence that this symposium devoted to interpretation should bring together psychologists, linguists and interpreters. Interpreting is a human performance in which cognitive activity is first and foremost; it therefore leads us into the field of psychology with no need to resort to special experiments; in this field the connection between thinking and speaking can be observed as it materializes with each segment of speech so that investigations into interpretation also pertain to psycholinguistics. Since it implies a comparison of speech acts in different languages it also obliges us to tread on linguistic ground. Thus interpreters can rejoice in having the opportunity of comparing their results with those obtained by psychologists, linguists and psycholinguists.

For a number of years, our research team at Paris University (Sorbonne Nouvelle) has been recording speeches and discussions at multilingual international conferences and comparing not only speeches and their interpretations but also speeches in different languages. We have collected a wealth of evidence which is as yet far from being entirely exploited; yet a number of conclusions seem now sufficiently ascertained for me to try and present a short extract of a speech and its simultaneous interpretation and to discuss some of the evidence obtained.

As a preface however, I should like to stress how important it is to consider what interpretation is supposed to achieve before embarking on a detailed study of the processes involved. Everything that is spoken in a booth in response to speakers' utterances is interpreting and representative of the state of the art; in a study that would propose to survey the present state of the profession, all types of interpretation would have to be taken into consideration. This, however, is not the purpose of our research team: we concentrate on the process of interpretation that establishes communication. We believe that in doing so, we determine not only what such interpretation is, but also what speech behaviour consists of. Seen from this angle it becomes a truism to state that interpretation, to be taken as an object for investigation, has to establish communication.

A fundamental precept has therefore guided our selection of recordings at international conferences: we have always checked that discussions in the meeting room have developed unhampered by the variety of languages used. Delegates speaking different languages and listening to the interpretation of languages they do not know must be able to understand each other as if they were communicating directly through one and the same language: that is a basic prerequisite for interpretation to be considered worth studying as a process. The best way of judging the quality of interpretation is to listen to a discussion period where people put questions to each other. If all this is carried out in two or three languages, and people prove satisfied with the replies, it can be said that communication was established, that the interpretation was successful and that the process involved was representative.

We also have to bear in mind that the findings on any process under investigation can be distorted if extraneous factors confuse the basic issue. Interpreting is free speech and it should be investigated in connection with spontaneous speech, i.e. extemporaneous interventions and not prepared statements or papers being read out. When we speak simultaneously, our thoughts are paramount in our minds and words follow suit without our paying attention to them. We think as we speak and so does the interpreter listening to us. When we read out a text however our thinking has already taken place and our thoughts, instead of controlling our words, are merely aroused by them, sometimes we even by-pass thinking altogether. The interpreter's performance is not the same in both cases; when translating from texts being read out he has to overcome problems that are quite different from the process of understanding and stating that which was understood which he carries out normally.

A further fact is worth mentioning before embarking on a more detailed account of some of my findings: it is a recurrent fact that at the beginning of any meeting there is much more language transposition or transcoding than later on. This constantly recurring phenomenon can be explained: as long as too much of what is meant remains unknown to the interpreters (although perfectly known to all participants, and therefore unsaid by the speaker) their only recourse is to lag as little as possible behind the speaker's words so as to translate his language. By and by, as the meeting goes on, interpreters analyse the tiniest bits of information, probe more and more deeply into the intended meaning of speakers and as this stored knowledge builds up, their interpretation departs from the linguistic meaning of the source language and consequently their rendering becomes more natural and their language more native.

The very short passage upon which I am going to comment – it took the speaker 36 seconds to utter it – has been extracted from a panel discussion which was part of a three day meeting organized last March by the Sugar Industry on the general theme: "*Sugar, Diet and Health*". This panel discussion took place on the afternoon of the second day; interpreters had already heard and translated papers on sugar and obesity, sugar and diabetes, sucrose and brain chemistry and sucrose and sports. They were therefore quite familiar with the various topics speakers might touch on.

This passage in English and its interpretation into French was chosen from a number of transcripts of recordings I made at that conference. It is intended to be an example of a few of the features that appear when studying simultaneous interpretation. It is of course not the sole basis for the conclusions I shall be presenting here, and not exhaustive as a substratum either. Much more can be said about simultaneous interpretation and its implications for language and memory than I could possibly say within this short time. I am preparing for publication an extensive study of 63 minutes of German–French interpretation, which I hope will be published in the not too distant future. It will contain more detailed observations and conclusions. This paper is meant as a typifying example of results obtained so far. The passage is taken from a panel discussion on the role of sugar in the soft drink and food industry; Mr Brooks from Canada is speaking; here are the first sentences of his statement:

> "I don't really want to get into the paper that I am presenting this afternoon, but it bears upon the matter that at present is being discussed. I think this is an extremely important point. Apart from certain necessary defensive work from sucrose manufacturers and sucrose users, there is a real need to identify where, within the normal society, sucrose and similar sugars are playing important positive roles. Dr Kingsbury's comments with regard to the sportsmen are pertinent. He is right also to identify the possibility of other needs at other times."

And here is the transcription of the recording showing the parallel development of original and translation:

APART FROM CERTAIN NECESSARY DEFENSIVE
Je crois que le problème est extrêmement

WORK FROM SUCROSE MANUF-
important. A part certains travaux

ACTURERS AND SUCROSE USERS
nécessairement défensifs

THERE IS A REAL NEED TO IDENTIFY
de la part des fabricants et des industries utilisatrices de saccha-

WHERE, WITHIN THE NORMAL SOCIETY
rose, il faut préciser

SUCROSE AND SIMILAR SUGARS ARE
le

PLAYING IMPORTANT POSITIVE ROLES.
rôle positif et important du saccharose et autres sucres

DR. KINGSBURY'S COMMENTS
chez les bien-portants.

WITH REGARD TO THE SPORTSMEN
Ce que Monsieur Kings –

ARE PERTINENT. HE IS RIGHT ALSO
bury vient de nous dire à propos des sportifs est

TO IDENTIFY THE POSSIBILITY
extrêmement pertinent. Il a aussi

OF OTHER NEEDS AT OTHER TIMES.
raison de dire qu'il y a

I DON'T THINK THE TOPIC IS A SIMPLE ONE
d'autres besoins à certains moments au plutôt chez d'autres

WHEN IT GETS DOWN TO IT. I . . . .
personnes.

The reader will notice that at the beginning of the transcription, the interpreter is still rendering the previous sentence and that, whilst he is still translating the end of the passage, the speaker is pronouncing a new sentence. This is a reminder that the interpreter receives a continuous stream of information and that interpretation, although shown here on paper, should not be analysed as if it was written translation.

I have arbitrarily subdivided the 36 seconds extract into segments of three seconds each in my presentation in order to present the way the speaker's and interpreter's parallel speeches develop. I have very roughly superimposed the words simultaneously pronounced by them in an effort to reproduce (although very sketchily) what can be heard when listening simultaneously to tape recordings of the two languages.

THE TIME LAG BETWEEN SPEAKER AND INTERPRETER

When looking at the transcript it can be observed that there are times when interpretation follows fluently upon the speaker's output with a delay of between 3 to 6 seconds. There are other times however when the interpreter pauses and lets the speaker get very much ahead of him. And there are still other times, usually following a pause in the interpreter's rendering when the flow of words coming out of his mouth increases to a very quick delivery. Why does this happen and how can it be explained? Let us look at the sentence: "*He is right also to identify the possibility of other needs at other times.*" Up to: "He is right also . . .", the interpretation is very fluid, developing smoothly and quickly.

"*Ce que Monsieur Kingsbury vient de nous dire à propos des sportifs est extrêmement pertinent. Il a aussi raison de . . .*" follows with no hesitation upon the previous sentence but then, upon hearing " . . . to identify the possibility . . .", there is a pause of over one second, quite a remarkable interruption in such a quick delivery.

I suggest that this pause was necessary for the interpreter to get the amount of information required for his understanding of the speaker's meaning. *To identify the possibility* does not mean anything; more is needed to give this set of words some sense: the interpreter needed to hear "*of other needs at other times*". With lightning speed he was then able to connect these words with the information stored in his cognitive memory. He had translated Dr. Kingsbury's statement approximately ten minutes before translating the Canadian delegate. We have a proof of his remembering, for upon hearing "*Dr. Kingsbury's comments* . . ." he said: "Ce que Monsieur Kingsbury *vient de nous dire* . . ." His words there stem quite normally from sense, a combination of previous knowledge and immediate language understanding. But understanding "*to identify the possibility of other needs at other times*" requires more than the mere recollection of having heard the speech a short while ago.

If interpreting was mere language transposition, nothing could have prevented the interpreter from saying: " . . .*d'identifier la possibilité d'autres besoins à d'autres moments*". The English sentence: "He is right also to identify the possibility of other needs at other times" contains nothing but familiar words, arranged in a syntactic order which can easily be transposed into French. The fact that in his rendering the interpreter chose to say something else ("Il a aussi raison de dire qu'il y a d'autres besoins à certains moments *ou plutôt chez d'autres personnes*") points to a more complex process than a mere understanding of language. To start with, the interpreter *does* translate literally " . . .*of other needs at other times*" with "*d'autres besoins à d'autres moments*"; he apparently wants to catch up with the speaker but having understood what was meant, he immediately corrects himself by adding: " . . *ou plutôt chez d'autres personnes*".

Understanding sense is adding a cognitive element to language meaning. What happened here is that the words "*other needs at other times*" merged with previously stored relevant knowledge, as evidenced by the addendum: " . . *ou plutôt chez d'autres personnes*", that refers to information that has been in store for about ten minutes. In going through Dr. Kingsbury's statement, I found the following sentence:

> "There are definitely times when there is a physiological need for sugar in the drinks, not only I think for athletes and sportsmen, but also in children, convalescents, people that aren't physically very active . . .".

Of course the interpreter could not have remembered this sentence word for word, but his recollection of the substance was aroused by the mention of "*other needs at other times*", and the conjunction of the two made sense.

THE CHOICE OF WORDS

Understanding is not the only process of the human mind that can be studied in interpretation. The interpreter is not only a listener, he is also a speaker and while his words are determined by his understanding of the speaker's intended meaning, to some extent they are also based on the speaker's language.

In our example, the words "*sucrose and similar sugars*" are translated into French: "*du saccharose et autres sucres*". Here a word in French (*saccharose*) appears to have been called up to match the English *sucrose*; the same can be said of *sugar* = *sucre*, or *important positive* = *positif et important*, etc.

Words that match in translation do so for a number of reasons that do not reflect identical psychological processes. In a previous publication (Lederer, 1973), I identified three ways which seem to underlie word matching in translation. The first one I called "glissement phonétique" (phonetic shift) : in the present case (E) *positive* = (F) *positif* or (E) *important* equating (F) *important*. A change in pronounciation brings a word from one phonological system over to another and the English word is turned into a French word. The "glissement phonétique" is in some cases fully justified, when controlled by sense as in the present case. At other times it is an important source of language contamination; thus (E) *material* becomes all too often (F) *matériel*, or (E) *to ignore*,*ignorer*, etc. In simultaneous interpreting where both languages are constantly present at the same time in short-term memory, it is a great temptation to take a shortcut and be contented with the change in phonetics under the misguided impression that words phonetically similar are semantically identical; fighting this natural trend is one of the main problems in the translation of languages that resemble each other, such as English-French or Italian-French.

The second way words can be matched in translation is through a translation of primary meanings : the word that comes first to mind as an equivalent to the English word is the word that fits the translation; here we find *sugar* = *sucre*, *needs* = *besoins, manufacturers* = *fabricants, sportsmen* = *sportifs*, etc. The process involved here is very much what most people think interpreting amounts to; the only mental processes appear to be the recognition and transposition of language meaning. Figures are the typical instance of that process in interpretation and yet they are the arch foes of many of the best interpreters who fail to hear and translate correctly even two digit figures, while having no problem in grasping the most intricate arguments. One finding of immediate interest in connection with figures is related to the interpreter's lagging behind the speaker : whenever figures are rendered correctly although they are embedded in a complex argument, the interpreter abruptly catches up with the speaker and pronounces the figure almost immediately after hearing it. It seems that figures have to be repeated while still within the span of short term memory.

Primary meaning translation is a process that often proves successful but that just as often can fail. In the present case, *sucre*, for *sugar* is appropriate but in numerous cases primary meanings translated with no regard to sense are not immediately intelligible; so for instance (E) *challenge* is always rendered in French by *défi* or (E) *account for* by *rendre compte,* although *expliquer* is available and much more to the point in French.

Finally a third way of matching words is the deliberate calling up of a specific term to match a given word. Thus (F) *saccharose* for (E) *sucrose*. There the interpreter not only has to find the specific term that does not automatically associate itself with the English, as *sucre* did with *sugar*; he also has to consciously refrain from "glissement phonétique" (*sucrose* would sound so natural in French!). In other cases he would have to repel the primary meaning translation; for instance in the case of "*a fleet of engines*", "*parc de locomotives*" has to replace the automatic urge to say "*flotte*" or "*flotille*" before becoming automatically associated with "*fleet*" after having been said a few times. In the case of *saccharose*, it can be assumed that since this interpretation took place on the second day of the meeting, the calling up of the word did not require a conscious effort on the part of the interpreter, for whom the equivalent had probably by then become automatic reflex. But the phenomenon of having from time to time to summon consciously a word or an expression is too common in interpretation not to be mentioned here.

THE VERBAL MANIFESTATIONS OF SENSE IN INTERPRETATION

In our English-French extract it is striking to note a constant intertwining of what might appear to be a word for word translation and of phrases that, although initiated by the words of the speaker, do not resemble them literally. A number of the words and phrases heard in English by the interpreter are transposed into French: "*A part certains travaux nécessairement défensifs de la part des fabricants*"
is a literal translation of
"*Apart from certain necessary defensive work from sucrose manufacturers*". This does not mean that the interpreter, when doing that literal translation, puts his intellect at rest. That he understood and not only repeated "*defensive work*" comes out clearly in the way he later translates "*within the normal society*" with "*bien-portants*".

Here a few words of explanation may be necessary: sugar manufacturers are not only doing promotion and marketing work in order to boost their sales, they also subsidize a number of laboratories doing research on the role of sugar in diabetes, coronary diseases, dental caries, etc. in the hope that results will ultimately show that sugar is not as bad for health as currently held by public opinion. The meeting brings together a number of scientists who have submitted papers on their findings in those various fields. The interpreter knows all this; he therefore cannot but understand what "*necessary defensive work*" means. The verbal manifestation of his understanding is found in the French rendering :
"*il faut préciser le rôle positif et important du saccharose et autres sucres chez les bien-portants*".
There is nothing in this French sentence that resembles phonetically or semantically the phrase "*within the normal society*". No better example could be found of the way in which something that is understood not only can be rendered in a form that is entirely alien to the original form but also kept in store for a period exceeding the short term memory span, and rendered at a place that is adequate in French.

"*Defensive work*" meant research work on various diseases. "*Normal society*" where sugar is playing a positive role, means "*bien-portants*". The choice in French of words differing from the English words shows that the interpreter understood both this part of the sentence and the first part on defensive work. We find a similar example of language disparity in the same sentence, where "*sucrose users*" is rendered by "*industries utilisatrices de saccharose*". The speaker could not have meant the end users, the panel discussion is on *the role of sugar in the soft drinks and food industry*. This is obviously what the speaker meant by "*sucrose users*". The interpreter makes this even more obvious by stating it explicitly.

The difference between sense and linguistic meaning is clearly revealed in the two equivalents I have just shown : *users = industries utilisatrices, normal society = bien-portants,* or earlier, *comments = vient de dire.* This variance in the interpreter's expression as compared to the basic meanings of words is the tangible evidence that can be seized upon to probe into non-verbal thinking. The point here is not how interpreters arrange their phrases syntactically so as to fit the requirements of their own mother tongue, but the fact that their wording reflects more than the knowledge of two languages and the ability to establish equivalents between the two. It reflects the thinking process that goes on during interpreting, something which obviously is not unique to interpreters or interpretation but applies to the understanding processes in general.

UNITS OF MEANING

My investigations of recordings of interpretations led me to put forth the general concept of units of meaning. I suggest that such units are segments of sense appearing at irregular intervals in the mind of those who listen to speech with a deliberate desire to understand it. As long as there is nothing but words available, such as in our case: " . . *to identify the possibility* . ." recognition of language sounds is possible (at least in the most cases, even though recognition of sounds often requires the assistance of sense), but no additional mental operations can be carried out. With the appearance of "*other needs*", the words present in short-term memory seem to pull together and merge with the recollection of knowledge acquired since the beginning of the meeting, all of a sudden making sense.

A colleague of mine who is preparing her Doctor's degree at our University, Miss Bertone, has drawn a parallel between the emergence of sense and Jacques Lacan's *point de capiton*. For Lacan, understanding is achieved with the last word of sentences, when words seem to pull together to give birth to an idea. He compares the process of understanding with the mattress maker's pulling up his thread every few stitches, making the *point de capiton* that divides up his fabric at regular intervals. (Lacan, 1966).

Chunks of sense appear in interpretation whenever the interpreter has a clear understanding of a speaker's intended meaning. They can be preceded by a slight pause or come after a few probing words that are literally translated. At other times they are rendered immediately, as "*ce que Monsieur Kingsbury vient de nous dire*" for "*Dr Kingsbury's comment*". Units of meaning are the synthesis of a number of words present in short term memory associating with previous cognitive experiences or recollections; this merging into sense leaves a cognitive trace in the memory while the short-term memory is taking up and storing the ensuing words until a new synthesis occurs and a new cognitive unit adds up to those previously stored in the cognitive memory.

WORD PREDICTION AND SENSE EXPECTATION

Units of meaning are not a grammatical segmentation of language into syntactic units. It often happens in ordinary life that we grasp the intended meaning of a speaker before he finishes his sentence. This also happens to interpreters. Anticipation can take different forms: either the interpreter actually says a word (the verb for instance) before the speaker has uttered the corresponding word or, more commonly, he puts in a word at the correct place in his French sentence which, if compared in time, is uttered after the original, but so soon afterwards and at so correct a place in his own language that there is no doubt the interpreter summoned it before hearing the original.

When studying these anticipations a clear distinction should be drawn between anticipations based on sense expectation and anticipations based on language prediction. In the first case the interpreter who is piling up one unit of meaning after the other in his cognitive memory (they don't keep separate there, but they all contribute to his understanding of the speech as it unfolds) knows, rightly or wrongly, what the speaker is aiming at. In the other case he predicts the appearance of words that frequently occur together in speech. We have an example of this stochastic process in our passage here. The speaker, to wind up his sentence, says : "*. . . where, within normal society, sucrose and similar sugars are playing important positive roles*".

The interpreter who had been speaking rather quickly while the speaker was uttering the beginning of that sentence remains silent while hearing: "*. . society, sucrose and similar sugars are playing important. .* "; the only word he pronounces is "*le*"! Then he gets the hint and resumes speaking : " *. . .rôle positif et important du saccharose et autres sucres chez les bein-portants*".

(F) "*rôle*" is pronounced practically at the same time as the English word "*important*". It is a fact that anyone would expect the word "roles" (or any other word with a similar semantic content) after hearing: "*There is a real need to identify where, within the normal society, sucrose and similar sugars are playing important. . .*"

Sense expectation is different.

I shall have to resort to interpretation from German into French where evidence of sense expectation is easier to collect, since the syntactic structures of German and French are wide apart and literal translation less frequent. The following example is an extract from an extensive study of simultaneous interpretation which is now nearly completed.

At a railways meeting the representative of an international financial body with headquarters in Switzerland said the following sentence :
"*Die Schweizerischen Bundesbahnen haben uns angeboten diese Presseveranstaltung, die vom Vertreter des kommerziellen Dienstes . . .*"
I stop here to show what the interpreter said in French in the meanwhile :

"*Les CFF nous ont offert de nous aider à organiser . . .*"

The French word *organiser* coincides in time with the last German word quoted so far, *Dienstes*; so there is clear evidence that "*. . nous aider à organiser. . .*" is an anticipation. *Organiser* is language prediction : "*Die Schweizerischen Bundesbahnen haben uns angeboten diese Presseveranstaltung. . .*" calls for something semantically equivalent to *organiser*. We shall see that the German word was *durchzuführen.* But where does *nous aider* come from? "*Les CFF nous ont offert . . .*" is closely matching "*Die Schweizerischen Bundesbahnen haben uns angeboten. . .*" but why "*. . de nous aider* à organiser", where only the word *organiser* could be expected in association with *Veranstaltung?* The sense expectation *aider à* is vindicated by the end of the German sentence :
"Die Schweizerischen Bundesbahnen haben uns angeboten diese Presseveranstaltung, die vom Vertreter des kommerziellen Dienstes in der Gruppe Guignard vorgeschlagen worden war, gemeinsam mit uns durchzuführen".

So *aider à organiser* was anticipating " . . *gemeinsam mit uns durchzuführen*".

Sense anticipation is easy to explain. In our case, the speaker has been giving details for several minutes about the way his company intended to organise a presentation to the press of various new types of passenger cars. So obviously when he starts saying :
"*Die Schweizerischen Bundesbahnen haben uns angeboten diese Presseveranstaltung. . .*", this could not merely call for "*durchzuführen*", since his company was also involved. Once again we have here an example of the way cognitive memory constantly intervenes in communication.

In this short paper and with the few examples that could be drawn from 36 seconds of speech, I have tried to show some of the extraordinary complexity involved in speech understanding and oral translation. If interpreting was mere shadowing in another language, consisting of translating the individual meaning of each successive word in the speaker's output, or if it was just translation of language with only problems of syntactic restructuring and occasionally technical terms, it would be an interesting but limited field of investigation.

As it involves a complex series of cognitive activities, it offers I believe an avenue for an investigation of the thinking processes involved in understanding and speaking. This avenue might not have been opened up, and the thinking processes might have remained in their black boxes, had the comparison of interpretation and original speech yielded no different results than the comparison of languages as such.

Much that is revealed by interpretation is nothing other than normal speech mechanisms. I hope these few glimpses of how interpretation operates will contribute to their better understanding.

REFERENCES

Lacan, J., *Ecrits.* Paris: Seuil,1966.

Lederer, M. La traduction: Transcoder ou Réexprimer? *Etudes de Linguistique Appliquée*, Didier, Paris, 1973, *12*.

Language and Cognition

Danica Seleskovitch

Universite Paris III – Sorbonne Nouvelle

Paris

SENSE AND LANGUAGE

Conference interpreters use the term "*translation*" to describe the operation that turns a text written in one language into a text written in another language, and insist that for the oral transmission of oral messages the word "*interpretation*" should be used. Roughly speaking they argue on the grounds that written translation implies the translation of language, whilst oral transmission is based on cognitive memory that does not retain the fleeting passage of the phonemic, semantic or syntactic structures but implies grasping and rendering of sense. We shall see that there is much reason for this differentiation, though we do consider the basic process to be the same as in the East Germans' use of the all embracing concept of "*Translation*" which covers both "*Übersetzen*" and "*Dolmetschen*" in their basic aspect.

If we look at the issue at stake in the use of two separate words, interpretation and translation, we find it is *sense* that interpreters claim not to find in language alone. In wishing to keep a word that has connotations of hermeneutics, they claim that to understand a statement and to convey it to a person who is ignorant of the language he is being addressed in, it is not enough for the interpreter to understand the semantics of individual words, phrases or sentences but that it is necessary for him to get the ideas beyond the words and convey those ideas and not the word content of the original language.

The claim that interpreting is not translation of language calls for clarification since it is tantamount to saying that there is a difference between linguistic meaning and sense. In this paper we shall try to see what that difference amounts to and why it should be taken into consideration when interpreting.

First let us state that semantics is confined to language in isolation, whilst sense can be investigated only when language is being used in a communicative form. Let us take as an example a few words just addressed to me as I am writing these lines: "*La mer est forte*" says a friend looking out from our terrace onto the heavy sea below. By itself, in language not being used in communication, the word "*mɛr*" could mean "*mère*" (mother) or "*mer*" (sea), the word "*fort*" could mean strong (as in: *un homme fort*) or *fat* (as in: *une femme forte*) and yet it is "*a heavy sea*" that I understand immediately and not "*a fat mother*" or any other such nonsense.

So the first point to be made when drawing a distinction between linguistic meaning and sense is that words used in speech lose part of the potential meanings which are attached to their phonemic structures in language, and only keep their contextually *relevant meaning*.

The second point to be made in order to emphasize the difference between linguistic meaning and sense is that in human communication there is always a cognitive addition made to the relevant meaning associated with language sounds. This "complément cognitif" as we call it, stems from the knowledge aroused by the speech but not attached linguistically to the sounds heard. Let us take an example. If I said here and now: "*When the workshift changed, I was still waiting in that dingy room*", I would be uttering only language; listeners would recognize known sounds and draw semantic conclusions from their syntactic arrangements, but this understanding of language would leave them guessing as to what I might have meant when saying that. In communication, when a linguistic utterance is embedded in the listener's or reader's previously acquired knowledge, there is no such guessing; there is instead an immediate grasp of what is meant, i.e. of sense.

The sentence I just quoted was taken at random from a book also chosen at random, an autobiography. Just before writing this sentence the authoress, Angela Davis, tells us that she has been arrested on charges of murder and is spending her first night in prison. Here is the whole extract:

"I thought that I was on my way to the cells, but instead I found myself in a large windowless room, a dim bulb barely illuminating the centre of the ceiling . . . A robust matron was in charge . . .*When the workshift changed, I was still waiting in that dingy room.* A new officer was sent to guard me."

Now, *workshift* leaves no doubt as to what it means here and now: guards in charge of prisoners newly brought in. *I* is the authoress, and not anyone of the three billion inhabitants that crowd our planet; *dingy room* is a prison room, and so on. The sentence has become an act of speech, it is no longer mere language; it carries sense, it communicates ideas, not merely semantics.

The grasping of sense is always so immediate when we speak that it is no wonder it should so often have been confused with linguistic meaning. By separating language meaning from sense as I did, the difference between the two appears clearly.

Sense and linguistic meanings have been dissociated in the past but unwittingly so. Written translations dealing with ancient languages or with contemporary but little known ones require much pondering about language as such, and with each lingering of the eye on words and phrases, linguistic meanings tend stealthily to replace the sense of utterances. Thus, with language analysis, language penetrates into consciousness, and many of the cognitive processes normally involved in content analysis fall away.

One of the great advantages of interpreting is that it operates at the normal delivery rate of speech. The interpreter cannot toy with language, and sense therefore prevails in his grasping of speech, Much progress too has been achieved in the understanding of the processes involved in written translation, such as evidenced by Nida's or Kade's writings, (Nida, 1964; Kade, 1971). When there is no barrier in time or distance between the text offered for translation and the translator, and the latter feels no pangs of uneasiness about the language he works from and is familiar with the topic, there is not much difference between translating and interpreting – in both cases sense is made of the act of speech, and sense remains the guiding principle in the rewording of the text.

Now, some people dealing in linguistics or in semiotics, argue that context is all that is needed to turn language into an act of speech. This view, derived from work on machine translation, ignores the human mind and its response to speech or texts. Our minds are not programmed like a computer, they take little note of the distribution of words within sentences. Context as such is a dead matter and must be considered as part of the reader's or listener's knowledge, a very tiny part indeed of a very recently acquired knowledge that in most cases will not stay in the memory beyond a few hours or days, but a part that plays a vital role in the understanding of each succeeding sentence in speech and is, in that respect, indistinguishable from the listener's general knowledge.

Analysing the process involved in comprehending any sense-carrying sentence would show that, to the reader, context is medium term cognitive memory and that the role it plays in understanding is strictly the same as that of long term cognitive memory or general knowledge. We have all heard, however faintly, of Angela Davis, and most of us probably remember our students' uproar when she was sentenced to death. This is part of our long term memory, part of the huge amount of knowledge stored in our ten billion neurons with their innumerable synapses. But understanding that the room mentioned in that sentence was a prison room stems from knowledge very recently acquired, a knowledge that might not endure beyond the assistance it provided to the understanding of the ensuing sentences.

So we see that the process of understanding speech is based on long and medium term cognitive memory and that as a whole the process which results in sense is based on a cognitive addition to linguistic meaning, that stems from memory. Thus sense can be defined as a cognitive construction made by the addressee on the basis of the sounds he received from the addresser's mouth; he adds to them such cognitive rememberance as fits the sounds, and such additional knowledge, whether from his long or medium term memory, that fits the whole of a clause or sentence.

The cognitive remembrance that fits the sounds is never summoned separately from the calling up of other knowledge; in other words, linguistic meaning never appears alone in normal communication but always together with other knowledge. The evidence for this is that there never is any polysemy or ambiguity in speech, as there often is with words or phrases in isolation. Concurrent knowledge acts as a repressor to irrelevant semantics. You never hear *kernel* when Colonel Blimp is mentioned, but 'kɜrn'l' by itself may mean either one or the other.

A second point to be made in connection with sense is that remembrance drawn from long or medium term cognitive memory adds up to linguistic meaning without taking up any linguistic shape; we *know* the room Angela Davis is in, is a prison room, but while reading we do not verbalize *room* into *prison room*; as soon as the merging of previous knowledge with linguistic meaning is achieved and as soon as a sentence has been understood, it loses any linguistic form![1] Our remembering is not the result of rote learning but of comprehension. That is why we speak of cognitive memory as being the *nonverbal remembering* of speech contents.

A third point to be made in connection with sense and linguistic meaning, and a very important one, is that sense is always conscious. What Husserl calls the '*Meinung*' as opposed to '*das Gemeinte*', the *vouloir dire* as we say in French, that which we wish to be known, we are conscious of. To impart that intended meaning at the normal rate of speech however, we do not call up the words consciously: the linking up of sounds and semantics is reflex. Through speech we point to our ideas, we signal our feelings and our most intricate thoughts. These feelings we are conscious of as well as of our thoughts, but as long as speech serves our purpose and fits our thinking we are not conscious of how it does the signalling in spite of the highly elaborate mechanisms involved. The only conscious control we exercise over the words we use is through a feedback process; we become conscious of our language when we hear that we said something amiss. In a parallel manner we are conscious of what we understand but not of the words that triggered off that understanding. With the exception of poetics we do not keep in mind the words we hear when listening to somebody explaining his ideas.

Speech appears to be like any other of our acquired gestures. The conscious wish to light a cigarette controls the fine nerves and muscles that bring our hand to the exact position required for the match to light the cigarette; we do not directly control any of the sub-gestures involved. In the same way we are conscious of our intent when speaking, of the sense we want to put across, not of the individual words or the grammar used to that effect and we listen to sense and grasp sense without paying attention to words.

I can summarize my position regarding sense in the following way:

1. *sense is conscious* while linguistic meaning is a conditioned reflex; this applies both to surface *and* to deep structures. If such deep structures exist at all, the syntactic arrangements we make in constructing our sentences are just as reflex in nature as is the choice of lexical items;

2. *sense is made up of the linguistic meaning* aroused by speech sounds *and of a cognitive addition to it* that emerges together with that linguistic meaning;

3. *sense is non-verbal*, not only because the cognitive addition remains unvoiced, but also because sense as a whole is dissociated from any language form in cognitive memory as soon as it has been understood.

INTERPRETING AND SENSE

Why, if there is sense, should it be taken into account in interpreting? Why should the interpreter want to grasp more than the language meaning of the sentences he gets over his headphones? Why not let sense rest with the specialists who discuss their problems and leave the interpreter to his own expertise: his linguistic skill. After all, it would seem to stand to reason that interpreters should refrain from "interpreting" what they hear and on the contrary render faithfully the meaning of words and sentences without interfering in any way with the deeper meaning of utterances.

This point of view would be correct if a syntactically and lexically correct translation of language provided the listener of the translated language with the same ease of access to sense as is given those who listen to their own mother tongue flowing from the speaker's mouth.

I know that the prevailing opinion is that for interpreting no understanding other than of language is required, and that problems of terminology are the only problems facing interpreters. Problems of terminology do exist (how do you say (F)*risberme* in English or *scuffler* in French?), and often direct translation from one language to the other is needed, but most interpreters will agree that it is not sufficient to know languages in order to interpret from one into the other and that the crux of the matter lies in an ability to understand ideas, while linguistic skill is a mere prerequisite. This is the basis on which the curriculum at the Sorbonne Nouvelle School of Interpreters (ESIT) was built up.

In this part of my paper I shall endeavour to show briefly why translated words or phrases that seem all right as long as there is no communicative purpose attached to the translation are far from being intelligible in genuine acts of speech. The reasons for this have been described in detail in a recent publication (Seleskovitch, 1976) which sets forth the latest findings of my research team at Paris University; I can therefore limit myself here to a brief outline of the basic reason why, even if the impossible task of knowing all lexical items in several languages was mastered, that knowledge alone, together with grammatical competence would not suffice for adequate translation. In the main the reason is that *languages do not choose the same set of words to point to the same objects or concepts so that speakers in individual languages do not use the same words to express the same ideas.* Should interpreting be carried out on the basis of language and not of sense, listeners would have difficulties in discovering the ideas behind assemblies of words they themselves would never use in that way.

So for instance a Frenchman hearing somebody say "*Le sujet n'a rien de divertissant – aussi aimerais-je croire qu'il n'ennuiera pas*" would be nonplussed, whereas he would have no difficulty in understanding "*Il ne s'agit pas d'un sujet particulièrement drôle, j'espère néanmoins qu'il vous interéssera*" as a translation for "*the subject matter has nothing funny about it, so I'd like to believe it will not bore you*". This example is taken from recordings of our interpretation classes; if you look at the syntactic structure in French, there is nothing that you would wish to correct, neither are there any false cognates among the words; *aussi* is a normal word for *consequently* or *so,* and yet in that case, it is *néanmoins* that is required; *néanmoins* is no linguistic equivalent to *so* but it is far superior to *aussi* in rendering the idea. "*Il ne s'agit pas d'un sujet particulièrement drôle, j'espère néanmoins qu'il vous intéressera*" makes sense, while "*Le sujet n'a rien de divertissant, aussi aimerais-je croire qu'il n'ennuiera pas*" does not.

When I say that different languages do not choose the same set of words to point to the same objects or concepts, I refer to the fact that words that seem to possess the same meaning in two languages, as for instance *key* = *clé*, or *trou* = *hole*, or *bed* and *lit, driver* and *conducteur*, do not associate with the same words in different languages when pointing to identical things or concepts that require several words for designation! So, when you say in English *key*hole, we say trou de *serrure*, and where we say in French chambre à *coucher*, you prefer *bed*room; for screw*driver* we say *tourne*-vis and so on. Now of course this so-called collocational feature has been known for a long time; yet the underlying principle has so far remained unnoticed: the *key* that is missing in French *trou de serrure* is cognitively there, just as the *lock* is cognitively present in *keyhole*. A cognitive addition is always made to the semantics associated with word sounds; thus *bedroom*: you know that you *lie down* in your beds just as we know when we say *chambre à coucher* that there are *beds* there; or screw*driver* and *tourne*-vis: you know that you have to *turn* a screw to drive it in, and we know that our turning the screw will *drive it in*; in each language we only say part of what we know to communicate the whole thing.

Words that translate easily in isolation such as *key* = *clé*, *hole* = *trou* but can no longer be accepted as adequate equivalents when translated together, reveal a principle which I refer to as the *keyhole principle*. This principle means that under all circumstances the use of language requires cognitive additions on the part of both speakers and listeners, so that I am entitled to say that the missing key in *trou de serrure* is the key to sense! The keyhole principle (let us hope that in English the missing lock will not bar us from sense!) means that language could best be described as the explicit demonstration of *part* of our perceptions and knowledge, that leaves an implicit part unsaid and nevertheless meant by speakers and understood by listeners.

The fact that languages do not match word for word to express identical thinking is overwhelmingly apparent when you analyse the language used by speakers of various nationalities at international conferences. Let me take a few examples of utterances I jotted down at meetings where for days specialists discussed the same matters. Here is an example of what an English speaker said at a medical conference: "*This is a slide showing the fractured area. . .*" A French physician showing a similar slide said "*Voici la zone lésée, avec fracture. . .*" or at an agricultural conference: "*Cet engrais phosphaté est appliqué en couverture. . .*" "*The fertilizer is broadcast to place. . .*" said the American to express the same idea. Or this German sentence recorded at a conference of electricity suppliers discussing transformers: "*Wir wollten eine Beziehung aufstellen zwischen den in Zeitrafferverfahren herbeigeführten Isolationszuständen und den im natürlichen Zeitlauf erreichten. . .*" while the French discussed "*le vieillissement artificiel des isolations . . .*" and did not mention any *procédé de raccourcissement du temps*, which is the linguistic equivalent of the German words but sounds strange in French.

The differences in the propriety of expression of different languages have been given various names: Diderot for instance spoke of "*génie de la langue*"; more recently Vinay and Darbelnet wrote their *Stylistique Comparée du francais et de l'anglais*, Wandruszka uses words such as: *Technolect*, *sociolect*, etc., but nowhere is mention being made of the fact that words never mean a thing but only part of it so that differences in wording only reveal the differences in the signals used to point to the same thing. As a matter of fact, individual words do seem to denominate the whole thing. So (F) *lit* seems to equate (E) *bed*, and both are intuitively believed to cover their referent. But it should not be forgotten that most words are opaque to the ordinary user. This opacity means that synchronically words as such are meaningless to us; they are meaningful only in so far as they refer to an object or a concept. But if we are able to trace the etymology of all our words, we would find that same feature of language: the referent is pointed to by one of its characteristics only; just one example: Latin *equus* was derived from Indo-European EKWOS meaning: "*the one that runs*", expressing only one characteristic of the horse. Present day words are mistaken for the whole thing they refer to, because we are no longer aware of their initial meaning. When translated into another language they seem to carry with them the whole thing which they actually only point to and they translate without effort. But this ease is only due to the fact that they have become meaningless as such, *horse* becomes *cheval* without difficulty, but if it was called the *one that runs* we would be tempted to translate *celui qui court*, arousing doubts in our listeners' minds as to what was meant, while *cheval*, more difficult to find, would fit the génie de la langue.

We no longer see through individual words; that is why language translation was thought possible; but as soon as several words are threaded together it becomes manifest that translation cannot do without a cognitive addition. When speeches are being interpreted, it becomes abundantly clear that unless care is taken to understand the sense implied in the words, i.e. to take more than linguistic meaning into consideration when translating, the partial or linguistic meaning of the source language, if translated as such, may become an obstacle to correct understanding in the other language. For example take the expression "*row crops*": if you look at those words without looking for the meaning behind them, you might be tempted to see only their linguistic meaning and to translate "*cultures en rangées*" or "*cultures alignées*" whilst in French to express what is really meant, you would have to find the relevant aspect being used to designate it, which is "*plantes sarclées*". In both languages, the referent covered by these expressions is the way maize (U.S. corn) or potatoes are grown and cultivated.

The intrinsic linguistic meaning of words may become an obstacle to intelligibility in other languages if translated as such. Thus for instance the immediate meaning of (F) "*détendeur*" would at first sight be *stress reliever* or *expander*, etc. Actually, when used by the Air Liquide Company it designates a contraption that opens up a cylinder of liquid oxygen, thus reducing the pressure inside the cylinder and letting the liquid expand (*détendre*) into gas. The Union Carbide Company in the United States calls this apparatus a *regulator*, denominating another aspect to point to the same thing.

Again, it might be argued, why should the interpreter go to the trouble of adding cognitively to the words heard? If we have to accept the fact that primary linguistic meaning is insufficient as an object for translation, why not be satisfied with secondary meaning and just learn that "*plantes sarclées*" are "*row crops*", as we learned that "*chambre à coucher*" is a "*bedroom*", and again we are landed with terminology. A simple reply to that can be found in an exquisite phrase of the playwright Ionesco. In his play "La Leçon", a girl defeats all efforts made to teach her the multiplication tables, but one day her teacher is astounded to discover that she knows unhesitatingly that 235 multiplied by 927 is 217,845; As he probes further, she continues to give results at computer speed. To his astonished query, she replies: "*I learned all the results by heart*".

It would be as preposterous to try and learn all the possible speech equivalents as it would to learn the results of all multiplications. It is easier and more efficient when translating, to accept the all-embracing principle that the explicit part of our thinking that shapes itself into language is not the same according to whether we are German, American or French. In each case there is a large unsaid part that underlies our speaking; but that which emerges and that which remains beneath the words is not the same in different languages. This is why interpreters, to be successful, have to act as nearly as possible as normal speakers or listeners, using words that fit the sense they wish to convey, grasping the sense when hearing speech and discarding the explicit linguistic meaning voiced in the initial language, which if translated would yield a speech that would sound unnatural and non-native and which, at the normal delivery rate, would preclude anything but approximate understanding to a listener who is not cognizant of the original language.

When I was a student in Paris, many years ago, I used to laugh at the habit that some fellow Serbian students and myself had fallen into; that was of speaking a mixture of French and Serbian, and using French sentences directly translated from Serbian. I called it the "*merci joli sur la question*" way of speaking because in Serbian when somebody asks how you are, you reply by thanking him for his query, saying "*Hvala lepa na pitanju*" which is literally "*Thank nice on the question*"!

Everybody is now aware of the ridicule of literal translation but language translation remains at the heart of most discussions on translation and interpretation, as if the mishaps of machine translation had not shown that there is more to translation than language alone. Even worse, the difficulties confronting the machine were attributed to translation in general and you may read in almost all articles and treatises on translation that polysemy of words or ambiguity of phrases are a problem for translation. Now obviously the *machine* must be programmed to distinguish whether "clean" means in French the imperative *nettoyez* or the adjective *propre*, and the machine must be able to dispel the ambiguity of sentences such as "*Vendre une bicyclette pour jeune fille qui n'a jamais servi*". "*Who is brand new, the girl or the bicycle*?" asks the machine!

With a pityful lack of observation of real life speech acts (would any child be in semantic doubt if he heard: "Go clean your teeth"?) some people claimed in earnest that this kind of problem, which is a very real one for computer programmers, is a problem of translation in general. It would certainly have been more advisable to go the other way round: to examine the problems of human translating and try and adapt the machine to solutions found by the human mind.

Translating language meanings and obtaining the desired effect, i.e. a wording immediately intelligible to listeners is impossible, not because there are doubts as to the intended meaning of words or phrases, but because the resulting translation of such words and phrases would fail to carry sense adequately in the other language. This is why interpreters have to grasp sense, and render the ideas behind the words. There is some point in suggesting that there is no reason why interpreters should grasp sense for their own benefit, there is however no arguing against the need for them to say things that enable their listeners to make sense out of what they say.

REFERENCES

Kade, O., Zur Rolle des Sachverständnisses beim Übersetzen. *Fremdsprachen,* Leipzig, 1971, 14 - 26.

Nida, E. A., *Toward a science of translation.* Leiden: E. J. Brill, 1964.

Seleskovitch, D., Traduire: de l'expérience aux concepts. *Etudes de Linguistique Appliquée,* Paris, Didier, 1976, *24.*

Syntactic Anticipation in German-English Simultaneous Interpreting

Wolfram Wilss

Universität des Saarlandes

Saarbrücken

INTRODUCTION

Any transfer of a text from a source language (SL) into a target language (TL) is more or less characterized by structural asymmetry between the two languages. Structural asymmetries or divergences can occur on the morphemic, lexemic, syntagmatic and syntactic levels. Therefore, Jakobson is right in stating that "languages differ essentially in what they must convey and not in what they may convey" (1966, 236). Similar statements can be found in publications by Coseriu (1974, 81) and Hörmann (1970, 349).

Structural asymmetries are obvious even in quite simple clauses, as the following example shows:

1) Ich habe das Buch gelesen

2) I have read the book

3) J'ai lu le livre

The structural pattern of the German clause – with an embedding of the complement phrase between the two elements of the verb phrase – corresponds in English and French to a linear syntactic construction which represents the so-called SPO sentence structure in its purest form. Languages with predominantly parallel syntactic patterning, e.g. English and French, demand less syntactic restructuring than do languages which differ considerably in structure, e.g. German and English. Thus, a SL/TL transfer on the basis of parallel syntactic structures can – at least on the syntactic level of the interlingual transfer – be regarded as easier to accomplish. In addition, larger "chunks" of information can be recoded with little restructuring, as the "expectation patterns" (Mattern 1974, 69) are largely similar. The implications for the teaching of simultaneous interpreting (SI) are obvious.

On the other hand, structural asymmetries can lead to considerable transfer problems. This is particularly true in cases where sentences of a structurally complex type must be transfered from a SL, say German, into a TL, say English (I am using the word complex in an intuitive, rather undefined manner). Here is the following example:

4) Der Kultusminister hat heute die Kunstausstellung in der von vielen Polizisten scharf bewachten Stadthalle eröffnet

If we look at this sentence from a structural point of view, it is evident that we are dealing with a sentence consisting of a finite clause:

5) Der Kultusminister hat heute die Kunstaussetellung in der . . . Stadthalle eröffnet

and an embedded participle construction:

6) . . . von vielen Polizisten scharf bewachten . . .

Notice that functionally speaking the participle has the status of a clause. This can convincingly be shown, if we turn the participle construction, by way of an intralingual paraphrasing operation, into a finite main or relative clause:

7) Der Kultusminister hat heute die Kunstausstellung in der Stadthalle eröffnet. Diese wurde von vielen Polizisten scharf bewacht.

8) Der Kultusminister hat heute die Kunstausstellung in der Stadthalle eröffnet, die von vielen Polizisten scharf bewacht wurde

A clause-type corresponding to (4) is non-existent in English. This means that (4), in going from German to English, cannot be maintained, but must be rendered on the basis of a non-literal transfer procedure:

9) Today the Minister of Education opened the art exhibition in the City Hall which was sharply guarded by many policemen.

The fact that the translator cannot operate with syntactic one-to-one-correspondences entails – in Halliday's terminology – a "rank-shift" operation (1965, 27 ff.; see also Catford 1965, 24 f. and Back, 1973) with a shift up from the participle construction into a subordinate clause which is connected to the main clause by a relative pronoun. This clause-type can be re-translated into German on the basis of a rank-bound (Catford 1965, 24 f.) or literal transfer procedure. It is obvious from this that the German language – in the realm of certain syntactic constructions – allows for more variability than the English language. In other words, a transfer from German into English in such cases gains the dimension of a "decision process" (Levý, 1967). Here, the translator does not have to make a binary choice between two mutually exclusive possibilities, but he has to make a decision in favour of one of the two alternatives. This decision is stylistically motivated, according to the translator's individual structural preferences.

Syntactic divergences between SL and TL have clearly different implications for translation and for SI procedures. The translator can fairly easily, and at the same time rather effectively, cope with syntactic restructuring phenomena, e.g. in the form of rank-shift operations, because his access to the text to be translated is not subject to time limitations. As a rule, the translator has enough time to analyze the SL text on the syntactic, semantic and text-pragmatic level and to recode the decoded textual element adequately, e.g. in keeping with the syntactic restrictions imposed by the TL.

Shifts of expression of this type occur rather frequently in German-English transfer. Hence, for the experienced translator this type of transfer operation becomes, in due course, a routine operation which facilitates the transition from cognitive transfer procedures to associative transfer mechanisms and thus creates the precondition for a quantitative and qualitative improvement of his transfer performance.

Contrary to the case in translation, obligatory syntactic rearrangement procedures of the type discussed so far – and for that matter any rearrangement – can be the sourse of more serious transfer difficulties for the simultaneous interpreter. Following Mattern, "simultaneous interpreting can be described as an irreversible process in which the interpreter recodes perceived information contained in SL speech acts to TL speech acts, thus enabling communication in a specific situation" (1974, 6). According to Seleskovitch, in order to accomplish communication with the help of SI the simultaneous interpreter must be able to transfer the result of his SL textual analysis into a semantically and stylistically acceptable TL form (1968, 34; 1974, 40 ff.). In the field of SI, the task of providing an intelligible TL text is considerably hampered, if not worse, by three factors.

1. The text to be interpreted is available to the simultaneous interpreter only once, and only for a very limited span of time (Wirl 1958, 15 ff.; Kade 1964, 48; Kainz, 1965,415 ff.). Any piece of information which cannot be handled in the one and only transfer procedure allowed in SI is irretrievably lost.

2. Contrary to translation transfers, receptive and reproductive linguistic procedures overlap in SI; while producing previously received parts of the SL text, the simultaneous interpreter continues receiving the constantly offered SL text.

3. Once the simultaneous interpreter has decided in favour of a specific transfer strategy, he cannot, so to speak, change any more – at least not as easily as the translator – into another syntactic gear.

These three features of SI transfer permit three conclusions:

1. Contrary to the translation process with its successive SL decoding and TL encoding procedures, SI is a sequence of "telescoped processes" (Mattern 1974, 14). SL textual analysis and TL textual reproduction are interlocked; TL reproduction normally begins before SL perception has been completed. Metaphorically speaking, the simultaneous intepreter is con-

stantly engaged in a catching-up race with the aim of holding constant or, still better, reducing the time-lag between SL textual decoding and TL textual encoding and thus of guaranteeing a time continuum in SI.

2. The decisive factor in SI is the moment when the simultaneous interpreter actually sets his reproduction process going. "Opinions vary in as far as the ideal time for beginning interpreting is concerned. It appears that this optimal moment of interpretation may be established as a theoretical value, which, in turn, could possibly serve as a general guideline for I (= the interpreter). In practice, however, the optimal moment of interpretation will differ depending on the subjective and objective factors involved; the objective or speech-language-linked factors being those which originate from the SL text and from relations of equivalence existing between SL and TL, and the subjective factors being those which depend on the interpreter himself". (Mattern 1974, 28). Here, as we shall see immediately, the concept of syntactic anticipation plays a major role.

3. SI is an important object of a theory of interlingual transfer and as such can clearly be differentiated from the investigation of translation processes. As a subject of linguistic and psycholinguistic research, SI can be looked at from theoretical, descriptive and applied aspects of language-pairs. In this respect this paper presents an approach which is typical of the kind of interlingual research pursued in the field of translation and SI studies at the University of Saarbrücken. The following discussion is based on a Diplomarbeit (dissertation) made under my supervision by one of our former students (Mattern, 1974).

THE CONCEPT OF SYNTACTIC ANTICIPATION

I would now like to look more closely into the concept of syntactic anticipation. As a starting-point I shall use the example which I have previously referred to under (4). This sentence contains two embeddings, an obligatory one, which is due to the rule-governed division of the verbal phrase in the finite clause into two lexemes, an auxiliary form and a participial form, and an optional embedding, which is due to the insertion of a participial construction in the main clause. If someone tried to write down this sentence in the notation of the GTG, the result would be a rather complex tree structure which would turn the often-claimed elegance and simplicity of the GTG description into the opposite.

Both embeddings are, as previously pointed out, not allowable in the German-English transfer. The syntactic equivalence of the SL sentence is a structure consisting of a main clause and a relative clause or a sequence of two anaphorically connected main clauses. The resulting restructuring operations can be represented in various ways, e.g. by assigning numbers to the individual elements of the SL text and by reordering these numbers according to the syntactic rules of the TL:

10. Der Kultusminister / hat / heute / die Kunstausstellung / in / der /

Der Kultusminister	hat	heute	die Kunstausstellung	in	der
1	2_1	3	4	5	6_1

von vielen Polizisten / scharf / bewachten / Stadthalle / eröffnet //

von vielen Polizisten	scharf	bewachten	Stadthalle	eröffnet
7	8	9	6_2	2_2

11. $\underbrace{\text{Today}}_{3}\,/\,\underbrace{\text{the Minister of Education}}_{1}\,/\,\underbrace{\text{opened}}_{2+2_2}\,/\,\underbrace{\text{the art exhibition}}_{4}\,/\,\underbrace{\text{in}}_{5}\,/$

$\underbrace{\text{the City Hall}}_{6_1+6_2}\,/\,\underbrace{\text{which}}_{(6_3)}/\underbrace{\text{was}}_{9_1}/\,\underbrace{\text{sharply}}_{8}\,/\,\underbrace{\text{guarded}}_{9_2}\,/\,\underbrace{\text{by many policemen}}_{7}//$

The numerical notation shows the obligatory structural changes occurring in the German-English transfer, plus the resulting structural modifications, expansions and contractions. Syntactically most significant is the verbal-phrase restructuring, which at the same time is also an important cue for the evaluation of the TL structure under the aspect of syntactic transparancy. The German segment "hat eröffnet" is contracted to one lexeme, resulting in a left-right shifting of the verbal phrase towards the frontal position which considerably alters the structure so clearly characteristic of the German sentence.

The implications for German-English SI are of primary importance. Since the semantically relevant element of the verbal phrase is in the final position in the sentence, the interpreter is forced to postpone the interpreting act, until the decoding operation of the whole sentence is complete. The consequence of the late take-off is an extremely heavy stress on the short-term memory of the interpreter. The time-lag between SL decoding and TL encoding necessitated by the embedding syntax may entail the loss of information indispensible for the understanding of the text by the TL recipient. This is a danger which is particularly noticeable in texts with a low degree of redundancy and a correspondingly high degree of information density. In such cases the only way out for the interpreter (unless he is already familiar with the content of the text to be interpreted) is to develop strategies for delaying output – with all the obvious implications for the receptive and the reproductive time continuum.

The problems connected with the semantic disambiguation of our sentence example become even more apparent, if we replace the verb "eröffnen" by "besuchen":

12. Der Kultusminister hat haute die Kunstausstellung in der von vielen Polizisten scharf bewachten Stadthalle besucht.

It can convincingly be shown that a sentence or a sentence segment containing what, according to Mattern (1974), can vaguely be termed a "thought completed phrase" can be conceived of as a sort of syntactic and semantic narrowing-down process. Or expressed in another way, the increasing amount of information which becomes available in the course of the formulation of a sentence reduces the number of possible alternatives, i.e. the growing volume of syntactic and lexical data is inversely proportional to the number of syntactic and semantic alternatives.

In the present case, the analysis of the meaning of the sentence is a long-drawn-out filtering process, ending only when the last word of the sentence has finally been registered.

In comparison with the handicaps of German-English SI, the interpreter re-interpreting the English equivalent of the German sentence into German is in a much better position. Since he is informed relatively early about the content of the verbal phrase, and since he does not have to plan large-scale syntactic shifts of expression, the perceptive and reproductive input requirements are considerably less.

At this point we come to the fundamental question to be discussed in the third section of this paper: what are the ways in which the simultaneous interpreter copes with difficulties in German-English transfer, and develops interpreting methods and techniques which allow optimal synchronisation or telescoping of SL decoding and TL encoding operations? The example which we have discussed so far offers little or no room for manoeuvering. The only advice which one can give the simultaneous interpreter here is to keep abreast of political, economic and sociocultural events and to compensate, as far as possible, for the lack of co-textual cues for the early syntactic and semantic disambiguation of the text through the use of their store of extra-linguistic information.

In the area of German-English SI, however, there are also other, more pertinent ways and means of overcoming difficulties in interpretating. By this I mean that there are cases in which strategies of syntactic anticipation can fruitfully be activated, as is obvious from the following example (after Mattern, 1974, 3):

13. Namens meiner Fraktion darf ich den beiden Herren
On behalf of my political
Berichterstattern für die Arbiet, die sie aufgewendet
group I should like to thank the two
haben, sehr herzlich danken.
rapporteurs very cordially for their work.

The German segment "Namens meiner Fraktion darf ich . . . (danken)" is a standard phrase which is frequently used as an opening gambit in a follow-up speech statement of one or several EEC rapporteurs. Once the simultaneous interpreter has heard "Namens meiner Fraktion darf ich . . " he can legitimately infer from previous experience that some form of saying "thank you" can be expected. It is not necessary for him, especially when he has been working for the EEC for some time and is familiar with debate conventions, to wait until he has actually received the stimulus "danken" before he begins with his TL reproduction. He has, as it were, contextually anticipated the word "danken". The explanation for this is, as Mattern has pointed out (1974, 3 ff.), that all SI, is possible only because the interpreter can fall back upon previously received information; as a result, anticipation can basically be regarded as a response to previously received and processed structural and semantic stimuli. In contrast to end-of-sentence stimuli, which Mattern calls "T-stimuli" (= terminal stimuli), these stimuli can be called A-cues (= anticipation cues), i.e. cues which allow the syntactic and/or semantic anticipation of what the simultaneous interpreter actually perceives, while the TL reproduction of the SL message is already well under way.

Following Mattern (1974, 4), the interaction of cues and the anticipation process can be shown as follows.

1. Previous experience with debate-opening gambits is triggered by "Namens meiner Fraktion darf ich . . .".

2. This A-cue sparks off an anticipatory process "should like to thank".

3. The T-stimulus confirms – or negates for that matter – the result of the anticipatory process, depending on whether the A-cue has been interpreted correctly or incorrectly.

From the preceding discussion it is clear that syntactic anticipation normally is something quite different from blind textual hypothesizing. It is rather the result of intelligent textual prediction triggered by linguistic units (morphemes, lexemes or lexeme combinations) which, within the framework of specific communication situations, serve as important cues for the achievement of high-quality SI performance.

Such cues, indispensible for any kind of syntactic and/or semantic anticipation, can be of various types.

1. Cues can e.g. be of a co-textual (intralingual) nature, as can be shown by the following example (taken from Mattern 1974, 35):

14. SL Bei allem, was sonst umstritten ist, meine ich
TL In all that
SL mich also insoweit in sachlicher Übereinstimmung
TL1 has been contested otherwise, I think that
TL2 Despite all the other issues at stake,
SL mit der inhaltlichen Auffassung der Fraktion dieses
TL1 I am along the lines of the
TL2 I think that we are in agreement with all the other
SL Hohen Hauses zu befinden, (wenn ich hier mit Herrn Präsident . .)
TL1 general opinion of the parliamentary groups in the
TL2 party groups of this assembly in this particular question.
TL1 Bundestag.

Different though the two English versions of the German sentence may be, they make it none the less clear that the lexeme sequence "meine ich mich", at least statistically, serves as a cue providing the interpreter with important contextual information on the further semantic development of the sentence. This cue enables him to start off the transfer process before the SL speaker has actually finished the infinite clause "mich zu befinden". "Zu befinden" is nearly a formal T-stimulus (an "O-value T-stimulus", Mattern 1974, 34) or a pallid verb (Mattern 1974, 79), necessary no doubt for the formal completion of the Sl collocational verb pattern, but adding no further information to that already perceived by the interpreter.

2. Cues can also be of an extralinguistic, situational nature, e.g. "It is, clear, that in an age so dominated by steadily aggravating environment problems, the Federal Republic of Germany is morally bound to give support to all international efforts at the improvement of environmental protection." (cf. (14)). The maintenance of a time continuum is in this case additionally facilitated by the fact that there is an almost ideal complementary relationship between situational knowledge and intralingual presuppositions. The

phrase "ist bereit" allows an exhaustive syntactic and semantic disambiguation of the entire sentence (things would be different, if the finite clause contained the phrase "ist entschlossen" instead of "ist bereit"; in the latter case the infinite clause could – at lease theoretically – continuc like this: "..ist entschlossen, sich allen . . . zu widersetzen").

3. Thirdly and finally, cues can also occur in linguistically and situationally standardized communication processes. We have already discussed the occurrence of a standardized communication situation in connection with example (3). Other relevant cases of context-independent, and at the same time standardized ways of expression, are phraseologically petrified or idiomatic speech segments such as verb-complement collocations (e.g. "Beitrag leisten"). They provoke automatic responses or automatic associations which may greatly facilitate otherwise complex SI performance. "All of us are stuffed with memorized connections between words . . . Once a memorized pattern begins, it will run off according to form" (Millcr 1951, 94). Such cliché expressions can be discussed within an associationist model of linguistic behaviour. They show that a large proportion of verbal utterances is pre-programmed, allowing the language user either no, or only a very limited degree of, stylistic variation. Vermeer goes even so far as to claim that 99.9 per cent of interpersonal linguistic communication is predetermined (in Wilss/Thome ,1974). This statement is certainly an exaggeration, but it demonstrates that it is very important for the simultaneous interpreter to progressively build up and internalize large inventories of cliché expressions which he can activate without effort from long-term memory, and use for associative SI transfer procedures.

IMPLICATIONS FOR TRAINING

Reference to the role of associationist theory in the anticipatory exploitation of cues in SI leads us to applied aspects of a science of SI, and these aspects, in their turn raise the question of the didactic implications of what has been discussed so far. It probably goes without saying that the development of a subtle syntactic and semantic anticipatory ability is a useful goal for the linguistically and psychologically based teaching of SI. The following five hypotheses might serve as starting points for an investigation of theoretical aspects of teaching SI.

1. Any SI process is language-pair-specific; it contains objective and subjective factors, and the balance of these factors varies with the individual text, the type of text and the interpreter.

2. Any teaching of SI which is oriented toward attaining certain learning targets in a certain period of time must limit itself basically to the investigation of the language-pair-specific factors of the interpretation process. An approach geared to the needs of the individual student should be complementary because the interpretation student does not represent an abstract entity, but must be looked upon as a human being with a specific personality profile. As such, any interpretation student possesses specific abilities and strategies of SL textual analysis and TL textual synthesis.

3. Whether inter or intralingual, the objective factors in SI can, to a certain extent, be systematized.

4. Only those factors which can be systematized are teachable and learnable.

5. Only systematic teaching and learning is generalizable in terms of transfer of training, transfer understood, of course, here not in an interlingual sense, but as the application of what has been learnt to new SI transfer situations.

If a system for teaching SI is based on these five premises, it is advisable to devise a staggered program progressing from straightforward, easy-to-handle sentences with relatively high frequency contextual constraints, to syntactically more complicated structures. Within the framework of such a progressive system, the applied science of SI can identify significant problem areas and initiate learning processes which are organized on the principle of "contextual generalization" (List 1972,56) and help to drive home to the interpretation student the plausibility of syntactic anticipation strategies.

Statistical data as to how often an interpreter must fall back upon anticipatory situations in a text are unavailable. Studies aimed at collecting, and evaluating the use of, discourse cues as practical guidelines for determining the optimal moment for initiation of the interpretation process could be useful in the teaching of simultaneous interpreters. Moreover, such studies could help the interpreter to analyze his own performance and to increase the syntactic flexibility which he needs in order to cope adequately with what he hears. It is obvious that the investigation of cues could help to give the interpreter a specific awareness of potentially sensitive points in the transfer process. This, in its turn, could lead to the establishment of syntactic expectation patterns with the status of statistically relevant transfer regularities (in the sense of Catford's definition of "translation rules"). Such insights into the process of syntactic anticipation could then be used to work out a practical partly teacher-dependent, partly teacher-independent course which, on the basis of language-pair-specific material, could speed up the process of recognizing and assessing co-textual and contextual cues for the elimination of SI difficulties.

REFERENCES

Back, T. *Das Phänomen des RANK-SHIFT in der Übersetzung Englisch-Deutsch mit besonderer Berücksichtigung der Einheiten Gliedsatz und Wortgruppe.* Saarbrücken: Manuscript, 1973.

Catford, J. C. *A Linguistic Theory of Translation.* London: OUP, 1965.

Coseriu, E. Les universaux linguistiques. *Proceedings of the 11th International Congress of Linguistics (1972).* Bologna: 11 Mulino, 1974.

Halliday, M. A. K., *et. al. The Linguistic Sciences and Language Teaching.* London: Longmans, Green and Co., 1965.

Hörmann, H. *Psychologie der Sprache.* Berlin: Springer, 1970.

Jakobson, R. On Linguistic Aspects of Translation. In Brower, R.A., (Ed.). *On Translation.* New York: OUP, 1966, 232 - 239.

Kade, O. *Subjektive uds objektive Faktoren im Übersetzungsprozess.* Dissertation Leipzig: Polycopy, 1964.

Kainz, F. *Psychologie der Sprach V/I.* Stuttgart: Enke, 1965.

Levý, J. *Translation as a Decision Process. To Honor Roman Jakobson. Essays on the Occasion of his 70th Birthday II.* Den Haag: Mouton, 1967, 1171 - 1182.

List, G. *Psycholinguistik. Eine Einführung.* Stuttgart: Kohlhammer, 1972.

Mattern, N. *Anticipation in German-English Simultaneous Interpretation.* Saarbrücken: Manuscript, 1974.

Miller, G. A. *Language and Communication.* New York: McGraw-Hill, 1951.

Seleskovitch, D. Zur Theorie des Dolmetschens. In Kapp, V. (Ed.). *Übersetzer und Dolmetscher.* Heidelberg: UTB, 1974, 37 - 50.

Seleskovitch, D. *L'interprète dans les conférences internationales: problèmes de langage et de communication.* Paris: Minard, 1975.

Wilss, W. and Thome, G. (Eds.). *Aspekte der theoretischen, sprachenpaarbezogenen und angewandten Sprachwissenschaft (Übersetzungswissenschaft).* Saarbrücken, Heidelberg: Groos, 1974.

Wirl, J. *Grundsätzliches zur Problematik des Dolmetschens und Übersetzens.* Wien, Stuttgart : Braumüller, 1958.

Simultaneous Interpretation:

A Hypothetical Model and its Practical Application

Barbara Moser

University of Innsbruck

Innsbruck

1 INTRODUCTION

Research on simultaneous interpretation (SI) may be said to be in what Kuhn (1970) described as the pre-paradigm stage. According to Kuhn the invention of different models is one of the characteristics of such a period, since more than one theoretical construction can always be placed upon a given collection of data. Empirical research to date has been well reviewed by Gerver (1976), whose model of SI attempts to account for the data so far collected. The presentation of another model of SI may thus be seen as one of the consequences of the varied nature of research during the pre-paradigm period, since no model ever solves all the problems it defines and no two models leave all the same problems unsolved. Therefore, models need not even be in conflict with each other. As each of them usually emphasizes different aspects of the problem under investigation, they may potentially even complement each other. The tentative description of SI offered in this paper should thus be regarded as only one of a host of possible alternatives. My training and on-the-job experience as an interpreter may very well have prevented me from seeing and integrating various important aspects of the process into this model, a fact for which I would like to apologize in advance.

2 THE MODEL

The basic model, on which all further elaborations for the course of the process of SI are based, has been developed by Massaro (1975a, b). His model is an attempt to describe the temporal flow of auditory information, beginning with the acoustic signal (the speaker's message) that arrives at the ear of the listener and ending with some form of mental representation of that message in the mind of the listener. For reasons of space this basic model cannot be explained here in detail; the necessary processing stages will be explained in connection with the expanded model for SI. Such an information processing model tries to describe the activities involved in understanding and producing language. The special situation of the interpreter, who is both listener and speaker – and to complicate the matter further, he is both about 60 - 75% of the time (Barik, 1972, 1973; Gerver, 1972) – demands a rather complicated processing model.

The flow chart represents a theoretical model illustrating the sequence of processing steps in SI. The boxes represent STRUCTURAL COMPONENTS, describing the nature of the information stored at a given stage of processing, whereas the intermediate headings represent functional components, describing the individual operations performed at a particular stage of processing. Each diamond represents a decision point in the process; if the answer to a given question is YES, the process continues; if the answer is NO, this information is fed back to an earlier STRUCTURAL COMPONENT, from where a particular section of the process is iterated until a YES-reply allows the continuation of the process. Such an operation is carried out in a so-called rehearsal loop. At some decision points, however, such a rehearsal loop is initiated even if the decision furnished a YES-answer. This is because SI, as the term implies, involves a simultaneity of certain processing stages, i.e. attention is devoted to both the incoming message and to the operations involved in the target language output. STRUCTURAL and functional components will not be listed and explained separately, but according to their serial appearance. Double-headed arrows indicate how knowledge stored in long term memory (LTM) continuously interacts with (i.e. becomes available for) the ongoing language processing. (See Fig. 1.)

2.1 The Initial Processing Stages

The source language message (sound wave pattern) arrives at the ear of the interpreter; it is received in the AUDITORY RECEPTOR SYSTEM and becomes available for feature detection (readout process). Here it is only determined whether an acoustic feature is present or not; no indication is given as to what kind of feature has been detected. This is a passive process, which means that everything that is heard is processed and nothing is rejected or filtered out, an important fact which will be referred to in section 2.3.3. The information gained is then stored in PREPERCEPTUAL AUDITORY STORAGE. A primary recognition process, using the phonological rules of the source language (SL) stored in LTM, then synthesizes these acoustic features into a synthesized percept (a syllable) which is stored in SYNTHESIZED AUDITORY MEMORY (STRING OF PERCEPTUAL UNITS).

Secondary recognition transforms the sequence of synthesized syllables into words. Syntactic and semantic cues are necessary for word recognition to occur; their possible nature will be described together with the explanation given for concepts in LTM. The doubleheaded arrow pointing to syntactic and semantic context SL stored in LTM indicates that relevant information is accessed to allow the interpreter to make a response to the question WORD? According to Miller (1962) the preceding context facilitates word identification; this is also true if word identification is delayed across a number of words (Solberg, 1975) – as may be the case in poor listening conditions (e.g. mediocre transmission devices in SI-installations). The feed-back loop from WORD? back to the STRING OF PERCEPTUAL UNITS, which holds the subsequently incoming information, indicates that further context may be needed to facilitate word recognition. Lexical stress patterns may also be used for the correct identification of words. Such cues, however, may often lead to conflicting situations with the interpreter. Non-native speakers using one of the official conference languages often tend to shift stress to an inappropriate syllable (due to native language interference), thus leading the interpreter to an incorrect word identification. In such a case the interpreter has two alternatives: he is either able to make use of syntactic and semantic context to resolve the ambiguity,

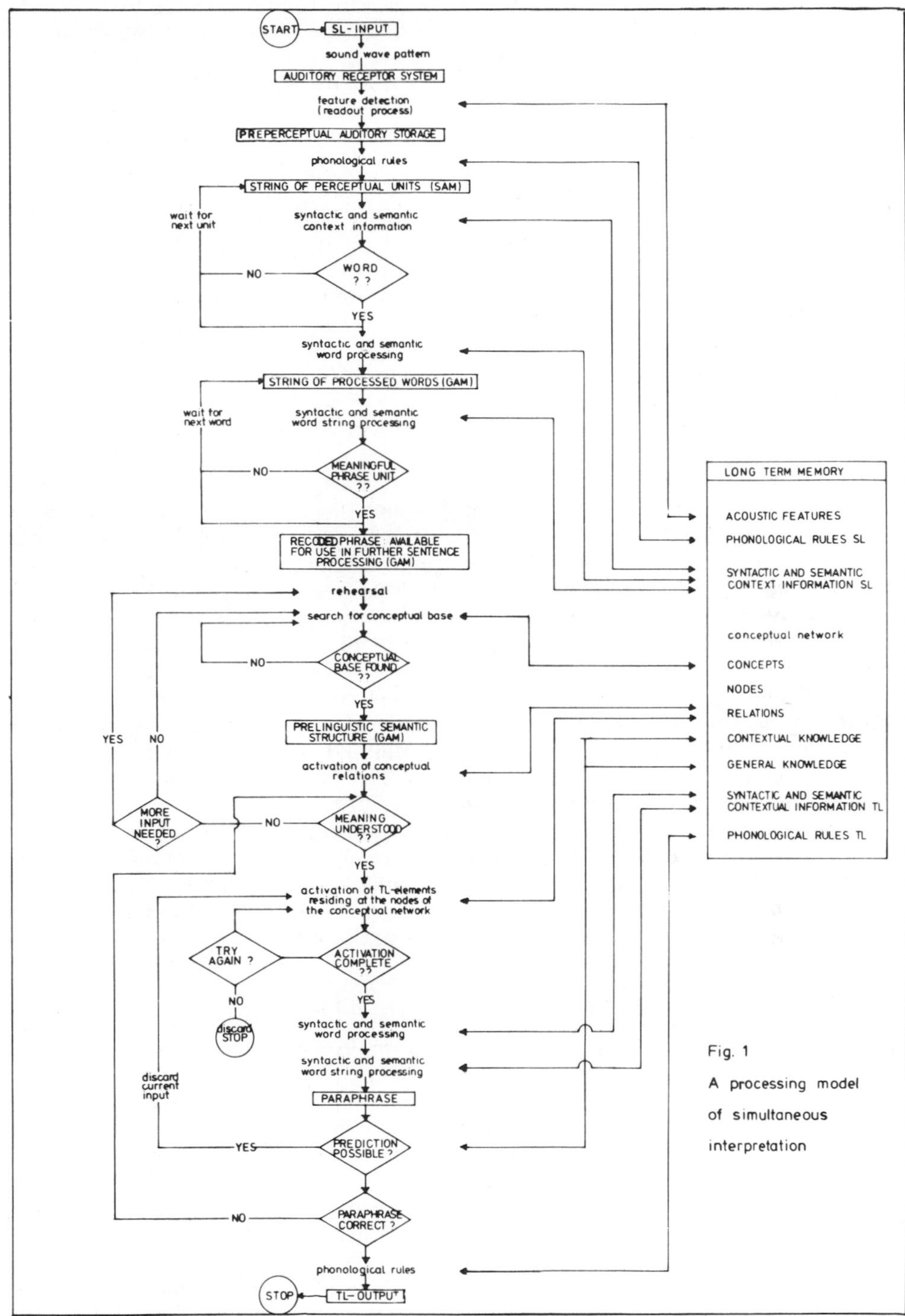
START
SL-INPUT
sound wave pattern
AUDITORY RECEPTOR SYSTEM
feature detection (readout process)
PREPERCEPTUAL AUDITORY STORAGE
phonological rules
STRING OF PERCEPTUAL UNITS (SAM)
wait for next unit
syntactic and semantic context information
NO
WORD ??
YES
syntactic and semantic word processing
STRING OF PROCESSED WORDS (GAM)
wait for next word
syntactic and semantic word string processing
NO
MEANINGFUL PHRASE UNIT ??
YES
RECODED PHRASE AVAILABLE FOR USE IN FURTHER SENTENCE PROCESSING (GAM)
rehearsal
search for conceptual base
NO
CONCEPTUAL BASE FOUND ??
YES
PRELINGUISTIC SEMANTIC STRUCTURE (GAM)
activation of conceptual relations
YES
NO
MORE INPUT NEEDED ?
NO
MEANING UNDERSTOOD ??
YES
activation of TL-elements residing at the nodes of the conceptual network
TRY AGAIN ?
ACTIVATION COMPLETE ??
NO
discard STOP
YES
syntactic and semantic word processing
syntactic and semantic word string processing
discard current input
PARAPHRASE
YES
PREDICTION POSSIBLE ?
NO
PARAPHRASE CORRECT ?
phonological rules
STOP
TL-OUTPUT
LONG TERM MEMORY
ACOUSTIC FEATURES
PHONOLOGICAL RULES SL
SYNTACTIC AND SEMANTIC CONTEXT INFORMATION SL
conceptual network
CONCEPTS
NODES
RELATIONS
CONTEXTUAL KNOWLEDGE
GENERAL KNOWLEDGE
SYNTACTIC AND SEMANTIC CONTEXTUAL INFORMATION TL
PHONOLOGICAL RULES TL
Fig. 1
A processing model of simultaneous interpretation

Figure 1

or else the NO-answer from WORD? is fed back to the STRING OF PERCEPTUAL UNITS, where the subsequently incoming units are used to disambiguate the word. One can see that the interpreter as a listener here may delay word identification across several words within the temporal limits of SYNTHESIZED AUDITORY MEMORY (1 - 2 seconds, Massaro, 1975a), in order to make use of subsequently incoming units.

2.2 The Stage of GENERATED ABSTRACT MEMORY (GAM)

The information now available for further processing is the STRING OF PROCESSED WORDS. We have now entered the domain of GAM, which is in a way equivalent to the short term memory referred to in other literature. Here, verbal information can be temporarily stored. A continuous recoding and rehearsal process, indicated by the feed-back loops, makes subsequently (or quasi-simultaneously) incoming information available for combined processing. Information is continuously chunked (to use the terminology of Miller, 1956) into more abstract units, which combine the essentials of meaning of the smaller units that are being recoded. Syntactic and semantic information will by necessity play a critical role in this process. This kind of information is stored in LTM where it can be accessed at different points in time during the processing sequence. The following stages presumably use this information: syntactic and semantic word string processing, search for conceptual base, and activation of conceptual relations. As can be seen from the flow chart, also the subsequent processing stages that are involved in the target language (TL) production have access to the same structural component in LTM. It should be noted that GAM (where the operations listed above are functional) can hold 7 ± 2 "chunks" of various sizes (Miller, 1956). This, however, may not be valid for the interpreter, since the more difficult secondary recognition is, the less capacity he can devote to the recoding and rehearsal process in GAM. Furthermore, the more capacity he has to devote to recoding information (i.e. transforming it into larger meaningful phrase units), the less capacity is available for him for storing already recoded information. This limitation demonstrates why inexperienced beginners in interpreting jump in with their translation at a very early point in the sentence, because they still devote most of their attention to the TL-production, thus decreasing their capacity in GAM. Moreover, they appear less efficient than experienced interpreters in "chunking" information, but rely more on a word-by-word representation. But 7 chunks in the form of individual words take up about the same storage capacity as 7 chunks in the form of somewhat larger units, such as word-pairs or short phrases.

2.2.1 The Role of Theoretical Linguistics

The crucial question for SI is of course, how syntactic (language-specific) and semantic (language-independent) information may be organized in a professional bilingual, such as the interpreter, and how this information is accessed and becomes available during the process. As for the syntactic organization we have been flooded with linguistic models of competence, none of which however has yet proven to be even a near approximation to actual linguistic performance (which, admittedly, none of them claims explicitly). The more recent work in generative semantics (McCawley, 1968, 1970, 1971; Lakoff, 1971, and also Fillmore, 1968, 1971), claiming the underlying structure of language to be a semantic representation, appears to be a promising approach. These linguists are beginning to accept as linguistic a great number of considerations that were formerly dismissed as cognitive. The generative semantics tradition holds that the underlying base of language is a semantic structure, where syntax is not independent of semantics, but interacts, as is proposed in the model for SI. For them semantics is not merely interpretive (cf. Chomsky, 1971; Katz, 1972; Jackendoff, 1972), but generative, implying an active generation of meaning. In the model for SI such an active generation is reflected e.g. in the processing stage of activation of conceptual relations. Generative semanticists argue for preliminary semantic representations which are believed to operate according to the principles of natural logic. This is to say that knowledge of the world (extra-linguistic knowledge, knowledge of a particular communication situation, of a subject matter under discussion in a conference, etc.) also determines the nature of the semantic representation and interacts with linguistic knowledge.

2.2.2 Effects of context on performance

This brings up the question of how context and knowledge of a certain subject matter under discussion in a conference can aid the interpreter in speeding up the process of accessing information in LTM. This accessing is performed within the framework of the recoding and rehearsal process in GAM, and as was pointed out before, the more capacity is saved within any processing stage, the more capacity becomes available for the interpreter to direct his attention to new incoming information and to TL-production.

Bransford and Johnson (1972), Johnson, et al. (1973), and Dooling and Mullet (1973) came to the conclusion, on the basis of data obtained, that a subject's understanding depends not only on what he hears but on the implications of received information in the light of relevant knowledge he already possesses. Bransford and Johnson (1972) point out in particular that, in order for prior knowledge to aid comprehension, it must become an activated semantic context (again cf. the processing stage – activation of conceptual relations). The effects of prior information on the performance of interpreters has been nicely illustrated by Chernov (1973), who demonstrated how interpreters can actually "get lost" if prior and actually received information are incompatible.

2.3 Organization of Semantic Information in an Interpreter

In the model proposed for SI mention is made of CONCEPTS, a CONCEPTUAL FRAMEWORK, and CONCEPTUAL RELATIONS. This particular view taken of the kind of deep and underlying structure involved in language understanding and production has become more popular with the publication of work in the generative semantics tradition mentioned above. There it was concluded that the end product/starting point for any language understanding/production is some form of prelinguistic structure. This appears to be a convenient starting/ending point for translation, where not only one language is at stake but two. It entails the storage of only one thought system and thus fulfills the principle of economy.

Schank (1972) argues for such a common conceptual base that is interlingual, onto which linguistic structures in a given language map during the understanding process. As support for his view he cites the fact that people can understand any given natural language and translate from that language into any other language they know, if they have been exposed to these languages long enough. He explains this phenomenon by saying that the conceptual base has in it the content of the thought that is being expressed and that during the translation process people invoke mapping rules for a given language from this conceptual base. The conceptual base is thus responsible for representing the concepts underlying an utterance without respect to the language in which that utterance was encoded. Such a conceptual base consists of concepts and formal relations that exist between them. According to Rumelhart, Lindsay, and Norman (1972) a concept can be thought of as a node in the memory system which corresponds to an object or idea that can be named and described. Thus one can say that concepts are neither words nor definitions of words. It is more plausible to assume that the content of a concept is everything that has been heard or read or seen about the concept (Collins and Quillian, 1972). One can readily deduce from this that it is important for the prospective interpreter to "hear, read, and see", hence learn the content of concepts in the country and from the people who speak the particular language in question. Concepts not only contain semantic information, which is assumed to be language-independent, but also sensory, phonetic and syntactic information (Kintsch, 1972), which is language-specific. Thus, source and target language "equivalents" may be regarded as being stored within the same concept, interconnected by relations.

A relation can be thought of as an association between any two points in the memory system. Relations exist between the different nodes within a concept, between individual concepts, and between clusters of concepts and other concepts in the memory system. In other words, one can picture LTM as a huge network of concepts (plus what they contain) and relations, a so-called associative network. There is no limit to the number of concepts in LTM, hence there is also no limit to the number of relations that can hold between them (Collins and Quillan, 1972). Because of everyday experience and the continuous acquisition of knowledge, we build up new relations all the time. In terms of preparation for a particular conference, the interpreter will thus try (if possible) to build up as many concepts and establish as many relations as possible, in order to facilitate and speed up the translation process.

2.3.1 The Process

Having stated, then, that concepts contain both source and target language nodes, the task of describing the kind of paraphrasing that takes place in SI becomes easier. During the phase of understanding the incoming message, the model shows that accoustic cues (the kind of sensory information stored at the SL-node), then phonological rules (the phonetic features stored at the SL-node), are contacted first, and the information is then stored in SAM (STRING OF PERCEPTUAL UNITS). It is then decided whether a word can be identified with these perceptual units or not. In this understanding process the interpreter thus connects words with certain conceptual constructions that exist, or are coming into existence, in his memory. In an interpreter these connections are assumed to be of a dual nature: intralingual links (between concept and word in one language) and interlingual links (between the language-specific nodes of the same concept) (cf. Riegel, 1968). Given the explicit task of translation, what the interpreter then does is to activate the conceptual relations and arrive at a certain conceptual arrangement, together with activating the necessary intra-lingual links and expressing this arrangement with target-language labels. It is not only important in this context that concepts must be combined in order to express the SL-meaning, they must be combinable in a way that is universal and not language-specific.

Such a model has been proposed by Fillmore (1968). Cases, to speak in his terminology, are a set of concepts which identify certain types of judgements human beings are capable of making about events that occur in their environment. For Fillmore the basics of deep structure are unordered case relations that are only indirectly evident in the surface structure. His concept of case already carries necessary information about the action communicated in the sentence. The combinability of cases depends on which cases can go along with a given verb. Fillmore illustrates this procedure by assigning a case frame (specifying this information) to each verb. Thus the verb emerges as an extremely powerful concept, as the one that in a way dominates the action. This is not surprising at all, if we consider that during the understanding process, i.e. when the interpreter hears the SL-message, the meaning of that message mostly does not become clear until the verb has been specified. Assuming, then, that the verb has been heard (as is mostly the case in translating from English to German), the case frame of the verb then specifies the role each of the concepts may take. In SI this means that the particular role specified by the verb is addressed in the SL-node, whereby the respective cases in the TL-node are activated as well. If this is successful, then there is hardly anything more in the way of combining concepts and proceeding with output according to the syntactic rules of the TL. If not, the system makes another try, if there is still enough time available. However, as time moves on (much of the time available in GAM has already been taken up by the processes described up to this point), the interpreter may decide to stop processing and discard the particular segment of information (cf. TRY AGAIN? – NO – discard STOP).

After syntactic and semantic word string processing the interpreter now has a paraphrase of the SL-message available. This is the very point where much of the processing capacity again becomes available for operating in like manner on the continuously presented SL-message. The more difficult the individual processes described up to this point were (e.g. under noisy listening conditions as described by Gerver, 1972, 1974) – and the search for the conceptual base, if the relations established between concepts are not very numerous, or do not exist, may take up more time and hence more capacity (because the search has to be repeated) – the greater is the influence on the speed of the TL-output, as well as on the amount of simultaneously presented input that can be processed. It becomes clear, then, that processes do interact at all stages in SI.

2.3.2 Prediction

In order to cope successfully with his task the interpreter will of course employ any strategies available to him that ultimately result in a saving of processing capacity. A YES-answer in the decision point PREDICTION POSSIBLE? enables the interpreter to discard current input, since he already "knows" what is coming in, and hence all the processing stages up to activation of TL-elements are eliminated. This does not eliminate feature detection, since it was stated that this is a passive process and goes on as long as the SL-message arrives at the ear of the interpreter. The remaining processing stages, however, are skipped as soon as prediction is possible, explaining the reason why the ability to predict so greatly facilitates the interpreter's task. The question remains how the interpreter "knows" what will come in. The phenomenon must clearly be explained from the nature of the organization of semantic information in an interpreter. Extensive exposure to a particular language, or two or more languages, relevant syntactic knowledge, contextual knowledge (knowledge of the subject matter under discussion in a conference, as well as knowledge of the ongoing discussion in a conference) appear to be the prime candidates responsible for prediction. Within the context of this model I propose that predictability is a function of how fast and how many conceptual relations can be activated. To put it bluntly, the more the interpreter knows, the more he can predict, and the better his knowledge is of anything (i.e. the more relations have been established between concepts to form conceptual clusters or ideas), the faster he can predict. The crux in SI, however, is that the interpreter has to predict for somebody else, namely the speaker. This entails that predictability is also a function of "shared knowledge", i.e. the compatibility of knowledge (of any kind) between the speaker and the interpreter.

In a more confined framework it would be interesting to know which concepts have a larger number of relations to other concepts or clusters of concepts, thus greatly facilitating prediction. In looking back on Fillmore's case grammar, the verb, supplying the greatest amount of information, has relations to all other cases, of which the agentive (mostly subject of a surface structure sentence) would be the next most important to know. This centrality of the verb and its importance in prediction should therefore be revealed in interpreting from a language in which it occurs at an early stage in the sentence (e.g. English) as opposed to a language where it appears late in the sentence (e.g. German, although German exhibits a rather loose word order). Prediction should thus be easier in working from English to German, than vice versa. Moreover, prediction should be much more reliable when translation is carried out in the former direction, and could thus lead to an elimination of the decision point PARAPHRASE CORRECT?

When working from German to English, however, the need for prediction is much greater, although the reliability of prediction is much lower. In recalling the limitations on GAM (time constraint 15 - 20 seconds, Massaro, 1975a), one realizes that the interpreter cannot always afford to wait for the verb. When working in the direction German-English he thus has to run the risk of an incorrect prediction, so as not to overload GAM. One should expect that interpreters working in this direction will always try to check their prediction for correctness against current input. For them the processing stages up to this point may thus have been carried out on a much more hypothetical basis, although a much greater time lag between SL-presentation and TL-output with interpreters working from English to German was found by Goldman-Eisler (1972), who explained that the former waits until a greater amount of input has been processed in order to make his prediciton.

One can see, then, that a number of factors are responsible for the phenomenon of prediction and that the interpreter always runs a certain risk. It appears to me that the willingness to run such a risk also depends on the individual interpreter. The advantages of prediction in SI are indicated in the flow diagram (cf. discard current input); the interpreter thus saves a considerable amount of processing capacity, which is made available for processing the simultaneously incoming SL-message.

2.3.3 Auditory Feedback

To conclude the "journey through the mind of the interpreter" a brief illustration shall be given on the possible effects of auditory feedback. As an interpreter, one not only hears the voice of the speaker, but also one's own voice, although the latter is very attenuated, since the SL-message (the voice of the speaker) arrives at both ears through the earphones. Voice-intensity (loudness) is an important factor in language processing. Primary and secondary recognition become extremely difficult, if a message is spoken and thus received in a very low voice. In interpreting this is even further complicated by the fact that rather two messages are perceived, namely, the SL-original as well as one's own output in the TL. In the course of this paper, however, it was stated that everything is processed that arrives at the ear of the interpreter; hence, one should expect some conflict between these two incoming messages, despite their qualitative difference.

For the interpreter, processing his own output as the second incoming message should be a function of the amount of capacity already taken up by the first (primarily attended) message. If this was difficult to process and thus completely exhausted the capacity available in GAM, processing the second message should stop at the STRING OF PERCEPTUAL UNITS (SAM – storage time available 1 - 2 seconds, Massaro, 1975a). If, however, the SL-message did not exhaust the capacity of GAM, the interpreter's TL-output should be processed much like the SL-message, and thus also be stored in GAM (where it remains available for further processing or comparison for 15 - 20 seconds).

I applied this reasoning during observations in a live conference with regard to interpreters' correcting their own output. Corrections (there were only 5 corrections within 45 minutes) were only made within the 15 - 20 seconds interval stated above. Unfortunately, I was unable to observe whether the input which was corrected was semantically more complicated than the remaining input. During this observation I also discovered that some errors in the TL-output were not corrected. I therefore asked the interpreters during a break whether they had noticed these uncorrected errors or not, and the answer was no, which indicates that processing of the TL-output stopped at SAM and that this output was not processed for meaning. A confident statement in this respect necessitates of course an experimental design where variables such as semantic complexity can be controlled.

Despite the endeavor to find consistent answers to a number of problems involved in the process of SI, many of them have remained unexplained and a great many need to be corroborated by respective experimental data, for which I hope this model supplies some material.

3 IMPLICATIONS FOR TRAINING

The model proposed in this paper pertains to an experienced and skilled interpreter, and not to the beginning student. Nevertheless, it seems possible to infer from such a model a "sequence of processing steps" for a beginners' course. The constraints inherent in the individual processing stages and storage components were illustrated, and in a course in interpreting it is thus necessary to try and push the limits of human processing ability. The purpose of the individual exercises is to develop the beginning students' abilities to handle linguistic material, to master the task of doing two things at the same time (listening and speaking), to train retention in GAM (necessary e.g. for German-English translation, because of the late occurrence of the verb), and to decrease reaction time.

These exercises fall under the main headings of abstraction of ideas, paraphrasing, probabilistic prognosis, decreasing reaction time, dual-task training, and shadowing.

3.1 Abstraction of ideas

For an interpreter this entails:

a) the abstraction (analysis) of ideas; and
b) the subsequent synthesis of ideas.

In consecutive interpretation the above two processes are separated in time (although note-taking also requires a certain degree of synthesizing). In SI they follow each other within 3 - 15 seconds.

Before the presentation of one (and subsequently a larger number of) sentence(s), students are instructed to report back the "keyword" immediately after presentation. This is to say, they should detect as quickly as possible what feature the sentences have in common.

Examples: Seat belts must be fastened.
Fall-out shelters are now commonplace.
Never forget to take a first aid kit.

Keyword: safety measures.

Es muss mit Stromabschaltungen gerechnet werden.
Die Temperatur darf in Büroräumen nicht mehr als 27° C betragen.
Es sollen verstärkt öffentliche Verkehrsmittel benützt werden.

Keyword: Energiekrise.

Syntactic and semantic complexity should be systematically increased, as well as the number and speed of successively presented sentences. In the beginning, exercises are in one language only, later they should be mixed, i.e. in analysis sentences should be presented in the foreign language, and the keyword reported back in the native language (and vice versa).

In another type of exercise under this heading students are presented with very long and wordy sentences and instructed to report back the essential idea as quickly as possible.

Example: People whose professional activity lies in the field of politics are not, on the whole, conspicuous for their respect for factual accuracy. (Swan, 1976, p. 42).

Answer: In general politicians are inaccurate.

Variations of this exercise with one and two languages as above.

3.2 Paraphrasing

Paraphrasing in this context does not overlap with the linguistic notion of paraphrasing, but rather the student's ability to render the basic meaning of a message in other words and in different sentence constructions should be developed. For this purpose almost any text can serve as course material. Again, speed of paraphrasing should be successively increased, as should the difficulty of the material presented. This is to say that texts presented in the beginning should exhibit a rather high degree of redundancy, whereas later on more information may be packed into certain passages. Exercises are again first carried out in the native language, then in the foreign language. Mixing two languages should not be introduced too early, since this already covers the full scope of SI.

3.3 Probabilistic Prognosis

For this kind of exercise it is necessary to introduce a context, since one can speculate only on things one knows something about. For this purpose texts should be handed out for preparation prior to class (later on this will be reduced to only a few minutes of preparation). In class, then, students are presented with a recorded passage containing various statements within the framework of the topic prepared, i.e. with the first couple of words from such statements, and are instructed to complete the statement as quickly as possible. Their answers must of course be compatible with the content of the material presented. Again, material should first be presented in the native language and then in the foreign language. There should be a systematic increase in difficulty of material presented, i.e. from more general texts to scientific and technical texts (possibility of integrating topics treated in courses for technical translation).

3.4 Decreasing Reaction Time

The exercises mentioned so far have already focussed on decreasing reaction time. Up to this point students more or less had to report the "same" information, either analyzing and synthesizing, or paraphrasing it. Before introducing the student to the dual task of both listening and speaking at the same time, another mental exercise can serve as a bridge for SI.

Students are first presented with questions that require either a yes or no answer; the response should again be given as quickly as possible. Questions should preferably draw on knowledge acquired in a special field (e.g. economics). Later on questions should require a complete answer; speed of presentation of successive questions is then increased, which will eventually result in a condition where the student is still thinking about an answer to the previous question, while already hearing the next one. The interval should, however, always be long enough to encourage the student to answer each question. Questions presented in the source language requiring an answer in the target language represent the final stage in this exercise. Such a procedure was also employed in an experiment by Pinter (1969).

3.5 Dual-task Training

One of the tasks should always be listening to a recorded passage, since this represents the basic skill in interpreting. The second task demanded of the student could be e.g. simultaneously counting backwards (first in the same language as the recorded passage, then in the target language). Another possibility for a second task could be reading aloud from a hand-out, whereby the topic of the hand-out should coincide with that of the recorded passage. Again, recording and hand-out are in the same language in the beginning, while later on, languages can be mixed. In order to ensure that students do actually listen to the passage, a recall test is given on the contents of the recorded passage afterwards, while successful counting can be monitored in the language lab. (Listening while reading is a condition one also meets on-the-job, when papers and documents are handed out prior to the conference.)

3.6 Shadowing

The central assumption underlying both the dual-task training and the shadowing exercises is that the difficulty of carrying out either the additional task or the shadowing will absorb much of the student's attention, while at the same time he is forced to listen. Shadowing exercises can be varied. Passages can either be in the native language or in the foreign language. In the beginning, input rates should be rather low (90 - 100 words per minute), with an intermediary input rate of up to 140 words per minute, but also with higher input rates of up to 170 words per minute, so as to push the limits of the students.

Another advisable variant would be to record passages for shadowing with added noise. Such listening conditions do occur for various reasons in live conferences. With an increasing level of noise, performance of students will necessarily drop, as was shown by Gerver (1972, 1974), but such exercises will increase their listening ability. The exercises proposed in this section are keyed to the student beginning interpreting. Their purpose is mainly to create and improve the student's abilities for coping with the final task of SI. The effectiveness of the individual exercises and of a combination of them can of course only be tested over time. A first attempt in this respect was made at the University of Innsbruck's department for translation and interpretation during the winter term 1976/77. The above exercises were integrated into a programmed course for students beginning interpreting.

4 PILOT STUDY

The programmed course consisted of fifteen one-hour sessions. Apart from monitoring the student's progress throughout the course, a final test was conducted for the participants of the course and for a control group.

4.1 Method

Subjects were five students enrolled in the course, all of whom had German as their A-language and English as B-language. They were all in their 5th semester and had never been enrolled in an interpreting course before. The control group consisted of five students from the same department in ther 5th semester, their A-language was German, their B-language English. They were currently enrolled in courses in the translation section.

4.2 Materials

There were 5 test conditions:

4.2.1 Décalage

8 blocks of 6 English sentences each (topic: conference proceedings) were recorded on tape. For blocks 1 and 2 subjects had to wait until the second sentence of a block had started before repeating the first one, and so on. For blocks 3 and 4 they had to wait until two sentences had passed before starting to repeat the first one, etc. The same procedure was applied for blocks 5 and 6, 7 and 8, instead of

repeating the original, however, subjects had to translate the sentence into German.

4.2.2 German passage – English counting

A passage in German (400 words) was recorded and presented at 100 words per minute. Subjects had to listen to the passage and simultaneously count backwards from 500 in English. The recall test consisted of 8 questions drawn from the German original at regular intervals; these were typed on cards and had to be answered within 8 minutes after the recoding had ended.

4.2.3 English passage – German counting

This test condition is identical to 4.2.2, only languages are reversed, and the English passage was different from the German one. Equal difficulty of the English and the German passage was judged by two independent judges.

4.2.4 Prediction

Subjects had 5 minutes to read an English text on acupuncture (500 words). This passage was recorded on tape with 8 blanks (at regular intervals); subjects had to listen and complete the statements as quickly as possible.

4.2.5 Shadowing

An English passage (300 words), recorded at 120 words per minute had to be shadowed; all words correctly shadowed were counted.

TABLE 1

Per cent correct response

TASK	TEST GROUP		CONTROL GROUP	
	MEAN	S.D.	MEAN	S.D.
Décalage: sentences correctly repeated/ translated	70.83	4.88	44.16	5.39
German passage-English counting correct answers	85.00	10.46	40.00	13.69
English passage-German counting correct answers	72.50	5.59	32.50	14.25
Prediction: correct predictions	88.00	13.04	36.00	11.41
Shadowing: words correctly shadowed	97.70	2.38	81.40	7.08

4.3 Results

All correct responses were counted and expressed in per cent of the total possible score for each test condition.

Comparison between the test and the control group revealed that on the whole the test group did significantly better in all test conditions.

Décalage	significant at the 0.01 level ($t = 4.19$, $df = 8$, two-tailed test)
German passage – English counting	significant at the 0.02 level ($t = 2.91$, $df = 8$, two-tailed test)
English passage – German counting	significant at the 0.02 level ($t = 2.92$, $df = 8$, two-tailed test)
Prediction	significant at the 0.02 level ($t = 3.35$, $df = 8$, two-tailed test)
Shadowing	significant at the 0.05 level ($t = 2.44$, $df = 8$, two-tailed test)

4.4 Discussion

As can be seen from the above breakdown into individual tasks, differences were most pronounced for the décalage task, in which the control group performed poorly, and least pronounced for the shadowing task, where the difference in performance was not as significant as for the other tasks. Although shadowing involves the dual task of listening and speaking, it does not involve simultaneous processing for meaning, as do the other tasks. The difference in performance may be attributed to this fact. The results of this pilot study may be viewed as an indication of the effects of the exercise program on the performance of tasks which approximate the SI-situation. One can say that the students involved in the experimental course had to a certain degree succeeded in improving the kind of perceptual abilities required for eventually coping with SI successfully. However, only follow-up studies with experimental tasks involving SI will definitely prove or negate the postive effects of such a program. The mobility in our student body (e.g. students going abroad for a year) and the difficulty of having a specific number of students with a particular language combination have so far prevented such follow-up studies. One of the side effects of the experimental course not deliberately intended was that, after having struggled through the course, two students decided to enter the translation section in our department, because they found it impossible to cope with the dual task of listening and speaking. This has inspired me to think about arranging this course as a kind of test course for students who are not yet sure whether they are qualified for interpreting or not. (The Austrian curriculum bifurcates after four semesters of basic course into another four semesters of main course in either translation or interpretation). Among other things, this program may eventually serve as one of a number of tools for the selection of interpreters.

5 CONCLUSION

The above section on implications for training and the results reported from the pilot study were intended to illustrate the fact that the kind of theoretical research offered in the first part of this paper may very well have practical application. After all, we want to equip the student with the best possible training, and didactic tools largely depend on how much we know about the skill we intend to teach. Obviously more detailed research is necessary to either validate or reject one or other processing stage outlined in the flow chart. The respective experiments will necessarily have to be carried out in lab conditions first, however distasteful this will appear to interpreters, who will of course object that such a procedure is a far cry from actual on-the-job conditions. But even if present and future research may not help today's interpreters in their task, one can hope it will be of advantage to the many more to come.

REFERENCES

Barik, H. C., *Simultaneous Interpretation: Temporal and Quantitative Data.* Chapel Hill, N.C.: The L.L. Thurstone Laboratory, University of North Carolina, 1972.

Barik, H. C., *Simultaneous Interpretation: Qualitative and Linguistic Data.* Chapel Hill, N.C.: The L.L. Thurstone Laboratory, University of North Carolina, 1973.

Bransford, J. D., and Johnson, M. K. Contextual prerequisites for understanding: Some investigations of comprehension and recall. *Journal of Verbal Learning and Verbal Behavior*, 1972, *11*, 717 - 726.

Chernov, G. V., Towards a psycholinguistic model of simultaneous interpreting (in Russian). *Linguistische Arbeitsberichte*, 1973, *7*, 225 - 260.

Chomsky, N., Deep structure, surface structure, and semantic interpretation. In: D. Steinberg and L. Jakobovits (Eds.). *Semantics: An Interdisciplinary Reader in Philosophy, Linguistics and Psychology* London: Cambridge University Press, 1971.

Collins, A. M. and Quillian, M. R. How to make a language user. In: E. Tulving and W. Donaldson (Eds.). *Organization of Memory*. New York: Academic Press, 1972.

Dooling, D. J. and Mullet, R. L. Locus of thematic effects in retention of prose. *Journal of Experimental Psychology*, 1973, *97*, 404 - 406.

Fillmore, C. J. The case for case. In: E. Bach and T. Harms (Eds.). *Universals in Linguistic Theory*. New York: Holt, 1968.

Fillmore, C. J. and Langendoen, D. T. (Eds.). *Studies in Linguistic Semantics*. New York: Holt, 1971.

Goldman-Eisler, F. Segmentation of input in simultaneous interpretation. *Psycholinguistic Research*, 1972, *1*, 127 - 140.

Gerver, D. The effects of source language presentation rate on the preformance of simultaneous conference interpreters. In: E. Foulke (Ed.). *Proceedings of the 2nd Louisville Conference on Rate and/or Frequency of Controlled Speech*. Louisville, KY: University of Louisville, 1969, 162 - 184.

Gerver, D. Simultaneous and consecutive interpretation and human information processing. London: *Social Science Research Council Report, HR 566/1.*, 1972.

Gerver, D. Simultaneous listening and speaking and retention of prose. *Quarterly Journal of Experimental Psychology*, 1974, *26*, 337 - 342.

Gerver, D. Empirical studies of simultaneous interpretation: A review and a model. In: R. Brislin (Ed.). *Translation. Applications and Research*. New York: Gardner Press, 1976.

Jackendoff, E. *Semantic Interpretation of Generative Grammar*. Cambridge, Mass.: MIT Press, 1972.

Johnson, M. K., Bransford, J. D., and Solomon, S., Memory for tacit implications of sentences. *Journal of Experimental Psychology*, 1973, *98*, 203 – 205.

Katz, J., *Semantic Theory*. New York: Harper, 1972.

Kintsch, W., Notes on the structure of semantic memory. In: E. Tulving and W. Donaldson (Eds.)., *Organization of Memory*. New York Academic Press, 1972.

Kuhn, T., *Structure of Scientific Revolutions*. 2nd edition. Chicago: University of Chicago Press, 1970.

Lakoff, G., On generative semantics. In: D. Steinberg and L. Jakobovits (Eds.). *Semantics: An Interdisciplinary Reader in Philosophy, Linguistics and Psychology*. London: Cambridge University Press, 1971.

Massaro, D. W. *Experimental Psychology and Information Processing*. Chicago: Rand McNally, 1975a.

Massaro, D. W., Language and information processing. In: D. W. Massaro (Ed.). *Understanding Language*. New York: Academic Press, 1975b.

McCawley, J. D. The role of semantics in grammar. In: E. Bach and T. Harms (Eds.). *Universals in Linguistic Theory*. New York: Holt, 1968.

McCawley, J. D. English as a VSO language. *Language*, 1970, *16*, 286 - 299.

McCawley, J. D., Where do noun-phrases come from? In: D. Steinberg and L. Jakobovits (Eds.). *Semantics: An Interdisciplinary Reader in Philosophy, Linguistics and Psychology*. London: Cambridge University Press, 1971.

Miller, G. A. The magical number seven, plus or minus two: Some limits on our capacity for processing information. *Psychological Review*, 1956, *63*, 81 - 97.

Miller, G. A. Some psychological studies of grammar. *American Psychologist*. 1962, *17*, 748 - 762.

Moser, B. *Simultaneous Translation: Linguistic, Psycholinguistic and Human Information Processing Aspects*. Unpublished Ph.D. thesis. University of Innsbruck, 1976.

Olson, D. Language and thought: Aspects of a cognitive theory of semantics. *Psychological Review*, 1970, *77*, 257 - 273.

Perfetti, C. Psychosemantics: Some cognitive aspects of structural meaning. *Psychological Bulletin*, 1972, *78*, 241 - 259.

Pinter, I. *Der Einfluss der Übung und Konzentration auf simultanes Sprechen und Hören*. Unpublished Ph.D. thesis. University of Vienna, 1968.

Riegel, K. F. Some theoretical considerations of bilingual development. *Psychological Bulletin*, 1968, *70*, 647 - 670.

Rumelhart, D. E., Lindsay, P. H., and Norman, D. A. A process model for long term memory. In: E. Tulving and W. Donaldson (Eds.). *Organization of Memory*. New York: Academic Press, 1972.

Schank, R. C. Conceptual dependency: A theory of natural language understanding. *Cognitive Psychology*, 1972, *3*, 552 - 631.

Solberg, K. B. Linguistic theory and information processing. In: D. W. Massaro (Ed.). *Understanding Language*. New York: Academic Press, 1975.

Swan, M. *Understanding Ideas*. Cambridge: Cambridge University Press, 1976.

Tulving, E. and Donaldson, W. (Eds.). *Organization of Memory*. New York: Academic Press, 1972.

Adult Simultaneous Interpretation: A Functional Analysis of Linguistic Categories and a Comparison with Child Development

Annette Karmiloff-Smith

University of Geneva

Geneva

INTRODUCTION

It may seem rather strange that a child psychologist would have anything of substance to say at a meeting devoted to adults – and particularly to a rather elite group of individuals who listen in one language and simultaneously speak in another! What could this have to do with the experimental study of a small child's acquisition of his first language? In the following pages, it will be argued first that some of the crucial problems faced by the investigator in developmental psycholinguistics could be clarified by carrying out a prior linguistic analysis of data available from simultaneous interpretation. It will also be suggested that many problems singled out as specific to the simultaneous interpreter's task are very similar to those with which a small child has to grapple when acquiring his first language. Both tasks fall under the heading of human problem-solving.

THE EXPERIMENTAL DILEMMA IN PSYCHOLINGUISTICS

First, let us review certain problems faced by researchers in psycholinguistics. In my view, psycholinguistics, be it developmental or adult-orientated, is faced with what could be termed an "experimental dilemma". If, in a comprehension task, the linguistic category to be tested is placed in its normal setting, with the usual extralinguistic and discourse clues, then the subject's decoding may simply be due to the accumulation of clues and not really to his understanding of the category under study. In production tasks with natural settings, adequate response patterns may be strongly context-tied. To avoid such problems, many psycholinguistic researchers explicitly remove from their experimental design all extralinguistic, intralinguistic and paralinguistic clues, as well as speaker/hearer presuppositional constraints. However, it would be a truism to assert that normally language *is* the interplay of syntax, semantics, pragmatics, intonation and so forth. Moreover, drawing strict distinctions between these different aspects is a far from obvious task. When experimental variables are narrowed down so that the interaction of these different factors is avoided, it may well be asked whether it is really "language" that is being studied. In my view, until the *functions* of various categories in different languages are known (and simultaneous interpretation data may help to provide this), then psycholinguistic research cannot avoid partially projecting preconceived grammatical concepts on to both experimental design and interpretation of results.

A few examples from developmental psycholinguistics may serve to make the point clearer. How would one go about discovering whether a young child understands the distinction between the spatial deictics "this" and "that"? A typical experiment would have the child seated for half the items next to the experimenter and the other half opposite him. A series of pairs of identical objects would be placed for half the items close to the speaker and the other half, say, 50 centimeters distant from him. In the most neutral voice possible, the experimenter would utter a series of test items of the following nature:

"give me this book"/"give me that book".

The experimenter would above all avoid paralinguistic clues, such as pointing, eye or head movements towards the object being referred to. The only clue for the child would lie in the lexical contrast between the two deictic terms. In other words, all redundant markers, or what may be called "contrastive emphasizers", are removed, to test in isolation how the child copes with the lexical contrast between "this" and "that". There have indeed been some excellent developmental studies on deictic contrasts (e.g. Clark and Sengul 1974; Macrae, 1976; Webb and Abrahamson, 1976) some of which were extended to cross-linguistic analyses (e.g. Garman, 1977). The avoidance of gestural clues is essential in such experimental approaches. However, in normal language usage, when a particular contrast is to be conveyed, rarely if ever would the lexical terms be used alone. Such contrast would usually be expressed by additional paralinguistic markers such as intonation and gestures.

Let us take another example. Much experimental work has been carried out on the so-called article contrast: "the" versus "a". The very use of the word "contrast" carries, in my view, theoretical assumptions which are not necessarily true of the articles' functions. How do we know that the articles actually do function as contrastive terms? Yet in experimental design, there is an a priori assumption that the articles are part of a common system. Thus, developmental psycholinguists (e.g. Maratsos, 1976) present children with a series of key test sentences such as examples 1 and 2 below, inserted into a short story:

1. "the girl stroked a dog, and then the boy stroked *a* dog"
2. "the girl stroked a dog, and then the boy stroked *the* dog".

If the child hears "a" dog in the second clause, he is expected to perform his action on another dog, whereas if he hears "the" dog, he is expected to understand it as an anaphoric reference to the same dog as in the first part of the utterance. In other words, the lexical contrast between the definite and indefinite articles is used in an experiment to refer to the situational contrast of action on the same referent as in the previous utterance, or on another member of the same class. The important point is that the articles *can* function in this way but, in my view, rarely if ever do they carry such a heavy communicative burden (Karmiloff-Smith, 1977a). Thus, if the essence of an utterance is to convey, for instance, that sometimes an action should take place on one and the same X, and other times on two different Xs, the weak article contrast will not be used, but rather linguistic emphasizers whose very function it is to mark contrasts of this nature. In the particular example discussed above, one would normally expect the addition of post-determiners as in examples 3 and 4 below:

3. "the girl stroked a dog and then the boy stroked the *same* dog"
4. "the girl stroked a dog and then the boy stroked *another* dog".

It has been shown that small children cannot perform above chance level on the article contrast alone. However, when the relevant linguistic emphasizers were added, children as of three years respond correctly with sentences containing the post-determiner "other" and as of five years with sentences containing the post-determiner "same" (Karmiloff-Smith, 1977b).

A similar problem arises with other so-called article contrasts. In French, for instance, the plural definite and indefinite articles "les" and "des" may be used to mark a class inclusion relationship; for example, "les voitures" can imply "all" the cars in the present context, whereas "des voitures" can function as a partative implying "some" of this totality. In previous child development studies, it was found that small children do not understand the class inclusion relationship expressed by "les" and "des" before roughly seven years of age (Inhelder and Piaget, 1959); However, it was subsequently shown that children perform significantly better if relevant linguistic emphasizers are added such as "toutes les voitures" stressing the totaliser function assumed to be conveyed by "les" (Karmiloff-Smith, 1976). In a similar production study, it became clear that when it is the child who produces the utterances covering such contrasts, never is the communicative burden of conveying the class inclusion relationship placed on the articles alone. Rather, children add relevant linguistic emphasizers. These considerations point to the fact that the articles do not alone function contrastively in normal language usage.

Hence the experimental dilemma. On the one hand, if the normal linguistic emphasizers are added, the task becomes almost too easy for the child and no developmental differences can be established. Yet, if unusual communicative burdens are placed on linguistic markers, it is never certain that the behavioural patterns observed are not ad-hoc, experiment-generated procedures, atypical of normal behavior.

INTRA-LINGUISTIC FUNCTIONS

This does not imply that the singular or plural definite and indefinite articles never appear alone without emphasizers in normal discourse. Of course they do. The essential point is that it is not the function of the articles to encode strong contrasts, whereas this is exactly how they are used in experimental design. But the articles alone obviously do have specific functions which are not necessarily identical from one language to another. Elsewhere it has been suggested that a distinction needs to be made between what might be termed the "primary assertive functions" of a marker and its "secondary assertive functions" (see Karmiloff-Smith, 1976 for full discussion). Later in this paper, a few suggestions will be made as to how simultaneous interpretation data might facilitate the linguistic analysis of these functions. At this juncture, it is suggested that in psycholinguistic experiments, distinctions are most often encoded by markers functioning in their secondary assertive functions to avoid specific clues, whereas in normal discourse those markers are chosen whose primary assertive function it is to convey specific semantic contrasts. In other words, to a certain extent it could be stated that many psycholinguistic experiments do not study "language" as it is normally used, but rather the way in which subjects cope with *unusual* uses of linguistic contrasts. This is of course part of subjects' competence and it is important to ascertain this fact. However, much caution needs to be exercised in extrapolating from such behavior to normal discourse.

Much of the discussion thus far rings the familiar bell of "armchair linguistics". How does one go about defining "*normal* discourse" or the "*normal* functions" linguistic categories have in any given language? Is the only solution the linguist's introspection, or the nigh impossible task of collecting representative naturalistic data? In fact, very few data are available to provide insight into the normal functions of a linguistic category. Data do exist, however, pointing to the misconceptions held about the way a category functions in a given language. They stem from difficulties investigators faced in trying to induce subjects to produce certain linguistic categories. A brief illustration will be given from the passive structure, since this has been so popular a terrain for psycholinguistic experimentation since the Chomskyan revolution of the late fifties.

Much of the initial experimentation on the passive structure was based on the erroneous assumption that the passive is merely a stylistic variation of the corresponding active sentence, i.e. that an active can be transformed into a passive without modifying meaning. Thus, for example, "the girl washed the car" was considered equivalent in meaning to "the car was washed by the girl". Numerous developmental studies were carried out in various languages to analyse how children cope with the passive voice (e.g. Hayhurst, 1967; Turner and Rommetweit, 1967; Bever, 1970; Sinclair and Ferreiro, 1970; Caprez et al, 1971; Sinclair et al, 1971; Baldie, 1976; Harris, 1976). All the studies indicated that comprehension of the active voice is developmentally earlier than the corresponding passive. In general, structures violating canonical order are more difficult for children to understand than those which adhere to it. Interestingly enough, it is from the problems arising in production tasks that clues emerge with respect to the intricate functions of the passive construction. What sort of situation induces a speaker to prefer a passive to an active structure?

A typical production experiment with children ran as follows: an action is performed in front of the child, e.g. a girl-doll is washing a car. The child is asked to describe the situation and produces: "the girl is washing the car". The experimenter then requests the child to repeat his utterance but starting with the words "the car . . ." in the hope that the child will produce a passive: "the car is being washed by the girl." However, rather than produce the passive, small children responded "the car is clean", or "the car, well it's the girl who is washing it", etc. (Sinclair and Ferreiro, 1971). Can one deduce from this that the child cannot produce the passive? Obviously not. It could be that the child has the capacity, but that we as researchers have not yet discovered the *functions* of the passive structure, i.e. which situations naturally elicit passive constructions in preference to active ones.

It is perhaps the discussion in the British Journal of Psychology, between Johnson-Laird (1968 and 1977) and Costermans and Hupet (1977) on the functions of the passive voice, which best illustrates how difficult it is experimentally, because of the need for a strict control of variables, to settle the issue of the functions a category has. Johnson-Laird experimented with English-speaking adults and Costermans and Hupet with French-speaking adults. Their disagreement hinges not on the results themselves, but on the interpretation of them. For Johnson-Laird, the passive voice is chosen by speakers to emphasize the importance of the logical *object* by placing it in the grammatical subject position, whereas for Costermans and Hupet the passive emphasizes the logical *subject* while the logical object is presuppositional. Both marshall convincing arguments in favor of their interpretation of similar results. Neither group of authors considered the possibility that both arguments may be partially correct in that the functions of the passive are different in French and in English.

Experimental tasks, however, were atypical of normal discourse, e.g. sentences such as "blue follows red/red is followed by blue" were to be matched by subjects to cards varying in the proportion of their two colored areas. In normal language, of course, the speaker's choice of the passive voice is part of a flow of discourse where presuppositional contraints exist between speaker and hearer with regard to the previous discourse, existing world knowledge, use of definite or indefinite determiners, present extralinguistic context, and so forth. Rarely, if ever, is discourse a series of juxtaposed sentences matched to isolated situations. The importance of the discourse context was highlighted in a recent study in developmental psycholinguistics on the passive (Dewart, 1975) where even the smallest amount of discourse sufficed to elicit better understanding of the passive voice in small children, perhaps because in such cases the choice of the passive is functionally meaningful. It may thus be useful to extend the concept of "grammaticality" to the functional aspects of language, e.g. a sentence reversing canonical order is only grammatical if such a reversal plays a meaningful function within the total discourse (see Karmiloff-Smith, in press, for discussion of child data in this respect).

It seems obvious that for psycholinguistic research, a clear understanding is required of the functions of various linguistic categories. Moreover, whilst endorsing the significance of the search for cross-linguistic universals, there is no reason to assume a priori that the same linguistic structure has the same function(s) in different languages. It is therefore suggested in this paper that simultaneous interpretation might provide rich and spontaneous, discourse-oriented data for a functional analysis of language, which might subsequently enhance the psycholinguist's task.

THE USE OF INTERPRETATION DATA FOR FUNCTIONAL ANALYSES

The following provides suggestions as to the type of linguistic analysis which might be carried out on simultaneous interpretation data, first to be taken from live interpretation situations, and later leading to manipulation of the source language input in order to observe reactions in the target language output. The suggestions are made in the form of a series of questions, picking up issues raised with regard to the experimental dilemma.

Do interpreters pick up a semantic contrast in the source language if it is conveyed solely by secondary assertive functions? If so, do they convey the contrast in the target language by the same means or do they add linguistic emphasizers, i.e. primary assertive functions? When the speaker uses a passive construction, does the interpreter keep to the same structure? When the interpreter modifies the linguistic category used in the target language, does this in turn provide clues to the interpreter's implicit knowledge of the function a structure is playing in the source language? What is the function, say, of pronominalisation? Is it a local economy of reference or does it announce a discourse theme? Clues to the functions of pronominalisation could be gleaned from whether the interpreter pronominalises as quickly as the speaker or tends to repeat the referent in full. Is this a cross-linguistic difference, or is it due to the fact that the speaker has a written text and the interpreter a spoken one and that the establishing of stable referents is a different process in writing and speaking? Does the fact that French has a grammatical gender category in any way affect the function of pronoun reference? In a study of gender acquisition amongst French-speaking children, it was shown that the gender category changes function with age: for the under six-year old it tends to be used predominantly for local lexical concord, whereas older children use gender in its morphological function of marking syntagmatic cohesion across noun and verb phrases (Karmiloff-Smith, 1978). For example, referring to a female called "bicron" in a picture, small children use "*le* bicron *elle* va sortir, le bicron vert, *celle-là*", whereas older children in the same situation use "le bicron il va sortir, *celui-là* . . .". The small child juxtaposes semantic and phonological procedures, whereas the older child bases his pronoun reference on the previous masculine *intralinguistic* marker, despite the fact that the extralinguistic referent is a female. Is this merely an experiment-generated pattern or is gender functioning as a cohesive discourse factor for older children and adults? If the latter is the function of grammatical gender category for French-speaking adults, by what linguistic or paralinguistic category is its function replaced in, say, English which only has natural gender markers? If we understand how one function is replaced in another language, will this in turn enable us to discern more clearly the function of categories in the original language? When the source language is from a written text, does the interpreter, conveying a spoken message, use the same proportion of verbal and nominal phrases in the target language? Is this a clue to the functions of the verbal and nominal phrase constructions? When canonical order is violated, does the interpreter pay heed to, say, the distinction between presuppositions and new information (Ducrot, 1972)? One could go on at some length. These few questions indicate the type of functional linguistic analysis which could be undertaken on the basis of simultaneous interpretation data, and why such an analysis may be a wise precursor to strictly controlled experimentation.

SIMULTANEOUS INTERPRETATION AND NORMAL DISCOURSE

One fundamental objection might be raised regarding the use of simultaneous interpretation data for a functional analysis of linguistic categories. Does the situation of simultaneously listening in one language and speaking in another, in any way resemble that of the usual monolingual dialogue? As far as can be gleaned from the literature, most experimental psychologists working in the field of simultaneous interpretation have focussed on the *unusualness* of the task (see Gerver, 1975, for review of recent research work). Much emphasis has been placed on the fact that simultaneous processing of two different languages is a rare occurrence in everyday life. Whilst this is true, simultaneous processing of more than one symbolic modality is not rare. Parallel processing would appear to be as frequent as sequential processing. As Gerver pointed out, "it is doubtful whether simultaneous listening and speaking per se is that much of a problem for experienced interperters"

(Gerver, 1975: 123). Indeed, experienced interpreters confirm that one can simultaneously listen in one language, speak in another, write down a page number and search through documents for table III on page 121, and look at one's watch to see when one's booth mate is due back! All this takes place while the interpreter continues to listen and speak about new information. In his review, Gerver goes on to point out that "difficulties are more likely to occur (for the interpreter) through the paced nature of the task, a speaker's particular accent or style of delivery, whether or not the interpreter can see the speaker, whether the subject matter or vocabulary are obscure" and so forth (Gerver, ibid). Surely all this holds true for monolingual discourse? Charniak (1972) and Schank (1976), for instance, have clearly demonstrated that monolingual understanding involves far more than the actual words uttered. Pronoun reference, for instance, is frequently based on extra-world knowlledge and on neither semantic nor syntactic clues in the actual discourse. Minsky (1975) and Schank (1976) have both put forward theories involving conceptual frames or scripts in which default knowledge plays an important anticipatory role in monolingual understanding. This is equally true for the interpreter who, most frequently, will opt in cases of ambiguity or noise for the most likely interpretation from *extralinguistic* knowledge. When such a decision is taken, some interpreters are aware of holding ready alternative paths to back up in the case of mis-anticipation. They are thus aware of the default status of their anticipation. It has been suggested that the successful interpreter has learned to block out the sound of his own voice (Welford, 1968). On the contrary, many interpreters can only perform adequately if they can monitor their own output. Experimental work on self-corrections (Gerver, 1974) demonstrates that simultaneous interpreters are continuously monitoring the flow of the target language. Psycholinguistic experiments on children have also shown self-corrections to be a clear indication not only of output monitoring but of the organization of linguistic categories into systems of relevant options for modulating meaning (Karmiloff-Smith, 1976a).

Several areas have been singled out by researchers as specifically relevant to the simultaneous interpreter's complex task. Amongst these are the following:

(i) The simultaneous processing of source language and target language;

(ii) the constant, partial anticipation of the semantics and even the syntactic form of a speaker's message, i.e. an understanding process which takes place frequently before the speaker has finished each of his sentences;

(iii) the need for prior general knowledge of the domain covered by speakers at a conference to enable rapid processing, i.e. the use of world knowledge, outside the specific discourse content, in the understanding process. For example, interpreters will tend to read documents in the target language to obtain basic knowledge, rather than merely seek translations of specific, technical terms in the source language;

(iv) the modulation of the speaker's message to the listener's culture (e.g. what is for, say, Western European culture a joke or a proverb, may represent an insult in, say, Oriental culture; the use of first and second person pronouns implying direct reference in one language may need to be replaced by indirect, third person pronouns in another language culture, etc);

(v) the gauging of the intralinguistic (rather than cultural) communicative burden that can be placed on a lexeme or morpheme, i.e. whether they can have plurifunctional status or whether linguistic or paralinguistic emphasizers need be added:

(vi) the need to create devices for role-taking and turn-taking in a dialogue. How, for instance, the interpreter holds the listener's continued attention for the end of his interpretation, by keeping a pronounced rising intonation when the original speaker has taken his seat and stopped speaking.

A COMPARISON WITH CHILD DEVELOPMENT

The purpose of the next paragraphs is to pursue a case for the fact that *all* of the above problems are not solely specific to the interpretation context. Rather, they are also faced constantly in the monolingual situation but, for the adult, they have become part of his automatized, implicit competence. Moreover, the above six areas in fact also represent some of the crucial aspects of how the small child goes about acquiring his first language. A few illustrations, mainly from child development data, will serve to discuss the issue at hand, i.e. that simultaneous interpretation is analogous in many important ways to the monolingual situation. Let us take up again each of the above six points.

(i) *Simultaneous processing.* Whilst it is indeed a rare occurrence to speak and listen simultaneously in two different languages, simultaneous processing of two different symbolic modalities is frequent. One example of this can be drawn from the fact that in reading the present paper aloud, I was able to process the content through the visual mode and take into account the written style, while simultaneously rendering it through the auditive mode in a spoken style. There are numerous other examples of simultaneous processing in our everyday life. In child development studies on cognitive strategies, the importance of multiple representations of a particular external reality has been shown to be an essential aspect of the way in which the young child comes to grips with a specific, goal-oriented problem (Blanchet et al., 1977; Karmiloff-Smith and Inhelder, 1975; Piaget and Karmiloff-Smith, in press). In general, the capacity to carry out simultaneous processing, rather than merely sequential processing, is a subject of crucial discussion amongst psychologists studying young infants (e.g. Mounoud, 1976).

(ii) *Anticipatory processes.* Anticipation of a speaker's message is clearly part of normal dialogue. It would be impossible to explain the rapidity with which the understanding process takes place if the hearer were not anticipating much of the content of the speaker's discourse. In naturalistic data from child development, it can be seen that children frequently fill in what is about to be said before it is actually pronounced. To my knowledge, there is no experimental literature on how this capacity develops as far as language is directly concerned.

However, the development of anticipation as a general cognitive capacity has been analysed by many authors, and particularly by Piaget (1936). A striking example of the infant's development of anticipation can be seen in their crying in the crib: whereas initially the infant continues crying until this provokes a response from the caretaker, very quickly the infant begins to introduce short pauses in the crying as if, in anticipation, he leaves a "slot" for the caretaker's response. Work on children's goal-oriented strategies also bears witness to the fact that children anticipate their next moves or next sub-goals (Inhelder et al., 1976).

(iii) *Prior world knowledge.* It is perhaps Schank (1976) and Charniak (1972) who have most clearly illustrated how the understanding process does not rely solely or even essentially on the actual words in the discourse. Rather, understanding involves inferences made from the hearer's general knowledge about the topic under discussion. For these authors, the subject brings into the understanding situation "scripts", or "scenarios", or in Minsky's (1975) terms "frames", which he uses to infer essential elements which have not been explicitly stated in the text. Whilst such "scripts" do not suffice alone to explain the understanding process (see Wilks, 1978 for critical analysis) there is no doubt that just as the interpreter requires knowledge outside the particular content of the discourse being interpreted, this holds equally true for the monolingual dialogue. The formation of these "scripts" in child development has not yet been reported on, although work in this respect is in progress at Yale (Nelson, personal communication).

(iv) *Communicative modulation of message.* Clearly in the monolingual situation, the speaker must modulate the content and style of his message according to the characteristics of his audience. Much will depend on the presuppositions which exist between speaker and hearer. Studies in child development on how children gradually develop code-switching capacity are particularly relevant in this respect (Brami-Mouling, 1977; Shatz and Gelman, 1973). Brami-Mouling has, for instance, shown that children dispose of a large repertory of verbal devices (both lexical and syntactic) which they put to use in dialogic situations where they feel that the hearer does not possess the same world knowledge or linguistic knowledge as they do. Thus, twelve-year olds addressing their message to six year olds (as compared to the same message addressed to their peers) will either give a definition of a difficult lexical term or use a simpler one, and tend to pronominalise less, use less indirect and anaphoric reference, etc. In other words, their lexicon and syntax vary according to whether they are talking to a six year or twelve year old. Moreover, these children are not necessarily aware of the code-switching devices they are using until considerably later in development. The in-depth analysis in progress by this author (Brami-Mouling, in preparation) will show how this capacity originally develops in younger children, some aspects of which seem already to be part of the competence of four year olds (Shatz and Gelman, 1973).

It is also of interest to note that work in brain pathology suggests that the "appropriateness" of the message (when one can joke, etc.) may be placed in a separate brain locus from other aspects of language. There are patients whose semantics and syntax are intact, but who lose the capacity to judge "appropriateness".

(v) *Gauging the intralinguistic communicative burden.* As discussed in the first part of this paper, morphemes and lexemes are most frequently plurifunctional, but in many cases it is necessary to add linguistic emphasizers if a particular contrast is to be conveyed. Here child development data shows that the understanding of the plurifunctional status of morphemes and the communicative burden a morpheme can carry are very essential facets of language acquisition. A study on the child's use and understanding of nominal determiners in French (Karmiloff-Smith, 1976a) demonstrated that morphemes are initially unifunctional for the child, and only gradually do they acquire their plurifunctional status. It is only approximately as of five years that children begin to use new procedures which introduce surface distinctions which do not exist in French but are part of the morphemic distinctions of other languages (Karmiloff-Smith, in press). For instance, children over five will use "une voiture" to mean "*a* car" but the slightly agrammatical "une de voiture" to mean "*one* car". It is not until later that one single form has explicitly a dual function for the child. Moreover, with development, children become aware of the presuppositions conveyed by using one determiner in the place of another, or by the absence or presence of a particular marker, e.g. typical statements from nine to ten year olds are of the following nature: "if I say *my* cars, you'll think yours are there, so it's better to say *the* cars even if they belong to me". Younger subjects always used the possessive adjective in such circumstances. Such examples not only point to the fact that children gradually organize morphemes into systems of relevant options for modulating meaning, but also that the interpreter's complex task of giving just enough information but not more than required (an important Gricean principle in language use, Grice, 1968) is something that the child acquires very gradually in development.

(vi) *Role-taking and turn-taking*. Much research and theoretical focus have recently been placed on mother-child dialogic interaction before the onset of speech (e.g. Bruner, 1975 and 1978; Ninio and Bruner, in press,; Ryan, 1978). Bruner, for example, has studied how infants learn to take turns and change roles of agent/recipient in ritualized games (hide and seek, take and give-back, construct and knock down, etc.) and how mother and infant guage one another's eye movements and gestures in order to reach joint attention on the same topic of interest. The mother is constantly updating her theory about her infant's capacities. For Bruner, these early dialogic interactions provide the matrix for the acquisition of language and give language its distinctive structure. Ryan (1978) has shown how the mother uses, like the interpreter, intonational patterns in order to change or hold her infant's attention.

The above points all indicate that some of the issues singled out as particularly relevant to the simultaneous interpreter's difficulties in performing his task are, in fact, important facets of child language development and therefore represent part of the implicit competence of every speaker and listener, be he monolingual, bilingual or multilingual. They are an inherent part of the behavioural patterns of dialogic situations. In the simultaneous interpretation situation, however, what is implicit in normal dialogue often becomes particularly explicit and therefore more directly observable to the researcher. This does not imply, of course, that there are no differences between the interpreter's task and the monolingual situation, but rather that stressing the similarities may provide new insights from simultaneous interpretation into the various components of language behaviour in general.

Thus, in my view, there are sound arguments in favor of considering interpretation data to be close in some important respects to normal discourse, and therefore to be more appropriate for an analysis of linguistic functions than is often the case with experimental data. The interpreter is motivated to convey a message clearly, as is the normal speaker in most circumstances, whereas in experimentation, subjects often have no communicative motivation whatsoever in their reactions to a series of isolated sentences. In many cases, therefore, data available from experiments are almost metalinguistic in nature and rarely involve spontaneous language usage. Above all, the interpreter is plunged into the flow of extended discourse, involving all the presuppositional constraints of normal speech.

THE INTERPRETER'S COGNITIVE TASK

One way of characterizing cognitively the interpreter's behaviour (and which again can be held to be partially true of normal dialogic interaction) would be the following: the interpreter, while listening to a speaker, is constantly updating his mini-theory of the speaker's semantic intentions. Each speech act is not only the communication of new information, but the intricate interplay of new information and presuppositions based on the knowledge accumulated from the present discourse and on general extralinguistic knowledge. Thus, the content of each message unit enables the interpreter to form a temporary "knowledge framework" for the particular subject under discussion and to filter each new message through that framework. The figure below gives a schematic representation of some general aspects of the interpreter's understanding process rather than the particular characteristic of passing from source to target language.

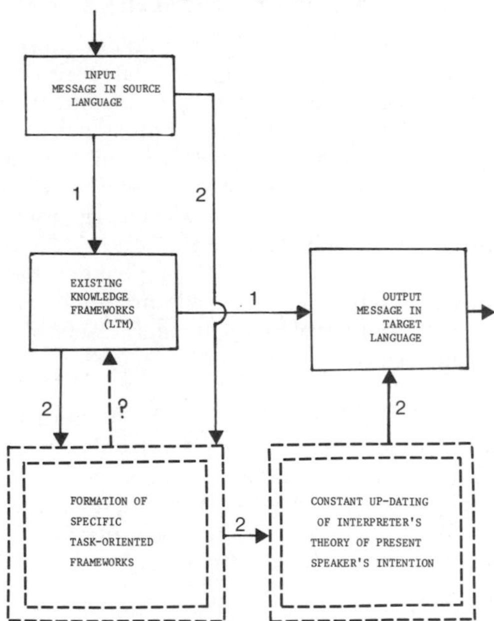

Figure 1 Schematic representation of the interpreter's understanding process.

As can be seen, when the interpreter perceives the input message in the source language, it is suggested that he first channels it through his own previous knowledge framework, i.e. what he already knows about the general subject under discussion. This would help him progressively to form an ad-hoc, specific task-oriented framework, useful for filtering the very specific discussion under way in that particular conference session. The task-oriented framework is obviously a very dynamic concept, whereas the previous knowledge frames are more stable in memory. The formation of specific, task-oriented frameworks enables the interpreter constantly to up-date his theory of what the *present* speaker is trying to convey in one particular flow of discourse. As the interpreter strengthens his task-oriented frame, his capacity to anticipate the present speaker's semantic intentions should increase. This very schematic representation is above all intended to stress the importance of both previous knowledge frameworks and the dynamic formation of task-oriented frameworks. Whether or not these task-oriented frameworks later become part of the interpreter's stable knowledge frameworks in memory, or whether he erases these task-oriented frameworks is an important issue for future research. It is perhaps in the rapid formation of task-oriented frameworks that the interpreter's task differs somewhat from the monolingual dialogic situation, although up-dating one's theory of a speaker's intention is nonetheless very much part of normal discourse. It may well be that these phenomena are more available to introspection on the part of the interpreter, because in the monolingual situation most of these procedures are automatized and much of dialogue is on known topics of shared knowledge. It should be added that sometimes children are more aware of their procedures when they are constructing them than when they have mastered them completely.

CONCLUDING REMARKS

Finally, I would reiterate that interpretation data may serve as a particularly relevant area for a functional analysis of linguistic categories which will prove useful for psycholinguistic research. If more were known about the *functions* various linguistic categories have in a language, and the relations between categories, a deeper insight would be gained into the sort of problems children face in coping initially with the daily input of their linguistic environment. It will also make possible the design of more realistic experimental situations, eliciting more naturally the particular category under study. Finally, it may be that knowledge of the functional links between linguistic categories could usefully complement the interpreter trainee's knowledge of semantic and syntactic links, all three being part and parcel of the competence underlying monolingual dialogue and essential facets of the child's acquisition of his first language.

If so much emphasis has been placed on the functional aspect of language in this paper, it is due to the fact that theoretically I fully endorse John Searle's position, and on this I shall conclude: "many of the purely syntactic rules of language will have a deeper explanation in terms of the functions that the syntactic forms serve" (Searle, 1976). I believe that simultaneous interpretation data may help to provide clues to these intralinguistic functions.

REFERENCES

Baldie, Brian, J. The acquisition of the passive voice, *Journal of Child Language* 1976, *3*: 331 - 348.

Bever, T. G. The cognitive basis for linguistic structures, in J. R. Hayes (Ed.), *Cognition and the development of Language*, New York: Wiley, 1970.

Blanchet, A., Ackerman-Valladao, E., Kilcher, H. and Robert, M., Une hypothèse sur les connaissances utilisees en situation de résolution de problème, *Proceedings of Symposium de l'Assoc. Francaise de Psychologie Scientifique*, 1977.

Brami-Mouling, Marie-Anne, Notes sur l'adaptation de l'expression verbale de l'enfant en fonction de l'age de son interlocuteur, Vol. XLV, *Archives de Psychologie*, 1977, *45*, 225 - 234.

Brami-Mouling, Anne-Marie. *La notion de présupposition et la place qu'elle occupe dans le discours chez l'enfant*, Ph.D. thesis, University of Geneva, in preparation.

Bruner, J. S. From communication to language: a psychological perspective, *Cognition*, 1975, *3/3*, 255 - 287.

Bruner, J. S., Joint attention and joint action: an analysis of dialogue, in R. N. Campbell and P. T. Smith (Eds.). *Stirling Conference on the Psychology of Language*, New York: Plenum Press, 1978.

Caprez, G., Sinclair, H., and Studer, B. Entwicklung der Passiveform im Schweizerdeutschen, *Archives de Psychologie*, 1971, *41*, 23 - 25.

Charniak, Eugene, *Toward a model of children's story comprehension.* Cambridge Mass.: M.I.T. Artificial Intelligence Lab. AI-TR-266, 1972.

Clark, E. V., and Sengul, C. J. Deictic contrasts in language acquisition, *Annual Meeting of the Linguistic Society of America*, New York, 1974.

Costermans J. and Hupet, M. The other side of Johnson-Laird's interpretation of the passive voice, *British Journal of Psychology*, 1977, *68* 107 - 111.

Dewart, M. H., *A psychological investigation of sentence comprehension by children*, Unpublished Ph.D. dissertation, University College London, 1975.

Ducrot, O., *Dire et ne pas dire: principes de sémantique linguistique*, Paris: Herman, 1972.

Garman, M, A cross-linguistic study of deixis acquisition, *4th Salzburg International Linguistics Meeting*, Salzburg, 1977.

Gerver, D., Simultaneous listening and speaking and retention of prose, *Quarterly Journal of Experimental Psychology*, 1974, *26*, 337 - 341.

Gerver, D. A psychological approach to simultaneous interpretation, *META*, 1975, 20.

Grice, H. P., Utterer's meaning, sentence-meaning, and word-meaning, *Foundations of Language*, 1968, *4*, 225 - 242.

Harris, M. The influence of reversibility and truncation on the interpretation of the passive voice by young children, *British Journal of Psychology,* 1976, *67*, 419 - 427.

Hayhurst, H., Some errors of young children in producing passive sentences, *Journal of Verbal Learning and Verbal behaviour*, 1967, *No. 6*. 634 - 639.

Inhelder, B., Blanchet, A., Ackerman, E., Karmiloff-Smith, A., Kilcher, H., Montangero, J., and Robert, M., (1976), Des structures cognitives aux procedures de decouverte, *Archives de Psychologie*, 1976, *Vol XLIV*, 173.

Inhelder, B., and Piaget, J. *La gènese des structures logiques élémentaires*, Neuchatel: Delachaux and Niestle, 1959.

Johnson-Laird, P. N. The interpretation of the passive voice, *Quarterly Journal of Experimental Psychology*, 1968, *20*, 69 - 73.

Johnson-Laird, P. N. The passive paradox: a reply to Costermans and Hupet, *British Journal of Psychology*, 1977, *68*, 113 - 116.

Karmiloff-Smith, A., *Little words mean a lot: the plurifunctionality of determiners in child language*, Ph.D. thesis, University of Geneva. (Revised version, forthcoming, London: C.U.P.) 1976.

Karmiloff-Smith, A. The interplay between syntax, semantics and phonology in language acquisition processes, in R. N. Campbell and P. T. Smith (Eds.). *Stirling Conference on the Psychology of Language,* New York: Plenum Press, 1978.

Karmiloff-Smith, A., Some aspects of the child's construction of a system of plurifunctionalmarkers, *Salzburg Fourth International Linguistics Meeting*, Salzburg, 1977a.

Karmiloff-Smith, A., More about the same: children's understanding of post-articles, *Journal of Child Language,* 1977b, *4*.

Karmiloff-Smith, A., Développement cognitif et plurifunctionalité des déterminants, in *Genèse de la Parole*, Paris: Presses Universitaires de France, 1977c.

Karmiloff-Smith, A, Language development after five, in Fletcher P. and Garman, M. *Studies in Language Acquisition*. London: Cambridge University Press, in press.

Karmiloff-Smith, A., and Inhelder, B., If you want to get ahead get a theory, *Cognition*, 1975, *3:3*, 195 - 212.

Macrae, A., *Meaning relations in language development: a study of some converse pairs and directional opposites*, Unpublished Ph.D. dissertation, University of Edinburgh, 1976.

Maratsos, M., *The use of definite and indefinite reference in young children*, London: Cambridge University Press, 1976.

Mounoud, P. Les révolutions psychologiques de l'enfant, *Archives de Psychologie*, Vol. XLIV, 1976,*No. 171*. 103 - 114.

Minsky, M., A framework for representing knowledge, in Winston, P. (Ed.) *The Psychology of Computer Vision*, New York: McGraw Hill, 1975.

Ninio, A., and Bruner, J. S., The achievement and antecedents of labelling, *Journal of Child Language*, 1978.

Piaget, J., *La naissance de l'intelligence*, Neuchatel: Delachaux et Niestle, 1936.

Piaget, J., and Karmiloff-Smith, A., (in press), Conflicts entre symmétries, in Piaget J., (Ed.), *Les morphismes*, Paris: Presses Universitaires de France, in press.

Ryan Maire, L., Contour in context: some situational variables associated with the use of prosodic feature in the speech of mothers to 12-month infants, in R. N. Campbell and P. T. Smith, (Eds.). *Stirling Conference on the Psychology on Language*, New York: Plenum Press, 1978.

Schank, R., Predictive understanding: plans, goals and inferences, as above *Stirling Conference on the Psychology of Language*, Stirling, June, 1976.

Shatz, M. and Gelman, R., "The development of communication skills: modification in the speech of young children as a function of listeners", *Monog. SRCD*, 1973, *38, No. 5*.

Searle, J., Rules of the language game, *Times Literary Supplement*, September, 1976.

Sinclair, Anne, Sinclair, H., and Marcellus, O., Young Children's comprehension and production of passive sentences, *Archives de Psychologie,* 1971, *41*, 1 - 22.

Sinclair, H., and Ferreiro, E., "Production et répétition des phrases au mode passif", *Archives de Psychologie*, 1970, *40*, 1 - 42.
Turner, E. A., and Rommetveit, R., The acquisition of sentence voice, *Child Development*, 1967, 649 - 660.
Webb, P. A., and Abrahamson, A., Stages of egocentrism in children's use of 'this' and 'that': a different point of view, *Journal of Child Language*, 1976, 349 - 365.
Welford, A. I., *The fundamentals of skill*,, London: Methuen, 1968.
Wilks, Y., Frames, scripts, stories and fantasies, in R. N. Campbell and P. T. Smith (Eds.). *Stirling Conference on the Psychology of Language*, New York: Plenum Press, 1978.

The Contribution of Cognitive Psychology to the Study of Interpretation

G. B. Flores d'Arcais

University of Leiden

Leiden, The Netherlands

The aim of this paper is to comment on some of the problems discussed during this symposium. No attempt will be made towards a systematic discussion of all papers presented at the Symposium and included in this book: instead, a selection will be made of the issues which seemed more interesting and provocative and seemingly capable of stimulating future research and useful discussions.

The Symposium has been an attempt to bring together two categories of professions, namely the behavioral scientists and the professional interpreters, in order to provide a better framework for the study of the skill of interpretation. The papers presented, the discussion carried out, and the scientific and social interaction which has taken place during the Conference, the ideas debated and the conclusions reached, all reflected the heterogeneity of the two main groups of participants. It would therefore be extremely difficult to provide a discussion paper capable of integrating the different and often distant points of view, and of presenting a balanced approach to the issues. It is better to recognize that this paper is heavily biased towards the orientation of the psychologists. As the title of the paper indicates, it will be an attempt to see to what extent modern psychology – particularly cognitive psychology – has contributed, or might contribute, to a knowledge of the processes taking place during the complex and amazingly skilled performance of simultaneous interpretation.

The main question this discussion will pose, with reference to the papers presented at the conference, is the following: what kind of contribution can the behavioral sciences make to our knowledge of the processes involved in language interpretation? In particular, one can ask the following questions:

a) What kind of work has been carried out so far in the area by behavioral scientists, and what kind of knowledge is available?

b) Of the material presented at the Symposium by behavioral scientists, what has been useful for a better knowledge of the processes of interpretation, for good selection and training procedures, for better performance of the interpreters and more efficient and less stressful working conditions?

These questions clearly concern only or mainly the psychological and sociological papers, be they presented by behavioral scientists or by teachers in schools for interpreters. On the other hand, several papers presented at the Symposium concerned applications and practical issues more of an educational character, namely selection and training of conference interpreters. Some of these issues will also be briefly commented upon.

The present contribution, then, will be structured as follows. First, a quick overview of the type of approach taken by the papers presented at the Symposium with reference to the above questions. Then an attempt will be made to sketch in which direction research and theoretical work might develop, as a result of the increased interest shown by behavioral scientists, professional interpreters, and schools for interpreters in the psychological processes involved in interpretation, and hopefully also as a result of the Venice Symposium.

As is apparent even from the table of contents of this book, the papers presented at the Symposium cover a broad range of basic and applied problems. Many of the contributions are indicative of the still very initial stage of our knowledge of the psychological processes of interpretation. Given the fascinating aspects of the skill of the interpreter, one is amazed by the lack of interest of the behavioral sciences at large for this skill. As Gerver points out in his review of research on interpretation (1976), experimental psychological studies on this area are extremely rare. There is an abundance of psychological and linguistic literature on bilingualism, as there is for the field of second language learning. But there are extremely few papers dealing specifically with the skill of simultaneous interpretation. Yet, the task could be a paradigmatic case for testing theories on language understanding, on language production, etc. It is probably because of the complexity of the situation, that, until very recently, no one has really tried to produce a full model of the processes of interpretation. However, it should be possible to put together pieces of knowledge about the different "subtasks" involved in the complex task in question, in order to produce at least some ideas about the processes taking place during interpretation.

THE CONTRIBUTION OF THE BEHAVIORAL SCIENCES TO THE SYMPOSIUM

The papers presented at the Symposium by behavioral scientists offer a rather good sample of a wide range of approaches to the study of interpretation. The work discussed has shown the Symposium participants several of the methods and theoretical points of view of psychology, namely the following: a) the psychometric approach; b) the human information processing approach; c) the approach of psycholinguistics; d) semantic memory; e) artificial intelligence; f) human factors; g) the social psychological approach. Let us briefly consider the basic issues involved in these approaches, as they were presented at the Symposium.

Psychometrics

Professor Carroll's paper was a beautiful example of a psychometric approach to the study of interpretation. As is well known to every student in psychology, the psychologist typically starts with an analysis of the task or skill to be investigated, and with a list of the possible psychological variables involved. He then chooses, or constructs, measuring instruments for these variables, checks whether these instruments work, and whether the predictions made through their usage are accurate or not: to the extent to which this is not the case, the hypotheses about the relevant psychological variables, and the characteristics of the measuring instruments, can respectively be changed and improved. Notice that this approach, with the several methods involved, enables us to reach two goals. First, it provides us with a set of measuring instruments which can be used for the prediction of future performance, and which therefore might be used for orientation or selection. Second, it gives us information about the abilities involved in a given task, and allows us to construct and empirically test a theory about these mental abilities.

Some procedures for the selection of students to be enrolled in courses for conference interpreters have been illustrated in the Symposium and are described in this book – e.g., in the papers by Keiser and by Longley. Batteries of psychological tests do not seem to be much in favor in the selection programs for interpreters – the main exception apparently being the Polytechnic of Central London – nor do psychometric concepts in general seem to seriously affect the selection procedures of the schools for conference interpreters. Whether some battery of tests might contribute or not, and how much, to a good selection program for prospective students of a course in conference interpretation, and whether the tests should represent a good solution for the selection, is not the most important issue, perhaps. But the main psychometric concepts could be of enormous importance in devising selection procedures. Good validation studies based on solid psychometric evidence could contribute in an efficient way to the programs for selection and training for interpreters. Teachers in these schools should be very careful before claiming that they know perfectly well what kind of skills are necessary for a good interpreter, and that the contribution of psychology is more or less superfluous. Decades of studies in tests and selection have taught psychologists at least to be very careful before taking decisions which affect selection and training. I think that this is one of the areas where the contribution of psychology for the interpreter schools can be of great value, especially if this work will be accompanied by a better knowledge about the nature of the skill of interpretation.

Human information processing

This approach is clearly the most characteristic aspect of contemporary cognitive psychology. One of the typical features of this point of view consists in the attempt to offer models of the *processes* which take place during performance of a particular task. Such models usually try to specify in detail the mental operations involved in a given process, and to outline the stages through which information is coded and transformed from the input to the appropriate response. This approach is exemplified by the papers of Massaro and Moser. Massaro has convincingly illustrated his model of human information processing with special reference to the perception of a speech signal, while Moser has essentially tried an extension of Massaro's model to the description of processing of information in the task of interpreting a message from one language into another.

One of the essential features of this type of model consists in the fact that they permit specific predictions about certain stages during processing, as well as empirical tests of such predictions: in this sense, such models can be extremely powerful. This approach will certainly contribute to the advance of our knowledge of the skill of interpretation. We shall return to this point further on.

To the present knowledge of the author, so far only two attempts have been made to offer process models for interpretation, namely the one presented by Gerver in his review of the literature on interpretation (Gerver, 1976) and the model introduced in Moser's paper. It is very likely that within a couple of years new empirical evidence and further thinking will oblige both authors to modify their models in several details, or perhaps even to throw them away as completely wrong: this is one of the nice features of the approach – namely, that one has to test the components of the model, and might be obliged to modify or even reject it. To be sure, a careful consideration of available theoretical and empirical evidence in cognitive psychology could probably already necessitate certain substantial modifications in Moser's model as described in this book. In the present author's opinion, the value of the model does not lie in the details of the solution offered, but in the attempt to apply a particularly fruitful approach to the study of a complex skill.

Psycholinguistics

As a first guess, one could have expected to find a number of studies of interpretation in the psycholinguistic literature, and in the contribution of psycholinguistics to the Symposium. So far, this has not been the case, nor have many of the theoretical ideas about language processing affected the approaches to interpretation: the contribution of psycholinguistics to this field is yet to come. However, the Symposium has already revealed that some very interesting ideas from cognitive psycholinguistics can be applied to the domain of language interpretation. This is particularly clear in Le Ny's attempt at utilizing notions of psychosemantics and cognitive psychology at large in the construction of a theoretical frame for the study of the processes involved in interpretation. Also, the contribution of the theoretical concepts and methodological experience of developmental psycholinguistics, as outlined in Karmiloff-Smith's paper, seems extremely promising for the study of interpretation.

A not inappropriate criticism of many psycholinguistic studies, especially of a consistent trend of research in the sixties, concerns the typical approach of studying perception, comprehension and memory of sentences in isolation: both in terms of ecological validity and of a general value of the models developed within such an approach for language processing at large, this line of research had and has clear limitations. During the last few years, however, the situation has changed much. The intentions of the speakers, the whole communicative situation, the linguistic and extralinguistic context, the different presuppositions implicit in the act of exchange of communication, all these as well as several other variables have been given a central place in psycholinguistic studies during recent years. This trend makes psycholinguistic theory more "available" for an attempt to study the complex process of interpretation, especially if we agree with a claim made several times during the Symposium especially from the interpreters, that interpretation is more than a change of code of a simple sequence of sentences.

It was interesting to see how the theoretical linguistic ideas expressed by

Uhlenbeck, and his proposal to integrate pragmatics more closely with linguistics, fit very nicely into this new trend in contemporary psycholinguistics. It is also important to point out how the notions expressed in his paper can be a useful framework for the development of a psycholinguistic and a sociolinguistic approach to the study of interpretation.

Semantic memory

There is an extremely lively trend in psychology and artificial intelligence, with research aiming at the development of satisfactory theories about the way we represent knowledge in our mind, relate new pieces of information to our existing knowledge, and retrieve the appropriate information from memory. Put more generally, the questions asked here refer to the structure of our internal encyclopedia, to procedures used in adding new information to it and in searching for the stored one, and to methods for efficient interactions between the available information and the use of new linguistic or non linguistic data. This area has been given the rather inappropriate term of *semantic memory*. Close to this trend is a recent line of work on the ways in which we comprehend connected discourse and text. The relation to psycholinguistics on the one hand and, to the psychology of memory and of thinking on the other are obvious. Long and Harding-Esch's paper, which included aspects of text analysis and text comprehension was an example of this approach. The contribution of this area is certainly central for the development of good psychological models of interpretation, because the process of comprehension and of integration of old and new information is clearly essential in the interpretation process.

Artificial intelligence

This is a very fashionable, exciting, productive and rapidly changing field which attracts many brilliant psychologists and linguists. The Symposium participants enjoyed a very lively imaginative presentation by Wilks. This topic is considered here separately from semantic memory, although as far as the problems of interest for interpretation, namely the comprehension, storage and retrieval of knowledge are concerned, the two fields overlap very much. At first, the field may only seem important for the study of interpretation because of the possible contributions to machine translation. In this area, as Wilks has pointed out, we are more cautious and less ambitious than we were in the fifties, when considerable amounts of money and scientific energy were put into large projects with a lot of naive optimism, but we are also less pessimistic than a few years ago, after the apparent failure of the main goals of the "first generation" projects. Between the notion of a machine capable of daily translating all Russian newspapers into perfect English, and the more modest idea of a system capable of finding in French the lexical equivalents of a small set of German lexical entries from within a restricted semantic domain, several alternatives are possible. The progress here is slow but rather substantial. Leaving aside for now possible technological developments such as machines capable of analyzing spoken speech in one language and of synthesizing spoken speech in a second language, developments which still belong more to the domain of science fiction than to the real possibilities of a technology based on what we know about langauge comprehension and speech perception and production, the advances in machine translation might suggest very useful notions for the study of human interpretation, and may constitute ways of testing critical assumptions and features of a model of interpretation. But A.I. might contribute to the study of language interpretation in a perhaps more substantial way, namely through theoretical notions about the organization and the representation of information in the mind, and the models of comprehension of linguistic material, and through powerful tests of these notions with computer simulation. The method of computer simulation should, and probably will, become a useful tool for testing models of language interpretation.

Human performance and human factors

We should distinguish here the field of *human performance*, which deals with the study of skills, and *human engineering* and *ergonomics* (the two terms are often used synonymously). Both the more basic and the applied field have grown enormously during recent years. We have, for example, a large amount of data and good models on performance under stress, on the characteristics of time on- and off-duty, etc.. for several rather delicate and difficult tasks, such as for example, tasks requiring quick detection of a signal which comes very quickly and then disappears, and in which an appropriate and very rapid decision is extremely important. Think, for example, of the radar operator in flight control: where detection of a rapid change in the signal, wrong identification of a pattern, lack of response or inappropriate decision can have tragic consequences for several individuals or even for an entire community.

Within the basic studies of skill and human performance, the discussion of interpretation given in a classic treatment of human skills, namely the book by Welford (1968) is rather brief and once more indicative of the lack of interest in psychology for this type of performance. Yet, probably much of what is known about performance under stress, or on the effect of arousal on correct performance in difficult tasks, etc., could be used to make predictions about performance in the interpretation booth, or to construct models of the interpretation process capable of accounting for critical variables such as rate of linguistic input, or maximum span between input and output, etc. Human performance research in interpretation can profit from the kind of experimental studies exemplified by Dornic's paper, that is, from studies of performance in non-dominant language under stress, with a high load on memory, etc.

More from the applied corner, the potential contribution of human factors studies to an exploration of the whole situation in which interpretation takes place is obvious. In this respect, Parson's paper is very interesting and some of his results are very useful. However, beside *questionnaire* data, *direct evidence* from actual performance or experimental studies with careful manipulation of possible critical variables should be even more illuminating and are badly needed in this field.

Social psychology and bilingualism

The paper by Lambert gives some beautiful examples of the possible contributions of social psychology to the study of interpretation: the study of cultural and attitudinal differences in bilingual subjects for concepts in the two different linguistic domains can offer important conclusions for the construction of a general theory of language interpretation.

Bilingualism is a very popular area of research in psycholinguistics and social psychology. Most of the studies are of a descriptive character, with the main goal being to find out what kinds of linguistic interference are common in bilingual speakers, what are the attitudes towards the two cultures and what are the effects of bilingualism on linguistic performance or in different cognitive domains. Almost all of the studies are on social bilinguals. Can the conclusions of these studies be extended to professional bilinguals? There are several areas where the answer might be positive. First, probably much of the evidence on interlinguistic interference can be used to make at least some good guesses about sources of difficulty in interpretation. Second, several questions about performance in professional bilinguals could be answered by taking the results of experiments with social bilinguals at least as good working hypotheses. For example, the results presented by Dornic give us some evidence about decrements in performance under stress in the less dominant language: this could offer some suggestions about the direction in which interpretation can be performed more easily, for example from an A language to a B language, or vice versa. Even the ample evidence on differences in the associative structures of words in two languages, or in semantic differential ratings for concepts from the two languages, as emerged in several studies by Lambert, among others, can be very useful. What these studies tell us is mainly something about attitudes. Semantic differential ratings, which concern the "affective" meaning of words, measure nothing but the attitude or the whole set of emotions associated with a particular concept. A French-English Canadian bilingual can give different semantic differential ratings to the concepts *church* and *église*, and this might reflect differences in the cultural experience within the two cultures (although the subject might well be aware that both words *mean* the same, in the sense that they express the same concept – and can be used for the same set of referents, to be sure). Even if associative structures and semantic differential ratings do not tell us much about meaning, the knowledge of the different emotional connotation associated with particular terms, or of the clear cultural differences bound to what a dictionary would give as equivalent lexical entries in two languages, is certainly of importance for conference interpreters. A possible conclusion which one might try to offer on the basis of differences in the use of the two linguistic systems in bilinguals would be that in order to be a really good interpreter it is not enough to be functionally bilingual but it would be necessary to be *bicultural*!

Contributions to psychological theory

Most of the psychological papers which have been "classified" in one way or another under the headings so far introduced in this section had obvious direct relevance for the study of conference interpretation. Some of them, however, have a more general relevance for psychological theory, in particular for comprehension and memory for language. Beside being contributions towards the study of interpretation, they bear on current psychological issues. For example, the study of Kolers, interesting as it is for interpretation studies, is particularly relevant for an old and much debated issue in the psychology of memory. The question involved is whether we encode experience in memory in a very abstract form – as many psycholinguistic studies seemed to indicate, among others – or in a language-specific form. Kolers brings evidence from studies on bilinguals in favor of the second alternative towards which much of his work seems to point. The papers by Massaro and Dornic, among others, again can be seen as a general contribution to psychological theory, although not new for the authors, in this sense. But it might be interesting for the reader of a book on studies on language interpretation to find that contributions which are more specific in character are related to more general theoretical issues in information processing.

Sociology, cultural anthropology and sociolinguistics

As compared with psychology, sociology, cultural anthropology and sociolinguistics probably have less to say about the *process* of interpretation. Still, if one wants to take into account, in the the study of interpretation, the whole communicative situation, then the contribution of sociology and sociolinguistics is essential as one can see from the few papers on these topics, such as Anderson's presentation. If we want to place the whole situation of conference interpretation in a wide social and sociolinguistic context, we can look at social psychological and sociological variables such as the attitudes and role perception of the interpreters, the social characteristics of the situation in which interpretation takes place, and take into consideration the whole dynamics of the social process which is an essential part of the communication exchange in interpretation. Similarly, the study of interpretation can certainly profit from anthropological data, such as those presented by Lang, and cross-cultural studies involving anthropological, social psychological and sociological variables such as the work exemplified by Brislin. Besides offering some extremely fascinating aspects of the roles of interpreters in different cultures, this type of study can offer new perspectives in the approach to interpretation, and suggests ways in which the interpretation situation might be improved.

Sign Language

The program of the Symposium included, as does this book, a whole section dedicated to studies on sign language and on sign language interpretation. This section would deserve a lengthy discussion at an analytic level. Only a couple of remarks will be made here, however.

First, the papers can be seen from a linguistic and a psycholinguistic perspective, and in this sense they represent fascinating contributions to our knowledge of the linguistic function as expressed in a non-verbal form. Given the different modality involved, with obvious differences in the organization of the morphological and syntactic structure of the utterances, the study of sign language would permit critical tests of several aspects of linguistic and psycholinguistic theories.

The second important contribution is a practical one: advances in the psycholinguistic theory of sign language might become the basis for educational programs for the deaf. A third, more specific and for the Symposium more central aspect, is the knowledge about the process of interpretation that one might gain from studies on sign language interpretation: given the differences in the parameters involved in the language – e.g., the possibility of encoding information more in a parallel than in a serial manner – sign language might suggest interesting hypotheses about levels of processing and of organization in the recoding of information from one langauge to the other. Finally, obviously, the construction of specific models for the process of interpretation for sign language will be of importance for the advance of techniques of training of sign language interpreters.

Research and programs in conference interpretation

So far, the different papers by behavioral scientists have been briefly commented upon. With a couple of exceptions, these authors are not directly involved in the work of conference interpreting; they have looked at language interpretation as at any other psychological skill, or as a linguistic or social phenomenon worth precise study. Several papers at the Symposium came from participants directly involved *in* the area of conference interpretation (interpreters, teachers in schools of interpreters, or scientists directly connected with interpretation schools). To distinguish the types of contribution on the basis of the professional affiliation of the authors is certainly not a very appropriate way of discussing papers. On the other hand, these contributions were clearly more applied in their goals, or emerged from the daily experience of interpreters or from careful studies based on the real performance of interpreters. We can distinguish two types of papers. First, there are studies which report findings and research on specific aspects of interpretation. Second, a group of papers bring evidence, data and proposals about selection and training of conference interpreters.

Studies in simultaneous interpretation

The results of some studies on the performance of interpreters in "normal" situations have been reported at the Symposium. Studies of this type can be based on collections of transcriptions of samples of the verbal behavior of interpreters (e.g., through recording of first language input on one track and of second language output – the interpreter's production – on the other track of a tape-recorder) as in Lederer's paper. Such studies certainly have a good face validity, and might clearly have ecological validity and represent a very useful way of coming to know more about the process of interpretation. In the same way as careful analyses of errors in language production can tell us much about the processes of language production (a typical example of this approach is given, for example, in a study by Garrett, 1975) analysis of properties of linguistic output of the interpreter as compared to the speaker's input can allow important conclusions on the process of interpretations. Variables such as time lag between speakers and the interpreter's translation, omission or corrections and so on, can be extremely important sources for constructing good models of the interpretation process. Notice that this kind of data can also be very useful for the study of language comprehension and language production in general. In a way, we have here the possibility of controlling the semantic structure of the linguistic production, for the task of the interpreter is exactly that of giving in a language the meaning of the message in another language: we can take advantage of such a situation to study structural variables in language production. Lederer's paper represents a good example of a useful and promising approach to the study of interpretation.

It is perhaps appropriate to make a point here. A claim often made in the discussions during the Symposium, especially from the professional interpreters, was that studies based on laboratory experiments cannot tell us very much about language interpretation, because they are too far from the real situation in which interpretation takes place, and from "real life". On this argument, research based on data obtained directly from performances in the translation booth should be the only good way of making progress in the study of interpretation. This point of view is clearly wrong. It is not because a situation is "closer" to "real life" that a study becomes good; it obviously depends on the questions asked, on the methods used to get an answer, and so forth. The point, however, has to be kept in mind when making generalizations from laboratory experiments to the "real" situation of the interpreter's work. But after all, there are probably very few "real life" situations which are more similar to a laboratory of psychological experimentation than the situation of the interpreter in a conference booth, both for the control of external variables and for the "artificiality" of the task in comparison to normal linguistic performance.

The paper by Wilss is an interesting example of an analysis of a typical problem in language interpretation: the kind of problem for interpretation which might emerge from correspondence or lack of correspondence in the surface structure forms of two languages. As Wilss shows, the study of such problems can benefit from linguistic analysis and a close examination of certain psycholinguistic principles involved in the translation process. This is clearly another example of how research might proceed: starting from the examination of specific problems, such as those related to differences in the structure of two languages across which interpretation has to take place, and making generalizations about the possible ways in which it might be possible to solve the difficulties which arise from such differences. This approach can be a good way of getting at the strategies used by interpreters to "compensate" for these difficulties, such as anticipations based on extralinguistic information. The knowledge obtained by these studies can have interesting practical applications for teaching interpreters appropriate ways of dealing with problems dependent on the structures of the languages involved in the translation process.

Selection and training-programs for interpreters

The experiences of different schools and of teachers of interpreters were presented at the Symposium. These provided very valuable information, which will be useful for future attempts at designing good selection and training programs, and for possible integration among the schools. Personal experience of many years of professional activity and of teaching certainly constitute an excellent basis for starting with the lay-out of a selection and training program, as is the case with Keiser's proposal. However, as has been pointed out before, the methods suggested reflect very little concern with psychometric methods and with the experience accumulated in decades of educational research. At first, selection criteria such as those proposed by Keiser have an excellent face validity. To be sure, intuitions about the aptitudes, skills and personality traits to be possessed by the interpreters are a good way of starting: it is, after all, what every psychologist does. But definitive selection programs should be based on careful control of such intuitions through serious psychometric studies. Little or no consideration for construct validity of the procedures devised for selection – nor even for simple predictive validity – seem to have been given in the program described by Keiser. He rightly asserts that students do not enrol in a course to be used as guinea pigs for psychological experiments. In this spirit, it would obviously be bad practice to admit students from whom we can expect a bad performance, in order to see whether they really perform badly, and in this way acquiring additional evidence for the predictive validity of the selection programs used. The same problems, however, concern selection programs for any school or job, and psychologists have been well aware of these. There are several ways of getting around the problem. To indicate a simple and obvious one, a factor analysis of correlations of a series of measures on task performance of good and less good conference interpreters could be a way to start making hypotheses about relevant variables – or as a way of testing certain intuitions. And obviously, modern psychometric and educational methodology offers much more for a good study on selection.

Also the training programs described, interesting as they are, seem to have been rather little affected by educational research. The psychological variables selected as important targets of the program again have a good face validity – and probably are the relevant ones. Most programs include techniques to teach pupils to improve comprehension for stories, summarize and repeat verbal material, to improve speech comprehension, to train social skills, empathy, self-confidence.

Certain programs, such as the one described by Longley, do already show some concern for validation. A possible favorable result of the Symposium will be an increased attention to the psychological problems involved in selection and training programs, and a more specific interest in procedures designed to improve the validity of such programs. After all, most programs are still only at a very initial stage.

TOWARDS A MODEL OF LANGUAGE INTERPRETATION

The experimental psychologist interested in linguistic processing, the teacher from an interpreter's school eager to utilize evidence available from psychological, psycholinguistic and sociolinguistic studies on interpretation in order to appropriately shape the training program for future interpreters, or the linguist interested in the interaction of two languages in contact during interpretation, all these will be a little disappointed to find out that so little is still known about the process and the skill of interpretation, and that the material presented at the Symposium, new and interesting as it was, still reveals the very early state of our knowledge in this topic. This being the case, one can conclude that research is badly needed in this field, and that future studies will fill the gap.

However, it is not necessary to wait for more work restricted to the domain of interpretation in order to make progress in this area. Progress would certainly result from a careful and skilled attempt to integrate knowledge from a number of areas in cognitive psychology. Some of these areas, capable of contributing to a plausible model of interpretation, have already been mentioned, as treated or touched upon in the Symposium papers. Some others are topics for which there is good experimental evidence, interesting and clear models: their contribution to a model of interpretation is obvious if one just considers the different phases and the skills involved in the process of interpreting.

It is certainly not the place, in a discussion paper, to try to propose a model of language interpretation and to show how the contribution from the different areas of cognitive psychology could be integrated in it. In the following only a very rough framework of how such a model could be constructed is attempted, and few of the many relevant topics are listed, as entries in an encyclopedia of cognitive psychology where one could start with a fruitful search.

Any model of simultaneous interpretation from one language (L_1) to the second language (L_2) would have to include two essential components, namely *decoding* of L_1, and *encoding* in L_2. The task of the interpreter certainly requires mechanisms and procedures for *language comprehension* and for *language production*. The amount of knowledge available within psycholinguistics about the two processes is extremely unbalanced. We do have some clear ideas and some reasonable hypotheses about stages and processing in language comprehension, but our knowledge of the processes underlying language production is still extremely limited. During the last few years, on the other hand, this topic has become a rapidly expanding area of psycholinguistic research.

Any models of interpretation one can try to construct will include procedures for the analysis and comprehension of the input language and for planning and uttering the output language. The two sets of procedures should account for the following *levels* of processing. The input side includes a level of *sensory processing*, namely the level of transformation of acoustic energy into a phonological representation, a level of *perceptual segmentation* of the incoming speech signal into words, clausal and sentence units, at which the signal, in other words, is given a structure with an internal representation, and a level of *message comprehension*, at which full semantic analysis is being carried out. Notice that this order does not imply serial processing. The isolation of a phonemic unit in perception is guided by our knowledge of the syntactic and morphological structure of the language, by our expectations about the content of the message, by the processing of the preceding linguistic information, and by other "top-down" constraints, and does not, in this sense "precede" sentence segmentation as a processing stage which has to be completed before passing on to the "following" stage.

At the output side, the model should include procedures to account for the levels of *conceptualization*, at which conceptual contents are selected and organized, of *formulization*, at which the conceptualized content is given a syntactic structure, and of *articulation* at which the structure is given an appropriate phonological interpretation and is overtly executed through the articulatory mechanisms (this distinction in three headings of the processes of sentence production is made by Kempen, 1977. Similar levels are proposed by Schlesinger, 1977). Once more, the levels should not be taken as indicative of serial processing: we normally certainly do not wait to formulate a syntactic structure until the procedures for conceptualizing have finished their job.

Notice that the interpretation process does probably not always require at every moment full processing of the input up to an abstract representation of meaning which then guides the conceptualization procedures of the output processing mechanism. It is reasonable to think of strategies capable of allowing the formulation procedures to be directly accessed by syntactic segmentation procedures, as will be suggested further on.

The levels of processing proposed are only broad categories for different processing stages and for different procedures. They can be taken as a framework for the use of knowledge available within cognitive psychology, and for the indication of topics in which our knowledge is still very limited.

Let us briefly consider a couple of typical areas where the advance in theory and research could already be used in the study of intepretation. One area is *speech perception*. In this domain, the available evidence at the level of perception of the phoneme or of the syllable is rather large, and could be easily used in constructing hypotheses or planning experiments on discrimination learning of speech sounds in second language acquisition.

The process of language comprehension and of language production during interpretation certainly involves a heavy load on *memory*. If the procedures of language production fall much behind language input processing, it is rather likely that important information gets lost. Both theoretical models of interpretation and practical suggestions for training, could use (at least to restrict the range of workable hypotheses) the body of knowledge cognitive psychology has produced on memory. For example, *sensory memory* for acoustic material is an area in which very precise evidence is available and where predictions about span of availability of surface material in language comprehension could be made.

An important area of research in contemporary cognitive psychology is *selective attention*. There are at least two ways in which the field can be very useful for a psychological model of interpretation. The first is the most obvious, and has to do with the fact that interpretation requires simultaneous execution of procedures for language comprehension and for execution of a linguistic response which might interfere with the linguistic material being processed in comprehension. The second and perhaps more interesting aspect of the studies in selective attention is the question of the level of processing of one source of information while monitoring another type of information: in this sense the notions proposed in models for selective attention have been extended to the most general information processing models. Former models of selective attention, developed for situations of dichotic listening, such as Broadbent's original filter model (1958), claimed that when two messages are presented simultaneously, only one can be processed at a time, while the other can wait only for a very brief period of time in a kind of sensory buffer and decays quickly if it is not allowed to enter into processing. Later evidence has shown that information of the "rejected" message is available at a much "higher" level than it was originally thought, and that selection of information probably takes place just prior to response execution. The notion of *level of processing* and of *availability of information* during processing is extremely important for a model of simultaneous interpretation and for the practical consequences it might have in interpretation tasks: imagine, for example, that noise or speed of speaking affects processing to some extent, and that one part of the message might seem to get "lost": still the hearer might be able to process the information because this is still available at some level.

We could continue with an extensive list of topics. There are several domains of study within the psychology of language, memory, speech perception, attention, human performance, which will give an important contribution to the cognitive study of interpretation. Some are topics which have only been recently studied. An example of an area which could have important implications for the study of interpretation is *prosody*. In most psycholinguistic studies intonation and the various suprasegmental aspects of the speech signal have been considered a kind of disturbing variable, to be kept "constant" or neutralized in research. Prosody has been disregarded as a powerful means for the hearer to take syntactic and semantic decisions. Sentence perception is driven by several variables, of which prosody is certainly an important one, as several recent experiments, (see e.g. Cohen and Nooteboom, 1975) have shown. The extent to which prosodic information is used in language comprehension by the interpreter is obviously a question to be answered by research, but undoubtedly the topic has something to say for a model of language interpretation. There are some new directions in the work done by modern psycholinguists which seem to offer promising developments for the study of language interpretation. One such direction is the study of strategies in language processing, which will be briefly mentioned here.

Strategies in language interpretation

An interesting line of research will be the attempt to specify some of the strategies which can be used by hearers in language comprehension and by speakers in language production. There is a considerable flow of work in contemporary psycholinguistics which sees language perception and comprehension as the result of an interaction of "bottom up" and "top down" processes. Among the conceptually driven elements of the process there are several strategies which are applied by the hearer to the incoming signal in order to "make up" strings with a meaningful representation. Strategies of this type have been proposed by Bever (1970) and Slobin (1973). Several examples of the strategies which can be used in the process of constructing an internal representation for a sentence are described by Clark and Clark (1977). To clarify this notion here, consider the process of language segmentation. An important stage in constructing a representation for a sentence consists in segmenting the speech signal in units like constituents or clauses. In this process listeners may use several clues to obtain a given representation. Several strategies can be used at this stage. For example, as soon as the input signals the presence of an element which may be segmented as an article, the hearer immediately waits for a noun or adjective-noun element, and as soon as it becomes possible to segment a noun-phrase unit, the hearer might take it, as a good guess, as the subject of the sentence. Such a strategy could be described as follows:

Strategy 1: The first part of the speech signal which can be represented as an article-noun or an article-adjective-noun is likely to be the subject of the sentence. Of course, the information coming immediately after may require the hearer to change the perceptual decision taken on the basis of such a strategy,and other strategies might be applied. The process of language perception would be considered in this way as the result of the utilization of the incoming information by some procedure which has available the knowledge of the syntactic and semantic system of the language involved, and utilizes as subroutines strategies of the type just exemplified. It seems possible to construct rather plausible models of language processing with this kind of notion, at least insofar as language comprehension is concerned. It is probably more difficult to handle language production with the notion of strategies: these cannot be conceived of as kinds of "shortcuts" or heuristics of the type exemplified (one can hardly produce a sentence by kinds of "approximations" without a full knowledge of the rules of a language). So, the form of such strategies in production probably has to be different. Still, the plans for formulation and execution of utterances might include production strategies to guide the search for a syntactic structure and word selection.

A full model of interpretation might include, as essential components, strategies of the type just proposed. These would be the strategies useful for language comprehension and production in general, without specific reference to the process of interpretation. However, it is clearly possible to postulate special strategies in language interpretation which would be used in the translation process. Consider, for example, two languages L_1 and L_2 which are characterized by a considerable amount of similarity in the syntactic structure as, for example, Spanish and Italian, or German and Dutch. To express the same content in two such languages it is possible to use very similar sentence forms, such as the two following utterances, in German and in Dutch respectively.

1) Peter ist sehr müde, und will gerne nach Haus gehen.

2) Pieter is erg moe, en wil graag naar huis gaan.

If one is given the task of interpreting into Dutch sentence (1), it can be done in a variety of ways, with different syntactic devices and a wide choice of lexical items. But the interpreter might also profit from the structural similarities between the two languages to utter directly a sentence like (2). In other words, the interpreter has the possibility of using the surface frame of L_1 and the similarity of the words in the two languages to avoid a search among several alternative structures in L_2. The formulation stage of the sentence in L_2 is in these cases directly monitored by the syntactic form of L_1. This kind of utilization of structural properties of the two languages involved in the interpretation process can be guided by strategies such as strategy 2.

Strategy 2: When the languages L_1 and L_2 bear a consistent amount of similarity in their syntactic structures, then start by preparing in L_2 the same surface syntactic "frame" as in L_1. Then retrieve in L_2 the dictionary entries corresponding to L_1 and fill in the frame from left to right.

Strategies of this kind are probably not the most frequent ways of making the interpretation. However, it is reasonable to suggest that interpreters might behave not too rarely according to strategies such as the one just tentatively suggested. The construction of models of interpretation could benefit from the use of such constructs. In this respect, studies such as the ones reported by Lederer and Wilss can be extremely useful.

Applied research and language interpretation

The development of cognitive psychology has been in part stimulated by careful and intelligent applied research, such as work on human performance, on vigilance, etc. In turn, the expansion of cognitive psychology has directly inspired useful research in several applied areas, from fields such as the psychology of reading, to ergonomics, etc. The relation between basic research and the applied fields has been very important for the latter, because it offered a solid theoretical backbone which was very often absent from previous work. As has been pointed out in the first part of this paper, research in the applied aspects of language interpretation has been rather scarce. This is again rather surprising, especially if we compare this fact with the situation in several other applied fields, where research has been very abundant. Once more, the knowledge available in cognitive psychology and in the applied work carried out within this theoretical framework could be very useful for the study of language interpretation and for the design of training procedures, and of the technical facilities required by the task.

It could also be very useful, when devising training programs or making proposals about ergonomic problems for the simultaneous interpreter – e.g., questions about schedules of work, technical properties of the conference booth, and so on –

to access the knowledge available in the area of human performance from studies on performance under stress and speed constraints, noisy environment, etc. It would also be useful to know more about certain limits of the human information processor, which cannot be influenced or changed beyond a certain level through training. Two examples will clarify this point.

Suppose that an experimenter flashes three rows of 3 random letters for, the duration of, say, 50 msec, on a screen with the request for an observer to report as many as possible of the 9 letters, and after a few milliseconds he projects on the same position a thick combination of Xs and random letters – a kind of visual *noise*, as it is called in experimental psychology. The observer will start reporting, say, three or four letters and then have the dramatic phenomenological impression of an image being *erased* while he is trying to read it. "Masking" with the visual noise interrupts the kind of image which has been called the visual *icon*, and there is no way of retrieving the erased material. No training can change this. The human processor has here a clear limit in capacity for speed of processing of the sensory information.

Another example, perhaps more interesting because it has more to do with limitations in skilled performance, is based on research carried out in the Netherlands on the steering of mammoth tankers. Imagine you are sitting at the steering wheel of a huge oil tanker, and that you decide that you have to correct your course: you turn the steering wheel, and nothing happens: the ship continues for a couple of miles on the same course. Since you do not notice any change in direction, you keep turning the wheel, with the result that a few miles further the ship has turned 30° or 40° instead of 4° or 6°, as you wanted. The feedback required for the action of steering is simply coming too late. The task is beyond what we could call the "perceptual scale" of humans. Very little can be done with training. (What psychologists proposed was to use a computer simulating on a display the effect of the action and anticipating the necessary feedback).

The performance of the interpreter under conditions of speed, noisy environment, etc., will sometimes probably be very close to certain limitations of processing capacity. Once more, we could look at the human performance literature and at work in ergonomics to find the elements for some conclusions or at least for good hypotheses about studies to be done in the area.

Methodological and technical contributions of cognitive psychology

Another contribution of the existing body of knowledge could come from the use of the progress in the methods for experimental design and in the technology for experimentation. Psychologists have developed extremely sophisticated and precise methods of controlled presentation of stimuli and of recording of responses. We can now single out extremely short segments of a speech signal, filter out frequencies, synthesize speech in several ways. This can enormously help progress in the study of interpretation.

Consider, as an example, the question of optimal and of upper limit rates of the source language, and imagine that you want to study the effect of high input speech rate on interpretation performance. If we increase the speech rate of the speaker, we also increase the amount of syntactic and semantic information loaded on the interpreter, while we could only be interested in the effect of the *speed* of the speech signal, independently of the amount of linguistic information given. Can we manipulate speed of the speech signal independently of grammatical information? Techniques of *speech compression*, used in psycholinguistic and speech perception experiments, allow us to present speech at a faster rate by keeping approximately constant the structural, melodic and prosodic quality of the speech signal, but in a much shorter time. The technique essentially consists of cutting out short segments of speech at regular intervals— say, five msec every five msec — or in other more elegant ways in more recent developments. Notice that we reduce the time given for processing but we give the hearer the same information. Similarly, techniques of manipulating at will the intonational structure of the speech signal could allow careful study of the effects of suprasegmental information on interpreter performance. Perhaps some interaction between schools of interpreters and laboratories of experimental psychology could produce some interesting results.

CONCLUSION

The main argument attempted in the second part of this discussion should be apparent: there is a considerable amount of knowledge within contemporary cognitive psychology which could be integrated and used to give reasonable answers to theoretical and practical questions in the study of interpretation. This integration to a large extent remains to be done. Obviously, even new specific experimental studies, along some of the lines suggested by the papers of the Symposium or discussed here, will be necessary for the development of the field. But some priority should be given to utilizing available research in order to develop the theoretical side.

It is obviously impossible to predict which direction developments of theory and of research will take. This paper has only tried to sketch some possible interesting lines of work, and to put forward a few elements which might give rise to important developments. Simultaneous interpretation is a fascinating skill and the task is certainly worth investigation and attention in terms of basic and applied research.

It is a firm belief of the present discussant that good answers to many of the questions posed at the Symposiun and scattered throughout this book might come only from basic research with careful consideration of the relevant psychological variables involved. Cognitive psychology can have a clear impact on the study of the processes underlying language interpretation. Technological and educational advance in the training of conference interpreters will certainly gain from a clear development of basic research. The paths which still have to be taken should be clear from the papers in this book.

REFERENCES

Bever, T. The cognitive basis for linguistic structures. In J. R. Hayes (Ed.)., *Cognition and the development of language.* New York: Wiley, 1970.

Broadbent, D. *Perception and communication.* London: Pergamon Press, 1958.

Clark, H. H., and Clark, E. V. *Psychology and language. An introduction to psycholinguistics.* New York: Harcourt, Brace, Jovanovich, 1977.

Cohen, A., and Nooteboom, S. G. *Structure and process in speech perception.* Berlin, Heidelberg, New York: Springer, 1975.

Garrett, M. The analysis of sentence production. In G. H. Bower (Ed.)., *The psychology of learning and motivation,* Vol. 9. New York: Academic Press, 1975.

Gerver, D. Empirical studies of simultaneous interpretation: A review and a model. In R. W. Brislin (Ed.)., *Translation. Applications and research.* New York: Gardner Press, 1976.

Kempen, G. Conceptualizing and formulating in sentence production. In S. Rosenberg (Ed.)., *Sentence production: Developments in research and theory.* Hillsdale, N.J.: Lawrence Erlbaum, 1977.

Schlesinger, I. M. Components of a production model. In S. Rosenberg (Ed.)., *Sentence production: Developments in research and theory.* Hillsdale, N.J.: Lawrence Erlbaum, 1977.

Slobin, D. I. Cognitive prerequisite for the acquisition of grammar. In C. A. Ferguson and D. I. Slobin (Eds.)., *Studies in child language development.* New York: Holt, Rinehart and Winston, 1973.

Welford, A. I. *The fundamentals of skill.* London: Methuen, 1968.

APPENDIX A

Some Ideas for Further Research

The final session of the symposium included a lively discussion of topics for further research in language interpretation. The following list summarizes the main points.

1. Selection and training of conference interpreters: development of a taxonomy of interpretation skills; critical examination of student selection criteria in current use; review of methods used to assess interpretation ability; development of new interpretation aptitude tests and standards or norms for different levels of interpretation jobs.

2. Stress in interpretation: analysis and investigation of, for example, situational, psychological, and physiological factors.

3. Social psychological aspects of conference interpretation: analysis of interpersonal perceptions; determination of source language and target language effects on speaker, interpreter, and listener; study of non-verbal issues.

4. Micro-analytic studies of international conferences: development and application of methods for observing linguistic aspects of international meetings; conduct of experiments on simulated international meetings.

5. Validation of interpretation: conduct of quantitative studies on the extent to which professional interpreters accurately perform their tasks.

6. Textual factors and interpretation: performance of linguistic analyses of readability and semantic complexity, for example, and their impact on interpretation quality.

7. Accuracy and sources of error in interpretation: determination of the effects of personal motivation, work pace, and quality of source text on interpreters' outputs.

8. Language dominance and interpreter performance: experimental measurement of the effects of simultaneous interpretation into "B" languages vs. "A" languages.

9. Spoken and sign language interpretation: determination of areas of over-

lapping or mutual interest between the two types of interpreters, with an eye to establishing collaborative research.

In addition, symposium participants urged the establishment of a mechanism for collecting and disseminating information stemming from research on language interpretation and translation. There was also a strong consensus favoring the creation of a permanent working party to plan and co-ordinate multidisciplinary, multinational research and to propose subsequent symposia.

Appendix B

PARTICIPANTS

Australia	
Ranier Lang	(currently at) The Department of Linguistics University of California at Los Angeles Los Angeles
Austria	
Elisabeth Fischer	University of Graz Graz
Barbara Moser	(currently at) Monterey Institute of Foreign Studies Monterey, California
Belgium	
Jean-Pierre Barra	H.R.V.T. Ghent
H. Baetens-Beardsmore	Free University of Brussels Brussels
F. Bovy	Euro-Translation Service Liege
Andre Brisau	H.R.V.T. Ghent
D. Godfrind	H.I.V.T. Schilderstraat 41 Antwerp
Walter Keiser	142 Avenue de Mai B 1200, Brussels

*Session Chairmen

Georges Lurquin	Institut Libre Marie Haps Brussels
Joseph Nuttin, Jr.,	University of Louvain Louvain

Canada

Josiane F. Hamers	International Center for Research on Bilingualism Lavel University Quebec City
Brian Harris	School of Translators and Interpreters University of Ottowa Ottawa, Ontario
Volker Junginger	Parliament Interpreter's School 85 Sparks Street Ottawa, Ontario
Paul A. Kolers	Department of Psychology University of Toronto Toronto, Ontario
Wallace E. Lambert	Department of Psychology McGill University Montreal, Quebec
Vito Modigliani	Department of Psychology Simon Fraser University Burnaby, British Columbia
Lilian U. Nygren	Ontario Institute for Studies in Education Toronto, Ontario
Elyse Piquette	Department of Linguistics McGill University Montreal, Quebec

Commission of the European Communities

D. Berbille	French Translation Division Brussels
Edmee Gangler	Interpretation Division Brussels
F. Hurdis-Jones	Interpretation Division Brussels

Nanza Mattern — Interpretation Division
Brussels

Loll N. Rolling — Jean Monnet Centre
Luxembourg

Réné Van Hoof — Interpretation Division
Brussels

Council of the European Communities

P. J. Arthern * — English Translation Division
Brussels

Denmark

J. Schoildann — Department of Psychiatry
Odense University Hospital
Odense

European Parliament

Franco Prété — Interpretation Division, European Parliament
Luxembourg

France

Laura E. Bertone — 1 Quai de Montebello
Paris

Robert Faerber — University of Strasbourg
Strasbourg

Marianne Lederer — E.S.I.T.
University of Paris III
Paris

Jean-François Le Ny — Department of Psychology
University of Paris VIII
Paris

Maurice Pergnier — E.S.I.T.
University of Paris III
Paris

Danica Seleskovitch — E.S.I.T.
University of Paris III
Paris

Christopher Thiery	E.S.I.T. University of Paris III Paris
German Federal Republic	
Jean Bunjes	University of Mainz Germersheim
Werner Bunjes	University of Mainz Germersheim
Hella Kirchhoff	Applied Linguistics University of Heidelberg Heidelberg
Jurgen Stahle	University of Mainz Germersheim
Dieter Stein	University of Heidelberg Heidelberg
Heiner F. Sussebach	University of the Saarland Saarbrucken
Ruth Willett	University of Heidelberg Heidelberg
Wolfram Wilss	Fachrichtung Angewandte Sprachwissenschaft University of the Saarland Saarbrucken
Israel	
Batya Frost	School for Translators and Interpreters Bar-Ilan University Ramat-Gan
Ruth Levy-Berlowitz	School for Translators and Interpreters Bar-Ilan University Ramat-Gan
Italy	
Mary Cotton	Italian Translators Association Rome
Gerald Bartlett Parks *	Universita di Trieste Trieste

Palmiro Herrero Rodriguez	C.I.P.P.T. Turin
Giancarlo Trentini *	University of Venice Venice
Maria Christina Bolla Trentini	Syntagma Milan
Japan	
Mitsuko Saito-Fukunaga	International Christian University Tokyo
N.A.T.O.	
L. M. Ravet	Administration and Conference Division Brussels, Belgium
Netherlands	
G. B. Flores d'Arcais	Department of Psychology University of Leiden, Leiden
E. M. Uhlenbeck	Department of Linguistics University of Leiden Leiden
S.H.A.P.E.	
Ghislain Hondequin	S.H.A.P.E. Technical Centre The Hague
South Africa	
J. Coetzer	Victan Trust (PTY) Ltd Johannesberg
Sweden	
Stan. Dornic	Department of Psychology University of Stockholm Stockholm
Aubrey Kagan	Karolinska Institutet Stockholm
Switzerland	
Jean Herbert	La Luciole 1253 Vandoeuvres, Geneva

Annette Karmiloff-Smith — Department of Psychology
University of Geneva
Geneva

Dina Leveille — 1 rue Hoffman
Geneva

Claude A. Namy — Ecole de Traduction et d'Interpretation
University of Geneva
Geneva

Turkey

Aksit Gokturk — University of Istanbul
Istanbul

United Kingdom

Diarmuid Bradley — Heriot-Watt University
Edinburgh 1.

Eileen Brannan — University of London
London, N.W 3.

David Gerver * — Department of Psychology
University of Stirling
Stirling, Scotland

Edith Harding-Esch — Linguistics Department
University of Cambridge
Cambridge

John A. Henderson — Department of French
University of Bradford
Bradford, West Yorkshire

Sylvie-Michelle Lambert — School of Languages
Polytechnic of Central London
London N.W.1.

John Long — M.R.C. Applied Psychology Research Unit
15 Chaucer Road
Cambridge

Patricia Longley — School of Languages
Polytechnic of Central London
London N.W.1.

Margaret Moore — British Deaf Association
Carlisle

Edith Paneth	Goldsmith's College London S.E.14 6 N.W.
W. S. Paton *	Department of Languages Heriot-Watt University Edinburgh
Yorick Wilks	Department of Linguistics University of Essex Colchester, Essex
United Nations	
B. Yakoflev	United Nations Geneva
United States	
Jack A. Adams *	Office of Naval Research London N.W.1.
R. Bruce W. Anderson	Department of Sociology University of Texas Arlington, Texas
Etilvia M. Arjona	Monterey Institute of Foreign Studies Monterey, California
David Bowen	Division of Interpretation and Translation Georgetown University Washington, D.C.
Margareta Bowen	Division of Interpretation and Translation Georgetown University Washington, D.C.
Richard W. Brislin	Culture Learning Institute East-West Centre Honolulu, Hawaii
John B. Carroll	L. L. Thurstone Psychometric Laboratory University of North Carolina at Chapel Hill Chapel Hill, North Carolina
Rita L. Domingue	Gallaudet College Washington, D.C.
Jacob Gurin	Department of Defence Ford Meade Maryland

Betty L. Ingram	Deafness Research and Training Centre New York University New York
Robert M. Ingram*	Department of Linguistics Brown University Providence, Rhode Island
Harlan Lane	Department of Psychology Northeastern University Boston, Massachusetts
Dom. Massaro	Department of Psychology University of Wisconsin Madison, Wisconsin
Harry J. Murphy	Campus Services for the Deaf California State University Northridge, California
H. McIlvaine Parsons	Institute for Behavioral Research Silver Spring, Maryland
H. Wallace Sinaiko*	The Smithsonian Institution 801 North Pitt Street Alexandria, Virginia
Ryan D. Tweney	Department of Psychology Bowling Green State University Bowling Green, Ohio

NAME INDEX

Abbs, M.H. 306, 313
Aboud, F.E. 143
Abrahmson, A. 370, 383
Ackerman, E. 377, 381
Ackerman-Valladao, E. 376, 381
Ahlgren, I. 112, 116
Ahmar, H. 105, 108, 310, 314
AIIC. 223, 229
Allport, G. W. 223, 229
Allusi, E. A. 311, 313
ALPAC. 171, 182
Anderson, J. R. 246, 258
Anderson, R. B. W. 3, 115, 116, 157, 169, 217-230, 392
Anderson, S. 185, 197
Anthony, D. A. 105, 106
Arjona, E. 2, 35-44
Aronson, E. 216
Azores, F. 211, 216

Back, T. 344, 351
Bach, E. 367, 368
Baldie, B. J. 372, 381
Balonov, L. J. 190, 197
Bar-Hillel, Y. 172, 182, 185, 197
Barik, H. C. 106, 353, 367
Barnard, F. A. P. 73, 78
Barnard, H. 71, 78
Barnard, P. J. 283, 284, 285, 286
Battison, R. 2, 57-79, 102, 106
Bavelas, A. 223, 229
Bello, W. 216
Bellugi, U. 63, 78, 88, 96, 101, 102, 103, 104, 105, 107, 108, 110, 115, 117
Bergman, B. 112, 116
Berkowitz, L. 229
Bernstein, L 299, 313
Bever, T. G. 102, 107, 372, 381, 398, 401
Biondi, L. 156, 169
Blanchet, A. L. 59, 78, 376, 377, 381
Bobrow, D. 182
Boese, R. J. 113, 116
Bolgar, M. 262, 271
Bowen, J. D. 275, 287
Bower, G. H. 402
Boyes-Braem, P. 103, 107
Braine, M. D. S. 147, 152
Brami-Mouling, M.-A. 377, 381
Bransford, J. D. 357, 367, 368
Brasel, B. B. 90, 96
Brault, G. J. 112, 116
Bresnan, J. 173, 182
Brislin, R. W. 3, 4, 106, 107, 108, 116, 118, 157, 159, 169, 205-216, 229 270, 313, 368, 392, 402
Broadbent, D. 397, 401
Brower, R. A. 107, 117, 204, 351
Bruderer, H. 182

Bruner, J. S. 286, 378, 381, 382
Bush, R. R. 197

Campbell, D. 213, 216
Campbell, R. N. 381, 382, 383
Caprez, G. 372, 381
Cariño, L. 211, 216
Carroll, J. B. 2, 119-129, 136, 142, 386
Carter, S. H. 89, 96
Casterline, D. 79
Catford, J. C. 164, 169, 258, 344, 351
Cattell, R. B. 125, 127, 128
Chandioux, J. 171, 182
Charniak, E. 171, 174, 182, 375, 377, 381
Charrow, V. 60, 78
Chase, W. G. 255, 256, 258
Chernov, G. V. 357, 367
Cherry, E. C. 126, 128
Chomsky, N. 186, 187, 197, 302, 313, 357, 367
Christopherson, P. 147, 152
Cicourel, A. 115, 116
Clark, E. V. 102, 107, 370, 381, 398, 401
Clark, H. H. 102, 107, 255, 256, 258, 398, 401
Clement, R. 135, 142
Cohen, A. 397, 401
Cohen, M. 106, 107
Cohen, M. M. 302, 303, 314
Cohen, R. 216
Colby, B. 183
Cole, P. 197
Cole, R. A. 101, 108, 304, 307, 313
Collins, A. M. 358, 367
Colotla, V. A. 310, 314
Conklin, H. C. 40, 44
Conrad, R. 101, 107
Cook, V. J. 273, 286
Cooper, F. S. 307, 313
Cordier, F. 297, 298
Coseriu, F. 343, 351
Costermans, J. 372, 381
Crammatte, A. B. 117
Crammatte, F. B. 117
Cromer, R. 285, 286
Croneberg, C. 79
Crosby, C. 133, 143
Cutting, J. E. 107, 314

Darbelnet, J. 25, 33
Davies, A. 287
Deese, J. 136, 142
Deneberg, G.-B. 264, 270, 273, 287
Deglin, V. L. 190, 191
Denhiere, G. 297, 298
Denison, J. 77, 78
de Saussure, F. 44, 186, 189
Dewart, M. H. 373, 381
Dien, T. A. 275, 287
Domingue, R. L. 2, 81-85
Donaldson, W. 367, 368
Dooling, D. J. 357, 367
Dornic, S. 3, 259-271, 273, 274, 275, 286, 287, 312, 313, 314, 319, 390, 391
Ducrot, O. 374, 381
Dumas, G. 167, 170
Dunn, L. M. 275, 287

Eastman, G. C. 104, 107
Eco, U. 110, 111, 113, 117
Eden, M. 313
Ekstrom, R. B. 125, 126, 127, 128
Ekvall, R. 222, 229
Elkind, D. 287
Enriquez, V. 210, 211, 216
Epée, Abbé de l' 70, 78
Epstein, W. 284, 287
Ervin, S. M. 137, 138, 142, 222, 229, 262, 270, 312, 313
Ervin-Tripp, S. M. 226, 229
Estes, W. K. 127, 128

Fant, C. G. M. 302, 313
Fant, L. J. 88, 96
Fay, E. A. 79
Ferguson, C. A. 402
Ferreiro, E. 372, 383
Fiedler, F. 206, 216
Fillmore, C. J. 182, 356, 367
Fischer, S. D. 63, 78, 105, 108, 114, 117
Fishman, J. A. 149, 152, 229
Flagg, P. W. 138, 143
Flavell, J. H. 287
Fleischer, L. 91, 96
Flores d'Arcais, G. B. 3, 385-402
Fodor, J. A. 102, 107
Foss, B. 286

Foulke, E. 367
Freedle, R. O. 287
French, J. W. 125, 128, 208, 216
Friedman, L. A. 114, 117
Frishberg, N. 78
Fromkin, V. A. 101, 107

Gaarder, A. B. 149, 152
Galanter, E. 197
Gallaudet, E. M. 77, 78
Gallaudet, T. H. 72, 78
Gardner, R. C. 134, 135, 142, 262, 268, 271
Garman, M. 370, 381
Garrett, M. F. 102, 107, 393, 402
Gelman, R. 377, 382
Genesee, F. 140, 142
Gerver, D. 1-4, 106, 107, 158, 169, 223, 224, 229, 269, 270, 295, 296, 298, 312, 313, 321, 353, 359, 364, 367, 368, 374, 375, 381, 386, 388, 402
Ghiselin, B. 125, 129
Giles, H. 135, 143
Givon, T. 182, 183
Glaser, R. 128
Godel, R. 184, 197
Goldman-Eisler, F. 106, 107, 360, 367
Gomes da Costa, B. 122, 128
Goodman, N. 256, 258
Goodrich, S. 60, 78
Goodwin, C. 231, 242
Gordon, D. 188, 197
Gordon, J. G. 77, 78
Grice, H. P. 182, 189, 196, 197, 378, 381
Grossman, R. E. 198
Gruber, F. A. 142
Guburina, P. 41, 44
Gutiérrez-Marse, L. 262, 270
Guthrie, G. 211, 216
Guttman, E. 149, 152
Guzman, A. de. 216

Haberland, R. 189, 197
Haber, R. N. 101, 108
Hägglund, M. 264, 270, 273, 287
Halle, M. 302, 313
Halliday, M. A. K. 167, 170, 344, 351
Hamayan, E. 105, 108, 310, 314
Hamers, J. 140, 141, 142, 261, 271
Hansen, B. 112, 117, 118
Harding-Esch, E, 3, 273, 287, 389
Harms, T. 367, 368
Harnad, S. 107
Harris, B. 3, 155-170
Harris, M. 372, 281
Havelka, J. 133, 143, 262, 268, 271
Hayes, J. R. 381, 401
Hayhurst, H. 372, 381
Hays, D. 182
Hebb, D. O. 135, 142
Heiman, G. W. 103, 108
Hennrikus, D. 126, 129
Henry, R. 4
Herbert, J. 2, 5-10, 41, 44
Hewes, G. W. 99, 107
Hoemann, H. W. 100, 101, 103, 104, 106, 107, 108, 109, 118
Horman, H. 343, 351
Housholder, K. 44
Huff, K. 81, 85
Hull, S. E. 76, 78
Hunt, E. 126, 127, 128
Hupet, M. 372, 381
Hymes, D. 110, 117, 226, 229

Ignatow, M. 274, 287
Ilg, G. E. 41, 44
Ingram, B. L. 2, 81-85
Ingram, R. M. 84, 85, 109-118
Inhelder, B. 371, 376, 377, 381, 382
Isard, S. 5, 103, 108

Jacano, F. 216
Jackendoff, E. 357, 368
Jacobs, L. R. 93, 96
Jacobs, R. A. 198
Jakimik, J. 304, 313
Jakobovits, L. A. 138, 143, 367, 368
Jakobson, R. 99, 105, 107, 109, 110, 117, 199, 204, 302, 313, 343, 351
James, C. V. 274
Jefferson, G. 231, 242, 243
Jenkins, J. J. 136, 142
Johnson-Laird, P. N. 372, 382
Johnson, M. K. 357, 367, 368
Johnson, N. S. 286, 287
Jones, R. L. 89, 96
Just, M. 229

Kade, O. 335, 341, 345, 351
Kainz, F. 345, 351
Kapp, V. 4, 352
Karmiloff-Smith, A. 3, 369-383, 388
Katz, J. 357, 368
Kavanagh, J. F. 107, 314
Keenan, J. M. 297, 298
Keiser, W. 2, 11-24, 387, 394
Kempen, G. 396, 402
Kendon, A. 231, 242
Keyser, S. J. 308, 313
Kilcher, H. 376, 377, 381
Kimura, D. 115, 117
King, H. 176, 182
Kintsch, E. 313
Kintsch, W. 246, 258, 275, 279, 285, 287, 297, 298, 313, 358, 368
Kirsner, R. S. 193, 194, 197
Klima, E. S. 63, 78, 88, 96, 101, 102 103, 104, 105, 107, 110, 115, 117
Kloss, H. 68, 75, 78
Kolers, P. A. 3, 137, 143, 245-258, 260, 261, 273, 275, 287, 313, 391
Krauthammer, M. 262, 271, 274, 287
Kuhn, T. 353, 368
Kuschel, R. 112, 117

Labov, W. 189, 197
Lacan, J. 330, 332
Lachman, R. 126, 129
Ladefoged, P. 302, 313
Lakoff, G. 188, 197, 356, 368
Lakoff, R. 188, 197
Lambert, S. M. 132, 141, 143
Lambert, W. E. 2, 131-143, 149, 152, 229, 260, 261, 262, 268, 271, 274, 287, 307, 314, 390
Lane, H. 2, 57-79, 103, 107
Langendoen, D. T. 356, 367
Lang, R. 3, 231-244, 392
Lansman, M. 126, 127, 128
Lasswell, H. D. 229
Lederer, M. 3, 323-332, 393
Lehman, W. 172, 173, 182
Lenneberg, E. H. 149, 152
Le Ny, J.-F. 3, 289-298, 388
Leopold, W. F. 161, 162, 163, 167, 168, 170
Lerner, D. 229
Le Taillanter, D. 297, 298
Levelt, W. J. M. 188, 197
Levin, J. 181, 182
Levý, J. 344, 352
Liberman, A. M. 307, 313
Li, C. 117
Liddell, S. K. 101, 103, 107, 108
Lieberman, P. 304, 313
Lieth, L. v.d. 112, 113, 115, 117
Lindsay, P. H. 358, 368
Lindzey, G. 216
List, G. 351, 352
Ljudskanov, A. K. 160, 169, 170
Longacre, R. 213, 216
Long, J. 3, 273-287, 389
Longley, P. 2, 45-56, 387, 395
Luce, R. D. 197

Macnamara, J. 137, 143, 260, 262, 268, 271
Macrae, A. 370, 382
Major, L. J. 135, 142
Maki, R. H. 262, 270, 273, 287
Makowsky, B. 113, 118
Mallery, G. 99, 107
Mandler, J. M. 286, 287
Maratsos, M. 370, 382
Marcellus, O. 372, 382
Marsh. L. G. 273, 287
Markowicz, H. 113, 117
Marslen-Wilson, W. D. 126, 129, 308, 309, 313
Marton, W. 285, 287
Mason, V. W. 275, 287
Massaro, D. W. 3, 299-314, 353, 360, 361, 368, 387, 391
Mathias, J. 182
Mattern, N. 343, 345, 346, 347, 348, 349, 352
Matthews, P. H. 187, 188, 197
Mattingly, I. G. 107
McCawley, J. D. 192, 197
McCormack, P. D. 273, 287, 356, 368
McNeill, D. 209, 216
McNulty, J. 170
Meade, R. D. 143
Meadow, K. P. 87, 88, 96, 97, 113, 117
Metz, C. 111, 117
Mey, J. L. 189, 197
Miller, G. A. 78, 101, 103, 108, 209, 216, 350, 352, 254, 356, 368

Mindel, E. D. 88, 96, 115, 117
Minsky, M. 172, 174, 175, 179, 182, 183, 357, 379, 382
Mitchell, S. 74, 79
Mitchell, T. 206, 214
Moerman, M. 231, 242
Mononen, L. 140, 142
Moore, J. 181, 182
Moore, N. 136, 143
Montangera, J. 377, 381
Morales-Goulet, R. 211, 216
Morgan, J. L. 197
Morris, C. 185, 197
Moser, B. 3, 353-368, 387, 388
Mounoud, P. 376, 382
Mullet, R. L. 357, 364
Murphy, H. J. 2, 87-97

Naiman, N. 167, 170
Namy, C. 2, 25-34
Narrol, R. 216
Newport, E. 79
Nicely, P. E. 101, 108
Nida, E. A. 38, 39, 44, 210, 216, 335, 341
Nilski, T. 319, 321
Ninio, A. 378, 382
Nooteboom, S. G. 379, 402
Norman, D. A. 246, 258, 358, 368
Novell, J. A. 273, 287

O'Barr, J. F. 242
O'Barr, W. M. 242
Oden, G. C. 302, 303, 314
Oller, J. W. 375, 387
Olson, D. 362
O'Rourke, T. J. 97, 117
Osgood, C. E. 137, 138, 142, 222, 229

Padden, C. 113, 117
Paenson, I. 41, 44
Paneth, E. 41, 44, 274, 286, 287
Parsons, H. M. 3, 141, 143, 315-321, 390
Pearson, C. 39, 44
Pederson, N. P. 205, 207, 216
Peet, H. P. 71, 72, 73, 79
Penfield, W. 149, 152
Perfetti, C. 368
Pergnier, M. 3, 199-204
Perren, G. E. 274, 287
Piaget, J. 149, 153, 371, 374, 381, 382
Picard, O. 135, 143
Pinter, I. 363, 368
Pope, B. 342, 343
Postman, L. 223, 229
Powell, J. W. 107
Preston, M. S. 261, 271
Preston, M. W. 137, 143
Price, L. A. 125, 128
Puhvel, J. 143
Putnam, H. 187, 197

Quillian, M. R. 358, 367

Rabbitt, P. M. A. 314
Rao, R. S. 260, 271
Rawlings, C. 139, 143
Reed, C. E. 152
Reich, C. M. 113, 117
Reich, P. A. 113, 117
Reichling, A. 197
Resnick, L. 128
Reynolds, A. G. 135, 138, 143
Riegel, K. F. 358, 368
Ries, J. 186, 197
Roberts, L. 149, 152
Robert, M. 376, 377, 381
Rommetveit, R. 191, 197, 198, 372, 383
Ronjat, J. 164, 166, 167, 168, 170
Rose, D. E. 117
Rosenbaum, P. S. 198
Rosenberg, S. 307, 314, 402
Ross, J. R. 188, 196, 198
Rouve, S. 274, 287, 304, 314
Rudy, L. H. 90, 97
Rumelhart, D. E. 246, 258, 358, 368
Russell, W. A. 136, 142
Ryan, M. L. 378, 382

Sacks, H. 231, 242, 243
Sadock, J. 188, 196, 198
Saegert, J. 105, 108, 310, 314
Sales, B. D. 101, 108
San, L. J. 198
Saporta, S. 44
Schank, R. C. 171, 174, 183, 189, 195, 196, 198, 317, 357, 368, 382
Scheflen, A. E. 235, 242

Schegloff, E. A. 231, 242, 243
Schein, J. 113, 114, 115, 117
Scherer, G. A. C. 260, 271
Schlesinger, H. S. 88, 97, 113, 115, 117
Schlesinger, I. M. 112, 117, 396, 402
Searle, J. 380, 382
Sebeok, T. A. 108, 299
Segalowitz, N. 229
Segalowitz, S. J. 142
Seitz, M. 140, 142
Selescovitch, D. 3, 27, 28, 33, 111, 118, 151, 153, 200, 204, 217, 222, 229, 333-341, 345, 352
Sengul, C. J. 370, 381
Shaffer, J. F. 126, 129
Schankweiler, D. P. 307, 313
Shatz, M. 377, 382
Sherwood, B. 155-170
Sherzer, D. 114, 118
Sicard, R. A. 71, 79
Siegman, A. 242, 243
Siertsema, B. 189, 198
Sinaiko, H. W. 1-4
Sinclair, A. 372, 382
Sinclair-de-Zwart, H. 285, 287
Sinclair, H. 372, 381, 382, 383
Siple, P. 79, 105, 107, 108
Slobin, D. I. 398, 402
Smith, J. M. 82, 85
Smith, P. T. 381, 382, 383
Smith, T. M. F. 122, 128
Smythe, P. C. 135, 142
Solberg, K. B. 354, 368
Solomon, S. 357, 368
Sorensen, R. K. 112, 118
Spearman, C. 123, 129
Sperry, R. W. 149, 153
Stachowitz, R. 172, 173, 182
Starck, R. 140, 142
Steinberg, D. 368
Steiner, G. 104, 108, 174, 183
Stenning, K. 283, 287
Stevens, S. S. 153
Stokoe, W. C. 61, 79, 88, 97, 100, 105, 109, 118
Strain, G. S. 311, 313
Strickland, L. 198
Stubbs, J. B. 275, 287
Studdert-Kennedy, M. 307, 313
Studer, B. 272, 381
Sudnow, D. 242, 243
Supalla, R. 79
Swan, M. 368
Swain, M. 167, 170

Tanokami, R. 112, 118
Taylor, C. W. 125, 129
Theios, J. 311, 314
Thiery, C. 2, 145-153, 158, 170, 223, 229
Thome, G. 350, 352
Thompson, S. A. 193, 194, 197
Thorndyke, P. W. 284, 287
Thurmond, J. B. 311, 313
Thurstone, L. L. 126, 129
Thurstone, T. G. 126, 129
Triesman, A. M. 273, 287, 307, 314
Triandis, H. 206, 216
Trifonovitch, G. 207, 216
Tucker, G. R. 135, 142, 229, 275, 287
Tulving, E. 310, 314, 367, 368
Turner, E. A. 372, 383
Tweney, R. D. 2, 99-108, 109, 118

Uchtomski, A. A. 266, 271
Uhlenbeck, E. M. 3, 185-198, 389
Umeda, N. 304, 316
Underwood, B. J. 127, 129

Valentine, E. G. 59, 79
Vance, T. J. 198
Van Dijk, T. A. 279, 283, 284, 287
Van Slype. 171, 183
Verhaar, J. W. M. 198
Vernon, M. 88, 96, 113, 115, 117, 118
Verstiggle, J. C. 292, 298
Vinay, J. P. 25, 33
Von Raffler-Engel, W. 160, 170
Vygotsky, L. S. 149, 153

Webb, P. A. 370, 383
Weeks, W. 207, 216
Weinreich, U. 137, 143
Welford, A. I. 375, 383, 390, 402
Werner, O. 213, 216
Wertheimer, M. 260, 271
Wheeler, F. R. 76, 79
Whitaker, H. A. 117
Whitely, D. 122, 128
White, M. N. 126, 128

Wilbur, R. 60-78
Wilks, Y, 3, 171-184, 198, 383, 389
Williams, J. 73, 79
Wilss, W. 3, 343-352, 394
Winograd, T. 174, 182, 183
Winston, D. 183
Wirl, J. 345, 352
Woodward, J. C. 104, 108
Wunderlich, D. 198
Wurms, S. A. 242, 243

Yaki, K. 125, 129
Yngve, V. H. 189, 198

Zadeh, L. A. 303, 314

SUBJECT INDEX

Acoustic features
in fluent speech, 303-304
Affective content
measurement in language of, 210-215
American Sign Language (A.S.L.)
contrasted with manual English, 68; contributions to linguistics of studies of, 112; as a distinct language, 88; errors in memory for signs in, 101; hierarchical linguistic structure in, 105-106; iconic character of, 104; linguistic analysis of, 61-67; linguistic structure of, 100-102; long-term memory for, 105; modulation of meaning in, 102; and morphological process, 102; morphology of, 63-67; psycholinguistic properties of, 102-103; and rate of conveyance of information in, 63; residual effects of dialectizing on, 74; and Signed English, 91
Anticipation of meaning
in understanding interpretation, 294-296
Artificial Intelligence (A.I.) theory
definition of, 174; frames in, 174; knowledge structures in, 175; and language understanding, 174; meaning boundaries in, 175
Behavioral sciences, the
contributions to the study of interpretation of, 386-395
Bilingual
aphasics, 138-139; Stroop Color Word Test, 139
Bilingualism
"associational meaning" systems in, 135-137; encoding efficiency in, 261-262; and individual differences, 268-270; input or decoding in, 260-262; language processing in, 137-142; language processing strategies in, 140; meaning structures in, 246; psychological approaches to, 131-142; and representation of experience, 245-252; symbol systems in, 255-257
Bilinguals
compound, 137-139; co-ordinate, 137-139; ear preference in, 141; E.E.G. activity in, 140; hemisphere preference in, 140-141; memory for details in, 248-255; memory in, 246; "true", 145-152; visual field preference in, 141
Bilinguals' performance
and extraversion, 269; effects of mental fatigue on, 267; and the effects of stress, 259-270; and individual differences, 259-270; and language domin-

ance, 259-270; and language switching, 270; and neuroticism, 269

Cognition
and language, 333-341
Cognitive psychology
and bilingualism, 245; contribution to study of interpretation of, 385-401
Communication
interplay of elements in, 38-39; and language interpretation, 1-4; pragmatic aspects of, 85
Conference interpretation
consecutive (definition of), 123; development of, 5-9; difficulties encountered in research into, 11-12; and general translation theory, 199-201; previous research into (sources), 3-4; research programs in, 392-395; simultaneous (definition of), 123; training in, 49-51
Conference interpreter
definition of, 14
Conference interpreters
aptitude tests for, 16-20; assumptions underlying selection for training of, 12-14; bodies making use of, 5-9; as communicators, 9; curriculum for training, 21; desirability of standardized tests in the selection of, 20; entrance exams for, 16-17; language proficiency tests for, 16-17; and their need for general knowledge, 18-19; requirement for, 9; role of, 157; selection and training of, 11-24; selection of candidates for, 16-20; selection tests for, 19; status of, 9; training of, 20-24
Conference interpreting
definition of, 14; and recovery time, 318-319
Consecutive interpretation
definition of, 14-15; notetaking in, 22; at the United Nations, 8
Conversation
analysis of, 231
Cross-cultural orientation programs
attribution training in, 206; behavior modification in, 207; cognitive training in, 206; contributions to translation/interpretation from, 205-215; experiential training in, 207; self-awareness training in, 206-207

Deaf, the
attitudes of the hearing to, 60; interpreters for, 81-86, 87-88
Deafness
as a cultural distinction, 112-113
Deaf students, 88-91
Definitions : see under subject

Extraversion
and bilinguals' performance, 269

Feature detection
in understanding speech, 301, 304
Fluency
associational, 125; expressional, 125; ideational, 125
Fluent speech
acoustic features in, 303-304
Folk taxonomies
in interpreter training, 40-41
Foreign language aptitude
factors in, 127
Functional analysis of language
use of interpretation data for, 373-374

Human factors
approach to Simultaneous Interpretation (S.I.), 315-321
Hushaphone, 7

Individual differences
in bilingualism, 259-270
Information processing
model of understanding speech, 299-312; research and theory in, 299
Intelligence
models and theories of, 123-125
Intercultural communication
and the training of interpreters, 40-43
Interpretation
anticipation of meaning and understanding during, 294-296; applied research in, 399-401; aptitude for, 17-18; Artificial Intelligence (A.I.) and the study of, 389-390; aspects of

performance in, 122-123; bibliography on, 4; contribution of cognitive psychology to the study of, 385-401; contribution of cross-cultural orientation programs to, 205-215; contribution of power analysis to, 205-215; contribution of the behavioral sciences to the study of, 386-395; contribution to psychological theory of the study of, 391; definition of, 35; human information processing in the study of, 387-388; human performance and human factors in the study of, 390; a model of, 395-398; and oral messages, 333; psycholinguistics in the study of, 388-389; psychometrics in the study of, 386-387; selection of students of, 120-127; the concept of semantic memory in the study of, 389; sense in, 329-330; of sign language, 81-84; and sign language, 103-106; sign language in the study of, 392; social psychology and the study of, 390-391; sociology, cultural anthropology and sociolinguistics in the study of, 392; strategies in, 389-399; suggestions for future research in, 403-404; units of meaning in, 330; word prediction and sense expectation in, 330-332

Interpretation situations
typologies of, 217-229

Interpreter
cognitive task of the 379-390; roles, 225-228; time-lag behind speaker of the, 326-327

"Interpreter" and "conference interpreter"
distinction between, 217

Interpreter roles
typologies of, 217-229

Interpreters
characteristics of candidates for training as, 46-47; characteristics of sign language, 114-115; characteristics of teachers of, 53-54; clients perception of, 227-228; examination of student, 54-55; factors affecting performance of, 219-225; use of folk taxonomies in the training of, 40-41; identification of, 319-320; identification with clients of, 220; an integrated training program for, 45-56; linguistic abilities in, 119-127; as listeners, 131; organization of semantic information in, 357-358; and modeling behavior, 320-321; monitoring of performance of, 220-221; "role-playing" in the training of, 39; selection for training of, 47-48; selection and training programs for, 394-395; use of Simultaneous Interpretation exercises in the training of, 41-43; training as intercultural communicators of, 40-43; training in conference interpretation of, 49-51; training in Simultaneous Interpretation of, 51-53; training of, 40-43, 48-53; training programs for, 45-46

Interpreters' output
factors affecting quality of, 11-12

Interpreters' performance
and neuroticism (measured by Eysenck Personality Inventory (E.P.I.)), 269

Interpreting
"metalinguistic" approach to, 28-29; and sense, 337-341

Language
A (definition of), 15; analysis of the semantic aspect of, 192-196; B (definition of), 15; C (definition of), 15; and cognition, 333-341; and culture, 209-215; dialectization of, 67-74; replacement of a, 74-78; and sense, 333-341; as a sorting device, 246-247; and translation, 209-245; ways of annihilating a, 67-68

Language boundaries
and projection, 178-181

Language categorization, 15

Language combination
definition of, 15

Language dominance
and bilingual balance, 134; and covert pronounceability of words, 262-263; and emotional stress, 266; and environmental stress, 266; free association

and, 133; measurement of, 133-142; reaction times and, 133; and recall of text, 273-286; speed factors in, 260-263; and stress, 263-268; and task stress, 264-265; and translation speed, 134; and unexpected events, 266

Language interpretation
and communication, 1-4

Language meaning, 201
and message meaning, 199-203

Language performance
processing stages in, 299-312

Language proficiency
cloze test in, 275; and dominance, 275; reading test in, 275; vocabulary test in, 275

Languages
asymmetry between, 343-346

Language switching
bilinguals' performance of, 270

Langue:parole dichotomy, 186

Liaison interpreters
behavioral aspects of, 231-242; nonverbal behavior of, 231-242; turntaking behavior of, 233-234; visual monitoring by, 236-241

Linguistics
limitations of, 110-111; and pragmatics, 185-196

Linguistics and pragmatics
distinction between, 185-196

Long term memory
in understanding speech, 311-312

Machine Translation (M.T.)
and background knowledge, 172; and the METEO system, 173; research in, 171-182; and syntax analysers, 172; and SYSTRAN, 173

"Make-sense" principle, 190-191

Manual language
the role of oral language in the evolution of, 57-58

Meaning
and semantic "satiation", 138; units of, 323-332

Memory
nature of semantic information in, 290-291

Message meaning, 201-202

National Interpreter Training Consortium (N.I.T.C.)
goals of, 83

Natural Language Understanding System (N.L.U.S.)
extensions of word sense in, 175-182; preference-violating use of language in, 175; pseudo-texts (P.T.) in, 175

Natural Translation (N.T.)
and associative memory, 169; and autotranslation, 165-167; and bilingual response, 167; and conservation of meaning across languages (C.O.M.A.L.), 169; and culture switching, 157; and diglossic translation, 161; and direct/indirect speech switching, 164; and elicited translation, 158-161; general theory of, 155; as an innate skill, 168-169; and linguistic translation, 165; and morphological translation, 164; and one-way translation, 163; and phonological translation, 164; and free translation, 166; psycholinguistic development of, 167-169; and spontaneous translation, 162; and transduction, 163

Neuroticism
and bilinguals' performance, 269

Normal discourse
and Simultaneous Interpretation, 374-376

Preperceptual Auditory Storage (P.A.S.)
acoustic features held in, 302-303; in understanding speech, 305-306

Perceptual units
in speech, 306-307

Power analysis
attraction power in, 208; coercive power in, 209; contributions to translation/interpretation from, 205-215; expert power in, 208; legimate power in, 209; reward power in, 208

Primary recognition
in understanding speech, 304-307; probabilistic prognosis, 363

Processing stages
in language performance, 299-312

Psycholonguistic development
anticipatory processes in, 376-377; communicative modulation of message in, 377; guaging the interlinguistic communicative burden in, 377-378; prior world knowledge in, 377; role taking and turn taking in, 378; simultaneous processing in, 376
Psycholinguistic process
and the relevance of laboratory studies, 99; and sign language, 99-106
Psycholinguistics
the experimental dilemma in, 369-371
Psychosemantics
and Simultaneous Interpretation, 289-297

Recall of text
factors in, 273; and language dominance, 273-286
Recordings
use in research of, 324
Reference
separate and common, 247-248
Reference semantics, 175-177
Registry of Interpreters for the Deaf, 82
Rehearsal and recoding
in understanding speech, 310-311

"Sapir-Whorf" hypothesis, 209
Secondary recognition
perceptual and contextual contributions to, 307-310; in understnading speech, 307-310
Second language deficit, 273-286
errors in, 273; "selection and organization" hypothesis in, 283-284; summary and recall of text in, 278-286
Semantic information
nature of memory for, 290-291
Semantics
and syntax, 194-196
Sense
and consciousness, 336; in interpretation, 329-330, 337-341; and linguistic meaning, 336; non-verbal nature of, 336
Shadowing
experiments in, 308; as a measure of aptitude for interpreting, 126-127
Signifié and *sens*
distinction between, 201
Sign language
formational analysis of, 63; history of the teaching of, 70-73; and interpretation, 103-106; interpretation of, 81-84; linearizing of, 69-70; and linguistic solipsism, 57-61; as linguistic systems, 110; nature of, 100; and the oralist movement, 75-77, 87; and psycholinguistic process, 99-106; relation to the structure of oral language of, 59; repression of, 57-58; in schools for the deaf, 75; as a source language, 113-114; transliteration of, 81; and neurolinguistic and psycholinguistic studies, 115-116
Sign language interpreters
characteristics of, 114-115; education of clients of, 83-84; employment opportunities and legislation concerning, 84
Sign language interpreting
research in, 87-96
Sign language interpretation
and attending behavior, 89-90; current research in, 91-96; fatigue in, 90; general theories of language, interpretation and communication, 109-116; models of the transmission and reception of messages in, 91-93; research in, 89-96
Simultaneous Interpretation (S.I.)
anticipation and décalage in, 23; auditory feedback during, 360-361; "cases" in, 359; compared with psycholinguistic development, 369-380; definition of, 15, 22-26; effects of context on performance in, 357; exercises for the training of interpreters in, 41-43; factors affecting target language (T.L.) production in, 345-346; human factors approach to, 315-321; a hypothetical model of, 353-367; an information processing model of, 353-361; introduction of, 7; memorizing and forgetting during, 291-293; and normal discourse, 374-376; out-of-booth (definition of), 15;

prediction in, 359-360; the process of, 358-359; and psycholinguistic development, 376-379; and psychosemantics, 289-297; and restructuring of language, 343-346; sources of stress in, 316-318; studies in, 393-394; and syntactic anticipation, 343-351; temporal factors in, 106; temporal regulation in, 296-297; temporal variables in, 318; theoretical aspects in the teaching of, 350-351; theoretical linguistics in the understanding of, 356-357; training of interpreters in, 51-53; typology of settings for, 29; understanding during, 293-296; at the United Nations, 8; units of meaning in, 323-332

Simultaneous interpreters
effect of the speaker's accent on the performance of, 31; and their perception of the listener, 33; and their perception of the speaker, 32; use of recordings in the training of, 28; training of, 25-33

Simultaneous interpretation training
abstraction of ideas in, 362; decreasing reaction time in, 363; dual task training in, 363-364; implications of an information processing model for, 361-367; paraphrasing in, 362-363; probabilistic prognosis in, 363; research in, 364-366; shadowing in, 364

Sociolinguistics
and translation theory, 202-203

Speech
perceptual units in, 306-307

Stress
effects in bilinguals of, 259-270; and language dominance, 263-268; and sources in Simultaneous Interpretation, 316-318; task, 264-265

Syntactic anticipation
concept of, 346-350; and Simultaneous Interpretation, 343-351

Syntax and semantics, 194-196

Synthesised Auditory Memory (S.A.M.)
percepts in, 302-303

Temporal regulation
in Simultaneous Interpretation, 296-297

Temporal variables
in Simultaneous Interpretation, 318

Time lag
between interpreter and speaker, 326-327

Transformational-generative grammar
recent development of, 186-189

Translating
as an innate skill, 155-169

Translation
aspects of performance in, 122-123; bibliography on, 4; choice of words in, 327-329; contribution of power analysis to, 205-215; contribution of cross-cultural orientation programs to, 205-215; definition of, 35; evaluation of quality of, 119-120; linguistic versus semiotic, 109-110; measure of adequacy in, 200-201; selection of students of, 120-127; sociolinguistic approach to, 199-203; time taken in, 135; and written language, 333

Translation process
and the speech chain, 37-40; types of cultural knowledge entering into, 39-40

Translation theory
and sociolinguistics, 202-203

Translators
as listeners, 131; linguistic abilities in, 119-127

"True" bilingualism
definition of, 145-146; and linguistic relativity, 150-151; and non-verbal thought, 150-151; research into, 147-152; second language learning and, 145-152

Typologies
of interpretation situations, 217-229; of interpreter roles, 217-229

Understanding
during Simultaneous Interpreting, 293-296; role of inference in, 194

Understanding speech
acoustic features in, 301-304; feature detection in, 301-304; Generated Abstract Memory (G.A.M.) in, 310; information processing model of, 299-

312; and long term memory, 311-312; Perceptual Auditory Storage (P.A.S.) in, 301, 305-306; primary recognition in, 304-307; rehearsal and recoding in, 310-311; secondary recognition in, 307-310
Units of meaning
in interpretation, 320

Venice Symposium
aims of, 1-2; topics covered by, 2-3

Whispered interpretation
definition of, 15
Whispering interpreter, 7
Working languages
at the United Nations, 8-9